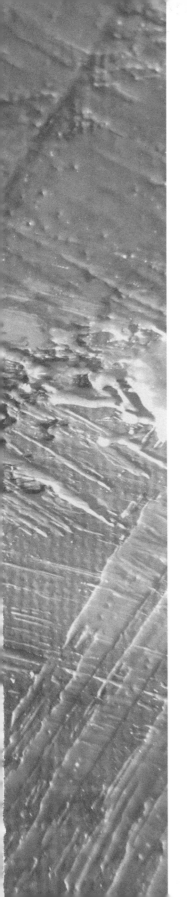

Social Research Methods

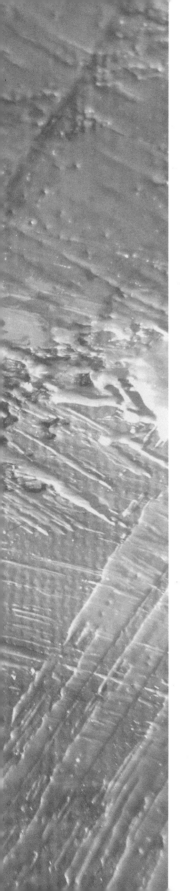

Social Research Methods

Canadian Edition

ALAN BRYMAN

AND JAMES J. TEEVAN

OXFORD
UNIVERSITY PRESS

OXFORD
UNIVERSITY PRESS

70 Wynford Drive, Don Mills, Ontario M3C 1J9
www.oup.com/ca

Oxford University Press is a department of the University of Oxford.
It furthers the University's objective of excellence in research, scholarship,
and education by publishing worldwide in

Oxford   New York

Auckland   Cape Town   Dar es Salaam   Hong Kong   Karachi
Kuala Lumpur   Madrid   Melbourne   Mexico City   Nairobi
New Delhi   Shanghai   Taipei   Toronto

With offices in

Argentina   Austria   Brazil   Chile   Czech Republic   France   Greece
Guatemala   Hungary   Italy   Japan   Poland   Portugal   Singapore
South Korea   Switzerland   Thailand   Turkey   Ukraine   Vietnam

Oxford is a trade mark of Oxford University Press
in the UK and in certain other countries

Published in Canada
by Oxford University Press

Library and Archives Canada Cataloguing in Publication

Bryman, Alan
Social research methods / Alan Bryman and James Teevan. — Canadian ed.

Includes bibliographical references.
ISBN-13: 978-0-19-541941-2   ISBN-10: 0-19-541941-3

1. Social sciences—Research—Textbooks. 2. Social
sciences—Methodology—Textbooks. I. Teevan, James J., 1942- II. Title.

H62.B78 2005   300'.72   C2005-901843-7

Cover Image: Photodisc/Getty Images

1 2 3 4 – 08 07 06 05
This book is printed on permanent (acid-free) paper ⊖.
Printed in Canada

Contents

Guide to the Book

Focus of the book

This book was written for undergraduate students taking a research methods course, most often in sociology departments but also in other social science disciplines such as social work and education. It covers a wide range of methods, approaches to research, and ways of carrying out data analysis. Research methods are not tied to a particular nation; many if not most of the principles transcend national boundaries. However, the genesis of this particular book gives it a particularly wide-ranging and international sensibility. The original text by Alan Bryman was written with the needs of UK post-secondary students in mind, but was widely adopted in Europe and Canada as well. Feedback from adopters and reviewers suggested the book could be made even more useful for Canadian instructors and students through the addition of Canadian and, more broadly, North American examples, sources, and research studies. James Teevan's adaptation of the book has preserved the qualities that contributed to its success—its clarity, comprehensiveness, and presentation of social research methods as an international enterprise—while at the same time incorporating elements that are integral to North American and Canadian courses in the discipline.

Many students taking a research methods course will also be asked, either as part of that course or later in their undergraduate careers, to carry out a small-scale research project. The focus in Parts Two, Three, and Four of the text is on the practice of social research, and as each research method is examined, its uses and limitations are explored. These sections should help students carrying out their own projects make informed decisions about their research. In Part Five, Chapter 17 provides advice on writing up research and Chapter 18 specifically addresses students conducting research projects. This chapter builds on earlier discussion of research questions in Chapter 1, reinforcing a topic central to the entire research process.

In addition to providing students with practical advice on doing social research, the book explores the nature of social research and the fundamental issues it raises. For example:

- Is a natural science model of the research process applicable to the study of people and society? If not, why not?

- Does the use of a natural science model imply certain assumptions about the nature of social reality?

- Equally, do those writers and researchers who reject such a model have an alternative set of assumptions about the nature of social reality?

- What kinds of research findings are regarded as legitimate and acceptable?

- To what extent do values affect the research process?

- Should researchers worry about the feelings of people outside the research community concerning what they do to people during their investigations?

These and many other issues impinge on social research in a variety of ways and will be confronted at different stages throughout the book. While knowing how to do research—how to design a questionnaire, how to observe, how to analyze the mass media, and so on—is crucial to an education in research methods, so too is a broad appreciation of the wider issues that affect the practice of social research.

An education in research methods involves more than teaching specific skills for doing research. Thus this text also provides tools for a critical appreciation of how and with what assumptions research is done. Even if this is the only time a student conducts research, that knowledge should make for a lifetime of critical reading of social research.

Structure of the book

One of the most fundamental distinctions in social research occurs between its quantitative and qualitative varieties. This distinction lies behind the structure of the book and the way in which issues and methods are approached. The book is divided into five parts.

Part One comprises two scene-setting chapters. It deals with basic ideas about the nature of social research.

- Chapter 1 examines such issues as the nature of the relationship between theory and research and the degree to which a natural science approach is an appropriate framework for the study of society. It is here that the distinction between quantitative and qualitative research is first encountered. They are presented as different *research strategies* with different ways of conceptualizing how people and society should be studied. As previously noted, this chapter also includes a discussion of *research questions*—what they are, their importance, and how they come to be formulated.
- In Chapter 2, the idea of a *research design* is introduced. This chapter introduces the basic frameworks within which social research is carried out, such as social survey research, case study research, and experimental research. These two chapters provide the basic building blocks for the rest of the book.

Part Two contains five chapters concerned with quantitative research.

- The first chapter explores the nature of quantitative research and provides a context for the later chapters. The next two chapters are largely concerned with aspects of social survey research.
- Chapter 4 is concerned with the kind of interviewing that takes place in survey research, that is, structured interviewing, and with the design of questionnaires. This involves a discussion of how to devise self-completion questionnaires.
- Chapter 5 examines the issue of how to ask questions for questionnaires and structured interviews.
- Chapter 6 covers structured observation, a method developed for the systematic observation of behaviour.
- Chapter 7 looks at the analysis of data collected by other researchers or by official bodies.

Part Three contains three chapters on aspects of qualitative research.

- Chapter 8 plays the same role in relation to Part Three as Chapter 3 plays in relation to Part Two. It provides an overview of the nature of qualitative research and as such provides the context for the other chapters in this Part.
- Chapter 9 is concerned with ethnography and participant observation. The two terms are often used interchangeably and refer to the immersion of the researcher in a social setting, the source of some of the best-known studies in social research.
- Chapter 10 deals with the kinds of interviewing that qualitative researchers conduct—typically semi-structured interviewing or unstructured interviewing—and with focus groups in which groups of individuals are interviewed on a specific topic.

Part Four looks at sampling in both quantitative and qualitative research and then at data analysis, including computer aids.

- Chapter 11 deals with sampling – how to select a sample and the considerations involved in assessing what can be inferred from different kinds of samples. Most texts place sampling near their discussion of survey research. The placement here reflects how sampling is also crucial in qualitative research.
- Chapter 12 presents a range of basic non-technical tools for quantitative analysis. The emphasis is on how to choose a method of analysis and how to interpret findings. No formulae are presented. Instead SPSS, the most widely used social science computer software for analysing quantitative data, is explained; mastering it means the computer performs the actual calculations.
- Chapter 13 explores some approaches to the analysis of qualitative data and also includes an introduction to using computer software in qualitative research analysis.

Part Five contains chapters that go beyond the quantitative/qualitative research contrast.

- Chapter 14 deals with some of the ways in which the distinction between quantitative and qualitative research is less fixed than sometimes supposed.
- Chapter 15 presents some ways in which they can be combined to produce what is referred to as multi-strategy research.

- Chapter 16 then applies these principles to content analysis, a method that provides a framework for the analysis of things like letters, documents, newspapers, movies, chat lines, books, radio and television, etc. and usually seen as the domain of quantitative research. It also examines two ways to analyse language: conversation analysis and discourse analysis.

- Chapter 17 provides guidance on writing up research, an often-neglected area in the teaching of the research process.

- Chapter 18 offers advice on conducting a research project, taking readers through the main steps involved.

Special features of the book

Several special features make the text more helpful:

- *Examples.* Students can learn by reading how others have carried out research and what lessons they seem to have learned. In view of this, most major points include an example or two, most from published research. Students generally do not have the resources to conduct a similar level of research. In these instances the most that can be asked of them is an awareness of how their early efforts are governed by the principle of looking for what is satisfactory, rather than what is optimal, and the implications of doing so.

- *Boxes.* The text is full of them. Boxes do a variety of things, besides creating a break in the text, making it less imposing and more readable. Sometimes they provide examples; sometimes they define key terms ('What is . . .?'); sometimes they list series of important points. They also provide a focus for definitions and key examples.

- *Ethics boxes.* Several chapters contain a special type of box that considers how ethical issues impinge on researchers and the kinds of principles involved.

- *Practical tips.* Most chapters have at least one box of practical tips, special points to think about or to watch out for, on certain recurring but easily avoidable mistakes which students make.

- *Checklists.* Most chapters include checklists of issues that should be borne in mind when engaging in certain activities, like doing a literature review, devising a structured interview schedule, or conducting a focus group. They are meant to highlight key points encountered in the text, to remind students what to look out for or consider when doing their own research.

- *Chapter overviews.* Each chapter begins with a chapter overview that alerts readers to what they can expect to have learned by the end of each chapter, a route map of what is to follow.

- *Key points.* At the end of each chapter is a summary of points that are particularly significant. They are meant to jog student memory on issues that are especially important.

- *Questions for review.* At the end of each chapter there is also a series of questions to help test understanding of key concepts and ideas.

- *Glossary.* At the end of the book is a glossary of definitions of central terms. Many repeat definitions in the "What is . . .?" boxes, but they also provide a convenient way of recalling the meaning of key terms.

Companion website

Social Research Methods is accompanied by an interactive website (**www.oup.com/ca/he/companion/brymanteevan**). The website provides additional teaching and learning material, including:

- Instructor's guide;

- PowerPoint slides;

- Examples, drawn from real research, of the main methods outlined in the book;

- Links to social research websites; and

- Summaries of key debates and controversies in social research.

The website also contains a **Methods and Skills Toolkit** designed to help guide students through the research process. This resource provides a guide to the practicalities and problems that students face when asked to do a research project. The toolkit covers a range of issues, from dealing with a supervisor to ways of organizing and writing a paper or thesis for maximum effect. The toolkit also shows students how the larger research issues and controversies dealt with in *Social Research Methods* may have an impact on their own experiences of conducting a research project.

How to use the book

The book can be used in many ways. Some instructors, for reasons of time or preference, may not want to include all chapters or all sections of a specific chapter.

- *Wider philosophical and methodological issues.* If a full appreciation of the wider philosophical context of enquiry in social research is not needed, Chapter 1 can largely be ignored, except for the part on formulating a research question. If an emphasis on such issues *is* of interest, Chapter 1 along with Chapter 14 should be a particular focus of attention.

- *Practical issues concerned with doing quantitative research.* This is the province of the whole of Part Two. Chapter 2 is a good introduction as it maps out the main research designs employed, such as experimental and cross-sectional designs, used by quantitative researchers.

- *Practical issues concerned with doing qualitative research.* This is the province of the whole of Part Three. Again, Chapter 2 maps out the research designs frequently employed, such as the case study, in qualitative research.

- *Analyzing data.* Chapters 12 and 13 explore the analysis of quantitative and qualitative research data respectively, including an introduction to the use of computer software for this analysis. Even if the module is taught without actual computer applications, exposure to them is useful for later work and for reinforcing the textual material.

- *The quantitative/qualitative research contrast.* The distinction between quantitative and qualitative research is used in two ways: to organize the discussion of current research methods and methods of analysis and to introduce some wider philosophical issues about social research. Chapter 1 outlines the chief areas of difference between quantitative and qualitative research. Some of the limitations of adhering to an excessively strict demarcation between the two research strategies is presented in Chapter 14, while Chapter 15 explores ways of integrating them. If time is an issue these chapters can be skimmed.

- *Writing.* Writing up research is as much a part of the research process as is data collection. Chapter 17 discusses a variety of issues to do with writing up research and should be read.

- *Doing a research project.* As already mentioned in this Guide, the whole book is relevant to student research projects or mini-projects, but Chapter 18 is where specific advice relating to this issue is located along with a discussion of writing a thesis or similar product.

Acknowledgments

Many people have helped me with this book, many of them unwittingly. Generations of research methods students at the University of Western Ontario have tested its contents. I wish to thank several people at or connected with OUP: David Stover, who had to persevere to initiate the project, Phyllis Wilson, who guided its early phases and never complained of my missing deadlines, and to a dedicated copy editor, Pamela Erlichman, for her suggestions. I am grateful to Sarah Pink for her permission to use an image from her research on women and bullfighting.

Two people deserve the greatest appreciation: Alan Bryman and my wife, Bonnie. He wrote the British text on which this book is based. He put into clear prose the many things I tried to impart to my students in lectures, from philosophy of science issues to showing the common aspects of qualitative and quantitative methods, making my adaptation so much easier. My wife put up yet again with the late nights and daily tensions that a book like this entails. Thank you both.

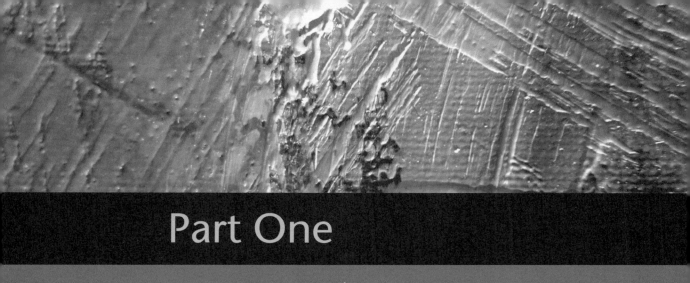

Part One

Part One of this book is concerned with two ideas that recur again and again throughout the text—the idea of research strategy and the idea of research design. Chapter 1 outlines a variety of considerations that affect the practice of social research and relates them to the issue of research strategy. Two research strategies are identified: quantitative and qualitative research. Chapter 2 then presents different kinds of research design and identifies criteria used to evaluate research evidence. Together these chapters provide basic conceptual building blocks that are returned to at many points in the book. Some of the issues may seem remote from research practice but they are in fact crucial aspects of how to think about social research.

Social research strategies

CHAPTER OVERVIEW

The aim of this chapter is to present some of the philoso-phy of science issues that are considered in the process of conducting social research. An important distinction com-monly drawn among practitioners of social research—be-tween *quantitative research* and *qualitative research*—is explored in relation to these considerations, including:

- the nature of the relationship between theory and re-search, in particular whether theory guides research (a *deductive* approach) or whether theory is an outcome of research (an *inductive* approach);

- *epistemological* issues—whether or not a natural sci-ence model of the research process, like the one used in chemistry or biology, is suitable for the study of the social world;

- *ontological* issues—whether the social world is re-garded as something external to social actors or as something that actors are in the process of fashioning into their personal realities;

- how *values* and *practical issues* impinge on the research process;

- the ways in which these issues relate to both quantita-tive and qualitative research; there is also a preliminary discussion, followed up in Chapters 14 and 15, that suggests that while quantitative and qualitative re-search represent different approaches to social research, a wedge should not be driven between them.

Introduction

This book is about social research. It would be easy to 'cut to the chase' and explore the nature of social re-search methods and then provide advice on how best to choose among them and then to implement them. But the practice of social research does not exist in a bubble, sealed off from the various philosophical al-legiances of their practitioners. For example, do the researchers view people as relatively passive reactors to the social world or as more active creators? Do they agree that the methods of natural science can be applied to the social world or do the practitioners think that social science needs unique methods ap-propriate to its unique subject matter? Must past re-search be the source for current research?

Two points are of particular relevance here. First, methods of social research are closely tied to differ-ent visions of how social reality should be studied. Methods are not simply neutral tools; they are linked with how social scientists envision the con-nection between different viewpoints about the na-ture of social reality and how it should be examined. However, it is possible to overstate this point. While methods are not neutral, they are not entirely sub-jective either. Second, there is a question of how re-search methods and practice connect with the wider social scientific enterprise. Research data are invari-ably collected in relation to something. The 'some-thing' may be a burning social problem or, more usually, a theory, such as a theory of prejudice or one of crime.

This is not to suggest that research is entirely dic-tated by theoretical concerns. One sometimes finds simple 'fact-finding' exercises being published. I once did a study on the plusses and minuses of sabbaticals. Yes, there is a downside: leaving a pet, children uprooted, returning to a damaged home. In other instances, research is motivated by what is seen as a pressing social problem. Hier (2002) investigated raves when they became an area of official concern following the 1999 Ecstacy-related deaths of three young adults in Toronto. Yet another stimulus for re-search is personal experiences (Lofland and Lofland 1995). For example, Sugiman's (2004), a third-generation Sansei, investigation of Japanese-Canadian women's experiences of internment during World War II stemmed from hearing the experiences of family and friends. By and large, however, research data achieve significance in sociology when viewed in relation to theoretical concerns, raising the issue of the relationship between theory and research.

Theory and research

Characterizing the nature of the link between theory and research is not straightforward. There are several issues at stake here, but two stand out: first, the form of theory; and second, the relationship between data and theory.

Degree of abstraction

The term 'theory' is used in a variety of ways (see Box 1.1), but its most common meaning is as an *explanation of observed regularities or patterns*, for example, explaining why schizophrenia is more common in the working class than in the middle class, or why more men than women are alcoholic. Theories of this type are often called *theories of the middle range* (Merton 1967) to contrast them with *grand theories*, which are more general and abstract.

Courses in sociological theory typically focus on grand theories such as structural-functionalism, symbolic interactionism, critical theory, post-structuralism, and so on. Grand theories generally offer few indications on how to collect the empirical evidence needed for testing them. So, if someone wanted to test a theory or to draw a testable inference from one, the level of abstraction would likely make it difficult to link the theory with the real

---

Box 1.1 The construction of theories

Theories are composed of interrelated, generally verified, statements or propositions. The statements and propositions come in varying forms and different types are often combined in the same research. Here are the most common:

1 DEFINITION: specifies what a thing is, giving its attributes; for example, 'Crime is any violation of the Canadian *Criminal Code* and includes arson, embezzling, etc.'

2 DESCRIPTION: portrays a phenomenon; for example, 'Arson involves the setting of fires and is often done at night, either to abandoned buildings or houses when no one is home. There were 438 cases last year with estimated damage over $2 billion, etc.'

3 RELATIONAL STATEMENTS: connect two or more variables; knowing the value of one conveys information about the value of the other variable; for example, 'As the economy experiences a downturn, the arson rate increases.' Relational statements can be:

(a) DETERMINISTIC, which means the two variables go together all of the time. If well-done research uncovers an instance in which they are not related, the relational statement is no longer true. It is disproved and must be modified.

(b) PROBABILISTIC, which means the two variables go together with some degree of regularity; for example, 40 per cent of the time, 80 per cent of the time, etc. Here, finding a case in which they are not related does not disprove the theory. This could be one of the times they are not related.

world. For research purposes, then, Merton argued that grand theories are of limited use in connection with social research, although, as the example in Box 1.2 suggests, an abstract theory like Giddens' structuration theory (1984) can have some payoff in research terms.

By and large, then, it is not grand theory that typically guides social research. Middle-range theories are much more likely to be the focus of empirical inquiry. They operate in a limited domain whether it is juvenile delinquency, sexist attitudes, educational attainment, or the labour process (see Box 1.3). For example, labelling theory represents a middle-range theory in the sociology of deviance. Its exponents examine the effects of societal reaction to deviance, to see if punishment deters or whether it sometimes backfires, leading to alienation and even more deviance by those punished. Merton's (1938) classic anomie theory, positing that crime is more common when a society instills lofty goals in everyone but provides insufficient means for all to achieve them,

---

Box 1.2 Grand theory and social research

Giddens' (1984) structuration theory attempts to bridge the gulf between notions of structure and agency in social life and could have formed the theoretical backdrop to empirical research by Dinovitzer *et al.* (2003) on the educational attainment of immigrant youth. The specific focus of their research was suburban Toronto immigrants, tracing their lives from 1976 to 1995. The data were quantitative, generated through structured interviews. The goal of the researchers was to tease out the relative influence of structural variables (such as class, gender, and relationship with parents of the students) and individual variables more under their control (such as studying and cutting classes) on achieving higher education.

The authors found both structural (gender and father's occupation) and individual (intellectual investment) variables affect higher education and that (essentially bilingual) ESL students do better than those immigrants for whom English is a first language. They are not brighter, nor do they work harder, but they have greater parental supervision and, perhaps partly as a result, plan better.

Box 1.3 Labour process theory: a middle-range theory

In the sociology of work, labour process theory can be regarded as a middle-range theory and has been the focus of considerable empirical research. Part of the theory examines the trend towards greater and greater control over manual workers and 'de-skilling,' the reduction in skill requirements for their labour. With respect to the former, Rinehart *et al.* (1998) showed how Total Quality Management programs borrowed from Japan have been met with suspicion by Canadian workers, and therefore are unsuccessful. On the topic of de-skilling, Rinehart (1996) found in a study of auto manufacturing plants that tasks are increasingly broken down into smaller pieces, resulting in repetitive and boring work, and to a blurring in the distinction between skilled and unskilled labour.

---

is another example. Middle-range theories, then, fall somewhere between grand theories and straight empirical findings. They represent attempts to understand and explain a limited aspect of social life.

Even the grand/middle-range distinction does not entirely clarify the issues involved in asking the deceptively simple question of 'what is theory?' This is because the term 'theory' is frequently used to mean little more than the background literature in an area of social inquiry, used either to set a context or to illustrate a void. For example, Beagan's (2001) study of everyday inequalities, based on gender, race, or sexual orientation, experienced by students in a Canadian medical school began this way. Thus, in many cases, the relevant background literature relating to a topic acts as the equivalent of a theory, as with the research referred to in Box 1.4 on delinquency.

In articles like the one reported in Box 1.4, there may be no, or virtually no, allusions to theories. Instead, the literature on a certain topic acts as the spur to an inquiry. It can serve as an impetus in a number of ways: (1) the researcher may seek to resolve an inconsistency between different research results or between different interpretations of the same result; (2) the researcher may spot a neglected aspect of a topic or recognize that certain ideas have not previously been tested, perhaps because a new

Box 1.4 Background literature as theory: first-person accounts of delinquency

Teevan and Dryburgh collected data from 57 male adolescents concerning their frequency of engaging in various deviant activities, such as truancy, theft, vandalism, and fighting, and asked them why they so acted. Then the boys were read specially adapted sociological explanations of such behaviour, like labelling theory or anomie theory, both previously mentioned in this chapter. The goal was to let them be sociologists and evaluate those theories. The idea was tied to giving marginalized groups a voice and to qualitative research, with its emphasis on seeing from the point of view of those studied.

The trouble arose when trying to get the results published. The idea was great, said some reviewers, but there was little theory *per se*. Eventually, Teevan dug up and fashioned the minimal amount that would let the piece be published. It can be found in the *Canadian Review of Sociology and Anthropology* (2000), 37: 77–93.

Box 1.5 Generating research ideas from the literature

Let's say you read an article that reports: other things being equal, the greater the division of labour in a society (the more jobs are broken down to be done by different people), the lonelier people are. What hypotheses can be derived from that finding?

1 Since a greater division of labour often involves a greater dependence on technology, then one can hypothesize: other things being equal, as dependence on technology increases, loneliness increases. *Note that the variable deemed the cause should come first, a rule that will help in later data analysis.*

2 If the literature suggests that loneliness is often related to drinking, another hypothesis is: other things being equal, the greater the division of labour in society, the more drinking that occurs.

3 Third, these two can be combined, thus predicting: other things being equal, as dependence on technology increases, drinking increases.

The process can continue with other things related to loneliness and thus perhaps affected by the division of labour, like suicide? Anything else?

This type of exercise has another benefit besides deriving new hypotheses. It can also suggest other areas for a literature search, should a topic have only a few available references.

social phenomenon has arisen or a new connection has been made (see Box 1.5); or (3) the researcher may feel that existing approaches to research on a topic are deficient, and so provide an alternative approach; and so on.

Many social scientists are prone to dismiss research that has no obvious connections with theory—in either the grand or middle-range sense of the term. Such research is often dismissed as *naive empiricism*, thus rejecting an accumulation of 'facts' as a sufficient justification for research. It would be harsh, not to say inaccurate, however, to brand as naive empiricism the numerous studies in which the publications-as-theory strategy is employed, simply because their authors have not been preoccupied with theory. Such research is conditioned by and directed towards research questions that arise out of an interrogation of the literature. The data collection and analysis are subsequently geared to the illumination or resolution of the research issue or problem that has been identified at the outset. The literature acts as a proxy for theory; in many instances, theory is latent or implicit in the literature.

Indeed, even research characterized as a 'fact-finding exercise' should not be prematurely dismissed as naive empiricism either. McKeganey and Barnard's (1996) research on prostitutes and their clients is a case in point. On the face of it, even if one strips away their concern with HIV infection, the research can be construed as naive empiricism and perhaps of a rather prurient kind. However, this is a harsh and probably inaccurate judgment. For example, the authors related their research findings to investigations of prostitutes in a number of other countries. They also illuminated their findings by drawing on ideas that are very much part of the sociologist's conceptual tool kit. One example is Goffman's (1963) notion of 'stigma' and the way in which stigmatized individuals, here prostitutes and clients, manage a spoiled identity; another is Hochschild's (1983) concept of 'emotional labour,' a term she coined to denote how flight attendants feign friendliness when dealing with difficult passengers.

It is not possible to tell from McKeganey and Barnard's (1996) report whether the concepts of stigma and emotional labour influenced their data collection. However, raising this question invites consideration of another question: insofar as any piece of research is linked to theory, what is the role of that theory? Up to this point, the chapter has implied that theory is something that guides the collection and analysis of data. In other words, research is done to answer questions posed by theoretical considerations. An alternative position is to view theory as something that arises after the collection and analysis of some or all of the data associated with a project. One begins to see here the significance of a second factor in considering the relationship between theory and research—whether it is deductive or inductive theory.

Deductive and inductive theory

Deductive theory represents the most common type of theory in social research. In it a researcher, on the basis of what is known about in a particular topic and of theoretical considerations in relation to it, deduces a hypothesis (or hypotheses) that must then be subjected to empirical scrutiny. Embedded within the hypothesis are concepts that need to be translated into researchable entities, to specify how empirical data can be collected in relation to the concepts that make up the hypothesis.

This view of the role of theory in relation to research is very much the kind of role that Merton (1967) had in mind in connection with middle-range theory, which, he argued, serves to guide empirical inquiry. Theory and the hypothesis deduced from it come first and drive the process of gathering data (see Box 1.6 for an example of a deductive approach to the relationship between theory and data). There is a comforting logic to the idea of developing theories and then testing them. In everyday contexts, people commonly think of theories as things that are quite illuminating but in need of testing before they can be considered valid and useful. The sequence can be depicted as one in which the steps outlined in Figure 1.1 take place.

Box 1.6 A deductive study

Based on their readings of previous studies of what affects religious beliefs—things like parents, schools, and friends—Kelley and De Graaf (1997) argued that there are good grounds to think that the nation into which one is born is also an important factor. These reflections constitute what they referred to as the 'theory' that guided their research and from which the following hypothesis was derived: 'People born into religious nations will, in proportion to the orthodoxy of their fellow-citizens, acquire more orthodox beliefs than otherwise similar people born into secular nations' (1997: 641). The authors hypothesized further that the religious orientation of the individual's family (whether devout or secular) would affect the nature of the relationship between national religiosity and religious orthodoxy.

To test the hypotheses, Kelley and De Graaf examined large-sample survey research from 15 nations. Religious orthodoxy was measured by four survey questions about religious belief: (1) whether the person believed in God; (2) past beliefs about God; (3) how close the individual felt to God; and (4) did they have a belief that God cares about everyone. To measure national religiosity, the 15 nations were classified into one of five categories, from secular to religious. The classification was derived by averaging parental religious attendance measured on a scale of five levels and religious belief in the nation as a whole (1997: 647).

The hypothesis was broadly confirmed and the authors concluded that the 'religious environment of a nation has a major impact on the beliefs of its citizens' (1997: 654).

Note how this study demonstrates the process whereby a hypothesis is deduced from existing theory and then guides the process of data collection so that it can be tested.

The last step involves a movement away from deduction—it involves *induction*, when researchers examine their data and evaluate the implications of their findings for the theory that first prompted the whole exercise. This can be seen in the case of Dinovitzer *et al.*'s (2003) final reflections on the implications of their findings for ideas related to educational attainment theory. They concluded that both the structure beyond an individual's direct control

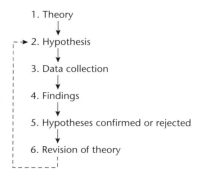

1. Theory
↓
2. Hypothesis
↓
3. Data collection
↓
4. Findings
↓
5. Hypotheses confirmed or rejected
↓
6. Revision of theory

Figure 1.1 The process of deduction

(younger age at immigration to Canada and parental supervision, and other things called social capital) and agency (individual variables like time spent studying and not cutting classes) affect the likelihood of continuing one's education.

It is also important to bear in mind that when this deductive approach, usually associated with quantitative research, is put into operation, there are many instances in which a researcher does not follow the exact linear sequence shown in Figure 1.1, with its clear logical sequence. For example, a researcher's view of the theory or literature may be changed by the data analysis; or the relevance of a set of data for a *second* theory may become apparent *after* the data have been collected. In fact, while the process of deduction outlined in Figure 1.1 often occurs, it is better considered as a general orientation to the link between theory and research. As a general orientation, its broad contours may frequently be discernible in social research, but there are often departures from it.

Finally, in some research *no* attempt is made to follow the sequence outlined in Figure 1.1. Some researchers prefer an approach that is primarily *inductive*, in which theory is the *outcome* of research. In other words, the process of induction involves drawing generalizable inferences out of observations. Figure 1.2 attempts to capture the essence of the difference between induction and deduction. And just as deduction entails an element of induction, the inductive process is likely to entail a modicum of deduction. Once the phase of theoretical reflection on a set of data has occurred, a researcher may want to

collect further data to establish the conditions in which the newly emerged theory does and does not hold. Such a general strategy is often called *iterative*: it involves a weaving back and forth between data and theory.

Moreover, as is true in the deductive approach, one also has to be cautious about the use of the term 'theory' in the context of the inductive strategy. While some researchers using induction undoubtedly try to develop theories, sometimes the result of research is little more than empirical generalizations of the kind Merton (1967) wrote about, such as the recent Statistics Canada finding that women are more frequently absent from work than men, 2.2 more days in 2002, and not a real theory (Statistics Canada, CANSIM, Table 279-0029). Box 1.7 gives an example of research that can be classified as inductive in the sense that it derives five explanations for participation in raves and relates them to earlier theories on the topic.

Wilson's (2002) research on raves (see Box 1.7) is an interesting illustration of an inductive approach. Two points are particularly worth noting about it. First, it uses the analysis of data to generate what is called a *grounded* theory, not just insightful empirical generalizations as do many others. Second, in much the same way that the deductive strategy is associated with a quantitative research approach, an inductive strategy of linking data and theory is typically associated with a qualitative research approach. It is not a coincidence that Wilson's research is based on in-depth, semi-structured interviews that

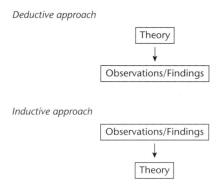

Figure 1.2 Deductive and inductive approaches to the relationship between theory and research

---

Box 1.7 An inductive study

Wilson (2002) examined the experiences of young adults who attend raves and in one phase of his research conducted semi-structured interviews with 10 females and 27 males. He also looked at underground magazines, flyers advertising raves, and recordings of raves. He found that reasons for going to raves varied from something as simple as escape, to intentional rejection of the traditionally gendered and racially segregated bar scene, to in reality a shallow resistance. This last turned out to be a support of the dominant culture as some ravers, in their disdain of the rave spinoffs and rave clubs, try to maintain an elite status. Concerning the use of Ecstacy, one male university student

asked: 'Do we really need social barriers, do we really need the defenses that we have and would life be better of if we didn't have some of the[m]?' (Wilson 2002: 396).

Therefore, in this inductive study Wilson's explanations came after, rather than before, the data. This was his expressed preference when he sought 'the meanings that youth give to their activities' (2002: 399). He began with subcultural and postsubcultural theory and sought to understand raves from the participants' points of view, an issue on which the existing literature was inconsistent. The qualitative data then led him to offer his five explanations of their behaviour.

---

produced qualitative data in the form of detailed answers to his questions. However, as shown in Box 1.7, this characterization of the inductive strategy as associated with qualitative research is not entirely straightforward either: not only does much qualitative research *not* generate theory, but also theory is often used, at the very least, as a background to qualitative investigations. Indeed, Wilson used theory as a departure point.

It is useful to think of the relationship between theory and research in terms of deductive and inductive strategies. However, as the previous discussion implies, the issues are not as clear-cut as sometimes presented. To a large extent, deductive and inductive strategies are possibly better thought of as tendencies rather than as binary choices, one *or* the other. The next section turns to other issues that impinge on the conduct of social research.

Epistemological considerations

An epistemological issue concerns the question of what is (or should be) regarded as acceptable knowledge in a discipline. A particularly central issue in this context is whether the social world can and should be studied according to the same principles and procedures as the natural sciences. The position that affirms the importance of imitating the natural sciences is invariably associated with an epistemological position known as *positivism* (see Box 1.8).

A natural science epistemology: positivism

The doctrine of positivism is extremely difficult to pin down and therefore to outline in any precise manner because it is used in different ways by differ-

ent authors. Worse, while for some, it describes a philosophical position in research, for others, it is a pejorative term used to refer to crude and often superficial data collection.

It is possible to see in the five principles in Box 1.8 a link with some of the points already raised about the relationship between theory and research. First, positivism includes a fairly sharp distinction between theory and research and includes elements of both deduction and induction. Second, the role of research is to test theories and to provide material for the development of laws, somewhat similar to the laws of science, like Boyle's law. There is also an implication that it is possible to collect observations in a manner not influenced by pre-existing theories. Finally, theoretical terms not directly susceptible to

Box 1.8 ⌁⌁ *What is positivism?*

Positivism is an epistemological position that supports the application of natural science methods to the study of social reality. But the term stretches further than this principle, though the constituent elements vary between authors. However, positivism is also generally taken to entail the following:

1 Only phenomena and regularities confirmed by the senses (usually sight and hearing) can genuinely be warranted as knowledge (the principle of *empiricism*). In other words, ideas must be subjected to the rigours of testing before they can be considered knowledge.

2 The purpose of theory is to generate hypotheses that can be tested and thereby allow explanations of laws to be assessed (the principle of *deduction*).

3 Knowledge is arrived at through the gathering of facts that provide the basis for generalizations or laws (the principle of *induction*).

4 Science must (and presumably can) be conducted in a way that is value-free. Researchers used to call this *objectivity*; today they are more likely to call it *intersubjectivity*, meaning that different researchers, even those with different values, would reach the same conclusions given the same data.

5 There is a clear distinction between scientific statements and normative or 'should' statements and a belief that the former are the true domain of science. This last principle is implied by the first principle above, because the truth of normative statements cannot be confirmed by the senses.

Box 1.9 ⌁⌁ *What is realism?*

Realism shares two features with positivism: first, a belief that the natural and the social sciences can and should use the same approach to the collection of data and to explanation and second, a commitment to an external reality, *separate from descriptions of it*, to which scientists should direct their attention. There are two major forms of realism:

- *Empirical realism* simply asserts that, through the use of appropriate methods, reality can be understood. This version of realism is sometimes referred to as *naive realism* to reflect its frequent assumption of a perfect (or at least very close) correspondence between reality and the terms used to describe it. When writers employ the term 'realism' in a general way, it is invariably this most common meaning to which they refer.

- *Critical realism* is a specific form that holds that deeper structures, generative mechanisms, lie beneath the observable patterns: 'We will only be able to understand—and so change—the social world if we identify the structures at work that generate those events . . .' and this is the domain of social science theory and research (Bhaskar 1989: 2).

Critical realism thus implies two things: first, that a scientist's conceptualization of reality may not correspond to any actual reality, and that categories employed to understand reality are temporary and provisional. Second, unlike naive realists, critical realists recognize a distinction between the objects that are a focus of inquiry and the terms used to describe, account for, and understand it. Therefore, critical realists, unlike positivists, admit theoretical terms not directly observed into their explanations, including the generative mechanisms that they infer from their observable effects. Its second implication is that the identification of generative mechanisms offers the prospect of introducing changes to transform the status quo. This is what makes critical realism *critical*.

the rigours of observation are often considered not to be genuinely scientific. All of this carries with it the implication of a greater epistemological status being given to observation than to theory.

A common mistake is to treat positivism as synonymous with science and the *scientific*. In fact, philosophers of science and social science differ quite sharply over how best to characterize scientific practice, and since the early 1960s there has been a drift away from viewing it in positivist terms. *Realism* (in particular, *critical realism*), for example, is another philosophical position that purports to provide an alternative account of the nature of scientific practice (see Box 1.9).

The crux of the epistemological considerations presented here is the rejection by some writers and traditions of the application of the canons of natural science to the study of social reality. It is difficult sometimes to disentangle the natural science model from positivism, as the butt of their criticisms. In

Box 1.10 ⚡ *What is interpretivism?*

Interpretivism denotes an alternative to the positivist orthodoxy that has held sway for decades. It maintains that a research strategy for the social sciences must respect the differences between people and the objects studied in the natural sciences. While billiard balls move without any thought on their part, humans do not, and it is the role of social scientists to grasp the subjective meaning of that movement or social action. Interpretivism's intellectual heritage includes Weber's notion of *Verstehen* or understanding, the phenomenological tradition, and symbolic interactionism.

other words, it is not always clear whether they are rejecting the application of a general natural scientific approach or positivism in particular.

Interpretivism

Interpretivism (Box 1.10) is a contrasting epistemology to positivism. The term subsumes the views of writers critical of the application of a natural science model to the study of the social world and who have been influenced by different intellectual traditions. For example, they share a view that the subject matter of the social sciences—people and their institutions—is fundamentally different from that of the natural sciences. For them it follows that the study of the social world requires a different logic of research procedure, one that reflects the distinctiveness of humans as against the world of nature. This clash reflects a division between an emphasis on the *explanation* of human behaviour that is the chief ingredient of the positivist approach to the social sciences and the preference for an empathetic *understanding* and an interpretation of human behaviour for those who reject positivism. This contrast reflects long-standing debates that precede the emergence of modern social science but find their expression in such notions as Max Weber's (1864–1920) *Verstehen* approach. Weber described Sociology as a 'science which attempts the interpretive understanding of social action in order to arrive at a causal explanation of its course and effects' (1947: 88). Weber's definition seems to embrace both explanation *and*

understanding here, but the crucial point is that the task of 'causal explanation' is undertaken with reference to the 'interpretive understanding of social action.' This is a different emphasis than in the more Durkheimian view in which the external forces that affect behaviour may have no meaning for those involved. For a Marxist view, see Box 1.11.

One of the main intellectual traditions responsible for the anti-positivist position has been *phenomenology*, a philosophy concerned with the ways individuals make sense of the world around them

Box 1.11 Marxist research methods

Almost all who adopt a Marxist approach reject positivism. But they are also critical of subjective perspectives on social life, like that of Weber, and argue that people are not the makers of social reality. Instead, those who own the means of production are; they deceive, constrain, and exploit the weak. The masses could be free if social scientists, by asking embarrassing questions, would uncover exploitation, expose hypocrisy, and reveal to them their oppression. This would transform the masses from what Marx called a *class an sich* (a class in itself, an objective reality) into a *class für sich* (a class for itself, one with a subjective reality).

Thus, Marxists reject Weber's recommendation, that it is the role of the scientist to be detached, as too passive. Instead they see the role of social science specifically as one of unmasking the unjust conditions in the world, thus allowing the downtrodden to see the sources of their ills. Thus, research should be action-oriented, what they call *praxis*, to empower the weak. Smashing myths and uncovering contradictions are just the first part of that process (cf. Neuman 2003).

There is no single type of action research, but broadly it can be defined as an attempt to diagnose a problem and then develop a solution based on the diagnosis. Action research can involve the collection of both quantitative and qualitative data; in action research, the investigator becomes part of the field of study. Action research should not be confused with *evaluation research* (see Box 2.10), which usually denotes studying the impact of an intervention, such as a new social policy or an innovation in an organization.

and in particular how philosophers should acknowledge their own personal preconceptions of that world. The initial application of phenomenological ideas to the social sciences is found in Schutz, whose works did not come to the notice of most English-speaking social scientists until they were translated from German in the 1960s, some twenty years after they had been written.

Schutz's work was profoundly influenced by Weber's concept of *Verstehen*, as well as by other phenomenological philosophers. Two of his points are particularly noteworthy. First, he saw a fundamental difference between the subject matter of the natural sciences and the social sciences, thus requiring an epistemology that reflects and capitalizes on that difference. The fundamental difference is that while molecules, atoms, and electrons do not think about their natural reality, humans do think about their social reality. Human action is meaningful; humans act on the basis of the meanings that they attribute to their acts and to the acts of others. Using their own common-sense constructs, individuals interpret the reality of their daily lives and it is these thoughts that motivate their behaviour.

This leads to the second point—namely, that it is the job of the social scientist to gain access to people's 'common-sense thinking' and hence to interpret their actions and their social world *from their point of view*. Thus any thoughts constructed by the social scientist to grasp this social reality must be founded upon the common-sense interpretations of those they study, people living their daily lives within their own social world (Schutz 1962: 59). It is this particular feature that social scientists claiming allegiance to phenomenology have typically emphasized.

In this exposition of *Verstehen* and phenomenology, it was necessary to skate over some complex issues. In particular, Weber's use of *empathy* to understand the behaviour of others is far more complex than the above suggests, and the question of what is and is not a genuinely phenomenological (sometimes called *hermeneutic*) approach to the social sciences is a matter of some disagreement. There is consensus, however, that their common emphasis on social action as meaningful to actors (and therefore needing an interpretation from their point of view) coupled with the rejection of positivism, con-

tributed to a stream of thought often referred to as *interpretivism* (e.g., Hughes 1990).

Verstehen and the phenomenological tradition, however, do not exhaust the intellectual influences on interpretivism. Many, but not all, also regard *symbolic interactionism* as an influence. The implications for empirical research of the ideas of the founders of symbolic interactionism, in particular George Herbert Mead (1863–1931), whose discussion of the way in which one's *self-concept* emerges through an appreciation of the perceptions of others, have been hotly debated. However, the general tendency has been to view symbolic interactionism as occupying similar intellectual space to the phenomenological tradition and so broadly interpretative in approach. Symbolic interactionists argue that interaction takes place in such a way that individuals are continually interpreting the symbolic meaning of their environment (including the actions of others) and act on the basis of this imputed meaning (cf., Collins 1994). In research terms, according to Blumer (1962: 188), 'the position of symbolic interaction requires the student to catch the process of interpretation through which [actors] construct their actions.'

There are other intellectual currents with affinities to an interpretative stance, but the phenomenological, *Verstehen*, and symbolic interactionist traditions can be considered major influences. Taking an interpretative stance can result in surprising findings, or at least findings that appear surprising, if a position from outside the particular social context being studied is adopted. Box 1.12 provides an interesting example of this possibility.

Of course, as the example in Box 1.12 suggests, when social scientists adopt an interpretative stance, they are not simply laying bare how members of a social group interpret the world around them. The social scientist almost certainly aims to place those interpretations into a social scientific frame. Thus there is a double interpretation going on: the researcher is providing an interpretation of others' interpretations. Indeed, there is a third level of interpretation going on, because the researcher's interpretations have to be further interpreted in terms of the concepts, theories, and literature of a discipline. Thus, taking the suggestion from Box 1.12 that Riverside is not perceived as a high-crime area by residents is Foster's interpretation

---

Box 1.12 Interpretivism in practice

Foster (1995) conducted ethnographic research using participant observation and semi-structured interviews in a housing estate in East London, referred to as Riverside, one experiencing a high level of crime, as indicated by official statistics. However, she found that residents did not perceive the estate to be a high-crime area. This perception can be attributed to a number of factors, but a particularly important reason is the existence of 'informal social control.' People expect a certain level of crime, but feel fairly secure because informal social control allows levels of crime to be contained.

Informal social control comprises a number of different aspects. One is that neighbours often look out for each other. In the words of one of Foster's interviewees: 'If I hear a bang or shouting I go out. If there's aggravation I come in and ring the police. I don't stand for it.' Another aspect of informal social control is that people often feel secure because they know each other. Another respondent said: 'I don't feel nervous . . . because people do generally know each other. We keep an eye on each other's properties. . . . I feel quite safe because you know your neighbours and you know they're there . . . they look out for you' (Foster 1995: 575).

---

of her subjects' interpretations. She then had the additional job of placing her interesting findings into a social scientific frame, which she accomplished by relating them to existing concepts and discussions in criminology, things like informal social control, neighbourhood watch schemes, and the role of housing as a possible cause of criminal activity.

The aim of this section has been to outline how epistemological considerations—especially those relating to the question of whether a natural science, and in particular a positivist approach, can supply legitimate knowledge of the social world—are related to research practice. There is a link with the earlier section in that a deductive approach to the relationship between theory and research is typically associated with a positivist position. Box 1.8 does try

to suggest that inductive logic is also a feature of positivism (third principle), but, in its implementation in social research, it is the deductive element (second principle) that tends to be emphasized. Similarly, the third level of interpretation that a researcher engaged in interpretative research must bring into operation is very much part of the kind of inductive strategy described in the previous section. However, while such interconnections between epistemological issues and research practice exist, it is important not to overstate them, since they represent tendencies rather than definitive points of correspondence. Thus, particular epistemological principles and research practices do not necessarily go hand in hand in a neat unambiguous manner. This point will be made again on several occasions.

Ontological considerations

Questions of social ontology are concerned with whether social entities can and should be considered objective entities with a reality external to specific social actors, or whether they can and should be considered temporary social constructions built up from the perceptions and actions of these actors. These positions are frequently referred to respectively as *objectivism* and *constructionism*. Their differ-

ences can be illustrated by reference to one of the most central terms in social science—organization.

Objectivism

Objectivism is an ontological position that implies that social phenomena confront individuals as external facts beyond their reach or influence. For example, an organization has rules and regulations and adopts standardized procedures for getting things done. A division of labour assigns people to different jobs. There is a hierarchy of authority, a mission statement, and so on. Objectivists see any organization as possessing a reality external to any of the specific individuals who inhabit it; they may leave but it will stay. Moreover, the organization represents a social order in that it exerts pressure on individuals to conform to organizational requirements. People learn and apply the rules and regulations and follow the standardized procedures. They do the jobs to which they are appointed. If they do not do these things, they may be reprimanded or even fired. The organization is therefore a constraining force that acts on and inhibits its members. To a large extent, this is the 'classic' way of conceptualizing an organization.

Constructionism

An alternative ontological position, *constructionism* (see Box 1.13), challenges the suggestion that things like an organization are external realities confronting social actors with limited power to influence or change them. Strauss *et al.* (1973), for example, carried out research in a psychiatric hospital and proposed that its organization is best conceptualized as one of 'negotiated order.' Instead of viewing order as a pre-existing characteristic, they argued that it is worked at and that rules are far less extensive and less rigorously imposed than might be supposed from an objectivist account of organization.

Indeed, Strauss *et al.* viewed rules more like general understandings than as commands (1973: 308). Precisely because relatively little of the spheres of action of doctors, nurses, and other personnel is specifically set down or prescribed, the social order of a hospital is an outcome of agreed-upon patterns of action that are themselves the products of negotiations among the different parties involved. The official rules may say that only a doctor can increase medication, but some nurses, though it is never actually stated, are routinely given this power. The social order is in a constant state of change because the hospital is 'a place where numerous agreements are continually being terminated or forgotten, but also

---

Box 1.13 *What is constructionism?*

Constructionism is an ontological position (often also referred to as constructivism) asserting that social phenomena and their meanings are produced by social actors through their social interaction and that they are in a constant state of negotiation and revision.

In recent years, the term has come also to include the notion that researchers' own accounts of the social world are constructions. In other words, researchers present a specific version of social reality, rather than one that can be regarded as definitive. Knowledge is viewed as indeterminate. (The discussion of postmodernism in Chapter 16 further examines this viewpoint.) This sense of constructionism is usually allied to the ontological version of the term. In other words, these are linked meanings, both antithetical to *objectivism*, but the second meaning is also antithetical to *realism* (see Box 1.9). The first meaning might usefully be thought of as constructionism in relation to the social world, the second as constructionism in relation to the nature of knowledge of the social world (and indeed the natural world). In this book the term is used in relation to the first meaning, an ontological position, one that views social objects and categories as socially constructed.

---

as continually being established, renewed, reviewed, revoked, [and] revised. . . . In any pragmatic sense, this is the hospital *at the moment* [our emphasis]: this is its social order' (1973: 316–17). The authors argued that a preoccupation with the formal properties of organizations (rules, organizational charts, regulations, and roles) neglects the degree to which order in organizations has to be *accomplished* in everyday interaction. This *informal* organization arises because there cannot be rules for every possible contingency, though this is not to say that the formal properties have *no* element of constraint on individual action.

Although Strauss *et al.* stressed the active role of individuals in the social construction of social reality, they did not push the argument to an extreme. But not all writers adopting a constructionist position are similarly prepared to acknowledge the existence or at least importance of an objective reality. It is precisely this apparent split between viewing the social world as an objective reality, and seeing it as a subjective reality in a continuous state of flux, that Giddens sought to straddle in formulating his idea of structuration (recall Box 1.2).

Constructionism also suggests that the categories people employ to help them understand the natural and social world are in fact social products. The categories do not have built-in essences; instead, their meaning is constructed in and through social interaction. Thus, a concept like 'masculinity' should be treated as a social construction. This notion implies that, rather than being treated as a distinct, timeless, and universal entity, the meaning of masculinity is built up during interaction. That meaning is likely to be ephemeral, in that it will vary over time and place. This tendency can be seen particularly in discourse analysis, examined in Chapter 16. As Potter (1996: 98) observed: 'The world . . . is *constituted* in one way or another as people talk it, write it, and argue it.' This sense of constructionism is highly antithetical to realism (see Box 1.9) and frequently leads to an interest in how social phenomena are represented. Box 1.14 provides an illustration of this idea in relation to the breast cancer 'epidemic.'

Constructionism is also frequently used as a term to reflect the indeterminacy of knowledge of the social world (see Box 1.14). However, this book uses the term in connection with the notion that social phenomena and categories are social constructions.

Relationship to social research

Questions of social ontology cannot be divorced from issues concerning the conduct of social research. Ontological assumptions and commitments affect how research questions are formulated and

---

Box 1.14 Constructionism in action

Lantz and Booth (1998) showed that a rise in the incidence of breast cancer since the early 1980s, and its depiction as epidemic, can be treated as a social construction. They analyzed a variety of popular magazines (a topic in Chapter 16) and noted that many of the articles draw attention to the lifestyles of modern women, such as delaying first births and having careers. The authors argued also that the articles ascribe blame: 'Women are portrayed as victims of an insidious disease, but also as victims of their own behaviours, many of which are related to the control of their own fertility' (Lantz and Booth 1998: 915).

This article concludes that, as a social category, the breast cancer epidemic is represented in popular magazines in a particular way—one that blames the victims and the lifestyles of modern women in particular. This is in spite of the fact that fewer than 20 per cent of cases of breast cancer are in women under the age of 50.

Lantz and Booth's study is fairly representative of a constructionist ontology in suggesting that the epidemic is not simply being construed as a social fact but is being ascribed a particular meaning (one that blames the victims of the disease). In this way, the representation of the disease in popular magazines forms an important element in its social construction.

---

how research is carried out. For example, if organizations are viewed as objective social entities that act on individuals, the researcher is likely to emphasize their formal properties. Alternatively, if the researcher emphasizes the daily changing nature of organization, it is likely that research will focus on the active involvement of people in reality construction. In each case, a different research design is required.

Research strategy: quantitative and qualitative research

Many writers on methodological issues distinguish between quantitative and qualitative research, but some writers see it as a fundamental contrast, whereas others see the distinction as no longer useful or even simply as 'false' (Layder 1993: 110). Most of the evidence suggests, however, that the quantitative/qualitative distinction, although vigorously debated, is still valid. It will be employed often in this book because it represents a useful means to classify different research methods and because it is a helpful umbrella for a range of issues concerned with the practice of social research.

On the face of it, there seems to be little to the quantitative/qualitative distinction other than that quantitative researchers employ more measurement than qualitative researchers do. Indeed, there is a predisposition among researchers along these lines; but many suggest that the differences are deeper than the superficial issue of the amount of quantification. For many writers, quantitative and qualitative research differ in their epistemological foundations and in other respects too. Indeed, examining the areas that were the focus of the last three sections—the connection linking theory and research, epistemological considerations, and ontological considerations—quantitative and qualitative research can be seen as forming two distinctive *research strategies,* or general orientations to the conduct of social research. Table 1.1 outlines the differences between quantitative and qualitative research in terms of the three areas.

Thus, quantitative research can be construed as a research strategy that emphasizes numbers and statistics in the collection and analysis of data and that:

- entails a deductive approach to the relationship between theory and research, in which an accent is placed on theory testing;

- incorporates the practices and norms of a natural science model and of positivism in particular; and

- embodies a view of social reality as an external, relatively constant, objective reality.

By contrast, qualitative research can be construed as a research strategy that usually emphasizes words rather than quantification in the collection and analysis of data and that:

- predominantly emphasizes an inductive approach to the relationship between theory and research, and the generation of theories;

- rejects the practices and norms of the natural scientific model and of positivism in particular, for an emphasis on how individuals interpret their social world; and

- embodies a view of social reality as a constantly shifting and emergent property of individuals' creations.

There is, in fact, considerably more to the quantitative/qualitative distinction than this contrast. In Chapters 3 and 8 the nature of quantitative and then qualitative research respectively will be outlined in greater detail. Then in Chapters 14 and 15 their contrasting features will be further explored, examining the effects of a commitment in quantitative research to a positivist epistemology and the rejection of that epistemology by qualitative researchers.

Finally, although it is useful to contrast the two research strategies, it is important not to hammer a wedge too deeply between them. It may seem perverse to introduce a basic set of distinctions and then suggest that they are problematic, but a recurring theme of this book is that discussing the nature of social research is just as complex as conducting research in the real world. One can discover general tendencies, but they are precisely that, tendencies. In reality, the picture becomes more complicated the deeper one goes.

Table 1.1 Fundamental differences between quantitative and qualitative research strategies

	Quantitative	Qualitative
Role of theory in research	Deductive; testing of theory	Inductive; generation of theory
Epistemological orientation	Natural science model; positivism	Interpretivism
Ontological orientation	Objectivism	Constructionism

For example, it is common to describe qualitative research as concerned with the generation rather than the testing of theories. However, there are many studies in which qualitative research tests rather than generates theories, like Hier's (2002) investigation of Ontario rave scenes (see also Box 1.7), with their all-night dancing and amphetamine use. Hier wanted to show how the regulation of raves was a contest between a city that feared increased drug use and supporters who eventually won the day by arguing that banning them would drive the drugs underground with even worse consequences. Also, although the Wilson (2002) study of the same topic is broadly interpretivist in epistemological orientation, with its emphasis on how ravers view their social situation, it includes some objectivist, rather than constructionist, overtones. For example, in examining the effects of technology, including the Internet, and the impending millennium on the scene, he was positing a world that is 'out there' and as having a formal, objective quality. It is thus another example of qualitative research that does not have *all* the qualitative features outlined in Table 1.1.

The point being made here is that quantitative and qualitative research represent different research strategies and that each carries with it striking differences in terms of the role of theory, epistemological issues, and ontological concerns. However, the distinction is not a hard-and-fast one: studies that have the broad characteristics of one research strategy may have a characteristic of the other. Also, many writers argue that the two can be combined within an overall research project, and Chapter 16 examines precisely this possibility.

Influences on the conduct of social research

Readers should now be seeing how social research is influenced by a variety of factors. Figure 1.3 summarizes the influences examined so far, but has added three more—the impact of *values*, *politics*, and of *practical considerations*.

Values

Values reflect the personal beliefs or feelings of a researcher. On the face of it, one would expect social scientists to be value-free and objective in their research. Research that simply reflects the personal views of its practitioners would appear biased and invalid, thus unscientific, because it is bound up with the subjectivities of its practitioners. Durkheim

(1858–1917) wrote that *social facts* are objects whose study requires that all 'preconceptions must be eradicated' (1938: 31). Since values are a form of preconception, his point at least implicitly means to suppress them when conducting research. Such a view is held with less and less frequency among social scientists today; there is a widespread recognition that it is not feasible to keep researcher values totally in check. Indeed, values can intrude at any or all of a number of points in the process of social research, such as:

- choice of research area;
- formulation of research question;
- choice of method;
- formulation of research design and data collection techniques;
- data collection;
- analysis of data;
- interpretation of data; and
- conclusions.

There are, therefore, numerous points at which bias and the intrusion of values can occur during the

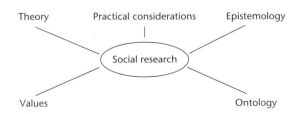

Figure 1.3 Influences on social research

Ethical issue 1.1 *Ethics: an introduction*

Ethical issues arise at every stage of social research and affect the integrity of the specific research as well as the discipline. Because they apply to so many decisions, this book inserts ethical issues boxes in the chapters where they are most appropriate. These boxes will include:

- some (in)famous cases in which transgressions of ethical principles occurred, though it is important to recall that ethical concerns arise not only in such extreme cases;
- stances taken on ethics in social research;
- the significance and operation of four overlapping areas of ethical concern: informed consent; deception; harm to participants; and invasion of privacy. Each is relevant to defining the activities no researcher should engage in and in specifying how to treat the people that provide the data upon which the researcher is dependent.

But writings on ethics in social research are often frustrating. There are differences of opinion on what is and is not ethically acceptable; indeed, some arguments made in the 1960s are still being rehashed. Even the professional ethical principles provided by the Canadian Sociology and Anthropology Association (current CSAA codes and guidelines can be found at www.csaa.ca/structure/ethics.htm) contain some ambiguity.

These debates about ethics cannot be resolved. What *is* crucial is to be aware of the ethical principles involved and of ethical practice in social research so that informed decisions about the implications of the various choices can be made. If nothing else, readers of these boxes will become aware of the possible disapproval coming their way if they make certain choices.

While the codes and guidelines of professional associations provide some guidance, their potency is ambiguous and they often leave the door open for some autonomy with regard to ethical issues.

---

course of research. For example, a researcher may develop an affection or sympathy, not necessarily present at the outset of an investigation, for the people being studied. It is quite common, for example, for researchers working within a qualitative research strategy, in particular when they use very intensive interviewing, to become so close to the people they study that they find it difficult to disentangle their stance as social scientists from their subjects' perspectives. This possibility may be made worse by the

---

Box 1.15 Taking sides in social research

Forty years ago, an interesting dispute occurred between Becker and Gouldner, leaders in US sociology and beyond. It raised many issues concerning the role of *values* in research, but here the issue of taking sides in research is the concern. Becker (1967) argued that it is almost impossible to do research unaffected by personal sympathies. For example, much research is undertaken in the context of hierarchical relationships (police/criminal, managers/workers, doctors/patients, or teachers/students). Becker felt it would be difficult in such instances not to take sides but the bigger dilemma is deciding *which* side.

Becker recognized that within his field, the sociology of deviance, the sympathies of many practitioners lay with the underdogs in these hierarchical relationships, leading them at a minimum to seek to express or represent their point of view. However, when sociologists of deviance do this, Becker argued, they are more likely to be accused of bias than are those who side with the more powerful. Becker offered two reasons for this bias in attributing bias: because members of the higher group are widely seen as having an exclusive right to define the way things are in their sphere and because they are regarded as having a more complete picture. In other words, credibility is differentially distributed in society.

Gouldner (1968) argued that Becker exaggerated these issues in that by no means must all research involve a need to take sides. He also wanted to distinguish the taking of the point of view of a section of society seriously, from sympathizing with that group. More recently, Liebling (2001) added that it is possible to see the merits of more than one side. Taking the case of prison research, she showed that not only is it possible to recognize the virtues of different perspectives, but also to do so without incurring too much wrath from either side, in her case, prison officials and prisoners.

tendency for sociologists to be sympathetic to underdogs (Becker 1967).

Equally, social scientists may be repelled by those they study. In his research into an African tribe known as the Ik, a social anthropologist was appalled by what he saw: a loveless (and for him unlovable) tribe that left its young and very old to die (Turnbull 1973). Although he was able to point to the conditions lying behind these practices, he was very honest in his disgust for what he witnessed, particularly during his early time with the tribe.

One way of dealing with the whole question of values and bias is to recognize that research cannot be value-free and thus try to ensure that values in the research process are acknowledged and so exhibit what is called *reflexivity* about the part played by such factors. As Turnbull (1973: 13) put it at the beginning of his book on the Ik: 'The reader is entitled to know something of the aims, expectations, hopes, and attitudes that the writer brought to the field [in his case, Western values about the family], for these will surely influence not only how he sees things but even what he sees.' Researchers are increasingly prepared to forewarn readers of their biases and assumptions and how these may have influenced their subsequent findings. There has been a growth since the mid-1970s in collections of inside reports of what doing a piece of research is really like, as against the generalities presented in social research methods textbooks (like this one). These collections frequently function as 'confessions' about personal biases and reveal the pride researchers take in telling the readers how open they are in revealing them.

Still another approach is to argue for consciously value-laden research. This is a position taken by some feminist writers who argue that only the research on women intended *for* women will be consistent with the wider political needs of women. Mies (1993: 68) argued that in feminist research the 'postulate of *value free research*, of neutrality, and indifference towards the research objects, has to be replaced by *conscious partiality*, which is achieved through partial identification with the research objects' [emphases in original]. For example, Tastsoglou and Miedema (2003) clearly proclaimed a feminist anti-racist approach for studying immigrant women in the Maritimes. The significance of feminism in relation to values goes further than this, however. In particular, several feminist social researchers in the early 1980s proposed that quantitative research is incompatible with feminist research on women. For writers such as Oakley (1981), quantitative research is bound up with male values of *control*, as seen in the researcher's control of the research subject/respondent and of the research context and situation. Moreover, the research process is seen as one-way, in which researchers extract information from those studied and give little or, more usually, nothing in return. For many feminists, such a strategy borders on exploitation and is incompatible with feminism's values of sisterhood and non-hierarchical relationships among women.

Their antipathy towards quantitative research resulted in a preference for qualitative research among feminists. Not only was qualitative research seen as more consistent with the values of feminism, but it was also seen as more adaptable to those values. Thus, feminist qualitative research came to be associated with an approach in which the investigator denied a value-neutral approach and engaged with the people being studied as people and not simply as respondents to research instruments. This stance of feminism in relation to both quantitative and qualitative approaches demonstrates how values have implications for the process of social investigation. In more recent years, there has been a softening of the attitudes of feminists towards quantitative research, especially when it is employed in conjunction with qualitative research (Oakley 1998). This issue will be revisited in Chapters 9, 15, and 16.

There are, then, different positions in relation to values and value-free research. Fewer writers today overtly subscribe to the position that the principle of objectivity can fully be put into practice. And although quantitative researchers sometimes seem to suggest an aura of objectivity (Mies 1993), there are little data for knowing how far they subscribe to such a position. There is a greater awareness today of limits to objectivity, so that some of the highly confident, not to say naive, pronouncements on the subject, like those of Durkheim, have fallen into disfavour.

Politics in social research

In the section on 'influences on the conduct of social research,' it was noted that values intrude in all phases of the research process, from the choice of a research area to the formulation of conclusions. This means that the social researcher is never working in a moral vacuum but is influenced by a whole variety of presuppositions that in turn have implications for the conduct of social research. This view is increasingly accepted among social researchers and one rarely hears today claims that social research, even the quantitative variety, can be conducted in a wholly objective, value-neutral way.

For some writers on social research, a 'conscious partiality,' as Mies (1993: 68) called it, is celebrated. This view may have allowed Pratt and Valverde (2002) to refer to a large Canadian newspaper as a 'notorious tabloid' and 'obsessed' with what it called bogus refugees. Particularly among feminist researchers, attempting research on women in an objective, value-neutral way would be undesirable (as well as being difficult to achieve) because it would be incompatible with the values of feminism. Instead, many feminist researchers advocate a stance that extols the virtues of a commitment to women and exposes the conditions of their disadvantage in a male-dominated society.

Considerations of this kind draw attention to how *politics* become important in different contexts and ways.

- Social researchers sometimes *take sides*. This is precisely what many feminist researchers do when they focus on women's disadvantages and on the possibilities for improving their position. But taking sides is more widespread than this.

- Related is the issue of *funding* research. Much social research is funded by organizations such as firms and government departments with a vested interest in the outcomes of the research. The very fact that some research is funded, while other research is not, suggests that political issues may be involved, in that such organizations may seek to invest in studies that will be useful to them, perhaps supportive of their operations and worldviews. Frequently, they launch a call for researchers to tender bids for an investigation in a certain area. When social researchers participate in such exercises, they are participating in a political arena because their research concerns and even research questions will be influenced by the funding body. As a result, as Hughes (2000) observed in relation to research in the field of crime, an investigation of gun crimes among the 'underclass' is more likely to be looked upon favourably for funding than one concerned with state-related misdemeanours. Morgan (2000) pointed out that research funded by government typically: is empirical; adopts quantitative research; is concerned with short-term costs and benefits of a policy or innovation; and is uncritical (in the sense that the underlying government policy is not probed, just its effective implementation). Such features can be related to the fact that a funding agency itself may be involved in a political process of seeking to secure a continuous stream of government funding; demonstrating relevance is one way of indicating standing in this regard.

- Gaining *access* is also a political process. Access is usually mediated by gatekeepers concerned not only about the researcher's motives but also about what the organization can gain from the investigation, what it will lose by participating in the research in terms of staff time and other costs, and potential risks to its image. Often, gatekeepers seek to influence how the investigation will take place: what kinds of questions can be asked, who can and cannot be a focus of study, the amount of time to be spent with each research participant, the interpretation of findings, and the form of any reports, even asking to approve drafts.

- Public institutions, such as the police, schools, hospitals, and probably most commercial firms, are concerned with how they are going to be represented in publications. Consequently, gaining access is almost always a matter of negotiation and as such inevitably turns into a political process. The results of this negotiation are often referred to as 'the research bargain' and it turns out that the term really should be plural. Once in the organization, researchers often discover a constant process of negotiation and renegotiation of what is and is not permissible, and layers of gate-keepers. For example, let's say permission to talk to the boys in a group home is given by the provincial government. Before research can begin, the head of the home has to be brought onside, then the staff, and then the actual adolescents. Frequently, one of the staff is then given the responsibility for dealing with the fieldworkers. A suspicion that they are really working for management then also has to be overcome. Thus, it is unwise to assume that simply because gatekeepers have given a researcher access, a smooth passage will ensue in subsequent dealings with the people to be studied. Even then, the most powerful of the boys may turn out to be the *key* gatekeeper. Researchers may even find themselves used as pawns if subgroups attempt to enlist them in advancing a particular viewpoint, and some research participants, because they doubt the utility of social research, may obstruct the research process. Some of Beagan's (2001) medical students refused to participate when they heard she was asking about 'gays and lesbians.' Even a cooperating student wrote on the questionnaire of being sick of being asked about sexual preference.

- There may be pressure to restrict the *publication* of findings. Hughes (2000) cited the case of a study of plea-bargaining in the British criminal justice system as a case in point. The researchers had uncovered what were deemed at the time to be disconcerting levels of informal plea-bargaining, concluding that the formal judicial process was being weakened. The English legal establishment sought to thwart the dissemination of the findings and was only persuaded to allow publication when a panel of academics confirmed the validity of the findings.

These are just a small number of ways politics intrudes in the research process.

Practical considerations

Nor should the importance and significance of *practical issues* in decisions about how to carry out social research be neglected. There are a number of different dimensions to this subject. For one thing, choices of research strategy, design, or method have to be dovetailed with the specific research question being investigated. If one is interested in the relative importance of a number of different causes of a social phenomenon, a quantitative strategy is probably appropriate because, as will be shown in Chapter 3, the assessment of cause is one of its keynotes. Alternatively, if the focus is on the worldviews of members of a certain social group, a qualitative research strategy—one sensitive to how participants interpret their social world—may be the way to go. If a researcher is interested in a topic on which no or little research has been done, the quantitative strategy may be difficult to employ because there is little prior literature from which to draw leads. A more exploratory stance may be preferable and, in this connection, qualitative research may serve the researcher's needs better, since it is typically associated with the generation rather than the testing of theory (see Table 1.1) and with a relatively unstructured approach to the research process (see Chapter 8).

Another dimension may have to do with the nature of the topic and of the people being investigated. For example, if a researcher wants to study individuals involved in illicit activities such as price fixing, pilfering, or drug dealing, it is unlikely that a social survey could gain the confidence of those involved or achieve the necessary rapport. It is not surprising, therefore, that the researchers in these areas tend to use a qualitative strategy. However, it's unlikely that the hypothesis in Box 1.6 on the effects of societal religiosity on individual religious orthodoxy in 15 nations could have used a qualitative approach.

Although practical considerations may seem rather mundane and uninteresting compared with the lofty realm inhabited by the philosophical debates surrounding epistemology and ontology, they are important ones. All social research is a coming together of the ideal and the feasible. Because of this, there are many circumstances in which the nature of the topic or of the subjects of an investigation and the constraints on a researcher loom large in decisions about how best to proceed.

Research questions

The last practical consideration is that of choosing a *research question*, which is not the same as a hypothesis—a hypothesis is a specific type of research question. Research questions set realistic boundaries for research; having none or poorly formulated research questions results in poor and unfocused research. It does not matter how well designed a questionnaire is or how skilled interviewers are; clear research questions are required to avoid going off in unnecessary directions and tangents. Research questions are crucial because they guide:

* the literature search;
* decisions about the kind of research design to employ;
* decisions about what data to collect and from whom;
* analysis of the data; and
* writing up the data analysis.

Unfortunately, the process of formulating and assessing research questions is difficult to spell out, but here are some general thoughts.

Research often starts out with a general area of interest, for example, homosexuality. This broad research area has to be narrowed to a tighter focus, moving from a general research area down to specific research questions. Thus, a move to homosexual lifestyle, then even more specifically to sexual practices, and finally to number of sexual partners would be appropriate. Even this last topic is a bit too broad, but the successive narrowing of the topic should illustrate the process.

This movement acknowledges that the research cannot answer all the research questions that occur, but must select one or two at most. This narrowing of focus is not just a limit placed by the time and cost of doing research. It is also due to the need for a clear focus, ensuring that research questions are related to form a coherent set of issues. If they do not, the research will probably lack focus and not make much contribution to understanding the topic. For more suggestions, see Box 1.16.

Research questions in quantitative research are sometimes more specific than those in qualitative research. Indeed, some qualitative researchers advocate a very open approach with *no* research questions. This is a very risky approach and can be a recipe for collecting masses of data without a clear sense of what to observe or what to ask interviewees. There is a growing tendency for qualitative researchers to advocate a somewhat more focused approach to their craft, as for example in Parnaby's (2003) study of Toronto's squeegee kids.

Box 1.16 Considerations when developing research questions

Research questions for a project should:

* be clear—they must be understandable to others;
* be researchable—they should be capable of development into a research design and allow data to be collected in relation to them; this means that extremely abstract terms are not suitable;
* connect with established theory and research—this means that there should be a literature to draw upon to show how the research questions should be approached. Even with a topic scarcely addressed by social scientists there will probably be some relevant literature (e.g., on related or parallel topics; recall Box 1.5); making connections with theory and research also demonstrates how the research contributes to knowledge and understanding;
* be linked to each other—unrelated research questions are unlikely to be acceptable, since a paper for publication should develop a single argument, one hard to make with unrelated research questions;
* have potential to make a contribution, however small, to knowledge on the topic;
* be neither too broad (needing a large grant) nor too narrow (unable to make a reasonably significant contribution to an area of study).

If unsure about how to formulate research questions (or indeed other phases of research), look at journal articles or research monographs to see how other researchers have formulated them.

K KEY POINTS

- Quantitative and qualitative research constitute different approaches to social investigation and carry with them important epistemological and ontological considerations.

- Theory can be depicted as something that precedes research (deductive, as in quantitative research) or as something that emerges out of it (inductive, as in qualitative research).

- Epistemological considerations loom large in considerations of research strategy. To a great extent, these revolve around the desirability of employing a natural science model (and in particular positivism) versus interpretivism.

- Ontological considerations, concerning objectivism versus constructionism, also constitute important dimensions of the quantitative/qualitative contrast.

- Feminist researchers have tended to prefer a qualitative approach, a situation that is changing now.

- Values can impinge on the research process at different times. There are political dimensions to the research process that link with values.

- The political dimensions of research are concerned with issues to do with the role and exercise of power at the different stages of an investigation.

- Practical considerations also can affect decisions about research methods. Clear research questions improve chances of success.

- Important ethical issues for social research arise in collecting data.

- The main areas of ethical concern relate to: harm to participants; lack of informed consent; invasion of privacy; and deception.

Q QUESTIONS FOR REVIEW

Theory and research

- If you had to conduct some social research, what would the topic be and what factors would have influenced your choice?

- Can you find, in your other courses, additional examples of middle-range theory?

- What are the differences between inductive and deductive theory and why is the distinction important?

Epistemological considerations

- What is meant by each of the following terms: positivism, realism, and interpretivism? Why is it important to understand each of them?

- How might a positivist and an interpretivist differ in conducting research on illegal drug use?

Ontological considerations

- What are the main differences between epistemological and ontological considerations?

- What do the terms objectivism and constructionism mean?

- Which theoretical ideas have been particularly instrumental in the growth of interest in qualitative research?

Research strategy: quantitative and qualitative research

- Outline the main differences between quantitative and qualitative research in terms of: the relationship between theory and data; epistemological considerations; and ontological considerations.

- Under what circumstances is qualitative research more concerned with testing theories and quantitative research with generating theories?

Influences on the conduct of social

- What are some of the main influences on social research?

Politics in social research

- What is meant by the suggestion that politics play a role in social research?

- In what ways are politics manifested in social research?

Research questions

- Why are research questions so important in the overall research process?

- What are the main characteristics of good research questions?

2 Research designs

CHAPTER OVERVIEW

A research design is a framework for the collection and analysis of data. It is designed for generating evidence, suited both to a certain set of criteria and to a research question, and thus defensible. This chapter is structured as follows:

- It begins with reliability, replication, and validity—criteria for assessing the quality of social research. Validity entails an assessment of several forms: measurement validity, internal validity, and external validity.

- The suggestion that such criteria are relevant mainly to quantitative research is examined, along with the

proposition that alternative criteria should be employed for qualitative research. One alternative set, concerned with the issue of *trustworthiness*, is outlined briefly.

- Four prominent research designs are then outlined:
  — experimental and related designs (such as the quasi-experiment);
  — cross-sectional design and survey research, its most common form;
  — longitudinal design and its various forms, such as panel and cohort studies; and
  — case study design.

Introduction

In the previous chapter, the idea of *research strategy* was introduced as a broad orientation to social research with a focus on the distinction between quantitative and qualitative research strategies. But the decision to adopt one or the other strategy is only a

beginning; two other key general decisions also have to be made: choosing a *research design* and choosing a *research method*. On the face of it, these two terms would seem to mean the same thing, but there is a crucial distinction between them (see Box 2.1).

Box 2.1 🔆 *What is a research design?*

A *research design* provides a framework for the collection and analysis of data. A choice of research design reflects decisions about the priority being given to a range of dimensions of the research process, including the importance attached to:

- expressing causal connections between variables;

- having a temporal (i.e., over time) appreciation of social phenomena, their interconnections, and process;

- understanding behaviour and the meaning of that behaviour in its specific social context, including validity; and

- generalizing to larger groups of individuals other than those actually forming part of the investigation; deciding on sample size.

A *research method*, on the other hand, is simply a technique for collecting data. It can involve a specific instrument, such as a self-completion questionnaire or a structured interview schedule, or participant observation in which the researcher listens to and watches others, even lives among them for a time.

Research designs are broad structures that guide the execution of a specific research method and the analysis of the subsequent data. For example, one of the research designs to be covered in this chapter—the case study—entails a detailed exploration of a specific case, which could be a community, organization, or person. But once a case has been selected, a research method(s) is still needed to collect data. Simply selecting an organization and deciding to study it intensively are not going to provide data. Do you observe? Do you conduct interviews? Do you examine documents? Do you administer questionnaires? In fact any or all of these *research methods* can be used, and the point to remember is that choosing a design is only a first step.

In this chapter, four research designs are examined: experimental design and its subtypes, including the quasi-experiment; cross-sectional or survey design; longitudinal design; and case study design. However, before embarking on the nature of and differences among them, a few of the recurring issues in social research that cut across some or all of them are first considered.

Criteria in social research

Three of the most prominent criteria for the evaluation of social research are *reliability*, *replication*, and *validity*. Each will be examined in much greater detail in later chapters, but a brief treatment here is helpful.

Reliability

Reliability is concerned with whether the results of a study would be the same if the study were repeated. The quantitative researcher is particularly concerned with whether measures devised for social science concepts (such as poverty, racial prejudice, and religious orthodoxy) are consistent or not. For example, if results on a new intelligence test are unstable and fluctuate, so that people's scores are quite different when administered on two or more occasions or by different psychometrists, that inconsistency would mean that the new test is an unreliable measure. Chapter 3 will look at the idea of reliability in greater detail, in particular at its different forms.

Replication

The idea of reliability is related to another criterion of research—*replicability*, whether others are able to repeat part or all of a study. There may be many reasons for doing so, such as a feeling that the results do not match prior evidence on the same topic. For replication to take place, the initial researcher must have spelled out all research procedures in great detail.

Validity

A further and in many ways the most important criterion of research is *validity*, which is concerned with the integrity of the conclusions generated by a piece of research. Like reliability, the idea of validity will be examined in greater detail in later chapters, but in the meantime it is important to be aware of the main types of validity typically distinguished:

- *Measurement validity.* This criterion, sometimes referred to as *construct validity*, applies primarily to quantitative research and its measures of social concepts. Essentially, it refers to whether a measure really reflects the concept it is supposed to denote. Does an IQ test really measure intelligence? In the study reported in Box 1.6, three concepts needed to be measured: national religiosity, religious orthodoxy, and family religious orientation. The question then is do the measures really represent the concepts they are supposed to be tapping? If they do not, the study's findings are questionable. Moreover, measurement validity is related to reliability: if a measure of a concept is unstable and hence unreliable, it simply cannot be a valid measure of the concept in question. One of the measures might be valid, but a researcher would not be able to know which one. In other words, the assessment of measurement validity presupposes that a measure is reliable.

- *Internal validity*. This form of validity relates mainly to causality, dealt with in greater detail in Chapter 3. For example, in the study examined in Box 1.6, the authors concluded that a nation's religious environment affects the religious beliefs of its citizens (Kelley and De Graaf 1997). Internal validity asks whether the religious environment is really responsible for variation in religious beliefs: could the cause be something else? In discussing issues of causality, it is common to refer to the factor that has a causal impact as the *independent variable* and the corresponding effect as the *dependent variable* (see Box 2.2). In the case of Kelley and De Graaf's research, the 'religious environment of a nation' is the independent variable, and religious belief is the dependent. Thus, internal validity raises the issue of degree of confidence that the independent variable really is, at least in part, responsible for the variation in the dependent variable.

- *External validity*. This criterion asks whether social scientific findings are applicable to people's everyday, natural, social settings or whether social research sometimes produces findings that, while technically valid, are artificial and would not occur in real life. The more the social scientist intervenes in natural settings or creates unnatural ones, such as a laboratory (or even just a special room to carry out interviews), the greater the chance that findings will be externally *in*valid. Measurement validity and a reasonable level of internal validity cannot guarantee external validity.

External validity is also concerned with whether the results of a study can be generalized beyond the specific research context in which the data were collected. The study in Box 1.5 asked 57 male, adolescent volunteers about their delinquency and if any of the currently popular sociological theories of delinquency could explain their behaviour. How far can these findings be generalized: to other male adolescents at the school attended, to all Canadian male adolescents? If they are fully externally valid, they can. If they possess no external validity, their findings apply to just the 57 boys studied and to no others. Usually external validity falls between these extremes and it is in this context that the issue of how people are selected to participate in research becomes crucial. This is one of the main reasons why quantitative researchers are so keen to generate *representative* samples (see Chapter 11).

Box 2.2 ⌇◉⌇ *What is a variable?*

A variable is simply an attribute on which cases differ from one another—on religion, for example, with Catholics, Protestants, Jews, Muslims, etc. 'Cases' can be people, but they can also be households, cities, organizations, schools, and nations. If an attribute does not vary but is the same for all, it is a *constant*. Constants are rarely of interest to social researchers. For example, according to a recent news item, more German motorists stuck in traffic (33 per cent of them) think about sex than about other things like alternative routes, running out of gas, or a bathroom stop. Interesting, but social researchers would want to compare men and women perhaps, or those drivers with some from France in order to understand variation and thus to know why. It is common to distinguish between different types of variables. The most basic distinction is between an *independent* and *dependent variable*. The former is deemed to have a causal influence on the latter.

Relationship with research strategy

One striking feature of the discussion so far is that it seems to somewhat ignore qualitative research. Both reliability and measurement validity are essentially concerned with the adequacy of measures, which are more of a concern in quantitative research. Internal validity is concerned with the soundness of the causal connection, an issue also of greater concern to quantitative researchers. The issue of external validity relates to the naturalness of the research approach and seems to have considerable relevance to both qualitative and quantitative research; but the representativeness of samples of research subjects has a more obvious application to quantitative research.

Some qualitative researchers even argue that applying the concepts of reliability and validity to their research is inappropriate, that the basis of these ideas in quantitative research renders them inapplicable to qualitative research. They propose that their

---

Box 2.3 ⌣ᣰᣰᣰ *What is naturalism?*

Naturalism is a term that not only has different meanings, but also has meanings that can be contradictory. It is possible to identify three different meanings:

- With clear affinities to positivism, one meaning essentially proposes a unity between the objects of the natural and the social sciences and because of this, no reason for social scientists to go beyond the traditional natural science approaches.

- *Naturalism means being true to the nature of the phenomenon being investigated.* This meaning represents a fusion of elements of an interpretivist epistemology and a constructionist ontology, examined in Chapter 1. Here naturalism recognizes that people attribute meaning to behaviour and are authors of their social

world rather than passive objects. Thus, they require a unique research design.

- *Naturalism is a style of research that seeks to minimize the use of artificial methods of data collection.* This meaning implies that the social world should be as undisturbed as possible when being studied (Hammersley and Atkinson 1995: 6).

The second and third meanings overlap and are incompatible with, and indeed opposed to, the first, which ignores the human capacity to interpret the social world and to be active agents, and also uses artificial methods of data collection, like asking questions rather than actually observing behaviour. When writers are described as *anti-naturalists*, it is invariably this first meaning they reject.

---

studies should be judged or evaluated according to different criteria. For example, Lincoln and Guba (1985) proposed *trustworthiness* as a criterion of how good a qualitative study is. Each aspect of trustworthiness has a parallel with the previous quantitative research criteria.

- *Credibility*, which parallels measurement and internal validity—that is, how believable are the findings? Did the investigator allow personal values to ruin any chance of intersubjectivity?

- *Transferability*, which parallels external validity—that is, do the findings apply to other contexts?

- *Dependability*, which parallels reliability—that is, are the findings likely to be consistent over time?

- *Confirmability*, which parallels replicability—that is, will another investigator reach the same conclusions?

These criteria will be returned to in Chapter 8 and the distinctive features of qualitative research further examined in later chapters.

While external validity may have been formulated largely in the context of quantitative research, it is actually a criterion on which qualitative research fares rather well. Qualitative research often involves a *naturalistic* stance (see Box 2.3). This means that the researcher collects data in naturally occurring situations and environments, as opposed to artificial ones. Living with people for months to observe their behaviour and intensive interviewing both may allow greater external validity of results.

By and large, these issues have been presented because some of them will emerge in the context of the discussion of research designs in the next section. But in a number of ways they also represent background considerations for some of the issues to be examined and then revisited later in the book.

Research designs

In this discussion of research designs, four different types are examined: experimental design; cross-sectional or survey design; longitudinal design; and case study design. Variations on these designs are examined in their relevant subsections.

Experimental design

True experiments are quite unusual in sociology, but are employed in certain areas, such as social psychology and studies of organizations. Researchers in social policy may also use them to assess the impact of reforms or new policies. As they are uncommon, then why introduce experimental designs at all in a book about social research? The chief reason is that *a true experiment is often used as a yardstick against which non-experimental research is assessed*. Experimental research is frequently held up as a touchstone, because it engenders considerable confidence in the robustness and trustworthiness of causal findings. In other words, true experiments tend to be very strong in terms of internal validity.

Manipulation

If experiments are so strong in this respect, why do social researchers not make more use of them? The reason is simple: to conduct a true experiment, it is necessary to do something to people and look for any effects, or more formally, to *manipulate* an independent variable to determine its influence on a dependent variable. More specifically, subjects are allocated to one of two or more experimental groups, each representing a different type or level of the independent variable, and then watched for corresponding types or levels of the dependent variable. However, the vast majority of independent variables of concern to social researchers cannot be manipu-

lated. If interested in the effects of gender identity on work experiences, some people cannot be made masculine and others feminine. If the topic is the effects of different religions on political attitudes or on health, people cannot be forced to practice or to convert to a different religion. As with the huge majority of such variables, ethical issues would not permit this social engineering (see Ethical issue 2.1).

Before moving to a more complete discussion of experimental design, it is important to introduce a basic distinction between *laboratory* and *field experiment*. The former takes place in an artificial setting, the latter in real-life settings such as in classrooms and factories. Box 2.4 describes a well-known example of a field experiment.

Classic experimental design

The research in Box 2.4 includes most of the essential features of what is known as classical experimental design. Students are randomly assigned to two groups. The experimental manipulation (the independent variable)—in this case, teacher expectations—is given to what is known as the *experimental group* or *treatment group* (the spurters); the other group is not given any expectations and thus forms a *control group*. The dependent variable—student performance—is meas-

---

Ethical issue 2.1 *The infamous case of the psychologist as Nazi concentration camp commandant*

Milgram (1963) was concerned with the use of brutality in the Nazi concentration camps of the Second World War. In particular, he was interested in how a person can be induced to cause extreme harm to another and if being ordered to do so would be sufficient. Milgram devised a laboratory experiment asking volunteers to act as 'teachers' who punished 'learners' (actually accomplices of the experimenter) by giving them electric shocks for incorrect answers to questions. The shocks were not, of course, real, but the teachers/volunteers were not aware of this nor did they know that the learners had been trained to respond to the rising level of electric shock with simulated but appropriate howls of pain. Some teachers were further disadvantaged in that they could not see, only hear, their 'students' who were hidden from them. In all instances teachers were told that shocking was part of

the study and that they were not causing permanent harm, in spite of the increasingly shrill cries of pain. The experiment continued until the teacher/volunteer refused to administer more shocks; most had great difficulty when the learner loudly complained of heart trouble, this followed by ominous silence.

Milgram's study showed that people can be induced to cause considerable pain to others. Further, in one variant of the experiment, the subject did not have to administer the shock directly but could order another (actually an accomplice of Milgram's) to shock the learner. In this instance more than 90 per cent of the subjects ordered the greatest shocks. Milgram saw these results as shedding light on the circumstances leading to the horrors of the concentration camp. Could he have told the volunteers he wanted to see if they would act like Nazis?

Box 2.4 A field experiment

Rosenthal and Jacobson (1968) suspected that teachers' expectations influence their students' school performance. The research was conducted in a poor US school with many minority group children enrolled. In the spring all students completed a test presented to them as a means of identifying 'spurters'—that is, students who were likely to excel academically. At the beginning of the following academic year, the teachers were given the names of the spurters in their class. In fact, a random 20 per cent of the schoolchildren had been identified as spurters. The test was re-administered eight months after the original one, allowing the authors to compare the so-called spurters and the other students for changes in academic performance, such as IQ scores, reading ability, and intellectual curiosity. Since there was no initial difference in ability between the spurters and the others, any improvements could be attributed to the fact that the teachers had been led to expect the former would perform better. The findings did show such differences, but they tended to be concentrated in the first two or three years of schooling.

ured before the experimental manipulation to make sure that the two groups really are equal, on average, at the start (see Figure 2.1). If they are, and because of random assignment they should be, the researchers can feel confident that any differences in student performance found between the two groups *after* the manipulation is teacher expectation that the spurters would fare better at school than the others. Everything else in the two groups is the same, leaving that the only explanation.

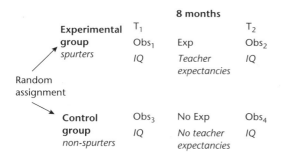

Figure 2.1 Classical experimental design

To capture the essence of this design, the following simple notation is used:

- **Obs:** an **obs**ervation made of the dependent variable; there may be more than two observations but, to simplify, the design shows the most common configuration: a *pre-test* and a *post-test,* here perhaps, IQ test scores and reading levels before the experimental manipulation and after.

- **Exp:** the **exp**erimental treatment (independent variable), such as the creation of teacher expectancies. **No Exp** refers to the absence of an experimental treatment and represents the experience of the control group.

- **T:** the **t**iming of the observations made in relation to the dependent variable, such as when an IQ test is administered.

Classic experimental design and validity

What is the purpose of the control group? Surely it is what happens to the spurters (the experimental group) that is really of concern. But for a study to be a true experiment, it must control (in other words, eliminate) rival explanations of a causal finding, leaving teacher expectations alone as having an impact on student performance. Of course, student performance is a much more complex phenomenon, but the present study only wants to examine one factor (teacher expectation) in it. The presence of a control group *and* the random assignment of subjects to both the experimental and control group eliminate such rival explanations and give the study its internal validity. To see this, consider some of the rival explanations that might occur if there were *no* control group, each a potential threat to internal validity (see Box 2.5). These threats are taken from a longer list (see Cook and Campbell 1979). In each, the prospect of a rival interpretation of a causal finding is offered, but the presence of a control group coupled with random assignment allows its elimination as a threat. As a result, confidence in the causal finding, that teacher expectations influence student performance, is greatly enhanced.

However, simply because research is deemed to be internally valid does not mean that questions cannot be raised about it. First, there is the question of measurement validity. In the case of the Rosenthal and

---

Box 2.5 Threats to internal validity (and their application to Rosenthal and Jacobson's 1968 study)

- *History*. This refers to events other than the manipulation of teacher expectations that also occurred and thus may have caused the spurters' scores to rise. The action of the school's principal to raise standards in the school is one such event. Without a control group, one cannot be sure if it was the teachers' expectations or the head's actions that produced the increase in spurters' grades. With the control group there, one can say that history should have an effect on the control subjects too and therefore differences between the experimental and control groups can be attributed to the effect of teacher expectations alone.

- *Testing*. This threat refers to the possibility that subjects may become more experienced at taking a test or sensitized to the aims of the experiment as a result of the pre-test. The presence of a control group, which presumably would also experience the same things, diminishes this possibility.

- *Instrumentation*. This threat refers to the possibility that changes in the way a test is administered can account for an increase (or decrease) in scores between a pre-test and post-test, for example, the teachers knowing their students better or being more friendly the second time they give the test. Again, if there is a control group, this should affect the control group as well.

- *Mortality*. This relates to the problem of attrition found especially in studies that span a long period of time; here subjects may have moved to a different school. Since this problem is likely to afflict the control group too, it is possible to account for its threat relative to the impact and importance of teacher expectancies.

- *Maturation*. Quite simply, people change and the ways in which they change may have implications for the dependent variable. The spurters may have improved anyway, just because they are older, regardless of the effect of teacher expectancies. The control group who ages the same amount casts doubt on this possibility.

- *Selection*. When students are not assigned by a random process to the experimental and control group, variations between them in the post-test may be due to any pre-existing differences in their membership. However, since a random process of assignment to the experimental and control groups was employed here, this possibility is reduced.

Jacobson (1968) study, there are potentially two aspects to this. One is the question of whether academic performance is adequately measured. Measures like reading scores seem to possess *face validity*, in the sense that they appear to exhibit a correspondence with what they are measuring. However, given the controversy surrounding IQ tests and what they measure, one may feel somewhat uneasy about how far gains in IQ test scores can be regarded as indicative of academic performance. Similarly, to take another of the authors' measures, intellectual curiosity—is that a valid measure of academic performance? Does it really measure what it is supposed to measure?

Another question relating to measurement validity is whether the experimental manipulation really worked. In other words, did the random identification of some schoolchildren as spurters adequately create the conditions needed for the self-fulfilling prophecy to be examined? The study very much relies on the teachers being duped by the procedure, but it is possi-ble that they were not all equally fooled, thus contaminating the manipulation.

Second, is the research externally valid? This issue is considered in Box 2.6. The fact that the research is a field experiment in a real school rather than a laboratory experiment enhances this aspect of the Rosenthal and Jacobson research. Also, the fact that the students and the teachers seem to have had little if any appreciation of their participation in an experiment may also have enhanced external validity, though at the same time this deception raises enormous *ethical* concerns (see Ethical issues 2.2 through 2.4).

A third issue relates to the question of replicability. The authors laid out very clearly their procedures and measures and anyone carrying out a replication could obtain further information from them. Consequently, the research is replicable, although there has not been an exact replication. Clairborn (1969) conducted one of the earliest replications and followed a

Box 2.6 Threats to external validity (and their application to Rosenthal and Jacobson's 1968 study)

Cook and Campbell (1979) identified five major threats to the external validity and hence generalizability of an investigation:

- *Interaction of selection and treatment*. This threat raises the question: to what social and psychological groups can a finding be generalized? Can it be generalized to a wide variety of individuals who differ in ethnicity, social class, region, gender, and type of personality? In the case of the Rosenthal and Jacobson study, the students were largely from poorer groups and a large proportion from ethnic minorities. This is a limitation on the generalizability of the findings.

- *Interaction of setting and treatment*. This threat relates to confidence that the results of a study can be applied to other settings, in Rosenthal and Jacobson's case, to other schools. There is then the wider issue of confidence that the operation of self-fulfilling prophecies can also be discerned in non-educational settings. In fact, Rosenthal and others have been able to demonstrate the role and significance of the self-fulfilling prophecy in a wide variety of different contexts (Rosnow and Rosenthal 1997), though this still does not answer the question of whether their specific findings can be generalized. One set of grounds for being uneasy about generalizing Rosenthal and Jacobson's findings is that they were allowed an inordinate amount of freedom for conducting their investigation from school authorities, indicative of the school being atypical.

- *Interaction of history and treatment*. This threat raises the question of whether the findings can be generalized to the past and to the future. The Rosenthal and Jacobson research was conducted 40 years ago. Would the findings still apply today? Also, their investigation was conducted at a particular juncture in the school academic year. Would the same results have obtained if the research had been conducted at different points in the year?

- *Interaction effects of pre-testing*. As a result of being pre-tested, subjects in an experiment may become sensitized to the experimental treatment, affecting their responses as they become more test-wise. Consequently, the findings may not be generalizable to groups *not* pre-tested, and, of course, in the real world people are rarely pre-tested. This may have occurred in the Rosenthal and Jacobson research, since all students were pre-tested at the end of the previous academic year.

- *Reactive effects of experimental arrangements*. People are frequently, if not invariably, aware of the fact that they are participating in an experiment. Their awareness may influence how they respond to the experimental treatment and therefore affect the generalizability of the findings. Since Rosenthal and Jacobson's subjects do not appear to have been aware of their participating in an experiment, this problem is unlikely to have been significant. The issue of *reactivity* and its potentially damaging effects is a recurring theme in many methods of social research.

procedure very similar to Rosenthal and Jacobson's. The study was carried out in three, middle-class, suburban schools and the timing of the creation of teacher expectancies was different from the original study. Clairborn failed to replicate Rosenthal and Jacobson's findings, casting doubt on the external validity of the original research and suggesting that the first three threats referred to in Box 2.6 may have played important parts in the differences between the two sets of results. Finally, was there some of inadvertently seeing what they wanted to see?

The laboratory experiment

One of the main advantages of laboratory over field experiments is the researcher's greater control over the experiment; it is easier to randomly assign subjects to different experimental conditions in the laboratory than in a real-life organization. This enhances the internal validity of the study. For example, Walsh *et al.* (1999) could tell some university students in Eastern Canada that previous results on the mathematics test they were about to take showed that women perform less well than men. Others were not told this. The data showed that women scored lower than men when informed of this 'fact.' When told that the test was to compare Canadians and Americans, there was no gender difference. Laboratory experiments also are more easily replicated because they are less bound to a specific milieu that would be difficult to reproduce.

Ethical issue 2.2 *Informed consent for experiments*

Homan (1991: 73) observed that implementing the principle of informed consent 'is easier said than done.' At least two major points stand out here.

- It is extremely difficult to present prospective participants with absolutely all the information required to make an informed decision about their involvement. In fact, relatively minor ethical transgressions probably pervade most social research, such as not giving absolutely all the details about the research for fear of contaminating people's answers to questions. On the other hand, Hessler *et al.*'s study of adolescent risk behaviour (2003) included what they described as a consent form that read like the sheets a pharmacist hands out when dispensing strong prescription medications.

- In ethnographic research, the researcher is likely to come into contact with a wide spectrum of people, and ensuring that absolutely everyone has the opportunity for informed consent is not practicable. Even when all research participants in a certain setting are aware that the ethnographer is a researcher, it is doubtful whether they are all similarly (let alone identically) informed about the nature of the research.

Outright deception is another issue. *Most experiments involve deception* because researchers want to limit participants' understanding of what the research is about so that they respond more naturally to the experimental treatment. For example, Goode (1996) placed four fake and slightly different dating advertisements in periodicals. He received nearly 1,000 replies and was able to analyze how each advertisement led to different results.

It is rarely feasible or desirable to provide participants with a totally complete account of what the research is about. Could students be told that half of them would meet an experimenter with a 'gay and proud' button, the other half no button, to investigate campus homophobia? Thus there are bound to be instances such as this where deception is deemed not only justifiable but if not done would make the research useless.

There are only two rules about deception. One is that it should be allowed only as a very last resort. The Nazi study would not work as a questionnaire. But could not students just fill in an anonymous questionnaire about their homophobia? The other rule is that anyone deceived must be debriefed as quickly as possible, and told of the deception. How did Milgram's subjects feel after their debriefing, to know that they were in a study about Nazis?

However, laboratory experiments like the one described in Box 2.7 also suffer from a number of limitations. First, the external validity is probably low, since the laboratory setting is unlikely to mirror real-world experiences and contexts, despite the fact that the subjects are very involved in most experiments and take them very seriously.

Also, there is likely to be an interaction of selection and treatment (see Box 2.6). In the case of Howell and Frost's (1989) study described in Box 2.7, for example, there are a number of difficulties. The subjects were students and not representative of the general population, if only for their youth, so that their responses to the experimental treatment may have been distinctive. They were volunteers, who generally differ from non-volunteers (Rosnow and Rosenthal 1997: ch. 5); as well, they were given incentives to participate, which may further separate them from others because not everyone will be

equally motivated to earn the money and thus participate. See Ethical issue 2.5. There was no effect of pre-testing because, like many experiments, there was none. However, it is quite feasible that reactive effects may have been set in motion by the experimental arrangements themselves.

Quasi-experiments

Quasi-experiments have certain characteristics of experimental designs but do not fulfill all the internal validity requirements. A large number of different types of quasi-experiments have been identified (Cook and Campbell 1979) and all of them cannot be covered here. A particularly interesting form is the case of 'natural experiments,' entailing the manipulation of an independent variable but in a real social setting, in an attempt to alter real social arrangements. In such circumstances, it is almost impossible to randomly assign subjects to experimental

Ethical issue 2.3 *Harm to participants*

Research likely to harm participants is regarded by almost everyone as unacceptable. But what is 'harm'? Harm can entail a number of facets: physical harm, loss of self-esteem, stress, and making subjects do things they will later be embarrassed to have performed. Then, what does 'is likely' mean: a 1 per cent chance, .01 per cent, 5 per cent? Researchers should anticipate and guard against consequences for research participants that are expected to be harmful or disturbing. Still:

- In the Rosenthal and Jacobson (1968) study (Box 2.5), it is at least possible that the pupils not identified as spurters but who could have excelled in their studies were adversely affected in their intellectual development by the greater attention received by the spurters;

- In the Festinger *et al.* (1956) study of a religious cult, the researchers (joining the group at a crucial time, close to the projected end of the world), encouraged delusions of group members who thought they were being successful in recruiting converts;

- In the Milgram experiment (1963) on obedience to authority, many of the participants experienced high levels of stress and anxiety after being incited to administer electric shocks.

The issue of harm to participants is further addressed in ethical codes advocating care over maintaining confidentiality of the identities and records of individuals. This injunction also means ensuring that when findings are published the individuals are not identifiable. The study of an American town, 'Springdale' (a pseudonym), by Vidich and Bensman (1968) is instructive in this regard. The published book on the research was uncomplimentary about the town and many of its leaders, and was written in what many people felt was a rather patronizing tone. To make matters worse, it was possible to identify individuals in the published account. The town's inhabitants responded with a Fourth of July Parade in which many of them wore badges citing their book pseudonyms, and an effigy of Vidich was set up so that it was peering into manure. The townspeople also announced their refusal to cooperate in any more social research; they were clearly upset by the publication and to that extent were harmed by it.

One of the problems with the no-harm-to-participants principle is that it is not possible to identify in all circumstances whether harm is likely, though that fact should not be taken to mean that there is no point in seeking to protect them. Kimmel (1988) noted in this connection the example of the 1939 Cambridge–Summerville Youth Study, an experiment conducted on 506 boys aged 5 to 13 who were identified either as likely to become delinquent or to be just average in this regard. The boys, equally divided in terms of this characteristic, were randomly assigned to either an experimental group to receive preventive counselling or to a no-treatment control group. In the mid-1970s the boys (by then men) were examined and results were quite shocking. 'Treated subjects were more likely than controls to evidence signs of alcoholism and serious mental illness, died at a younger age, suffered from more stress-related diseases, tended to be employed in lower-prestige occupations, and were more likely to commit second crimes' (1988: 19).

In other words, the treatment brought negative consequences to the group. This is an extreme example and relates to an experiment, not common in social research, but it does illustrate the difficulty of anticipating harm to respondents. For another example, most students would not think that a questionnaire on marital happiness might start a respondent thinking, then questioning, and finally leaving a marriage. Could asking a grade eight boy in gym class about steroid use, something unknown to him, encourage experimentation? Some interviewees even find the questions asked them unsettling or find the cut and thrust of a focus group discussion stressful, especially if they inadvertently reveal more than they might intend. How should they be informed?

All ethical codes suggest that when there is any prospect of harm to participants, if the risks of research are greater than the risks of everyday life, informed consent, the focus of Ethical issue 2.2, is essential. If uninformed participants are harmed as a result of the research, the investigator is more culpable than if they were informed and knew some of the risks involved in their participation.

Ethical issue 2.4 *Who defines harm?*

Who is the final arbiter of harm? It is probably up to the local ethics committee housed at universities and other places of research, and made up of researchers and perhaps a layperson or two. As an aside, do the former have a conflict of interest as they too will eventually face a similar body, even some of their co-members? How likely is it that the lay members will overrule the experts?

Pretend those two issues are well handled, though certainly the latter is often not. The rule of thumb when harm is expected is that it should not outweigh the bene-

fits of the research. Again, who defines these terms and what is the benefit of a publication for a researcher? Most social scientists are not curing cancer or ending racism. A tongue-in-cheek ethics report of 40 years ago pointed out the risks of a clinical trial of an 'umbrelly' contraceptive for males, measured against the benefits of unencumbered sex for females. The all-female ethics committee agreed to the project despite such potential 'small' risks as a 5 per cent chance of male impotence, some bleeding, and if all goes wrong, even perhaps a death.

and control groups. An example is provided in Box 2.8. The absence of random assignment casts doubt on the study's internal validity, since the groups may not have been equivalent before the independent variable was introduced. However, the results of such studies are still compelling because they are real rather than artificial interventions in social life; therefore, they possess stronger external validity and occasionally one comes across a single-group natural experiment that is particularly striking (see Box 2.9).

Quasi-experimental designs have been particularly prominent in *evaluation research* studies (see Box

2.10). Sometimes the results are surprising. A quasi-experimental investigation of the effect of support for caregivers of the elderly (Demers 1996) showed that the extra support makes caregivers feel less depressed; but they feel *more* and not less burdened. She was not sure why—perhaps the help offered is seen as something else to be coordinated and managed.

Significance of experimental design

As stated at the outset, the chief reason for introducing the experiment as a research design is because of its frequent use as a yardstick against which quantita-

Box 2.7 A laboratory experiment

Howell and Frost (1989) were interested in whether charismatic leadership is more effective in organizations than two other leadership approaches—considerate and structuring. They conducted a laboratory experiment to test a number of hypotheses, including one that individuals working under a charismatic leader have higher task performance than those under a considerate leader (Howell and Frost 1989: 245). Course grades were enhanced by 3 per cent for the 144 students who volunteered for the experiment (what ethical issue does that raise?). They were randomly assigned to work on a simulated business task under one of the three types of leadership, all three performed by two female actresses. In broad conformity with the hypotheses, subjects working under charismatic leaders score generally higher in terms of measures of task performance than those working under other leaders, particularly the considerate leader.

Ethical issue 2.5 *A monetary incentive*

The participants in the Dinovitzer *et al.* (2003) study on educational attainment among immigrants were offered five dollars to participate. Probably no one answered the questionnaire simply for the small amount of money involved. Still, many ethics review boards do not allow paying subjects for their participation except to cover actual costs such as parking, etc. They do so to protect the poor from 'selling' themselves to researchers. And few would be too critical of Beagan's (2002) offer to medical students for a chance at a $200 draw (which technically gets around the payment idea) for taking part in her study of discrimination. But would offering $10,000 for testing a promising drug with potentially dangerous side effects be acceptable? What about selling a kidney for research purposes? You get the idea.

Box 2.8 Quasi-experiments

A common type of quasi-experiment is to compare data taken before and after a policy shift by government or industry. For a hypothetical example, the number of car accidents before and after the lowering of a speed limit can be examined. If the number goes down, this can be interpreted as a success of the change, but one cannot be sure because there is no control group not experiencing the change. Perhaps it is just the publicity surrounding the policy change that reduces the rate.

In the case of the installation of cameras to detect speeding, if the cameras are placed only in randomly selected places and not in others, the research is changed from a quasi- to a real experiment. This gives the two groups (camera and control) and the before and after structure needed to examine cause and effect.

Governments find it difficult, however, to subject some people to one condition and others to another; therefore, they often make do with quasi-experimental evaluations of policy changes. A criminologist may want to randomly assign criminals to jail or home custody and then compare the two forms of detention, but the potential for some of the at-homes to re-commit crimes would be seen as too great a cost. Because minor criminals are more likely to get home custody than are more serious criminals, a fair test is not possible. The prison system is part of the real social world, just as the school is. It is not an artificial laboratory and therefore assignment is determined not by scientific but by government and civil needs. For example, when Canada abolished the death penalty, it was not meant as an experiment but as a significant policy decision. The resulting data could be examined as if the change were part of a quasi-experiment, but the legislation was definitely not set up for that purpose.

Box 2.9 A natural (quasi-) experiment

The effect of television violence on children is one of the most contested areas of social research. St Helena in the South Atlantic provided a fascinating laboratory for the examination of the various claims, when television was introduced to the island for the first time in the mid-1990s. The findings—from 15 hours of video footage observing children at play during school breaks, from diaries kept by about three hundred of the children, and from ratings by teachers—reveal that children do not copy the violence they see on TV (Midgley 1998: 5). A report of the findings in *The Times* in April 1998 found that 'the shared experience of watching television made them less likely to tease each other and to fight, and more likely to enjoy books' (Frean 1998: 7). The reports of the research in academic journals confirm that there is no evidence that the introduction of television leads to an increase in anti-social behaviour (e.g., Charlton *et al.* 1998, 1999).

amination of experiments reveals. A central feature of any experiment is a *comparison*: at the very least it compares results obtained from an experimental group with those of a control group. In the case of the Howell and Frost (1989) experiment in Box 2.7, although there is no control group, the research still compared the effects of three different forms of leadership. The advantage of any kind of comparison like this is that there is a better understanding of the phenomenon at question than looking at it alone. The case for arguing that charismatic leadership is an effective, performance-enhancing form of leadership is much more persuasive when viewed in relation to forms of leadership that are less effective. Thus, while the experimental design is typically associated with a quantitative research strategy, the specific logic of comparison provides lessons of broad applicability and relevance.

Cross-sectional design

The cross-sectional design is often connected in people's minds with questionnaires and structured interviewing. But other research methods also are used in cross-sectional research, including structured observation and analysis of official statistics or diaries.

tive research is judged. This occurs largely because a true experiment reduces doubts about internal validity and can determine causality. As seen in the next section, cross-sectional designs of the kind associated with survey research are frequently regarded as limited for being the opposite—because of greater problems of imputing causality unambiguously.

Logic of comparison

Before exploring such issues, it is important to draw attention to an important general lesson that an ex-

Box 2.10 ⚙ *What is evaluation research?*

Evaluation research examines the effects of organizational innovation, such as a longer school day or greater worker autonomy in a plant. A more specific example comes from examining a report from the Pivot Legal Society in BC, urging repeal of Canadian prostitution laws. Based on interviews with 91 prostitutes, the society found, for example, that the law against communicating for the purpose of prostitution (prostitution itself is not illegal) is problematic. It forces prostitutes to make their arrangements in back alleys, where they are vulnerable to assault by their clients and others, or to jump into cars before they have fully ascertained how safe they will be. Others will object to any change in the law, saying it will increase the numbers of prostitutes, make them more of a public nuisance, and even that underage boys will become vulnerable to their lure. Which side wins is a political issue, a 'should' question, but the validity of the claims is for evaluation research to resolve.

The essential question usually asked by such studies is whether the new policy initiative or organizational change achieved its anticipated goals? A typical design has one group that is exposed to the treatment, that is the new initiative, and a control group that is not. Since it is often not feasible or ethical to randomly assign research participants to the two groups, certainly not in the situation just described, such studies are usually quasi-experimental. Or data from everyone before a change may be compared with data from after; the before becomes the control group, before intervention, the after the experimental group and there is the added advantage that the

two groups are basically the same, making random assignment unnecessary. That would be the case for the prostitution study, or more realistically, if Ontario reintroduces photo radar and the number of red lights run is compared before and after its implementation.

Experimental designs are fairly entrenched in evaluation research, but in recent years evaluations based on qualitative research have emerged. Although there are differences of opinion about how qualitative evaluation should be carried out, there is consensus on the importance of a full understanding of the context in which an intervention occurs and the diverse viewpoints of the stakeholders (Greene 2000). For example, Pawson and Tilley (1997) advocated a *critical realism* approach (see Box 1.9) and a focus on the factors that inhibit or promote change after any intervention. Tilley (2000) later outlined an early example of the approach in an evaluation of closed-circuit television (CCTV) in car parks. He observed that there are several ways in which CCTV can deter car crime, including a direct deterrence of offenders and a greater usage of car parks that in itself increases surveillance. These are the causes. Examples of contexts are: time (such as periods of constant use, while the car park fills up and empties during rush-hour periods or slow times during the day); blind spots in car parks; and the availability of other nearby venues for offenders to commit car crimes. The kind of evaluation research advocated by Pawson and Tilley maps the different combinations of cause and context in relation to different outcomes.

Box 2.11 Description, explanation, prediction, and control

This discussion of cause is also related to the issues of description and explanation. Quantitative research often explains a phenomenon in terms of inferred causes and effects. Qualitative research, on the other hand, is often content to describe a phenomenon. Cause cannot be seen and is therefore not described. Feminist researchers especially may avoid causal inference, seeing it as a first step to prediction and even control. Their preference for lack of hierarchy in scientific investigation would preclude such a process.

A local paper (*London Free Press*, 19 February 2004) reported a 20-year study that related marital conflict resolu-

tion to chance of divorce in more than six hundred couples. Matches involving two conflict avoiders, or two constant fighters, or two who respect one another despite an occasional argument have marriages that last. Mixing any of those three styles in one marriage spells trouble, as when a constant fighter marries an avoider. But that is not the main point. The main point is that the researchers developed a simple graphic formula for predicting marital outcome. Couples could be tested and then act on the basis of their scores.

Each will be covered in later chapters, but in the meantime the basic structure of the cross-sectional design is outlined. For any method, the difference between a cross-sectional design and an experiment is that there is only one measure, not a before and after—a snapshot taken at one point in time. In the case of the Rosenthal and Jacobson (1968) study, eight months separated the pre- and post-testing of the schoolchildren in the study.

The cross-sectional design is defined in Box 2.12. Two elements related to this definition should also be emphasized:

- *More than one case*. Researchers employing a cross-sectional design are interested in variation in respect of people, families, nation states, or whatever, and variation can be established only when more than one case is being examined. Usually researchers employing this design select many cases, for a variety of reasons. First, the larger number makes it more likely to encounter variation in *all* of the variables of interest and permits finer distinctions between cases. Ten cases may allow a high–low comparison, but 100 will allow a very high, high, average, low, and very low comparison. Second, requirements of statistical techniques are likely to require larger numbers (see Chapter 12).

- *Patterns of association*. With a cross-sectional design, only *relationships* between variables can be examined, not causes. There is no time-ordering to the variables, because the data on them are collected more or less simultaneously, and the researcher does not, usually, cannot, manipulate any of them. This creates the problem referred to in Box 2.12 as 'ambiguity about the direction of causal influence.' All that can be said for certain is that the variables 'go together.' As will be shown in Chapter 12, there are a number of ways for researchers to draw cautious inferences about causality, but they rarely have the credibility of causal findings deriving from an experimental design. As a result, cross-sectional research invariably lacks the internal validity that one finds in

---

Box 2.12 Cross-sectional design and internal validity

A cross-sectional design entails the collection of data (usually quantitative) on *more than one case* (usually many more than one) and at *a single point in time,* on two or more variables (usually more than two), which are then examined to detect *patterns of association*. The practice makes it difficult to show cause because the independent and dependent variables are measured simultaneously, making any demonstration of temporal order, that the cause actually precedes the effect, harder to specify.

For example, there is a well-supported negative relationship between social class and serious forms of mental illness—more poor people are mentally ill. But there is also a debate about that relationship: does being poor lead to stress and therefore to mental illness (called *social causation*)? Or does being mentally ill lead to difficulties in holding down a job and thus poverty (called *social selection*)? Or is it a bit of both?

A study of 1,000 men found that those who have two or more orgasms a week exhibit a 50 per cent reduced mortality risk compared with men who have on average fewer than one orgasm per week. Most men will make the obvious conclusion (that orgasms lead to long life), but it is also possible that the causal arrow points in the other direction: men who are ill are less likely to be sexually active in the first place (Houghton 1998: 14). This finding and the preceding one are similar, showing what Blaxter (1990) called 'an ambiguity about the direction of causal influence.' There is only an association between the two variables—no clear causal link.

For one final illustration, the *Globe and Mail* reported a Statistics Canada study on smoking and grades in school (15 June 2004). The headline proclaimed that young smokers get lower grades. However, the rest of the text suggested that poor grades lead to smoking, that low self-esteem is a cause of smoking, that learning difficulties cause low self-esteem, that need for peer approval leads to smoking, and that smoking and skipping classes are correlated. An experiment could clear this up, except for the ethical issues. . . . On the other hand, the article right next to this one was about ailing seniors and suicide. Sicker people take their lives more often. Now, here there is no question about temporal order. Still, perhaps both illness and suicide are caused by loneliness?

most experimental research (see the examples in Box 2.12).

Reliability, replicability, and validity

How does cross-sectional research measure up in terms of the previously outlined criteria for evaluating quantitative research: reliability, replicability, and validity?

- The issues of reliability and measurement validity primarily relate to the quality of the measures employed to tap the concepts in which the researcher is interested, rather than to a research design. This will be covered in the next chapter.

- Replicability characterizes most cross-sectional research, so long as the researcher spells out procedures for: selecting respondents, administering research instruments (structured interview or self-completion questionnaire, etc.), and the analysis of data.

- Internal validity is typically weak. As just suggested, it is difficult to establish causal direction from the resulting data. Cross-sectional research designs generally produce associations rather than causal connections.

- External validity is strong when the sample is a random one. When non-random methods of sampling are employed, external validity becomes questionable, an issue specifically addressed in Chapter 11.

- Since much cross-sectional research uses research instruments, such as self-completion questionnaires and structured observation schedules, external validity is jeopardized because the very intrusion of the instruments can change some peoples' behaviour in subtle (becoming less sure of themselves) and not so subtle (lying) ways.

Variables that cannot be manipulated

As noted in the section on experimental design, in much (if not most) social research it is not possible to manipulate the variables of interest. This is why most quantitative social research employs a cross-sectional design rather than an experimental one. To more or less all intents and purposes, ethnicity, age, gender, and social backgrounds are 'givens' and not really amenable to the kind of manipulation necessary for a true experimental design (but see Boxes 2.13 and 2.14). For example, an experimenter with makeup and a fake accent can create a fictional man or a woman—say, a Scot or a Swede—perhaps to see the effects on job offers, but the manipulation is limited to the external signs of gender and ethnicity, missing the more subjective and experiential aspects.

Box 2.13 Manipulating non-manipulable variables: body weight, ethnicity, and race

A researcher was interested in how people respond to 'overweight' as against 'normal weight' people. She could have compared accounts told by people of different body weights or even directly observed responses by others to them. Instead, because she had gorged herself, filling her short frame to almost 100 kilograms, she conducted a personal experiment. She gradually slimmed down and at the same time looked for changes in the reactions of others to her as she did. Apparently, the effects of being fat were not as negative as anticipated, because she claimed that early on she 'had the most unbelievably good-looking man chat her up' (reported in Wilkinson and Whitworth 1998: 3). The experiment could be made less personal by showing pictures of individuals, first fat and then slim, and asking respondents for their opinions and then comparing those offered for the fat and those for the slim picture.

Ethnicity too can be studied experimentally. Identical résumés could be sent out to prospective employers, but the names and birth places would vary. The researcher could then monitor the calls for personal interviews. This is a watered-down version of what Griffin (1961) did in the 1950s when he blackened his face and visible parts of his body and travelled around the American South as a person of colour, always keeping his eyes averted to show due deference to whites. He was treated as a black man in a number of ways, such as having to use segregated water fountains. Griffin's aim was to experience what it was like being a black person in a period and region of racial segregation. While Griffin's study is interesting, it is doubtful whether a brief sojourn as a person of colour could adequately have captured the experience of being black in the American South, one that is formed by many years of personal encounters and the knowledge that they will be ongoing. This point draws attention to the external validity of his study.

point in time, T_1. The effect is to create a data set that comprises variables Obs_1 to Obs_n and cases $case_1$ to $case_n$, as in Figure 2.2. For each case (which may be a person, household, city, nation, etc.) data collected at one point are available for each of the variables, Obs_1 to Obs_n. Thus, each cell in the matrix has data in it.

Longitudinal design(s)

With a longitudinal design, cases are examined at time 1 and again on at least one further occasion,

---

Box 2.14 Sex offender treatment questioned: again the independent variable is not manipulated

Treating sex offenders in custody apparently has little effect on their re-offending after release. A group of 724 men serving time in a BC federal prison were analyzed and then divided into two groups, by whether they took or did not take treatment. For ethical reasons there could be no random assignment, so the control group consisted of men incarcerated before the treatment was available. The experimental group were those who chose the treatment; this was not the perfect assignment to groups but better than occurs in most studies, and less of a problem because their motivation should only help show the effectiveness of the treatment.

The results showed equal re-offending in both groups, around 20 per cent. This statistic held for non-sexual crimes too—not very encouraging for the professionals who treat inmates. Cynics are wondering, however, about the timing. Could the national debt and current fiscal-responsibility measures have had any unintended effect on the analysis? The critics will be looking carefully at the reliability and validity of the study. That is easy. The hard thing is to do the same when the data support one's values.

Adapted from an article by Jane Armstrong, *Globe and Mail*, 31 March 2004.

However, the very fact that certain variables are givens provides a clue as to how to make causal inferences in cross-sectional research. Many of the variables of interest can be *assumed* to be temporally prior to other variables. For example, in a relationship between ethnic status and alcohol consumption, the latter cannot be the independent variable because it occurs after ethnicity. Ethnicity still cannot be said with certainty to be the cause, however— just a possible cause. In other words, even though unable to manipulate things like ethnic status or gender, causal inferences still can be cautiously drawn from cross-sectional data.

Structure of cross-sectional designs

A cross-sectional design collects data on a series of variables (Obs_1 Obs_2 Obs_3 Obs_4 Obs_5 . . . Obs_n) at a single

---

Box 2.15 Qualitative research within a cross-sectional design

The current discussion of the cross-sectional design places it firmly in the context of quantitative research. But qualitative research can also use a form of cross-sectional design. Beardsworth and Keil (1992) carried out a study of the dietary beliefs and practices of vegetarians. The authors carried out 'relatively unstructured interviews,' which were 'guided by an inventory of issues' with 76 vegetarians and vegans (1992: 261). The interviews were taped and transcribed, yielding a large corpus of qualitative data.

The research was not preoccupied with quantitative criteria like internal and external validity, replicability, measurement validity, and so on. In fact, the conversational interview style made the study more externally valid than research using more formal instruments of data collection. It is also striking that the study was concerned with the factors that influence food selection, like vegetarianism. The very notion of an 'influence' carries a strong connotation of causality, suggesting that qualitative researchers are also interested in the investigation of causes and effects, albeit not in the language of quantitative research with its talk of independent and dependent variables. As well, the emphasis was much more on understanding the *experience* of something like vegetarianism than is often the case with quantitative research. However, the chief point in providing the illustration is that it bears many similarities to the cross-sectional design in quantitative research. It entailed interviewing quite a large number of people and at a single point in time. And just as with many quantitative studies using a cross-sectional design, the examination of early influences on people's past and current eating behaviour can be based on their retrospective accounts of factors that earlier influenced them.

	Obs$_1$	Obs$_2$	Obs$_3$	Obs$_4$	. . .	Obs$_n$
Case$_1$						
Case$_2$						
Case$_3$						
Case$_4$						
Case$_5$						
. . .						
Case$_n$						

Figure 2.2 The data rectangle in cross-sectional research

but with no manipulation like there is in experimental design (see Box 2.16). It thus allows insight into the time order of variables and is better able to deal with the problem of 'ambiguity about the direction of causal influence' that plagues cross-sectional designs. Because certain potentially independent variables can be identified at T1, the researcher is in a better, if not perfect, position to infer that the effects identified at T2 or later occurred *after* the independent variables. In all other respects, the points made above about cross-sectional designs are the same as

those for longitudinal designs. Because of the time and cost involved, a longitudinal design is somewhat infrequent in social research but it is important, especially to show cause and effect.

But longitudinal is a term that is used in different senses. Sometimes it really means an update. Goyder *et al*. (2003) were doing that when they examined how evaluations of occupational prestige had changed over 25 years. Some of the earlier male advantage had disappeared; indeed, some occupations showing a female incumbent were later rated more highly than the same occupation with a male incumbent. Sometimes it is to detect trends as in the Baer *et al*. (2001) 15-nation study of joining clubs and associations of the early 1980s and early 1990s. And sometimes it is a specific application to examine cause and effect as above. For example, Kerr (2004) could investigate the decline in hyperactivity of Canadian children as they get older and its sources in poverty and family structure.

In all, it is common to distinguish two types of longitudinal design: the *panel study* and the *cohort study*. With the former, data are collected from a sample of people, households, or schools, and so on, often a randomly selected national one, on at least two (and often more) occasions. Illustrations are presented in Box 2.17, a study of value differences. A cohort is made up of people who share a certain characteristic, such as all being born in the same years (see Box 2.18) or having a certain experience, such as being unemployed or getting married in the same month. A cohort study selects either an entire cohort of people or a randomly selected sample of them as the focus of data collection. For example, Brannigan *et al*. (2002) using the National Longitudinal Survey of Children and Youth found that in every age cohort tested, childhood hyperactivity and aversive (hostile) parenting practices are related to childhood misconduct and aggression.

Panel and cohort studies share similar features. In social sciences like sociology, social policy, and human geography, both are usually in the form of repeated cross-sectional survey research using a self-completion questionnaire or structured interview. They have a similar design structure and are concerned both with illuminating social change and improving the understanding of causal influences.

Box 2.16 Longitudinal research and the case study

Case study research frequently includes a longitudinal element. The researcher is often a participant of an organization or member of a community for many months or years or may conduct interviews with individuals over a lengthy period. Moreover, the researcher may be able to inject an additional longitudinal element by analyzing archival information and asking respondents to recall things that occurred before the study began, thus discovering some history.

A longitudinal element also occurs when a case that has been studied is returned to at a later stage. A particularly interesting example of this occurred in 'Middletown,' a pseudonym for an American Midwest town first studied by Lynd and Lynd (1929) in 1924–25 and restudied in 1935 during the Depression to determine changes (Lynd and Lynd 1937). In 1977, the community was again restudied, this time in a post–Vietnam War setting (Bahr *et al*. 1983), using the same research instruments but with minor changes.

Box 2.17 Canadian–American differences gleaned from panel survey data

Michael Adams's 2003 book *Fire and Ice: The United States, Canada and the Myth of Converging Values* is based on value surveys of Americans and Canadians in 1992, 1996, and 2000. The main purpose of such panel studies is to detect change, and Adams certainly did. He found that as the economies of the two countries have become more integrated (through NAFTA, etc.), the younger people in each country, those in their twenties, are growing apart. On one side of the border he found people interested in personal creativity, spontaneity, personal control, ecological concerns, global consciousness, and a 'flexible gender identity.' On the other side he found people interested in consumption and financial security, with greater confidence in big business, a penchant for risk, and a fear of never acquiring sufficient social status. These are oversimplified generalizations; but it is not hard to guess which country is which.

Panel and cohort designs differ in important respects too. A panel study that continues for many years can distinguish between age effects (the impact of the ageing process on individuals) and cohort effects (effects due to being born at a similar time) because its members will have been born at different times. A cohort study, however, generally can only distinguish ageing effects, since all members of the sample will have been born at more or less the same time. Also, a panel study, especially one at the household level, needs rules for handling new entrants to households (e.g., as a result of marriage or elderly relatives moving in) and exits from households (e.g., as a result of marriage break-up or children leaving home).

Panel and cohort studies share similar problems. First, there is the problem of sample attrition through death, moving, and so on, or through subjects choosing to withdraw at later stages of the research. The study by Dinovitzer *et al.* (2003) on the educational attainment of immigrant youth talked to only 65 per cent of those originally surveyed 19 years earlier (and 54 per cent of those originally sought). Still comparing those later found to those lost, the authors found no significant differences that would explain the loss. That comparison is a common practice and when no difference is found, the losses are treated as random and thus acceptable to ignore. The main problem with attrition is that those who leave the study may differ in some important respects from those who remain, so that the latter do not form a representative group. Those immigrants who stayed in Canada, for example, may be the easiest to find; those who went on, perhaps home or to the US, may be the hardest to find, thus biasing later databases. However, there is also some evidence from panel studies that attrition declines with time (Berthoud 2000*a*); in other words, those who do not drop out after the first wave or two of data collection tend to stay on the panel.

Second, there are few guidelines for determining the best timing for further waves of data collection. Finally, there is evidence of a *panel conditioning* effect, whereby continued participation in a longitudinal study affects respondent behaviour. Menard (1991) cited a study of family caregiving in which 52 per cent of respondents indicated a change, as a result of their participation in the research, in how they cared for relatives.

Surveys, like the General Social Survey (see Chapter 7), carried out on a regular basis on *different*

Box 2.18 The National Longitudinal Survey of Children and Youth

This cohort study is a long-term effort to monitor child development and the well-being of Canada's children as they mature from infancy to adulthood. It began with a representative sample of children 11 years or younger in 1994–95 being interviewed, with follow-ups every two years. Statistics Canada collects the data with directions provided by HRDC (Human Resources Development Canada). The study hopes to follow them until they are 25 years old and at the same time develop policies to help children to live healthy, active, and rewarding lives.

The first cycle was cross-sectional by definition. The second allowed some longitudinal research comparing the first and second cycles and the third even more. The response rate in cycle 1 was 86 per cent; of those who cooperated in cycle 1, 92 per cent participated in cycle 2 and 88 per cent in cycle 3, a good retention rate. See Michaud's 2001 article in *Canadian Studies in Population*, 28: 391–405 for more information.

samples of the population, are not truly longitudinal designs because they do not involve the same people being interviewed on each occasion. They are perhaps better thought of as involving a repeated cross-sectional design or trend design in which samples are selected on each of several occasions. They are able to chart change, but they are less able to address this issue of the direction of cause and effect because the samples are always different.

It is easy to associate longitudinal designs more or less exclusively with quantitative research. However, qualitative research sometimes incorporates elements of a longitudinal design. This is especially noticeable in ethnographic research when the ethnographer is in a location for a lengthy period of time or when interviews are carried out on more than one occasion in order to address change. As an example of the latter, Smith *et al.* (2004) described a study of the experiences of citizenship for 110 young people. They were interviewed in depth in 1999 and then re-interviewed at two-year intervals to examine changes in their lifestyles, feelings, opinions, and future ambitions in relation to citizenship issues. Only 64 young people participated in all three waves of data collection, suggesting the high level of sample attrition in this style of research.

Case study design

The basic case study entails the detailed and intensive analysis of a single case. Some of the studies in sociology using this kind of design, included:

- a single community, such as Hughes's classic study of Drummondville, a textile town in Quebec (1943), and Pratt and Valverde's (2002) research on Somalis in Toronto;
- a single family, such as Lewis's (1961) study of the Sánchez family in Mexico;
- a single organization, such as a study of an automobile factory by Rinehart (1996) or of nurses in a Hamilton hospital to clarify their reasons for disaffection (White 1990);
- a person, like Walt Disney; such studies are characterized by use of the life history or biographical approach (see Chapter 10); and

- a single event, like the fight against locating a home for recovering addicts in a Richmond, BC, neighbourhood (Huey 2003).

What is a case?

Most commonly, a case study is defined by its location, such as a community or organization, and its intensive examination of the setting. The Toronto Somali community served as a case study for the wider topic of how refugees come to be defined as 'bogus,' as 'drains' on Canada's welfare system. There is a tendency to associate case studies with qualitative research (true above, Pratt and Valverde 2002) because exponents of the case study design often favour methods like participant observation and unstructured interviewing, each viewed as particularly helpful in generating an intensive, detailed examination of a case. However, case studies are frequently sites for the employment of *both* quantitative and qualitative research, a topic examined in Chapter 15.

With a case study, the case is an object of interest *in its own right* and the researcher aims to provide an in-depth elucidation of it. Unless a distinction of this or some other kind is drawn, it becomes impossible to distinguish the case study as a special research design, because almost any kind of research can be construed as a case study. Even research based on a national, random sample of Canadians could be considered a case study of Canada. Similarly, Beagan's (2001) investigation of bias in one (unnamed) medical school is better described as employing a cross-sectional design rather than a case study, because the case itself is little more than a location that forms a backdrop to the findings. What distinguishes a true case study is the goal to elucidate the unique features of the case and so collecting in-depth, often qualitative, data that may be unique to time and place. This is known as an *idiographic* approach and can describe Shalla's (2002) study of how Air Canada's customer and service agents became victims under airline restructuring. A research design like cross-sectional is generally more quantitative and *nomothetic*, that is, seeking generalizations that apply regardless of time and place.

With both experimental and cross-sectional designs, the typical orientation is deductive. However, when a qualitative research strategy is employed within a cross-sectional design the approach tends to be inductive. In other words, whether a cross-sectional design is inductive or deductive tends to depend on whether a quantitative or a qualitative research strategy is employed. The same point can be made of case study research. When the predominant research strategy is qualitative, a case study tends to take an inductive approach to the relationship between theory and research; if a predominantly quantitative strategy is taken, it tends to be deductive, guided by specific research questions derived from theoretical concerns.

Reliability, replicability, and validity of case studies

The question of how the case study fares on the research design issues of measurement validity, internal validity, external validity, reliability, and replicability depends in large part on whether the researcher feels these criteria are appropriate for evaluating case study research. Writers of qualitative case study research tend to play down or ignore the salience of these factors (cf. Stake 1995). Writers strongly influenced by the quantitative research strategy tend to depict them as more significant, even making efforts to develop case studies that more easily can meet the criteria.

However, one question on which a great deal of discussion has centred concerns the *external validity* or *generalizability* of case study research. How can a single case possibly be so representative that it yields findings applicable to other cases? For example, how can findings from a case study of the Toronto police department be generalizable to all large urban police departments in Canada? The answer, of course, is that they probably cannot. It is important to appreciate that case study researchers do not delude themselves that it is possible to identify typical cases that can represent a class of objects, whether it is factories, mass media reporting, police services, or communities. In other words, they do *not* think that a case study is a sample of one.

Types of case

Related to the issue of external validity, Yin (1984) distinguished three types of case:

- The *critical case*. Here the researcher has a clearly specified hypothesis, and a case is chosen on grounds that it will allow a better understanding of the circumstances under which the hypothesis does and does not hold. The classic study by Festinger *et al.* (1956) of a religious cult whose members believed that the end of the world was about to happen is an example. The fact that the world did not end allowed the researchers to test propositions about how people respond to thwarted expectations. What did they do after quitting their jobs, leaving their homes, and waiting on a mountaintop when nothing happened? Sneak down and move to another town? No, actually they decided that their faith had saved humankind and that their new role was to tell others of that miracle and to convert them to their religion.

- The *extreme*, even *unique*, case is a common focus in clinical studies. Margaret Mead's (1928) well-known study of growing up in Samoa seems to have been motivated by her belief that it represented a unique case and thus could challenge the currently popular nature-over-nurture hypothesis. She found that, unlike adolescents in most other societies, Samoan youth do not suffer a period of anxiety and stress in their teenage years. She explained this by their culture's strong, consistently enforced standards of conduct and morality. These factors, associated with this relatively trouble-free period in their lives, were of interest, because she thought they might contain lessons for Western youth and its 'everyone decide for him- or herself' ideology.

- The *revelatory case*. The basis for the revelatory case exists 'when an investigator has an opportunity to observe and analyse a phenomenon previously inaccessible to scientific investigation' (Yin 1984: 44). In most instances today, these would be new phenomena, since there are few places sociologists have not penetrated.

- But cases are also often chosen because of mundane reasons, such as being close and willing, and still provide an adequate context for certain research questions to be answered, for key social processes to be examined. The case merely provides an apt context for the working through of these research questions. To take a concrete example, Russell and Tyler's (2002) study of one store in the UK clothing chain Girl Heaven, for 3- to 13-year-old girls, was not motivated by its being critical, unique, or providing a context never before studied. It was selected for its capacity to illuminate the links between gender and consumption and the commodification of childhood in modern society. Indeed, often it is only at a very late stage in the research that the singularity and significance of the case becomes apparent (Radley and Chamberlain 2001).

As previously mentioned, one of the standard criticisms of the case study is that its findings cannot be generalized. Case study researchers argue strenuously that this is not the purpose of their craft. A valid picture of one case is more valuable than a potentially less valid picture of many. Their aim instead is to generate an intensive examination of a single case and then to engage in a theoretical analysis. Pratt and Valverde (2002) studied only Somalis and declared a hope that others would study other immigrant groups in other places. Their central concern is the quality of the theoretical reasoning the case study allows. How well do the data support the theoretical arguments generated? Is the theory complete, clear, *parsimonious*—a word meaning uncomplicated and clean? Such a view places case study research firmly in the inductive tradition of the relationship between theory and research. However, a case study design is not necessarily associated with an inductive approach and there are examples of case study design using deductive logic.

However, not all writers are convinced about the merits of multiple-case study research. Dyer and Wilkins (1991), for example, argued that a multiple-case study approach tends to lead to paying less attention to the specific context and more to the ways in which the cases can be contrasted. Moreover, the need for comparisons tends to mean that the researcher requires an explicit focus at the outset, whereas it may be advantageous to adopt a more open-ended approach in many instances. These concerns about retaining contextual insight and a rather more unstructured research approach are very much associated with the goals of the qualitative research strategy (see Chapter 8 and Boxes 2.19 and 2.20).

Box 2.19 Comparative research

Cross-cultural research may be realized in a quantitative or qualitative context; it is usually done within a cross-sectional design. Phenomena such as voting behaviour or crime victimization in two or more countries can be compared using the same research instruments, seeking similarities and differences and a deeper understanding of social reality in different national contexts. At the least it supplies a replication. The research by Kelley and De Graaf (1997) referred to in Box 1.6 is an illustration of cross-cultural survey evidence collected in 15 nations.

Cross-cultural research has problems, apart from it being more expensive. When using existing data such as official statistics or survey evidence, the researcher must ensure that the data are comparable in terms of categories and data-collection methods; when new data are being collected, the researcher must ensure that the need to translate data-collection instruments (e.g., interview schedules) does not undermine genuine comparability. Even when translation is carried out competently, there is still the potential problem of an insensitivity to specific national and cultural contexts, for example, whether the London tube performs the same function as the Toronto subway. Switching 'tube' for 'subway' in a question is only a start because the experiences in the two cities may be different in terms of use, safety, etc.

As well, cross-cultural research helps to reduce the risk of failing to appreciate that social science findings are often, if not invariably, culturally specific. For example, Wilson's (2002) qualitative examination of Ontario raves made frequent comparisons to the earlier rave scene in Britain. However, the UK scene was more a result of working-class oppression than Canada's middle-class, but culturally alienated, experience. For a quantitative example Baer *et al.* (2001) found that joining clubs and voluntary organizations increased towards the end of the last century in the US, West Germany, and the Netherlands, was stable in Canada and 10 other countries, but decreased in Spain.

Box 2.20 Managing cross-cultural research

As its name implies, cross-cultural research entails the collection and/or analysis of data from two or more nations. Possible models include:

1 A researcher, perhaps in conjunction with a research team, collects data in a number of countries. A related option is for a coordinator to recruit researchers in participating nations with common interests to coordinate their own investigations in their own country. The work is coordinated to ensure comparability of research questions, survey questions, and procedures for administering the research instruments (as done for the study in Box 3.1). The foreign team leaders have total autonomy in deciding which companies they choose as long as they meet predetermined criteria (e.g., industry type, size, and so on). The

specifics of the case study method (e.g., web survey and the qualitative guidelines for employee interviews) were developed by the team and also need to be followed.

2 A lone researcher or small team replicates work done in a foreign country using the same instruments, directions, etc., but in his or her own country, thus requiring less coordination. A 2004 Ipsos-Reid survey for Canadian Blood Services found that 3.7 per cent of Canadians are blood donors, with the over-forties giving the most. This is less than half of the rate in Taiwan and below the US rate of about 5 per cent. The latter figure is interesting given the usual depictions of Canadian–US value differences referred to in Box 2.17.

The strength of comparative design is to allow distinguishing characteristics of two or more cases to act as a springboard for theoretical reflections about the contrast. Comparative design is something of a hybrid: in quantitative research it is frequently an extension of a cross-sectional design and in qualitative research it is frequently an extension of a case study design. It even exhibits certain features similar to experiments and quasi-experiments, which also rely on the capacity to forge a comparison.

Bringing research strategy and design together

Finally, we can bring together the two research strategies covered in Chapter 1 with the research designs outlined in this chapter. Table 2.1 shows the typical form associated with each combination of research strategy and research design along with a number of examples that either have been encountered so far or will be covered in later chapters. Table 2.1 refers also to research methods to be encountered in later chapters, but not referred to so far. The Glossary provides a quick reference for unfamiliar terms.

The distinctions are not always perfect. In particular, in some qualitative research it is not obvious whether a study is an example of a longitudinal design or a case study design. Life history studies, research that concentrates on a specific issue over time, and ethnography, in which the researcher charts change in a single case, contain aspects of both designs. Such studies are perhaps better conceptualized as longitudinal case studies rather than as belonging to one category of research design or another. A further point is that there is no typical form in the qualitative research strategy/experimental research design cell. Qualitative research in the context of true experiments is very unusual, with a quasi-experimental design being a less valued but more realistic alternative.

Table 2.1 Research strategy and research design

Research design	Research strategy	
	Quantitative	Qualitative
Experimental	*Typical form:* Most experimenters employ quantitative comparisons between experimental and control groups on the dependent variable. *Examples:* Boxes 2.4, 2.8	No typical form. Quasi or evaluative research more usual than others forms? No example.
Cross-sectional	*Typical form:* Survey research or structured observation on a sample at a single point in time; content analysis on a sample of documents. Sometimes there is a comparison, as in cross-cultural research *Examples:* Boxes 1.4, 1.6, 2.12, 3.1, 7.7, 12.2, 12.6, 16.1, 16.3	*Typical form:* Qualitative interviews or focus groups at a single point in time; qualitative content analysis of a set of documents relating to a single period. *Examples:* Boxes 2.15, 12.2, 12.9, 12.10, 16.2, 16.6, 16.7
Longitudinal	*Typical form:* Survey research on a sample on more than one occasion, as in panel and cohort studies; content analysis of documents relating to different time periods. *Examples:* Boxes 2.17, 2.18	*Typical form:* Ethnographic research over a long period, qualitative interviewing on more than one occasion, or qualitative content analysis of documents relating to different time periods. Such research is longitudinal when the main focus is to map change. *Examples:* Boxes 2.16, 16.6
Case study	*Typical form:* Survey research on a single case with a view to revealing important features about its nature. No example.	*Typical form:* The intensive study by qualitative interviewing of a single case, which may be an organization, life, family, or community. In Boxes 5.5 and 16.7 more than one case is used to facilitate comparison. *Examples:* Boxes 1.11, 3.1, 7.1, 7.5, 12.4, 12.6

K   KEY POINTS

- There is an important distinction between a research method and a research design.

- It is necessary to become thoroughly familiar with the meaning of technical terms used as criteria for evaluating research: reliability, replicability, and validity (measurement, internal, and external).

- It is also necessary to be familiar with the differences among the four major research designs covered: experimental; cross-sectional; longitudinal; and case study. The term 'experiment' has a specific technical meaning here.

- There are various threats to validity in non-experimental research.

- Although the case study is often thought to be a single type of research design, it has several forms. It is also important to be concerned with case study evidence in relation to issues like external validity (generalizability).

- The boundaries between ethical and unethical practices are not clear-cut and certain notorious studies have been a particular concern.

- Related to this last point, extreme cases of ethical violation tend to be associated with two particular research methods—notably disguised observation and the use of deception in experiments. Do not infer from this that ethical concerns primarily reside in some methods but not others.

Q   QUESTIONS FOR REVIEW

- What are the chief differences among the following: a research method; a research strategy; and a research design?

Criteria in social research

- What are the differences between reliability and validity and why are they important criteria for the evaluation of social research?

- Give an example of each of the following: measurement validity, internal validity, and external validity.

- Why have some qualitative researchers sought to devise alternative criteria for reliability and validity when assessing their investigations?

- Why have some qualitative researchers *not* sought to devise alternative criteria for reliability and validity when assessing the quality of investigations?

Research designs

- Which research design would be good for examining the use of illegal drugs in a local high school?

- A researcher reasons that people who read *broadsheet* newspapers (wider than they are tall) are likely to be more knowledgeable about personal finance than readers of *tabloid* newspapers (taller than they are wide). One hundred people are interviewed about which type they read and their level of financial knowledge: 65 readers of tabloids and 35 of broadsheets. The latter are on average considerably more knowledgeable about personal finance than tabloid readers and the researcher concludes that reading broadsheets enhances knowledge of personal finance. Assess that conclusion.

Experimental design

- 'The main importance of the experimental design for social research is that it comes closest to demonstrating causal connections between variables.' Discuss.

- Following from the last question, if it is so useful and important, why is it not used more?

- What is a quasi-experiment?

Cross-sectional design

- What is meant by a cross-sectional research design?

- In what ways does the survey exemplify the cross-sectional research design?

- Assess the degree to which survey research can achieve internally valid findings.

- To what extent is the survey design exclusive to quantitative research?

Longitudinal design(s)

- Why might a longitudinal research design be superior to a cross-sectional one?
- What are the main differences between panel and cohort designs?

Case study design

- What is a case study?
- Is case study research exclusive to qualitative research?
- What are some of the principles by which cases might be selected?

Ethical principles

- Why are ethical issues important in relation to the conduct of social research?
- Does 'harm to participants' refer to physical harm alone?
- What are some difficulties with following this ethical principle?
- Why is the issue of informed consent so hotly debated?
- What are the main difficulties of following this ethical principle?
- Why is the privacy principle important?
- Why does deception matter?
- How helpful are studies like Milgram's electric shock experiments for understanding ethical principles in social research?

The difficulties of ethical decision-making

- How easy is it to conduct ethical research?

Part Two

Part Two of this book is concerned with quantitative research. Chapter 3 sets the scene by exploring the main features of this research strategy. Chapter 4 focuses on the structured interview, one of the main methods of data collection in quantitative research and in survey research in particular and on a second prominent method of gathering survey research data—questionnaires that people complete themselves. Chapter 5 provides guidelines on how to ask questions for structured interviews and questionnaires. Chapter 6 discusses structured observation, a method that provides a systematic approach to the observation of people. Chapter 7 addresses other data sources and approaches to examining them, including the possibility of using data collected by other researchers and official statistics. These chapters provide the essential tools for doing quantitative research, from the very general issues to do with its basic features to the very practical issues of conducting surveys.

3

The nature of quantitative research

CHAPTER OVERVIEW

This chapter is concerned with quantitative research, until recently the dominant strategy in social research. Its influence has waned slightly since the mid-1970s, when qualitative research became increasingly influential, but it continues to exert a powerful influence. The emphasis in this chapter is on what quantitative research typically entails, though later in the chapter departures from this ideal type are outlined. This chapter explores:

- the main steps of quantitative research, presented as a linear succession of stages;

- the importance of measurement in quantitative research and the ways in which measures are devised for concepts; this discussion includes a look at *indicators*, an indirect way of measuring concepts for which there are no direct measures;

- procedures for checking the reliability and validity of the measurement process;

- the main preoccupations of quantitative research: measurement, causality, generalization, and replication; and

- some common criticisms of quantitative research.

Introduction

In Chapter 1 quantitative research was outlined as a distinctive research strategy. In very broad terms, it was described as entailing the collection of numerical data, a deductive relationship between theory and research, a predilection for a natural science approach (and of positivism in particular), and an objectivist conception of social reality. This chapter examines the strategy in more detail.

It should be abundantly clear by now that much more than the presence of numbers distinguishes a quantitative from a qualitative research strategy. It has a distinctive epistemological and ontological position. In this chapter, the main steps in quantitative research are outlined. It also examines some of its principal concerns, such as measurement validity, and how they are addressed.

The main steps in quantitative research

Figure 3.1 outlines the main steps in quantitative research. This is very much an ideal account of the process: it is probably never or rarely found in this pure form, but it represents a useful starting point for getting to grips with the main ingredients of the approach and the links between them. Research is rarely as linear and as straightforward as the figure implies.

Some of the chief steps were covered in the first chapters. The fact that the model starts off with theory signifies a broadly deductive approach to the relationship between theory and research. It is common for outlines of quantitative research to suggest that a hypothesis is deduced from a theory and is tested. This notion has been incorporated into

1. Theory
   ↓
2. Hypothesis
   ↓
3. Research design
   ↓
4. Devise measures of concepts
   ↓
5. Select research site(s)
   ↓
6. Select research subjects/respondents
   ↓
7. Administer research instruments/collect data
   ↓
8. Process data
   ↓
9. Analyze data
   ↓
10. Findings/conclusions
   ↓
11. Write up findings/conclusions

Figure 3.1 The process of quantitative research

Figure 3.1. However, a great deal of quantitative research does not specify a hypothesis; instead, theory acts loosely as a set of concerns in relation to which the social researcher collects data. This was the case for Gazso-Windlej and McMullin's (2003) study of how time, resources, and patriarchy affect the continued unequal spousal sharing of domestic labour in Canada. The specification of testable hypotheses is most common in experimental research, less so in other research designs. Return to Box 1.6 to see a cross-sectional social survey design involving hypothesis testing.

In step 3 a research design is selected, a topic explored in Chapter 2; this choice has implications for a variety of issues, such as the external validity of findings and ability to impute causality. Step 4 entails devising measures of concepts, a process often referred to as *operationalization*, a term derived from physics to refer to the operations by which a concept (such as temperature or velocity) is measured (Bridgman 1927). Further aspects of this issue are explored later in this chapter.

The next two steps are the selection of a research site or sites and then the selection of subjects/respondents. (Experimenters tend to call the people on whom they conduct research 'subjects,' whereas

social survey researchers typically call them 'respondents.') Thus, in social survey research an investigator must establish an appropriate setting for the research. Box 1.4 provided a recent example of research that involved similar deliberations about selecting research sites and sampling respondents. First a school was chosen, one where the researcher had connections. Then there was an issue of permission slips and thus the study focused on boys old enough to give their own permission. Finally, because of a less-than-eager response, all boys who were willing became part of the study. See Box 3.1 also. In experimental research, these two steps are likely to include the assignment of subjects into control and treatment groups.

Step 7 is the administration of the research instruments. In experimental research, this usually means pre-testing subjects, manipulating the independent variable for the experimental group only, and post-testing. In cross-sectional research using social survey research instruments, it involves interviewing the members of the sample with a structured interview schedule or distributing a self-completion questionnaire. In research using structured observation, this step involves an observer(s) watching the setting and

Box 3.1 Selecting research sites and sampling respondents: the IT study

The 'Workforce Aging in the New Economy' comparative study of information technology employment examines, among other things, age discrimination in hiring in the IT sector and forced early retirement. The project involves research in four sites: Canada, the US, Australia, and the EU. It will eventually involve between 17 and 22 case studies in each locale. A large firm (100+) and a mid-sized firm will be selected in each locale. The rest of the firms will be small (20 or fewer employees). In the small firms all employees will be interviewed. In the mid- and large-sized firms the researchers will talk to a random sample.

The website www.wane.ca has more useful information about the project, but this brief description should clearly demonstrate how researchers are involved in decisions about selecting both research site(s) and respondents.

the behaviour of people and then assigning each element of behaviour to a category.

Step 8 simply refers to the fact that information collected must be transformed into 'data.' In quantitative research, this usually means to prepare it so it can be quantified. With some information this can be done in a relatively straightforward way—for example, for information relating to such things as people's ages, incomes, number of years spent at school, and so on. For other variables, quantification entails *coding* the information—that is, transforming it into numbers to facilitate a quantitative data analysis. Codes act as tags placed on data to facilitate computer processing. This consideration leads into step 9—the analysis of the data. In this step, the researcher chooses among quantitative techniques to summarize the data, to test for relationships between variables, to develop ways of presenting the results to others, and so on.

Next, the researcher must interpret the results of the analysis and it is at this stage that 'findings' emerge. The researcher considers the connections between the findings from step 8 and the various preoccupations that acted as the impetus of the research. If there is a hypothesis, is it supported? What are the implications of the findings for the theoretical ideas that were the background to the research?

Then the research must be written up. Until it enters the public domain in some way, as a paper to be read at a conference, a report to the agency that funded the research, or as a book or journal article for academic social researchers, it cannot take on significance beyond satisfying the researcher's personal curiosity. In writing up the findings and conclusions, the researcher is doing more than simply relaying results to others: readers must be convinced that the research conclusions are important and the findings robust. Thus, a significant part of the research is convincing others of the significance and validity of one's findings.

Once the findings have been published they become part of the stock of knowledge (or 'theory' in the loose sense of the word) in their domain. Thus, there is a feedback loop from step 11 back to step 1. The presence of both an element of deduction (step 2) and induction (the feedback loop) is indicative of the positivist foundations of quantitative research. The emphasis on the translation of concepts into measures (step 4) is also a feature of positivism. It is to this important phase of translating concepts into measures that the discussion turns. As will be seen, certain considerations follow from the stress placed on measurement in quantitative research; by and large they relate to the validity and reliability of the measures.

Concepts and their measurement

What is a concept?

Concepts are the building blocks of theory and represent the points around which social research is conducted. Just think of the numerous concepts that have already been mentioned in relation to research examples cited so far in this book:

> de-skilling, emotional satisfaction, religious orthodoxy, religious orientation, hyperactivity, academic achievement, teacher expectations, charismatic leadership, and healthy lifestyle.

Each represents a label given to elements of the social world that seem to be significant and to have common features. As Bulmer succinctly put it, con-cepts 'are categories for the organisation of ideas and observations' (1984: 43). One item mentioned in Chapter 2 but missing from the list is IQ. It has been omitted because it is not a concept! It is a *measure* of the concept of intelligence. This is a rare case for social science, a measure so well known that the measure and the concept are almost synonymous. (Examples in the physical world are temperature and the centigrade scale, and length and the metric scale.)

For a concept to be employed in quantitative research, it has to be measured, and then it can be an independent or a dependent variable. In other words, a concept can provide an explanation of a certain aspect of the social world (independent), or it can be something needing an explanation (dependent). A concept like social mobility can be used in either capacity: as a possible explanation of certain attitudes (are there differences between the downwardly mobile and others in their political attitudes?) or as something to be explained (why are some people upwardly mobile and others not?). Equally, one may be interested in changes in the amount of social mobility or in variations among comparable nations in their levels of social mobility.

Why measure?

There are three main reasons for the preoccupation with measurement in quantitative research:

- Measurement allows a delineation of *fine differences* between people in terms of the characteristic in question. This is very useful, since, although it is often easy to distinguish between people in terms of extreme categories, finer distinctions are much more difficult to recognize. Clear variations in levels of job satisfaction—people who love their jobs and people who hate their jobs—are easy to see, but small differences are much more difficult to detect.

- Measurement gives a *consistent device* or yardstick for gauging such distinctions. This consistency relates both to time and to other researchers. In other words, a measure should be something not influenced by when or whom it is administered. Saying that a measure is uninfluenced by time does not mean that measurement readings do not change; they do, if only because people exhibit natural rhythms and also age. What it means is that the measure should generate consistent results, *other* than those that occur as a result of natural changes. Whether a measure actually possesses this consistency is related to the issue of *reliability*, introduced in Chapter 2 and examined again below.

- Measurement provides the basis for *more precise estimates of the degree of relationship between concepts* (e.g., through correlation analysis, which will be examined in Chapter 12) when variables are broken down into more categories. Nine levels of stress and six of job satisfaction are more useful than if each had only three levels—low, moderate, and high.

Indicators

To provide a measure of a concept (often referred to as an *operational definition*, a term deriving from the idea of operationalization), it is necessary to have an indicator or indicators that can stand for the concept (see Box 3.2). There are a number of ways to devise indicators:

- through a question(s) that is part of a structured interview schedule or self-completion questionnaire. The question(s) can be concerned with the respondents' attitude (e.g., job satisfaction), or their social situation (e.g., stress), or a report of their behaviour (e.g., leisure pursuits);

Box 3.2 ⎯◯⎯ *What is an indicator?*

It is worth making two distinctions here, first between an *indicator* and a *measure*. The latter refers to things that can be relatively unambiguously *counted*, such as personal income, age, number of children, number of years spent at school. Measures in other words are quantified in a reasonably direct way. Indicators stand for concepts less directly quantifiable, such as job satisfaction (see Box 3.3). These indicators allow job satisfaction to be measured and to treat the resulting quantitative information as if it were a measure. An indicator, then, is something employed *as though it were a measure of a concept*; thus IQ tests are a battery of *indicators* to measure the *concept* of intelligence.

Indicators may have a *direct* or *indirect* relationship to the concepts for which they stand. Thus, an indicator of marital status ('Are you currently married?') has a much more direct relationship to its concept than an indicator (or set of indicators) relating to job satisfaction. Sets of attitudes always need to be measured by batteries of indirect indicators. So too do many forms of behaviour. Directness and indirectness are not qualities inherent to an indicator: data from a survey question on amount earned per month may be a direct measure of personal income, but, if used as an indicator of social class, it becomes an indirect measure. The issue of indirectness raises the question of where an indirect measure comes from—that is, how does a researcher devise an indicator of something like job satisfaction? Usually, it is based on seeing how others have measured it and, failing that, on common-sense understandings of the forms the concept takes or on anecdotal or qualitative evidence relating to it.

- through recording behaviour using a structured observation schedule (e.g., pupil behaviour in a classroom);

- through official statistics (e.g., police statistics on crime);

- through an examination of mass media content (e.g., Wilson's (2002) looking in underground magazines for the ideals and philosophy that support the rave scene).

Thus, indicators can be derived from a wide variety of sources and methods. Very often the researcher, especially one engaged in survey research, has to consider whether one indicator of a concept suffices. Rather than having just a single indicator, the researcher may ask a number of questions to tap a concept (see Boxes 3.3 and 3.5 for examples).

Using multiple-indicator measures

The main advantage in using a multiple-indicator measure of a concept is that there are potential problems in relying on just a single indicator:

- A single indicator may misclassify some individuals, due to the wording of the question or a misunderstanding of its meaning. But if there are a number of indicators and someone is mis-classified through a particular question, it is possible to offset its effects.

- One general, broad indicator may capture only a portion of the underlying concept. Asking people how satisfied they are with their work may miss the complexity of the situation. Someone saying 'not satisfied' may like some parts or work, just as someone 'satisfied' can dislike a specific aspect. Alternatively, a question may cover only one aspect of the concept in question. For example, to measure job satisfaction, is it sufficient to ask people how satisfied they are with their pay? Almost certainly the answer is no, because for most people there is more to job satisfaction than just satisfaction with pay. A single indicator like this misses things like satisfaction with benefits, with the work itself, and other aspects of the work environment. By asking a number of questions the researcher can get access to a wider range of aspects of the concept.

- One can make much finer distinctions. Take the Westergaard *et al.* (1989) measure of commitment

---

Box 3.3 A multiple-indicator measure of a concept

The research on the effects of redundancy by Westergaard *et al.* (1989) was conducted by structured interviews with 378 laid-off steelworkers. One interest was whether their commitment to work varied according to whether they were still unemployed at the time of the interview, or had found work, or had retired. To measure commitment to employment, the authors gave respondents 10 statements and asked them to indicate their level of agreement or disagreement on a seven-point scale running from 'Yes, I strongly agree' to 'No, I strongly disagree.' A midpoint on the scale allowed a neutral response. This approach to investigating an attitude is a *Likert scale*, though in many cases researchers use a five-point rather than a seven-point scale for responses. See Box 3.4 for a description of what a Likert scale entails. Examples of the statements included:

- Work is necessary, but rarely enjoyable.

- I regard time spent at work as time taken away from the things I want to do.

- Having a job is only important to me because it brings in money.

- Even if I won a great deal of money I'd carry on working.

- If unemployment benefits were really high I would still prefer to work.

- I would soon get bored if I did not go to work.

- Any past feelings I've had of achieving something worthwhile have usually come through things I've done at work.

The authors found that whether their respondents had found work since being made redundant, or were still unemployed, or had taken retirement made little difference in their attitudes.

---

to work as an example (see Box 3.3). Focusing on just one of the indicators as a measure, and assuming that answers indicating no commitment are assigned 1 and answers indicating a very high level a 7 and the five other points 2, 3, 4, 5, and 6, a group of people could vary from 1 to 7. But with a multiple-indicator measure of 10 indicators the range is 10 (10×1) to 70 (10×7). Box 3.4 provides some information about the Likert scale used in the study by Westergaard *et al.*

Box 3.4 ☼ What is a Likert scale?

The investigation of attitudes is a prominent area in much survey research. One of the most common techniques for investigating attitudes is the *Likert scale*, named after Rensis Likert who developed the method. It is essentially a multiple-indicator measure of intensity of feelings about the area in question. In its most common format, it comprises a series of statements (known as 'items') on an issue or theme. Each respondent is then asked to indicate level of agreement with the statement. Usually, the format for indicating level of agreement is a five-point scale going from 'strongly agree' to 'strongly disagree,' but seven-point and other formats are used too. There is usually a middle position of 'neither agree nor disagree' or 'undecided' indicating neutrality on the issue. A respondent's reply on each item is scored and then the scores are aggregated to form an overall score (as is done in Box 3.3). Variations on the typical format on agreement are scales referring to frequency (e.g., 'never' through 'always') and evaluation (e.g., 'very poor' to 'very good').

There are several points to remember in constructing a Likert scale. The following are particularly important:

- The items must be statements and not questions.
- The items must all relate to the same object (job, organization, ethnic groups, unemployment, sentencing of offenders, etc.).
- The items that make up the scale should be interrelated (see the discussion of 'internal reliability' in this chapter and Box 3.7).
- It is useful to vary the phrasing so that some items imply a positive view of the phenomenon of interest and others a negative one. Thus, in the example in Box 3.3, some items imply a negative view of work (e.g., 'Having a job is not very important to me') and others a positive view of work (e.g., 'I would soon get bored if I did not go out to work'). This variation is advised in order to identify respondents who exhibit 'response sets' (see more in Chapters 4 and 5).

Box 3.5 A multiple-indicator measure of another concept

In Kelley and De Graaf's (1997) research on religious beliefs, national religiosity and family religious orientation were each measured by a single indicator (see Box 1.6). However, religious orthodoxy was measured by four survey questions; answers to each of the four were given a value and then added together to form a religious belief score for each respondent. The questions were as follows:

- Please indicate which statement below comes closest to expressing what you believe about God:
  — I don't believe in God. (1)
  — I don't know whether there is a God and don't believe there is a way to find out.
  — I don't believe in a personal God, but I do believe in a higher power of some kind.
  — I find myself believing in God some of the time, but not at others.
  — While I have doubts, I feel that I do believe in God.
  — I know God really exists and I have no doubts about it. (6)
- Which best describes your beliefs about God?
  — I don't believe in God and I never have. (1)

  — I don't believe in God, but I used to.
  — I believe in God now, but I didn't used to.
  — I believe in God now and I always have. (4)
- How close do you feel to God most of the time?
  — Don't believe in God. (1)
  — Not close at all.
  — Not very close.
  — Somewhat close.
  — Extremely close. (5)
- There is a God, one personally concerned with every human being.
  — Strongly agree. (5)
  — Agree.
  — Neither agree nor disagree.
  — Disagree.
  — Strongly disagree. (1)

Notice the values attached to each answer. A person whose answers add to 20 (6+4+5+5) is the most religious, a person with a sum of 4 the least, getting a 1 on each question, showing low religiosity.

Dimensions of concepts

Another possibility is for the concept of interest to have different dimensions, often revealed in other theory and research associated with that concept. Thus, in developing a measure for a concept, its different aspects or components should be considered. Bryman and Cramer (2001) demonstrated this approach with reference to the concept of 'professionalism.' The idea is that people scoring high on one dimension (like respecting confidentiality) may not necessarily score high on other dimensions (like fiscal honesty or continuing education), so that for each respondent you end up with a multidimensional 'profile.' Box 3.6 demonstrates the use of dimensions in connection with the concept of 'de-skilling' in the sociology of work.

However, in much quantitative research, there is a tendency to rely on a single indicator for each concept. For many purposes this is quite adequate and it is wrong to think that investigations relying on single indicators are somehow deficient. In any case, some studies, like Kelley and De Graaf (1997; see Box 3.5), employ both single- and multiple-indicator

> ### Box 3.6 Specifying dimensions of a concept: the case of de-skilling
>
> Recall the issue of de-skilling (Box 1.3). Based on a reading of the literature on the topic, Marshall *et al.* argued that there are two important components or *dimensions* of de-skilling: 'skill as complexity and skill as freedom,' which 'are central to the thesis that work is being proletarianized through the de-skilling of tasks' (1988: 116). 'Skill as complexity' was measured by a single interview question asking respondents whether their current jobs require more, less, or about the same amount of skill as when they first started. 'Skill as freedom' was measured by seven indicators treated separately and not aggregated. The questions asked about such things as whether respondents can reduce the pace or initiate new tasks in their work. Neither dimension comprised measures that offered significant support for the de-skilling thesis.

measures of concepts. What *is* crucial is that measures be reliable and valid representations of the concepts they are supposed to be tapping. It is to this issue that the discussion now turns.

Reliability and validity

Although the terms *reliability* and *validity* almost seem to be synonyms, they have quite different meanings in evaluating measures of concepts, as seen in Chapter 2.

Reliability

Reliability is fundamentally concerned with consistency of measures. There are at least three different meanings of the term, outlined in Box 3.7 and elaborated on in the following sections.

Stability

The most obvious way of testing for the stability of a measure is the *test–retest* method. This involves administering a test or measure on one occasion and

then re-administering it to the same sample on another occasion, that is:

$$T_1 \qquad T_2$$
$$Obs_1 \qquad Obs_2$$

One would expect to find a high correlation between Obs_1 and Obs_2. Correlation is a measure of the strength of the relationship between variables. This topic will be covered in Chapter 12 in a discussion about quantitative data analysis. For now, imagine a multiple-indicator measure supposed to tap a concept called 'designerism' (a preference for buying goods and especially clothing with 'designer' labels). The measure would be administered to a sample of respondents and then later re-administered. If the correlation is low, the measure is unstable, implying that respondents' answers cannot be relied upon.

Box 3.7 ⌁⊙⌁ What is reliability?

Reliability refers to consistency in the measure of a concept. It involves three prominent factors:

- *Stability*. This entails asking whether a measure is steady over time and whether results from that measure fluctuate. This means that, if one administers a measure to a group and then re-administers it perhaps an hour later, there should be little variation in the results obtained. Thermometers have this kind of reliability.

- *Internal reliability*. The key issue is whether the indicators that make up the scale or index are consistent—in other words, whether respondents' scores on any one indicator tend to be related to their scores on the other indicators. For example, people who agree with a statement that voting is a basic requirement of democracy should actually vote more often than those who disagree.

    Cronbach's alpha coefficient is a commonly used test of internal reliability. It varies between 1 (denoting perfect internal reliability) and 0 (denoting none). The figure .80 is typically employed to mark the bottom acceptable level

of internal reliability, though many writers work with a slightly lower figure. Berthoud (2000*b*: 169) wrote that a minimum level of .60 is 'good.' In the case of the commitment to work scale devised by Westergaard *et al.*, alpha was .70, which they referred to as 'a satisfactory level' (1989: 93). In the case of Kelley and De Graaf's (1997) measure of religious orthodoxy, which used four indicators, alpha ranged from .79 to .95 for each of the 15 national samples that made up the data (see Boxes 1.6 and 3.4 for more information about this research).

- *Inter-observer consistency*. When subjective judgment is involved in activities like the recording of observations or the translation of data into categories, and where more than one 'observer' is involved in such activities, there is the possibility for a lack of consistency in their decisions. This can arise in a number of contexts, for example: when answers to open-ended questions have to be categorized or in structured observation when observers have to decide how to classify subjects' behaviour. For example, is the observed person afraid, concerned, or just thinking when reading about the spread of yet another new deadly virus in the paper?

However, there are a number of problems with this approach to evaluating reliability. Respondents' answers at T_1 may influence how they reply at T_2. This may result in greater consistency between Obs_1 and Obs_2 than is in fact the case. Second, events may intervene between T_1 and T_2 that influence the degree of consistency. For example, if a long span of time is involved, changes in the economy or in respondents' personal financial circumstances can influence their views about and predilection for designer goods. On the other hand, Berthoud (2000*b*) was pleased that an index of illness achieved high test–retest reliability. Because 'some of the variation between tests (a year apart) was caused by genuine changes in people's health' (2000*b*: 170), there would have been no easy way of disentangling the effects of a lack of stability in the measure from 'real' changes in people's health over the year in question. There are no clear solutions to these problems, other than by introducing a complex research design and so turning the investigation of reliability into a major project in its own right. Perhaps for

these reasons, many, if not most, reports of research findings do not appear to carry out tests of stability. Indeed, longitudinal research is often undertaken precisely in order to identify the social change and its correlates absent in cross-sectional research.

Internal reliability

This meaning of reliability also applies to multiple-indicator measures like those examined in Boxes 3.3 and 3.5. With a multiple-item measure in which each respondent's answers to each question are aggregated to form an overall score, the possibility is raised that the indicators do not relate to the same thing; in other words, they lack coherence. All of the designerism indicators should be related to each other. If some are not, they may actually be indicative of something else.

One way of testing internal reliability is the *split-half* method. Take the commitment-to-work measure developed by Westergaard *et al.* (1989) as an example (see Box 3.3). The 10 indicators would be divided into two halves of 5, allocated on a random or an odd–even basis. The degree of correlation be-tween scores on two halves would then be calcu-lated. If the 10 are consistent, a respondent's score on the two groups of indicators should be similar, perhaps high on both, or low on both. The calcula-tion of a correlation yields a figure that varies be-tween 0 (no correlation and therefore no internal consistency) to 1 (perfect correlation and therefore complete internal consistency). Currently, most re-searchers use a test of internal reliability known as *Cronbach's alpha* (see Box 3.7). Its use has grown as a result of its incorporation into computer software for quantitative data analysis.

It is usually expected that alphas of .80 and above imply an acceptable level of internal reliability. Sometimes lower levels have to suffice; the study of domestic labour by Gazso-Windlej and McMullin (2003) could only achieve alpha's averaging .50 for its Likert-style items measuring gender ideology, but recall the study was also exploratory. The meaning of correlation will be explored in much greater detail later on. The chief point at this stage is that the cor-relation establishes how closely a respondent's scores on the two groups of indicators are related.

Inter-observer consistency

The idea of inter-observer consistency is briefly out-lined in Box 3.7. The issues involved are too ad-vanced to be dealt with at this stage and will be briefly touched on in later chapters. Cramer (1998: ch. 14) provides a very detailed treatment of the is-sues and appropriate techniques.

Validity

As noted in Chapter 2, measurement validity has to do with whether a measure of a concept really meas-ures that concept (see Box 3.8). When people argue about whether a person's IQ score really measures or reflects that person's level of intelligence, they are raising questions about the measurement validity of the IQ test in relation to the concept of intelli-gence. Whenever students and their teachers debate whether multiple-choice examinations provide an accurate measure of academic ability, they too are raising questions about measurement validity.

Box 3.8 What is validity?

Validity refers to whether an indicator (or set of indica-tors) devised to gauge a concept really measures that concept. Several ways of establishing validity are ex-plored in the text: face validity; concurrent validity; predictive validity; construct validity; and convergent validity. Here the term is being used as shorthand for the *measurement validity* of Chapter 2. Validity should therefore be distinguished from the other terms in-troduced in Chapter 2, internal validity and external validity.

Writers on measurement validity of concepts dis-tinguish among a number of different types of valid-ity, outlined below.

Face validity

At the very minimum, a researcher who develops a new measure should establish that it has *face validity*—that is, that the measure on appearance re-flects the content of the concept in question. Face validity can be established by asking those with ex-pertise in a field to act as judges to determine whether, *on the face of it*, the measure seems to reflect the concept concerned. Face validity is, therefore, an essentially intuitive process.

Concurrent validity

The researcher can also seek to gauge the *concurrent validity* of the measure. Here the researcher employs a *criterion* relevant to the concept in question, one on which cases (e.g., people) are known to differ. Assuming that as job satisfaction goes down absen-teeism goes up, to establish the concurrent validity of a new measure of job satisfaction, a researcher may look to see if people who are satisfied with their jobs are less likely than those who are not satisfied to be *absent* from work. If a lack of correspondence is found, such as no difference in levels of job satisfac-tion between frequent and infrequent absentees, doubt is cast on whether the new measure is really addressing job satisfaction.

Construct validity

Some writers advocate that the researchers estimate the *construct validity* of a measure, involving a deduction of hypotheses from a theory relevant to the concept. For example, drawing on ideas about the impact of technology on the experience of work, a researcher may anticipate that people who do routine jobs are less satisfied with their jobs than those who have a greater chance for variety, complexity, and creativity. Accordingly, this theoretical deduction of the relationship between job satisfaction and job routine would be examined. If there is a correlation, then the measure in question has construct validity. On the other hand, some caution is required if the relationship is weak or non-existent. The measure of job routine may be an invalid measure of that concept or the theory or the deduction that is made from it may have been misguided. Either way, it is probably best to seek another measure.

Convergent validity

In the view of some methodologists, the validity of a measure ought to be gauged by comparing it to measures of the same concept developed through other methods. For example, if a questionnaire asks how much time managers spend on various activities (such as attending meetings, touring their organization, in-

formal discussions, and so on), its validity may be determined by observing a number of managers to see how much time is actually spent in various activities.

An interesting instance of convergent *in*validity is described in Box 3.9. Crime surveys were consciously devised to act as a check on official police statistics. The two sets of data are collected in quite different ways: official crime statistics are collected as part of the bureaucratic processing of offenders in the criminal justice system, whereas crime victimization surveys collect data from interviews of national samples of citizens. In the case reported in Box 3.9 a lack of convergent validity was found. The problem with the convergent approach to testing validity is that it is not easy to establish which of the two measures represents the more accurate picture. They are really measuring several different things: (1) the crimes people experience, including some things that may not be crimes and omitting others that are, as when a stolen item is presumed 'lost'; (2) crimes that people are willing to call the police about, plus the crimes the police themselves discover; (3) crimes the police actually record. In any case, the 'true' volume of crime at any one time is an almost entirely metaphysical notion (Reiner 2000*a*).

Box 3.10 provides a brief account of a newly derived scale using the Likert procedure and some of the ways in which reliability and validity are assessed.

Box 3.9 A case of convergent *in*validity: crime statistics

Toronto police are routinely questioned about the crime statistics on which they base their claims to an increased budget. But across Canada there are different 'crime rates' generally, as any comparison of official police reports and national crime victimization data will show. As part of the General Social Survey (GSS), Canadians are asked about their victimization. It is widely accepted that the victimization data show more crime than the police data because many Canadians do not report their experiences to the police, for a variety of reasons (such as the bother, the embarrassment, etc.). Therefore, for robbery the victimization rate is almost three times the official rate. But in auto theft this is less likely because insurance claims require a police report and so the two rates should

be close. Actually the police data show 50 per cent more thefts, because the GSS, which shows personal victimization, does not include company cars or cars taken from car dealerships (Silverman *et al.* 2000: 58). So there will probably always be a discrepancy. In a similar instance, police uncover (15 per cent) more homicides in Canada than does the Mortality Database drawn from death certificates (Gabor *et al.* 2002), where some officials may try to lessen the pain for relatives of murder victims.

The victimization data are not measured in a true panel design, because different people are interviewed in each wave of data collection, but the categories of crime used in the survey are generally close enough to look for changes over time.

Box 3.10 Developing a Likert Scale: the case of attitudes to vegetarians

Noting that some non-vegetarians see vegetarianism as deviant and sometimes treat vegetarians with suspicion if not hostility, Chin *et al.* (2002) developed a scale to measure pro- or anti-vegetarian attitudes. It was comprised of 33 statements to which respondents are asked to indicate strength of agreement or disagreement on a seven-point scale. The items were chosen from the following: interviews with both vegetarians and non-vegetarians, reviewing the literature on vegetarianism, field observations, brainstorming within the team, and examining attitude scales on other forms of prejudice for possible wording and presentation. The items were meant to tap four areas:

- forms of behaviour among vegetarians viewed as irritating, for example, 'Vegetarians preach too much about their beliefs and eating habits' (possibly a double-barrelled item—see Chapter 6 because it includes both beliefs and eating habits, which may not be the same);
- disagreement with vegetarians' beliefs, for example, 'Vegetarians are overly concerned with animal rights';

- health-related aspects of being a vegetarian, for example, 'Vegetarians are overly concerned about gaining weight'; and
- appropriate treatment of vegetarians, for example, 'It's okay to tease someone for being a vegetarian.'

The scale was tested on a sample of US undergraduates. Some items were dropped because of poor internal consistency with other items. Cronbach's alpha for the remaining 21 items was .87 (see Box 3.7).

The construct validity of the scale was also tested. Students completed other scales on variables thought to be associated with pro- or anti-vegetarian attitudes. For example, the authors hypothesized that people scoring high on an authoritarian attitude scale are more likely to be anti-vegetarians. This was confirmed, although the relationship is weak. Worse, contrary to their hypothesis, their attitude-towards-vegetarianism score is *not* related to political conservatism measures. They had thought liberals would be more tolerant of vegetarians. Thus their scale emerged as internally reliable but of slightly questionable construct validity.

Reflections on reliability and validity

There are, then, a number of ways to investigate the merit of measures devised to represent social scientific concepts. However, the discussion of reliability and validity is potentially misleading, because it is wrong to think that all new measures of concepts are submitted to the rigours just described. In fact, many measures are simply asserted. There may be a test for internal reliability when a new multiple-indicator measure is devised and an examination of face validity, but in many cases no further testing takes place, a point elaborated later.

It should also be remembered that, although reliability and validity are analytically distinguishable, they are related: if a measure is not reliable, it cannot be valid. This point can be made with respect to each of the three criteria of reliability just discussed. If the measure is not stable over time, it may be measuring different things on different occasions. Similarly, a multiple-indicator measure lacking internal reliability is actually measuring two or more different things and therefore cannot be valid. Finally, if observers cannot agree on the meaning of what they are observing, there is a lack of inter-observer consistency, which means a valid measure cannot be in operation.

The main preoccupations of quantitative researchers

Both quantitative and qualitative research exhibit a set of contrasting preoccupations, reflecting epistemologically grounded beliefs about what constitutes acceptable knowledge. In this section, four distinctive preoccupations of quantitative research are examined: measurement, causality, generalization, and replication.

Measurement

The most obvious preoccupation is with measurement, a feature that is scarcely surprising since that has been the focus of much of the discussion in the present chapter. From the position of quantitative research, measurement carries a number of advantages previously outlined. It is not surprising that, therefore, issues of reliability and validity are a concern for quantitative researchers, though this is not always manifested in research practice.

Causality

There is a very strong concern in most quantitative research with explanation. Quantitative researchers are rarely concerned merely to describe how things are, but are keen to say *why* things are the way they are, an emphasis also frequent in the natural sciences. Thus researchers examining prejudice may want not only to describe it, for example, in terms of how much prejudice exists in a certain group of individuals, or what proportion of people in a sample are highly prejudiced, but also to explain it, which means examining its causes. They may seek to explain prejudice in terms of personal characteristics (such as levels of authoritarianism, with those less flexible and rule-bound being more prejudiced) or in terms of social characteristics (such as amount of social mobility, increased levels leading to less prejudice). In the resulting reports, prejudice is the dependent variable, the one to be explained, and authoritarianism and social mobility are independent variables, the ones that have a causal influence upon prejudice.

When an experimental design is being employed, the independent variable is the variable that is manipulated. There is little ambiguity about the direction of causal influence (see Box 2.7). However, with cross-sectional designs of the kind used in most social survey research, there is ambiguity about the direction of causal influence because the data on all variables are simultaneously collected, meaning one cannot say with full confidence that an independent variable preceded the dependent one. To refer to independent and dependent variables in the context of cross-sectional designs, one must *infer* the temporal sequence of variables based on common sense or prior theory, that one causes the other, as in the example concerning authoritarianism and prejudice in the previous paragraph. However, there is always the risk that the inference is wrong (see Box 3.11).

The concern about causality is reflected in the preoccupation with internal validity referred to in Chapter 2. There it was noted that a frequent criterion of good quantitative research is the extent of confidence in the researcher's causal inferences. Research that exhibits the characteristics of an experimental design is often more highly valued than cross-sectional research because of the greater confidence that can be placed in the causal findings associated with the former. For their part, quantitative researchers who employ cross-sectional designs are invariably concerned to develop techniques that allow causal inferences to be made. Moreover, the rise of longitudinal research almost certainly reflects a desire on the part of quantitative researchers to improve their ability to generate findings that permit a causal interpretation.

Generalization

In quantitative research, researchers usually want to generalize their findings beyond the confines of the particular context in which the research is conducted. Thus, if a study of prejudice involves people filling out a questionnaire, can the results apply to individuals other than those who actually participated in the study? Given that it is rarely feasible to send questionnaires to or interview whole populations (such as all members of a town, or the whole population of a country, or even everyone in an organization), those studied are only a *sample*. A sample should be as representative as possible of a population in order to say that the results are not unique to the particular group upon whom the research is conducted, those who provide the data. The preoccupation with generalization can be viewed as an attempt to develop the lawlike findings of the natural sciences. According to Archimedes' principle, water rises in any bathtub, anywhere and

---

Box 3.11 The case of displayed emotions in convenience stores

Following a review of the literature, Sutton and Rafaeli (1992) hypothesized a positive relationship between the display of positive emotions to retail shoppers (smiling, friendly greeting, eye contact) and the level of retail sales. In other words, when retail staff are friendly and give time to shoppers, higher sales follow. Sutton and Rafaeli had data from 576 convenience stores in a US national retail chain. Structured observation of the retail workers provided data on the display of positive emotions, and quantitative sales data provided information for the other variable.

The hypothesis was not supported; indeed, stores in which retail workers are *less* inclined to smile, be friendly, and so on, have better sales. Sutton and Rafaeli (1992: 124) considered restating their hypothesis to make it seem that they had found what they had expected (see Ethical issue 15.1), but fortunately resisted the temptation. Instead, they conducted a qualitative investigation of four stores to help understand what was happening. They used a number of methods: unstructured observation of interactions between staff and customers; semi-structured in-

terviews with store managers; casual conversations with store managers, supervisors, executives, and others; and data gathered through posing as a customer in stores. The qualitative investigation suggested that the relationship between the display of positive emotions and sales *is* indeed negative, but that sales are likely to be a cause rather than a consequence of the display of emotions. In stores with high levels of sales, staff are under greater pressure and encounter longer queues at checkouts. Staff therefore have less time and inclination for the pleasantries associated with the display of positive emotions.

Thus, instead of the causal sequence being

More positive emotions → More retail sales

it is

More retail sales → Less positive emotions

This exercise also highlights the main difficulty associated with inferring causal direction from a cross-sectional research design (see Box 2.12 and Figure 2.2).

---

anytime someone steps into it, and any sample will do.

Probability sampling, explored in Chapter 11, is the usual first choice among researchers seeking a representative sample. This procedure largely eliminates bias by using a process of random selection to choose a sample. The use of a random selection process does not guarantee a representative sample, however, because as will be seen in Chapter 11, even there, factors that operate over and above the selection system can jeopardize the representativeness of a sample. A related consideration is that even with a representative sample, of what is it representative? The simple answer is that it is representative of the population from which it is selected and, strictly speaking, one cannot generalize beyond that population. This means that, if the population from which a sample is taken are all inhabitants of one town, or city, or province, or are all members of an organization, generalizations should be made only to the inhabitants or members of the specific town, city, province, or organization. But it is very tempting to see the findings as having a more pervasive applicability, so that even results from a sample se-

lected from a large city like Toronto are thought relevant to similar cities. Thus, while one should not make inferences beyond the population from which the sample is selected, many researchers do so, expanding the limits on generalizing findings.

The concern with generalizability or external validity is particularly strong among quantitative researchers using cross-sectional and longitudinal designs. Experimental researchers are concerned about generalizability, as the discussion of external validity in Chapter 2 suggested, but users of this research design usually give greater attention to internal than to external validity issues.

Replication

The natural sciences are often depicted as wishing to reduce to a bare minimum the contaminating influence of the scientist's biases and values, characteristics, and expectations. Were biases pervasive, the claims of the natural sciences to provide a definitive picture of the world would be seriously undermined. To check on the influence of these potentially damaging problems (and others), scientists believe that they should be able to replicate each other's experiments. If a scientist's findings repeatedly cannot be reproduced, serious questions are raised about the validity of the findings. Likewise, quantitative researchers in the social sciences often regard the ability to replicate as an important ingredient of their activity. It is easy to see why: the possibility of the intrusion of the researcher's values would appear to be much greater when examining the social world than when a natural scientist investigates the natural order. Consequently, it is often regarded as important that the researcher spells out clearly all research procedures so that they can be replicated by others, even if the research does not end up being replicated.

Actually, replication is not a high-status activity in the natural and social sciences, often regarded as a pedestrian and uninspiring pursuit. Moreover, standard replications are not easily publishable in the minds of many academic journal editors. Consequently, replications of research appear in print far less frequently than might be supposed. A further reason for the low incidence of published replications is that it is difficult to ensure, especially in social science research, that the conditions in a replication are precisely the same as those of the original study. So long as there is some ambiguity about whether the conditions relating to a replication are the same as those in the initial study, any differences in findings may be attributable to the design of the replication rather than to some deficiency in the original study. Nonetheless, it is crucial that the methods used in generating a set of findings are made explicit, so that it is *possible* to replicate a piece of research. Thus, it is *replicability* that is often regarded as an important quality of quantitative research.

The critique of quantitative research

Over the years quantitative research, along with its epistemological and ontological foundations, has been the focus of a great deal of criticism, particularly from exponents of qualitative research. They include criticisms of quantitative research in general as a research strategy and criticisms of specific methods and research designs with which quantitative research is associated.

Criticisms of quantitative research

To give a flavour of the critique of quantitative research, four criticisms are covered briefly:

- *Quantitative researchers fail to distinguish people and social institutions from 'the world of nature.'* Phenomenologists charge social scientists employing a natural science model with treating the social world as if it were no different from the natural order. In so doing, they draw attention to one of positivism's central tenets—namely, that the principles of the scientific method can and should be applied to any phenomenon investigated. More particularly, as observed in Chapter 1, it means riding roughshod over the fact that people interpret the world around them, whereas this capacity for self-reflection cannot be found among the objects of the natural sciences, such as chemical elements, photosynthesis, and the circulation of blood.

- *The measurement process possesses an artificial and false sense of precision and accuracy.* There are a number of aspects to this criticism. For one thing, the connection between the measures developed by social scientists and the concepts they are supposed to be revealing is assumed rather than real. Testing for validity in the manner described in the previous section cannot really address this problem, because the very tests themselves (concurrent, construct, etc.) have the same flaws—no assurance that they are really measuring their concepts or the original ones. A further way in which the measurement process is regarded as flawed is that it presumes, for example, that different individuals responding to the same question are interpreting the key terms in the question similarly. For example, 'What is your social class?' can mean current wealth to one person; to another it can mean ancestry as in how many generations the family has been wealthy. For many methodologists, respondents simply do not interpret such terms similarly. An often attempted solution to this problem is to use questions with fixed-choice answers—'Are you upper class, middle class, working class, etc.?'—but this approach merely provides 'a solution to the problem of meaning by simply ignoring it' (Cicourel 1964: 108).

- *The reliance on instruments and procedures hinders the connection between research and everyday life.* This issue relates to the question of external validity raised in Chapter 2. Many methods of quantitative research rely heavily on administering research instruments to subjects (such as structured interviews and self-completion questionnaires) or on controlling situations to determine causal connections (such as in experiments). However, as Cicourel (1982) asked, how do researchers know if survey respondents have the requisite knowledge to answer a question or whether they share a common sense of the importance of the topic in their everyday lives? Thus, if

respondents answer a set of questions designed to measure prejudice, are they all equally aware of what it is and its manifestations? One can go even further and ask how well their answers relate to their everyday lives. People may answer a question designed to measure racial prejudice, but respondents' actual behaviour may be at variance with their answers (LaPiere 1934). For more on the discrepancy between attitudes and behaviour, see Box 3.12.

- *The analysis of relationships between variables creates a static view of social life that is independent of people's lives.* Blumer argued that studies that aim to bring out the relationships between variables omit 'the process of interpretation or definition that goes on in human groups' (1956: 685). This symbolic interactionist assessment incorporates the first and third criticisms above, that the meaning of events to individuals is ignored and that the connection to everyday contexts is missing, but adds a further element. Quantitative research creates a sense of a static social world separate from the individuals who make it up. In other words,

---

Box 3.12 Gap between stated and actual behaviour

A study of racial prejudice conducted many years ago by LaPiere (1934) illustrates this issue. He spent two years travelling with a young Chinese student and his wife and then observing from a distance if they were refused entry at hotels and restaurants. Of 66 hotels approached, they were refused entry once; of 184 restaurants and diners, none refused entry.

LaPiere then allowed six months to elapse before sending questionnaires to the hotels and restaurants visited. One question asked: 'Will you accept members of the Chinese race as guests in your establishment?' Of the establishments *that replied*, 92 per cent of restaurants and 91 per cent of hotels said no. LaPiere's simple though striking study clearly illustrates a gap between reports of behaviour and actual behaviour. It should also be noted that the question asked was somewhat unclear, a feature not usually noted in connection with this widely cited study. 'Will you . . .?' can be interpreted as asking about the future or to state the establishment's policy. Why the more obvious formulation of 'Do you . . .?' was not used is not clear, though it is unlikely that this point had a significant

bearing on the findings and their implications for survey research. On the other hand, the results may be just another example of the widespread difference between holding a prejudiced attitude and engaging in a discriminatory act. An experimental study of prejudice among college students (Frazer and Wiersma 2001) showed that in hypothetical situations the students hire black and white applicants of varying abilities equally, but a week later recall the black applicants as less intelligent than whites though both groups were equal. Indeed, one old study showed that people did not want certain groups in their neighbourhoods, the catch being that the groups were fictional! In the real world, peer pressure can make an unprejudiced person discriminate, to 'go along,' while a prejudiced person may not discriminate for fear of a lawsuit.

The gap is usually worst when predictions of future behaviour are involved. The Canadian Blood Services pointed out that 28 per cent of Canadians intend to give blood in any given year, but only 3.7 per cent do. Literally millions intend to vote—many even revealing their preferences to pollsters—and then do not vote.

it is seen to carry an objectivist ontology with a reality, here a social world, that exists outside of human consciousness.

These criticisms reflect a set of concerns associated with a qualitative research strategy combining an interpretivist epistemological orientation (an emphasis on meaning from the individual's point of view) and a constructionist ontology (an emphasis on viewing the social world as the product of individuals rather than as something beyond them). The criticisms may appear very damning, but, as will be seen in Chapter 8, quantitative researchers have a powerful battery of criticisms of qualitative research in their arsenal as well.

Is it always like this? Reality and practice

One of the problems with characterizing any research strategy, design, or method is that to a certain extent each is presented as an ideal, one rare in actual research practice. This gap between the ideal and actual can arise as a result of at least two major considerations. First, it arises because those who write about and teach research methods cannot cover every eventuality that can arise in the process of social research. Thus, a model of the process of quantitative research, such as that provided in Figure 3.1, is really a general *tendency* rather than a definitive description of all quantitative research. A second reason for the gap is that, to a great extent, writing and teaching about research methods essentially provide an account of *good practice*. These practices are often not followed in the published research that students are likely to encounter in their substantive courses. This failure to follow the procedures associated with good practice is not necessarily due to incompetence on the part of social researchers, though in some cases it is. More likely it is associated with matters of time, cost, and feasibility—in other words, the unavoidable pragmatic concerns of conducting research.

Reverse operationalism

For an example of the first source of the gap between ideal and actual research practice, take the case of 'reverse operationalism' (Bryman 1988*a*: 28). The model of the process of quantitative research in Box 3.1 implies that concepts are specified and then measures are provided for them. As noted, this means that indicators must be devised. This is the basis of 'operationalism' implying a deductive view of how research should proceed. However, this view neglects the fact that measurement can entail more of an inductive element than Box 3.1 implies. Sometimes, measures are developed that in turn lead to conceptualization. One way in which this can occur is when a statistical technique known as *factor analysis* is employed. This technique is employed in relation to multiple-indicator measures to determine whether groups of indicators tend to bunch together to form distinct clusters, referred to as *factors*. Gazso-Windlej and McMullin (2003) did this to measure gender ideology.

To measure the concept of 'charismatic leadership,' a term that owes a great deal to Weber (1947), Conger and Kanungo (1998) generated 25 items to provide a multiple-item measure of the concept. These items came from their reading of existing theory and research on the subject, particularly in connection with charismatic leadership in organizations. When the items were administered to a sample of respondents and the results analyzed, the items bunched into six factors, each of which to all intents and purposes represents a dimension of the concept of charismatic leadership:

- strategic vision and articulation behaviour;
- sensitivity to the environment;
- unconventional behaviour;
- personal risk;
- sensitivity to organizational members' needs; and
- action orientation away from the maintenance of the status quo.

The point to note is that these six dimensions were not specified at the outset: the link between conceptualization and measurement was inductive. Nor is this an unusual situation in social research. Johnson *et al.* (2003) read transcripts of unstructured interviews with Canadian adolescents on their need to smoke in order to identify the words they used to describe tobacco dependence, and from this reading the researchers developed questions they used in subsequent interviews to compile 60 key phrases that describe the reasons for smoking. Some smoked for pleasure, others for emotional reasons, and still others for empowerment because it made them feel more adult. Here not only was the theory grounded, but the measures also came from the data.

Reliability and validity testing

A second reason for a gap between ideal and actual research practice is because researchers do not follow some of the recommended practices. Analyses of published quantitative research in organization studies (Podsakoff and Dalton 1987) revealed that writers rarely report tests of the stability of their measures and even more rarely evidence of measurement validity (only 3 per cent). The one exception is a large proportion of articles that use Cronbach's alpha, a gauge of internal consistency for multiple-item measures, but for non-scale items the stability and validity of many measures in the field of organization are unknown. This is not to say that this research is necessarily *un*stable and *in*valid, but simply unknown or not demonstrated. The reasons for this omission are almost certainly the cost and time likely to be involved. Researchers tend to be more concerned with substantive issues and less in the work required for thoroughly determining measurement quality. Thus as Cicourel (1964) said, much measurement in sociology is 'measurement by fiat.'

The remarks on the lack of assessment of the quality of measurement should not be taken as a justification for readers to neglect this phase in their work. The aim here is merely to draw attention to some ways in which practices described in this book are not always followed and to suggest some reasons for this shortcoming.

Sampling

A similar point can be made in relation to sampling, the topic of Chapter 11. As will be seen, good practice is strongly associated with *random* or *probability sampling*. However, quite a lot of research is based on inferior alternatives. Sometimes the use of non-probability samples is due to the impossibility or extreme difficulty of obtaining probability samples. Yet another reason is that the time and cost involved in securing a probability sample are too great relative to the level of resources available. And yet a third reason is that sometimes the opportunity to study a certain group arises and represents too good an opportunity to miss. Again, such considerations should not be viewed as a justification for ignoring the principles of sampling, not least because not following the principles of probability sampling carries implications for the kind of statistical analysis that can be employed (see Chapter 12). Instead, the purpose as before is to draw attention to the ways in which gaps between recommendations about good practice and actual research practice can arise.

K   **KEY POINTS**

- Quantitative research can be characterized as a linear series of steps moving from theory to conclusions, but the process described in Figure 3.1 is an ideal from which there are many departures.

- The measurement process in quantitative research generally entails a search for indicators.

- Establishing the reliability and validity of measures is important for assessing their quality.

- Quantitative research can be characterized as exhibiting certain central preoccupations: measurement, causality, generalization, and replication.

- Quantitative research has been subjected to many criticisms by qualitative researchers. These criticisms tend to revolve around rejecting the view that a natural science model is appropriate for studying the social world.

Q QUESTIONS FOR REVIEW

The main steps in quantitative research

- What are the main steps in quantitative research?

- To what extent do the main steps follow a strict sequence?

- Do the steps suggest a deductive or inductive approach to the relationship between theory and research?

Concepts and their measurement

- Why is measurement important to a quantitative researcher?

- What is the difference between a measure and an indicator?

- Why may multiple-indicators of a concept be preferable to one using a single indicator?

Reliability and validity

- Are some forms of reliability more important than others?

- 'Whereas validity presupposes reliability, reliability does not presuppose validity.' Discuss.

- What are the main criteria for evaluating measurement validity?

The main preoccupations of quantitative researchers

- Outline the main preoccupations of quantitative researchers. What reasons can be given for their prominence?

- Why is replication especially important to quantitative researchers, in spite of the tendency for replications in social research to be very rare?

The critique of quantitative research

- 'The crucial problem with quantitative research is its failure to address adequately the issue of meaning.' Discuss.

- How central is the quantitative researchers' use of a natural science model of research to the critique by qualitative researchers of quantitative research?

4

Structured interviewing and questionnaires

CHAPTER OVERVIEW

The structured interview is one of a variety of forms of the research interview, but it is the one most commonly employed in survey research. The goal of the structured interview is standardization, with many guidelines developed to minimize variation in the conduct of interviews within a particular project. Many of the same rules apply also to self-completed questionnaires. The chapter explores:

- reasons for the widespread use of the structured interview in survey research, entailing a consideration of the importance of standardization to the process of measurement;

- the different contexts of interviewing, such as the use of more than one interviewer, and whether the interview is administered in person, by telephone, or via the computer;

- various prerequisites of structured interviewing, including: establishing rapport with the interviewee; asking questions exactly as they appear on the interview schedule; keeping to the question order as it appears on the schedule; and recording exactly what is said by interviewees;

- problems with structured interviewing, including: influence of the interviewer on respondents and the possibility of systematic bias in answers (known as *response sets*);

- the advantages and disadvantages of the questionnaire compared with the structured interview;

- the use of diaries as a form of questionnaire; and

- a feminist critique of structured interviews and questionnaires.

Introduction

The interview is a common occurrence in social life; there are job interviews, media interviews, and police interviews. And then there are research interviews, the topic of this chapter. These different kinds of interviews share some common features, such as the eliciting of information by an interviewer from an interviewee and the operation of rules, of varying degrees of formality or explicitness, concerning the conduct of the interview.

In a social research interview, the aim is for the interviewer to elicit from *respondents*, as they are frequently called in survey research, all manner of information: the interviewees' own behaviour (or that of others), attitudes, norms, beliefs, and values. There are many different styles of research interview, but the kind primarily employed in survey research is the structured interview, the focus here. Other kinds of interviews are also briefly mentioned, but their discussion is saved for later chapters.

The structured interview

The research interview is a prominent data-collection strategy in qualitative research, but it is in quantitative research, specifically survey research, that it is most common and thus the current focus

Box 4.1 *What is a structured interview?*

A structured interview, sometimes called a *standardized interview*, entails the administration of an interview schedule by an interviewer. Interviewers are supposed to read out questions exactly and in the same order as they are printed on the schedule. All interviewees thus experience the same context of questioning and receive exactly the same interview stimulus. The goal is to allow interviewees' replies to be aggregated (added together to form group rates) and this can be achieved reliably only if those replies are in response to identical cues. Questions are usually very specific and offer the interviewee a fixed range of answers from which to choose. The structured interview is the typical form of interview in survey research.

Box 4.2 Some prominent sources of error in survey research

This is a list of the principal sources of error in survey research.

1 A poorly worded question.
2 How a question is asked by the interviewer.
3 Misunderstanding on the part of the interviewee.
4 Interviewee lapses in memory.
5 The way the information is recorded by the interviewer.
6 How the information is processed, either when answers are coded or when data are entered into the computer.

(see Box 4.1). The structured interview is one of the two main ways of administering a survey research instrument. The other, self-administered questionnaires, is the topic of the end of the chapter.

The main reason why survey researchers typically prefer the structured interview is that it promotes standardization of *both* the asking of questions *and* the recording of answers. This feature has two closely related virtues from the perspective of quantitative research: reducing error due to variation in the asking of questions and greater accuracy in and ease of processing respondents' answers.

Reducing error due to interviewer variability

Properly executed, standardization in both asking questions and recording answers means that variation in people's replies are due to 'true' or 'real' variation and not to the interview context. Still there is always a chance that some respondents will be inaccurately classified and there are a number of possible reasons for this (see Box 4.2).

To take a simple illustration, a question on alcohol consumption among students will show that they vary in amount of alcohol they consume (see Figure 4.1). Most measurement will contain an element of error, so that it is helpful to think of varia-

tion as made up of two components: true variation and error. In other words: variation = true variation + variation due to error. The aim is to keep the error portion to a minimum (see Figure 4.1), since error reduces the validity of a measure. Standardization in the structured interview means that two sources of variation due to error—the second and fifth in Box 4.2—are likely to be less pronounced.

Variability can occur in either of two ways. First is *intra-interviewer variability*, whereby an interviewer is not consistent in the asking of questions and recording answers either of different respondents or even the same respondent over the duration of the interview. Second, when there is more than one interviewer (the usual case), there may be *inter-interviewer variability*, whereby interviewers are not consistent with each other in the ways they ask questions and/or record answers. Needless to say, these two

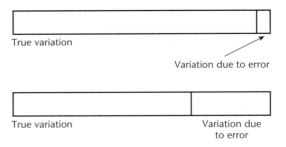

Figure 4.1 A variable with little error and one with considerable error

sources of variability are not mutually exclusive; they can coexist, compounding the problem even further. In view of the significance of standardization, some prefer to call the structured interview a *standardized interview*.

Accuracy and ease of data processing

Like self-completion questionnaires to be discussed next, most structured interviews contain mainly questions that are variously referred to as *closed*, *closed ended*, *pre-coded*, or *fixed choice*. With a closed question, the respondent is given a limited choice of possible answers and asked to select which one(s) apply. This issue will be covered in detail in Chapter 5. Ideally, this procedure simply entails the interviewer placing a tick in a box by the answer(s) selected by a respondent or circling the selected answer. The advantage is that the potential for interviewer variability is reduced: there is no problem of whether the interviewer can write down everything that the respondent says or misinterpret the reply given. If an *open* or *open-ended* question is asked, the interviewer generally cannot write down everything said, may embellish what is said, or may misinterpret what is said.

However, the advantages of this type of question in the context of survey research go further than this. One advantage particularly significant in the current context is that closed questions greatly facilitate the processing of data. When an open question is asked, the answers need to be sifted and *coded* before the data can be analyzed quantitatively. Not only is this laborious, particularly if there are many open questions and/or respondents, but it also introduces the potential for another source of error (the sixth in Box 4.2), variability in the coding of answers. When open questions are asked, answers can be in the form of several sentences. These answers have to be examined and then categorized, so that each person's answer can be aggregated with other respondents' answers to the same question. A number can then be allocated to each category of answer for quantitative analysis. This general process is known as *coding* and will be examined in greater detail in Chapter 5.

Coding introduces yet another source of error. First, if the rules for assigning answers to categories, collectively known as the *coding frame*, are flawed, any observed variation may not reflect the true variation in interviewees' replies. Second, there may be variability in the ways in which answers are categorized. As with interviewing, there can be two sources: *intra-coder variability*, whereby a coder varies over time in applying the rules for assigning answers to categories, and *inter-coder variability*, whereby coders differ from each other in how to categorize the same answer. If either (or both) source(s) of variability occurs, at least part of the variation in interviewees' replies does not reflect true variation, instead caused by error.

The closed question sidesteps this problem neatly, because respondents' allocate *themselves* to categories. The coding process is then a simple matter of attaching a different number to each category of answer and entering the numbers into a computer database, as in: Strongly agree = 1, Agree = 2, etc. It is not surprising, therefore, that this type of question is often referred to as pre-coded, because coding decisions are typically undertaken before any respondent has actually been asked questions. There is very little opportunity for interviewers or coders to differ in how they record answers. Of course, if some respondents misunderstand any terms in the answers presented, or if the answers do not adequately cover the appropriate range of possibilities, the question cannot provide a valid measure. However, that is a separate issue, another one for later. The chief point to register about closed questions for the moment is that, when compared to open questions, they reduce one potential source of error *and* are easier to process for quantitative analysis.

Other types of interview

The structured interview is by no means the only type of interview, but it is certainly the main type encountered in survey research and in quantitative research generally. Unfortunately, a host of different terms have been employed by writers on research methodology to distinguish the diverse forms of research interview. Box 4.3 represents an attempt to capture some of that variety.

Box 4.3 Other types of interviews

- *Semi-structured interview.* This is a term that covers a wide range of instances. It typically refers to a context in which the interviewer has a series of questions in the general form of an interview schedule but is allowed to vary the sequence of questions. The questions are frequently somewhat more general in their frame of reference from that typically found in a structured interview schedule. Also, the interviewer usually has some latitude to ask additional questions in response to what are seen as significant replies.

- *Unstructured interview.* The interviewer typically has only a list of topics or issues to be covered, often called an *interview guide.* The style of questioning is usually informal and the phrasing and sequencing of questions can vary from interview to interview. *Intensive interview* is a term employed by Lofland and Lofland (1995) as an alternative term; it's also called *ethnographic interview.*

- *Qualitative interview.* For some writers, this term seems to denote an *unstructured interview* (e.g., Mason

1996), but more frequently it is a general term that embraces interviews of both the semi-structured and unstructured kind (e.g., Rubin and Rubin 1995). Today, this is increasingly called an *in-depth interview.*

- *Focus group.* This refers to an interview using predominantly open questions, to ask interviewees *in a group setting* about a specific situation or event that is relevant to them and of interest to the researcher. Chapter 11 has more on this.

- *Oral history interview.* This is an *unstructured* or *semi-structured interview* in which the respondent is asked to recall events from his or her past and to reflect on them (see also Box 11.4). There is usually a cluster of fairly specific research concerns relating to a particular epoch or event.

- *Life history interview.* Similar to the *oral history interview,* the aim of this type of *unstructured interview* is to glean information on the entire biography of each respondent (see also Box 11.4).

All the forms of interview outlined in Box 4.3, with the exception of the *structured interview* and the *standardized interview,* are primarily used in qualitative research and it is in that context that they will be encountered again later in this book. They are rarely used in quantitative research and survey research in particular, because the absence of standardization in asking questions and recording answers makes respondents' replies more difficult to aggregate. This is not to say that they have no role at all. For example, as will be seen in Chapter 5, the unstructured interview can have a useful role in developing the fixed-choice alternatives with which respondents are provided in the kind of closed question that is typical of the structured interview.

Interview contexts

In a traditional interview, an interviewer stands or sits in front of the respondent asking the latter a series of questions and writing down the answers. However, there are several possible departures from this archetype.

More than one interviewer or interviewee

More than one interviewer is a very unusual situation in social research because of the considerable cost involved in dispatching two (or indeed more than two) people to interview someone. In the case of focus groups it is more common, but in that instance there is more than one interviewee too. However, it is very unusual for structured interviews to be used in this connection. In survey research, it is almost always a specific individual who is the object of questioning by one interviewer. Indeed, in survey interviews it is advisable to discourage as far as possible the presence and intrusion of others during the course of the interview. Investigations in which more than one person is being interviewed tend to be in qualitative research, though this is not always the case; Pahl's (1990) study of patterns of control of money among couples employed structured interviewing of couples, and then of husbands and wives separately.

In person or by telephone?

While it is more customary in academic social research not involving national samples to conduct research with face-to-face interviews, telephone interviewing is the norm in fields like market and government research, where it often takes the form of computer-assisted telephone interviewing (see later). There are several advantages of telephone over personal interviews:

- They are far cheaper and also quicker to administer. This arises because interviewers have to spend a great deal of time travelling between respondents for personal interviews, a factor even more pronounced when a sample is geographically dispersed. Of course, telephone interviews take time and hired interviewers have to be paid, but the cost of conducting a telephone interview is still lower than a comparable face-to-face one. Moreover, the general efficiency of telephone interviewing has been enhanced with the advent and widespread use in commercial circles of computer-assisted telephone interviewing (CATI).

- The telephone interview is easier to supervise than the personal interview. This is a particular advantage when there are several interviewers because it becomes easier to check on interviewer errors in asking questions, such as rephrasing them or probing inappropriately. Face-to-face interviews can be tape-recorded so that data quality can be assessed, but this raises issues of confidentiality, so that this procedure has to be treated cautiously.

- Telephone interviewing has a further advantage that has to do with some evidence suggesting that in personal interviews, respondents' replies are sometimes affected by characteristics of the interviewers (e.g., gender, class, and ethnicity). Indeed their mere physical presence may encourage interviewees to reply in ways they feel will be

deemed desirable by interviewers. The remoteness of the interviewer in telephone interviewing removes this potential source of bias to a significant extent. The interviewer's personal characteristics, race, and appearance (but not gender) cannot be seen and, being physically absent, may offset the likelihood of respondents' answers being affected by the interviewer.

Box 4.4 Dealing with interviewer effects

It makes sense that some interviewer characteristics will affect the data collected. After all, polling companies do not just hire anyone to collect data. Check any mall: the interviewers tend to be middle-aged women. In general, sex and race are the key reactive issues that affect responses. The good news is that their effects are mostly confined to sexual and racial issues and have less effect on other areas.

For example, take the topic of whether jobs should be set aside for female applicants only. Here are the results (percentage who approve): male talking to male interviewer, 37; male talking to female interviewer, 48; female talking to either male or female interviewer, 58. Something is wrong, but where? One might assume some men are lying to the woman interviewer, but it could be men lying to a man interviewer just as males may lie to other males on their incomes, sex lives, etc. A man may believe in employment equity but, knowing it is controversial, not admit it. Some of the women who say they agree may not really. They may feel that the time for employment equity is past and it is time for women to make it strictly on their merits, but they may lie to another woman so they don't appear to be deserting the feminist cause. Sharing a common status does not always lead to candour. Indeed, Kusow (2003) concluded that insider status compared to outsider (here being a Somali in Canada) is less important than the experiences of the actual research situation.

What can be done? A first step is to train interviewers carefully to be professional and clinical, to stress that any answer is acceptable, and in the pilot to see if any interviewers stand out. The data collected by any one interviewer should be similar to the data of the others, at least roughly. So if one interviewer is finding that 88 per cent of men agree with reserving jobs just for women, something may be wrong. Check early for this problem and if found retrain the individual. As a last resort replace the interviewer.

Telephone interviewing suffers from certain limitations when compared to the personal interview:

- People who do not own or who are not contactable by telephone obviously cannot be interviewed by telephone. Since this characteristic is most likely to be a feature of poorer households, the potential for sampling bias exists. Also, many people choose to be ex-directory—that is, they have paid to have their telephone numbers not listed in a telephone book. Again, these people cannot be interviewed by telephone. One likely solution to this last difficulty is *random digit dialling*. With this technique, the computer randomly selects telephone numbers within a predefined geographical area. This procedure can catch ex-directory households, though it cannot, of course, gain access to those without a telephone. In some areas laws prevent contacting cell phones in this way.

- Respondents with hearing impairments are more likely to find telephone interviewing difficult for them than personal interviewing.

- The length of a telephone interview is unlikely to be sustainable beyond 20–25 minutes, whereas personal interviews can be much longer (Frey 2004).

- There is some evidence that telephone interviews fare less well in asking about sensitive issues, such as drug and alcohol use, income, tax returns, and health. However, the evidence is not entirely consistent on this point, though it is probably sufficient to suggest that when many questions of this kind are to be used, a personal interview may be superior (Shuy 2002).

- Telephone interviewers cannot engage in observation. This means that they are not in a position to respond to signs of puzzlement or unease on the faces of respondents. In a personal interview, the interviewer may respond to such signs by restating the question or attempting to clarify the meaning of the question, though this has to be handled in a standardized way as far as possible. A further issue is that sometimes interviewers are asked to collect subsidiary information in connection with their visits (e.g., whether a house is in need of repair). Such information cannot be collected when telephone interviews are employed.

- Frequently, a specific individual in a household or firm is the target of an interview, for example, a person in a certain role or position or with particular characteristics. In other words, simply anybody will *not* do. It is probably more difficult to ascertain by telephone interview whether the correct person is replying.

- The telephone interviewer cannot employ visual aids such as show cards (see Box 4.7) from which respondents select their replies, or use diagrams or photographs.

- There is some evidence that the quality of data derived from telephone interviews is inferior to that of comparable face-to-face interviews. A series of experiments in the US using long questionnaires, reported by Holbrook *et al.* (2003), found that respondents interviewed by telephone are more likely to: express no opinion or 'don't know'; to give the same answer to a series of linked questions; to express socially desirable answers; to be apprehensive about the interview; and to be dissatisfied with the time taken by the interviews (even though they were invariably shorter than in the face-to-face mode). Also, telephone interviewees tend to be less engaged in the interview process. While these results should be viewed with caution, since studies like these are affected by things like the length and topic of the questionnaire, they do provide interesting food for thought.

Computer-assisted interviewing

Today the use of computers in the interviewing process is common, especially in commercial survey research conducted by market research and opinion-polling organizations. There are two main formats for computer-assisted interviews: computer-assisted personal interviewing (CAPI) and computer-assisted telephone interviewing (CATI). Among commercial survey organizations, almost all telephone interviewing is CATI. The main reason for the growing use of CAPI has been the increased portability and affordability of 'laptop' computers and the availability of quality software packages for devising interview schedules.

With computer-assisted interviewing, the questions that comprise an interview schedule appear on the screen. As interviewers ask each question, they 'key in' the appropriate reply using a mouse and proceed to the next question. This process has the great advantage that, when *filter questions* (see Box 4.6 later in the chapter) are asked, so that certain questions may be skipped as a result of a person's previous reply —for example, if there are no siblings then there's no need to ask about sharing the care of a dependent parent—computers can be programmed to 'jump' to the next relevant question. This removes the possibility of interviewers inadvertently asking inappropriate questions or failing to ask some that should be asked. As such, computer-assisted interviewing enhances the degree of control over the interview process and can therefore improve standardization of the asking and recording of questions.

However, there is very little evidence to suggest that the quality of data deriving from computer-assisted interviews are demonstrably superior to comparable paper-and-pencil interviews (Couper and Hansen 2002). If interviewers are out in the field all day, they can either take a disk with the saved data to the research office or use a modem to send the data over a telephone line. It is possible that technophobic respondents may be a bit alarmed by their use, but, by and large, the use of computer-assisted interviewing seems destined to grow. The money saved will outweigh any concern by interviewers that they can see only part of the schedule at any one time.

CAPI and CATI have not infiltrated academic survey research to the same degree that they have commercial survey research, although that picture is changing because of their many advantages. In any case, many of the large datasets available for analysis (see Chapter 7 for examples) come from computer-assisted interviewing studies by large social research organizations. One further point in connection with computer-assisted interviewing is that this section has not included Internet surveys. The reason for this is that such surveys are more properly considered as self-completion questionnaires than structured interviewing, because there really is no interviewer. Internet surveys are covered later.

Using online personal interviews

Although online interviews run a higher risk of respondent dropout, Mann and Stewart (2000: 138–9)

have suggested that in fact it is possible to develop a relationship of mutual trust. This can be accomplished by regularly sending messages to respondents reassuring them that their written utterances are helpful and significant, especially since interviewing through the Internet is still an unfamiliar experience for most people and takes longer than other forms. It is also worth the trouble, because online interviews make it easier for the researcher to go back to interviewees for further information or reflections, something difficult to do with face-to-face interviews.

A further issue for the online personal interviewer is whether to send all the questions at once or to conduct the interview on a question-followed-by-reply basis. The problem with sending all at once is that respondents may read through them and only reply to the most interesting. Thus, asking one question at a time is likely to be more reliable. Bampton and Cowton (2002) reported their experiences of conducting e-mail interviews by sending questions in small batches. They argued that this approach takes pressure off interviewees to make a quick reply, gives them the opportunity to provide considered replies (although the authors recognized that there can be a loss of spontaneity), and gives the interviewers greater opportunity to respond to interviewee answers.

There is evidence that prospective interviewees are more likely to agree to participate if agreement is solicited prior to sending the actual questions. Another aid to seeking compliance is for the researcher to use some form of self-disclosure, such as directions to the researcher's website that contains personal information, even a picture, and particularly information relevant to the research issue (Curasi 2001; O'Connor and Madge 2001, 2003). Unsolicited e-mails, often referred to as 'spamming,' are regarded as a nuisance by online users and can result in an immediate refusal to take the message seriously.

Curasi (2001) conducted a comparison in which 24 online interviews carried out through e-mail correspondence were contrasted with 24 parallel face-to-face interviews. The interviews were concerned with shopping on the Internet. She found that:

- face-to-face is better than online for maintaining rapport with respondents;

- because greater commitment and motivation are required for completing an online interview, replies are often more detailed than in face-to-face interviews; and

- online interviewees' answers tend to be more considered and grammatically correct because they have more time to ponder and tidy up answers before sending them. Whether this is a positive feature is debatable: there is the obvious advantage of a 'clean' transcript, but there may be some loss of spontaneity.

On the other hand, Curasi found that the least detail also comes from online interviews, perhaps because replies must be typed not just spoken. The full significance of this difference in the nature of the respondent's mode of answering has not been fully appreciated.

The webcam may offer further possibilities for online personal interviews, making the online interview similar to the telephone version but also similar to an in-person interview since those involved in the exchange can see each other. However, one of the main advantages of the online interview is lost: respondents' answers need to be transcribed.

Conducting interviews

Issues concerning the conduct of interviews are examined here in a very general way. In addition to these matters, there is clearly the important issue of how to word the interview questions themselves. This area will be explored in Chapter 5 after discussing self-completion questionnaire techniques because many of the rules of question asking relate to both. One further general point is that the advice concerning the conduct of interviews provided in this chapter relates to structured interviews. The framework for conducting interviewing in qualitative research (such as unstructured and interviewing and focus groups) will be handled in later chapters.

Know the schedule

Before interviewing anybody, an interviewer should be fully conversant with the schedule and know it inside out. Interviewing can be stressful for interviewers and it is possible that under duress, standard interview procedures such as filter questions (see Box 4.6 later in the chapter) can cause interviewers to get flustered and leave questions out or ask the wrong questions. All interviewers need to be fully trained to reduce interviewer variability in asking questions, a potentially important source of error.

Introducing the research

Prospective respondents have to be provided with a credible rationale for the research in which they are

being asked to participate and for giving up their valuable time. This aspect of conducting interview research is of particular significance at a time when response rates to survey research appear to be declining, though the evidence on this issue is the focus of some disagreement. The introductory rationale may be either spoken by the interviewer or printed for the respondent to read. It usually is spoken when interviewers make first contact with respondents, on the street or when they 'cold call' respondents in their homes in person or by telephone. A written rationale is common to alert respondents that someone will be contacting them to request an interview. In many cases, respondents may be presented with both modes—for example, when they are sent a letter and then later ask the interviewer who turns up to interview them what the research is all about. It is important for the two accounts to be consistent, since this could be a test.

Rapport

It is frequently suggested that it is important for the interviewer to achieve *rapport* with the respondent. This means that a relationship must be established (very quickly) to encourage respondents to want (or at least be prepared) to participate in and persist with the interview. Unless an element of rapport is established, some respondents may initially agree to be interviewed but then decide to terminate participation because of the length of time the interview is taking

Box 4.5 Topics and issues to include in an introductory statement

There are several issues to include in an introductory statement to a prospective interviewee. The following are important considerations:

- Make clear the identity of the person who is contacting the respondent.
- Identify the auspices under which the research is being conducted (e.g., a university, a market research agency).
- Mention where any funding of the research came from, or, if you are a student doing research for a thesis, make this clear (see Ethical issue 4.1).
- Indicate what the research is about in broad terms and why it is important, and give an indication of the kind of information to be collected.
- Indicate how the respondent has been selected (e.g., by a random process, by convenience, because of special characteristics).

- Provide reassurance about the confidentiality of any information provided.
- Make it clear that participation is voluntary.
- Reassure respondents that they will not be identified or identifiable. This can usually be achieved by pointing out that data become anonymous when entered into the computer, and analysis is then conducted at an aggregate or group level.
- Provide the respondent with the opportunity to ask any questions (e.g., provide a contact telephone number if the introduction is a written statement). If in person, simply ask if the respondent has any questions.

These suggestions are also relevant to the covering letter that should accompany mailed questionnaires, along with a stamped, pre-addressed envelope.

or perhaps because of the nature of the questions being asked. While this injunction essentially invites the interviewer to be friendly with respondents and to put them at ease, it is important that this quality is not stretched too far. Too much rapport can result in the interview going on too long and the respondent suddenly deciding that too much time is being spent on the activity. Also, the mood of friendliness can result in the respondents tailoring their responses to please the interviewer. The achievement of rapport between interviewer and respondent is therefore a delicate balancing act. Moreover, it is probably some-

what easier to achieve rapport in a face-to-face interview rather than the telephone interview. In the latter the interviewer is unable to offer obvious visual cues of friendliness, like smiling or maintaining good eye contact, which are frequently regarded as conducive to gaining and maintaining rapport.

Asking questions

It was suggested earlier that one aim of the structured interview is to ensure that each respondent is asked exactly the same questions, removing a poten-

Ethical issue 4.1 *Mentioning sponsorship*

At one Ontario university, ethical rules prohibit including the name of the sponsor of the research in the cover letter. The rule is based on the feeling that people may feel pressured or coerced by reading, for example, that the research is sponsored by the Canadian Cancer Society. At another university, it is unethical *not* to supply that information as it is thought to be part of *informed consent*. For example, some people may not want the government to know anything about them and seeing the federal Ministry of Fisheries as funding the study would lead to

their refusal to reply. Ethical issues are never straightforward.

Even listing the sponsor does not guarantee informed consent, however. Rushton (2000), who studies racial differences, for example, would have listed the 'X' Foundation as his sponsor. To most respondents, this would not have triggered any recognition of its controversial status. Should he have been required to add that for many people 'X' is considered conservative at best, racist at worst? Again ethical issues are never straightforward.

tial source of error in survey research and leading to a variation in replies that does not reflect 'true' variation. The structured interview is meant to reduce the likelihood of this occurring, but it cannot guarantee it will not occur, because there is always the possibility that some interviewers will embellish or otherwise change a question when it is asked. There are many reasons why interviewers may vary the question wording, such as a reluctance to ask certain questions, perhaps because of embarrassment (Collins 1997). Therefore, training interviewers, paying them well, and monitoring them is very important.

Does it really matter? Do small variations to wording make a significant difference to people's replies? While the impact of variation in wording obviously differs from context to context, and in any case is difficult to quantify exactly, three experiments suggested that even small variations in wording can affect replies, up to 2 per cent of the total variation in each question (Collins 1997). On the face of it, this is a small amount of error, but researchers still regard it as a concern.

Recording answers

An identical warning for identical reasons can be registered in connection with the recording answers; interviewers should write down respondents' replies as exactly as possible. Not to do so can distort respondents' answers and introduce errors. Such errors are less likely to occur when the interviewer has merely to allocate respondents' replies to a category, as in a closed question. That error is far less frequent than in the case when answers to open questions are being written down (Fowler and Mangione 1990).

Clear instructions

In addition to instructions about the asking of questions and the recording of answers, interviewers need instructions about how to progress through an interview schedule. *Filter questions* require the interviewer to ask questions of some respondents but not others. For example, the question 'For which political party did you vote at the last general election?'

presumes that the respondent did in fact vote. This option can be reflected in the fixed-choice answers provided, so that one is a 'did-not-vote' alternative. However, another solution is not to presume anything about voting behaviour but to ask respondents whether they voted in the last general election and then to filter out those who did not vote. The foregoing question about the political party voted for can then be asked only of those who did in fact vote. Similarly, in a study of meals, there is no point in asking vegetarians lots of questions about eating meat. It is probably best to filter vegetarians out and then perhaps ask them a separate series of questions.

Box 4.6 Instructions for interviewers in the use of a filter question

1 Have you consumed any alcoholic drinks in the last twelve months?

Yes _____

No _____

(if **No** proceed to question 4)

2 (*To be asked if interviewee replied* **Yes** *to question 1*)

Which of the following alcoholic drinks do you consume most frequently?

(Ask respondent to choose the category that he or she drinks most frequently and tick one category only.)

Beer _____

Spirits _____

Wine _____

Liqueurs _____

Other _____   (specify) _____

3 How frequently do you consume alcoholic drinks?

(Ask interviewee to choose the category that comes closest to his or her current practice.)

Daily _____

Most days _____

Once or twice a week _____

Once or twice a month _____

A few times a year _____

Once or twice a year _____

4 (*To be asked if interviewee replied* **No** *to question 1*)

Have you ever consumed alcoholic drinks?

Yes _____

No _____

Box 4.6 provides a simple example in connection with an imaginary study of alcohol consumption. The chief point to register about this example is that it requires clear instructions for the interviewer. If such instructions are not provided, there is the risk that either respondents will be asked inappropriate questions (which can be irritating for them) or the interviewer will inadvertently fail to ask a question (which results in missing information) because of misreading a filter response.

Question order

Interviewers should also be alerted to the importance of keeping to the order of asking questions. For one thing, varying the question order can result in certain questions being accidentally omitted, because the interviewer may forget to ask those that have been leapfrogged during the interview. Also, variation in question order can have an impact on replies. If some respondents have not been asked a question that they should have been, on unemployment for example, and others have, their responses will reflect this. A source of variability and error may be introduced in a later question on causes of increasing crime, for example, with those previously asked mentioning unemployment as a cause more often than those who were not asked.

Probing

A highly problematic area for researchers employing a structured interview method is *probing* respondents who need help with their answers. It may occur if respondents do not understand the question—they may either ask for further information or it may be clear from what they say that they are struggling to understand the question or to provide an adequate answer. The second kind of situation the interviewer faces occurs when the respondent does not provide a complete answer and has to be probed for more information. The problem in both situations is obvious: the interviewer's intervention may influence the respondent and different interviewers' interventions may differ. A potential source of variability in respondents' replies that does not reflect 'true' variation is introduced—that is, an error.

Some general tactics with regard to probes are as follows:

- If further information is required, usually in the context of an open-ended question, standardized probes can be employed, such as 'Can you say a little more about that?' or 'Are there any other reasons why you think that?' or simply 'hmm . . . .'

- If, with a closed question, the respondent replies in a way that does not allow the interviewee to select one of the pre-designed answers, the interviewer should repeat the fixed-choice alternatives and make it apparent that the answer needs to be chosen from those provided.

- When the interviewer needs to know about something that requires quantification, such as the number of visits to a doctor in the last four weeks or the number of banks in which the respondent has accounts, but the respondent answers in general terms ('quite often' or 'I have several'), the interviewer needs to persist for a clearer answer. This will usually entail repeating the question. The interviewer should not offer a guess on the basis of the respondent's reply and then suggest an answer, since the latter may be unwilling to disagree with the interviewer's suggested figure or to embarrass the interviewer.

Prompting

Prompting is very rare and should be used only as a last resort. It occurs when the interviewer suggests a possible answer to a question to the respondent. The key prerequisite here is that all respondents receive the same prompts. All closed questions entail standardized prompting, because the respondent is provided with a list of possible answers from which to choose. Unacceptable prompting would be to ask an open question and to suggest possible answers only to some respondents, such as those who appear to be struggling to think of an appropriate reply.

Another form of prompting occurs during the course of a face-to-face interview when the interviewer uses 'show cards' (see Box 4.7) rather than reading out a series of fixed-choice alternatives. Sometimes called 'flash cards,' they display all the answers from which the respondent is to choose and are handed to the respondent at different points of the interview. Three kinds of context in which it may be preferable to employ show cards rather than to read out the entire set of possible answers are as follows:

- When there is a very long list of possible answers. For example, respondents may be asked which magazines they each read most frequently. To read out a list of magazines would be tedious and it is probably better to hand the respondent a list from which to choose.

- Some people are not keen to divulge personal details such as their age or their income. One way of neutralizing the impact of such questioning is to present respondents with age or income ranges with a letter or number attached to each. Such a procedure may be extendable to sensitive areas such as number of sexual partners or sexual practices for the same reasons. They can then be asked to say which letter applies to them (see Box 4.7). This procedure will obviously not be appropriate if the research requires *exact* ages, incomes, or number of sexual partners.

- Sometimes, during the course of interviews, respondents are presented with statements to which they are asked to indicate their levels of agreement and given the same possible answers for each of 'strongly agree, agree, neutral, disagree, and strongly disagree.' The components are often referred to as *items* rather than as *questions*, since respondents are not being asked. See Boxes 3.3

and 3.10 for examples. It is time-consuming and off-putting to read out all seven possible answers 10 times. Also, it may be expecting too much of respondents to read out the answers once and then require them to keep the possible answers in their heads for the entire batch of questions to which they apply. A show card that can be used for the entire batch and to which respondents can constantly refer is an obvious solution. Most Likert scales of this kind comprise five levels of agreement/disagreement and it is this more conventional approach that is illustrated in the second show card in Box 4.7.

Leaving the interview

Do not forget common courtesies like thanking respondents for giving up their time. But the period immediately after the interview is one in which some care is necessary in that some respondents try to engage the interviewer in a discussion about the purpose of the interview. Interviewers should resist elaboration beyond their standard statement because respondents may communicate what they are told to others, which may bias the responses of these others.

Training and supervision

On several occasions, reference has been made to the need for interviewers to be trained. Fowler (1993) cited evidence to suggest that training shorter than one full day rarely creates good interviewers. For most readers of this book planning to do research, such situations are unlikely to be relevant because they will be 'solo' researchers who must in a sense train themselves to follow the procedures and advice provided below. The references are intended more for students who plan to become interviewers for a large research institute or market research agency. There they will need training and supervision, especially in the following areas:

- contacting prospective respondents and providing an introduction to the study;

- reading out questions as written and following instructions in the interview schedule (e.g., in connection with filter questions);

Box 4.7 A show card and a second one reusable as appropriate

Card 4 (Age)	Card 6 (various)
(a) Less than 20	Strongly agree
(b) 20–9	Agree
(c) 30–9	Undecided
(d) 40–9	Disagree
(e) 50–9	Strongly disagree
(f) 60–9	
(g) 70 and over	

- appropriate styles of probing;
- recording exactly what is said; and
- maintaining an interview style that does not bias respondents' answers.

Supervision of interviewers in relation to these issues can be achieved by:

- checking individual interviewers' response rates;
- tape-recording at least a sample of interviews;
- examining completed schedules to determine whether any questions are being left out or if they are being completed properly; and
- making call-backs on a sample of respondents (usually about 10 per cent) to determine whether they were interviewed and to ask about interviewers' conduct.

Self-administered questionnaires

Self-administered questionnaires (from hereon simplified to 'questionnaire') are in many respects structured interviews without an interviewer. They can be delivered in several different ways. Probably the most common is the mailed questionnaire, whereby a questionnaire is sent via post to respondents who, following completion of the instrument, are asked to return it by post (e-mailed questionnaires are discussed below). Alternatively, respondents can deposit their completed questionnaires in a certain location, such as the supervisor's office in a business organization. The term also includes researchers handing out questionnaires to students in a class and collecting the completed versions. For example, Smith and McVie (2003) used such an instrument in their longitudinal cohort study on crime among a large sample of adolescents. Desks were spread out as much as possible and supervisors oversaw the completion of the questionnaires under examlike conditions: no talking or looking at the answers of others (2003: 183).

In many ways the questionnaire and structured interview are very similar. The obvious difference is that in questionnaires respondents must read and answer each question themselves. Because there is no interviewer to administer it, the research instrument has to be especially easy to follow and questions particularly easy to answer. As a result, questionnaires compared with structured interviews tend to:

- have fewer 'essay' type questions (*open*) because short (*closed*) are easier to answer;
- have easy-to-follow designs to minimize risk that a respondent will inadvertently omit a question or a part of one; and
- be shorter to reduce the risk of 'respondent fatigue,' since it is so much easier for a tired respondent facing a long questionnaire to throw it out than it is for a tired interviewee to ask the interviewer to leave.

Advantages of questionnaire over the structured interview

Cheaper, quicker, more convenient to administer

Interviewing is expensive, and the cheapness of the questionnaire is especially advantageous if a sample is geographically dispersed. When this is the case, a mailed questionnaire is much cheaper, saving the time and cost of interviewer travel. This advantage is obviously less pronounced in the use of telephone interviews, but even here the mailed questionnaire enjoys cost advantages.

A thousand questionnaires can be sent through the post in one batch; two classes of four hundred students each can fill out a questionnaire in one class period. Even with a team of telephone interviewers, it takes a long time to conduct personal interviews with samples of that size. However, it is important to remember that the questionnaires do not all come back immediately (respondents fill them in at *their* convenience) and may take several weeks to be returned. Also, there is invariably a need to send out follow-up letters and/or questionnaires to those who fail to return them initially.

Absence of interviewer effects

It was already noted that interviewer characteristics may affect respondent answers. While the findings from this research are somewhat equivocal, with few consistent patterns to suggest which interviewer characteristics bias answers, some suspect that things like ethnicity, gender, and the social background of interviewers may combine to bias respondent answers. In some cases this is obvious—a woman versus a man asking about need for further efforts toward employment equity—but generally it is not. Obviously, without an interviewer present when a questionnaire is being completed, interviewer effects are eliminated. Also, no one is there to read the questions in a different order, in a different way, or with a different emphasis.

Probably of greater importance is the tendency for people to exhibit a social desirability bias when an interviewer is present, giving 'politically correct' responses. There is also a tendency for respondents to underreport activities that induce anxiety or about which they are sensitive. Research summarized by Tourangeau and Smith (1996) strongly suggests that respondents tend to report more drug use and alcohol consumption and a higher number of sexual partners and abortions in questionnaires than in structured interviews.

Advantages of structured interview over the questionnaire

Cannot explain

It is always important to ensure that the questions asked are clear and unambiguous, but this is especially so with the questionnaire, since there is no interviewer to help respondents with questions they find difficult to understand and hence to answer. Also, great attention must be paid to ensure that the questionnaire is easy to complete; if instructions are unclear questions may be inadvertently omitted.

Greater risk of missing data

Partially answered questionnaires are more likely, because of a lack of prompting or supervision, than is possible in interviews. It is also easier for respondents to decide not to answer a question when on their own than being asked by an interviewer. For example, questions that appear boring or irrelevant to the respondent may be especially likely to be skipped.

Cannot probe

There is no opportunity to probe respondents to elaborate an answer. Interviewers are trained to get more from respondents. However, this problem largely applies to open questions, which are not used a great deal in questionnaire research.

Increased risk if questions not salient to respondents

Respondents to questionnaires are more likely than in interviews to become tired of answering questions that are not fully salient to them and throw away the questionnaire. Put positively, when a research issue *is* salient to the respondent, a high response rate is feasible. This means that, when questions are salient, the questionnaire may be a good choice, especially for its much lower cost.

Difficult to ask a lot of questions

As signalled above, because of the possibility of 'respondent fatigue,' long questionnaires are rarely feasible. They may even result in a greater tendency for questionnaires not to be answered in the first place, since they can be off-putting.

Difficulty of asking other kinds of question

It is also important to avoid asking more than a very small number of open questions (because respondents frequently do not want to write a lot). Questions with complex structures, such as filters, should be avoided as far as possible (because some respondents may find them difficult to follow).

Questionnaire can be read as a whole

Respondents are able to read the whole questionnaire even before answering the first question. When this occurs, none of the questions asked is truly independent of the others. It also means that one cannot be sure that questions have been answered in the correct order, raising the earlier possibility of question order effects.

Not appropriate for some kinds of respondent

Respondents whose literacy is limited or whose facility with English is restricted may not be able to answer the questionnaire. The second of these difficulties cannot be entirely overcome when interviews are being employed, but the difficulties are likely greater with mailed questionnaires.

One last problem: who filled out the questionnaire?

With mailed questionnaires, one can never be sure who answered the questions, the designated respondent or someone else. It is also impossible to have any control over other members of a household helping the respondent to answer the questions. Similarly, if a questionnaire is sent to a manager in a firm, the task may simply be delegated to someone else. This advantage of the structured interview over the mailed questionnaire does not apply when the former is administered by telephone, since the same problem applies.

Online social surveys

There has been a considerable growth in the number of surveys being administered online. It is questionable whether the research instruments should be regarded as structured interviews or as self-completion questionnaires—in a sense they are both. So far as online social surveys are concerned there is a crucial distinction between surveys administered by e-mail (e-mail surveys) and surveys administered via the web (web surveys). In the case of the former, the questionnaire is sent via e-mail to a respondent, whereas with a web survey, the respondent is directed to a website in order to answer a questionnaire. Sheehan and Hoy (1999) suggested that there has been a tendency for e-mail surveys to be employed with 'smaller, more homogeneous groups of on-line user groups,' whereas web surveys have been used to study 'large groups of on-line users.'

E-mail surveys

With e-mail surveys it is important to distinguish between embedded and attached questionnaires sent by e-mail. In the case of the embedded questionnaire, the questions are to be found in the body of the e-mail. There may be an introduction to the questionnaire followed by a graphic that partitions the introduction from the questionnaire itself. Respondents have to indicate their replies using simple notations, such as an 'X,' or they may be asked to delete alternatives that do *not* apply. If a question is open, they are asked to type in an answer. When finished, they simply need to select the reply button to return the completed questionnaire. With an attached questionnaire, the questionnaire arrives as an attachment to an e-mail that introduces it. As with the embedded questionnaire, respondents must select and/or type their answers. To return the questionnaire, it must be attached to a reply e-mail, although respondents may also be given the opportunity to fax or send the completed questionnaire by mailed mail to the researcher (Sheehan and Hoy 1999).

The chief advantage of the embedded questionnaire is that it requires less computer expertise. Knowing how to read and then return an attachment requires a certain facility with handling online communication that is still not universally applicable. Also, the recipients' operating systems or software may present problems with reading attachments, while many respondents may refuse to open one because of concerns about a virus. On the other hand, the limited formatting possible with most e-mail software, such as using bold, variations in font size, indenting, and other features, makes the appearance of embedded questionnaires rather dull and featureless, although this limitation is rapidly changing. Furthermore, it is slightly easier for the respondent to type material into an attachment that uses well-known software like Microsoft Word, since if the questionnaire is embedded in an e-mail, the alignment of questions and answers may be lost.

Dommeyer and Moriarty (2000) compared the two forms of e-mail survey in connection with an attitude study. The attached questionnaire was given a much wider range of embellishments in terms of appearance than was possible with the embedded one. Before conducting the survey, undergraduate students were asked about the relative appearance of the two formats. The attached questionnaire is deemed to be better-looking, easier to complete, clearer in appearance, and better organized. The two formats were then administered to two random samples of students, all active e-mail users. The researchers found a much higher response rate with the embedded than with the attached questionnaire (37 per cent versus 8 per cent), but little difference in terms of speed of response or whether any questions are more likely to be omitted with one format rather than the other. Although Dommeyer and Moriarty (2000: 48) concluded 'the attached e-mail survey presents too many obstacles to the potential respondent,' it is important to appreciate that this study was conducted during what were still early days in the life of online surveys. It may be that as prospective respondents become more adept at using online communication methods and virus-checking software improves in terms of accessibility and cost, the concerns that led to the lower response rate for the attached questionnaire will be less pronounced.

Web surveys

Web surveys invite prospective respondents to visit a website where the questionnaire can be found and completed online. The web survey has an important advantage over the e-mail survey in that it can use a much wider variety of embellishments in terms of appearance. Plate 4.1 presents part of the questionnaire from the Gym Study from Chapter 12 in a web-survey format and answered in the same way as in Box 12.2. Common features include 'radio buttons' (whereby the respondent makes a choice between closed-question answers by clicking on a circle in which a dot appears—see question 8 in Plate 4.1) and pull-down menus of possible answers (see Plate 4.2). There are also greater possibilities to use colour. With open questions, the respondent is invited to type directly into a boxed area (e.g., question 2 in Plate 4.1).

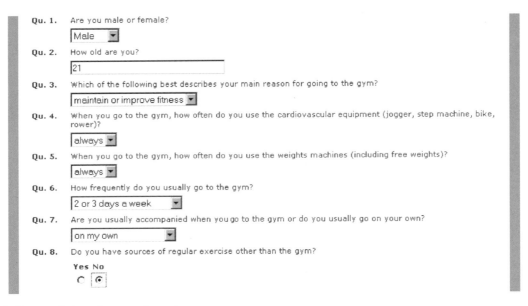

Plate 4.1 Gym study in web survey format

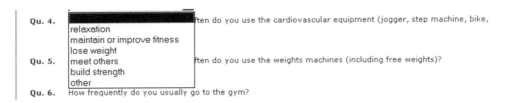

Plate 4.2 A pull-down menu for Qu. 3

However, the advantages of the web survey are more than its appearance. The questionnaire can be designed so that when there is a filter question (e.g., 'if yes, go to question 12; if no, go to question 14'), it skips automatically to the next appropriate question. The questionnaire can also be programmed so that only one question ever appears on the screen or so that the respondent can scroll down and look at all questions in advance. Finally, respondents' answers can be automatically programmed to download into a database, thus eliminating the daunting task of coding of a large number or questionnaires. There is a growing number of software packages designed to produce questionnaires with all the features just described.

Potential respondents need to be directed to the website containing the questionnaire. Where there are possible problems to do with restricting who may answer the questionnaire, it may be necessary to set up a password system to filter out people for whom the questionnaire is not appropriate.

Diaries as a form of questionnaire

When the researcher is specifically interested in precise estimates of behaviour, the diary warrants serious consideration, though it is still a relatively underused method. Unfortunately, the term 'diary' has somewhat different meanings in social research (see Box 4.9). It is

---

Box 4.8 Advantages and disadvantages of online surveys compared to mailed questionnaires

This box summarizes the main advantages and disadvantages of online surveys, both e-mail and web varieties, compared to mailed questionnaires. All three share one disadvantage relative to personal and telephone interviews, namely, that the researcher can never be certain of who is actually answering the questions.

Advantages

1 *Low cost.* Even though mailed questionnaires are cheap to administer, online surveys are even cheaper. There is no postage, paper, envelopes, and time taken to stuff covering letters and questionnaires into envelopes.

2 *Faster response and processing.* Online surveys can be returned considerably faster than mailed questionnaires. Also, automatic skipping when using filter questions and an opportunity for immediate downloading of replies into a database make this kind of survey quite attractive for researchers.

3 *Fewer unanswered questions.* There is evidence that online questionnaires are completed with fewer unanswered questions than mailed questionnaires.

4 *Better response to open questions.* Open questions are more likely to be answered online and to result in more detailed replies.

Disadvantages

1 *Low response rate.* Typically, response rates to online surveys are lower than for comparable mailed questionnaires.

2 *Restricted to online populations.* Only people who are available online can reasonably be expected to participate in an online survey. This restriction should gradually ease over time but since the online population differs in significant ways from the non-online population, it will likely remain a difficulty.

3 *Requires motivation.* Because online survey respondents must pay for the connection and perhaps are tying up their telephone lines, they may need a higher level of motivation than mailed questionnaire respondents. This suggests that the solicitation to participate must be especially persuasive.

4 *Confidentiality and anonymity issues.* It is normal for survey researchers to indicate that respondent replies will be kept anonymous. However, with e-mail surveys, since the address of respondents is known, they may find it difficult to believe that their replies really are anonymous.

5 *Multiple replies.* With web surveys, there is a risk that some people may mischievously complete the questionnaire more than once. There is much less risk of this with e-mail surveys.

Adapted from Cobanoglu *et al.* (2001); Kent and Lee (1999); Schaeffer and Dillman (1998); Sheehan and Hoy (1999); Tse (1998).

the first of the three meanings—what Elliott (1997) called the *researcher-driven diary*—which is the focus of attention here, especially its use in quantitative research. When employed in this way, the researcher-driven diary functions in a similar way to the questionnaire. Equally, it can be said that the researcher-driven diary is an alternative to structured observation (see Chapter 6) in quantitative research, or of ethnography (see Chapter 9) in qualitative research.

Corti (1993) distinguished between 'structured diaries' and 'free text diaries.' Either can be employed by a quantitative researcher. The research on the domestic division of labour by Sullivan (1996) is an illustration of a structured diary (see Box 4.9). The diary has the general appearance of a questionnaire with largely closed questions. The kind of diary employed in this research is often referred to as a 'time-use' diary, in that it is designed for diarists to record, more or less at the time of the actual behaviour, how long they engage in certain activities, such as food preparation, childcare, eating, and so on. Sullivan asked couples, at the same time, to record on a five-point scale, like a Likert scale, the amount of enjoyment they derive from the different activities.

Such records of the time spent in different activities are often regarded as more accurate than those done at the end of the day, perhaps because the events are less subject to memory problems or to the tendency to round up or down. However, the method is more intrusive than answering a questionnaire because it is a constant interruption and it can be argued that it changes behaviour. For example, one can become more aware of the fleeting of time and thus skip an activity.

An example of a free-text diary is provided in Coxon's (1994) study of how the risk of HIV/AIDS affects the sexual activities of gay men. One of several advantages of the diary method for this research is that it provided information on the time sequencing of events (e.g., which practice followed which) and context, information more difficult to glean from questionnaires. The method allowed recording, for one week, of the following information:

- location of the activity;
- nature and sequence of each separate sexual act (who did what to whom);
- whether drugs accompanied the practice;
- what activities—sexual or otherwise—preceded each item of sexual activity;
- whether any aids were employed; and
- whether the diarist or his partner achieved orgasm.

Crook and Light (2002) employed what are often referred to as *time-use diaries* within a free-text format. University students were asked to keep a diary for a week, divided into 15-minute intervals, of the different kinds of study and learning activity in which they engaged at different times of the day, their location, and study resources used (e.g., when during the day do most of your library visits take

---

Box 4.9 The diary in social research

There are three major ways in which the term 'diary' is used in social research:

- *As a method of data collection.* Here the researcher devises a structure for the diary and asks diarists to record what they do more or less contemporaneously with their activities and can be employed for the collection of data in quantitative and qualitative research. One example of such researcher-driven diaries is an e-mail qualitative study of adolescent risk behaviour (Hessler *et al.* 2003) that resulted in rich narratives of everyday life as perceived by adolescents. Sometimes, the collection of data in this manner is supplemented by a personal interview in which the diarist is asked questions about such things as what was meant by certain remarks.

- *As a document.* The diary in this context is written spontaneously by the diarist and not at the behest of a researcher. Such diaries are often used by historians, but have potential for other researchers too. As Scott (1990) observed, the diary in this sense often shades into autobiography. Diaries as documents will be further addressed in Chapter 7.

- *As a log of researcher activities.* Researchers sometimes keep a record of what they do at different stages as an *aide mémoire*. For example, the social anthropologist Malinowski (1967) kept a log of his activities, 'infamous' because it revealed his distaste for those he studied and his inappropriate involvement with females. This kind of diary often shades into the writing of field notes by ethnographers, about which more is written in Chapter 9.

place?) (2002: 162). The various activities were grouped into three types: classes, private study, and social study (i.e., study with a peer). They were able to show the very different patterns and amounts of study typically undertaken during a day.

Using free-text recording of behaviour carries the same kinds of problem as those associated with coding answers to structured interview open questions—namely, the time-consuming nature of the exercise and the risk of introducing error associated with coding answers (see Chapter 5 for a discussion of these issues). However, the free-text approach is less likely to be problematic when, as in the case of Coxon's (1994) research, diarists are instructed about what is required and when the kinds of behaviour of interest are specific. It would be much more difficult to code free-text entries relating to a more general arena of types of behaviour such as the domestic arena studied by Sullivan (1996).

Corti (1993) recommended that the person preparing the diary should:

- provide explicit instructions for diarists;
- be clear about the time periods within which behaviour is to be recorded (e.g., daytime, twenty-four hours, or week);
- provide a model of a completed section of a diary;
- provide brief checklists of 'items, events or behaviour' to jog the memory; and
- include fixed blocks of time or columns showing when the designated activities start and finish (e.g., in diaries of the kind used by Sullivan that show how people budget their time).

Advantages and disadvantages of the diary as a method of data collection

The two studies illustrating the use of diaries also suggest potential advantages:

- When fairly precise estimates of the frequency and/or amount of time spent in different forms of behaviour are required, the diary may provide more valid and reliable data than questionnaires.
- When information about the sequencing of different types of behaviour is required, it is likely to perform better than questionnaires or interviews.
- These first two advantages can suggest that structured observation is just as feasible, but structured observation is probably less appropriate for producing data on behaviour that is personally sensitive, such as sexual behaviour. Moreover, although data on such behaviour can be collected by structured interview, respondents are less likely to divulge details of the kind revealed in Coxon's (1994) research. If such information is collected by questionnaire, there is greater risk of recall and rounding problems (as in 52 minutes being recorded as an hour).

On the other hand, diaries may suffer the following problems:

- They tend to be more expensive than personal interviews (because of costs related to recruiting diarists and checking that diaries are being properly completed).
- Diaries can suffer from a process of attrition, as people tire of the task of completing a diary.
- This last point raises the possibility that diarists become less diligent over time about their record keeping, raising a reliability issue.
- There is sometimes a failure to record details sufficiently quickly, so that memory recall problems set in.

However, diary researchers such as Coxon and Sullivan argue that the resulting data are more accurate than equivalent data based on interviews or questionnaires.

Respondent problems

While structured interviews, questionnaires, and diaries are commonly used in social research, certain problems associated with them have been identified, some of which can apply even to semi-structured interviewing in qualitative research.

Response sets

This problem is especially relevant to multiple-indicator measures (see Chapter 3), where respondents reply to a battery of related questions or items, of the kind found in a Likert scale (see Box 3.3). A response set occurs when people respond to a series of items not according to how they actually feel about them but in some other way. Two of the most prominent types of response set are the 'acquiescence' effect and the 'social desirability' effect.

Acquiescence

Acquiescence refers to a tendency among some people either to agree or to disagree consistently with a set of questions or items, regardless of content. Imagine a respondent agreeing to all items in Box 3.3. Agreement with some of the items implies a low level of commitment to work (items 1–4), whereas agreement with items 5–10 implies a high level of commitment to work. At least some of those responses are probably not valid opinions. Therefore, researchers who employ this kind of multiple-item measure use wordings that imply opposite stances to weed out those respondents who appear to have an acquiescence response set. Thus an item, 'Retirement 55 is too late for me. I want Retirement 35', can be paired with one saying: 'For me, I hope the government abolishes mandatory retirement.' People without an acquiescence problem may agree with one, but not both.

Social desirability

The social desirability effect refers to evidence that some respondents' answers to questions are related to their perception of the social desirability of those answers. An answer perceived as socially undesirable is less likely to be endorsed than one perceived as desirable. This phenomenon has been demonstrated in studies on mental health using psychiatric invento-ries on minor neuroses and anxieties. Many respondents will choose not to admit to such problems. This could imply adding a correction factor in order to get more true figures, but the problem is compounded by the fact that some groups may lie less than others or in different directions. Women conceal their illness less, for example, than do men. In studies of sexual intercourse, even today, an opposite measurement error occurs.

When these forms of response error go undetected, they represent sources of error in concept measurement. Some have suggested that the structured interview is particularly prone to them. Awareness of them has led to measures to limit their impact (e.g., by weeding out cases obviously affected by them) or by instructing interviewers to not become overly friendly with respondents and to avoid appearing judgmental about their replies.

The issue of meaning

A phenomenological critique of survey-interview data revolves around a 'problem of meaning,' the fact that when humans communicate they not only draw on commonly held meanings but also simultaneously create new ones. 'Meaning,' in this sense, is something worked at and achieved—not simply given. In structured interviewing this requires drawing attention to the presumption that interviewers and respondents have the same meanings for the terms employed in the interview questions and answer options. In fact, this issue is simply side-stepped in most structured interview research, with the problem of meaning resolved by ignoring it. This means that respondents who dramatically say they 'hate' body piercing may have strong opinions on everything, and thus their hate is the same as a milder person's 'dislike.' When a mild person says 'hate' in an interview or on a questionnaire, this may be real cause for concern.

A feminist critique

A feminist critique of the methods discussed in this chapter is difficult to disentangle from the general critique launched against quantitative research, briefly outlined in Chapter 1. However, for many feminist social researchers they symbolize more than other methods the limitations of quantitative research, partly because of its nature. By 'its nature' is meant that the methods epitomize the asymmetrical relationship between researcher and subject integral to quantitative research: the researcher extracts information from the research subject and gives nothing in return. For example, standard textbook advice, of the kind provided also in this chapter, says that *rapport* is useful to interviewers, but they should guard against becoming too familiar. This often means that questions asked by respondents (e.g., about the topic or about the research process) should be politely but firmly rebuffed on the grounds that they can bias the respondents' subsequent answers.

This is perfectly valid and appropriate advice from the canons of structured interviewing with its quest for standardization and for valid and reliable data. However, from the perspective of feminism, when women interview women in that way, a wedge is hammered between them that, in conjunction with the implication of a hierarchical relationship between the interviewer and respondent, is incompatible with the feminist value of helping all women. An impression of exploitation arises,

precisely what feminist social science seeks to eliminate.

It was this kind of critique of quantitative research in general that ushered in a period in which many feminist social researchers found qualitative research more compatible with their goals and norms. In terms of interviewing, this resulted in a preference for forms of interviewing such as unstructured and semi-structured interviewing and focus groups, discussed in later chapters. However, as noted in Chapter 1, there has been some softening of attitudes towards the role of quantitative research among feminist researchers. For example, by paying more attention to issues like greater privacy in the interview and special training in sensitive interviewing, dedicated surveys in some countries have proved highly instructive about the causes and incidence of violence against women (cf. Walby and Myhill 2001). Such research, based on structured interviews, would seem consistent with the goals of most feminist researchers and indeed of potentially great significance for many women. Nonetheless, there is still a tendency for qualitative research to remain the preferred research strategy for many feminist researchers.

K KEY POINTS

- The structured interview is a research instrument used to standardize the wording and order of questions and often the recording of answers too, to minimize interviewer-related error.

- It can be administered in person, over the phone, or online.

- It is important to keep to the wording and order of questions when conducting survey research by structured interview. Training in the asking of questions, recording of answers, and establishing rapport are essential parts of conducting interviews.

- Self-administered questionnaires reduce some of the problems encountered in structured interviews. On the other hand, they have their own weaknesses.

- Online surveys may be either of two major types: web surveys and e-mail surveys.

- The researcher-driven diary is an alternative to using questionnaires and interviews, especially when the research questions are concerned with specific behaviour rather than attitudes or opinions.

- Steps need to be taken to reduce response sets, a potential problem in structured interviews and questionnaires.

- These methods symbolize the characteristics of quantitative research that feminist researchers find distasteful, in particular the lack of reciprocity and the taint of exploitation.

Q QUESTIONS FOR REVIEW

The structured interview

- Why is it important for survey research to keep interviewer variability to a minimum?

- How successful is the structured interview in reducing interviewer variability?

- Why may a survey researcher prefer a structured to an unstructured interview?

- Why do structured interview schedules typically include mainly closed questions?

Interview contexts

- In what circumstances is it preferable to conduct structured interviews with more than one interviewer?

- 'Given the lower cost of telephone interviews as against face-to-face interviews, the former are generally preferable.' Discuss.

Conducting interviews

- Prepare an opening statement for a school study of student shoplifting.

- To what extent is rapport an important ingredient of structured interviewing?

- What is the difference between probing and prompting? What danger does each pose?

Self-administered questionnaires

- What advantages do they have over structured interviews?

- What disadvantages do they have in comparison with structured interviews?

- What ethical issues are involved when professors ask their current students to fill out a questionnaire in class?

Online social surveys

- What is the significance of the distinction between e-mail and web surveys?

- Are there circumstances in which embedded e-mail questionnaires are more likely to be effective than attached questionnaires?

- What advantages do online surveys have over traditional research methods for collecting such data?

- What disadvantages do they have in comparison with traditional research methods for collecting such data?

Diaries as a form of questionnaire

- What are the main kinds of diary used in the collection of social science data?

- Are there circumstances when a diary approach is preferable to a questionnaire?

Problems with structured interviewing

- What are response sets and why are they potentially important?

Feminist responses to these methods

- What are the main issues behind the feminist critique of structured interviewing, questionnaires, and diaries as described in this chapter?

5 Asking questions

CHAPTER OVERVIEW

This chapter is concerned with the questions used in the structured interviews and questionnaires discussed in the previous chapter. The focus is still on social survey research as it explores:

- issues involved in deciding when to use open or closed questions;

- different kinds of question that can be asked in structured interviews and questionnaires;

- rules to bear in mind when designing questions;

- question order;

- how questionnaires should be designed to reduce error and to make answering easier for respondents;

- projection or vignette questions in which respondents are asked to reflect on a scenario presented to them;

- the importance of pre-testing questions in a pilot study; and

- using questions taken from previous survey research.

Introduction

As suggested in Chapter 4, there is much more involved in survey research than an optimal phrasing of questions. However, that issue is a crucial concern and it is not surprising that this aspect of designing survey instruments has been a major focus of attention.

Open or closed questions?

One of the most significant considerations for many researchers is whether to ask a question in an open or closed format, a distinction introduced in the last chapter, and relevant to the design of both structured interview and self-administered questionnaire research.

With an open question respondents can reply however they wish. With a closed question they are presented with a set of fixed alternatives from which they have to choose an appropriate answer. All of the questions in Box 5.7 are of the closed kind. So too are the Likert-scale items in Box 5.9, a particular kind of closed question. What, then, are some of the advantages and limitations of this format?

Open questions

Open questions present both advantages and disadvantages to a survey researcher; however, as the following discussion suggests, problems associated with the processing of answers to open questions tend to reduce their use.

Advantages

Still, open questions have certain advantages over closed:

- Respondents can answer in their own terms, not just those chosen by the researchers.

- They allow unusual responses, replies that the survey researcher may not have contemplated and therefore not offered as a fixed-choice alternative.

- The questions do not suggest answers to respondents. Therefore, their level of knowledge and understanding of issues can be tapped. The salience of issues for respondents can also be explored.

- They are useful for exploring new or changing areas.

- They can generate fixed-choice format answers, a point returned to later in this chapter.

Disadvantages

However, open questions also present problems for a survey researcher:

- They are time-consuming; interviewees are likely to talk longer than with a comparable closed question.

- Answers have to be 'coded,' which is very time-consuming. Box 5.1 outlines the nature of coding and some of its considerations: reading through answers, deriving themes to form the basis for codes, and then going through the answers again so that the answers can be coded for entry into a computer spreadsheet. It is sometimes called *post-coding* to distinguish it from *pre-coding*, whereby the researcher designs a coding frame in advance of administering a survey instrument and often includes the pre-codes in the questionnaire (as in Box 5.4). However, in addition to being time-consuming, post-coding can be an unreliable process,

---

Box 5.1 ⌦ *What is coding?*

Coding is a key stage in quantitative research. Many forms of social science data are essentially unstructured, including answers to open questions in interviews and questionnaires, newspaper articles, and behaviour in a school classroom. To quantify and analyze such materials, the social researcher has to code them. Coding entails two main stages. First, the unstructured material must be categorized. For answers to an open question, this means examining people's answers and grouping them into different categories. Box 5.2 provides examples of this process. Second, the researcher usually assigns numbers to the categories so created. This is a largely arbitrary process, in the sense that the numbers themselves are simply tags to allow the material to be processed quantitatively. Thus, when Schuman and Presser (1981, see Box 5.5) asked a question about the features of a job that people most prefer, answers could be grouped into 11 categories: pay; feeling of accomplishment; control of work; pleasant work; security; opportunity for promotion; short hours; working conditions; benefits; satisfaction; other responses. Each of these 11 categories then needs to be assigned a number, such as: 1 for pay; 2 for feeling of accomplishment; 3 for control of work; 4 for pleasant work; etc.

There is an important distinction between *pre-coding* and *post-coding*. Many closed questions in survey research instruments are pre-coded (as in Box 5.5). This means that respondents are being asked to assign themselves to a category with a number already assigned. Post-coding occurs when answers to an open question are coded or when themes in newspaper articles con-

cerned with a certain topic are counted, as in content analysis (see Chapter 16).

When coding, three basic principles need to be observed (Bryman and Cramer 2004):

- The categories generated must not overlap. If they do, the numbers assigned to them will not denote distinct categories.

- The list of categories must be complete and therefore cover all possibilities. If it is not, some material will not be capable of being coded. This is why coding, such as answers to an open question, sometimes includes a category of 'other.'

- There should be clear rules about how codes should be applied, with examples of the kinds of answers that should be subsumed under a particular code. Such rules are meant to ensure that coders are consistent over time in how they assign the material to categories and, if more than one person is coding, are consistent with each other. The term 'coding frame' is often employed to describe the lists of codes that should be applied to unstructured data and the rules for their application. In content analysis and structured observation, the term 'coding manual' is often preferred to describe the lists of codes for each item of information and the rules to be employed.

Coding also occurs in qualitative research but the role it plays and its significance are somewhat different there from quantitative research. The procedure for coding with a qualitative data analysis computer program is described in Chapter 13.

Box 5.2 Coding an open question

Coding an open question usually entails reading and re-reading transcripts of respondents' replies to discover distinct themes in them. A subsequent *coding frame* is then designed to identify the types of answer associated with each question and their respective codes (i.e., numbers). The numbers allocated to each answer can then be used in the computer processing of the data. A coding schedule also helps to keep a record of rules followed in identifying certain kinds of answer in terms of a theme.

Charles and Kerr (1988) conducted interviews concerning the consumption of food in the home with 200 women. Their interviews were of the semi-structured kind (see Box 5.3), so that the questions were open-ended. Charles and Kerr were working within a qualitative research strategy, but, for several of their questions, they found it helpful to quantify respondents' answers. For example, one of their concepts was responsibility for meal preparation. It was coded into five categories of responsibility: self prepares all meals; self mainly, partner sometimes; either or both (50/50); self mainly with help from partner and/or children sometimes; and other.

Thus, while the bulk of the presentation of their findings is in the form of passages from interview transcripts, which is the conventional way of presenting such findings in qualitative research (see Chapter 10), some of their findings are similar to those encountered in quantitative research. As the authors said: 'The material is . . . qualitative, as we included many open-ended questions which gave the women the chance to talk freely, and quantitative, as the sample was large enough to produce useful statistical data' (Charles and Kerr 1988: 7).

Box 5.3 Coding a very open question

Foddy (1993) reported on asking a small sample of his students, 'Your father's occupation is (was) . . .' and requested three details: nature of business, size of business, and whether owner or employee. In answer to the size of business issue, the replies were particularly variable in kind, including: 'big,' 'small,' 'very large,' '3000 acres,' 'family,' 'multinational,' '200 people,' and 'Philips.' The problem here is obvious: one simply cannot aggregate and therefore compare the replies. In a sense, the problem is only partly to do with the difficulty of coding an open question; it is also due to a lack of specificity in the question. If, instead, Foddy had asked 'How many employees are (were) there in your father's organization?' a more comparable set of answers should have been forthcoming. Whether his students would have known this information is, of course, yet another issue. However, the exercise illustrates potential problems of asking an open question, particularly one that lacks a clear reference point.

answers recorded in structured interviews. One obvious solution is to employ a tape recorder, but this can make some respondents nervous and the transcription of answers to tape-recorded open questions is immensely time-consuming. The problem of transcription is one continually faced by qualitative researchers using semi-structured and unstructured interviews (see Chapter 10) but they solve it by asking only a small number of respondents, unlike the large numbers typical of survey research.

Closed questions

The advantages and disadvantages of closed questions are in many respects implied in the considerations relating to open questions.

Advantages

Closed questions offer the following advantages to researchers.

because it introduces potential variability in the coding of answers by different coders and therefore of both measurement error and lack of validity. Boxes 5.2 and 5.3 deal with coding open questions.

- Because of the greater time and effort required, many prospective respondents are likely to be put off by the idea of having to write extensively, which may exacerbate the problem of low response rates with mailed questionnaires in particular (see Chapter 11).

- Because of the difficulty of writing down verbatim what respondents say, there is variability in the

- It is easy to process answers. For example, the respondent in a self-completion questionnaire or the interviewer using a structured interview schedule can place a tick or can circle an answer for the appropriate response. The mark can then

Box 5.4 Processing a closed question

What do you think of the prime minister's job performance since taking office?

(*Please tick the appropriate response.*)

Very good	____	5
Good	____	4
Fair	____	3
Poor	____	2
Very poor	____	1

be scanned by an optical reader from the pre-codes placed to the side of the fixed-choice answers. See Box 5.9 for an example.

- Closed questions enhance the comparability of answers. As mentioned, post-coding can be unreliable (see the sixth point in Box 4.2), even with inter-coder reliability checks and intra-coder checks to insure that coders do not vary their coding conventions. Closed questions essentially circumvent this problem.

- Some respondents may not be clear about what a question is getting at; the availability of answers may help to clarify the situation.

- Because interviewers and respondents are not expected to write extensively and instead to place ticks or circle answers, closed questions are easier and quicker to complete.

- In interviews, closed questions reduce the possibility of variability in the recording of answers. As noted in Chapter 4, if interviewers cannot write down exactly what respondents say, a source of bias and hence of invalidity is introduced. Closed questions reduce this possibility, though there is still the potential problem that interviewers may have to *interpret* what is said to them in order to assign answers to a category, as when a person says he works full-time but later adds that he has been home a lot and not been too busy lately.

Disadvantages

However, closed questions exhibit certain disadvantages:

- There is a loss of spontaneity in respondents' answers. There is always the possibility that they may come up with interesting replies not covered by the fixed answers provided. One solution here is to use an open question to generate the categories (see Box 5.5). Also, there may be a good case for including 'other' as a possible response category and to allow respondents to elaborate on this choice.

- The fixed answers provided should not overlap, for example, when the age categories offered are '20–30,' '30–40,' and '40–50.' Here the forced-choice answers are not mutually exclusive and 40-year-old respondents do not know whether to choose the second or the third category; therefore they must arbitrarily select one or the other or even tick both answers. Generally, if a respondent ticks more than one answer when only one is required, the answer is coded as an error response. The arbitrary selection of one or the other is a bigger problem, as it would not be detected. Pre-tests usually sort out this problem, but when money is scarce and they are not done, these problems can arise.

- It is difficult to make forced-choice answers exhaustive. All possible answers should really be provided, but a common compromise is to list the most common and then an 'other' category, so to avoid excessively long lists of possible answers. Should a common 'other' response appear frequently in the pre-test, it can be added to the actual list.

- There may be differences among respondents in their interpretation of forced-choice answers and thus validity is jeopardized. For example, the understanding of the word 'soon' in a question can vary immensely from person to person.

- Closed questions may irritate those respondents unable to find a category that they feel applies to them.

- In interviews, a large number of closed questions reduces conversation and gives the interview an impersonal feel, thus reducing rapport. On the other hand, the value of rapport in structured interviewing is in some dispute (does it lead to respondents giving answers they think will please the interviewer?) and thus it may not be a real problem. In fact, closed questions may represent a welcome break.

Box 5.5 A comparison of results for a closed and an open question

Schuman and Presser (1981) conducted an experiment to determine if responses to closed questions can be improved by asking the questions first as open questions and then developing categories of reply from respondents' answers. They asked a question about what people look for in work in both open and closed format. Different samples were used. They found considerable disparities between the two sets of answers (40 per cent of the open format categories were not capable of being subsumed by the closed format answers). They then revised the closed categories to reflect the answers they received from people's open-ended answers. They re-administered the open question and the revised closed question to two large samples of Americans. The question and the answers they received are as follows.

'This next question is on the subject of work. People look for different things in a job. Which one of the following five things do you most prefer in a job? [closed question]. What would you most prefer in a job? [open question].'

Closed format			Open format	
Answer	%		Answer	%
Work that pays well	13.2		Pay	16.7
Work that gives a feeling of accomplishment	31.0		Feeling of accomplishment	14.5
Work where there is not too much supervision and you make most decisions yourself	11.7		Control of work	4.6
Work that is pleasant and people who are nice to work with	19.8		Pleasant work	14.5
Work that is steady with little chance of being laid off	20.3		Security	7.6
	96% of sample			57.9% of sample
			Opportunity for promotion	1.0
			Short hours/lots of free time	1.6
			Working conditions	3.1
			Benefits	2.3
			Satisfaction/liking a job	15.6
Other/DK/NA	4.0		Other responses	18.3
	100%			100%

With the revised form of the closed question, Schuman and Presser found a much higher proportion of the sample whose answers to the open question correspond to the closed one. They argued that the new closed question is superior to its predecessor and also superior to the open question. However, it is still disconcerting that only 58 per cent of respondents answering the open question can be subsumed under the same categories as those answering the closed one. Also, the distributions are somewhat different: for example, twice as many respondents answer in terms of a feeling of accomplishment with the closed format than with the open one. Nonetheless, the experiment demonstrates the desirability of generating forced-choice answers from open questions.

Types of questions

Structured interviews and self-completion questionnaires generally contain several different types of question. There are various ways of classifying these, but here are some prominent forms:

• *Personal factual questions*. These are questions that ask the respondent to provide *personal information*, such as age, occupation, marital status, income, and so on. This kind of question also includes questions about *behaviour*. Such factual questions often have to rely on the respondents' memories, as when asked about frequency of religious service attendance, how often they go to a movie, or when they last ate out in a restaurant.

- *Factual questions about others*. These ask for personal information about others. They should be used very sparingly, as a last choice, in that they not only may have problems of recall as above but they also rely on possibly distorted views of respondents concerning others' behaviour (Beardsworth and Keil 1997). If interested in perceptions of how another acts or feels, such a question is acceptable. If interested in the actual behaviour or attitudes of another, it is not.

- *Informant factual questions*. Sometimes, those interviewed or who complete a questionnaire act as informants about an entity with which they are familiar, rather than as respondents answering questions about themselves. Asking employees about such things as the size of the firm for which they work, whether it employs certain technologies, whether it has a union, and whether workers engage in labour slowdowns as a form of protest are examples. Although more defensible than the previous type of questions because the information may not be readily available, they may lead to problems.

- *Questions about attitudes*. Questions about attitudes are very common in both structured interview and self-completion questionnaire research. A five-point Likert scale (See Box 5.9) is one of the most frequently encountered formats for measuring attitudes.

- *Questions about beliefs*. Respondents are frequently asked about their beliefs, possibly social and political beliefs. This can be in the form of Likert scales too, for example, asking whether the respondent believes Canada is better off since signing the NAFTA agreement: definitely yes, yes, unsure, no, definitely no. Or a survey about crime may ask respondents about crime. Is it skyrocketing, rising, staying about the same, lowering, hitting new lows? (Which of those choices is inappropriate?) This question does *not* measure crime but it can give insight into perceptions about crime, and perhaps thus indirectly into fear of crime and even likelihood of support for an increase to the police budget.

- *Questions about knowledge*. Questions can sometimes 'test' respondents' knowledge in an area. For example, the *Globe and Mail* asked undergraduates in 2004 to rate Canada's professional schools. Their ratings made general sense but were marred by the very high ratings given to the University of Waterloo's medical and law school. Neither exists.

Most structured interview schedules and self-completion questionnaires include more than one of these types of question. It is important to bear in mind the distinction between them because:

- They force a clarification of what is being asked, albeit in rather general terms.

- It guards against asking questions in an inappropriate format. For example, a Likert scale is entirely unsuitable for asking factual questions about behaviour.

- When building scales like a Likert scale, it is best not to mix different types of question, as measurement validity may be threatened. For example, attitudes and beliefs sound similar and one may be tempted to mix them, but it is best to have separate scales for attitudes and beliefs.

Rules for designing questions

Over the years, numerous rules have been devised in connection with the dos and don'ts of asking questions. In spite of this, frequent mistakes persist. So here are three simple rules of thumb as a starting point; beyond that the rules act as a means of avoiding further pitfalls.

General rules of thumb

Always bear in mind the research questions

The questions asked in a self-completion questionnaire or structured interview should be geared to answering research questions. This first rule of thumb has at least two implications. First, it means to ensure that questions allow the research questions to be fully addressed; it is painful to find at a later stage that a crucial question was omitted. Second, it means that there is little point in asking questions that do not relate to research questions. It is also not fair to waste respondents' time answering them.

What do you want to know?

Rule of thumb number two is to decide exactly what you want to know. Consider the seemingly harmless question:

> Do you have a car?

What is that question seeking to tap? Is it car ownership? If so, the question is inadequate, largely because of the ambiguity of the word 'have.' The question can be interpreted as: personally owning a car; having access to a car in a household; and 'having' a company car or a car for business use. Thus, an answer of 'yes' may or may not be indicative of car ownership. To know whether a respondent owns a car, ask directly about this matter. Similarly, there is nothing wrong with the question:

> How many children do you have?

However, if what you are trying to address is the standard of living of a person or household, the crucial issue may be how many are living at home.

How would *you* answer it?

Rule of thumb number three is to put yourself in the position of the respondent. Ask yourself the question and try to work out a reply. If you do this, there is at least a possibility that the ambiguity inherent in the 'Do you have a car?' question will manifest itself, and its inability to tap car ownership become apparent. Assume also that there is a follow-up question to the previous one:

> Have you driven the car this week?

Again, this looks harmless, but to a respondent, the phrase 'this week' is vague. Does it mean the last seven days or does it mean the week in which the questioning takes place, which is, of course, affected by such things as whether the question is being asked on a Monday or a Friday? In part, this issue arises because the question designer has not decided

what the question is about. Putting yourself in the position of the respondent can reveal the difficulty of answering this question.

Taking account of these rules of thumb and the following rules about asking questions may help to avoid the more obvious pitfalls.

Specific rules when designing questions

Avoid ambiguous terms in questions

Avoid terms such as 'often' and 'regularly' as measures of frequency. They are ambiguous; different respondents will operate with different frames of reference when employing them. Sometimes, it is unavoidable, but when there is an alternative allowing actual frequency to be measured, this will nearly always be preferable. So, a question such as:

> How often do you usually go to the movies?
>
> Very often   _____
>
> Quite often   _____
>
> Not very often   _____
>
> Not at all   _____

suffers from the problem that, with the exception of 'not at all,' the terms in the response categories are ambiguous. Instead, ask about actual frequency, such as:

> How frequently do you usually go to the movies?
> *(Please tick whichever category comes closest to the number of times you visit the cinema.)*
>
> More than once a week   _____
>
> Once a week   _____
>
> 2 or 3 times a month   _____
>
> Once a month   _____
>
> A few times a year   _____
>
> Once a year   _____
>
> Less than once a year   _____

Alternatively, simply ask respondents about the number of times they have gone to the movies in the previous four weeks.

It is also important to bear in mind that certain common words, such as 'dinner' and 'book,' mean different things to different people. For some, dinner is a midday snack, whereas for others it is a substantial evening meal. Similarly, some people refer to magazines or to catalogues and brochures as books, whereas others work with a more restricted definition. In such cases, it is necessary clearly to define such terms.

Avoid long questions

Most methodologists agree that long questions are undesirable. In a structured interview the interviewee can lose the thread of the question and in a self-completion questionnaire the respondent may be tempted to omit such questions or to skim them and therefore not give them sufficient attention. However, Sudman and Bradburn (1982) have suggested that this advice is more applicable to attitude questions than to those asking about behaviour. They argued that, when the focus is on behaviour, longer questions have certain positive features in interviews—for example, they are more likely to provide memory cues and facilitate recall because of the time taken to complete the question. However, by and large, it's best to keep questions short.

Avoid double-barrelled questions

Double-barrelled questions ask about two things, making respondents unsure about how best to respond. Take the question:

> How satisfied are you with your pay and conditions in your job?

The problem here is obvious: the respondent may be satisfied with one but not the other. Not only will the respondent be unclear about how to reply, but also any answer is unlikely to be a good reflection of satisfaction with pay *and* conditions. Similarly:

> How frequently does your husband help with cooking and cleaning?

suffers from the same problem. A husband may provide extensive help with cooking but be totally uninvolved in cleaning, so that any stipulation of frequency of help is going to be ambiguous and create uncertainty for respondents.

The same rule applies to fixed-choice answers. In Box 5.5, one of Schuman and Presser's (1981) answers is:

> Work that is pleasant and people are nice to work with.

While there is likely to be symmetry between the two ideas in this answer—pleasant work and nice people—there is no *necessary* correspondence. Pleasant work may be important for someone who is relatively indifferent to the issue of pleasant co-workers. A further instance of a double-barrelled question is provided in Box 5.6.

Box 5.6 Matching question and answers in closed questions (and some double-barrelled questions too)

A publisher had inserted a feedback questionnaire within a novel's pages, including a series of Likert-style items regarding the book's quality. In each case, the respondent is asked to indicate whether the attribute being asked about is: poor; acceptable; average; good; or excellent. However, in each case, the items are presented as questions. For example:

> Was the writing elegant, seamless, imaginative?

The problem here is that an answer to this question is 'yes' or 'no.' At most, respondents might have gradations of yes and no, such as: definitely; to a large extent; to some extent; not at all. However, 'poor' or 'excellent' cannot be answers to this question. The questions should have been presented as statements, such as:

> Please indicate the quality of the book in each of the following criteria:
>
> The elegance of the writing:
> Poor Acceptable Average Good Excellent
>
> The seamlessness of the writing:
> Poor Acceptable Average Good Excellent
>
> The imagination of the writing:
> Poor Acceptable Average Good Excellent

This also fixes the extra problem of the 'treble-barrelled' question as the original form actually asks about three attributes of the writing. The reader's views about the three qualities may vary.

It may be argued that the issue is a nit-picking one: someone reading the question obviously knows that he or she is being asked to rate the quality of the book in terms of each attribute. The problem is that the impact of a disjunction between question and answer is simply not known, so the publisher may as well get the connection between question and answers right. People whose first language is not the one used in the question will appreciate the extra care.

Avoid very general questions

It is easy to ask a very general question when in fact what is wanted is a response to a specific issue. The problem with questions that are very general is that they lack a frame of reference. Therefore:

> How satisfied are you with your job?

seems harmless, but it lacks specificity. Does it refer to pay, conditions, the nature of the work, or all of these? Respondents are likely to vary in their interpretations and this will be a source of error. A favourite general question comes from Karl Marx's *Enquête Ouvrière*, a questionnaire sent to 25 000 French socialists and others (though there is apparently no record of any being returned). The final (one-hundredth) question reads:

> What is the general, physical, intellectual, and moral condition of men and women employed in your trade? (Bottomore and Rubel 1963: 218).

Avoid leading questions

Leading or loaded questions push respondents in a particular direction, although invariably they do have the ability to rebut any implied answer. Questions of the kind 'Do you agree with the view that . . .?' fall into this class as it is suggesting a particular reply to respondents. A question like:

> Would you agree to cutting taxes further even though welfare provision for the most needy sections of the population might be reduced?

is also likely to make it difficult for some people to answer in terms of fiscal probity. But once again, Marx is the source of a favourite leading question:

> If you are paid piece rates, is the quality of the article made a pretext for fraudulent deductions from wages? (Bottomore and Rubel 1963: 215).

Avoid questions that actually ask two questions

The double-barrelled question is a clear instance of the transgression of this rule, but in addition there are questions such as:

> Which political party did you vote for at the last general election?

What if the respondent did not vote? It is better to ask two separate questions:

> Did you vote at the last general election?
>
> Yes ＿＿＿
>
> No ＿＿＿
>
> If YES, for which political party did you vote?

Another way in which more than one question can be asked is with a question like:

> How effective have your different job search strategies been?
>
> Very effective ＿＿＿
>
> Fairly effective ＿＿＿
>
> Not very effective ＿＿＿
>
> Not at all effective ＿＿＿

The obvious difficulty is that, if respondents use more than one job search strategy, estimates of effectiveness may vary for each strategy. A mechanism is needed to assess the success of each strategy rather than forcing respondents to average out their sense of how successful the various strategies are.

Avoid questions that include negatives

The problem with questions with 'not' or similar formulation in them is that some respondents may miss the word 'not' and answer opposite to what was intended. There are occasions when it is impossible to avoid negatives in a question, but those like the following should be avoided as far as possible:

> Do you agree with the view that students should not have to take out loans to finance higher education?

Instead, the question should be asked in a positive format (Should students have to take out loans?). Questions with double negatives are never appropriate, because it is difficult to know how to respond to them. Take the following example:

> Would you rather not drink non-alcoholic beer?

It is difficult to know what a 'yes' or 'no' answer would actually mean in this case.

One context in which it is difficult to avoid using questions with negatives is when designing Likert-scale items. Identifying respondents with response sets may even require reversing the direction of some questions (more on this later in the chapter), making negatives difficult to avoid.

Minimize technical terms

Use simple, plain language and avoid jargon. Do not ask a question like:

Do you sometimes feel alienated from work?

The problem here is that many respondents do not know the meaning of 'alienated,' and even if they do, are likely to have different views of what it means.

Consider the following question:

The influence of the CAUT on national politics has declined in recent years.

Strongly agree _____ Agree _____ Undecided _____
Disagree _____ Strongly disagree _____

The use of acronyms, such as CAUT, is a problem because many people are unfamiliar with what the initials stand for.

Does the respondent have the requisite knowledge?

There is little point asking about matters of which respondents have no knowledge. For example, it is very doubtful that meaningful data about computer use can be extracted from respondents who have never used one.

Ensure symmetry between a closed question and its answers

A common mistake is for a question and its answers to be out of phase with each other. Box 5.6 describes such an instance.

Ensure answers provided for a closed question are balanced

A fairly common error when asking closed questions is for the provided answers to be unbalanced. For example, imagine being given a series of options like:

Excellent _____ Good _____ Acceptable _____
Poor _____

The response choices are weighted towards a favourable response. Excellent and Good are both positive; Acceptable is a neutral or middle position; and Poor

is a negative response. A second negative response choice like 'Very poor' is needed.

Memory problems

Do not overstretch people's memories. Although it would be nice to have accurate replies to a question about the number of times respondents have gone to the movies in the previous 12 months, it is highly unlikely that most people can in fact recall events accurately over such a long time (other perhaps than those who have not gone at all or only once or twice in the preceding 12 months). It is for this reason that, in the similar question referred to above, the usual time frame is just one month.

Don't know

One area of controversy when asking closed questions is whether to offer a 'don't know' or 'no opinion' option. The issue chiefly relates to questions concerning attitudes. The main argument for including a 'don't know' option is that *not* to include one risks forcing people to express views that they do not really hold. Many advocate offering survey respondents the 'don't know' option in the form of a filter question to remove those who do not hold an opinion on a topic. This means that the interviewer needs to ask two questions, with the second question just for those who have an opinion.

The alternative argument in connection with 'don't know' is that making it an option allows some respondents to select it when they cannot be bothered to do the required thinking on an issue. A series of experiments conducted in the US found that many respondents who express a lack of opinion on a topic do in fact hold one (Krosnick *et al.* 2002). Respondents with lower levels of education are especially prone to selecting the 'don't know' option; later questions in a questionnaire are more likely to elicit a 'don't know' response. The latter finding implies a kind of question order effect, a topic addressed later in the next section; respondents may become increasingly tired or bored as the questioning proceeds and therefore more lazy in their answers. The researchers concluded that data quality is not enhanced by the inclusion of a 'don't know' option and that some respondents become inhibited from expressing an opinion that they probably hold.

Consequently, these researchers would *not* offer a 'don't know' option unless absolutely necessary.

Question order

Quite a lot of research has been carried out on how asking questions at different points in an interview schedule affects people's responses. Few if any consistent effects of question order have been unveiled, with different results demonstrated on various occasions. Mayhew (2000) provided an interesting anecdote on question order in relation to a crime survey. The question 'Taking everything into account, would you say the police in this area do a good job or a poor job?' appeared twice by mistake for half of the respondents, once early on, but also later in the context of questions on contact with the police. Almost a quarter (22 per cent) gave a more positive rating the second time. Mayhew suggested that as the interview wore on, respondents became more sensitized to crime-related issues and more sympathetic to the pressures on the police. As nice as this explanation sounds, it cannot explain the 13 per cent who gave a lower rating. That is quite a reliability issue; also see Box 5.7.

It is difficult to draw general lessons from such research, however, at least in part because experiments in question order do not always reveal clear-cut effects of varying the order in which questions are asked, even in cases where effects might legitimately have been expected. There are two general lessons:

- All respondents in a survey should receive questions in the same order.

- Researchers should be sensitive to the possible effects of earlier questions on answers to subsequent questions.

The following rules about question order are sometimes proposed:

- Early questions should be directly related to the announced research topic. This removes the possibility that respondents will be wondering at an early stage in the interview why they are being asked apparently irrelevant questions. This injunction also means that personal questions about age, social background, and so on should *not* be asked at the beginning of an interview.

- As far as possible, questions more likely to be salient to respondents should be asked early in the interview schedule, so that their interest and attention are more likely to be secured. This suggestion may conflict with the previous one. Questions specifically on the research topic may obviously not be salient to respondents, but it implies that, as far as possible, questions relating to the research topic that are more likely to grab their attention, should be asked at or close to the start of the interview.

- Potentially embarrassing questions or ones that may be a source of anxiety should be left, if at all possible, until later in the schedule, but not to the very end.

- With a long schedule or questionnaire, questions should be grouped logically and into related sections, since this allows for a better flow than jumping from one topic to another.

- Within each group of questions, general questions should precede specific ones. When a specific question comes first, the aspect of the general question covered by the specific one may be discounted in the minds of respondents, who feel they have already covered it. Thus, if a question about how people feel about their salary precedes a general question about job satisfaction, some respondents may discount the issue of pay when responding about job satisfaction, having already answered it. If items about abortion, where the mother's life is threatened or the pregnancy is a result of incest or rape, come first, they may affect answers to the later item: 'Abortion is a matter of individual personal choice. Under all circumstances a woman should be in control of her own body.' Some who agree with the statement may become neutral, having exhausted their support earlier.

It is sometimes recommended that questions dealing with opinions and attitudes precede questions about behaviour and knowledge. This is because behaviour and knowledge questions may be less affected by question order than questions that tap opinions and attitudes. Once a person has admitted to a behaviour, a need for consistency may then affect the attitude. This way a husband can reveal his support for equal housework early in an interview and then later report less than ideal actual involvement.

Box 5.7 About question order

Most political pollsters try to be fair, and for the moment ignore that this term has not been precisely defined and is instead open to interpretation. And it is true that most outright fraud would be detected. But imagine two pollsters, one who wanted the Liberals to win and the other the Conservatives. The key question in both surveys is: 'On Election Day, for whom do you intend to vote?' This is followed by an alphabetical list of the main political parties. Look below at the two sets of Likert items (five options from strongly agree to strongly disagree) immediately preceding that one and decide if replies will be biased.

Set One:

1 It is time that someone really helped the homeless.

2 Tax cuts should wait until we clean up the environment.

3 I hope there will be a hospital bed available when I need it.

4 I am fearful that Canada Pension will run out of money before I am eligible.

Set Two:

- In the end, tax cuts usually mean more for all.
- Canada's mounting debt is mortgaging the future of its children.
- If Canada did not have to pay so much interest on the national debt it could afford good health care for all.
- The government should register criminals not guns.

    It should not have taken long to answer the earlier question about bias correctly. Also, did you also notice the problem of response set? In any event, this is an interesting exercise because it connects the roles of values and bias in social research and question order.

- Because of a possible question order effect, even if a respondent provides an answer to a question to be asked later in the interview, when the interviewer arrives at the actual question, it should be repeated.

However, question order effects remain one of the more frustrating areas of structured interview and questionnaire design, because of the inconsistent evidence and thus difficulty in formulating general rules.

Designing the questionnaire

Clear presentation

Make sure that the layout is easy on the eye and that it facilitates answering all questions relevant to the respondent. At the very least a variety of print styles (e.g., different fonts, print sizes, bold, italics, and capitals) can enhance the appearance *so long as they are used in a consistent manner*. This last point means, for example, using one style for general instructions, one for all headings, perhaps one for all specific instructions (like 'Go to question 7'), one for broad essay questions, and one for shorter answers. Mixing print styles, so that one style is sometimes used for both general instructions and then specific questions, can confuse respondents.

Vertical or horizontal closed answers?

Bearing in mind that most questions in a questionnaire are likely to be closed, one consideration is whether to arrange the fixed answers vertically or horizontally. Very often, the nature of the answers dictates a vertical arrangement because of sheer length. Many writers prefer a vertical format whenever possible because of the greater potential for confusion in horizontal format (e.g., see Box 5.8). There is a risk, especially if the questionnaire is being answered in haste, that the required tick will be placed in the wrong space—for example, indicating Good when Fair is the intended response. Also, a vertical format more clearly distinguishes questions from answers. To some extent, these potential problems can be reduced through the judicious use of spacing and print variation, but they represent significant considerations. A further reason why vertical alignments can be superior is that they are probably easier to code, especially when pre-codes appear on the questionnaire. Very often, questionnaires are arranged so that to the right of each question are two columns: one for where the data relating to the question will appear in the full data set; the other for the codes assigned to possible responses. The latter allows the appropriate code to be circled for later computer entry. Thus, not only is there less ambiguity about where to place the tick, but the coding is also easier. However, when there is a battery of questions with identical answer formats, as in a Likert scale, a vertical format takes up too much space. One way of dealing with this is to use abbreviations with an accompanying explanation. An example is found in Box 5.8; the four items presented there are taken from an 18-item Likert scale designed to measure job satisfaction (Brayfield and Rothe 1951).

Box 5.8 Closed question with a horizontal or a vertical format?

What do you think of the prime minister's performance since taking office?

(Please tick the appropriate response.)

Very good ____ 5   Good ____ 4   Fair ____ 3
Poor ____ 2   Very poor ____ 1

What do you think of the prime minister's performance since taking office?

(Please tick the appropriate response.)

Very good	____	5
Good	____	4
Fair	____	3
Poor	____	2
Very poor	____	1

Box 5.9 Formatting a Likert scale

In the next section you are presented with a set of statements. Please indicate your level of agreement or disagreement with each by indicating whether you: Strongly Agree (SA), Agree (A), are Undecided (U), Disagree (D), or Strongly Disagree (SD).

(Please indicate your level of agreement by circling the appropriate response.)

3 My job is like a hobby to me.
   SA A U D SD

4 My job is usually interesting enough to keep me from getting bored.
   SA A U D SD

5 It seems that my friends are more interested in their jobs than I am in mine.
   SA A U D SD

6 I enjoy my work more than my leisure time.
   SA A U D SD

Identifying response sets in a Likert scale

One of the advantages of using closed questions is that they can be pre-coded, thus simplifying the data entry for computer analysis. However, some thought has to go into the scoring of the items of the kind presented in Box 5.9. One can, for example, score question 23 as follows:

   Strongly agree = 5

   Agree = 4

   Undecided = 3

   Disagree = 2

   Strongly disagree = 1

Accordingly, a high score for the item (5 or 4) indicates satisfaction with the job and a low score (1 or 2) indicates low job satisfaction. The same applies to question 24. However, for question 25, the picture is different. Here, agreement indicates a *lack* of job satisfaction and disagreement job satisfaction.

Practical tip *Common mistakes when asking questions*

Over the years, Bryman read many projects and dissertations based on structured interviews and self-completion questionnaires. A small number of mistakes recurred regularly, including:

- An excessive use of open questions. While a resistance to closed questions is understandable, although not something we would agree with, open questions are likely to reduce the response rate and cause analysis problems. Keep the number to an absolute minimum.

- An excessive use of yes/no questions. Sometimes students include lots of questions that provide just a yes/no form of response. This is usually the result of lazy thinking and preparation. The world rarely fits into this kind of response. Take a question like:

    Are you satisfied with opportunities for promotion in your firm?

    Yes _____ No _____

  This does not provide for the probability that most respondents are not simply satisfied or not. People invariably vary in their intensity of feelings about such things. So why not rephrase it as:

    How satisfied are you with opportunities for promotion in the firm?

    Very satisfied   _____

    Satisfied   _____

    Neither satisfied nor dissatisfied   _____

    Dissatisfied   _____

    Very dissatisfied   _____

- Students often fail to give clear instructions on self-completion questionnaires about how the questions should be answered, with a tick, something to be circled, or whatever. If only one response is allowed, clearly indicate it, for example, 'tick the ONE answer that comes closest to your view.'

- Generally, do not let respondents choose more than one answer. Sometimes unavoidable, replies to such questions are often more difficult to analyze.

- In spite of constant warnings about the problems of overlapping categories, students still formulate response choices that are not mutually exclusive or omit some categories. For example:

    How many times per week do you use public transport?

    1–3 times _____   3–6 times _____

    6–9 times _____   More than 10 times _____

  Not only do respondents not know which to choose if the answer is 3 or 6 times, there is no answer for someone who would want to answer 10.

- Students sometimes do not make answers correspond to questions. For example:

    Do you regularly go to your gym?

    More than once a week   _____

    Once a week   _____

    2 or 3 times a month   _____

    Once a month   _____

  The problem here is that the answer to the question is logically either 'yes' or 'no.' However, the student quite sensibly wants to gain some idea of frequency (a good idea in light of the second point in this list). The problem is that the question and the response categories are out of kilter. A better question is:

    How frequently do you go to your gym in any month?

    More than once a week   _____

    Once a week   _____

    2 or 3 times a month   _____

    Once a month   _____

If you have never committed any of these 'sins,' you are well on the way to being able to produce a questionnaire that would stand out from the rest, provided you also take into account the other advice given here and in Chapter 4.

One would have to reverse the coding of this item, so that:

    Strongly agree = 1

    Agree = 2

    Undecided = 3

    Disagree = 4

    Strongly disagree = 5

The point of including such items is to identify people who exhibit response sets, mentioned in the last chapter, like acquiescence. If someone were to agree with all 18 items, when some of them indicated *lack* of job satisfaction, the answers are unlikely to provide a valid assessment of job satisfaction for that person.

Clear instructions about how to respond

Always be clear about how respondents should indicate their replies to closed questions. Are they supposed to place a tick by, or circle, or underline the appropriate answer? Is choosing more than one answer acceptable? If not, this should be indicated in the instructions, for example:

> *(Please choose the ONE answer that best represents your views by placing a tick in the appropriate box.)*

If this is not made clear and some respondents choose more than one answer, their replies will have to be treated as if they had not answered. If choosing more than one category is acceptable, this too must be made clear, for example:

> *(Please choose ALL answers that represent your views by placing a tick in the appropriate boxes.)*

It is a common error for such instructions to be omitted and for respondents either to be unsure about how to reply, or to make inappropriate selections.

Keep question and answers together

This is a simple and obvious, though often transgressed, requirement—namely, that a question should not be split so that it appears on two separate pages. A common error is for a closed question to appear at the bottom of a page and the closed answers on the next page. Doing so carries the risk of the respondent failing to answer the question or paying insufficient attention to the whole question and giving a superficial answer (a problem that is especially likely when a series of questions with a common answer format is being used, as with a Likert scale).

Vignette questions

A form of closed question often used in examining people's normative standards is the vignette technique. It essentially comprises presenting respondents with one or more scenarios and asking them how they would respond if confronted with the circumstances depicted in the scenario. For example, Achille and Ogloff (1997) used vignettes of dying patients (self or stranger and different forms of assisted suicide) in their study of assisted suicide and found lethal injection less acceptable (79 per cent) than withdrawal of life support (90 per cent) among BC respondents. Box 5.10 describes a vignette employed in a study of family obligations. It sought to measure normative judgments about how family members should respond to relatives who are in need and indeed *who* should do the responding.

The vignette was designed to tease out respondents' norms concerning several aspects of family obligations: the nature of the care (whether long or short term and whether direct involvement or just the provision of resources); the significance of geo-graphical propinquity; the dilemma of paid work and care; and the gender component of who should give up a job if necessary to oversee care. There is a gradual increase in the specificity of the situation facing Jim and Margaret as the vignette develops. Initially, unaware of whether Jim and Margaret are prepared to move, then one sees they are and they do in fact move, which leads to whether one of them should become a full-time caregiver.

Many aspects of the issues being tapped by the series of questions can be accessed through attitude items, such as

> When a working couple decide that one of them should care for parents, the wife should be the one to give up her job.
>
> Strongly agree _____ Agree _____ Undecided _____
>
> Disagree _____ Strongly disagree _____

The advantage of the vignette over such an attitude question is that it anchors the choice in an actual

---

Box 5.10 A vignette to establish family obligations

Jim and Margaret Robinson are a married couple in their early forties. Jim's parents, who live several hundred miles away, have had a serious car accident and they need long-term daily help. Jim is their only son. He and his wife both could get transfers to work nearer his parents.

CARD E

(a) From the card, what should Jim and Margaret do?

Move to live near Jim's parents

Have Jim's parents move to live with them

Give Jim's parents money to help them pay for daily care

Let Jim's parents make their own arrangements

Do something else (SPECIFY)

Don't know

(b) In fact, Jim and Margaret are prepared to move and live near Jim's parents, but teachers at their children's school say that moving right now could have a bad effect on their children's education.

What should Jim and Margaret do? Should they move or should they stay?

Move

Stay

(c) Why do you think they should move/stay?
PROBE FULLY VERBATIM

(d) Jim and Margaret *do* go to live near Jim's parents. A year later Jim's mother dies and his father's condition gets worse so that he needs full-time care.

Should Jim or Margaret take an extended leave from work to take care of Jim's father? *IF YES*: Who should, Jim or Margaret?

Yes, Jim should give up his job

Yes, Margaret should give up her job

No, neither should give up their jobs

Don't know/Depends

Adapted from Finch (1987: 108)

---

situation and thus reduces the possibility of an un-reflective reply. Finch (1987) also argued that for a sensitive area like this, some respondents may feel threatened and judged on their replies. Recall the study of assisted suicide. The fact that the questions are about other people (and imaginary ones at that) permits a certain, if sometimes only small, distance between the questioning and the respondent and hence a more candid answer. One obvious requirement of the vignette technique is that scenarios must be believable; considerable effort needs to go into their construction.

Finch also pointed to some limits to this style of questioning. It is more or less impossible to establish what assumptions are being made about the characters in the scenario (such as their age, ethnicity, and number of children at home) and the significance of those assumptions for the validity and comparability of people's replies. It is also difficult to establish how far people's answers reflect their own normative views or indeed how they themselves would act when confronted with the kinds of choices revealed in the scenarios. In spite of these reservations, the vignette technique warrants serious consideration.

Pilot studies and pre-testing questions

It is always desirable to conduct a pilot study before collecting data from respondents, not just to ensure that individual questions operate well but also that the research instrument as a whole is appropriate. Pilot studies may be particularly crucial in research based on self-completion questionnaires, since there is no interviewer to clear up any confusion and, since they are distributed in large numbers, considerable wastage may occur prior to a problem becoming apparent.

Here are some uses of pilot studies in survey research:

- If the main study is going to employ mainly closed questions, open questions in pilot qualitative interviews can be asked to generate the fixed-choice answers.

- Piloting an interview schedule can provide interviewers with experience of using it and can infuse in them greater confidence.

- If everyone (or virtually everyone) who answers a question gives the same answer, the resulting data are less likely to be of interest. A pilot study allows such questions to be identified and modified into one with variable answers.

- In interview surveys, it may be possible to identify questions that make respondents feel uncomfortable and to detect any tendency for interest to be lost at certain junctures.

- Questions that seem not to be understood (more likely to be realized in an interview than in a self-completion questionnaire context) or questions that are often not answered should become apparent. The latter problem of questions being skipped may be due to confusing or threatening phrasing, poorly worded instructions, or confusing positioning in the interview schedule or questionnaire (see Box 5.11). Whatever the cause, missing data are undesirable and a pilot study may be instrumental in identifying the problem.

- Pilot studies allow the researcher to determine the adequacy of instructions to interviewers, or to respondents completing a self-completion questionnaire.

- It may be possible to consider how well the questions flow and whether it is necessary to move some of them around to improve this feature.

Box 5.11 A bad questionnaire

How would you fix this questionnaire?

_____

'Hello. I am taking a Sociology course on research methods and would like to ask you some questions. Would that be OK?'

1 Were you ever scared that you were HIV-positive?

Yes _____   No _____

For questions 2 to 6, please answer Agree or Disagree.

2 As a religious person, I feel sorry for AIDS victims.

3 I think victims of any disease deserve compassion.

4 I think the new legislation will be a boon to AIDS victims.

5 The government should not allocate more money to AIDS research.

6 People with AIDS and other sexual diseases should be quarantined.

If agree, has your viewpoint changed since the 1980s when AIDS first widely emerged?

Yes _____   No _____

Now there are just a few more questions.

7 If one were planned, would you fight having an AIDS hospice on your street?

Yes _____   No _____

8 How does your spouse feel about AIDS victims?

Compassionate _____   Sympathetic _____

Concerned _____   Angry _____   Don't know _____

9 Elizabeth Taylor has raised much money for AIDS research. Should people be doing more fund-raising in this area?

Yes _____   No _____

10 Do you know any AIDS victims? Yes _____   No _____

Finally I need a few facts for comparison purposes.

11 How old are you? _____

12 Did you graduate high school? Yes _____   No _____

13 Did you ever have yourself tested for AIDS?

Yes _____   No _____

Thank you for your cooperation.

Practical Tip 👉 *Getting help in designing questions*

When designing questions, try to imagine someone who will be asked to answer the questions. This can be difficult, because some (if not all) questions may not apply—for example, to a young student doing a survey of retired people. However, try to think about how *you* would reply. This means concentrating not just on the questions themselves but also on links between the questions. For example, do filter questions work in the expected way?

Then try the questions out on some friends or class-mates, as in a pilot study. Ask them to be critical and to consider how well the questions connect to each other. Also, look at the questionnaires and structured interview schedules experienced researchers have devised. They may not have asked questions on your topic, but how they have asked questions should give an idea of what to do and what to avoid.

Checklist of issues to consider for a structured interview schedule or self-completion questionnaire

✓ Is there a clear and comprehensive way of introducing the research to respondents?

✓ Can questions used by other researchers of this topic be used?

✓ Do the questions allow answers to all of the research questions?

✓ Can any questions not strictly relevant to the research questions be dropped?

✓ Has the questionnaire been pre-tested with some appropriate respondents?

✓ If a structured interview schedule, are the instructions clear (e.g., with filter questions, is it clear which question(s) should be omitted)?

✓ Are instructions about how to record responses clear (e.g., whether to tick or circle; whether more than one response is allowable)?

✓ Has the number of open questions been limited?

✓ Can respondents indicate levels of intensity in their replies, not forced into yes or no answers with intensity of feeling appropriate but not indicated?

✓ Have questions and their answers been kept on the same page?

✓ Have sociodemographic questions been left until close to the end of the questionnaire?

✓ Are questions relating to the research topic at or very close to the beginning?

✓ Have the following been avoided:
  — Ambiguous terms in questions or response choices?
  — Long questions?
  — Double-barrelled questions?
  — Very general questions?
  — Leading questions?
  — Questions that include negatives?
  — Questions using technical terms?

✓ Do respondents have the requisite knowledge to answer the questions?

✓ Is there an appropriate match between questions and response choices?

✓ Are the response choices properly balanced?

✓ Do any of the questions depend too much on respondent memory?

If using a Likert scale approach:

✓ Are some items that can be reverse-scored, to minimize response sets, included?

✓ Is there evidence that the items really do relate to the same underlying cluster of attitudes, so that they can be aggregated?

✓ Are the response choices exhaustive and not overlapping?

✓ Is there a category of 'other' (or similar category such as 'unsure' or 'neither agree nor disagree') so that respondents are not forced to answer in a way that is not indicative of what they think or do?

The pilot should not be carried out on people who may become members of the sample in the full study, as the selecting-out of a number of members of the population affects the representativeness of any subsequent sample. If possible, find a small set of respondents comparable to members of the population from which the sample for the full study will be taken. Beagan (2002) did this in her study of medical students.

Using existing questions

One final observation regarding the asking of questions is to consider using questions employed by other researchers for at least part of the questionnaire or interview schedule. This may seem like stealing but use of existing questions means that the questions have in a sense been already piloted and investigated for their reliability and validity. A further advantage of using existing questions is that they allow comparisons with other research, showing whether change has occurred or whether location makes a difference in findings. At the very least, examining questions used by others gives ideas about how best to approach the research questions, even if a later decision is to modify them.

The use of existing questions is a common practice among researchers. For example, the researchers who developed the scale designed to measure attitudes to vegetarians (Box 3.10) used several existing questions devised for measuring other concepts in which they were interested, such as measures of authoritarianism and political conservatism. These other measures had known reliability and validity. Similarly, Walklate (2000: 194) described how in developing a survey instrument for victims of crime, she and her colleagues used 'tried and tested questions taken from pre-existing criminal victimization surveys amended to take account of our own more localized concerns.'

K KEY POINTS

- While open questions undoubtedly have advantages, closed are typically preferable for a survey, because of the ease of asking questions and recording and coding answers.

- This point applies particularly to the self-completion questionnaire.

- Open questions of the kind used in qualitative interviewing have a useful role in formulating fixed-choice answers and pilot studies.

- Learning rules of question-asking avoids some of the obvious pitfalls.

- Question order is very important and some general rules should be followed.

- Presentation of closed questions and the general layout are important considerations for the questionnaire.

- Remember always to put yourself in the position of the respondent when asking questions and to ensure generating data appropriate to the research questions.

- A pilot study/pre-testing can clear up problems in question formulation.

Q QUESTIONS FOR REVIEW

Open or closed questions?

- Why are closed questions preferred to open questions in survey research?
- What are the limitations of closed questions and how can each be reduced?

Types of question

- What are the main types of question likely to be used in a structured interview or self-administered questionnaire?

Question order

- How strong is the evidence that question order and interviewer characteristics can significantly affect answers?

Question layout

- Why is a vertical format for presenting answers to closed questions preferable to a horizontal format?

Vignette questions

- In what circumstances are vignette questions especially appropriate? Make up one to examine an addiction of your choice.

Pre-testing questions

- Why is it important to pre-test questions?

Using existing questions

- Why should using questions devised by others be considered?

6 | Structured observation

CHAPTER OVERVIEW

Structured observation is a relatively underused method in social research. It entails the direct observation of behaviour that is then recorded in categories devised prior to the start of data collection. This chapter explores:

- limitations of survey research for the study of behaviour;

- different forms of observation in social research;

- the potential of structured observation for the study of behaviour;

- how to devise an observation schedule;

- different strategies for observing behaviour in structured observation;

- issues of reliability and validity in structured observation;

- field studies, whereby a researcher intervenes in actual social life and records, using structured observation, what happens as a consequence of the intervention;

- ethical issues in the above; and

- some criticisms of structured observation.

Introduction

Structured observation is a technique in which the researcher employs explicitly formulated rules for the observation, categorization, and recording of behaviour. One of its main advantages is that behaviour is observed directly, unlike in survey research, which allows behaviour only to be inferred from reports. In survey research, respondents report their behaviour, but there are good reasons for thinking that such reports are not entirely accurate. Structured observation constitutes a possible solution in that it entails the direct observation of behaviour.

Problems with survey research on social behaviour

Chapter 4 dealt with several different aspects of survey research, including problems typically associated with it. Box 6.1 summarizes briefly some of the main elements. Also recall that practitioners have developed, with varying degrees of success, ways of dealing with them or at least of reducing their impact.

Box 6.1 Problems with using survey research to investigate behaviour

- *Problem of meaning.* People vary in their interpretations of key terms in a question. Does 'watching television' include having it on while making dinner or must one be concentrating?

- *Problem of memory.* Respondents may not remember certain aspects of behaviour. Or they may falsely remember others. For example, crime victims try to report crimes that happened to them long before the time period (usually one year) in question, just because the victimization was so traumatic.

- *Social desirability effect.* Respondents often give answers they think reflect well on them, perhaps the most important shortcoming of the method. This means, for example, overestimating the amounts given to charity and underreporting traffic tickets.

- *Question threat.* Threatening questions may lead to a dishonest reply. Men who recently underwent surgery for prostate cancer may not want to admit to any incontinence.

- *Gap between stated and actual behaviour.* How people say they are likely to behave and how they actually behave is often inconsistent (see Box 3.12). Husbands, for example, traditionally overestimate how much time they will give (versus actually give) in sharing housework. It need not be a lie as much as a difference between a wish and reality. On the other hand, Perrucci *et al.* (2000) found two quite different pictures of racial relations on a predominantly white university campus—what they called 'front stage' and 'back stage.' The latter only became fully apparent when direct observation supplemented questionnaires and showed less acceptance of racial minorities.

So why not observe behaviour?

An obvious solution to the problems just identified is to observe people's behaviour directly rather than to rely on research instruments like questionnaires to elicit such information. This chapter outlines a method called *structured observation* (see Box 6.2). Much like the interview (see Box 4.3), there are many different forms of observation in social research and Box 6.3 outlines some of them.

It has been implied that structured observation is an alternative to survey methods of research. After all, in view of the various problems identified in Box 6.1, it would seem an obvious solution to observe people instead. However, structured observation has not attracted a large following and instead tends to be used only in certain research areas, such as classrooms, courts, and hospitals.

Central to any structured observation study is the *observation schedule,* specifying the categories of behaviour to be observed and how behaviour should be allocated to those categories. This is best illustrated by looking at examples. One of the classic schedules for the observation of small group behaviour was developed by Bales (1951) (see Figure 6.1).

From such data a number of features can be derived. For example, it becomes possible to compare leaders' and followers' styles in terms of such things as the relative emphasis on asking questions and an-

---

Box 6.2 🔅 **What is structured observation?**

Structured observation, often called *systematic observation,* and typically cross-sectional, is a technique in which the researcher formulates explicit rules for observers about what behaviour they should look for and how they should record it. Each person who is part of the research (or *participant*) is observed for a predetermined period using the same rules. These rules are articulated in what is usually referred to as an *observation schedule*, which bears many similarities to a structured interview schedule using closed questions. The ultimate aim of the observation schedule is to aggregate each type of behaviour being recorded for everyone in the sample. The resulting data resemble questionnaire data considerably, in that the information collected on different aspects of behaviour can be treated as variables for analysis.

Box 6.3 Major types of observation research

- *Structured observation.* See Box 6.2.

- *Participant observation.* This is one of the best-known methods of social science research. It is primarily qualitative and entails the relatively prolonged immersion of the observer in a social setting to observe the behaviour of members of that setting (group, organization, community, etc.) and to elicit the meanings they attribute to their environment and behaviour. Participant observers vary considerably in how much they participate in the social settings in which they locate themselves. See Chapter 8 for a more detailed treatment.

- *Non-participant observation.* This term, used to describe the most frequent kind of structured-observation, applies to a situation in which the observer does not participate in what is going on in the social setting other than to observe it. This can be called *unobtrusive observation* if the observed are unaware that they are being observed. Either can entail structured or unstructured observation (see below).

- *Unstructured observation.* As its name implies, unstructured observation does not use an observation schedule for recording behaviour. Instead, the aim is to record, in as much detail as possible, the behaviour of participants and then to develop a narrative account (story) of that behaviour. In a sense, most participant observation is unstructured but the term unstructured observation is usually employed in conjunction with non-participant observation.

1   Helps, rewards, affirms others
2   Tension release, jokes, shows satisfaction
3   Agrees, concurs, complies
4   Gives direction
5   Gives opinion, evaluation
6   Gives orientation, repeats, clarifies
7   Asks orientation, for repetition/clarification
8   Asks opinions
9   Asks for direction, possible ways of action
10 Disagrees, withholds help
11 Shows tension, withdraws
12 Shows antagonism, deflates, defends self

Sum of 13: Balancing task areas (neutral affect)
   6 + 7 Communication
   5 + 8 Evaluation
   4 + 9 Decision

Sum of 13: Balancing socioemotional reactions
   (−) (+)
   10 + 3 (Dis)agreement
   11 + 2 Tension (reduction)
   12 + 1 (Dis)integration

Adapted from Bales (1951)

Figure 6.1 Small group interaction process

relief in an authoritarian or in a shared leadership style? It is interesting to think about how a scheme like this could help leadership trainees become aware of their styles, and possibly to begin questioning their appropriateness.

One might want to code what is happening every 15 seconds. The coding for a 12-minute period might then look like Figure 6.2. Notice how questions tend to be followed by answers and negative affect by smoothing positive affect (sum of 13). Two types of leaders often emerge, a task specialist and a socioemotional leader, one more responsible for feelings.

swering them, upon silence and talking. Age and gender differences in tension reduction efforts, categories 1 and 12 can be explored. It also becomes possible to compare different groups in terms of these categories, information that then can be useful in developing effective leadership styles. For example, is there less tension and thus less need for tension

7	7	6	6	6	7	6	6	8	5	10	2
5	8	5	12	1	9	9	4	4	5	4	4
10	11	12	12	2	1	1	11	2	8	8	5
5	10	10	2	1	3	2	1	3	6	2	1

Figure 6.2 Coding sheet for imaginary study of small group

Note: Each cell represents a 15-second interval and each row is 3 minutes.

The observation schedule

Devising a schedule for recording observations is clearly a crucial step in a structured observation project. The considerations are very similar to those involved in producing a structured interview schedule; these include things like:

- A clear focus is necessary, meaning that the research problem also needs to be clearly stated. The observer must know exactly who is to be observed and which of the many things going on in any setting are to be recorded.

- As with the production of a closed question for a structured interview schedule, the categories of behaviour must be both mutually exclusive (i.e., not overlap) and inclusive (everything must have a category). Taking the earlier example, what if someone knocks on the door to ask about emptying the trash can? Perhaps the best approach is to have another category of behaviour coded 'other' or 'interruption.' Pilot studies help to reveal possible problems associated with a lack of inclusiveness.

- The recording system must be easy to operate. Complex systems with large numbers of types of behaviour will prove undesirable. Much like interviewers using a structured interview schedule, observers need to be trained, but even so it is easy for an observer to become flustered or confused if faced with too many options.

- A problem can arise if the observation schedule requires too much interpretation on the part of the observer. For example, it can be difficult to distinguish between a Category 10, withholds help, and a Category 11, withdraws. If interpretation is needed, clear guidelines for the observer and considerable training and experience are required.

Strategies for observing behaviour

There are different ways of conceptualizing how behaviour should be recorded:

- One can record in terms of *incidents*. This means waiting for something to happen and then recording what follows from it. Essentially, this is what LaPiere (1934) did as he waited for the Chinese couple to negotiate entry to each hotel or restaurant and then recorded whether they were allowed entry or not.

- One can observe and record a wider variety of behaviours, in either short or long periods of time. In the research reported in Box 2.10, children in St Helena were videotaped over a two-week period during their morning, lunch, and afternoon breaks. The tapes were then coded using 'the Playground Behaviour Observation Schedule, an instrument for recording the occurrence of 23 behaviours (e.g., games; fantasy play; character imitation; anti-social and pro-social behaviour) and their behaviour groupings (i.e., whether the behaviour was undertaken by an individual, a pair, by 3 to 5 children, or 6 or more). . . . A separate schedule was completed for each 30-second segment' (Charlton *et al.* 1998: 7).

- *Time sampling* is another approach to the observation of behaviour. In the Rosenhan study the 'patients' could be in the ward at 9 a.m. for an hour, at the nurses' desk at 11 a.m. for 15 minutes, and in the chapel for 5 minutes at 3 p.m., etc., making notes of what occurred in terms of the observation schedule.

Issues of reliability and validity

Compared with interviews and questionnaires, structured observation 'provides (*a*) more reliable information about events; (*b*) greater precision regarding their timing, duration, and frequency; (*c*) greater accuracy in the time ordering of variables; and (*d*) more accurate and economical reconstruction of large-scale social episodes' (McCall 1984: 277). This is a very strong endorsement, but there are still several issues of reliability and validity that confront practitioners of the method. Some of them are similar to those faced by any researcher seeking to develop measures in social research in general (see Chapter 3) and by survey research in particular. However, certain concerns are specific to structured observation.

Reliability

Practitioners of structured observation have been concerned with *inter-observer consistency*. Essentially, this entails considering how closely two or more observers of the same behaviour agree on the code for that behaviour on the observation schedule.

A second consideration is the degree of consistency of the application of the observation schedule over time—that is, *intra-observer consistency*. This is clearly a difficult undertaking because of the capacity for people to behave in different ways on different occasions and in different contexts. The procedures for assessing this aspect of reliability across all possibilities are broadly similar to those applied to the issue of inter-observer consistency.

It is clearly not easy to achieve reliability in structured observation, a point of some significance

---

Box 6.4 A study of shoplifting

Buckle and Farrington (1994) reported a replication of a study of department store shoplifting. Customers were selected at random as they entered the store and followed by two observers until they left. The observers recorded such details as: cost of items bought; gender, race, and estimated age; and shopping behaviour. In the original study of 486 people, 9 people shoplifted; in the replication it was 6 out of 502. Most shoplifting was of small items of relatively little monetary value and most shoplifters purchased other goods at the same time, just not the shoplifted one. In each instance shoplifters were more likely to be male but under 25 (in the first study) and over 55 (in the replication). Does this discrepancy mean that the study should be redone? Would younger men predominating in two out of three studies be conclusive?

Box 6.5 Cohen's kappa

Cohen's kappa is a measure of agreement when two people code items beyond that which would occur by chance. It can be applied to any coding, textual information, as in the content analysis of newspaper articles, answers to open interview questions, as well as to coding observations. Much like Cronbach's alpha (see Box 3.7), the coefficient varies between 0 and 1. The closer it is to 1, the higher the agreement and the better the inter-observer consistency. A coefficient over .75 is considered very good; between .6 and .75, good; 'fair' ranges from .4 up to .6.

---

since validity presupposes reliability (see Chapter 3). Reliability may be difficult to achieve on occasion, however, because of the effects of such factors as observer fatigue and lapses in attention. This should not be exaggerated, because observers can be trained to use even complex coding schedules with high reliability. It just takes time and money.

Validity

Measurement validity relates to the question of whether a measure is measuring what it is supposed to measure. The validity of any measure is affected by:

- whether the measure reflects the concept it is designed to measure (see Chapter 3); and
- error that arises from the use of the measure in the research process (see Chapter 4).

The first of these issues simply means that in structured observation it is necessary to attend to the same kinds of issues concerning the checking of validity (assessing face validity, concurrent validity, and so on) encountered in interviews and questionnaires. The second aspect of validity—error in implementation—relates to two matters in particular.

- Is the observation schedule administered as directed? This is the equivalent of ensuring that structured interviewers follow the research instrument and its instructions exactly as indicated. Variability between observers or over time makes the measure unreliable and therefore it cannot be valid. Ensuring that observers have as complete

Box 6.6 Reactive effects

Webb *et al.* wrote about 'reactive measurement effect' (1966: 13). It occurs whenever a research subject's knowledge of participating in scholarly research leads to a change in behaviour, thus confounding the investigator's data. Response sets, social desirability, and political correctness, reducing bad attributes and increasing good—each has been mentioned. When a respondent reacts to characteristics of the interviewer is another example. Here are a few more:

- *The guinea pig effect—awareness of being tested.* The classic study was the Hawthorne factory, which showed that each time the working conditions improved productivity went up. But then it went up after working conditions deteriorated! The workers detected the change, and thinking they should react, changed their behaviour. A well-known general problem in experimental research (but which may have a broader applicability) is for some individuals to seek out cues about the aims of the research and adjust what they say and do in line with their perceptions (which may of course be false) of those aims.

- *Role selection.* Webb *et al.* argued that participants are often tempted to adopt a particular kind of role in research. Some people with no strong opinion on an item may develop one when asked, feeling they should be knowledgeable. Even telling them how important they are to the research can encourage some 'expertise.' Other, fairly opinionated individuals, may back off a bit, scared by the tape recorder perhaps, or not wanting to come on too strong to a stranger.

- *Measurement as a change agent.* The very fact of researcher presence may itself cause things to be different. For example, the fact that there is an observer sitting in a classroom means a chair is being used that otherwise would be unoccupied, with resulting changes in space and privacy to those at close hand. This very fact may influence behaviour. When Whyte (1955) in his study of Cornerville joined one of the bowling teams, he in effect removed one of his subjects from that role and turned that person into a rival on an opposing team.

- *Trying to help or be nice to the researcher.* Too often it is assumed that research participants are passive. But even in experiments this is not true. They are not just sitting their awaiting independent variables; they are also trying to please. An old saying says that if you ask five friends to do push-ups they will say 'what?' or 'why?' Five subjects in an experiment, especially students, the usual pool from which subjects are drawn, say 'where?' In fact, subjects generally try to do what they think they are supposed to do (a few are deliberately mean and do the opposite). Some even ask 'Was I good?' at the end of the experiment. Chemical elements, rocks, and cadavers in the science lab never are so affected. But either way, help or hinder, something besides the independent variable is partially causing the effect.

- The first four dealt mainly with the participant in social research. The researcher can also be an issue. The premise is that different researchers elicit different data and get the data they want by communicating, often unconsciously, their expectations. This is why experiments are supposed to be *double blind* so no one knows the hypothesis (*single blind* means that just the subject is in the dark). Here, hiring others to collect the data can help.

Reactive effects are likely to occur in any research in which participants know they are the focus of investigation. Webb *et al.* called for greater use of what they called *unobtrusive measures* or *non-reactive methods* that do not entail a participant's knowledge of research involvement. See Box 7.11 for more ethical issues; records can be checked, for instance, at hospitals and courts, removing the reactivity, but permission to inspect those records should be obtained; otherwise the ethical issue of invasion of privacy becomes relevant. Then comes the issue of who will and who will not give that permission. Ethical social research is never easy.

Alternatively, the usual tools of social research can be used. The things like a confidentiality guarantee and reminders of it may help, as can anonymous questionnaires (versus interviews) and phone versus personal interviews, which then bring their own downsides (recall Chapter 4). Perhaps try to phrase questions to be as non-threatening and non-judgmental as possible: 'Many people did not have time to vote in the referendum or could not make up their minds. Did you vote?' To allow more men to admit fear of being out late at night, do not ask how afraid they are. Use a vignette: 'John does not like to walk alone at night in his neighbourhood. There is a lot of crime and police officers are rarely if ever seen there. Is John almost a copy of you, a lot like you, a bit like you, not at all like you?'

Sociological information is often very useful and to give up because it is not perfect is not really an option. As a consumer of that information, be skeptical. Maybe there were reactive errors. But be skeptical both when the results please you as when they displease you. Research showing that university women are more violent than university men on dates (Katz *et al.* 2002) should be frowned on to the same degree as research showing that men are the bigger problem.

Checklist for structured observation research

✓ Are the research questions clearly defined?

✓ Does the observation schedule indicate precisely the kinds of behaviour to be observed?

✓ Have observation categories been designed to minimize the need for observers to interpret what is going on?

✓ Has overlap in the categories of behaviour been eliminated?

✓ Are the categories of behaviour inclusive?

✓ Do the different categories of behaviour allow an answer to the research questions?

✓ Has a pilot study of the observation schedule been conducted?

✓ Are the coding instructions clear?

✓ Is it easy to log the behaviour immediately while it is happening?

---

an understanding as possible of how the observation schedule should be implemented is therefore crucial.

• Do people change their behaviour because they know they are being observed? This is an instance of what is known as the 'reactive effect' (Box 6.6). After all, if people adjust the way they behave because they know they are being observed (perhaps because they want to be viewed in a favourable way by the observer), their behaviour would have to be considered atypical, not what happens in reality. As McCall (1984) noted, there is evidence that participants become accustomed to being observed and most continue their regular lives, so that the researcher essentially becomes less intrusive the longer he or she is in the field. This of course applies less to sensitive areas, such as sexual or deviant behaviour.

Field experiments as a form of structured observation

Part of LaPiere's study was a field experiment; he arranged for the Chinese couple to seek entry to the hotels and restaurants in order to observe the effects of their attempts. A field experiment, therefore, is a study in which the researcher directly intervenes in and/or manipulates a natural setting to observe the consequence of that intervention. However, unlike most structured observation, in a field experiment participants do not know they are being studied. A famous field experiment is described in Box 6.7. The LaPiere study (1934) was an imperfect experiment because there was no control group of non-Chinese people to see how they were treated. But other field experiments do take the form of an experimental design (see Chapter 2).

While such research provides some quite striking findings and gets around the problem of reactivity by not alerting research participants to their being observed, like the pseudo-patient study in Box 6.7, ethical concerns (see Ethical issue 6.1) are often raised because of the use of *deception*. Moreover, employing an observation schedule is inevitably limited because excessive use will blow the observer's cover. The most that can usually be done is limited coding, as in the Rosenhan (1973) research.

Box 6.7 A field experiment

Rosenhan (1973) was one of eight researchers who gained entry as patients to mental hospitals in the US. Some of them—they are referred to as 'pseudo-patients'—sought entry to more than one hospital, so that 12 hospitals were approached. Each pseudo-patient was instructed to claim 'hearing voices.' All successfully gained entry—in 11 of the 12 cases with a diagnosis of schizophrenia. As soon as they had gained entry, the pseudo-patients were instructed to cease exhibiting any symptoms. In spite of the fact that the pseudo-patients were all 'sane,' it took many of them quite a long time to be released. The length of hospitalization varied between 7 and 52 days, with an average of 19 days. In four of the hospitals, pseudo-patients approached psychiatrists and nurses with a request for release, but no member of a staff was approached more than once on any day. The pseudo-patients recorded the nature of the response to their requests: 71 per cent of psychiatrists responded by moving on with their heads averted and 88 per cent of nurses did likewise. To Rosenhan this indicated that a mental patient becomes powerless and depersonalized. The study has been highly controversial because many psychiatrists questioned its implications, while others have raised ethical issues such as its use of deception.

Ethical issue 6.1   *Ethics of covert observation*

In spite of the widespread condemnation of violations of informed consent and the view that covert observation is especially vulnerable to accusations of unethical practice in this regard, studies using the method still appear periodically. The defence is usually of the 'end-justifies-the-means' kind, the benefits outweigh the risk or harm and virtually all codes of ethics allow covert research as a last resort. It should be avoided 'as far as possible' but may be necessary both to stop research participants from changing their behaviour because they know they are being studied and to get around secretive gatekeepers. Still, it should be only a last resort and where informed consent has not been obtained prior to the research it should be obtained post-hoc. That is a general rule and probably often broken in dealing with dangerous subjects, like pimps and other criminals. In such studies it is absolutely crucial to safeguard the anonymity of research participants.

Another difficulty here is how researchers decide whether it is in fact impossible to obtain data other than by covert work. They define 'benefit greater than harm.' I suspect that, by and large, covert observers typically make their judgments in this connection on the basis of the *anticipated* difficulty of gaining access to a setting or of encountering reactivity problems, rather than as a response to difficulties actually experienced. For example, Homan justified his use of covert participant observation of a religious sect on the grounds that sociologists are viewed very negatively by group members and therefore: 'It seemed probable that the prevalence of such a perception would prejudice the effectiveness of a fieldworker declaring an identity as sociologist' (Homan and Bulmer 1982: 107).

Perhaps another of the most famously controversial cases of covert research is Humphreys (1970) *Tea Room Trade*, made less offensive and then replicated in Canada many years later by Desroches (1990). In these instances the researcher (Humphreys himself and police acting for Desroches) observed homosexual encounters in public toilets ('tearooms'), taking the role of 'watch queen'—that is, someone who watches out for possible intruders while men meet and engage in sexual activity there. The style of observation was closer to structured than to participant observation.

Such 'voyeurism' was offensive to some critics. But as part of his research Humphreys also recorded the participants' car licence numbers. He was then able to track down their names and addresses, thus further invading their privacy, and ended up with a sample of 100 active tearoom-trade participants. To reduce the risk of being remembered, Humphreys waited a year before contacting his respondents and he also changed his hairstyle. After this deception, he then conducted an interview survey (Desroches did not do this) of a sample of those who had been so identified about their health issues (a lie) including some questions about marital sex. He neither told them he knew about their activity nor did he debrief them when finished. This is generally unethical but here probably a good idea as it would have caused pain to many of his married respondents who then would have feared the potential costly consequences of arrest or being exposed publicly (outed).

Criticisms of structured observation

Although not extensively used in social research, structured observation has often been controversial. Some problems have been implied in some of the previous discussion of reliability, validity, and generalizability. However, other criticisms warrant further discussion:

- There is a risk of imposing an inaccurate framework on the setting observed. This point is similar to the problem of a closed question, a risk especially great in settings about which little is known. One solution is for the structured observation to be preceded by a period of unstructured observation, so that appropriate variables and categories can be specified in advance.

- Because it concentrates on directly observable behaviour, structured observation is less able to get at the *intentions* behind behaviour. When intentions are of concern, observers must impute them. Essentially, the problem is that structured observation does not readily allow the observer to get a grasp of the meaning of behaviour, which according to Weber is what makes human behaviour different from the subject matter of natural scien-

tists. In a similar vein, the context of the behaviour, the setting, what is going on in the larger world, etc., are given insufficient attention as factors that are affecting the observed behaviour.

- There is a tendency for structured observation to generate many small bits of data. The problem can then be one of finding general themes to link the fragments to see the bigger picture that lies behind them. This is compounded by the last criticism, that observers may not know the meanings of the behaviours observed to the actors.

On the other hand . . .

It is clear from the previous section that there are limitations to structured observation. However, it also has to be remembered that, when overt behaviour is the focus of analysis and perhaps issues of meaning are less salient as in crowd behaviour, structured observation is almost certainly more accurate and effective than getting people to report their behaviour on a questionnaire. Structured observation also may work best when accompanied

---

Ethical issue 6.2 *Random response technique*

Originally designed for interview situations, one impetus for developing the random response technique was to protect both respondents and researchers so police could not use researcher records and bring them into court as witnesses. (Can some harm be anticipated here, as when the still-free criminals repeat their crimes?)

The process involves respondents flipping a coin but not revealing the results. About half of them should get a head, half a tail. All respondents are then instructed: 'For the following question, if you have a head you must say yes, regardless of whether it is true or not. Tails should answer the question truthfully.' Then comes the question: 'Have you ever used cocaine?' Even if no one used it, about 50 per cent have to say yes because they got a head.

Assume 60 per cent of respondents say yes. The excess over the 50 per cent (heads who had to say yes) reveals how many of the tails used cocaine, here 10 per cent. But

that figure must be doubled because one would expect the same number of cocaine users in the heads condition forced to say yes anyway. (They were yes two times, once for head and once for cocaine.)

I did this as a class exercise and had students raise their hands to say yes or no. When the behaviour in question was shoplifting after the age of 16, the data revealed 80 per cent 'yes,' meaning a 60 per cent (30 per cent plus another 30 per cent) shoplifting rate. The exercise did not work when the topic was post-puberty homosexual behaviour, which came out at only 50 per cent yes. Here there are three possibilities: no one had engaged; one or two had, but the behaviour is not that widespread and heads and tails rarely come out exactly 50–50, so they were concealed in the fluctuation; students may have been too afraid that their classmates would think a raised hand was an admission and not a head.

by another method, for example, one that can probe reasons.

In laboratory experiments in fields like social psychology, observation with varying degrees of structure is quite commonplace, but in social research generally structured observation has not been frequently used. Perhaps one major reason is that, although interviews and questionnaires are limited in terms of their capacity to tap behaviour accurately, as noted above, they do offer the opportunity to reveal information about both behaviour *and* attitudes plus demographic data on social background. They can also investigate the explanations that people offer to explain their behaviour. As a result, researchers using questionnaires are able to gain some information about the factors that are behind the uncovered patterns of behaviour. Also, not all forms of behaviour are accessible to structured observation and sometimes survey research or researcher-driven diaries (see Box 4.9) are the only likely means of gaining access to them.

K   KEY POINTS

- Structured observation is an alternative to survey-based measures for the study of behaviour.

- It contains explicit rules for recording behaviour.

- Structured observation has generally been applied to a narrow range of behaviour, such as that occurring in schools.

- It shares with survey research many common problems concerning reliability, validity, and generalizability.

- Reactive effects have to be taken into account but not exaggerated.

- The field experiment is a form of structured observation of real life but suffers from ethical difficulties.

- Problems with structured observation revolve around a difficulty in imputing meaning of behaviour and ensuring that the framework for recording is valid.

Q   QUESTIONS FOR REVIEW

Observing behaviour

- What are the chief characteristics of structured observation?

- To what extent does it provide a better approach to the study of behaviour than questionnaires or structured interviews?

The observation schedule

- 'An observation schedule is much like a self-completion questionnaire or structured interview except that it does not entail asking questions.' Discuss.

- With a partner, devise an observation schedule for observing an area of social interaction in which both of you are regularly involved, for example, studying in the library. Ask others with whom you normally interact in those situations how well they think the schedule matches what goes on and especially if it missed anything.

Strategies for observing behaviour

• What are the main ways to record behaviour in structured observation?

Issues of reliability and validity

• How do the considerations of reliability and validity in structured observation mirror those encountered in the asking of questions in structured interviews and self-completion questionnaires?

• What is a reactive effect and why can it be especially important in structured observation research?

Field experiments as a form of structured observation

• What are field experiments and what ethical concerns do they pose?

Criticisms of structured observation

• 'The chief problem with structured observation is that it does not give access to the intentions that lie behind behaviour.' Discuss.

• Design an argument against the view that structured observation works best when used in conjunction with other research methods.

Other sources of data

CHAPTER OVERVIEW

This chapter examines other sources of data, including documents, state records, and data collected by other researchers. It explores:

- personal documents in both written form (such as diaries and letters) and visual form (such as photographs);

- official and state documents;

- official documents from private sources;

- mass media outputs such as radio or television scripts;

- virtual outputs, such as Internet resources;

- the criteria for evaluating each of the above sources;

- secondary analysis, the use of data collected by other researchers or of official statistics collected by government departments in the course of their work;

- the advantages and disadvantages of secondary analysis;

- the growing recognition in recent years of the potential of official statistics, following a period of neglect because of criticisms levelled at them; and

- the notion that official statistics are another *unobtrusive method* because research participants are unaware of being studied and thus act naturally.

Introduction

This chapter is concerned with a fairly heterogeneous set of data sources, such as letters, diaries, autobiographies, newspapers, television shows, websites, and photographs. They are collectively referred to here as documents, for ease of presentation. Using data that already exist, such as these, does not mean that the research will be less time-consuming than research that collects primary data. On the contrary, the search for relevant data can often be a frustrating and highly protracted process. Moreover, once they have been collected, considerable interpretative skill is required to ascertain the meaning of the materials uncovered.

Documents in this chapter are relevant materials that:

- can be read (though the term 'read' has to be understood in a looser fashion than normally when it comes to visual materials like photographs);

- have not been produced specifically for the purpose of social research; and

- are preserved so that they become available for analysis.

Documents are important because they provide an unobtrusive measure. They are non-reactive, thus removing one common threat to the validity of the data.

In discussing the different kinds of documents used in social science, Scott (1990) usefully distinguished between personal documents and official documents and further classified the latter in terms of private as opposed to state documents. These distinctions are employed in much of the discussion that follows. Scott also enumerated four criteria for assessing the quality of documents (1990: 6):

- *Authenticity*. Is the evidence genuine and of unquestionable origin?

- *Credibility*. Is the evidence free from error and distortion?
- *Representativeness*. Is the evidence typical of its kind, and if not, is the extent of its uniqueness known?

- *Meaning*. Is the evidence clear and comprehensible?

This is an extremely rigorous set of criteria against which documents should be gauged, and frequent reference to them is made in the discussion.

Personal documents

Diaries, letters, and autobiographies

Diaries and letters have often been used by historians, but given less attention by other social researchers (see Box 7.1). Whereas a letter is a form of communication with other people, diarists invariably write for themselves. When written for wider consumption, diaries are difficult to distinguish from another kind of personal document—the autobiography. Used with a life history or biographical method, letters, diaries, and autobiographies (whether solicited or unsolicited) can either be the primary source of data or adjuncts to another source, such as life story interviews. However, it is with extant (that is, unsolicited) documents that this chapter is primarily concerned.

The distinction between biographies and autobiographies can sometimes break down, and Walt Disney provides a case in point. The first biography of Disney, written by his daughter, Diane Disney Miller (1956), would almost certainly have included information from Mr Disney himself. Moreover, several have noted the 'sameness' about subsequent biographies, a feature attributable to tight control by the Walt Disney Corporation of the primary materials in their Disney archive (letters, notes of meetings, and so on) out of which biographies are fashioned. As a result, although Walt Disney never wrote an autobiography in the conventional meaning of the term, his hand, and subsequently that of the company, can be seen in the biographies written.

In evaluating personal documents, the *authenticity* criterion is clearly of considerable importance. Is the purported author of the letter or diary the real author? In the case of autobiographies, this has become a growing problem in recent years as a result of the increasing use of 'ghost' writers. But the same is potentially true of other documents. For example, in the case of Augustus Lamb (see Box 7.1), Dickinson (1993: 126–7) noted that there are 'only three letters existing from Augustus himself (which one cannot be certain were written in Augustus's own hand, since the use of amanuenses was not uncommon).' This raises the question of how far Augustus was in fact the author of the entirety of the letters, especially in the light of his apparent learning difficulties.

Box 7.1 Using historical personal documents: the case of Augustus Lamb

Dickinson (1993) provided an interesting account of the use of historical personal documents in the case of Augustus Lamb (1807–36), an only child of Lady Caroline Lamb and William Lamb, the second Viscount Melbourne. It is possible that the boy suffered throughout his short life from epilepsy, though he seems to have suffered from other complaints too. Dickinson was drawn to him because of her interest in nineteenth-century reactions to people with mental handicaps but who were never institutionalized. In fact, Dickinson doubted whether the term 'mental handicap' is applicable to Augustus and suggested the somewhat milder description of learning difficulties. At the same time, she showed the problems that people around him experienced in coming to terms with his conditions, in large part because of their difficulty in finding a vocabulary consistent with his high social status.

The chief sources of data are 'letters from family and friends; letters to, about and (rarely) from Augustus' (1993: 122). Other sources included the record of the post-mortem examination of Augustus and extracts from the diary of his resident tutor and physician for the years 1817–21. Despite the many sources, Dickinson still could not conclude with certainty that she gave a definitive portrayal of what the boy was like.

Turning to the issue of *credibility*, Scott (1990) observed that there are at least two major concerns with respect to personal documents: the factual accuracy of reports and whether they do in fact report the true feelings of the writer (see Box 7.2). The case of Augustus Lamb, in which clear differences were found in views about him and his condition, suggests that a definitive factually accurate account is at the very least problematic. Scott recommended a strategy of healthy skepticism regarding the sincerity with which the writer reports his or her true feelings. Famous people may be fully aware that their letters or diaries will be of considerable interest to others and may, therefore, have one eye firmly fixed on the degree to which they truly reveal themselves in their writings, or alternatively ensure that they convey a 'front' that they want to project. In another context, adolescents may write their diaries with an eye to the possibility of a parent 'accidentally' reading their words. Finally, in a particularly interesting illustration, sometimes what is not there is of importance. Sugiman (2004) suggested that the Japanese-Canadian women interned in World War II often did not write down their experiences, to shield their children from that painful knowledge.

Box 7.2 Letters: a dying art in hard copy

The potential of letters in historical and social research is limited to a certain time period. As Scott (1990) observed, letter writing became a significant activity only after the introduction of an official postal service in the nineteenth century. The emergence of the telephone in the twentieth reduced letter writing, and it is likely that the growth of e-mail communication, especially in so far as e-mails are not kept in electronic or printed form, is likely to mean that the role of letters for historical purposes will continue to decline in the twenty-first.

On the other hand, there is growing interest in e-mail in its own right by social researchers. For example, Sharf (1999) reported how, while conducting research into rhetoric about breast cancer, she joined a listserv (a managed list of e-mail addresses around a specific theme) on breast cancer and gradually realized that electronic communications had considerable potential for her research.

Representativeness is clearly a major concern for these materials. Since literacy was far lower in the past, letters, diaries, and autobiographies are likely to be the preserve of the literate and not the working classes. Moreover, since boys were often more likely to receive an education than girls, the voices of women tend to be underrepresented in these documents. Women are also less likely to have had the self-confidence to write diaries and autobiographies. Therefore, such historical documents are likely to be biased in terms of authorship. A further problem is the selective survival of documents like letters. Why do any survive at all and what proportion are damaged, lost, or thrown away? One does not know, for example, how representative suicide notes are. Quite aside from the fact that only a relatively small percentage of suicide victims leave notes, some of those few that do exist may be destroyed by family members, especially if they contain accusations blaming them.

Finally, the question of meaning is often rendered problematic by things like damage to letters and diaries and the use by authors of abbreviations or codes that are difficult to decipher. Also, as Scott (1990) observed, letter writers leave much unsaid in their communications because they share with their recipients common values and assumptions that are taken for granted and thus not included.

Visual objects

There is a growing interest in the visual in social research, with photographs the most obvious manifestation of this trend. Rather than being thought of as incidental to the research process, photographs and other visual objects are becoming objects of interest in their own right (see Box 7.3). Once again, there is a distinction between those produced as part of fieldwork and those that are extant (the focus of attention here). One of the main ways in which photographs may be of interest to social research is in terms of what they reveal about families. As Scott (1990) observed, many family photographs are taken as a record of ceremonial occasions (weddings, christenings) and of recurring events such as Christmas, annual holidays, or a new uniform at the start of the school year. Scott distinguished three

Box 7.3 Photographs in social research

Photographs can play a variety of roles in social research. While often seen in relation to qualitative research, there is no reason not to use them in quantitative research as some have done, for example, in a questionnaire or as prompts in connection with an experiment. Again the topic is *extant* photographs, not *research-generated* photographs taken at a researcher's behest. Three prominent roles photographs can play are:

- *Illustrative*. Photographs may illustrate points and therefore enliven what might otherwise be a rather dry discussion of findings. In some classic reports by anthropologists, photographs played such a role.

- *As data*. Photographs may be viewed as data in their own right. When based on research-generated photographs, they become essentially part of the researcher's *field notes* (see Box 9.12 for an example). When based on extant photographs, they become the main source of data about the field in which the researcher is interested. The examples in this section of Blaikie and Sutton (Box 7.4) are of this kind.

- *As prompts*. Photographs may be used as prompts to entice people to talk about what they see in them. Both research-driven photographs and extant photographs may be used in this way. Sometimes, research participants may volunteer their own photographs for this use. For example, Riches and Dawson (1998) found in their interviews with bereaved parents that unsolicited photographs of the deceased children were often shown to them, just as they were previously shown to neighbours and friends in efforts by parents to handle their grief.

types of home photograph: *idealization*, a formal pose—for example, the wedding photograph or a photograph of the family in its finery; *natural portrayal*, which entails capturing actions as they happen, though there may be a contrived component to the photograph; and *demystification*, capturing a subject in an untypical (and often embarrassing) situation. Scott suggested a need to be aware of these different types in order not to be exclusively concerned with the superficial appearance of images and to probe beneath that surface. He wrote:

There is a great deal that photographs do not tell us about their world. Hirsch [1981: 42] argued, for example, that 'The prim poses and solemn faces which we associate with Victorian photography conceal the reality of child labour, women factory workers, whose long hours often brought about the neglect of their infants, nannies sedating their charges with rum, and mistresses diverting middle class fathers' (Scott 1990: 195).

As Scott argued, this means not only that the photograph must not be taken at face value when used as a research source, but it is also necessary to have considerable knowledge of the social context in order to probe beneath the surface. In fact, one may wonder whether the photograph in such situations can be of any use to a researcher. A researcher does not need a photograph to uncover the ills that formed the underbelly of Victorian society, for example; its only purpose seems to be to suggest a gap between the photographic image and the underlying reality. Sutton (1992) made a similar point in Box 7.4.

Scott saw the issue of *representativeness* as a particular problem for the analyst of photographs. As he suggested, photographs that survive the passage of time—for example, in archives—are very unlikely to

Box 7.4 Photographs of the Magic Kingdom

Sutton (1992) noted a paradox about people's visits to Disney theme parks. On the one hand, the Magic Kingdom is supposed to be 'the happiest place on Earth' with employees ('cast members') being trained to enhance that experience. However, it is clear that some people do not enjoy themselves while visiting. Time spent waiting in lines, in particular, is a gripe for visitors ('guests') (Bryman 1995). Nonetheless, people expect their visit to be momentous and therefore take photographs that support their anticipation that the Disney theme parks are happy places. When they return home, they 'discard photographs that remind them of unpleasant experiences and keep those that remind them of pleasant experiences' (Sutton 1992: 283). In other words, positive feelings are a post-visit reconstruction substantially aided by one's photographs. Thus the photographs provide not accurate recollections of a visit but distorted ones.

be representative; instead, they have been subject to selective retention. The example provided in Box 7.4 of photographs of visits to Disney theme parks suggests that the process of discarding photographs may be systematic rather than random. The other problem relates to the issue of what is *not* photographed, as suggested by the quotation by Hirsch, and Sutton's suggestion that unhappy events at Disney theme parks may not be photographed at all. An awareness of what is not photographed can reveal the 'mentality' of the person(s) behind the camera. This is the point Sutton was making: the absence of photographs depicting less happy experiences at the park suggests something about how the prospect of a visit to a Disney theme park is viewed and therefore about the influence of one powerful corporation in the culture industry. It is clear that the question of representativeness is much more fundamental than the issue of what survives, because it points to how the selective survival of photographs may be part of a reality that family members (or others) deliberately seek to fashion. As in Sutton's example, that very manufactured reality may then become a focus of interest for the social researcher in its own right.

The real problem for the user of photographs is that of recognizing the different ways in which the image may be comprehended. Blaikie (2001) found some fascinating photographs in the local museums of the Northern Isles of Orkney and Shetland from local photographers and donated family albums. As Blaikie observed, in the images themselves and the ways in which they are represented by the museums the 'apparently raw "reality" of island culture has already been appropriated and ordered' (2001: 347). For example, the image of a crofter standing by his home can suggest respectability or poverty. Was the photographer providing a social commentary, or depicting a disappearing way of life, or merely providing an image with no obvious subtext? Any or a combination of these different narratives may be applicable. While acknowledging the diversity of interpretations that can be bestowed on the images he examined, Blaikie argued that in his case, as they were organized by the museums, they provide a perspective on the emergence of modernity and the sense of loss of a past life. Coming to this kind of understanding requires being sensitive to the contextual nature of images and the variety of interpretations that can be made about them.

Government documents

The state is a source of much information of potential significance for social researchers. It produces a great deal of quantitative statistical information but in addition the state is the source of a great deal of textual material of potential interest, such as official reports. For example, in his study of the issues surrounding synthetic bovine growth hormone, Jones (2000) used transcripts of the Canadian Senate inquiry on the topic. Briefly, Monsanto, the manufacturer, lost the battle to have it accepted; its 'scientific facts' lost to health groups claims that the hormone is unnecessary and worse, poses a health risk both to cows and to humans who drink their milk. Similar materials, but in a different context, were employed by Abraham (1994) in his research on the medical drug Opren. The research was concerned with the role of self-interest and values in scientists' evalua-

tions of the safety of medicines. The author described his sources as 'publicly available transcripts of the testimonies of scientists, including many employed in the manufacture of *Opren*, Parliamentary debates, questions and answers in *Hansard*, and leaflets, letters, consultation papers and other documentation disposed by the [drug regulatory authority]' (Abraham 1994: 720). His research showed inconsistencies in the scientists' testimonies, suggesting that self-interest can play an important role in such situations. He also used his findings to argue that an 'objective' scientific ethos, influential in the sociology of science, has limited applicability in areas in which self-interest arises.

In terms of Scott's (1990) four criteria, such materials can certainly be seen as authentic and as having meaning (in the sense of being clear and comprehensible to the researcher), but the two other standards require somewhat greater consideration. The question of credibility raises the issue of whether the documentary source is biased. This is exactly the point of Abraham's (1994) research. In other words, such documents can be interesting precisely because of the bias they reveal. Equally, this point suggests that caution is necessary in attempting to treat them as depictions of reality. The issue of representativeness is complicated in that materials like these are in a sense unique and it is precisely their official or quasi-official character that makes them interesting in their own right. There is also, of course, the question of whether the case itself is representative, but in the context of qualitative research this is a less meaningful question, because no case can be representative in a statistical sense. The issue in qualitative research is sometimes one of establishing a cogent theoretical account and the *possibility* of examining that account in other contexts. This is what Pratt and Valverde (2002) suggested in their study of Somali refugees—that others would study other groups.

Official documents from private sources

This is a very heterogeneous group of sources, but a common one is company documents. Companies (and indeed organizations generally) produce many documents, some in the public domain, such as annual reports, press releases, advertisements, and public relations material in printed form and on the World Wide Web. Other documents are not (or may not be) in the public domain, such as company newsletters, organizational charts, minutes of meetings, memos, internal and external correspondence, manuals for new recruits, and so on. This kind of material is often used by organizational ethnographers in their investigations, but the difficulty of gaining access to it means that many other researchers have to rely on public domain documents alone. Even if the researcher is an insider with access to an organization, certain private documents may still remain unavailable.

Private documents also need to be evaluated using Scott's four criteria. As with the materials considered in the previous section, documents deriving from private sources like companies are likely to be authentic and meaningful (in the sense of being clear and comprehensible to the researcher), though this is not to suggest that the analyst of documents should be complacent. Issues of credibility and representativeness are still likely to require scrutiny.

People who write documents generally want to convey a particular point of view. An interesting illustration of this simple observation is provided by a study of career development issues in a major retail company (Forster 1994). Forster extensively analyzed company documentation primarily relating to human resource management issues, as well as interviews and a questionnaire survey. Because he was able to interview many of the authors of the documents about what they had written, 'both the accuracy of the documents and their authorship could be validated by the individuals who had produced them' (1994: 155). In other words, the authenticity of the documents was confirmed and apparently the credibility as well. However, Forster also said that the documents revealed divergent interpretations among different groupings of key events and processes:

> One of the clearest themes to emerge was the apparently incompatible interpretations of the same events and processes among the three sub-groups within the company—senior executives, HQ personnel staff, and regional personnel managers. . . . These documents were not produced deliberately to distort or obscure events or processes being described, but their effect was to do precisely this (1994: 160).

In other words, members of the different groupings expressed, in the documents, perspectives that reflected their positions in the organization. Consequently, although authors of the documents could confirm their contents, those contents could not be regarded as 'free from error and distortion,' as Scott put it. Therefore, documents cannot be regarded as providing objective accounts of a state of affairs. They have to be interrogated and examined in the context of other sources of data. As Forster's case suggests, the different stances taken by the authors of documents can be used to develop insights into the processes and factors that lie behind divergence, in this instance, the significance of subcultures.

Issues of representativeness are also important. Did Forster have access to a total set of documents? It could be that some had been destroyed or that he was not allowed access to certain sensitive documents. This is not to say that such documents necessarily exist but that a healthy skepticism and good detecting are important tools.

Mass media outputs

Newspapers, magazines, television programs, films, and other mass media are potential sources for social scientific analysis. Parnaby's (2003) study of how Toronto tried to deal with its squeegee kids, for example, examined 200 newspaper articles appearing from 1995 until 2000, mostly from the *Toronto Star, Sun,* and *Globe and Mail*—what he deemed a popular, a mass, and a quality newspaper. Similarly, Hier's study of the Ecstacy panic surrounding raves in Toronto looked at hard-copy newspaper stories in all four major Toronto newspapers (2002).

Films, television shows, and magazines provide similar potential for research, as the example in Box 7.5 suggests. For example, Coté and Allahar (1994) concluded in their examination of magazines aimed at adolescents, that these 'teenzines' turn adolescents into uncritical consumers at the same time as they divert them from protesting against their lack of adult privileges.

Authenticity issues are sometimes difficult to ascertain in the case of mass media outputs. While the outputs can usually be deemed to be genuine, the authorship of articles is often unclear (e.g., editorials, some magazine articles), so that it is difficult to know whether the account was written by someone in a position to provide an accurate version. Credibility is frequently an issue, but in fact, as the examples used in this section show, it is often the uncovering of error or distortion that is the objective of the analysis. Representativeness is rarely an issue for analyses of newspaper or magazine articles, since

the corpus from which a sample is drawn is usually ascertainable, especially when a wide range of newspapers is employed, as in Hier's (2002) investigation. Finally, the evidence is usually clear and comprehensible but may require considerable awareness of contextual factors, such as Giulianotti's need to be aware of the symbolic significance of sheep to Aberdeen football supporters (see Box 7.5).

Box 7.5 Aberdeen football fanzines

Giulianotti (1997) wrote about the fan[maga]zines that emerged in connection with Aberdeen's football club, one of the clubs that were the focus of his ethnographic research (see Box 9.4). He showed how the fanzines help to create a sense of identity among supporters, especially during a period of the sport's decline. He showed, for example, that 'the fanzines combine the more traditional sense of cultural differences from the rest of Scotland with the North-East's self-deprecating, often self-defeating humour' (1997: 231). An illustration of this tendency concerns sheep. Rival fans insist that Aberdeen supporters have an interest in this creature that extends beyond its potential as a provider of food and wool. This is revealed in the repetitive chant of rival supporters: 'Sheep-shagging bastards, you're only [etc.] . . .' (1997: 220). This allegation of bestiality is turned by the supporters upon themselves in their fanzines, so that a sheep is frequently used in cartoons and stories about sheep are common.

Virtual outputs and the Internet as objects of analysis

There is one word avoided in the chapter so far—text. It is frequently employed as a synonym for 'written document,' but not here in that photographs and films have also been examined. But, in relatively recent times, the word 'text' has been applied to an increasingly wide range of phenomena, so that theme parks, technologies, and a wide range of other objects are treated as texts out of which a 'reading' can be fashioned, with virtual text a recent source.

The relative newness of the Internet means that websites and webpages as potential sources of data are still fairly underused by social researchers, although Wilson's look at Toronto's rave scene did use Internet newsgroups (2002). However, the vastness of the Internet and its growing accessibility make it a likely source of documents for future both quantitative and qualitative data analysis. Hier (2000), for example, examined a Toronto-based racial supremacy website and found that it allows people to be exposed to its ideas in a relatively anonymous way, without, for example, subscribing to a hard-copy newsletter. He thus feared that ordinary citizens may become susceptible to its messages.

The use of images in websites is also potentially interesting. Crook and Light (2002) analyzed the photographs in 10 university prospectuses. The authors noted that the images that accompany departmental entries often include photographs of students apparently studying; however, they are rarely shown in the typical contexts of formal university learning, such as at lectures or alone in their rooms. Instead, they are usually shown in 'social' forms of learning where they are also active, engaged, and frequently out of doors. The authors argued that these less typical learning contexts are chosen because they are more seductive.

In addition, other forms of Internet-based communications (such as listservs, discussion groups, and chat rooms) have been used as objects of analysis. For their study of online social support groups, Nettleton *et al.* (2002) examined interactions in newsgroups, discussion lists, chat rooms, etc. In a study of the use of e-mail in two organizations, Brown and Lightfoot (2002) found that online communication is strongly influenced by pre-existing, non-online forms of communication (such as written memos) meaning that previous ways of working are not fully displaced. In addition, they noted that e-mail is often employed as a means of establishing who is responsible (and not responsible) for certain actions. As such, the internal politics of organizations in terms of establishing personal responsibility may loom large in the use of e-mail.

There is clearly a huge potential with Internet documents, but Scott's criteria need to be kept in mind. First, authenticity: anyone can set up a website so that matters such as financial predictions may be given by someone who is not an authority. Second, credibility: are there possible distortions? For example, some websites encourage people to buy or sell particular stocks held by the website authors, so that the prices of stocks can be manipulated. Third, given the constant flux of the Internet, it is doubtful whether one can ever know how representative websites on a certain topic are. As Ho *et al.* (2002) pointed out, new websites are continually appearing, others disappearing, still others being modified. Searching on the Internet is like trying to hit a target that not only continually moves, but is also in a constant state of metamorphosis. In a related vein, any one search engine provides access to only a portion of the web and there is evidence that even the

Practical tip *Referring to websites*

There is a growing practice in academic work that when referring to websites the date they were consulted should be included. This convention is very much associated with the fact that websites often disappear and frequently change, so that if subsequent researchers want to follow up any findings, or even to check on them, they may find that they are no longer there or that they have changed. Citing the date(s) of consulting the website may help to relieve any anxieties about such problems.

Checklist for evaluating documents

Have the following questions been answered?

☑ Who produced the document?

☑ Why was the document produced?

☑ Was the person or group that produced the document in a position to write authoritatively about the subject or issue?

☑ Is the material genuine?

☑ Did the person or group have an axe to grind or a particular slant?

☑ Is the document typical of its kind and if not is it possible to establish how untypical it is and in what ways?

☑ Is the meaning of the document clear?

☑ Can the events or accounts presented in the document be corroborated?

☑ Are there different interpretations of the document from the one you offer and if so what are they and why have you discounted them?

---

combined use of several search engines gives access to just under a half of the total population of websites and no way of knowing if they are a biased sample. Finally, websites are notorious for a kind of 'webspeak,' so that it can be difficult to comprehend what is being said without some insider knowledge.

Researchers basing their investigations on websites need to recognize these limitations as well as the opportunities offered. Scott's suggestions invite consideration of why a website is constructed; in other words, why is it there at all? Is it there for commercial reasons? Does it have an axe to grind? In other words, be no less skeptical about websites than about any other kind of document. Employing both printed and website materials can provide a basis for cross-validating sources.

Introduction to secondary analysis

Survey research and structured observation can be extremely time-consuming and expensive to conduct, well beyond the means of most students. This is where *secondary analysis* comes in. Large amounts of quantitative data already exist, collected by individual social scientists, and many organizations, most notably government departments and university-affiliated research centres, such as the Institute for Social Research at York, the Population Research Library at the University of Alberta, and the Institute of Urban Studies at the University of Winnipeg, which specializes in applied research aimed at ameliorating urban problems. Many make it available, in statistical aggregate form, on such things as income, fertility, crime, and unemployment, and sometimes of the individual cases with identifiers removed. Using such data rather than collecting new has the additional advantage of not bothering an already over-surveyed public. For

this reason, secondary analysis should be considered not just by students but by all social researchers, and, indeed, some granting agencies require applicants proposing to collect new data to demonstrate that relevant data are not already available in a data archive. On the other hand, the use of official statistics for social research has been controversial, and aspects of the ensuing debate are addressed later.

Advantages of secondary analysis

There are several reasons for considering secondary analysis as a serious alternative to collecting new data. Its advantages have been enumerated by Dale *et al.* (1988).

- *Cost and time.* As noted at the outset, it offers good quality data like those listed in Box 7.6 for a tiny fraction of the resources involved in collecting new data.

- *High-quality data.* Most of the data sets employed for secondary analysis are of extremely high quality. First, the sampling procedures have been rigorous, in most cases resulting in samples that are as close to being representative as is reasonably possible. Although those responsible for these studies suffer the same problems of survey non-response as anybody else, well-established procedures are usually in place for following up non-respondents and thereby keeping this problem to a minimum. Second, the samples are often national samples or at least cover a wide variety of regions. Their geographical spread and size are attained only in research with substantial resources. Third, many data sets have been generated by highly experienced researchers and, in the case of some of the

large data sets, gathered by social research organizations with strong control procedures to check on data quality.

- *Opportunity for longitudinal analysis.* Secondary analysis can offer a chance for longitudinal research, which, as noted in Chapter 2, is less frequent in the social sciences because of the time and costs involved. Sometimes, as with the General Social Survey (GSS) (see Box 7.7), a panel design has been employed and it is possible to chart trends and connections over time. Such data are sometimes analyzed cross-sectionally, but there are obviously opportunities for longitudinal analysis as well. Also, with data sets such as the GSS survey, because certain interview questions are recycled each year, shifting opinions or changes in behaviour can be identified. With such data sets, actual respondents differ from year to year, so that causal inferences cannot be readily established, but nonetheless it is still possible to gauge trends. See Box 7.8 for an example of the creative use of longitudinal secondary data.

- *Subgroup analysis.* When large samples are the source of data (as in the GSS) there is the opportunity to study what can often be quite sizeable subgroups. In a sample of 100 people, one may find only three seniors over age 85. No quantitative researcher wants to talk about those three seniors, as in 'only 33 per cent of the aged is in good health.' That is one person. Make it a national sample of 2000 and the numbers are increased twentyfold to 60. With this number, which is still small, estimates of seniors still enjoying good health are more meaningful. It is impossible to get numbers like those in a small study unless those groups are the specific focus and others omitted.

Myles and Hou (2004), by using a 20 per cent sample of 1996 census data, could study 18 000 blacks and similar numbers of Chinese and South Asian respondents in their investigation of the spatial assimilation of new racial minority immigrants to Toronto. They found a traditional pattern for the blacks and South Asians: first moving into ethnic enclaves when they come to Canada, and then as they become more affluent, moving into the wider society. Chinese immigrants are different. They buy houses earlier than the other two groups and choose

Box 7.7 General Social Survey features

INTRODUCTION

In 1985, Statistics Canada initiated the General Social Survey (GSS), which over a five-year period would cover major topics of importance, especially the health of Canadians and their level of social support. The GSS has two principal objectives: first, to gather regular data on Canadian social trends so to monitor changes, and sec- ond, to provide information on specific policy issues of current interest. The GSS is a continuing program with a survey cycle each year. Each cycle classifies subjects by age, sex, education, and income. Core content areas, however, cannot be treated adequately in each survey cycle. Instead, they are covered usually every five years. The content by cycle is as follows:

Cycle	Year	Topics
1	1985	Health, Social Support
2	1986	Time Use, Social Mobility, Language
3	1988	Personal Risk, Victim Services
4	1989	Education and Work
5	1990	Family and Friends
6	1991	Health (Various Topics)
7	1992	Time Use, Culture, Sport and Unpaid Activities
8	1993	Personal Risk, Alcohol and Drug Use
9	1994	Education, Work, Transition into Retirement
10	1995	Family Effects of Tobacco Smoke
11	1996	Social Support, Tobacco Use
12	1998	Time Use
13	1999	Victimization, Spousal Violence, Senior Abuse and Public Perceptions of Alternatives to Imprisonment
14	2000	Access to and Use of Information Communication Technology
15	2001	Family History
16	2002	Social Support and Aging

COLLECTION METHODS

Telephone interviewing is the major form of data collection, due to its lower cost, ease of monitoring interviewers, and data quality. Only 3 per cent of Canadians do not have a phone. Sample size for each cycle of the GSS is approximately 10 000 households, generally one person per household. Respondents in smaller provinces are oversampled.

AVAILABILITY

The GSS provides a series of publications that present national and some regional-level summary data, primarily in the form of tables and charts, along with initial analyses and findings. But the interest here is in the availability of the data for secondary analysis. Public-use microdata files, together with supporting documentation, are available. These files contain individual records, screened to ensure confidentiality. Files come on 9-track tape, tape cartridge, and diskettes, or on CD-ROM (for an additional cost). The Data and Users Guide for GSS Cycles 1–15 can be retrieved from the Data Archive. For further information or assistance, contact the Coordinator, Data Services.

Source: 'Delivering Information—Supporting Learning.' File last modified on 6 April 2004. Accessed on 24 June 2004, http:// library.usask.ca/data/social/gss.html

to stay in or form new Chinese communities. It is easy to see how a wide range of different subgroups can be identified for similar kinds of analysis. Box 7.9 provides a further example of subgroup analysis based on married women over age 40.

- *Opportunity for cross-cultural analysis.* Cross-cultural research has considerable appeal at a time when social scientists are more attuned to globalization. It is easy to forget that many findings may not apply to countries other than that in which

Box 7.8 Labour market outcomes of different fields of study: an example of secondary analysis

Walters (2004) was interested in post-secondary education and specifically in the issue of whether Canada needs graduates with highly specialized technical skills more than those with a liberal arts background. Pooling national graduate surveys from 1982, 1986, 1990, and 1995 he found that fine arts make the least money after graduation, followed by humanities, then social science and that engineers and math and business graduates make more. But he found that the gap was generally consistent, that the liberal arts are not losing ground to more technical areas. His work was not applied research, but it probably has some policy implications, for example, in the areas of paying back student loans and variable tuition. A study like this allows an important topic to be illuminated using a relatively large representative sample that would be beyond the reach of most individual researchers.

Box 7.9 The labour force participation of women in mid-life: an example of secondary analysis

Ginn and Arber (1995) were interested in the declining labour force participation of married women in the 15 or so years before reaching pensionable age. To explore some of the factors behind this tendency, national surveys for 1988, 1989, and 1990 were 'pooled' to provide a sample of more than 11 000 women aged 40 to 64 and living in private households. The authors were especially interested in the relative importance of women's personal characteristics (such as age, health, and class) and the characteristics of their households (whether husband is employed and if so his income and number of children). One of the most significant variables for women of all mid-life ages is whether the partner is employed; if partner is not in paid employment, women also tend not to be in employment. The authors also noted the significance of not having information on certain issues: 'The correlation between partners' non-employment may be due to several factors, which cannot be distinguished with these data; husbands and wives may synchronise their retirement in order to avoid the wife being employed when the husband is at home, or their joint non-employment may reflect the [similar] local labour market conditions faced by couples' (1995: 90).

the research is conducted. But cross-cultural research presents barriers to the social scientist in addition to its obvious cost—barriers to do with practical difficulties of doing research when language and cultural differences are likely to be significant. The research on religiosity described in Box 3.5 by Kelley and De Graaf (1997) provides an example of using cross-cultural secondary data. The authors describe the process as follows:

> Data are from the 1991 'Religion' module of the International Social Survey Programme (ISSP) . . . a module containing exactly the same questions, answer categories, and sequencing for all countries surveyed. . . . The samples are all large, representative national samples of adults. The most common procedure is to hold face-to-face interviews . . . followed by a leave-behind self-completion questionnaire containing the ISSP module . . . (Kelley and De Graaf 1997: 642).

Kelley and De Graaf's results were based on a secondary analysis of the data from the 15 nations involved in the research. Opportunities for such cross-cultural analysis appear to be increasing. For example, common core questions may be used in national surveys conducted in several countries.

Both the US and Britain have the equivalent of our GSS. This allowed Grabb and Curtis (2004) to create a whole literature comparing the US and Canada, revealing cross-national regional differences where national differences were popularly expected.

- *More time for data analysis.* Precisely because data collection is time-consuming, the analysis of data is often rushed. It is easy to perceive data collection as the difficult phase and to view the analysis as relatively straightforward, but this is not the case. Working out what to make of the data requires considerable thought and often a preparedness to learn unfamiliar techniques of data analysis. While secondary analysis invariably entails a lot of data management—partly to get to know the data and partly to get it into a proper form (see later in this chapter)—the analysis phase should not be underestimated. Freed from having to collect fresh data means it can be better planned and executed.

- *Reanalysis can offer new interpretations.* It is easy to think that once a set of data has been analyzed, the data have in some sense been drained of further insight. In fact, data can be analyzed in so many different ways that it is very unusual for all possible analyses to be exhausted. For one example, a secondary analyst may look at relationships between variables not envisaged, or which could not have been envisaged by the initial researchers, prompting a reconsideration of the relevance of the data (see Box 7.10). Second, new methods of quantitative data analysis, offering the prospect of a rather different interpretation of the data, are continuously emerging in disciplines such as statistics and even within the social sciences themselves. As awareness of such techniques spreads, and potential relevance recognized, researchers want to apply them to other, even existing, data sets.

- *The wider obligations of the social researcher.* For all types of social research, research participants give up some of their time, usually for no reward. It is not unreasonable that the public should expect the data they generate to be mined to the fullest. Indeed, much social research is chronically under-

analyzed because primary researchers often want to look at data only with respect to central research questions or lose interest as they imagine a new set of research questions. Making data available for secondary analysis enhances the chance of a fuller use.

Limitations of secondary analysis

The foregoing list of benefits of secondary analysis sounds almost too good to be true. In fact, there are not very many limitations, but the following warrant some attention.

- *Lack of familiarity with data.* With data collected by others, a period of familiarization is necessary, to get to grips with the range of variables, the ways in which they were coded, and various aspects of their organization. This period can be quite substantial with large complex data sets and should not be underestimated.

- *Complexity of the data.* Some of the best-known data sets employed for secondary analysis, such as the GSS, are very large both in number of respondents and variables. Sometimes, the sheer volume of data can present problems with the management of the information at hand, and again, a period of acclimatization may be required. Also, some of the most prominent data sets employed for secondary analysis are known as *hierarchical* data sets, meaning that the data are collected and presented at the level of both the household and the individual (and sometimes other levels). Different data may apply to each level. Thus, at the household level, data on such variables as number of cars may appear, while at the individual level, data on income and occupation are found. The secondary analyst must decide which level of analysis to use; if the decision is to analyze individual-level data, the individual-level data must then be extracted from the data set. There is also the potential for making an *ecological fallacy* (see Box 7.11).

- *No control over data quality.* The point has been made on several occasions that secondary analysis offers the opportunity for students and others to examine data of far higher quality than they could collect themselves. However, this point applies

---

Box 7.10 Secondary analysis and new research questions

Secondary analysis can involve topics that in all likelihood were not envisaged by those responsible for the data collection. In a secondary analysis of data on dietary choices, attitudes, and practices, Beardsworth *et al.* (2002) added gender as a focus, one not examined in previous analyses. The analysis showed that women are more likely than men to adopt a 'virtuous' pattern of eating, one that acknowledges a sensitivity and preparedness to act in terms of Western ethical and nutritional principles. The article also showed that these principles have a sinister component in that they frequently come to be associated among women with feelings of guilt, disordered eating patterns, and concerns about body shape. This work serves as an example of a profitable extension of prior research using existing data.

Box 7.11 ⌾ *What is the ecological fallacy?*

The ecological fallacy is the error of assuming that inferences about individuals can be made from aggregate data. Coleman and Moynihan (1996) provided the example of the relationship between ethnicity and crime. They observed that findings showing a higher incidence of crime in neighbourhoods with high concentrations of ethnic minorities have been used to imply that members of such minority groups are more likely to commit crimes.

However, individual data are needed to examine this relationship, which may or may not be true. For example, it may not be the members of the minority groups who are responsible for the high levels of offending, but their non-minority neighbours who resent their presence. Similarly, people could be coming from adjoining neighbourhoods to commit crimes on victims they perceive as more vulnerable. Aggregate data cannot evaluate these possibilities.

---

mainly to data sets such as the GSS and others (see Box 7.6). With lesser-known data sets, somewhat more caution may be necessary in connection with data quality, although certain fundamental checks on quality are usually made by the archives in which such data are deposited.

- *Absence of key variables.* Because secondary analysis entails the analysis of data collected by others for their own purposes, it may be that one or more of the secondary analysts' key variables is not present or the same variable was measured differently in different years. For the study in Box 7.8, for example, Walters (2004) had this problem so he had to make some omissions and to modify some of the original data. Or analysts may, for example, want to see if a known relationship between two variables holds even when *other* variables are taken into account. Such an analysis is known as *multivariate analysis*, an area to be touched on in Chapter 12. The inability to examine the significance of these theoretically important variables can arise when, for example, a theoretical approach, one that emerges after the collection of the data, suggests its importance.

Official statistics

Agencies of the state, in the course of their business, are required to keep a running record of their activities and when these records are aggregated, they form official statistics. Thus, in Canada, the police compile data that form the crime rate and Statistics Canada collects data that form the basis for the estimates of the level of unemployment. These are just two, as it happens high profile, sets of statistics that can be subsumed under the general category of 'official statistics.'

The use of official statistics for social research has been controversial for many years. Still, official statistics offer the social researcher certain advantages over some other forms of quantitative data, such as data based on surveys:

- The data are often based on populations, not samples, allowing a complete picture to be obtained.

- Since the people who are the source of the data are not being asked questions as part of a research project, the problem of *reactivity* is less pronounced than when data are collected by interview or questionnaire.

- There is a greater prospect of analyzing the data both longitudinally and cross-culturally. Because the data are compiled over many years, it is possible to chart trends over time and perhaps to relate them to broader social changes. As well, official statistics from different nations can be compared for a specific area of activity. Durkheim's 1897 study of suicide (reprinted in 1952) was the result of a comparative analysis of official statistics from several countries.

However, readers who recall Box 3.9 will already be on guard. The official statistics concerned with an area of social life like crime can be very misleading, because they record only those individuals who are processed by the agencies that have the responsibility for compiling the statistics. Crime and other forms of deviance have been a particular focus of attention and concern among critics of the use of official statistics. Figure 7.1 illustrates, in connection with crime and the crime rate, some of the factors of concern.

Taking a criminal offence as the starting point (step 1), consider the factors that affect its becoming part of the crime rate. An offence may become a candidate for inclusion in the crime rate if its victim is aware of being victimized or if not, if a witness becomes aware (step 2). Would you be aware that $5 is missing from your wallet? Then a crime has to be recognized as such before it can be reported to the police (step 3). Did you lose that money or was it stolen? Next, if it is recognized as a criminal offence, the victim or the witness still must choose to bring the crime to the notice of the police (step 4). Male victims of sexual assault rarely report their experiences. So far this means that, if a criminal act goes unnoticed, or is noticed but not recognized as criminal, or is noticed and recognized as criminal but not reported to the police, it does not enter the official statistics.

Even then the crime may not be entered into the crime statistics, because the police have considerable discretion about whether to proceed officially and may choose to let a suspect off with a warning (step 6). They may be influenced by such factors as: the severity of the crime, the perpetrator's previous record, the perpetrator's demeanour or suggestions of contrition, even the victim's demeanour (do argumentative drunks get as much attention as sober victims?), and the officer's volume of work at the time or how close it is to quitting time.

Alternatively, a crime may be observed by the police during their patterns of surveillance, itself a product of decisions about how best to deploy police officers (step 5). Once again, the crime may not become part of the crime rate because no police are available to witness it. Overall, this means that only after the police exercise discretion in such a way as to lead them to seek a prosecution (step 6), is the offence recorded (step 7) and becomes a part of the crime rate (step 8).

The general implication of this process for the crime rate and for criminal statistics is that a substantial amount of crime undoubtedly goes unrecorded, frequently referred to as 'the dark figure' (Silverman *et al.* 2000). Nor can crime be regarded as alone in this problem. Suicide statistics almost certainly fail to record many potential cases for inclusion. Deciding whether the deceased was involved in an accident or intended to commit suicide can sometimes be difficult to determine in the absence of a suicide note. Moreover, those responsible for concluding whether a death is a suicide or not may come under considerable pressure not to record it as

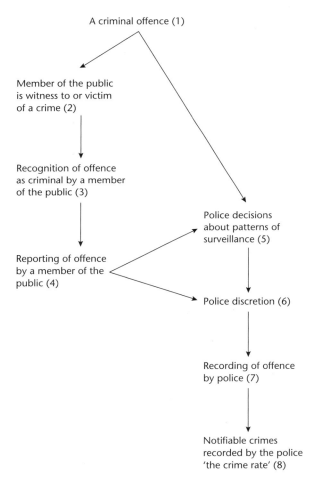

Figure 7.1 The social construction of crime statistics—eight steps

Adapted from a figure in Beardsworth *et al.* (n.d.)

such, possibly because of the potential stigma or because of religious taboos concerning suicide.

To push the point even further, the deficiencies of official statistics extend beyond things like crime and suicide. For example, official levels of unemployment may misrepresent the 'real' level of unemployment. People who have given up trying to get jobs are often missed in the statistics, while those who form part of the 'underground or informal economy' (thus not really unemployed) are included in the unemployment statistics. In addition, definitions of apparently similar or identical terms (such as unemployment or socioeconomic class) used by those responsible for compiling official statistics may not be commensurate with the definitions created by social researchers.

Reliability and validity

Issues of reliability and validity seem to loom large in the official statistics just discussed. Reliability is jeopardized when definitions and policies regarding the phenomena to be counted vary over time. For example, local governments may decide to place more police services into surveillance of a certain crime, such as drugs, prostitution, or driving while intoxicated, thus 'increasing' these rates. Moreover, as part of such crackdowns, police officers may be less likely to use their discretion and thus not let off perpetrators with a warning. Zero tolerance programs have the same result. Thus, variations over time in levels of particular crimes may not be due to variations in levels of transgression but to variations in the propensity to expend resources on surveillance and to proceed with prosecution. For one final point, a further factor that can impair the reliability of crime statistics is 'fiddling' by police officers (see Boxes 3.9 and 7.12). To the extent that such factors operate, the reliability of the crime data is adversely affected and, as a result, validity is similarly impaired.

Problems with official statistics extend to the examination of variables associated with crime. Variations in criminal activity among ethnic groups or social classes may be a product of such factors as: variations in the likelihood of members of the public reporting a crime when the perpetrator is of one ethnic group or class rather than another (are First

> ### Box 7.12 Fiddling the crime figures
>
> An article in *The Times* (Leake 1998) reported growing evidence that senior police officers frequently massage crime statistics. The author argued that many officers deliberately 'lose' crimes in order to make their detection rates look better. As a result, official crime rates are often lower than they should be. The article cited the following methods of suppressing crimes:
>
> - classifying multiple offences as a single incident;
> - excluding common assaults, when people are not seriously injured, from the figures for violent crime; and
> - excluding drug offences in which people admitting guilt are only cautioned.
>
> These methods of reducing the crime rate adversely affect their reliability and thus their validity (recall Chapter 3), but they also hurt longitudinal analysis. Variations over time in the propensity to massage the data make it impossible to compare figures from different time periods.

Nations people more often noticed and reported?); variations in the surveillance activities of the police so that areas with a high concentration of members of one ethnic group or class rather than others are more likely to be the focus of activity (do patrols favour some areas more than others?); variations between ethnic groups or social classes in the propensity of police officers to exercise discretion; and problems for the police of learning about and investigating certain crimes that are themselves related to ethnicity or class (e.g., white-collar crime). In another area, variations among ethnic groups in suicide rates may be partly due to how much power each has to pressure officials like coroners not to treat a death as a suicide. Religious groups view suicide differently and this affects the probability of leaving suicide notes, which in turn affects official labels.

Condemning and resurrecting official statistics

In the 1960s, in particular, there was a torrent of criticism of official statistics, especially those connected with crime. In fact, so entrenched was the belief in many quarters that official statistics were of dubious value to social researchers that it was recommended that social researchers instead investigate the organizational processes that produce such deficient official data. An effect of this view was to consign official statistics to the sidelines of social research; although some work continued, it was more sensitive to the fact that official statistics are invariably not tailored to the needs of social researchers.

An important article by Bulmer (1980) questioned the relative neglect of official statistics and marked a turning point in the views of many towards this source of data (Levitas and Guy 1996). For one thing, Bulmer argued that the critique of official statistics had largely revolved around statistics relating to crime and deviance. Both are subject to special well-known problems, making it wrong to generalize these problems to the full range of official statistics. Moreover, the flaws in many of the official statistics not concerned with crime and deviance are probably no worse than the errors that occur in much measurement deriving from methods such as surveys based on questionnaires and structured interviews, if only due to the latter's higher non-response rates. Indeed, some forms of official statistics are probably very accurate by almost any set of criteria, such as those relating to births, marriages, and deaths. All social measurement is prone to error; what is crucial is taking steps to keep that error to a minimum.

However, even here some caution is necessary. Crime *victimization* data, for example, are still not error-free (see Box 3.9). Silverman *et al.* (2000) pointed to several measurement errors that afflict them, such as an overestimation of serious incidents through a process known as 'telescoping.' This means that serious incidents outside the recall period of 12 months (the period respondents are questioned about) are erroneously considered to have occurred during that period. Additional problems arise from other factors; for example, women are more likely to report sexual offences and domestic violence to the police (step 4 in Figure 7.1) than to a survey interviewer. In other words, dismissing official statistics on crime on the basis of survey evidence generated by victimization studies, not free of error itself, is inappropriate.

Today, the wholesale rejection of official statistics by social researchers has been tempered. While there is widespread recognition and acknowledgment that problems remain with certain forms of official statistics, each set has to be evaluated for the purposes of social research on its own merits.

Official statistics as a form of unobtrusive method

One of the most compelling and frequently cited bases for the continued use of official statistics is that they are an unobtrusive measure, although now many writers prefer to use the term 'unobtrusive method' (Lee 2000). Official statistics fit fairly squarely in the second of the four types of unobtrusive measures outlined in Box 7.13. As noted there, this second grouping covers a very wide range of sources of data including statistics generated by non-government organizations. An interesting use of such data is described in Box 7.14.

However, social researchers often do not use such data and it is not irrelevant that the author referred to in the research presented in Box 7.14 is an economist. Indeed, there may be potential for searching out and mining statistical data produced by organizations that are relatively independent of the state.

Box 7.13 ☼ *What are unobtrusive measures?*

An unobtrusive measure removes the observer from the behaviour being studied. Here are three main types (Webb *et al.* 1966):

1 *Physical traces*. These are the 'signs left behind by a group' and include such things as graffiti and trash.

2 *Archive materials*. This category includes statistics collected by governmental and non-governmental organizations, diaries, the mass media, and historical records.

3 *Simple observation*. This refers to 'situations in which the observer has no control over the behaviour . . . in question, and plays an unobserved, passive, and non-intrusive role in the research situation' (1966: 112).

Official statistics belong in Category 2, as does most of the content analysis of media of the kind described in Chapter 16. Structured observation of the kind covered in Chapter 6 typically does not fall into Category 3, because the observer is usually known to those being observed.

It is important to realize that Webb *et al.* did not want unobtrusive methods to supplant conventional methods. Instead, they wanted to highlight the then current almost exclusive reliance upon methods likely to be affected by reactivity. They sought greater 'triangulation' in social research, with conventional (reactive) and unobtrusive (non-reactive) methods employed in conjunction. For example, they wrote that their inventory of unobtrusive methods 'demonstrates ways in which the investigator may shore up reactive infirmities of the interview and questionnaire' (1966: 174).

It is worth noting that unobtrusive methods or measures encapsulate at least two kinds of ways of thinking about the process of capturing data. First, many so-called unobtrusive measures are in fact *sources* of data, such as graffiti, diaries, media articles, and official statistics. Such sources require analysis in order to be rendered interesting to a social scientific audience. Second, it includes *methods* of data collection, such as simple observation. Here the data are not simply out there awaiting analysis in the way in which diaries or newspaper articles are (although, of course, a great deal of detective work is often necessary to unearth such sources). This means that neither of the terms 'unobtrusive methods' or 'unobtrusive measures' captures the variety of forms terribly well. A further disadvantage of the term 'unobtrusive measure' is that it seems to imply a connection to quantitative research alone, while certain qualitative approaches may qualify as well.

Box 7.14 ☼ *Using unofficial statistics? The case of New York taxi drivers*

Following his informal observation on the behaviour of New York taxi drivers (cabbies), Camerer (1997) tested two theories about the relationship between the number of hours a cabby works and average hourly earnings. One theory—the law of supply—predicted that cabbies would want to work more when their average hourly earnings are high (e.g., during bad weather or on weekdays when more businesspeople are around), rather than when they are low. The second theory—daily income targeting—suggests that cabbies set an income target for the day and once that target is attained they stop work for the day. On good days (when hourly wages are higher) this theory simply means that they will go home earlier.

Camerer obtained taximeter readings from the New York Taxi and Limousine Commission. The data allowed 3000 observations of cabbies' behaviour for 1988, 1990, and 1994. Tips are not recorded, so a guess had to be made about them. The data provided unequivocal support for the daily income targeting theory. However, further analysis revealed a difference between newer and more experienced drivers: the former behave very much in line with income targeting theory; the experienced drivers are more varied and their overall behaviour closer to the law of supply theory, though not entirely in conformity with it. Overall, if cabbies obey the law of supply, mean incomes would rise by around 15 per cent.

Secondary analysis of qualitative data

Although secondary analysis of quantitative data has been done for many years, similar use of qualitative data has only recently become popular. There is no obvious reason why qualitative data cannot be the focus of secondary analysis, though undoubtedly such data present certain problems not fully shared by quantitative data. Hammersley (1997) suggested, for example, that reusing qualitative data may be hindered by the secondary analyst's lack of an insider's understanding of the social context within which the data were produced, a problem perhaps more an issue in ethnographic field notes than with interview transcripts. Such problems seem to afflict even researchers revisiting their own data many years after the original research had been carried out (Mauthner *et al.* 1998: 742). Still, it was secondary analysis of unstructured interviews that formed the basis of the study by Johnson *et al.* (2003) of the reasons why adolescents smoke.

There are also distinctive ethical issues involved. The difficulty of making settings and people anonymous is one. Qualitative data invariably contain detailed accounts of contexts and people that can make it difficult to conceal the identities of institutions and individuals in the presentation of raw data (as opposed to publications in which such concealment is usually feasible). For example, Coleman *et al.* (2001) performed a secondary analysis of case files, coupled with community worker follow-up information, of 78 Canadian aboriginal children treated for inhalant abuse (usually gasoline and started generally before age 10), to discover that the majority suffered a relapse. A second issue is confidentiality. The original researcher(s) may not have obtained the consent of research participants for the analysis of data by others. Nonetheless, in spite of such difficulties, secondary analysis offers rich opportunities, especially because qualitative researchers can by themselves rarely examine all of the facets of their large data sets meaning that much of the material remains underexplored.

K   KEY POINTS

- Documents constitute a heterogeneous source of data, including personal documents, official documents from state or private sources, and output from mass media.

- Such materials can be the focus of both quantitative and qualitative enquiry but the emphasis in this chapter has been upon the latter.

- Documents may be in printed, visual, digital, or indeed any other retrievable format.

- For many researchers, just about anything can be 'read' as a text.

- Criteria for evaluating the quality of documents include: authenticity; credibility; representativeness; and meaning. Their relevance varies somewhat according to the kind of document being assessed.

- Secondary analysis of existing data offers the prospect of being able to explore research questions without having to collect new data.

- Very often, secondary analysis offers the opportunity of being able to employ high-quality data sets from large, reasonably representative samples.

- Secondary analysis presents few disadvantages.

- The analysis of official statistics may be thought of as a special, more controversial form of secondary analysis because of unease about the reliability and validity of certain types of official data, especially those relating to crime and deviance.

- The problems associated with official data relating to crime and deviance should not be generalized to all official statistics. Many forms of official statistics are less prone to the kinds of errors detectable in crime and deviance data, but there still remain possible divergences of definition between compilers of such data and social researchers.

- Official statistics represent a form of unobtrusive method and enjoy certain advantages (especially lack of reactivity) because of that.

- Secondary analysis of qualitative data is more common now.

Q QUESTIONS FOR REVIEW

- What is meant by a document?
- What might Scott consider as a fifth criterion for assessing documents?

Personal documents

- List the different kinds of personal documents and rank how each fares in terms of Scott's four criteria.
- What is the role of personal documents in a life history method?
- What uses can family photographs have in social research?

Official government documents

- What does the study by Abraham suggest about the potential for social researchers of official state documents?
- How do such documents fare in terms of Scott's criteria?

Official documents deriving from private sources

- What kinds of documents may be considered private official documents?
- How do such documents fare in terms of Scott's criteria?

Mass media outputs

- What kinds of documents are mass media outputs?
- How do such documents fare in terms of Scott's criteria?

Virtual outputs

- Can anything be treated as a text?
- Do Internet documents and other virtual outputs raise special problems in satisfying Scott's criteria?

Other researchers' data

- What is secondary analysis?

- Outline the main advantages and limitations of secondary analysis.

- Examine recent issues of a Canadian sociology journal such as *Canadian Journal of Sociology*. Locate an article that uses secondary analysis. How well do the advantages and limitations just outlined fit with this article?

Official statistics

- What reliability and validity issues do official statistics pose?

- What other unobtrusive methods or measures can be used in secondary analysis?

Secondary analysis of qualitative data

- How feasible is it for researchers to analyze qualitative data collected by another researcher?

Part Three

Part Three of this book is concerned with qualitative research. Chapter 8 explores the main features of this research strategy. Chapter 9 deals with ethnography and participant observation, which are among the main ways of collecting qualitative data. Chapter 10 is concerned with the kind of interviewing carried out in qualitative research and the focus group method, an increasingly popular technique that allows people to be interviewed in groups. These chapters will provide essential tools for doing qualitative research. They range from general issues to do with the generic features of qualitative research to practical issues of conducting observational studies or interviews.

8 The nature of qualitative research

CHAPTER OVERVIEW

Qualitative research usually emphasizes words rather than quantification in its data analysis. As a research strategy it is inductivist, constructionist, and interpretivist; but qualitative researchers do not always subscribe to all three of these features. This chapter is concerned with outlining the main features of qualitative research, an increasingly popular approach to social research. The chapter explores:

- the main steps in qualitative research; delineating the sequence of stages in qualitative research is more controversial than with quantitative research, because it exhibits less standardization;

- the relationship between theory and research;

- the nature of concepts in qualitative research and how they are different from those in quantitative research;

- whether reliability and validity are appropriate criteria for qualitative researchers, and if alternative criteria, more tailored to qualitative research, are necessary;

- five main preoccupations of qualitative researchers: seeing through the eyes of research participants; description and context; process; flexibility and lack of structure; and concepts and theory as outcomes of the research process;

- some common criticisms of qualitative research;

- the main contrasts between qualitative and quantitative research; and

- the stance of feminist researchers on qualitative research.

Introduction

In Chapter 1 it was suggested that qualitative research is a distinctive research strategy and differs from quantitative research in several ways. Most obviously, qualitative research tends to be concerned with words rather than numbers, but three further features are particularly noteworthy:

- an inductive view of the relationship between theory and research, with the former generated out of the latter;

- an epistemological position described as interpretivist, meaning that, in contrast to the adoption of a natural scientific model in quantitative research, the stress is on understanding the social world by examining the participants' interpretations of their world; and

- an ontological position described as constructionist, which implies that social life is an outcome of the interactions between individuals, rather than a phenomenon 'out there' and separate from those involved in its construction.

As Bryman and Burgess (1999) observed, although there has been a proliferation of writings on qualitative research since the 1970s, stipulating what it is and is not as a distinct research strategy, is by no means straightforward, for at least three reasons:

- As a term, 'qualitative research' is sometimes taken to imply an approach to social research in which no quantitative data are collected or generated. Many writers on qualitative research are critical of this view, because (as will be seen) what distinguishes qualitative research is much more than an absence of numbers.

- Writers like Gubrium and Holstein (1997) have suggested that several different traditions in qualitative research can be identified (see Box 8.1).

- Too often qualitative research is described by how it differs from quantitative research. A potential problem with this tactic is that qualitative research ends up addressed not in terms of what it is but in terms of what quantitative research is not.

Silverman (1993) has been particularly critical of accounts of qualitative research that do not acknowledge the variety of forms that the research strategy can assume. In much the same way that in Chapter 3 it was recognized that quantitative researchers employ different research designs, the discussion of the characteristics of qualitative research must be sensitive to the different orientations of qualitative researchers. Indeed, qualitative research subsumes several diverse research methods that differ from each other considerably. The following are the main research methods associated with qualitative research:

- *Ethnography/participant observation.* While some caution is advisable in treating ethnography and participant observation as synonyms, in many respects they refer to similar, if not identical, approaches to data collection. In both a researcher is immersed in a social setting for some time observing and listening to behaviour with a view to gaining an appreciation of the culture of a social group. It has been employed in such social research classics as Whyte's (1955) study of street corner life in a slum community and Gans's (1962) research on residents in the throes of urban redevelopment.

- *Qualitative interviewing.* This is a very broad term to describe a wide range of interviewing styles (see Box 4.3 for an introduction). Moreover, qualitative researchers employing ethnography or participant observation typically also engage in a substantial amount of qualitative interviewing.

- Focus groups (see Box 4.3).

- Language-based approaches such as discourse and conversation analysis (see Chapter 16).

- The collection and qualitative analysis of texts and documents.

Each of these approaches to data collection will be examined in Part Three. The picture of the very different methods and sources that comprise qualitative research is then made even more complex by the fact that a multi-method approach is frequently employed. As noted above, researchers employing ethnography or participant observation frequently conduct qualitative interviews. Often they analyze texts and documents as well. Thus, there is considerable variability in the collection of data in studies deemed to be qualitative. Of course, quantitative research also subsumes several different methods of data collection (covered in Part Two), but the inclusion here of methods concerned with the analysis of language as a form of qualitative research implies somewhat greater variability.

Box 8.1 Four aspects of qualitative research

Gubrium and Holstein (1997) suggested four traditions of qualitative research:

- *Naturalism*—seeks to understand social reality in its own terms; provides rich descriptions of people and interaction in natural settings.

- *Ethnomethodology*—seeks to understand how social order is created through talk and interaction; has a naturalistic orientation.

- *Emotionalism*—exhibits a concern with subjectivity and gaining access to the 'inside' experiences of humans.

- *Postmodernism*—sensitive to the different ways social reality is constructed.

The term 'naturalism' here is more or less the same as the second meaning in Box 2.3. Ethnomethodology will be encountered in Chapter 16 in a qualitative approach known as *conversation analysis*. The more recent postmodern standpoint will be addressed in Chapter 17. The third tradition—emotionalism—has not led to much research and is not emphasized in this book. However, the mere presence of four contrasting traditions points to the difficulty of creating a definitive account of the nature of qualitative research.

The main steps in qualitative research

The sequence outlined in Figure 8.1 provides a representation of the qualitative research process. To illustrate the steps, a published study by Foster (1995) of crime, previously encountered in Box 1.12, is used.

- *Step 1. General research question(s).* It is frequently assumed that communities with public housing and high levels of crime tend to have low levels of social control. But Foster (1995) argued that little is known about how informal social control operates in such communities and its significance for crime. Thus, Foster formulated a general set of concerns revolving around public housing and its crime-proneness and the possible role and dynamics of social control in the process. She also noted that some writers suggest that the propensity to crime is also attributable to flaws in the design of public housing, not just to tenants.

- *Step 2. Selecting relevant site(s) and subjects.* The research was conducted in one community (with the

1. General research questions

2. Selecting relevant site(s) and subjects

3. Collection of relevant data

5b. Collection of further data

4. Interpretation of data

5. Conceptual and theoretical work

5a. Tighter specification of the research question(s)

6. Write up findings/conclusions

Figure 8.1 An outline of the main steps of qualitative research

fictitious name 'Riverside'), that had a high level of crime and housing features frequently associated with a propensity to crime. Relevant research participants, such as residents, were identified.

- *Step 3. Collection of relevant data.* Foster described her research as 'ethnographic.' She spent 18 months 'getting involved in as many aspects of life there as possible from attending tenant meetings, the mothers and toddlers' group, and activities for young people, to socializing with some of the residents in the local pub' (1995: 566). Foster also reported 'extended interviews' with 45 residents of Riverside (and a few more from a contiguous area) and 25 'officials,' such as police and housing officers. Foster's account of her research methods suggests two types of data: fieldwork notes based on her ethnographic observation of life in the community and detailed notes (and most probably transcripts) of her interviews.

- *Step 4. Interpretation of data.* One of the key findings to emerge from the data is that, in spite of its high crime rate, crime is not perceived as a problem by Riverside residents. For example, she quoted from an interview with an elderly tenant: 'They used to say that they couldn't let the [apartments] here . . . but I mean as far as muggings or anything like that you don't hear of nothing like that even now' (Foster 1995: 568). Instead, housing problems loom larger in the minds of residents than crime. She also found 'hidden economy' crimes (cash transactions, hiding income from welfare inspectors) prevalent and that much crime is tolerated by residents. Finally, she observed that, contrary to expectations about places like Riverside, there is clear evidence of informal social control mechanisms at work, such as shaming practices.

- *Step 5. Conceptual and theoretical work.* No new concepts emerged from Foster's research, but her findings enabled her to tie together some of the elements outlined under step 1. For example, she wrote:

> Crime then need not be damaging *per se* providing other factors cushion its impact. On Riverside these

included support networks in which tenants felt that someone was watching out for their properties and provided links with people to whom they could turn if they were in trouble. Consequently while generalized fears about crime remained prevalent, familiarity and support went some way to reducing the potential for hostile encounters (1995: 580).

It is this step, coupled with the interpretation of data, which formed the study's findings.

- *Steps 5a. Tighter specification of the research question(s)*, and *5b. Collection of further data.* There is no specific evidence in Foster's account that she collected further data after making early interpretations of her data. When this occurs, as it sometimes does in research within a grounded theory framework, there can be an interplay between interpretation and theorizing, on the one hand, and data collection, on the other. Such a strategy is frequently referred to as *iterative*. She did write at one point that some residents and officials were interviewed twice and in some cases even three times in the course of her research. This raises the possibility that she was re-interviewing certain individuals in light of her emerging ideas, but this can only be a speculation.

- *Step 6. Writing up findings/conclusions.* There is no real difference between the significance of writing up quantitative research and qualitative research. An audience has to be convinced about the credibility and significance of the interpretations offered. Researchers are not and cannot simply be conduits for the things they see and the words they hear. Foster did this by making clear to her audience that her findings have implications for policies regarding public housing and crime and for understanding links among housing, community, and crime. A key point to emerge from her work, which she emphasized at several points in the article and hammered home in her concluding section, is that being an insider to Riverside allowed her to see that a community regarded by outsiders as having a high propensity towards crime should not be presumed to be seen in the same way by members of that community.

Two particularly distinctive aspects of the sequence of steps in qualitative research are the highly related issues of links between theory and concepts with research data. It is to these issues that the discussion now turns.

Theory and concepts in qualitative research

Most qualitative researchers when writing about their craft emphasize a preference for treating theory as something that emerges out of the collection and analysis of data. As will be seen in Chapter 13, practitioners of grounded theory—a frequent approach to the analysis of qualitative data—stress the importance of allowing theoretical ideas to emerge out of data. But some qualitative researchers argue that qualitative data can and should have an important role in the *testing* of theories as well. Silverman (1993), in particular, argued that qualitative researchers have become increasingly interested in testing theories, a reflection of the growing maturity of the strategy. Certainly, there is no reason why qualitative research cannot be employed to test theories specified in advance of data collection. In any case, much qualitative research entails the testing of theo-

ries in the course of the research process. So, in Figure 8.1, the loop back from step 5*a* 'tighter specification of the research question(s)' to step 5*b* 'collection of further data' implies that a theoretical position may emerge in the course of research that spurs the collection of further data to test it. This oscillation between testing emerging theories and collecting data is a particularly prominent feature of grounded theory. It is presented as a dashed line in Figure 8.1, because it is a more optional feature of the process of qualitative research than other steps. The generation of theory still tends to be the preferred approach.

A central feature of Chapter 3 was the discussion of concepts and their measurement. For most qualitative researchers, developing measures of concepts is not a significant consideration, but concepts are still very much part of the landscape in qualitative research. However, the way in which concepts are developed and employed is often rather different from that implied in the quantitative research strategy. Blumer's (1954) distinction between 'definitive' and 'sensitizing' concepts captures part of that difference.

Blumer (1954) argued stridently against a concept coming to be seen exclusively in terms of the indicators developed for it. Fine nuances in the form a concept can assume and alternative ways of viewing its manifestations are thus sidelined. Instead, Blumer recommended that social researchers view their concepts as sensitizing, providing 'a general sense of reference and guidance in approaching empirical instances' (1954: 7). For Blumer, then, concepts should give a very general sense of what to look for, and act as a means for uncovering the *variety* of forms the phenomena to which they refer can assume. In other words, his views entailed largely a critique of quantitative research and a programmatic statement that would form a springboard for an alternative approach that today would be recognized as qualitative research.

Blumer's distinction is not without its problems, however. It is not at all clear how far a very general formulation of a concept can serve as a useful guide to empirical inquiry. If it is too general, it will simply fail to provide a useful starting point because its guidelines are too broad; if too narrow, it is likely to repeat some of the difficulties Blumer identified in relation to definitive concepts. However, his general view of concepts attracted some support, because his preference for not imposing preordained schemes on the social world chimes with that of many qualitative researchers. Thus, a researcher frequently starts with a broad outline of a concept, which is then revised and narrowed during the course of data collection. For subsequent researchers, the concept may be taken up and revised again as it is employed in different social contexts or in relation to somewhat different research questions.

Reliability and validity in qualitative research

In Chapters 2 and 3 it was noted that reliability and validity are important criteria for establishing and assessing the quality of quantitative research. However, there has also been some discussion among qualitative researchers concerning their relevance for qualitative research (see Box 8.2). But even among writers who view the criteria as relevant, there is a sense for some that the meanings of the terms need to be altered. For example, since measurement is not a major preoccupation among qualitative researchers, the traditional issue of validity would seem to have little bearing on such studies. As foreshadowed briefly in Chapter 2, different stances have been taken by qualitative researchers on these issues.

Adapting reliability and validity for qualitative research

One stance is to assimilate reliability and validity into qualitative research with little change of meaning, other than playing down the salience of measurement issues. Mason, for example, in her book on qualitative research, stayed very close to the meanings that criteria like reliability, validity, and generalizability (external validity) have in quantitative research, where they were largely developed. Thus to her, validity refers to whether 'you are observing, identifying, or "measuring" what you say you are' (1996: 24).

Others also wrote about reliability and validity in relation to qualitative research but invested the terms with a somewhat different meaning from Mason. LeCompte and Goetz (1982) wrote about the following:

- *External reliability*, by which they meant the degree to which a study can be replicated. This is a difficult criterion to meet in qualitative research, since, as LeCompte and Goetz recognized, it is impossible to 'freeze' the social setting and circumstances of an initial study to make it replicable in the sense in which the term is usually employed (see Chapter 3). However, they pointed to several strategies that

---

Box 8.2 The emergence of a concept in qualitative research: the case of emotional labour

Hochschild's (1983) idea of emotional labour—labour that 'requires one to induce or suppress feelings in order to sustain the outward countenance that produces the proper state of mind in others' (1983: 7)—has become a very influential concept in the sociology of work and in the developing area of the sociology of emotions. (For a quick lay interpretation of this, it looked at how workers manage to keep smiling at some of their truly obnoxious customers.) Somewhat ironically for a predominantly qualitative study, Hochschild's initial conceptualization emerged from an earlier questionnaire she developed on a related topic. To develop the idea of emotional labour, Hochschild looked to the world of work and mainly at flight attendants. She gained access to Delta Airlines, a large American airline, and in the course of her investigations:

- watched sessions for training attendants and had many conversations with both trainees and experienced attendants during them;
- interviewed various personnel, such as managers in various sections and advertising agents;

- examined Delta advertisements spanning 30 years;
- observed the flight attendant recruitment process at Pan American Airways, since she had not been allowed to do this at Delta; and
- conducted 'open-ended interviews lasting three to five hours each with thirty flight attendants in the San Francisco Bay Area' (1983: 15).

For a contrasting occupational group also involved in emotional labour, she interviewed five debt collectors. In her book, she explored such topics as the human costs of emotional labour and the issue of gender in relation to it. It is clear that Hochschild's concept of emotional labour began with a somewhat imprecise idea that emerged out of a specific concern and was gradually developed to address its wider significance. The concept has been picked up by other qualitative researchers in the sociology of work. For example, Leidner (1993) used ethnography to study a McDonald's restaurant and an insurance company about how organizations seek to 'routinize' the display of emotional labour.

---

can be introduced to approach the requirements of external reliability. For example, they suggested that a qualitative researcher replicating ethnographic research needs to adopt a similar social role to that adopted by the original researcher in order to increase chances of seeing and hearing the same things as in the original research.

- *Internal reliability*, by which they meant whether, when there is more than one observer, members of the research team agree about what they see and hear. This is a similar notion to *inter-observer consistency* (see Box 3.7).
- *Internal validity*, by which they meant whether there is a good match between researchers' observations and the theoretical ideas they develop. LeCompte and Goetz argued that internal validity tends to be a strength of qualitative research, particularly ethnographic research, because the prolonged participation in the social life of a group over a long period of time allows the researcher to ensure a high level of congruence between concepts and observations.

- *External validity*, which refers to the degree to which findings can be generalized across social settings. LeCompte and Goetz argued that unlike internal validity, external validity represents a problem for qualitative researchers because of their tendency to employ case studies and small samples.

As this brief treatment suggests, some qualitative researchers have employed the terms 'reliability and validity' in very similar ways to quantitative researchers when developing criteria for assessing research.

Alternative criteria for evaluating qualitative research

However, a second position in relation to reliability and validity in qualitative research can be discerned. Some writers suggest that qualitative studies should be judged or evaluated according to quite different criteria from those of quantitative researchers. Lincoln and Guba (1985) and Guba and Lincoln

(1994) proposed that it is necessary to assess the quality of qualitative research in new ways and with new terms for reliability and validity. They proposed two primary criteria for assessing a qualitative study: *trustworthiness* and *authenticity*.

Trustworthiness is made up of four criteria, each of which has an equivalent criterion in quantitative research:

- *credibility*, which parallels internal validity;
- *transferability*, which parallels external validity;
- *dependability*, which parallels reliability; and
- *confirmability*, which parallels objectivity.

A major reason for Guba and Lincoln's unease about the simple application of quantifiable reliability and validity standards to qualitative research is that such criteria presuppose that a single absolute account of social reality is feasible. In other words, they were critical of the view (described in Chapter 1 as *realist*) that there are absolute truths about the social world that it is the job of the social scientist to reveal. Instead, they argued that there are many possible accounts.

Credibility

The significance of this stress on multiple accounts of social reality is especially evident in the trustworthiness criterion of *credibility*. After all, if there can be several possible accounts of an aspect of social reality, it is the feasibility or credibility of the researcher's account that determines its acceptability to others. The establishment of credibility entails both ensuring that research is carried out according to the canons of good scientific practice *and* submitting research findings to the members of the social world studied for confirmation that the investigator correctly understood their social world. This latter technique is often referred to as *respondent validation* or *member validation* (see Box 8.3). Another technique they recommend is *triangulation,* a topic saved until Chapter 15.

Transferability

Because qualitative research typically entails an in-depth, intensive study of a small group, or of individuals sharing certain characteristics, qualitative findings tend to be oriented to the contextual uniqueness and significance of the aspect of the social world being studied. As Guba and Lincoln put it, whether findings 'hold in some other context, or even in the same context at some other time, is an empirical issue' (Lincoln and Guba 1985: 316). Instead, qualitative researchers are encouraged to produce what Geertz (1973) called *thick description*—that is, rich accounts of the details of a culture. Guba and Lincoln argued that a thick description provides others with what they refer to as a database for making judgments about the possible transferability of findings to other milieus.

Dependability

As a parallel to reliability in quantitative research, Guba and Lincoln proposed the idea of dependability and argued that to establish it researchers should adopt an 'auditing' approach. This entails ensuring that complete records are kept of all phases of the research process—problem formulation, selection of research participants, fieldwork notes, interview transcripts, data analysis decisions, and so on—in an accessible manner. Peers would then act as auditors, possibly during the course of the research, and certainly at the end, to establish whether proper procedures had been followed and to assess the degree to which theoretical inferences can be justified. Auditing has not, however, become a popular approach to enhancing the dependability of qualitative research. A rare example is a study of behaviour at an American 'swap meet,' where second-hand goods are bought and sold (Belk *et al.* 1988). A team of three researchers collected data over four days through observation, interviews, photography, and video-records. The researchers conducted several trustworthiness tests, such as respondent validation and triangulation. But, in addition, they submitted their draft manuscript and entire data set to three peers, whose task 'was to criticize the project for lack of sufficient data for drawing its conclusions, if they saw such a void' (1988: 456). The study also highlights problems associated with auditing. One is that it is very demanding for the auditors, bearing in mind that qualitative research frequently generates extremely large data sets, and this may be the major reason auditing has not become a widespread approach to validation.

Box 8.3 ⟨💡⟩ *What is respondent validation?*

Respondent validation, sometimes called *member valida-tion*, is a process whereby a researcher provides the peo-ple on whom the research was conducted with the findings. The aim is to seek corroboration or criticisms of the researcher's account. Respondent validation has been particularly popular among qualitative researchers who generally want to ensure a good correspondence be-tween their findings and the perspectives and experiences of their research participants. They are, after all, describ-ing *their* reality. There are several different forms of re-spondent validation:

- The researcher provides each research participant with an account of what he or she said to the re-searcher in an interview or conversations and of what the researcher observed by watching that person in the course of a study. For example, Bloor (1997) reported that after he carried out observations of ear, nose, and throat (ENT) consultants concerning their assessment of patients, he submitted a report to each consultant on his or her practices and asked for feedback.

- The researcher provides impressions and findings to the group or organization studied. Bloor (1997) said that for his research on therapeutic communities, he conducted (taped) group discussions with community members to gauge reactions to draft research reports.

- The researcher shows pre-publication versions of arti-cles, books, etc. to those who were the subject of the

investigation. Skeggs (1994), for example, asked young working-class women, the focus of her ethnog-raphy, to comment on draft chapters (see Box 9.10 for further details).

In each case, the goal is to seek confirmation that the researcher's findings and impressions are congruent with those on whom the research was conducted and to seek out areas in which there is a lack of correspondence and the reasons for it. However, the idea is not without its practical difficulties:

- Respondent validation may lead to defensive reactions from some research participants and even demands for censorship.

- Bloor (1997: 45) observed that because some research participants develop relationships with the researcher of 'fondness and mutual regard,' there may be a reluctance to be critical.

- It is highly questionable whether research participants can validate *all* of a researcher's analysis, since it will include inferences made for an audience of social sci-ence peers, including concepts and theories and an appropriate social science frame for the resulting pub-lications. Hobbs (1993), for example, fed some of his scholarly publications to his informants and they made little sense of what he had written. Similarly, Skeggs (1994: 86) reported: *'Can't understand a bloody word it says* was the most common response' (see Box 9.10 for further details of this study).

Confirmability

Confirmability is concerned with ensuring that, while recognizing that objectivity is improbable in social research, the researcher can be shown to have acted in good faith. In other words, it should be ap-parent that personal values or theoretical inclina-tions were not overtly allowed to sway the conduct of the research and findings deriving from it. Guba and Lincoln proposed that establishing confirmabil-ity should be one of the objectives of auditors. However, the main point of discussing Guba and Lincoln's ideas is that they differ from writers like LeCompte and Goetz in their criteria for evaluating qualitative research.

In between quantitative and qualitative research criteria

Hammersley (1992*a*) lies midway between the two positions. He proposed that validity is an important criterion but reformulated it somewhat. For him, va-lidity means that an empirical account must be plau-sible and credible and take into account the amount and kind of evidence used in its developing. In pro-posing this criterion, Hammersley shared with real-ism (see Box 1.9) the notion of an external social reality accessible to the researcher. However, he si-multaneously rejected the empirical realist position that such access is direct and in particular that a researcher can reflect an image of the social world to an audience. Instead, he argued, the researcher is always engaged in representations or constructions of that world. The plausibility and credibility to other scientists of a researcher's 'truth claims' then become the main considerations in evaluating qualitative research. Hammersley's *subtle realist* account, as he called it, entails recognizing that one can never be absolutely certain about the truth of any account, since there exists no completely incontrovertible way of gaining direct access to the reality on which it is based. Therefore, he argued 'we must judge the validity of claims [about truth] on the basis of the adequacy of the evidence offered in support of them.' This means that an account can be held to be 'valid or true if it represents accurately those features of the phenomena that it is intended to describe, explain, or theorize' (1992a: 69).

Hammersley also suggested *relevance* as an important criterion of qualitative research. Relevance is assessed with respect to the importance of a topic in the literature on that field. Hammersley also discussed whether the concerns of practitioners (that is, people who are part of the social setting being investigated and who are likely to have a vested interest in the research question and the implications of its findings) might be an aspect of relevance. However, he recognized that the kinds of research questions and findings that may be of interest to practitioners and researchers are likely to be somewhat different. As Hammersley noted, practitioners are likely to be interested in research that helps them to understand or address the problems that confront them. These may not be (and perhaps are unlikely to be) at the forefront of a researcher's set of preoccupations. However, there are occasions when the two overlap and researchers can use this capability in efforts to secure access to organizations in which they wish to conduct research.

Overview of the issue of criteria

There is a recognition—albeit to varying degrees—that a simple application of the quantitative researcher's criteria of reliability and validity to qualitative research is not desirable, but writers vary in the degree to which they propose a complete over-haul of those criteria. Nor do the three positions outlined above—adapting quantitative research criteria, alternative criteria, and Hammersley's subtle realism—represent the full range of possible stances (Seale 1999). To a large extent, the differences among the three positions reflect divergence in the broad acceptance of a realist position. Writers on qualitative research who apply the ideas of reliability and validity with little if any adaptation broadly position themselves as realists—that is, as saying that social reality can be captured by qualitative researchers through their concepts and theories. Lincoln and Guba rejected this view, arguing instead that qualitative researchers' concepts and theories are representations and that there may be, therefore, other equally credible representations of the same phenomena. Hammersley's position occupies a middle ground in terms of the axis, with realism at one end and anti-realism at the other, in that, while acknowledging the existence of social phenomena as part of an external reality, he disavowed any possibility of reproducing that reality for the audiences of social scientific endeavour. Most qualitative researchers today probably operate around the midpoint on this realism axis, though without necessarily endorsing Hammersley's views. Typically, they treat their accounts as one of a number of possible representations rather than as definitive versions of social reality. They also bolster those accounts through some of the strategies advocated by Lincoln and Guba, such as thick descriptions, respondent validation exercises, and triangulation.

To some extent, traditional quantitative research criteria have made something of a comeback since the late 1990s. One reason is because to reject notions like reliability and validity can be taken by some constituencies (such as funding bodies) as indicating a lack of concern with rigour, not a desirable impression to create. Consequently, there has been some increased concern with such issues. Armstrong *et al.* (1997) reported the result of an exercise in what they called 'inter-rater reliability,' which involved the analysis of a transcript, by six experienced researchers, of a focus group made up of sufferers of cystic fibrosis (CF) examining links between perceptions of disability and genetic screening. The raters were asked to extract prominent

Box 8.4 Reliability for qualitative researchers

Gladney *et al.* (2003) reported an exercise in which two multi-disciplinary teams of researchers were asked to analyze qualitative interviews conducted with 80 Texas school students on three topics: violence on television, reasons for violence among some young people, and reasons for some young people *not* being violent. One group of raters read interview transcripts of the interviews; the other group listened to the audiotaped recordings. Thus, the dice were slightly loaded in favour of different themes being identified by the two groups. In spite of this there was remarkable consistency between the two groups in themes identified. For example, in response to the question 'Why are some young people violent?', Group One identified the following themes: family/parental influence; peer influence; social influence; media influence; and coping. Group Two's themes were: the way they were raised; media influence; appearance; anger, revenge, protection; and peer influence. Such findings are quite reassuring and are interesting because of the clear interest in reliability expressed in a qualitative research context.

themes from the transcript, one of the main ways of analyzing qualitative data (see Chapter 13). The six tended to identify similar themes but differed in how themes were 'packaged.' For example, one theme identified by all six was 'visibility': CF sufferers feel disadvantaged relative to other disabled groups because the public are more sympathetic to and more inclined to recognize more visible disabilities. However, two analysts linked it with stigma and one to managing invisibility. In a sense the results are somewhat inconclusive but interesting for this discussion because they reveal a concern among qualitative researchers in reliability. A more recent and similar exercise is described in Box 8.4.

The main preoccupations of qualitative researchers

As noted in Chapter 3, quantitative and qualitative research can be viewed as exhibiting a set of distinctive but contrasting preoccupations. These preoccupations reflect epistemologically grounded beliefs about what constitutes acceptable knowledge. In Chapter 1, it was suggested that whereas quantitative research is profoundly influenced by a natural science approach of what should count as acceptable knowledge, qualitative researchers are more influenced by *interpretivism* (see Box 1.10). This position can itself be viewed as the product of the confluence of three related stances: Weber's notion of *Verstehen*; symbolic interactionism; and phenomenology. In this section, five distinctive preoccupations among qualitative researchers are examined.

Seeing through the eyes of the people being studied

An underlying premise of many qualitative researchers is that the subject matter of the social sciences (people and their social world) differs from the subject matter of the natural sciences. A key difference is that the objects of analysis of the natural sciences (atoms, molecules, gases, chemicals, metals, and so on) cannot attribute meaning to events or their environment. However, people *do*. Consequently, many qualitative researchers see a need for research methods that reflect this fundamental difference. As a result, many qualitative researchers express a commitment to viewing events and the social world through the eyes of the people that they study, rather than as though those subjects were incapable of their own reflections on the social world. Hiller and DiLuzio (2004) took this so far as to analyze the interview experience itself from the perspective of the interviewees. Studying internal migrants in Canada, they sought to find what interviewees get out of the process and found, for example, that they like meeting someone who values them and validates their life experiences.

The epistemology underlying qualitative research has been expressed as involving two central tenets:

'(1) . . . face-to-face interaction is the fullest condition of participating in the mind of another human being, and (2) . . . you must participate in the mind of another human being (in sociological terms, "take the role of the other") to acquire social knowledge' (Lofland and Lofland 1995: 16). This tendency reveals itself in frequent references to *empathy* and seeing through others' eyes. Here are some examples:

- Armstrong carried out research on British soccer hooliganism through participant observation. He described his work as located in '*Verstehende* sociology—trying to think oneself into the situations of the people one is interested in . . . in this case the "hooligan." This approach involves recognizing social phenomena as due not to any single or simply identifiable cause and attempting to make sense from the [multi-causal] social actors' viewpoint' (Armstrong 1993: 5–6).

- For their research on teenaged girls' views on and experiences of violence, Burman *et al.* (2001: 447) 'sought to ground the study in young women's experiences of violence, hearing their accounts, and privileging their subjective views.'

This predilection in qualitative research for seeing through the eyes of the people studied is often accompanied by the closely related goal of probing beneath surface appearances. After all, by taking the position of those under study, the prospect is raised that they may view things differently from what an outsider with little direct contact would expect. This stance reveals itself in:

- Foster's (1995) research on a high-crime community thought safe by its inhabitants;

- Taylor's (1993: 8) study of intravenous female drug users, showing the people she studied are not 'pathetic, inadequate individuals' but 'rational, active people making decisions based on the contingencies of both their drug-using careers and their roles and status in society';

- Armstrong's (1993: 11) finding that, contrary to the popular view, hooligans are not a highly organized group led by a clearly identifiable group of ringleaders; and

- Atkinson's (2004) ethnography of tattooing, which rejected a widely held view that it represents

pathological self-injury and instead saw it as a pro-social and regulated act of communication.

The empathetic stance of seeking to see through the eyes of one's research participants is very much in tune with interpretivism and demonstrates well the epistemological links with phenomenology, symbolic interactionism, and *Verstehen*. However, it is not without practical problems; for example: the risk of 'going native' and losing sight of what is being studied (see Box 9.6); the problem of how far the researcher should go, such as whether to participate in illegal or dangerous activities, a risk in research like that engaged in by Taylor and Armstrong; and the possibility that the researcher will be able to see through the eyes of only some of the people in a social scene but not others, such as people of the other gender. These and other practical difficulties will be addressed in the chapters that follow.

Description and the emphasis on context

Qualitative researchers are much more inclined than quantitative to provide a lot of descriptive detail when reporting their research. This is not to say that they are exclusively concerned with description. They *are* concerned with explanation, and indeed the extent to which qualitative researchers ask the question 'why?' is frequently understated. For example, Skeggs (1997) wrote that her first question for young working-class women was 'why do women, who are clearly not just victims of some ideological conspiracy, consent to a system of class and gender oppression which appears to offer few rewards and little benefit?' (1997: 22; see Box 9.10 for further details of this study).

Many qualitative studies provide a detailed account of what goes on in the setting being investigated. On the surface, some of this detail may appear irrelevant, and, indeed, there is a risk of becoming too embroiled in descriptive detail. Lofland and Lofland (1995: 164–5), for example, warned against the sin of what they call 'descriptive excess' in qualitative research, whereby the amount of detail overwhelms or inhibits the analysis of data.

One of the main reasons why qualitative researchers are keen to provide considerable descriptive detail is their typical emphasis on a contextual understanding of social behaviour. This recommendation means that one cannot understand the behaviour of members of a social group other than in terms of the specific environment in which they operate. In this way, behaviour that may appear odd or irrational can make perfect sense when understood in the particular context within which that behaviour takes place. The emphasis on context in qualitative research goes back to many of the classic studies in social anthropology, which often demonstrated how a particular practice, such as the magical ritual that accompanies the sowing of seeds, makes little sense unless understood as part of the belief systems of that society. One of the chief reasons for an emphasis on descriptive detail is that it is often precisely this detail that provides the mapping of context in terms of which behaviour is understood. The propensity for description can also be interpreted as a manifestation of the naturalism that pervades much qualitative research (see Boxes 2.4 and 8.1), because it places a premium on detailed, rich descriptions of social settings.

Emphasis on process

Qualitative research tends to view social life in terms of processes. This tendency reveals itself in a number of different ways but the main one is in the concern to show how events and patterns unfold over time. As a result, qualitative evidence often conveys a strong sense of change and flux. As Pettigrew (1997: 338) usefully put it, process is 'a sequence of individual and collective events, actions, and activities unfolding over time in context.' Qualitative research using participant observation is particularly associated with this emphasis on showing process. Ethnographers are typically immersed in a social setting for a long time—frequently years. Consequently, they are able to observe how events develop over time or how the different elements of a social system (values, beliefs, behaviour, and so on) interconnect. Such findings can inject a sense of process by seeing social life in terms of streams of interdependent events and elements (see Box 8.5).

This is not to say, however, that ethnographers are the only qualitative researchers who inject a sense of

---

Box 8.5 Process in youth shelters

Karabanow (2002) described his experiences in street shelters for homeless and runaway youth. As a participant observer, he could observe routine activities there and describe the shelter culture. In addition to observation, he carried out in-depth interviews with three levels of shelter workers as well as using agency archival materials. As a result, he was able to highlight dramatic transformations, both in their external environment and internal operations over the years, leading to an understanding of organizational evolutionary processes. This example shows the development of a sense of process in at least two ways, first through observation of the shelter over time, so that developments and interconnections between events could be brought out. Second, by connecting these events with historical and other data, links with previous events and actions could be outlined.

---

process into attempts to understand social life. It can also be achieved through semi-structured and unstructured interviewing, when participants are asked to reflect on the processes leading up to or following on from an event. McKee and Bell (1985: 388), for example, showed, through the use of a 'largely unstructured, conversational interview style' with 45 couples in which the man was unemployed, the accommodations made over time by both husbands and wives to the fact of his unemployment. The various accommodations are not an immediate effect of unemployment but are gradual and incremental responses over time. The life history approach is another form of qualitative research that can be used to show process. One of the best-known studies of this kind is Lewis's (1961) classic study of a poor Mexican family. Lewis carried out extended taped interviews with family members to reconstruct their life histories. Thus, the emphasis on process in qualitative research can be seen in several of its approaches to data collection.

Flexibility and limited structure

Many qualitative researchers are disdainful of approaches to research that impose a predetermined format on the social world. This position largely relates to the preference for seeing through the eyes of the people being studied. After all, a structured method of data collection is bound to be the product of an investigator's *prior* ruminations, expectations, and decisions about the nature of a social reality yet to be encountered. Therefore, the researchers are limiting the degree to which they can genuinely adopt the worldview of those being studied. Consequently, most qualitative researchers prefer a research orientation that entails as little prior contamination of the social world as possible and thus avoids imposing an inappropriate frame of reference on people. Keeping structure to a minimum is supposed to enhance the opportunity of genuinely revealing the perspectives of the people being studied. Also, in the process, aspects of people's social world that are particularly important to them, but that might not even have crossed the mind of a researcher unacquainted with it, are more likely to be forthcoming. As a result, qualitative research tends to be a strategy that tries not to delimit areas of enquiry too much and to ask fairly general rather than specific research questions (see Figure 8.1).

Because of the preference for an unstructured approach to collecting data, qualitative researchers adopt methods of research that do not require highly specific research questions in advance; therefore, they don't need to devise instruments specifically for those questions. Ethnography, with its emphasis on participant observation, is particularly well suited to this orientation. It allows researchers to submerge themselves in a social setting with a fairly general research focus in mind and gradually to formulate a narrower emphasis after making as many observations of that setting as possible. They can then formulate more specific research questions out of their collected data.

Similarly, interviewing is an extremely prominent method in the qualitative researcher's armoury, but it is not of the kind encountered in most of Chapter 4—namely, the structured interview. Instead, qualitative researchers prefer less-structured approaches to interviewing, as will be seen in Chapter 10. Blumer's (1954) argument for sensitizing concepts rather than definitive ones (that is, the kind employed by quantitative researchers) is symptomatic of the preference for a more open-ended, and therefore less structured, approach.

Another advantage of the unstructured nature of most qualitative inquiry is that it offers the prospect of flexibility. The researcher can change direction in the course of the investigation much more easily than in quantitative research, which tends to have a built-in momentum once the data collection is underway. If one sends out hundreds of postal questionnaires and realizes after getting some back that there is another issue to investigate, it is not easy to retrieve the situation. Structured interviewing and structured observation can involve some flexibility, but the requirement to make interviews as comparable as possible limits it. O'Reilly (2000) wrote that her research on the British on the Costa del Sol shifted in two ways over the duration of her participant observation: from an emphasis on the elderly to expatriates of all ages; and from an emphasis on permanent residents to less-permanent forms of migration, such as tourism. These changes occurred be-

---

Box 8.6 Emerging concepts

Along with some colleagues, Bryman undertook an evaluation of new staff appraisal schemes in four universities. The research entailed collecting both quantitative and qualitative data, the former derived from large numbers of interviews with appraisers, appraisees, senior managers, and many others. In the course of conducting the interviews and analyzing the subsequent data, they became increasingly aware of a cynicism in many of those interviewed. For some it is a belief that nothing happens of any significance in the aftermath of an appraisal meeting; for others it is a feeling that some participants to the appraisal process are just going through the motions. As one of the interviewees said: 'It's like going through the motions of it [appraisal]. It's just get it over with and signed and dated and filed and that's the end of it' (Bryman *et al.* 1994: 180).

On the basis of these findings it was suggested that the attitudes towards appraisal and the behaviour of those involved in it are characterized by what the researchers coined, *procedural compliance*. This they defined as 'a response to an organizational innovation in which the technical requirements of the innovation . . . are broadly adhered to, but where there are substantial reservations about its efficacy and only partial commitment to it' (1994: 178).

cause the elderly and permanent migrants were not as distinctive as she supposed. See Box 8.6 for a further illustration of how the unstructured data collection style of qualitative research can suggest alternative avenues of inquiry or ways of thinking about the phenomenon being investigated.

The critique of qualitative research

Similar to the criticisms levelled at quantitative research, mainly by qualitative researchers, a parallel critique has been built up of qualitative research. Some of the more common ones follow.

Qualitative research is too subjective

Quantitative researchers sometimes criticize qualitative research for being too impressionistic and subjective. By these criticisms they usually mean that qualitative findings rely too much on the researchers' often unsystematic views (and values) about what is significant and important, and also on the close personal relationships that many researchers strike up with the people studied. Precisely because qualitative research often begins in a relatively open-ended way and entails a gradual narrowing-down of research questions or problems, the consumer of the research reports is given few clues as to why one area was the chosen focus rather than another. By contrast, quantitative researchers point to the tendency for the problem formulation stage in their work to be more explicitly stated in terms of such matters as the existing literature on the topic and key theoretical ideas.

Difficult to replicate

Most quantitative researchers also argue that these tendencies are even more of a problem because of the difficulty of replicating a qualitative study, although replication in the social sciences is by no means a straightforward matter, regardless of this particular issue (see Chapter 3). Precisely because it is unstructured and often relies on the qualitative researcher's ingenuity, it is almost impossible to conduct a true replication, since there are hardly any standard procedures to be followed. In qualitative research, the investigator is the main instrument of data collection, so that what is observed and heard and also what the researcher decides to concentrate upon is very much a product of personal predilection. There are several possible components of this criticism: what qualitative researchers (especially perhaps in ethnography) choose to focus on while in the field is a product of what strikes them as significant, whereas other researchers might empathize with other issues; the responses of participants (people being observed or interviewed) to qualitative researchers are likely to be affected by the characteristics of the researcher (personality, age, gender, and so on); and because of the unstructured nature of qualitative data, interpretation is profoundly influ-

---

Ethical issue 8.1 *Qualitative research and ethics committees*

Van den Hoonaard (2001) suggested that it is often harder to get ethical approval for qualitative than for quantitative research. The issue in crudest terms is that qualitative research is seen as less scientific and ethics committees prefer the epistemology of quantitative research, with its derived hypotheses and specific plans. And if the ethics committee says no, the research can neither be funded nor carried out.

On more ethical grounds, qualitative research is especially faulted for difficulties in confidentiality. There is a fear that the rich detail and small number of subjects may preclude that protection. Also, unlike in quantitative research where data are usually collected one on one, here a whole group may be watched, including some who may not have wanted the attention. Thus, one ethics committee suggested that a researcher go ahead with her work but to turn her head when someone who had not previously signed a consent form entered her field of vision.

enced by the subjective leanings of a researcher. Because of such factors it is difficult—not to say impossible—to replicate qualitative findings. The difficulties that ethnographers experience when they revisit grounds previously trodden by another researcher (often referred to as a 'restudy') do not inspire confidence in the replicability of qualitative research (Bryman 1994).

Problems of generalization

It is often suggested that the scope of qualitative investigations is restricted. When participant observation is used or when unstructured interviews are conducted with a small number of individuals in one organization or locality, many argue that it is impossible to know if findings can be generalized to other settings. How can just one or two cases be representative of all cases? In other words, can one really treat Karabanow's (2002) study of two shelters for homeless youth (Box 8.5) as generalizable to all youth shelters? In the case of research based on interviews rather than participation, are those interviewed representative? Are the prostitutes, from three Western provinces (Nixon *et al.* 2002) typical of prostitutes in other areas of Canada? Do prostitutes in Ontario, Quebec, and the East start out young (by age 15); were they sexually abused as children; and do they daily suffer what they come to see as 'normal'—abuse from pimps, johns, other prostitutes, intimate partners, and the police? Probably so in this instance, but additional data could confirm that suspicion.

The answer in much qualitative research about generalization is, of course, 'no.' A case study is not a sample of one drawn from a known population. Similarly, the people interviewed in qualitative research are not meant to be representative of a population; indeed, in the case of prostitutes, one may find it more or less impossible to enumerate the population in any precise manner. Instead, the findings of qualitative research are to develop theory rather than to generalize to populations. It is the logic and persuasiveness of the theoretical reasoning and the quality of the theoretical inferences made from the qualitative data, rather than statistical criteria, that are decisive in considering the generalizability of the findings of qualitative research.

However, not all writers on this issue in qualitative research (and case study research in particular) accept this view. Williams (2000) argued that qualitative researchers are often in a position to produce generalizations on those aspects of the focus of enquiry (a group of drug users, a group of football hooligans, a strike) that 'can be seen to be instances of a broader set of recognisable features' (2000: 215). In addition, Williams argued that not only can qualitative researchers make such generalizations, in fact they often *do* make them. Thus, when generating findings relating to the hooligans who follow a certain football club, a researcher will often draw comparisons with findings by other researchers relating to comparable groups. Indeed, the researcher may also draw comparisons and linkages with followers of other professional sports teams or to violent groups not linked to sport. Such generalizations will always be limited and somewhat more tentative than those associated with statistical generalizations of the kind associated with probability sampling (see Chapter 11). On the other hand, they do help to counter the view that generalization beyond the immediate evidence and the case is impossible in qualitative research.

These three criticisms reflect many of the preoccupations of quantitative research discussed in Chapter 3. A further criticism often made of qualitative research, but perhaps less influenced by quantitative research criteria, is that qualitative research frequently lacks transparency in how the research was conducted.

Lack of transparency

It is sometimes difficult to establish from qualitative research what the researchers actually *did* and how they arrived at their conclusions. For example, qualitative research reports are sometimes unclear about such matters as how people were chosen for observation or interview. This deficiency contrasts sharply with the sometime laborious accounts of sampling procedures in reports of quantitative research. But suggesting that readers have a right to know if research participants were selected to correspond to a wide range of people does not really constitute an inappropriate application of quantitative research criteria.

Also, the process of qualitative data analysis is frequently unclear (Bryman and Burgess 1994*a*). It is often not obvious how the analysis was conducted—in other words, what the researcher was actually doing when the data were analyzed and therefore how the study's conclusions were derived. To a large extent, this lack of transparency is increasingly being addressed by qualitative researchers.

Is it always like this?

This was a heading used in Chapter 3 in relation to quantitative research, but it is perhaps less easy to answer now. To a large extent, this is because qualitative research is less codified than quantitative research; that is, it is less influenced by strict guidelines and directions about how to collect and analyze the data. As a result, and this may be noticed by readers of the chapters that follow, accounts of qualitative research are frequently less prescriptive in tone than those found in quantitative research. Instead, they often exhibit more of a descriptive tenor, outlining the different ways qualitative researchers have gone about research or suggesting alternative ways of conducting research based on the writer's own experiences or those of others. To a large extent this picture is changing, in that a growing number of books seek to make clear-cut recommendations about how qualitative research should be carried out.

However, looking at some of the preoccupations of qualitative research just described, one can see departures from the practices implied by them. One of the main departures is that qualitative research is sometimes a lot more focused than is implied by the suggestion that the researcher begin with general research questions and narrow them down so that theory and concepts are arrived at throughout the data collection. There is no *necessary* reason why qualitative research cannot be employed to investigate a specific research problem. For example, Hammersley *et al.* wanted to examine the contention, based on other studies of schools, that 'external examinations lead to lecturing and note-taking on the part of secondary-school teachers and instrumental attitudes among their pupils' (1985: 58). This contention was examined by comparing two schools that varied considerably in the emphasis they placed on examinations. A related way in which qualitative research differs from the standard model is in the notion of a lack of structure in collecting and analyzing data. As will be seen in Chapter 16, techniques such as conversation analysis entail the application of a highly codified method for analyzing talk. Moreover, the growing use of computer-assisted qualitative data analysis software (CAQDAS), the subject of Chapter 13, is leading to greater transparency in the procedures used for analyzing qualitative data which in turn may lead to more frequent codification in qualitative data analysis.

Some contrasts between quantitative and qualitative research

Several writers have contrasted quantitative and qualitative research with tables that highlight their differences (e.g., Hammersley 1992*b*). Table 8.1 attempts to draw out the chief contrasts.

- *Numbers vs. Words.* Quantitative researchers are often portrayed as preoccupied with applying measurement procedures to social life, while qualitative researchers are seen as using words in their analyses of society.

- *Point of view of researcher vs. Points of view of participants.* In quantitative research, investigators are in the driving seat; their concerns structure the

Table 8.1 Common contrasts between quantitative and qualitative research

Numbers	Words
Point of view of researcher	Points of view of participants
Researcher distant	Researcher close
Theory testing	Theory emergent
Static	Process
Structured	Unstructured
Generalization	Contextual understanding
Hard, reliable data	Rich, deep data
Macro	Micro
Behaviour	Meaning
Artificial settings	Natural settings

investigation. In qualitative research, the perspective of those being studied—what they see as important and significant—provides the point of orientation.

- *Researcher is distant vs. Researcher is close.* In quantitative research, researchers are uninvolved with their subjects and in some cases, as in research based on mailed questionnaires or on hired interviewers, may have no contact at all. Often this lack of a relationship is regarded as desirable by quantitative researchers, because they fear compromising objectivity if too involved with the people they study. Qualitative researchers seek involvement with the people being investigated, so that they can genuinely understand the world through their eyes.

- *Theory and concepts tested in research vs. Theory and concepts emergent from data.* Quantitative researchers typically bring a set of concepts to bear on the research instruments being employed, so that theoretical work precedes the collection of data, whereas in qualitative research, concepts and theoretical elaboration emerge out of data collection.

- *Static vs. Process.* Quantitative research is frequently depicted as presenting a static image of social reality with its emphasis on relationships between variables. Change and connections between events over time tend not to surface, other

than in a mechanistic fashion. Qualitative research is often depicted as attuned to the unfolding of events over time and to the interconnections between the actions of participants of social settings.

- *Structured vs. Unstructured.* Quantitative research is typically highly structured enabling the investigator to examine the exact concepts and issues that are the focus of the study; in qualitative research the approach is invariably unstructured, so that the possibility of getting at actors' meanings and of concepts emerging out of data collection is enhanced.

- *Generalization vs. Contextual understanding.* Whereas quantitative researchers want their findings to be generalizable to the relevant population, the qualitative researcher seeks an understanding of behaviour, values, beliefs, and so on in terms of the context in which the research is conducted.

- *Hard, reliable data vs. Rich, deep data.* Quantitative data are often depicted as 'hard' in the sense of being robust and unambiguous, owing to the greater precision offered by measurement. Qualitative researchers claim, by contrast, that their contextual approach and their often-prolonged involvement in a setting engender rich data.

- *Macro vs. Micro.* Quantitative researchers are often depicted as involved in uncovering large-scale social trends and connections between variables, whereas qualitative researchers are seen as concerned with small-scale aspects of social reality, such as interaction.

- *Behaviour vs. Meaning.* It is sometimes suggested that the quantitative researcher is concerned with people's behaviour and the qualitative researcher with the meaning of that behaviour, a distinction respectively between what are called *action* and *agency*.

- *Artificial settings vs. Natural settings.* Whereas quantitative researchers conduct research in a contrived context, qualitative researchers investigate people in natural environments.

However, as will be seen in Chapters 14 and 15, while these contrasts depict reasonably well the differences between quantitative and qualitative research, they should not be viewed as constituting hard and fast distinctions.

Feminism and qualitative research

A further dimension that could have been included in the previous section is the view of some that qualitative research is associated with a feminist sensitivity, and that, by implication, quantitative research is viewed by many feminists as incompatible with feminism. This issue was briefly introduced in Chapter 1. The link between feminism and qualitative research is by no means a cut-and-dried issue, in that, although it became something of an orthodoxy among some writers, it has not found favour with all feminists. Indeed, there are signs that views on the issue are changing.

The notion of an affinity between feminism and qualitative research has at least two main components: a view that quantitative research is inherently incompatible with feminism and a view that qualitative research provides greater opportunity for a feminist sensitivity to come to the fore. Quantitative research is frequently viewed as incompatible with feminism because:

- According to Mies (1993), quantitative research suppresses the voices of women either by ignoring them or by submerging them in a torrent of facts and statistics.

- The criteria of valid knowledge associated with quantitative research turn women, when they are the focus of research, into objects. This means that women are again subjected to exploitation, in that knowledge and experience are extracted from them with nothing given in return, even when the research is conducted by women (Mies 1993).

- The emphasis on statistical control of variables in analysis further exacerbates this last problem, and indeed the very idea of control is viewed as masculine.

- The use of predetermined categories in quantitative research results in an emphasis on what is already known and consequently in 'the silencing of women's own [emerging] voices' (Maynard 1998: 18).

- The criteria of valid knowledge associated with quantitative research also mean that women are to

be studied in a value-neutral way, when in fact the goal of feminist research should be to conduct research imbued with value, specifically *for* women.

By contrast, qualitative research is viewed by many feminists as either more compatible with feminism's central tenets or as more capable of being adapted to them. Thus, in contrast to quantitative research, qualitative research allows:

- women's voices to be heard;

- exploitation to be reduced by giving as well as receiving during fieldwork;

- women *not* to be treated as objects to be controlled by the researcher's technical procedures; and

- the emancipatory goals of feminism to be realized.

For example, Skeggs (2001: 429) observed that one of the earliest principles on which feminist research is based is that it should 'alleviate the conditions of oppression.'

How qualitative research achieves these goals will be addressed more in the next two chapters, since the issues and arguments vary somewhat from one method to the other. Skeggs (2001: 429–30) argued that the political goals of feminist research lead to a preference for qualitative research 'to focus on women's experience and to listen and explore the shared meanings between women with an aim to reformulate traditional research agendas.' In fact, the issue of qualitative research providing the opportunity for a feminist approach has somewhat different aspects when looking at ethnography, qualitative interviewing, and focus groups—the topics of the next two chapters. However, it also should be recognized that there has been a softening of attitude among some feminist writers towards quantitative research in recent years. Examples include:

- There is a recognition that many of the worst excesses of discrimination against women might not have come to light so clearly were it not for the collection and analysis of statistics, as in data on salaries, revealing gender discrimination (Maynard 1994; Oakley 1998). The very presence of factual evidence of this kind allowed the case for equal opportunities legislation to be made much more sharply, although, needless to say, there is more that can be done in this field.

- As Jayaratne and Stewart (1991) and Maynard (1994, 1998) pointed out, at the very least it is difficult to see why feminist research that *combines* quantitative and qualitative research would be incompatible with feminism.

- There has also been a recognition that qualitative research is not *ipso facto* feminist in orientation. If, for example, ethnography, covered in the next

chapter, provided for a feminist sensitivity, one would expect disciplines like social anthropology, virtually founded on the approach, to be almost inherently feminist, which is patently not the case (Reinharz 1992: 47–8). Thus the question of appropriate approaches to feminist research seems to reside in the *application* of methods rather than something inherent in them. Consequently, some writers have preferred to write about *feminist research practice* rather than about *feminist methods* (Maynard 1998: 128). These issues will be returned to in the next two chapters.

K KEY POINTS

- There is disagreement over what precisely qualitative research is.

- Qualitative research does not lend itself to a clear set of linear steps. It tends to be a more open-ended research strategy than is typically the case with quantitative research.

- Theories and concepts are viewed as outcomes of the research process.

- There is considerable unease about the simple application of the reliability and validity criteria associated with quantitative research to qualitative research. Indeed, some writers prefer alternative criteria that have parallels with reliability and validity.

- Most qualitative researchers reveal a preference for seeing through the eyes of research participants.

- Several writers have depicted qualitative research as having a far greater affinity with a feminist standpoint than quantitative research can exhibit.

Q QUESTIONS FOR REVIEW

- What are some of the difficulties in providing a general account of qualitative research?

- What are some of the main quantitative research methods rejected by qualitative researchers and why?

The main steps in qualitative research

- Does a research question in qualitative research have the same significance and characteristics as one in quantitative research?

Theory and concepts in qualitative research

- Is the approach to theory in qualitative research inductive or deductive?

- What is the difference between definitive and sensitizing concepts?

Reliability and validity in qualitative research

- How have some writers adapted the notions of reliability and validity to qualitative research?
- Why have some writers sought alternative criteria for evaluating qualitative research?
- How far do Lincoln and Guba's criteria stray from quantitative criteria?
- What is respondent validation?

The main preoccupations of qualitative researchers

- How do the preoccupations of qualitative researchers differ from those of quantitative researchers, considered in Chapter 3?

The critique of qualitative research

- What are some of the main criticisms levelled at qualitative research?
- To what extent do they reflect the preoccupations of quantitative research?

Is it always like this?

- Can qualitative research be employed in hypothesis testing?

Some contrasts between quantitative and qualitative research

- 'The difference between quantitative and qualitative research revolves entirely around the concern with numbers in the former and with words in the latter.' To what extent do you agree with this statement?

Feminism and qualitative research

- Why have many feminist researchers preferred qualitative research?
- Is there no role for quantitative research in feminist research?

9   Ethnography and participant observation

CHAPTER OVERVIEW

Ethnography and participant observation entail the extended involvement of a researcher in the social life of those studied. The chapter explores:

- the problems of gaining access to different settings and suggestions about how to overcome them;

- whether a covert role is practicable and acceptable;

- the role of key informants for the ethnographer;

- the different roles ethnographers can assume in the course of their fieldwork;

- the role of field notes in ethnography and the varieties of forms they can assume;

- bringing ethnography to an end;

- the controversy about the nature of a feminist ethnography; and

- the role of visual materials and increasing use of them in ethnography.

Introduction

Discussions about the merits and limitations of participant observation were fairly standard in textbooks on social research. However, for some time, writers on research methods have preferred to write about ethnography rather than participant observation. It is difficult to date the point at which this change of terminology (though it is more than just this) occurred, but it was sometime in the 1970s. Before that, ethnography was primarily associated with social anthropology where the investigator visits a (usually) foreign land, gains access to a group (e.g., a tribe or village), spends a considerable amount of time (often many years) with that group with the aim of uncovering its culture, watches and listens to what people say and do, engages people in conversations to probe specific issues of interest, takes copious field notes, and returns home to write up the results.

Box 9.1 represents an attempt to deal with some of these issues and to arrive at a working definition of ethnography. The seven bullet points at the end of Box 9.1 that make up the definition of ethnography could be viewed as a simple process; in fact, ethnography is nowhere near as straightforward as this implies. This chapter outlines some of the main decisions ethnographers must make, along with some of the many contingencies they face. However, it is not easy to generalize about the ethnographic research process so as to provide definitive recommendations about research practice.

As prefigured at the end of the last chapter, the diversity of experiences that confront ethnographers and the variety of ways in which they deal with them does not readily permit clear-cut generalizations. The following comment in a book on ethnography makes this point well:

> Every field situation *is* different and initial luck in meeting good informants, being in the right place at the right time, and striking the right note in relationships may be just as important as skill in technique. Indeed . . . many unsuccessful episodes are due as much to bad luck as to bad judgement (Sarsby 1984: 96).

Box 9.1 ⌇(◉)⌇ *What are ethnography and participant observation?*

Ethnography and participant observation are often difficult to distinguish. In both, a researcher is immersed in a group for an extended period of time, observing behaviour, listening to what is said in conversations, and asking questions. Typically, participant observers and ethnographers gather further data through documents and in interviews, especially on issues not directly observable or about which the observer is unclear. Desroches (1990), for example, added interviews with 15 investigating officers to his hidden video-equipment recordings of sexual activities in public washrooms.

Ethnography also sometimes refers to a specific focus on the culture of the group (and an understanding of people's behaviour within the context of that culture) in which the ethnographer is immersed. On top of this, ethnography frequently simultaneously refers to both a method of research of the kind outlined above *and* the written product of that research. In this book ethnogra-

phy includes participant observation and encapsulates the notion of ethnography as a written product of ethnographic research. In it ethnography is a research method in which the researcher

- is immersed in a social setting for an extended period of time;
- makes regular observations of the behaviour of members of that setting;
- listens to and engages in conversations;
- interviews informants on issues not directly amenable to observation or that the ethnographer is unclear about;
- collects documents about the group;
- develops an understanding of the culture of the group and people's behaviour within the context of that culture;
- and writes up a detailed account of that setting.

Practical tip ☞ *Micro-ethnography*

If doing research for an undergraduate project or master's dissertation, it is generally too hard to conduct a full-scale ethnography, if only because of time difficulties. Nevertheless, it may be possible to carry out a form of *micro-ethnography* (Wolcott 1990), involving a focus on one specific aspect of a topic. For example, if interested in call centres,

one possibility is to focus on how staff manage to interact and discuss work problems with one another in spite of continuously receiving calls and being monitored. A shorter period of time (from a couple of weeks to a few months) can be spent in the organization—either on a full-time or a part-time basis—to achieve this more realistic goal.

However, this statement should not be taken to mean that forethought and an awareness of alternatives approaches are irrelevant. It is with this kind of

issue that the rest of this chapter is concerned. Issues to do with the conduct of interviews by ethnographers are reserved for Chapter 10.

Access

One of the key and yet most difficult steps in ethnography is gaining access to a social setting relevant to the chosen research problem. How to gain access differs along several dimensions, one of which is whether the setting is relatively open (public) or closed (see also Lofland and Lofland 1995). Closed,

non-public settings generally involve organizations of various kinds, such as firms, schools, cults, social movements, and so on. The open/public setting is likely to be everything else—that is, research involving communities, gangs, drug users, and so on. Obviously 'public' does not equate with easy access.

Overt versus covert ethnography

One way to ease the access problem is to assume a *covert* role—in other words, not disclose that you are a researcher. This strategy removes the need to negotiate access or to explain why one wants to intrude into peoples' lives and make them objects of study. Indeed, seeking access is a highly fraught business and the adoption of a covert role removes some of the difficulties. These two distinctions—the open/public versus closed setting and the overt versus covert role—suggest a fourfold distinction in forms of ethnography (see Figure 9.1; an example of recent Canadian work is given for each of the four types).

Three points should be noted about Figure 9.1. First, the open/public setting versus closed setting distinction is not hard and fast. Sometimes, gaining access to groups can have an almost formal quality—such as having to pacify a gang leader's anxieties about your goals. Also, organizations sometimes create contexts that have a public character—such as meetings arranged for members or prospective recruits by social movements like religious cults or political movements.

Second, the overt versus covert distinction is problematic. For example, although ethnographers may seek access through an overt route, there may be many people with whom they come into contact who are unaware of the ethnographer's status as a researcher. Atkinson (1981: 135) noted in connection with his research on the training of doctors in a medical school that, although he was 'an "open" observer with regard to doctors and students,' he was 'a "disguised" observer with regard to the patients.'

Box 9.2 Perils of covert observation: field notes in the lavatory

Ditton's (1977) research in a bakery provides an interesting case of the practical difficulties of taking notes during covert observation as well as an illustration of an ethnographer who shifted position from covert to overt observation at least in part because of those difficulties:

> Right from the start, I found it impossible to keep everything that I wanted to remember in my head until the end of the working day . . . and so had to take rough notes as I was going along. But I was stuck 'on the line,' and had nowhere to retire to privately to jot things down [except the washroom]. [Eventually] . . . my frequent requests for 'time out' after interesting happenings or conversations in the bakehouse and the amount of time I was spending in the lavatory began to get noticed. I had to pacify some genuinely concerned work-mates . . . and 'come out' as an observer—albeit in a limited way. I eventually began to scribble notes more openly, but still not in front of people when they were talking. When questioned about this, as I was occasionally, I coyly said that I was writing things down that occurred to me about 'my studies' (Ditton 1977: 5).

Also, some ethnographers move between the two roles (see Box 9.2).

Another interesting case is provided by Glucksman (1994), who in the 1970s left her academic post to work on a factory assembly line in order to shed light on the reasons why feminism appeared not to be relevant to working-class women. In a sense, she

	Open/public setting	Closed setting
Overt role	*Type 1* • Wilson's (2002) study of Toronto raves • Totten's (2001) study of youth gang members (Box 9.7)	*Type 2* • Karabanow's (2002) study of two Canadian youth shelters (Box 8.5) • Clancey's (2001) study of scientists in the Arctic (Box 9.12)
Covert role	*Type 3* • Desroches's (1990) updates on homosexual activities in public washrooms	*Type 4* • Lauder's (2003) discussion of covert research on the Heritage Front

Figure 9.1 Four types of ethnography

was a covert observer, but her motives for the research were primarily political not academic. At the time she was undertaking the research she had no intention of writing the book that subsequently was published under a pseudonym. Was she an overt or a covert observer (or neither or both)? Whichever description applies, this is an interesting case of what might be termed 'retrospective ethnography.'

A third point to note about Figure 9.1 is the preferred choice of an overt to a covert role. There are several reasons for this situation. As Box 9.3 reveals, this has to do with practical and ethical considerations, with the latter more important (recall Ethical issue 6.1). Because of the ethical problems that beset covert research (and indeed some of the practical difficulties), the bulk of the discussion of access issues that follows focuses on ethnographers playing an overt role (see Ethical issue 9.1).

Access to closed settings

Gaining access to most organizations requires strategic planning, hard work, and sometimes luck. In selecting a case study for an ethnographic investigation, the researcher may employ several criteria, each determined by the research area of interest. One may choose a certain case because of its 'fit' with the research questions, but there are no guarantees of success. Sometimes, sheer perseverance pays off. Leidner (1993) was determined that McDonald's be one of the organizations in which she conducted ethnographic research on the routinization of service work. She wrote:

> The company was a pioneer and exemplar of routinized interaction, and since it was locally based, it seemed like the perfect place to start. McDonald's had other ideas, however, and only after tenacious pestering and persuasion did I overcome corporate employees' polite demurrals, couched in terms of protecting proprietary information and the company's image (Leidner 1993: 234–5).

This kind of determination is necessary for any instance in which a specific organization is the target, such as a particular religious sect or social movement. Rejection too often can mean seeking a completely different research topic.

However, with many research questions, several potential cases are likely to meet the criteria. Organizational researchers have developed a range

---

Box 9.3 The covert role in ethnography

Advantages

- *Easier access.* Adopting a covert role largely gets around the access problem; no permission to gain entry to a social setting or organization is sought.

- *Less reactivity.* Because participants do not know of the study, they are less likely to adjust their behaviour because of that knowledge.

Disadvantages

- *The problem of taking notes.* It is difficult and sometimes impossible to take notes without revealing that research is being conducted. But notes are very important to an ethnographer, and it is too risky to rely on memory alone.

- *The problem of not being able to use other methods.* If the researcher is in a covert role, it is dangerous to steer conversations in a certain direction for fear of detection and it is essentially impossible to engage in interviewing.

- *Anxiety.* Ethnography is frequently a stressful research method and the worries about detection can add to those anxieties. Moreover, if the ethnographer *is* found out, the whole research project may be jeopardized.

- *Ethical problems.* Covert observation transgresses two important ethical tenets: deception of participants and their 'informed consent' (whereby they can agree or disagree to participate on the basis of information supplied to them). It can also be taken to be a violation of the principle of privacy. Indeed, many writers think covert research can harm the practice of research, with innocent researchers being tarred with the same brush as uncovered observers, of their being seen as snoops or voyeurs. On the other hand, in some situations, like investigating the neo-Nationalist Socialist organization, Heritage Front, Lauder (2003) concluded that covert participant observation may be justified.

Ethical issue 9.1 *Stances on ethics*

Writers on research ethics adopt different stances concerning ethical issues; the following can be distinguished:

- *Universalism.* It takes the view that ethical precepts should never be broken; infractions of ethical principles are morally wrong. This stance is not popular and the closest it gets to acceptance is when it admits to exceptions. For example, Van Maanen (1991*b*) wrote up his experiences as a ride operator in Disneyland many years after he had been employed there for school vacation jobs. He never got permission from those he described for this invasion of their privacy.

- *Situation ethics.* Goode (1996) argued for deception to be considered on a case-by-case basis, a 'principled relativism,' based on '*the end justifies the means.*' Some writers argue that without some breaking of ethical rules, one would never know about certain social phenomena like terrorists, cults, drug gangs, white-collar criminals, etc., which often require some kind of disguised observation. Liberal social reformers might add that exposing the sins of the powerful would

be another acceptable instance of lowering ethical standards but this can raise an even harder question. For example, do they have more right to deceive than more conservative researchers who engage in deception to expose the sins of the underclass and less powerful? Is lying to a priest to uncover paedophilia more acceptable than lying to an animal rights activist to reveal a plan to destroy a mink coat factory?

- *Ethical transgression is pervasive.* Virtually all research involves elements that are at least ethically questionable. This occurs whenever all participants are not given absolutely all the details on a piece of research. Punch (1994: 91), for example, observed that 'some dissimulation is intrinsic to social life and, therefore, to fieldwork.' He quoted Gans (1962: 44) in support: 'If the researcher is completely honest with people about his activities, they will try to hide actions and attitudes they consider undesirable, and so will be dishonest. Consequently, the researcher must be dishonest to get honest data.'

---

of tactics, some of which may seem rather unsystematic but still worth mentioning here:

- Use friends, contacts, and colleagues to help gain access; as long as the organization is relevant to the research question, the route should not matter.

- Try to get the support of someone within the organization to vouch for you and the value of the research. Such people are placed in the role of 'sponsors.'

- Even with a level of agreement lower down the hierarchy, clearance from top management/senior executives is still usually needed. Such senior people act as 'gatekeepers.'

- Offer something in return (e.g., a *final* report). It can help to create a sense of being *trustworthy*. This strategy carries a risk of making the researcher a cheap consultant. On the other hand, it must not lead to those studied dictating the findings. Some writers on research methodology do not recommend offering something in return, although, among researchers on formal organizations, it is commonplace.

- Provide a clear explanation of aims and methods. Suggest a meeting to deal with worries and concerns of the participants and provide an explanation of what will happen in terms that can readily be understood by the layperson.

- Be prepared to negotiate—almost no one gets complete access.

- Be reasonably honest about the amount of people's time likely to be needed. This question will almost certainly be asked in seeking access to commercial organizations and probably to many not-for-profit ones too.

Access to open/public settings

Gaining access to public settings shares many problems with access to closed settings. Sometimes ethnographers can have their paths smoothed by individuals who act as both sponsor and gatekeeper. In seeking access to one group of football hooligans, Giulianotti (1995; see Box 9.4) sought out someone who could adopt this role for him. Later in gaining access to a second group, he was able to draw upon existing acquaintances to ease his entrée into the group. These are two common methods of gaining access to groups—via gatekeepers and via acquaintances who then act as sponsors. In seeking access to intravenous female drug users, Taylor (1993) consciously used a gatekeeper strategy. She contacted a local detached drug worker in the area who introduced her to some local users and accompanied her on her first few research visits. A form of research bargain (see Box 9.4) was set up in which Taylor agreed to see any of his clients who preferred to discuss issues with a female.

Box 9.4 Access to football hooligans

Giulianotti (1995) sought access to two groups of football hooligans. Access to one was reasonably smooth in that he was a close friend of 3 of the 47 men caught by the police at a notorious prior match. He had also gone to school and socialized with many of them, and in terms of 'age, attire, and argot' his personal characteristics were similar to those he was studying. Gradually his contacts grew and eventually he 'began socializing freely with the gang at football matches, travelling to and from matches within the main grouping' (Giulianotti 1995: 4).

Access to the other group of supporters was much more difficult for three reasons: absence of prior acquaintanceships; his background and accent; and a high level of negative newspaper publicity about them at the time he was seeking access, making them sensitive to people writing about them. Giulianotti sought out a gatekeeper who could ease his entry into the group. After some abortive attempts, he was finally introduced to someone at a game and this contact gave access to more supporters and then even more. Eventually, he was able to negotiate access to the group by striking what he, following Becker (1970), called a 'research bargain': he would provide details of what rival fans thought of them. Giulianotti described his overall research strategy as:

> regularly introducing myself to new research acquaintances; renegotiating association with familiar casuals; talking with them, drinking with them, and going to matches with them; generally participating with them in a variety of social situations; but disengaging myself from . . . participating in violence, within and outside of football match contexts (Giulianotti 1995: 3).

'Hanging around' is another common access strategy, one that typically entails either loitering in an area until noticed or gradually becoming incorporated into or asking to join a group. An example of the difficulties that await the researcher is one of Whyte's (1955) early field encounters in Boston's North End in his classic case study *Street Corner Society*. The following incident occurred in a hotel bar:

> I looked around me again and now noticed a threesome: one man and two women. It occurred to me that here was a maldistribution of females that I might be able to rectify. I approached the group and opened with something like this: 'Pardon me. Would you mind if I join you?' There was a moment of silence while the man stared at me. He then offered to throw me downstairs. I assured him that this would not be necessary and demonstrated as much by walking right out of there without any assistance (1955: 289).

Wolf (1991) employed a hanging-around strategy to gain access to Canadian outlaw bikers. On one occasion he met a group of them at a motorcycle shop and expressed an interest in 'hanging around' with them. But he tried to move too quickly in seeking information about them, and was forced to abandon his plans. Eventually, a hanging-around strategy resulted in him being approached by the leader of a biker group (Rebels MC), who acted as his sponsor. To bring this off, Wolf ensured that he was properly attired. Attention to dress and demeanour can be a very important consideration when seeking access to either public or closed settings.

As these anecdotes suggest, gaining access to social settings is a crucial first step in ethnographic research, in that without access research plans are halted in their tracks. It is also fraught with difficulties and in certain cases with danger—for example, when the research is on groups engaged in violent or criminal activities. Therefore this discussion of access strategies can be only a starting point in knowing what kinds of approach to consider.

Ongoing access

But access does not finish with contact and entrée to the group; access to *people* is still needed. Securing access is in many ways an ongoing activity and is likely to prove a persistent problem in closed contexts like organizations.

- People will be suspicious, perhaps seeing the researcher as an instrument of top management (it is very common for members of organizations to believe that researchers are placed there to check up on them). When Sharpe (2000: 366) began research on prostitution in a red light area, she was quickly depicted as being 'anything from a social worker to a newspaper reporter with hidden cameras and microphones.' When conducting her research on the British on the Costa del Sol, O'Reilly (2000) was suspected of being a tax inspector.

- They will worry that what they say or do may get back to bosses or colleagues. Van Maanen (1991a) noted that when conducting ethnographic research among police officers, one is likely to observe activities that are deeply discrediting and even illegal. Credibility is determined by the researcher's reactions to situations and events like these.

- If they have these worries, they may go along with the research but in fact sabotage it, engage in deceptions, provide misinformation, and not allow access to 'back regions' (Goffman 1956).

There are three ways to smooth the path of ongoing access:

- Play up credentials—past work and experience; knowledge of the organization; understanding its problems.

- Pass tests—be non-judgmental when hearing about informal activities or about the organization; make sure information given does not get back to others, whether bosses or peers.

- Play a role—if research involves quite a lot of participant observation, the role will be part of the position in the organization; otherwise, construct a 'front,' by demeanour and dress, by explanations about being there, by helping out occasionally with work, or offering advice. Be consistent—do not behave ambiguously or inconsistently.

Similar considerations apply to research in public settings:

- Make sure a plan exists for how people's suspicions can be allayed. Giulianotti (see Box 9.4) simply said that he was doing research on football supporters for a book.

- Be prepared for tests of either competence or credibility. Taylor (1993) reported that at a meeting at a drop-in centre 'proper cups' for tea were put out. Afterwards, Taylor was told that, if she had crooked her 'wee finger' as the leader of the centre had done, her informant 'would have put [Taylor] down in such a way that you'd never want to speak to us again' (1993: 15). When doing research on gang members in a poor community, Horowitz (Gerson and Horowitz 2002; see Box 9.8) wrote that she was frequently told 'confidential' stories (which turned out to be fictional) to see if she could keep a secret.

- Be prepared for changes in circumstances. Both Giulianotti (Box 9.4) and Armstrong (1993) found that sudden newspaper exposés of football hooliganism and evidence of police infiltration led to worries that they were not what they said they were.

Key informants

One aspect of having sponsors or gatekeepers who smooth access for the ethnographer is that they may become *key informants* in the course of the subsequent fieldwork. The ethnographer relies a lot on informants, but certain informants may become particularly important to the research by developing an appreciation of the research and directing the ethnographer to situations, events, or people likely to be helpful to the investigation. Whyte's (1955) study is again an extreme example of this development. He reported Doc as saying to him at one point: 'You tell me what you want to see, and we'll arrange it. When you want some information, I'll ask for it, and you listen. When you want to find out their philosophy of life, I'll start an argument and get it for you. If there's something else you want to get, I'll stage an act for you' (Whyte 1955: 292). Doc was also helpful in warning Whyte that he was asking too many questions, when he told him to 'go easy on that "who," "what," "why," "when," "where" stuff' (1955: 303). Taylor (1993) said that in her participant observation of 50 female drug users, intensive interviews were carried out with 26 women, 8 of them key informants.

Key informants can clearly be of great help to the ethnographer and frequently provide a support that helps with the stress of fieldwork. However, it also needs to be borne in mind that they carry risks. An ethnographer may develop an undue reliance on the key informant and rather than seeing social reality through the eyes of members of the social setting, is seeing only part of it through the eyes of the key informant.

In addition, ethnographers encounter many others who will act as informants whose accounts may be solicited or unsolicited. Some researchers prefer the latter, because of greater spontaneity and naturalism. Very often, research participants develop a sense of the events or encounters the ethnographer wants to see. Armstrong (1993) said that he would sometimes get tip-offs while doing research on hooligans in a club called 'Blades' (see Chapter 8 for other references to this research):

> I often travelled on the same coach as Ray [an informant]; he would then sit with me at matches and in pubs . . . giving me background information. Sometimes

he would start conversations with Blades about incidents which he knew I wanted to know about and afterwards would ask 'Did you get all that down then?' . . . There was never one particular informant; rather, there were many Blades . . . who were part of the core and would always welcome a beer and a chat about 'It,' or tell me who I 'ought to 'ave a word wi' ' (Armstrong 1993: 24–5).

Such unsolicited sources of information are highly attractive to the ethnographer because of their relative spontaneity, although, as Hammersley and Atkinson (1995: 130–1) observed, they may on occasion be staged for the ethnographer's benefit.

Solicited accounts can occur in two ways: by interview (see Chapter 10) or by casual questioning during conversations (though in ethnographic research the boundary between an interview and a conversation is by no means clear). When the ethnographer needs specific information on an issue not amenable to direct observation or that is not cropping up during 'natural' conversations, solicited accounts are likely to be the only way forward.

Roles for ethnographers

Related to the issue of ongoing access is the question of the role an ethnographer adopts in relation to the social setting and its members. Several classifications describe the various roles in fieldwork as arrayed on a continuum of degrees of involvement with and detachment from members of the social setting (see Figure 9.2). It should also be noted that all of the roles are employed at different times in the course of ethnographic research and for different purposes.

For example, the participant observer can be a:

- *Complete participant:* a fully functioning member of a social setting but whose true identity is unknown to

members, thus a covert observer, like Humphreys in the tea room. The ethnographer is engaged in regular interaction with people and participates in their daily lives (but resumes a researcher stance to write down notes once the situation has unfolded).

- *Participant-as-observer:* same as above but members of the social setting are aware of the researcher's status as a researcher. All the studies referred to in Figure 9.1 as involving an overt role—whether in open/public or closed settings—are of this kind, as is Giulianotti's research (see Box 9.4).

- *Observer-as-participant:* the researcher is mainly an interviewer, with some observation but very little participation. Many of the studies covered in Chapter 10 are of this type. Ethnographic research on the police is often of this type, since the opportunities for genuine participation are few due to legal and safety limitations. Thus, as an observer-as-participant, Norris (1993) described how in this role he concentrated on gathering two types of

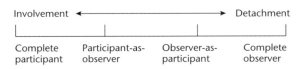

Figure 9.2 Classification of participant observer roles (Gold 1958)

data: 'naturally occurring inter-officer talk' and 'detailed descriptions of how officers handled "live" incidents' (1993: 126). See also Box 9.5 for a further illustration. (Some critics question whether research based on this role is genuine ethnography, but because it is necessary in some situations, like with the police, to dismiss it totally is rather restrictive.)

- *Complete observer:* the final possibility, no interaction with the observed (unobtrusive) and thus people need not take the researcher into account. Most writers do not include this as a form of ethnography since by definition there is no or minimal involvement and participation is more or less entirely missing. There is no *reactivity* but there is also greatly reduced potential for *understanding.*

Each role carries its own advantages and risks; those concerning a complete participant were covered in Box 9.3. The participant-as-observer role carries the risk of over-identification and hence of 'going native' (see Boxes 9.5 and 9.6), but offers an opportunity to get close to people. The observer-as-participant role carries the risk of not understanding the social setting and its people sufficiently and therefore making incorrect inferences. In an interesting variant of this problem (Hessler *et al.* 2003) cautioned observers, here of adolescent risk behaviour, against the temptation to act as a counsellor to respondents.

Gans (1968) would add that even were it possible, adopting a single ethnographic role over the entire course of a project is probably undesirable. There would be a lack of flexibility in handling situations and people, and risks of excessive involvement (and hence going native) or of detachment would loom large. The issue of the roles the ethnographer adopts is of considerable significance because of its implications for relationships with those being studied.

Box 9.5 What is 'going native'?

Ethnographers sometimes lose their sense of being a researcher and become wrapped up in the worldview of the people they are studying, a condition called 'going native.' The prolonged immersion of ethnographers in the lives of the people they study, coupled with a commitment to see the social world through their eyes, lie behind the risk of actually going native. Going native is a potential problem for several reasons but especially because the ethnographer may find it difficult to develop a social scientific angle on the collection and analysis of data. As Hobbs (1988: 6) wrote of his own fieldwork, he: 'often had to remind himself that [he] was not in a pub to enjoy [himself] but to conduct an academic inquiry, and repeatedly woke up the following morning with an incredible hangover, facing the dilemma of whether to bring it up or write it up.' He may have been on the brink of going native.

A related issue for him concerned illegal activity. Hobbs admitted that he engaged in some.

A refusal, or worse still an inquiry concerning the legal status of the 'parcel,' would provoke an abrupt conclusion to the relationship. Consequently, I was willing to skirt the boundaries of criminality on several occasions, and I considered it crucial to be willingly involved in 'normal' business transactions, legal or otherwise. I was pursuing an interactive, inductive study of an entrepreneurial culture, and in order to do so I had to display entrepreneurial skills myself. . . . [My] status as an insider meant that I was afforded a great deal of trust by my informants, and I was allowed access to settings, detailed conversations, and information that might not otherwise have been available (1988: 7, 15).

Box 9.6 Not going native

It should not be assumed that the risk of going native is inevitable in ethnography nor indeed that it is the only risk in participant observers' relations to the social situations in which they find themselves. Lee-Treweek (2000) carried out research on auxiliary caregivers in two homes for the elderly. She described how in one she had an almost completely opposite reaction to going native. She disliked the home and found the staff unappealing because of their lack of sympathy for and their uncaring approach to the elderly people for whom they were responsible. Nonetheless, she felt she 'was gathering good data, despite [her] feelings of being an outsider' (2000: 120). The lesson of this story is that going native is not inevitable and that in the final report, one must be careful to let neither liking nor distaste colour the results.

Active or passive?

A further issue raised about any situation in which the ethnographer participates is being more of an active or a passive participant. Even when the ethnographer is in an observer-as-participant role, sometimes participation is unavoidable or a compulsion to join in in a limited way may be felt. For example, Fine's (1996) research on the work of chefs in restaurants was carried out largely with semi-structured interviews. In spite of this limited participation, he found himself involved in washing up in the kitchens to help out during busy periods. In many instances, the researcher has no choice. In acting as a bouncer (Winlow *et al.* 2001), the participant observer is not going to have the luxury of deciding whether to become involved in fights, since these are likely to come with the territory.

Sometimes, ethnographers *feel* they have no choice about getting involved, because a failure to participate actively may indicate to members of the social setting a lack of commitment and lead to a loss of credibility. This situation can arise especially when the activities involved are illegal or dangerous. On the other hand, many writers counsel against active participation in criminal or dangerous activities (see Box 9.7). Both Armstrong (1993) and Giulianotti (see Box 9.4) refused to fight while doing their research into football hooliganism. The latter wrote: 'My own rules are that I will not get involved in fighting or become a go-between for the two gangs

in organizing fights' (1995: 10). Indeed, here is a strong argument against covert research on criminals or those involved in dangerous activities, since it is much more difficult for someone in such a role not to participate (see Box 9.5).

> **Box 9.7** Legal, ethical, and clinical implications of doing fieldwork with violent gang members
>
> In his ethnographic research, Totten (2001) was interested in how youth gang members accounted for the violence they perpetrated against their girlfriends and their racist and homophobic activities. One underlying factor he uncovered is their constructions of masculinity, which they had built on the limited resources at hand. Most had lived on the street, were themselves victims of severe child abuse and neglect, and had witnessed their mothers being beaten. Their violence is thus an attempt to affirm their masculinity.
>
> That was the sociology, but what about the boys themselves? Here the researcher had to act in some instances. By law, he had to report any abuse suffered by children under 16, whether by gang members or their victims. Second, those deemed at risk of suicide had to be referred to mental health providers. Finally, some of the gang members were on probation or living in treatment facilities. Authorities there also had to be informed. Totten handled this confidentiality issue by studying only those boys who agreed to these limits.

Field notes

Because of the frailties of human memory, ethnographers must jot down their observations. These should be fairly detailed summaries of events and behaviour and the researcher's initial reflections on them. The notes need to specify key dimensions of whatever is observed or heard. There are some general principles:

- Write down notes, however brief, as quickly as possible after seeing or hearing something interesting.

- Write up full field notes at the end of the day at the very latest and include such details as location, those involved, what prompted the exchange or event, date and time of the day, etc.

- Some may prefer using a tape recorder to record initial notes, but this may create a problem of having to transcribe a lot of speech.

- Notes must be vivid and clear and complete. If in doubt, write it down.

Obviously, it is good to take notes straightaway, that is, as soon as something interesting happens. However, wandering around with a notebook and pencil in hand and continually scribbling notes down runs the risk of making people self-conscious. It may be necessary, therefore, to develop strategies of taking small amounts of time out, though without making the participants anxious or suspicious (see Box 9.2).

To some extent, strategies for taking field notes are affected by the degree to which the ethnographer enters the field with clearly delineated research questions. As noted in Chapter 8, most qualitative research begins with general research questions, but there is considerable variation in their specificity. Obviously, when there is some clear focus to a research question, ethnographers have to orient their observations to it. At the same time they have to maintain a fairly open mind so that the element of flexibility—a strength of qualitative research—is not eroded.

In the context of her research on female drug users, Taylor (1993: 15) explained that in her early days in the field she tended to listen rather than talk because she 'did not know what questions [she] wanted to ask.' Armstrong (1993: 12) wrote in connection with his research on football hooliganism that his research 'began without a focus' and that as a result 'he decided to record everything.' Therefore a typical Saturday would mean 30 pages of handwritten notes. Such open-endedness usually cannot last long, because trying to record the details of absolutely everything is quickly tiring. Usually the ethnographer begins to narrow down the focus of research, perhaps relating the emerging findings to the social-scientific literature on the topic, and to match observations to that narrower focus. This approach is implied by the sequence suggested by Figure 8.1.

For most ethnographers, the main equipment needed for observation is a notepad and pen (e.g., Armstrong 1993: 28). A tape-recorder may be useful but, as suggested above, is likely to increase radically the amount of transcription and is possibly more obtrusive than writing notes. Most ethnographers report that after a period of time they become less obtrusive to participants in social settings, who become familiar with their presence. Speaking into a tape-recorder can rekindle an awareness of the ethnographer's presence

---

Box 9.8 Narrowing the focus of an ethnography

The process of narrowing down the focus of research, here on groups on the margins of society (Gerson and Horowitz 2002: 202), involved an initial interest in 'what is really going on' in such groups and communities? How do people make sense of their social worlds? In the early stages of her research on young people in a very poor community in Chicago, Horowitz used these general research questions to guide her data collection but 'began to focus on specifying the sociological issues only after some time in the field' (2002: 202).

She found a great deal of variety in the ambitions, orientations, patterns of interaction, attitudes towards street life, and behaviour in different settings among the young people she observed. Horowitz began to ask questions about how well the world of these young people fit with two prominent models used to explain the worlds of the poor, such comparisons a frequent justification for research. She concluded that neither model 'account[ed] for young people's creativity or for the struggles they mounted and the choices that they made in the face of great obstacles' (2002: 202).

Box 9.9 Virtual participant observation

Kanayama (2003) was interested in the nature of a virtual community formed by an Internet group of Japanese senior citizens, one that included 120 members by 1991. Kanayama described her 10-month study as follows:

> I had participated in this group as a technical volunteer supporter for two years to help senior members use PCs and the Internet and . . . took a position as a non-active participant. . . . Many members, including representatives of the group, knew of [my] personal background. I also conducted in-depth interviews with six female and seven male members . . . by telephone (Kanayama 2003: 274).

She found that members of this virtual community operated well with the medium and could construct real social relationships in cyberspace, and were thus able to provide a supportive environment for each other.

and in gatherings it may be difficult to use, because of the extraneous noise. Photography can be an additional source of data and helps to stir the ethnographer's memory, but it is likely that some kinds of research (especially involving crime and deviance) render taking photographs unworkable.

Types of field notes

Some writers have found it useful to classify the types of field notes generated in the process of conducting ethnography. The following classification is based on the similar categories suggested by Lofland and Lofland (1995) and Sanjek (1990):

- *Mental notes*: particularly useful when it is inappropriate to be seen taking notes. These should be written down at the earliest break.
- *Jotted notes* (also called scratch or rough notes): very brief notes written down on pieces of paper or in small notebooks to jog one's memory about events that should be written up later. Lofland and Lofland (1995: 90) referred to these as being made up of 'little phrases, quotes, key words, and the like.' They need to be jotted down inconspicuously, preferably out of sight, since taking detailed notes in front of people may make them self-conscious.
- *Full field notes*: as soon as possible make detailed notes, the main data source. They should be written at the end of the day or sooner if possible. Write as promptly and as fully as possible about events, people, conversations, etc. Write down, but in brackets, initial ideas about interpretation and impressions and feelings.

It is worth adding that in field notes the ethnographer's presence is frequently evident. This can be seen in Whyte's description of almost being thrown down the stairs reported earlier. Precisely because they record the mundane as observed and experienced by ethnographers, it is here that they come to the surface. In the finished work—the ethnography in the sense of a written account of a group and its culture—the ethnographer is frequently written out of the picture. Field notes, except for brief passages, are invariably for personal consumption (Coffey 1999), whereas the written ethnography is for public consumption and has to be presented as a definitive account of the social setting and culture in question. To allow the ethnographer to surface often in the text risks making the account look like an artifice rather than an authoritative chronicle. This issue will be addressed in further detail in Chapter 17.

Analytic memos

Most of the previous discussion focused on the mechanics of the notes. But content is even more important. There can be notes on the setting, the people, methodological problems encountered, etc. But one type of field note deserves special attention, the analytic memo. This represents not what the researchers see but some initial thoughts of their analysis of the meanings of what they see. It is a memo written to self that will bridge the gap between the data and more abstract theoretical models. The memos should be dated and then reviewed regularly. They should be kept separate from notes on actual observation as they are not data but comments on them.

The end

Knowing when to stop is not an easy or straightforward matter in ethnography. Because of its unstructured nature and the absence of specific hypotheses for testing (other than those that may emerge during data collection and analysis), there is a tendency for ethnographic research to lack an obvious end point. But clearly ethnographic research does come to an

end. It may be that there is an almost natural end to the research, such as investigations into the waning Toronto rave scene, but this is a fairly rare occurrence. Sometimes, the rhythms of the ethnographer's occupational career or personal and family life necessitate withdrawal from the field. Such factors include: the end of a period of sabbatical leave;

the need to write up and submit a doctoral thesis by a certain date; or funding for research drawing to a close. As regards family and personal commitments, for example, Taylor (1993) wrote that one instrumental factor in her departure from the field was a lengthy illness of her youngest son.

Moreover, ethnographic research can be highly stressful for many reasons: the nature of the topic, which places the fieldworker in stressful situations (as in research on crime); the marginality of the researcher in the social setting and the need constantly to manage a front; and the often necessary prolonged absence from one's normal life. Ethnographers may simply feel that they have had enough.

An important reason for beginning to bring fieldwork to a close is that the research questions are answered, so that there are no new data worth generating. The ethnographer may even feel a strong sense of *déjà vu* towards the end of data collection. In the language of grounded theory, all the researcher's categories are thoroughly *saturated*, although Glaser and Strauss's (1967) approach would invite making certain that there are no new questions to be asked and no new comparisons to be made.

Thus the reasons for bringing ethnographic research to a close can involve a wide range of factors, from the personal to matters of research design. Whatever the reason, disengagement has to be *managed*. For one thing, this means that promises must not be forgotten (was a report promised as a condition of entry?). It also means that ethnographers must provide good explanations for their departure. Members of a social setting always know that the researcher is a temporary fixture, but over a long period of time, and especially if there was genuine participation in activities within that setting, people may forget that the ethnographer's presence is finite. The farewells have to be managed and in an orderly fashion. Also, the ethnographer's *ethical* commitments must not be forgotten, such as the need to ensure that persons and settings are made anonymous—unless, of course, as sometimes happens, there has been an agreement that the social setting can be disclosed (as often occurs in the study of religious sects and cults).

Can there be a feminist ethnography?

This heading is in fact the title of a widely cited article by Stacey (1988). It rebuts the view that there can be a distinctively feminist ethnography that both draws on the distinctive strengths of ethnography and is informed by feminist tenets. Reinharz (1992) saw feminist ethnography as significant in terms of feminism, because:

- it documents women's lives and activities, which previously were often seen as marginal and subsidiary to men's;

- it understands women from their perspective, so that research that 'trivializes females' activities and thoughts, or interprets them from the standpoint of men in the society or of the male researcher' (1992: 52) is rejected; and

- it understands women in context.

Similarly, Skeggs (2001: 430) observed that ethnography 'with its emphasis on experiences and the words, voice and lives of the participants' has been viewed by many feminist researchers as well-suited to the goals of feminism.

However, such commitments and practices go only part of the way. Of great significance to feminist researchers is whether the research allows for a non-exploitative relationship between researcher and researched. One of the main elements of such a strategy is for the ethnographer not to treat the relationship as a one-way process of extracting information from others, but actually to provide something in return. Skeggs's (1994, 1997) account of her ethnographic research on young women, briefly mentioned in Chapter 8, represents an attempt to address this issue of a non-exploitative relationship

Box 9.10 A feminist ethnography

Skeggs's (1997) longitudinal ethnographic study of 83 white, working-class women was 'based on research conducted over a total period of 12 years including 3 years' full-time, in-the-field participant observation. It began when the women enrolled in a "caring" course at a local college and it followed their trajectories through the labour market, education, and the family' (1997: 1).

The elements of a distinctively feminist ethnography can be seen in the following comments:

- 'This ethnography was politically motivated to provide space for the articulations and experiences of the marginalized' (1997: 23).

- The 'study was concerned to show how young women's experience of structure (their class and gender positioning) and institutions (education and the media) frame and inform their responses and how this process informs constructions of their own subjectivity' (1994: 74). This comment, like the previous one, reflects a commitment to documenting women's lives and allowing their experiences to come through, while also pointing to the significance of context.

Skeggs also felt that her relationship with the women was not exploitative. For example, she wrote that the research enabled the women's 'sense of self-worth' to be 'enhanced by being given the opportunity to be valued, knowledgeable, and interesting.' She claimed she was able to 'provide a mouthpiece against injustices' and to listen 'to disclosures of violence, child abuse, and sexual harassment' (Skeggs 1994: 81).

when women conduct ethnographic research on other women (see Box 9.10).

Stacey (1988), however, argued, on the basis of her fieldwork experience, that the various situations she encountered as a feminist ethnographer placed her 'in situations of inauthenticity, dissimilitude, and potential perhaps inevitable betrayal, situations that I now believe are inherent in fieldwork method. For no matter how welcome, even enjoyable the fieldworker's presence may appear to "natives," fieldwork represents an intrusion and intervention into a system of relationships, a system of relationships that the researcher is far freer to leave' (Stacey 1988: 23). Stacey also argued that, when the research is written up, it is the feminist ethnographer's interpretations and judgments that come through and that have authority. Skeggs responded to this by acknowledging in the case of her own study that her academic career was undoubtedly enhanced by the research, but added that Stacey's views construe women as victims. Instead, she argued:

> The young women were not prepared to be exploited; just as they were able to resist most things which did not promise economic or cultural reward, they were able to resist me. . . . They enjoyed the research. It provided resources for developing a sense of their self-worth. More importantly, the feminism of the research provided a framework [for them to see] . . . that their individual problems are part of a wider structure and not their personal fault (Skeggs 1994: 88).

Similarly, Reinharz (1992: 74–5) argued that, although ethnographic fieldwork relationships may sometimes *seem* manipulative, a clear undercurrent of reciprocity often lies beneath them. The researcher, in other words, may offer help or advice to her research participants, or she may exhibit reciprocity by giving a public airing to normally marginalized voices (although the ethnographer is always the mouthpiece for such voices and may be imposing a particular 'spin' on them). Moreover, it seems extreme to abandon feminist ethnography because the ethnographer cannot fulfil all possible obligations simultaneously. Indeed, this would be a recipe for the abandonment of all research, feminist or otherwise. What is also crucial is transparency—transparency in the feminist ethnographer's dealings with the women she studies and transparency in the account of the research process, both of which are great strengths in Skeggs's work. Nonetheless, it is clear that the question of whether there is or can be a feminist ethnography is a matter of ongoing debate. The fact that female researchers are in careers that will put them into the top income categories and that their subjects are often taken from the bottom ones, is a nagging issue not yet resolved.

The rise of visual ethnography

The use of visual materials in social research is by no means new; for example, social anthropologists have used photographs of the tribes and villages in which they resided for many decades. However, there is a clear sense that their use in social research has entered a new phase, one that can be discerned in books on this area such as *Visual Ethnography* by Pink (2001).

A distinction can be made between the use of visual materials that are *extant* and those produced more or less exclusively for the purposes of research. The former was featured in Chapter 7 and takes the form of such artefacts as people's collections of photographs and images in newspapers and magazines. This chapter emphasizes research-driven visual images, mainly photographs but also video recordings and other visual media. The distinction between extant and research-driven visual materials is not an entirely satisfactory one, but for simplicity is used here.

It is also worth observing that although the term 'visual ethnography' is increasingly popular, it is sometimes used in a way that does not imply the kind of sustained immersion in a social setting that has been used in this chapter as a feature of ethnography. Sometimes, the term is used to include interviews of the kind covered in the next chapter in which visual materials figure prominently. However, to avoid splitting visual resources across too many chapters, the discussion of their use in qualitative research is presented here.

The following discussion emphasizes photographs, mainly because they are the visual medium that has received the greatest attention. There are a number of ways in which photographs have been employed by qualitative researchers:

1. As *aides mémoires* in the course of fieldwork where they essentially become components of the ethnographer's field notes.

2. As sources of data in their own right and not simply as adjuncts to the ethnographer's field notes.

3. As prompts for discussion by research participants. Sometimes the photographs may be extant; in other contexts, they are taken by the ethnographer or by research participants more or less exclusively for the purposes of the investigation.

Pink (2001) drew an important distinction between two positions on visual materials. The traditional framework is a *realist* one (see Box 1.9 on realism); the photograph simply captures an event or setting that then becomes a 'fact' for the ethnographer to interpret along with other data. The image and what it represents is essentially unproblematic and acts as a window on reality. This has been the dominant frame within which visual resources have been produced and analyzed. In contrast, Pink also drew attention to a position that she called *reflexive*. This entails an awareness of and sensitivity to the ways in which the researcher as a person had an impact on what a photograph reveals. This sensitivity requires a grasp of the way that one's age, gender, background, and academic proclivities influence what is photographed, how it is composed, and the roles that informants and others may have played in influencing the resulting image.

Additionally, this approach to the visual is frequently collaborative, in the sense that research participants may be involved in decisions about what photographs should be taken and later how they should be interpreted. Further, there is recognition of the fluidity of interpreting images, implying that they can never be fixed and are always viewed by different people in different ways. Thus, in Pink's research on Spanish bullfighters, enthusiasts interpreted the images she took of bullfights in terms of bullfighter performance. Canadian viewers of the images might employ a different interpretive frame, one to do with animal rights and cruelty.

Plate 9.1 presents an image, referred to as *The Bullfighter's Braid*, from Pink's research. It depicts a female bullfighter and appealed to many connoisseurs of the sport who read into it different artistic and other meanings and values. For Pink, it held additional significance in terms of her interests in gender and the broader discipline of social anthropology (see Pink 2001: 101 and http://sunsite.ualberta. ca/reflexive-frames/1_rprf/_E/gal_pink_1.html for

Plate 9.1 *The Bullfighter's Braid*

Box 9.11 Photographs in a study of hospital wards

Radley and Taylor (2003*a*, 2003*b*) were interested in the role played by the physical setting of a hospital ward in patient recovery. Nine patients in a ward were asked to take photographs on the ward a few days after their surgery. Each patient was supplied with a camera and asked to take up to 12 photographs of things that were personally significant in the hospital. The only constraint was not to include people in their photographs (because of hospital restrictions). The researchers stayed with the patients while they took their photographs. A day after they were developed, patients were interviewed and again a month or so later at home. On each occasion, patients were asked about all the photographs and which ones best expressed their stay in hospital. This approach to interviewing, namely, asking people to discuss photographs and their meaning and significance, is often referred to as *photo-elicitation*.

Most of the images taken appear very mundane and neither striking nor interesting. However, the photographs took on considerable significance for the interviewees' views on the positive and negative aspects of their stays. These fitted into a narrative of the kind that narrative analysts seek to uncover. As the authors expressed it: 'The camera engaged the patients with the hospital setting in a critical way. This meant that the photographic prints also became part of the passage . . . from hospital to home, something we have found to be important in how patients manage their recovery.'

Source: Accessed on 17 December 2002, www.lboro.ac.uk/departments/ss/visualising_ethnography/hospital.html.

more information about this photograph). A further example of the use of visual resources in ethnographic contexts is described in Boxes 9.11 and 9.12.

The various examples of the use of visual materials give a sense that they have great potential for ethnographers and qualitative researchers more generally. Their growing popularity should not entice readers into thinking that visual methods should be incorporated into their investigations: their use must be relevant to the research questions being asked. For her research on Niketown in Chicago, Peñaloza (1999) was interested in what she dubbed 'spectacular consumption,' that is, turning what could otherwise be a mundane consumption event (purchasing sportswear) into a spectacle through the use of sporting images, sounds, and atmospheres. In exploring research questions to do with this topic (e.g., the role of the environment in creating a sense of spectacular consumption), an approach that included photography was very appropriate, since spectacle is a visual phenomenon.

Box 9.12 Visual ethnography?

Clancey (2001) described a study in the Canadian High Arctic, which sought to use the extreme environment there to see how scientists might someday live and work on Mars. The research used a variety of methods: ethnography to understand how scientists like to work and live, experiments with various tools and procedures, and in the present context, systematic photography and time-lapse videos. He found this combination applicable to other multidisciplinary field expeditions that are spread over a large terrain.

As a data source, visual research methods require researchers to 'read' images while sensitive to: the context in which they were generated; the potential for multiple meanings that need to be worked through with research participants; and, where researchers are the source of the images, to the significance of their own social position. In other words, the analyst of visual materials needs to be skeptical about the notion that a photograph provides an unproblematic depiction of reality. In addition, researchers usually include non-visual research methods in their investigations (such as interviews). This leads to the question of the relative significance of words and images in the analysis of data and the presentation of findings. Since words are the traditional medium, it is easy to slip into seeing the visual as ancillary. Finally, visual research methods raise especially difficult ethical issues of invasion of privacy and anonymity.

K   KEY POINTS

- Ethnography refers to both a method and the written product of research based on that method.

- The ethnographer is typically a participant observer who also uses non-observational methods and sources such as interviewing and documents.

- The ethnographer may adopt an overt or covert role, but the latter carries great ethical difficulties.

- The method of access to a social setting depends in part on whether it is public or closed.

- Key informants frequently play an important role for the ethnographer but care is needed to ensure that their impact on the research is not excessive.

- There are several different ways of classifying the roles that the ethnographer may assume. These are not necessarily mutually exclusive.

- Field notes are important for prompting the ethnographer's memory.

- Ethnography with a feminist standpoint has become a popular approach to collecting data, but there have been debates about whether there really can be a feminist ethnography.

- Visual materials such as photographs and video have attracted considerable interest among ethnographers in recent years, not just as adjuncts to data collection but as objects of interest in their own right.

Q   QUESTIONS FOR REVIEW

- Is it possible to distinguish ethnography and participant observation?

- How does participant observation differ from structured observation?

- To what extent can participant observation and ethnography rely solely on observation?

Access

- 'Covert ethnography takes away the need to gain access to inaccessible settings and therefore has much to recommend it.' Discuss.
- Does the problem of access finish once initial access to a setting is achieved?
- What is the role of key informants in ethnographic research? Is there anything to be concerned about when using them?

Roles for ethnographers

- What is meant by going native?
- Should ethnographers be active or passive in their research?

Field notes

- Why are field notes important for ethnographers?
- Why is it useful to distinguish between different types of field notes?

The end

- How does one decide when to cease data collection in ethnographic research?

Can there be a feminist ethnography?

- What are the main ingredients of feminist ethnography?
- Assess Stacey's argument about whether feminist ethnography is possible in light of Skeggs's research or any other ethnographic study that describes itself, or can be seen, as feminist.

The rise of visual ethnography

- What roles can visual materials play in ethnography?
- Why don't photographs provide unproblematic images of reality?

Interviewing in qualitative research

CHAPTER OVERVIEW

This chapter is concerned with interviews in qualitative research which, as discussed in Chapter 4, tend to be far less structured than those associated with survey research. The two forms of qualitative interviewing discussed here are the unstructured and the semi-structured. This chapter is concerned mainly with individual interviews in qualitative research but the focus group method is also discussed. The chapter explores:

- differences between structured and qualitative interviewing;

- the main characteristics of and differences between unstructured and semi-structured interviewing; the two terms refer to extremes, and in practice a wide range of interviews with differing degrees of structure lies between them;

- how to devise and use an interview guide for semi-structured interviewing;

- the different kinds of questions that can be asked in an interview guide;

- the importance of recording and transcribing qualitative interviews;

- the potential and pitfalls of online interviewing;

- how focus groups should be conducted in such terms as the number and size of groups, how to select participants, and how direct questioning should be;

- the significance of interaction between participants in focus group discussions;

- some practical difficulties with focus group sessions, such as the possible loss of control over proceedings and the potential for unwanted group effects;

- the significance of qualitative interviewing and focus groups in feminist research; and

- the advantages and disadvantages of qualitative interviewing relative to participant observation.

Introduction

The interview is probably the most widely employed method in qualitative research. Of course, as seen in Chapter 9, ethnography usually involves a substantial amount of interviewing and this undoubtedly contributes to its widespread use. However, the flexibility of the interview and its economy of time and effort are what really make it so attractive. While interviewing, transcribing interviews, and the analysis of transcripts are all very time-consuming, they can

be more readily accommodated into researchers' personal lives.

In Box 4.3, several different types of interview were briefly outlined. Other than the structured and standardized interviews, they are associated with qualitative research. In spite of the apparent proliferation of terms describing interviews in qualitative research, the two main types are the unstructured and the semi-structured interview. Researchers sometimes employ the term 'qualitative interview' to include both. Focus groups and group interviewing are also examined in the chapter along with other forms of interview associated with qualitative research. There is clearly the potential for considerable confusion here, but the types and definitions presented in Box 4.3 should inject a degree of terminological consistency.

Differences between structured and qualitative research interviews

In a number of ways qualitative interviewing is usually quite different from interviewing in quantitative research:

- In quantitative research, the approach is structured to maximize the reliability and validity of measurement of key concepts. The researcher has a clearly specified set of research questions that the structured interview is designed to answer. Qualitative interviewing is much less structured with an emphasis on openness and a greater freedom to modify and add to initial research ideas once in the field.

- There is greater interest in the interviewee's concerns; in quantitative research, the interview mostly reflects those of the researcher.

- In qualitative interviewing, going off at tangents is often encouraged—it gives insight into what the interviewee sees as relevant and important; in quantitative research, it is usually regarded as a nuisance and discouraged.

- In qualitative interviewing, interviewers can depart significantly from any schedule or guide. They can ask new questions that follow up interviewees' replies and can vary the order and even the wording of questions. In structured interviews, none of these things is done, because they compromise the reliability and validity of measurement.

- As a result, qualitative interviewing tends to be flexible, responding to the direction in which interviewees take the interview and perhaps adjusting the emphases in the research as a result of

issues that emerge during the interviews. By contrast, structured interviews are typically inflexible, due to a need to standardize the interactions with all interviewees.

- In qualitative interviewing, the researcher wants rich, detailed answers; in structured interviewing the interview is supposed to generate answers that can be coded and processed quickly.

- In qualitative interviewing, the interviewee may be interviewed on more than one and sometimes even several occasions (see Box 10.1 for an example). In structured interviewing, unless the research is longitudinal in character, the person is interviewed only once.

Box 10.1 Unstructured interviewing

Malbon (1999: 33) described his strategy for interviewing 'clubbers' as follows:

> interviews were very much 'conversational' in style, although all interviews were taped. The first interview was designed . . . to put the clubber at ease while also explaining fully and clearly in what ways I was hoping for help; to begin to sketch in details of the clubbers clubbing preferences, motivations and histories; and to decide how to approach the night(s) out that I would be spending with the clubber. . . . The main content of the second [more relaxed] interview consisted of comments, discussion, and questions about the club visits . . . and the nature of the night out as an experience. . . . [D]iscussion occasionally diversified . . . to cover wider aspects of the clubbers' lives.

Unstructured and semi-structured interviewing

The two major types of qualitative interviewing are:

- The almost totally *unstructured interview:* here the researcher uses at most an *aide mémoire* as a brief set of self-prompts to investigate certain topics. There may be just a single question asked by the interviewer and the interviewee is allowed to respond freely, with the interviewer simply responding to points that seem worthy of follow-up. Unstructured interviewing tends to be similar in character to a conversation. See Box 10.1 for an illustration of an unstructured interview style.

- A *semi-structured interview:* the researcher has a list of questions or fairly specific topics to be covered, often referred to as an interview guide, but the interviewee still has a great deal of leeway in how to reply. See Box 10.2 for an illustration of a semi-structured interview. Questions may not follow the exact order on the schedule and some questions not included in the guide may be asked as the interviewer picks up on things said by interviewees. But, by and large, all of the questions are asked and a similar wording is used from interviewee to interviewee. Box 10.3 provides an example

---

Box 10.2 Semi-structured interviewing

Lupton (1996) investigated Australian food preferences using 33 semi-structured interviews conducted by four female interviewers (of whom she was one). She wrote:

Interviewees were asked to talk about their favourite and most detested foods; whether they thought there was such a thing as 'masculine' or 'feminine' foods or dishes; which types of foods they considered 'healthy' or 'good for you' and which not; . . . whether they liked to try new foods; which foods they had tasted first as an adult; whether there had been any changes in the types of food they had eaten over their lifetime; whether they associated different types of food with particular times, places or people; . . . whether they ate certain foods when in certain moods and whether they had any rituals around food (1996: 156, 158).

Box 10.3 Flexibility in semi-structured interviewing

Like Lupton (see Box 10.2), Beardsworth and Keil (1992) were interested in food-related issues, particularly in vegetarianism. They carried out 73 'relatively unstructured interviews':

guided by an inventory of issues to be covered in each session. As the interview program progressed, interviewees themselves raised additional or complementary issues, and these formed an integral part of the study's findings. In other words, the interview program was not based upon a set of relatively rigid pre-determined questions and prompts. Rather, the open-ended, discursive nature of the interviews permitted an iterative refinement, whereby lines of thought identified by earlier interviewees could be taken up and presented to later ones (Beardsworth and Keil 1992: 261–2).

---

of these features while Box 10.4 gives an example of the qualitative interviewing typical of life history research.

In semi- and unstructured cases, the interview process is not just flexible but also emphasizes how interviewees frame and understand issues and events—that is, what they view as important in explaining and understanding patterns and forms of their behaviour. Thus, Wilson (2002) wanted to understand the rave subculture from the participants' point of view and Tastsoglou and Miedema (2003) sought to derive the meaning of community from the immigrant women themselves, not *a priori*. Once again, recall that qualitative research is not just quantitative research with numbers missing.

There is a growing tendency for semi-structured and unstructured interviewing to be referred to collectively as in-depth interviews or as *qualitative interviews*. The two types are extremes and there is a lot of variability between them (the first example in Box 10.2 seems somewhat more structured than the one in Box 10.3, for example, though both are illustrative of semi-structured interviewing), but most qual-

Box 10.4 Life history interviews

One special form of interview associated with qualitative research is the life history interview. It is often combined with various kinds of personal documents like diaries, photographs, and letters, and it invites subjects to look back in detail across an entire life course and to report their experiences and how they understood their world. While there has been a trickle of studies using the approach over the years, until relatively recently it has not been popular. It has suffered because of an erroneous treatment of the life in question as a sample of one and hence of limited generalizability. However, it has certain clear strengths from the point of view of the qualitative researcher: its unambiguous emphasis on the point of view of the life in question and a clear commitment to the process of social life, showing how events unfold and interrelate in people's lives.

An example of the life history interview approach is provided by Lewis in his research on the Sánchez family and its experiences in a Mexican slum:

> I asked hundreds of questions of [the five members of the Sánchez family]. . . . While I used a directive approach to the interviews, I encouraged free association, and I was a good listener. I attempted to cover systematically a wide range of subjects: their earliest memories, their dreams, their hopes, fears, joys, and sufferings; their jobs; their relationship with friends, relatives, employers; their sex life; their concepts of justice, religion, and politics; their knowledge of geography and history; in short, their total view of the world. Many of my questions stimulated them to express themselves on subjects that they might otherwise never have thought about (Lewis 1961: xxi).

Miller (2000) has suggested a resurgence of interest in recent years and an increasing use of biographical methods like life story interviews and especially those referred to as narrative interviews. Moreover, the growing use of such interviews has come to be associated less and less with the study of a single life (or indeed just one or two lives) and are increasingly applied to studying several lives. Atkinson (2002, 2004), for example, conducted narrative interviews with women tattoo enthusiasts (see Box 13.11).

P. Atkinson (2004) observed that the length of the typical life story interview varies considerably but suggested

that it usually takes two or three sessions of between one hour and one-and-a-half hours each. He provided a catalogue of questions that can be asked and divided them into groups (1990: 43–53):

- Birth and family of origin, e.g., 'How would you describe your parents?'
- Cultural traditions, e.g., 'Was your family different from others in town?'
- Social factors, e.g., 'What were some of your struggles as a child?'
- Education, e.g., 'What are your best memories of school?'
- Love and work, e.g., 'How did you end up in the work you do or did?'
- Inner and spiritual life, e.g., 'What are the stresses of being an adult?'
- Major life themes, e.g., 'What were the crucial decisions in your life?'
- Vision of the future, e.g., 'Is your life fulfilled yet?'
- Closure questions, e.g., 'Have you given a fair picture of yourself?'

An *oral history* interview is usually somewhat more specific in tone in that the subject is asked to reflect on specific events or periods in the past. The emphasis is less upon the individual and his/her life than on the past and is sometimes combined with other sources, such as documents. The chief problem with the oral history interview (which it shares with the life history interview) is the possibility of bias introduced by memory lapses and distortions. Sugiman (2004) pointed out in her work on Japanese-Canadian women interned in the Second World War that memory is a social and even political act, involving recall, forgetting, transforming, and shaping to audience. On the other hand, oral history testimonies can provide a voice to groups that are typically marginalized in historical research (true also of life history interviews), either because of their lack of power or because they are typically regarded as unexceptional, both points made frequently by feminist researchers.

---

itative interviews are close to one type or the other. In neither case does the interviewer follow a strict schedule, as is done in quantitative research interviewing, although in semi-structured interviews the interviewer loosely follows a script. That choice of

whether to veer towards one type rather than the other is affected by a variety of factors.

- Researchers who feel that using even the most rudimentary interview guide hinders genuine access to the worldviews of members of a social setting are likely to favour an unstructured interview. But even here it is rarely so unstructured that the researcher cannot at least specify a research focus.

- If the researcher is beginning the investigation with a fairly clear rather than a general focus, it is likely that the interviews will be semi-structured, so that the more specific issues can be addressed.

- To ensure a modicum of comparability of interviewing style if more than one person is to carry out the fieldwork, semi-structured interviewing may be preferred. See Box 10.2 for an example.

- Multiple-case study research generally needs some structure to ensure cross-case comparability, a requirement of the Workforce Study on Aging mentioned in Box 3.1.

Preparing an interview guide

The idea of an interview guide is much less specific than the notion of a structured interview schedule. In fact, the term can be employed to refer to a brief list of memory prompts for areas to be covered in unstructured interviewing and the somewhat more structured list of issues to be addressed or questions to be asked in semi-structured interviewing. What is crucial is that the actual questioning is flexible, allowing interviewers to learn how research participants view their social world.

In preparing for qualitative interviews, Lofland and Lofland (1995: 78) suggested asking the question 'Just what about this thing is puzzling me?' This can be applied to each of the research questions generated or it may be a mechanism for generating research questions. They suggested that puzzlement may be stimulated by various activities: random thoughts in different contexts (written down as quickly as possible); discussions with colleagues, friends, and relatives; and, of course, reading the existing literature on the topic. The formulation of the research question(s) should not be so specific that alternative avenues of inquiry that arise during the collection of fieldwork data are closed. Such premature closure of the research focus would be inconsistent with qualitative research's (see Figure 9.1) emphases on the worldview of those being inter-

viewed and not starting out with too many preconceptions. Gradually, in the meandering around, an order and structure begin to emerge.

Basic elements in preparing the interview guide are to:

- create a certain amount of order, so that questions flow reasonably well, but still allow changing the order during the actual interview;

- formulate interview questions or topics in a way that answers the research questions (but do not make them too specific);

- try to use a language that is comprehensible and relevant to those being studied;

- not ask leading questions, just as in interviews in quantitative research; and

- remember to record 'face sheet' information of a general kind (name, age, gender, etc.) and a specific kind (position in company, number of years employed, number of years involved in a group, etc.), because such information is useful for putting people's answers into context.

There are also some practical details to attend to before the interview.

- Become familiar with the setting in which the interviewees engage in the behaviour of interest. This helps in understanding what they are saying.

- Get hold of a good-quality recording machine and microphone. Qualitative researchers nearly always record and then transcribe their interviews. This procedure is important for the detailed analysis required in qualitative research and to ensure that the interviewees' answers are captured in their own terms. If taking notes, it is too easy to lose phrases and language used. Also, because interviewers are not supposed to follow a strictly formulated schedule of questions of the kind used in structured interviewing, they need to be responsive to the interviewee's answers, not writing with head down, so that it is possible to follow up. A good microphone is very important; many interviews have been compromised because of being inaudible.

- Make sure as far as possible that the interview takes place in a setting that is quiet (so there is no or little outside noise to affect the quality of the recording) and private (so the interviewee does not worry about being overheard).

- Prepare for the interview by cultivating the criteria of a quality interviewer suggested by Kvale (1996) (see Box 10.5).

Box 10.5 Kvale's qualification criteria for an interviewer (plus two others)

Kvale (1996) proposed a useful list of ten criteria of a successful interviewer.

- *Knowledgeable:* is thoroughly familiar with the focus of the interview; pilot tests of survey interviews are a good idea.
- *Structuring:* gives purpose of interview; asks if interviewee has questions.
- *Clear:* asks simple, easy, and short questions; no jargon.
- *Gentle:* lets people finish; gives them time to think; tolerates pauses.
- *Sensitive:* listens attentively to what is said and how it is said; is empathetic.
- *Open:* responds to what is important to the interviewee; is flexible.
- *Steering:* knows what needs to be found out.
- *Critical:* is prepared to challenge what is said, for example, dealing with an inconsistency in interviewee's replies.
- *Remembering:* relates what is said to what has previously been said.
- *Interpreting:* clarifies and extends meanings of interviewees' statements but without imposing meaning on them.

To Kvale's list, please add the following:

- *Balanced:* does not talk too much, which can make interviewees passive, and does not talk too little, which can cause interviewees to feel their talk is not along the right lines.
- *Ethically sensitive:* for examples, ensures that the interviewee appreciates what the research is about and its purposes, and that all answers will be treated confidentially.

After the interview, make notes about:

- how the interview went (was interviewee talkative, cooperative, nervous, etc.?);
- where the interview took place;
- any other feelings about the interview (did it open up new avenues of interest?); and
- the setting (noisy/quiet, many/few other people in the vicinity).

Various guidelines that suggest a series of steps in formulating questions for an interview guide in qualitative research are presented in Figure 10.1.

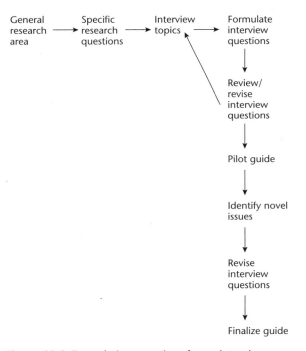

Figure 10.1 Formulating questions for an interview guide for social research

Kinds of questions

The kinds of questions asked in qualitative interviews are highly variable; Kvale (1996) suggested nine. Most interviews contain virtually all of them, although interviews that rely on lists of topics are likely to follow a somewhat looser format. Kvale's nine types are as follows:

- *Introducing questions:* 'Please tell me about when your interest in X first began?'; 'Have you ever . . .?'; 'Why did you go to . . .?'

- *Follow-up questions:* getting the interviewee to elaborate an answer, such as 'What do you mean by that . . .?'; even, 'Yeesss?' Kvale suggested repeating significant words in an answer to stimulate further explanation. See Box 10.6 for an example.

- *Probing questions:* following up what has been said through direct questioning, such as 'Can you say some more about that?'; 'You said earlier that you prefer not to do X. Can you say what kinds of things have put you off it?'; 'In what ways do you find X disturbing?'

- *Specifying questions:* 'What did you do then?'; 'How did (name) react to what you said?'; 'What effect did (event) have on you?' See Box 10.6 for an example.

- *Direct questions:* 'Do you find it easy to keep smiling when serving customers?'; 'Are you happy with the way you and your husband decide how money should be spent?' Such questions are perhaps best left until later in the interview, in order not to influence the direction of the interview too much.

- *Indirect questions:* 'What do most people around here think of the ways that management treats its staff?' but only after asking 'How do you feel?' in order to get at the individual's own view first.

- *Structuring questions:* 'I would now like to move on to a different topic.'

- *Silence:* allow pauses to signal to the interviewee an opportunity to reflect and amplify an answer; do not pause so long that it embarrasses the interviewee.

- *Interpreting questions:* 'Do you mean that your leadership role had to change from one of encouraging others, to a more directive one?'; 'Is it fair to say that you don't mind being friendly towards customers most of the time, but when they are unpleasant or demanding you find it more difficult?'

As this list suggests, one of the main ingredients of the interview is listening—being attentive to what the interviewee is saying or not saying. It means that the interviewer is active without being too intrusive—a difficult balance. But it also means that, just

---

Box 10.6 Using a semi-structured interview: research on female offenders

Two factors seem to have been instrumental in Davies' (2000) decision to employ semi-structured interviewing with female offenders. First, she felt that her research questions—'exploring the types of crimes individuals engaged in and details of the ways in which they conducted them' (2000: 85)—were an important factor in her decision. A second factor was the consistency of semi-structured interviewing with the principles of feminist research 'because such interviews seek not to be exploitative but to be appreciative of the position of women' (2000: 86). Davies interviewed female offenders both in prison, which necessitated a lengthy series of negotiations about access, and in the community. The latter were selected by already willing interviewees putting her in touch with others. She described her interview strategy as follows: 'Most important is to listen, then prompt and encourage when appropriate without "leading," and to steer the discussion back on track if it appears to be heading down a less promising avenue' (2000: 91). At one point, as a follow-up question, she repeated the interviewee's words,

a tactic mentioned by Kvale (1996), and then followed up the reply with what Kvale called a probing question (Davies is PD):

> PD: You mentioned security tags and foil?
>
> F: It depended on the shops—some shops we would just . . . when we just started out we didn't know about the foil so we used ter take in a pair of wire clippers, take them off, and dump them in the changing room but they made one hell of a crack—have you heard wire being cut? It made a hell of a bang so we just used ter take them off and shove them anywhere—yer know what I meant— somewhere they wouldn't be found like in a pocket of someone else's coat and . . . then we found out about the foil an we started doing that.
>
> PD: How did you find out about that? (2000: 91).

Interviews were transcribed and written up within a day or two of their taking place so that any particular nuances or impressions would not be forgotten.

because the interview is being recorded (generally recommended), the interviewer cannot take things easily. In fact, an interviewer must be attuned and responsive not just to what the interviewee is saying and not saying but also what the interviewee is doing. This is also important because something like body language can indicate that the interviewee is becoming uneasy with a line of questioning. An ethically sensitive interviewer does not place undue pressure on an interviewee and is prepared to cut short any line of questioning that is clearly a source of anxiety.

It is also likely that the kinds of questions asked will vary in terms of the different stages of a qualitative interview. Charmaz (2002) distinguished three types of questions in this connection. Note: the past and factual come first, then feelings, and finally questions of process and summing up.

- *Initial open-ended questions:* Examples are: 'What events led to . . .?'; 'What was your life like prior to . . .?'; 'Is this organization typical of others you have worked in?'

- *Intermediate questions:* 'How did you feel about . . . when you first learned about it?'; 'What immediate impact did . . . have on your life'; 'What do you like most/least about working here?'

- *Ending questions:* 'How have your views about . . . changed?'; 'What advice would you give to someone who is undergoing a similar experience . . .?'; 'If you had to do it over, would you choose to work for this organization?'

Most questions are likely to be of the intermediate kind and, in practice, some overlapping of categories is likely. Nonetheless it is a useful distinction to bear in mind.

Remember as well that interviews include different kinds of measures, such as:

- values—of interviewee, of group, of organization;

- beliefs—of interviewee, of individual others, of group;

- behaviour—of interviewee, of others;

- formal and informal roles—of interviewee, of others;

- relationships—of interviewee, of others;

- places and locales;

- emotions—particularly of the interviewee, but also possibly of others;

- encounters; and

- stories.

Try to vary the types of question asked (as suggested by Kvale's nine types outlined above) and the different phenomena just listed, if appropriate. It is also worth recalling that general questions are usually best avoided. Mason (2002) counselled against using them, arguing that when they are used, interviewees usually ask for clarification or try to contextualize the question. Vignette questions can be used in qualitative interviewing as well as in structured interviewing (see Chapter 4) and represent a way of asking specific questions. In qualitative research, vignette questions can help to ground interviewees' ideas and accounts of behaviour in particular situations (Barter and Renold 1999). By presenting interviewees with concrete and realistic scenarios, the researcher can elicit a sense of how certain contexts mould behaviour. Hughes (1998) employed the technique in a study of perceptions of HIV risk among drug injectors. In this field of research context is important, because injectors' willingness to engage in risky behaviour is influenced by situational factors. Scenarios were produced that presented risk behaviour and respondents were asked about the kinds of behaviour they felt the injectors *should* engage in (such as protected sex) and then how they felt the hypothetical injectors *would* behave (such as unprotected sex in particular situations). Hughes argued that a scenario approach is particularly valuable with sensitive topics and for eliciting a range of responses to different contexts.

Using an interview guide: an example

Box 10.7 is taken from a study of visitors to Disney theme parks (Bryman 1999). The interview is with a man in his sixties and his wife who is two years younger. They had visited Walt Disney World, and were very enthusiastic about the visit.

The sequence begins with the interviewer asking what is considered a 'direct question,' in terms of the nine question types suggested by Kvale (1996). The

Box 10.7 Part of the transcript of a semi-structured interview

Interviewer: OK. What were your views or feelings about the presentation of different cultures, as shown in, for example, Jungle Cruise or It's a Small World at the Magic Kingdom or in World Showcase at Epcot?

Wife: Well, I thought the different countries at Epcot were wonderful, but I need to say more than that, don't I?

Husband: They were very good and some were better than others, but that was down to the host countries themselves really, as I suppose each of the countries represented would have been responsible for their own part, so that's nothing to do with Disney, I wouldn't have thought. I mean some of the landmarks were hard to recognize for what they were supposed to be, but some were very well done. Britain was OK, but there was only a pub and a Welsh shop there really, whereas some of the other pavilions, as I think they were called, were good ambassadors for the countries they represented. China, for example, had an excellent 360-degree film showing parts of China and I found that very interesting.

Interviewer: Did you think there was anything lacking about the content?

Husband: Well I did notice that there weren't many black people at World Showcase, particularly the American Adventure. Now whether we were there on an unusual day in that respect I don't know, but we saw plenty of black Americans in the Magic Kingdom and other places, but very few if any in that World Showcase. And there was certainly little mention of black history in the American Adventure presentation, so maybe they felt alienated by that, I don't know, but they were noticeable by their absence.

Interviewer: So did you think there were any special emphases?

Husband: Well, thinking about it now, because I hadn't really given this any consideration before you started asking about it, but thinking about it now, it was only really representative of the developed world, you know, Britain, America, Japan, world leaders many of them in technology, and there was nothing of the Third World there. Maybe that's their own fault, maybe they were asked to participate and didn't, but now that I think about it, that does come to me. What do you think, love?

Wife: Well, like you, I hadn't thought of it like that before, but I agree with you.

---

replies are very bland and do little more than reflect the interviewees' positive feelings about their visit to Disney World. The wife acknowledges this when she says, '. . . but I need to say more than that, don't I?' Interviewees frequently know that they are expected to be expansive in their answers. This sequence occurred about halfway through the interview, so the interviewees were primed by then into realizing that more details were expected. There is almost a tinge of embarrassment that the answer is so brief and not illuminating. The husband's answer is more expansive but not particularly enlightening.

Then the first of two important prompts by the interviewer follows. The husband's response is more interesting in that he now begins to answer in terms of the possibility that black people are underrepresented at attractions like the American Adventure, which tells the story of America via a debate between Mark Twain and Benjamin Franklin. The second prompt yields further useful reflection, this time that Third World countries are underrepresented in

World Showcase in the Epcot Centre. The couple are clearly aware that the prompting has made them provide these reflections when they say: 'Well, thinking about it now, because I hadn't really given this any consideration before you started asking about it.' This is the whole point of prompting—to get the interviewee to think more about the topic and to provide an opportunity for a more detailed response. It is not a leading question, since the interviewees were not being asked 'Do you think that the Disney company fails to recognize the significance of black history (or ignores the Third World) in its presentation of different cultures?' There is no doubt that the prompts elicit the more interesting replies, precisely their role.

Recording and transcription

The point has been made several times that in qualitative research the interview is usually audio-recorded and then transcribed (not just listened to)

whenever possible (see Box 10.8). Qualitative researchers are frequently interested not just in what people say but also in the way they say it. If this aspect is to be fully woven into an analysis, the complete series of exchanges in an interview must be available. Also, because interviewers are supposed to be highly alert to what is being said—following up interesting points made, prompting and probing where necessary, drawing attention to any inconsistencies in the interviewee's answers—it is best if they do not also have to concentrate on writing down what is said.

As with just about everything in social research, there is a cost (other than the financial one of buying recording equipment and tapes or disks) in that the use of a recorder may upset respondents, who become self-conscious or alarmed at the prospect of their words being preserved. Most people will allow their interview to be recorded, though it is not un-

common for a small number to refuse, and these interviews can be done by writing down responses as an alternative. This advice also applies to cases of malfunctioning recording equipment. Among those who do agree to be recorded, some will not get over their fear at being confronted with a microphone, and as a result, their interviews may not be as interesting as others.

In qualitative research, there is often a large amount of variation in the time that interviews take. For example, in Wilson's rave study (2002), the interviews lasted between 45 minutes and 4 hours. It should not be assumed that shorter interviews are necessarily inferior to longer, with the exception of those marked by interviewee non-cooperation or anxiety about being recorded. Indeed, when a long interview contains very little of significance it may not be worth the time and cost of transcription. Thankfully, such occasions are relatively unusual. If people do agree to be interviewed, they usually do so in a cooperative way and loosen up after initial anxiety about the microphone. As a result, even short interviews are often quite revealing.

Transcribing interviews is very time-consuming—five to six hours of transcription for every hour of speech. Also, transcription yields vast amounts of text that then must be read. Beardsworth and Keil (1992: 262) reported that their 73 interviews on vegetarianism (see Box 10.3) generated 'several hundred thousand words of transcript material.' It is clear, therefore, that, while transcription has the advan-

---

Box 10.8 ☼ *Why record and transcribe interviews?*

With approaches that entail detailed attention to language, such as conversation analysis and discourse analysis (see Chapter 16), the recording of conversations and interviews is to all intents and purposes mandatory. However, researchers who use qualitative interviews and focus groups also see the following advantages in such recording:

- it allows public scrutiny by other researchers, who can evaluate the original analysis, even conduct a secondary analysis;

- it therefore helps to counter accusations that an analysis was influenced by a researcher's values or biases; and

- it allows the data to be reused in ways other than intended by the original researcher—for example, in the light of new theoretical ideas or analytic strategies.

However, it has to be recognized that the procedure takes a lot of time. Also, there is some debate on having the interviewer transcribe the data (more familiar with what actually was said) or hiring an outside contractor (less time-consuming) to transcribe the interviews (Rafaeli *et al.* 1997: 14).

Practical tip ☞ *Transcribing interviews*

A student doing research for a thesis may not have the resources to pay for professional transcription and unless an accurate touch typist, it can take a lot longer than the suggested five to six hours per hour of speech. Access to a transcription machine with a foot operated stop-start mechanism makes the task of transcription much easier. However, the important thing is to allow sufficient time for transcription and be realistic about how many interviews can be transcribed in the time available.

tage of keeping intact the interviewee's (and interviewer's) words, it does so by piling up the text to be analyzed. It is no wonder that writers like Lofland and Lofland (1995) advise that the analysis of qualitative data not be left until after all the interviews have been completed and transcribed. To procrastinate may create the impression that the task is overwhelming. Also, there are good grounds for making analysis an ongoing activity, because it allows the researcher to be more aware of the emerging themes that can then be investigated in a more direct way in later interviews (see Box 10.3 for an example).

It is easy to view transcription as a relatively unproblematic translation of the spoken into the written word. However, given the importance of transcripts in qualitative research, the issue should not be taken lightly. Transcribers need to be trained in much the same way that interviewers are. Moreover, even among experienced transcribers errors occur. Poland (1995) provided some fascinating examples of the mistakes in transcription that can result from many different factors (mishearing, fatigue, or care-

lessness). For example, one transcript contained the following passage:

> I think unless we want to become like other countries, where people have, you know, democratic freedoms . . .

But the actual words on the audio-tape were:

> I think unless we want to become like other countries, where people have no democratic freedoms . . . (1995: 294)

Steps clearly need to be taken to check on the quality of transcription.

Flexibility in the interview

A further point is the need for a flexible approach to interviewing in qualitative research. This advice is more than needing to be responsive to what interviewees say and following up the interesting points they make. Flexibility is important in such areas as varying the order of questions, following up leads, and clearing up inconsistencies in answers. It is important in other respects too, such as coping with audio-recording equipment breakdown and refusals by interviewees to allow a recording to take place. A further element is that interviewers often find that, as soon as they switch off their recording equipment, the interviewee continues to ruminate on the topic of interest and frequently says more interesting things than in the interview itself. It is usually not feasible to switch the machine back on again, so try to take some notes either while the person is talking or as soon as possible after the interview. Such 'unsolicited accounts' can often be the source of revealing

---

Practical tip ☞ *Transcribing sections of an interview*

Quite often whole interviews or at least large portions of them are not useful, perhaps because interviewees are reticent or they are not as relevant to the research topic as originally envisioned. There seems little point in transcribing such material. For example, Gerson and Horowitz (2002: 211) found some of their qualitative interviews 'uninspiring and uninteresting.' Therefore, one suggestion is to listen to the interviews closely, at least once or more usually twice, and then only transcribe those portions that seem useful or relevant. (What would the participants have to be told to make this ethical—or is that not an issue?) The same applies to focus group research, often more difficult and time-consuming to transcribe than personal interview recordings because of the number of speakers involved. The downside is missing things, thus requiring a going back to the tapes at a later stage of the analysis to find something that emerged as significant only later on.

Practical tip ☞ *Keeping the recorder going*

Since interviewees sometimes 'open up' at the end of the interview, just when the recording device has been switched off, there are good grounds for keeping it switched on as long as possible. So, when winding down the interview, do not switch off the tape-recorder immediately. How unethical is it just to pretend to turn it off? What if it is still running but the respondent thinks it is off and says, 'Now that the machine is off, let me add . . .'?

information. This is certainly what Parker, in his study of organizations, found with 'unrecorded comments prefixed with a silent or explicit "well, if you want to know what I really think." . . . Needless to say, a visit to the toilet to write up as much as I could remember followed almost immediately' (2000: 236).

Online interviews

Although online interviews run a greater risk than face-to-face interviews of a respondent dropping out of the exchange, Mann and Stewart (2000: 138–9) suggested that in fact a relationship of mutual trust can be built up. It requires interviewers to keep sending messages to respondents to reassure them that their written utterances are helpful and significant, especially since interviewing through the Internet is still an unfamiliar experience for most people. This kind of relationship also can make it easier for the longer-term commitment required in an online interview to be maintained. Taking longer also makes it easier for the researcher to go back to interviewees for further information or reflections, something that is difficult to do with the face-to-face personal interview.

A further issue for the online personal interviewer is whether to send all the questions at once or to interview on a question followed by reply basis. The problem with the former tactic is that respondents can read all the questions and may only reply to those that they feel interested in, so asking one question at a time is likely to be more reliable. Bampton and Cowton (2002) reported their conducting e-mail interviews by sending questions in small batches. They argued that this approach takes pressure off interviewees to reply quickly, gives them the opportunity to provide considered replies (although the authors recognized that there can be a loss of spontaneity), and gives the interviewers greater opportunity to respond to interviewees' answers.

Evidence shows that prospective interviewees are more likely to agree to participate if their agreement is solicited prior to sending them the actual questions. Another good idea is for the researcher to provide some self-disclosure, such as directing the person being contacted to the researcher's website that contains personal information and particularly information relevant to the research issue (Curasi 2001; O'Connor and Madge 2001, 2003). The reason for ob-

taining agreement from interviewees before sending them questions to be asked is that unsolicited e-mail, often referred to as 'spamming,' is regarded as a nuisance among online users and can result in an immediate refusal to take the message seriously. See Box 10.9 for more about online interviews.

Curasi (2001) compared 24 online interviews concerned with shopping on the Internet carried out through e-mail correspondence to 24 parallel face-to-face interviews and found that:

- face-to-face interviewers are better than online in maintaining rapport with respondents;

- because greater commitment and motivation are required for completing an online interview, replies are often more detailed than in face-to-face interviews; and

- online interviewees' answers tend to be more considered and grammatically correct because they have more time to ponder and tidy up their answers before sending them. Whether this is a positive feature is debatable: there is the obvious advantage of a 'clean' transcript, but there may be some loss of spontaneity.

On the other hand, Curasi found the least detail from online interviews, perhaps because replies must be typed not just spoken. The full significance of this difference in the nature of the respondents' mode of answering has not been fully appreciated.

The use of a webcam may offer further possibilities for online personal interviews, making the online interview similar to a telephone one, but also similar to an in-person interview because those involved in the exchange would be able to see each other. However, one of the main advantages of the online interview would be lost; respondents' answers would need to be transcribed, as in traditional qualitative interviewing.

Box 10.9 Online interviews

Markham's (1998) approach to life on the Net involved interviews. The interviews followed a period of 'lurking' (reading but not participating) in computer-mediated communication forums like chat rooms. The asking and answering of questions were in real time, rather than what might occur via e-mail, where a question might be answered several hours or days later. She used an interview guide and the interviews lasted between one hour and over four hours. Such interviews are a very real challenge for both interviewer and interviewee because neither party can pick up on visual cues (puzzlement, anxiety) or auditory cues (sighs, groans).

One of Markham's interests lay in the reality of online experiences. This can be seen in the following brief sequence (Markham is Annette):

> *Annette:* How real are your experiences in the Internet?
>
> *Sherie:* How real are experiences off the Internet? (1998: 115)

In fact, Markham noted how her notion of 'real' was different from that of her interviewees. For Markham 'real' carried a connotation of genuineness or authenticity but for her interviewees it was more to do with distinguishing experiences that occur offline (real) from those online (not real). It is likely that these distinctions between life online and life offline will become less significant as younger people growing up with the Internet conduct large portions of their lives online.

Kendall (1999: 62) would support this. She spent three years as an online participant observer along with conducting face-to-face interviews and attending face-to-face gatherings. She was interested in issues to do with identity and the online presentation of self; interestingly, she found (among other things) that the participants give higher status to embodied experiences (real) over mediated ones (online and not real).

Thus, while much research on the Internet treats the technology as a given, recent thinking on technology has preferred to examine how the technology is interpreted by users. Taking this position, Hine (2000: 9) located the Internet 'as a product of culture . . . shaped by the ways in which it is marketed, taught, and used.' Thus it can be 'not real' or inferior to embodied experience.

Focus groups: an introduction

Most people think of an interview as involving an interviewer and one interviewee. The focus group technique, however, involves more than one, usually at least four, interviewees. Essentially it is a group interview with an interest in how people, in conjunction with their interactions with one another, feel about selected general topics.

Most focus group researchers work within a qualitative research tradition and this is why the topic has been placed here. This means they explicitly want to reveal how group participants view issues and aim to provide a fairly unstructured setting with the person who runs the focus group session, usually called the *moderator* or *facilitator,* expected to guide each session but not intrude. What can distinguish focus groups from other qualitative approaches are:

- The technique allows the researcher to develop an understanding about *why* people feel the way they do. In a normal individual interview, the intervie-

wee is often asked about reasons for holding a particular view, but the focus group approach offers the opportunity of allowing people to probe each other's reasons for holding it. This can be more interesting than the sometimes-predictable question-followed-by-answer approach of normal interviews. For one thing, an individual may answer in a certain way in a focus group, but after hearing others may want to qualify or modify a view. Alternatively some may want to voice agreement to something that they probably would not have thought of without hearing the views of others. These possibilities mean that focus groups can elicit a wide variety of different views on an issue.

- In conventional one-to-one interviewing, interviewees are rarely challenged; they may say things that are inconsistent with earlier replies or that patently cannot be true, but interviewers are often reluctant to point out such deficiencies. In a focus group, individuals often argue with each other and challenge each other's views. Arguing means the researcher may get more realistic accounts of what people think, because they are forced to think about and possibly revise their views.

• The focus group offers an opportunity to study how individuals collectively make sense of a phenomenon and construct meanings around it. It is a central tenet of theoretical positions like symbolic interactionism, that coming to terms with and understanding social phenomena are not un-dertaken by an individual in isolation. Instead, it is something that occurs in interaction and discussion with others. In this sense, therefore, focus groups reflect the processes through which meaning is constructed in everyday life and to that extent can be more naturalistic (see Box 2.3 on the idea of naturalism) than individual interviews (Wilkinson 1998). On the other hand, whether these new insights will persist beyond the actual group session, which they would have to, to be called 'natural,' has not been studied.

Conducting focus groups

A number of practical aspects of conducting a focus group require some discussion.

How many groups?

How many groups are needed? Table 10.1 provides data on the number of groups and other aspects of the composition of actual focus groups (cf. Deacon et al. 1999). As it suggests, there is a good deal of variation in the numbers of groups used, but generally they range from 10 to 15.

Clearly, it is unlikely that just one group is sufficient, since the responses may be peculiar to that one group. Besides time and resources, there are also strong arguments for saying that having many groups is unnecessary. When the moderator can an-

Table 10.1 Composition of groups in focus group research

Authors	Frohlich et al. (2002)	Kitzinger (1993, 1994)	Lupton (1996)	Macnaghten and Jacobs (1997)	Miraftab (2000)	Schlesinger et al. (1992)
Area of research	A contextual understanding of pre-adolescent smoking behaviour	Audience responses to media messages about AIDS	Responses to diet and health controversies	Understanding and identification with sustainable development	Housing experiences of Kurdish and Somali refugees in Vancouver	Responses of women to watching violence
Number of groups	Not specified	52	12	8 (each group had 2 sessions)	Not specified	14
Size range of groups	Probably 12	Not specified but appears to be 3–9 or 10	3–5	6–10	10–15 '	5–9
Average (mean) size of groups	NA	6.75	4.1	approximately 8	NA	6.6
Criteria (if any) for inclusion	4 groups out of 32 Quebec communities	No, but groups made up of specific groups (e.g., retirement club members, male prostitutes)	Gender	Age, ethnicity, gender, occupation/ retired, rural/ urban location	None, except being recent immigrant	Experience of violence, Scottish/ English, ethnicity, class
Natural groups	No	Yes	Yes	No	No	Some

Practical Tip ☞ *Number of focus groups*

Focus groups take a long time to arrange and a long time to transcribe the recordings that are made. Most students will not be able to include as many focus group sessions for projects or dissertations as the studies cited in this chapter and will therefore need to make do with a smaller number of groups in most instances. Make sure to be able to justify the number of groups chosen and why the data are still significant.

ticipate fairly accurately what the next group is going to say, there are probably enough groups. This notion is similar to the *theoretical saturation* criterion briefly introduced in Chapter 9.

One factor that can affect the number of groups is whether the researcher thinks that the range of views is likely to be affected by sociodemographic factors, such as age, gender, class, and so on. Many focus group researchers like to ensure that different demographic groups are included, resulting in a larger number of groups. In connection with the research described in Box 10.11, Kitzinger (1994) wrote that a large number of groups is preferred, to capture as much diversity in perspectives as possible. On the other hand, more groups increase the complexity of

the analysis. For example, Schlesinger *et al.* (1992: 29; see Table 10.1 and Box 10.10) reported that their 14 tape-recorded hour-long sessions produced more than 1400 pages of transcription for analysis.

Size of groups and selecting participants

How large should groups be? Morgan (1998*a*) suggested 6 to 10 members. To control for the problem of 'no-shows,' overrecruiting is sometimes employed (e.g., Wilkinson 1999*a*: 188). This point aside, he recommended smaller groups when participants are likely to have a lot to say, as often occurs when participants are emotionally involved with the topic. He also suggested smaller groups for topics that are controversial or complex and when uncovering personal accounts is a major goal. Larger groups are appropriate when the researcher wants 'to hear numerous brief suggestions' (Morgan 1998*a*: 75).

Most topics do not require a particular kind of participant, except that the topic should be relevant to them. A wide range of people is often required, but they may be organized into separate groups in terms of criteria, such as age, gender, education, and having or not having had a certain experience. The aim is to then look for any systematic variation in how the different groups discuss a matter. For exam-

Box 10.10 Asking about violence

Some researchers want to inject some structure into their focus group sessions. An example of this is the research on the viewing of violence by women conducted by Schlesinger *et al.* (1992; see Table 10.1). For example, in relation to the rape scene, the reactions of the audiences were gleaned through 'guiding questions' under five main headings, the first three of which had several more specific elements:

- Initially, participants were given the opportunity to discuss the film in terms of such issues as: perceived purpose of the film, realism, and story line.

- The questioning then moved to reactions to the characters such as: the woman who is raped; the three rapists; the female lawyer; and the male lawyers.

- Participants were then asked about their reactions to scenes, such as: the rape; the female lawyer's decision

to support the case after initially not supporting it; and winning the case.

- Participants were asked for their reactions to the inclusion of the rape scene.

- Finally, they were asked about how they perceived the film's value, in particular whether the film being American made a difference to their reactions.

While the research by Schlesinger *et al.* (1992) clearly examined a lot of specific topics, initial questions were designed to generate relatively open-ended reactions. Such a general approach to questioning, fairly common in focus group research, allows the researcher to navigate between addressing the research questions and ensuring comparability between sessions and, on the other side, allowing participants to raise issues they see as significant and in their own terms.

ple, to examine responses of women to viewing violence, Schlesinger *et al.* (1992) showed 14 groups (see Table 10.1) four levels of visual mass-media violence: incidental violence, some violence, marital violence, and an extremely vivid sexual assault scene. The authors concluded:

> Having a particular experience or a particular background does significantly affect the interpretation of a given text. The four programs screened are obviously open to various readings. However, on the evidence, *how* they are read is fundamentally affected by various sociocultural factors and by lived experience (Schlesinger *et al.* 1992: 168; emphases in original).

A slight variation on this approach is Kitzinger's (1994) study of reactions to media representations of AIDS (see Box 10.11 and Table 10.1). Her groups were made up of people in a variety of different situations. Some were what she called 'general population groups' (e.g., a team of civil engineers working on the same site) but others were made up of those that might have a special interest in AIDS (e.g., male prostitutes or intravenous drug users). Increasingly, focus group practitioners try to discern patterns of variation by putting together groups with a particular attribute or cluster of attributes.

A further issue in selecting group participants is whether to select people who are unknown to each other or to use natural groups (e.g., friends, co-workers, or students in the same class). Some researchers prefer to exclude people who know each other, fearing that pre-existing styles of interaction or status differences may contaminate the session. Others prefer to select natural groups whenever possible (see Kitzinger, Box 10.11, and Table 10.1). Holbrook and Jackson (1996) reported that, for their research on shopping centres, they initially tried to secure participants unknown to each other, but this strategy attracted no takers. They then sought out participants in various social clubs in the vicinity of the centres. Their new view was defended by arguing that, because of their interest in research questions concerning shopping in relation to the construction of identity and how it relates to people's sense of place, recruiting people who know each other would be a highly appropriate strategy. See Ethical issue 10.1.

Opting to only recruit people from natural groups is not always feasible, however, because of difficul-

---

Box 10.11 Focus group in action: AIDS in the Media Research Project

Focus group research was part of a larger project on the representation of AIDS in the mass media. The focus groups were concerned with the examination of how 'media messages are explored by audiences and how understandings of AIDS are constructed. We were interested not solely in what people thought but in *how* they thought and *why* they thought as they did' (Kitzinger 1994: 104).

Details of the groups are given in Table 10.1. Since one goal of the research was to emphasize the role of interaction in the construction of meaning, it was important to provide a platform for enhancing this feature. Accordingly, 'instead of working with isolated individuals, or collections of individuals drawn together simply for the purposes of the research, we elected to work with pre-existing groups—people who already lived, worked or socialized together' (Kitzinger 1993: 272). As a result, the groups were made up of such collections of people as a team of civil engineers working on the same site, six members of a retirement club, intravenous drug users, and so on. The sessions themselves are described as having been 'conducted in a relaxed fashion with minimal intervention from the facilitator—at least at first' (Kitzinger 1994: 106). Each session lasted approximately two hours and was tape-recorded.

---

ties in getting everyone in the group to participate. In addition, Morgan (1998*a*) articulated a downside; people in natural groups know each other and may operate with taken-for-granted assumptions that they feel do not need to be brought to the fore. He

---

Ethical issue 10.1 *Changing one's mind*

Was the switch from saying that the research needed people unknown to each other to actually using natural groups, because of difficulty in getting the former, ethical? A similar question occurs when a researcher's deductive hypothesis is unsupported. Is it ethical to change the original approach to grounded theory, where the data come first, and thus establish congruence between theory and data?

suggested that if it is important for the researcher to bring out such assumptions, groups of strangers are better.

Asking questions and level of moderator involvement

There are different questioning strategies and approaches to moderating focus group sessions. Most seem to approximate a practice that lies between a rather open-ended approach and a somewhat more structured one. For example, Macnaghten and Jacobs (1997) employed a 'topic guide' and grouped topics to be covered into areas of discussion. Their middle-of-the road approach to question structuring can be seen in the following passage in which a group of working women reveal a cynicism about government and experts regarding the reality of environmental problems (in this passage 'F' is 'female' and 'Mod' is moderator):

> *F:* They only tell us what they want us to know. And that's just the end of that, so we are left with a fog in your brain, so you just think—what have I to worry about? I don't know what they're on about.
>
> *Mod:* So why do Government only tell us what they want us to hear?
>
> *F:* To keep your confidence going. (All together)
>
> *Mod:* So if someone provides an indicator which says the economy is improving you won't believe it?
>
> *F:* They've been saying it for about 10 years, but where? I can't see anything!
>
> *F:* Every time there's an election they say the economy is improving (Macnaghten and Jacobs 1997: 18).

In this passage, there is an emphasis on the topic to be addressed but also a capacity to pick up on what the group says.

How involved should the moderator/facilitator be? This question is similar to the considerations about how unstructured an interview should be in qualitative interviewing. In qualitative research, the aim is to get at the perspectives of those being studied. Consequently, the approach should not be intrusive and too structured. There is, therefore, a tendency for researchers to use a fairly small number of very general questions to guide the focus group session. Obviously, if the discussion goes off at a total tangent it may be necessary to refocus the participants' attention, but even then it is necessary to be careful, because what may appear to be digressions may in fact reveal something of interest to the group participants. More direction is also probably needed if the research questions are not picked up by participants or when a particularly interesting point made by one participant is not followed up by others (see Box 10.6).

Clearly, the moderator has to straddle two positions and each tactic—intervention and non-intervention—carries risks. The style of questioning and moderating depends on things like the nature of the research topic (is it embarrassing, for example, requiring more intrusion) and levels of interest and/or knowledge among participants in the research. A low level of participant interest may require a somewhat more structured approach. If in doubt the best advice is to err on the side of minimal intervention.

Recording and transcription

Even more important than in interviewing for qualitative research, the focus group session needs to be recorded. Writing down not only exactly what people say but also who says it is too difficult, especially if more than one person is speaking at once. In an individual interview one may be able to ask a respondent to 'hold on' while writing something down, but doing this in an interview involving several rapidly speaking people is generally too disruptive.

Transcribing focus group sessions is also more complicated and hence more time-consuming than transcribing traditional interview recordings. Sometimes people's voices are hard to distinguish, making it difficult to decide who is speaking. Also, people sometimes talk over each other, which can make transcription even more unreliable. Therefore, a very high-quality microphone, one capable of picking up even quite faint voices from many directions is a necessity. Focus group transcripts always seem to have more missing bits, due to lack of audibility, than transcripts from conventional interviews.

Group interaction in focus group sessions

Kitzinger (1994) observed that reports of focus group research frequently do not take group interaction into account. This is surprising, because it is precisely the forms of social interaction and their impact that would seem to distinguish a focus group session from an individual interview. Wilkinson reviewed over 200 studies, published between 1946 and 1996, based on focus groups and concluded: 'Focus group data is most commonly presented as if it were one-to-one interview data, with interactions between group participants rarely reported, let alone analyzed' (1998: 112).

In the context of her research on the coverage of AIDS in the mass media, Kitzinger (1994) drew attention to two types of interaction in focus groups: complementary and argumentative interactions. The former brings out those elements of the social world that provide participants their own frameworks of understanding. They are often an emergent product of the interaction, with each participant building on the preceding remark, as in the following passage taken from Morgan and Spanish's (1985: 414) research on heart attack victims:

No. 1: But I think maybe what we're saying here is that there's no one cause of heart attacks, there's no one type of person, there's probably umpteen different types of heart attacks and causes coming from maybe smoking, maybe obesity, maybe stress, maybe design fault, hereditary, overwork, change in life style. Any of these things in themselves could be . . .

No. 2: And when you start putting them in combination [unclear].

No. 3: Yeah, you may be really magnifying each one of these particular things.

No. 2: Yeah, and depending on how, and in each person that magnification is different. Some people can take a little stress without doing any damage, some people can take a little smoking, a little drinking, a little obesity, without doing any damage. But you take a little of each of these and put them together and you're starting to increase the chances of damage. And any one of these that takes a magnitude leap increases the chances.

This sequence brings out the emerging consensus around the question of who has heart attacks and why. No. 1 summarizes several factors that have been discussed; No. 2 then introduces the possible significance of some of these factors existing in combination; No. 3 agrees about the importance of combinations of factors; and No. 2 summarizes the position of the group on the salience of combinations of factors, raising at the same time the possibility that for each person there may be unique combinations of factors that are responsible for heart attacks.

However, as Kitzinger (1994) suggested, arguments in focus groups can be equally revealing and moderators can play an important role in identifying differences of opinion, and exploring with participants the factors that lie behind them. Disagreement can provide participants with a chance to revise their opinions or to think more about the reasons why they hold them. By way of illustration, a passage from Schlesinger *et al.* (1992; see Table 10.1) is presented. The group is made up of women with no experience of violence. The debate is concerned with the rape scene:

Speaker 1: I think . . . that they could've explained it. They could easily leave [out] that rape scene.

Speaker 2: But it's like that other film we watched. You don't realize the full impact, like, the one we were watching, the first one, until you've got the reconstruction.

Speaker 3: Yeah, but I think with that sort of film, it would cause more damage than it would good, I mean, if someone had been raped, would you like to have [to] sit through that again?

The debate then continued to consider the significance of the scene for men:

Speaker 1: Men would sit down and think, 'Well, she asked for it. She was enjoying it and look, the men around enjoyed it' (Schlesinger *et al.* 1992: 51–2).

One factor, then, that seems to be behind the unease of some of the women about the inclusion of the vivid rape scene is that men may enjoy it, rather than find it repulsive, and identify with the onlookers in the film. This account came about because of earlier disagreement within the group and allowed a rounded account of women's reactions to the scene to be forged.

In sum, as Kitzinger (1994) argued, drawing attention to patterns of interaction within focus groups allows a researcher to determine how group participants in their own terms view the issues with which they are confronted. The posing of questions by and then agreement and disagreement among participants help to bring out their own stances on these issues. The resolution of disagreements also helps to force participants to express the grounds on which they hold particular views.

At the time of writing, possibilities associated with conducing online focus groups have probably attracted greater attention than online personal interviews, perhaps because the potential advantages are greater with the former. For example, with focus groups, a great deal of time and administration can be saved by working online, whereas there is less comparable saving with online personal interviews, unless a great deal of travel is involved.

Limitations of focus groups

Focus groups clearly have considerable potential when the process through which meaning is jointly constructed is of particular interest. They also offer considerable potential for feminist researchers. What, then, are their chief limitations?

- The researcher probably has less control over proceedings than with the individual interview. As seen, not all writers on focus groups perceive this as a problem and indeed feminist researchers often see it as an advantage. However, the question of control raises issues for how far a researcher can allow focus groups to 'take over' the running of proceedings. There is clearly a delicate balance to be taken into account over how involved moderators should be and how far a set of prompts or questions should influence the conduct of focus groups. What is not clear is the degree to which it is appropriate to surrender that control, especially when there is a reasonably explicit set of research questions to be answered, as is commonly the case, especially in funded research.

- A huge amount of data can be very quickly produced. For example, Bloor *et al.* (2001) suggested that one focus group session can take up to eight hours to transcribe, somewhat longer than an equivalent personal interview, because of variations in voice pitch and the need to take account of who says what. Also focus group recordings are particularly prone to inaudible comments from those far away from the microphone, which affects transcription.

- The data are difficult to analyze. Developing a strategy of analysis that incorporates both the themes in what is said and patterns of interaction is not easy.

- They are difficult to organize both in terms of initial agreement and turning up at a particular time. Very small payments, such as book tokens, are sometimes made to induce participation, but nonetheless it is common for people not to turn up.

- There are possible problems of group effects. This includes the obvious problem of dealing with reticent speakers and with those who hog the stage. Krueger (1998) suggested making clear to group participants that other people's views are definitely required; for example, he suggested saying something like 'That's one point of view. Does anyone have another point of view?' (1998: 59). As for those who do not speak very much, it is recommended that they be actively encouraged to say something.

In another context, it would be interesting to know how far agreement among focus group participants is more frequently encountered than disagreement, perhaps due to group pressure to conform. Related is the fact that participants in a group setting may be more prone to expressing socially acceptable views than in individual interviews. Morgan (2002) cited a study in which group interviews, with boys discussing relationships with girls, were compared with individual interviews with them on the same topic. Alone, the boys express a degree of sensitivity

Box 10.12 Advantages and disadvantages of online focus group and personal interviews compared to face-to-face interviews in qualitative research

This box summarizes the main advantages and disadvantages of online focus groups and personal interviews compared to their face-to-face counterparts. The two methods are combined because the tally of advantages and disadvantages applies more or less equally well to both of them.

Advantages

- Online interviews and focus groups are extremely cheap to conduct compared to comparable face-to-face equivalents. They are likely to take longer.

- Interviewees or focus group participants otherwise normally inaccessible (e.g., in another country) or hard to involve in research (e.g., very senior executives, and other very busy people) are more easily involved.

- Interviewees and focus group participants are able to reread their (and in focus groups, others') previously written statements.

- The interviews do not have to be audio-recorded, thus eliminating interviewee apprehension about speaking and being recorded and time-consuming expensive transcription.

- The transcripts of the interviews are more accurate because mishearing and not hearing do not arise. This is a particular advantage with focus group discussions because it is clear who is contributing even when several are 'speaking' at the same time.

- Focus group participants can employ pseudonyms to conceal their identity making it easier for them to discuss embarrassing issues or to divulge potentially unpopular views. The same holds true for electronic interviews; they may make the discussion of sensitive issues easier than in face-to-face interviews.

- In focus groups, shy or quiet participants may find it easier to participate and overbearing participants are less likely to predominate, though variations in keyboard skills may militate against equal participation.

- Participants are less likely to be influenced by characteristics like the age, ethnicity, or appearance (and possibly even gender if pseudonyms are used) of other participants in a focus group.

- Similarly, interviewees and focus group participants are less likely to be affected by characteristics of interviewers or moderators respectively, so that interviewer bias is less likely.

- When interviewees and participants are online at home, they are essentially being provided with an 'anonymous, safe and non-threatening environment' (O'Connor and Madge 2002: 11.2) one that may be especially helpful to vulnerable groups.

- Similarly, researchers are not confronted with the potentially discomfiting experience of having to enter what may be unsafe environments.

Disadvantages

- Only people with access to online facilities and/or who find them relatively straightforward are likely to be in a position to participate.

- It is more difficult for the interviewer to establish rapport with interviewees. This is less of a problem when the topic is of greater interest to participants.

- Probing is more difficult, though not impossible. Curasi (2001) reported some success in eliciting further information from respondents but it is easier for interviewees to ignore or forget about these requests for further information or for expansion on answers given.

- There is less spontaneity of response since interviewees can reflect on their answers much more than is possible in a face-to-face situation. However, this can be construed as an advantage in some respects since interviewees are likely to give more considered replies.

- There is a tendency for non-response to be higher in online personal interviews.

- The researcher cannot be certain that the people who are interviewed are who they say they are (though this issue may apply on occasion to face-to-face interviews as well).

- Online interviews and focus groups from home require considerable commitment from interviewees and participants if they have to install software onto their computers and remain online for extended periods of time, thereby incurring expense (though offering remuneration for such costs is possible) and blocking their telephone lines.

- The interviewer/moderator may not be aware that the interviewee/participant is distracted by something and in such circumstances will continue to ask questions as if they had the person's full attention.

- Online connections may be lost and long breakdowns can undermine confidence and any momentum in interaction that has been built up.

- Interviewers cannot capitalize upon body language that might suggest puzzlement or in the case of focus groups a thwarted desire to contribute to the discussion.

Adapted from Adrianssens and Cadman (1999); Bampton and Cowton (2002); Clapper and Massey (1996); Curasi (2001); Mann and Stewart (2000); O'Connor and Madge (2001); Sweet (2001); Tse (1999).

not present in the group context, where more macho views tend to be forthcoming, suggesting that the boys are seeking to impress others and influenced by the norms of their peer group. However, this does not render the group interview data tainted, because it may be precisely the gulf between privately and publicly held views that is of interest.

- Madriz (2000) proposed that there are circumstances when individual interviews are more appropriate. One is when participants are likely to disagree profoundly with each other, a second when some participants may not be comfortable in each other's presence (e.g., bringing people in a pre-existing hierarchical relationship together). Finally, because of the potential for focus groups to cause discomfort among participants, for example, when intimate details of private lives need to be revealed, an individual interview, or even a self-completion questionnaire may be better, but see Box 10.12.

Online focus groups

Selecting participants for focus groups is always potentially difficult, complicated further for online groups in that all must have access to the necessary hardware and software. One source of participants for online focus groups is posting on appropriate special interest websites, special interest bulletin boards, or chat rooms.

Mann and Stewart (2000) advocated that an online focus group have between six and eight people, not larger because that can make it difficult for some people to participate, especially those with limited keyboard skills. Also, moderating the session can be more difficult with a large number and as Adrienssens and Cadman (1999) have suggested, large groups can present management problems.

Before starting an online focus group session, moderators are advised to send out a welcome message introducing the research and laying out some of the ground rules for the ongoing discussion. There is evidence that participants respond more positively if the researchers reveal something about themselves (Curasi 2001). This can be done in the opening message or by creating links to a personal website.

In online focus groups participants make contributions more or less immediately after a previous one (whether from the moderator or other participants). As all are simultaneously online, contributions can be responded to as soon as they are typed (and with some forms of software, the contributions can be seen as they are being typed). As Mann and Stewart (2000) observed, because several participants can type in a response to something at the same time, the convention of taking turns in regular conversations is largely sidelined.

Online focus groups are unlikely to replace their face-to-face counterparts but instead are likely to be used for certain kinds of research topics and/or samples. As regards the latter, dispersed or inaccessible people are especially relevant to online focus group research; slow typists are not. As Sweet (2001) pointed out, relevant topics are likely to be those involving sensitive issues or about Internet use itself, for example, Boxes 10.9 and 10.13.

Feminism and interviewing in qualitative research

Unstructured and semi-structured interviewing are prominent in feminist research, in part reflecting a preference for qualitative research. But their popularity also reflects a view that a qualitative interview realizes many of the goals of feminist research, and thus is especially appropriate. Indeed, it has been expressed that 'Whilst several brave women in the 1980s defended quantitative methods, it is nonetheless still

Box 10.13 An online focus group study

O'Connor and Madge (2001, 2003; see also Madge and O'Connor 2002) employed conferencing software in connection with a virtual focus group study of the use of one online information website for parents. Initially, the researchers set up a web survey on use of the parenting website. When respondents sent in their questionnaire, they were thanked for their participation and asked via e-mail by the researchers whether they were prepared to be interviewed in depth. Of the 155 respondents who returned questionnaires, 16 agreed to be interviewed. Interviewees were sent the software to install on their own machines. The researchers tried to ensure that each group was asked more or less the same questions, so the researchers worked in pairs whereby one cut and pasted questions into the discussion (or otherwise typed questions) and the other acted as a focus group moderator by thinking about the evolution of the discussion and about when and how to intervene. For each session, the researchers introduced themselves and asked participants to do likewise. In addition, they had placed descriptions and photographs of themselves on a website to which participants were directed. An important part of the process of building rapport was the fact that both of the researchers were mothers. One of the findings reported is that the greater anonymity afforded by the Internet gives participants greater confidence in asking embarrassing questions, a finding that has implications for online focus groups. This can be seen in the following extract:

Amy: I feel better asking BW [Babyworld] than my health visitor as they're not going to see how bad I am at housekeeping!!!

Kerry: I feel the same. Like the HV [health visitor] is judging even though she says she isn't

Kerry: Although my HV has been a lifeline as I suffer from PND [post-natal depression]

Amy: Also, there are some things that are so little that you don't want to feel like you're wasting anyone's time. Asking the HV or GP might get in the way of something mroe important, whereas sending an e-mail, the person can answer it when convenient

Amy: My HV is very good, but her voice does sound patronising. I'msure she doesn't mean it, but it does get to me . . .

Kerry: Being anon means that you don't get embarrassed asking about a little point or something personal (O'Connor and Madge 2001: 10.4).

It is striking that this brief extract reveals a good flow without intervention by the researchers. It contains several mistakes (e.g., 'I'msure') but these are retained to preserve the reality of the interaction. The researchers do not have to transcribe the material because it is already in textual form. Also, the fact that participants appear to relish the anonymity of the Internet as a source of information has implications for online focus groups because participants may find it easier to ask naïve questions or make potentially embarrassing comments than in face-to-face focus groups.

---

the case that not just qualitative methods, but the in-depth face-to-face interview has become the paradigmatic "feminist method"' (Kelly *et al.* 1994: 34). The point is not that such interviewing is somehow more in tune with feminist values than, say, ethnography (especially since interviewing is often an ingredient of ethnographic research), but that it is usually less invasive to participants and less time-consuming for researchers, than perhaps ethnography.

Moreover, it is specifically interviewing of the kind conducted in qualitative research that has potential for a feminist approach, not the structured interview associated with social survey research. Why would one type of interview be more consistent with feminism than the other? In a frequently

cited article, Oakley made the following points about the standard survey interview.

- It is a one-way process—the interviewer extracts information or views from the interviewee but offers nothing in return. For example, interviewers using a structured interview do not give their own views, even if asked. Indeed, they are typically advised not to because of fears of contaminating respondents' answers.

- The interviewer–interviewee relationship is a form of hierarchy, or power relationship. Interviewers assume the right to ask questions, implicitly placing their interviewees in a position of subservience. The element of power is also revealed in a structured interview seeking out information from the researcher's perspective.

Because of these points, the standard survey interview is inconsistent with feminism especially when women interview other women; it is seen as indefensible for women so to 'use' other women. Instead feminist researchers advocate a framework for conducting interviews that establishes:

- a high level of rapport between interviewer and interviewee;
- a high degree of reciprocity on the part of the interviewer;
- the perspective of the woman being interviewed; and
- a non-hierarchical relationship.

In connection with the reciprocity advocated, Oakley (1981) noted in her research on transition to motherhood that respondents frequently asked her questions. She argued that it was ethically indefensible for a feminist not to answer some, if not all, of them. For Oakley, therefore, the qualitative interview is a means of resolving some of the dilemmas encountered when a feminist interviews a woman. However, as noted in previous chapters, while this broad adher-

ence to a set of principles for interviewing in feminist research continues, it has been tempered with the greater recognition of the potential of quantitative research, and thus of the structured interview.

An interesting dilemma, perhaps not so easily resolved, is what feminist researchers should do when their own 'understandings and interpretations of women's accounts would either not be shared by some of the research participants, and/or represent a challenge or threat to their perceptions, choices, and coping strategies' (Kelly *et al.* 1994: 37). It is the first type of situation that is examined here, at least in part because its implications go beyond feminism to the tricky question of how far a commitment of seeing through the eyes of those being studied can and/or should be stretched. Two examples are relevant. Reinharz (1992: 28–9) cited a study by Andersen in which 20 'corporate wives' came across in their interviews as happy with their lot and supportive of feminism only in relation to employment discrimination. Andersen interpreted their responses as indicating a 'false consciousness'—in other words, she did not really believe them. When Andersen wrote an article based on her findings, the women wrote a letter rejecting her account, affirming that women can be fulfilled as wives and mothers. A similar situation confronted Millen (1997) when she interviewed 32

Box 10.14 Focus group: a model of women-centred research

A recent qualitative study of women's sexual arousal 'used focus group techniques to learn more about the factors affecting women's sexual interest, inhibition, and desire.' The purpose of the study was to develop a questionnaire on the topic for women. One already existed for men but the researchers did not want simply to adapt it and instead 'wanted to hear from women themselves.'

'The study was designed around a number of themes, including feelings about one's body; concern about reputation; unwanted pregnancy/contraception; feeling desired versus feeling used by a partner . . . and involved nine groups of women selected to represent a diverse range in terms of age, race, education, and sexual orientation.'

In Canada, recent feminist research using focus groups includes Ristock (2001), Little (2001), and Wachholz and Miedema (2000). Ristock examined how 70 feminist

counsellors respond to clients reporting abuse in a lesbian relationship, and revealed how even feminist models and therapies for heterosexual violence may need revision in such instances. Little looked at Ontario single mothers on welfare after they had experienced reduced support services and enhanced measures to force job seeking and participation. Specifically, she conducted a secondary analysis of 200 focus group interviews done by Ontario Workfare Watch. As a result she was able to dispel some myths about these women and to underscore some of the ways they were forced to cope, including not eating and moving in with abusive ex-partners. Finally, Wachholz and Miedema examined how immigrant women feel about the police intervention that follows official reports of spousal abuse. The 'solution' often brings with it the harm of extra economic hardships for immigrant women already faced with socioeconomic vulnerability.

female scientists using semi-structured, in-depth individual interviewing. As Millen (1997: 5.6, 5.9) put it:

> From my external, academically privileged vantage point, it is clear that sexism pervades these professions, and that men are assumed from the start by other scientists, to be competent scientists of status whilst women have to prove themselves, overcome the barrier of their difference before they are accepted. These women, on the other hand, do not generally view their interactions in terms of gendered social systems. There is therefore a tension between their characterisation of their experience and my interpretation of it . . .

Two interesting issues arise from these two accounts. First, how can such a situation arise? If researchers are genuinely seeing through other's eyes, the 'tension' to which Millen referred should not arise. However, it clearly can and does, and this strongly suggests that qualitative researchers are more affected by their own perspectives and research questions than would be expected from textbook accounts of the research process. Second, given that feminist research is often concerned with wider political goals of emancipation, a tension between participants' worldviews and the researcher's position raises moral questions about the appropriateness of imposing an interpretation not shared by the research participants themselves. Such an imposition can hardly be regarded as consistent with the principle of a non-hierarchical relationship in interviews.

Therefore, while qualitative interviewing has become a highly popular research method for feminist researchers because of its malleability into a form that can support the principles of feminism, questions persist about the relationship between researchers' and participants' accounts, questions that have a broader significance for the conduct of qualitative research.

The focus group as a feminist method

The use of focus groups by feminist researchers has grown considerably in recent years and Wilkinson (1998, 1999b) has argued for its great potential in this regard. Three aspects of the method stand out in terms of their compatibility with the ethics and politics of feminism. They go beyond the issues just discussed about qualitative interviews.

- Focus group research is less artificial than many other methods, because it emphasizes group inter-

---

Ethical issue 10.2 *Ethics and research on prostitution*

O'Connell Davidson and Layder (1994) discussed a small-scale ethnographic research on a prostitute, Desiree [a pseudonym], and her clients. While Desiree and the women who served as her receptionists by welcoming clients were fully aware of O'Connell Davidson's status, the clients were not. Both researchers acknowledged an invasion of client privacy and lack of informed consent but were 'untroubled' by the intrusion O'Connell Davidson's presence represented because the clients were anonymous to her and she was not 'in a position to secure, store or disclose information that could harm them' (1994: 214). Thus, the fact that there was no harm to participants was regarded as the litmus test of the ethical status of the research. They offered a further defence by saying that ethical transgression is pervasive: 'Virtually all social research is intrusive and exploitative to some degree' (1994: 215). There was an acknowledged commitment to and sympathy for Desiree and her receptionists, but these sentiments do not extend to clients:

I have . . . no personal liking and no real sympathy for them. I have a professional obligation to preserve their anonymity and to ensure that they are not harmed by my research, but I feel no qualms about being less than frank with them, and no obligation to allow them to choose whether or not their actions are recorded (1994: 215).

In other words, rights of informed consent and of not being deceived are differentially distributed in society according to these authors. In such circumstances, researchers set themselves up as the judge of which individuals or groups 'deserve' ethical treatment. This view has far-reaching implications and is more common than thought. Examine the following pairs for who would probably get the better ethical research treatment: religious clergy pedophiles and their young victims; First Nations people and the police; or minority students and majority teachers.

action, a normal part of social life. Moreover, the tendency to recruit participants from naturally occurring groups underpins the lesser artificiality, since people are able to discuss in situations that are quite normal for them. As a result, there is greater opportunity to derive understandings that chime with the 'lived experience' of women. However, not all writers accept the contention that focus groups are more natural than individual interviews. Even when pre-existing groups are used, gathering people to discuss a certain topic (such as a television program) is not inherently naturalistic, because the whole interaction is so unusual and to a significant extent contrived. Indeed, completing questionnaires or being interviewed may appear more natural, because such instruments are fairly commonplace, whereas being asked to discuss, in a group, an issue not necessarily of one's choosing is less so.

- Feminist researchers have expressed a preference for methods that study the individual within a social context. The tendency for most methods to treat the individual as a separate entity devoid of a social context is disliked by many feminist researchers who prefer to analyze 'the self as relational or as socially constructed' (Wilkinson 1999*b*: 229–30).

- As noted previously, feminist researchers are suspicious of research methods that exploit and create a power relationship between researcher and respondent. Wilkinson observed that the risk of this occurring is greatly reduced because focus group participants are able to take over much of the direction of the session from the moderator. Indeed, they may even subvert the goals of the session in ways that would be of considerable interest to the moderator. As a result, participants' points of view are much more likely to be revealed than in a traditional interview.

Wilkinson did not argue that focus groups, or indeed any method, can be described as inherently feminist. Instead, she argued that because of these three features and when sensitive to feminist concerns, the focus group method has considerable potential for feminist research. The focus group may even promote hearing the voices of highly marginalized groups of women. Madriz (2000: 843) argued, for example, that for a group like lower-socioeconomic-class women of colour, focus groups constitute a relatively rare opportunity for them to 'empower themselves by making sense of their experience of vulnerability and subjugation.'

Qualitative interviewing versus participant observation

The aim of this section is to compare the merits and limitations of interviewing in qualitative research with those of participant observation. They are probably the two most prominent methods of data collection in qualitative research, so there is some virtue in assessing their strengths, a debate actually begun many years ago. In this section, interviewing is compared with participant observation rather than ethnography, because the latter invariably entails a significant amount of interviewing. So too does participant observation, but the present discussion follows the principle outlined in Box 9.1—namely, that the term refers specifically to the observational activities of a participant observer. As

noted there too, the term 'ethnography' is reserved for the wide range of data collection activities in which ethnographers engage—one of which is participant observation—along with the written account that is a product of those activities.

Advantages of participant observation in comparison to qualitative interviewing

Seeing through others' eyes

As noted in Chapters 1 and 8, this is one of the main tenets of qualitative research, but on the face of it the participant observer would seem to be better placed for gaining a foothold on social reality in this way. Their prolonged immersion in a social setting would seem to make them better equipped to see as others see. Participant observers are not only in much closer contact with people for a longer period of time, they also participate in many of the same kinds of activity as those being studied. Research that relies on interviewing alone, on the other hand, is likely to entail more fleeting contacts, although qualitative research interviews can last many hours and re-interviewing is not unusual.

Learning the native language

Becker and Geer (1957) argued that the participant observer is like a social anthropologist visiting a distant land: to understand a culture the language must be learned. However, it is not simply the formal language that must be understood; often it is also the 'argot'—the special uses of words and slang—that are important for penetrating a group's culture. Such an understanding is arrived at through a prolonged observation of language use. See Chapter 16 for more on language analysis.

The taken for granted

The interview relies primarily on verbal behaviour, and thus things that interviewees take for granted are less likely to surface than in participant observation, where such implicit features are more likely to be revealed. This is due to the observer's continued presence and ability to observe behaviour, rather than relying on what is said.

Deviant and hidden activities

Much of what is known about criminal and deviant subcultures has been gleaned from participant observation. These are areas, including drug taking, violent gangs, pilferage, illegal commerce, and hooliganism, in which insiders are likely to be reluctant to talk about in a one-on-one interview. Ethnographers conducting participant observation are more likely to engage in the prolonged interaction that allows them gradually to infiltrate such social worlds and to insinuate themselves into the lives of people who might be sensitive to outsiders. For similar reasons, participant observers have

sought access to areas like resistance at work, such as work-to-rule practices and industrial sabotage, or to groups that support a deviant ideology, such as white supremacists.

Sensitivity to context and flexibility

The participant observer's extensive contact with a social setting allows the context of people's behaviour to be mapped out fully. The participant observer interacts with people in a variety of different situations and possibly roles, so that links between behaviour and context can be forged. Being so versatile, and because of the unstructured nature of participant observation, it is more likely to uncover unexpected topics or issues. Except with the most unstructured forms of interview, the interview process is likely to entail some degree of closure once the interview guide is put together, which can slightly blinker the researcher.

Naturalistic emphasis

Participant observation can come closer to a naturalistic emphasis, because the researcher confronts members of a social setting in their natural environments. Interviewing, by its nature a disruption of members' normal flow of events even when it is at its most informal, is less amenable to this feature. It is unsurprising that when referring to naturalism as a tradition in qualitative research, Gubrium and Holstein (1997; see Box 9.1) referred mostly to studies in which participant observation was a prominent component.

Advantages of qualitative interviewing in comparison to participant observation

Issues resistant to observation

Many issues are simply not amenable to observation, so that asking people about them is the only viable means of finding them out, even within a qualitative research strategy. For example, consider Beardsworth and Keil's (1992) research on vegetarianism (see Boxes 10.2 and 10.3). It was not feasible for investigators to insinuate themselves into the lives of vegetarians, to uncover issues like why they

Box 10.15 Information through interviews: research on prostitution

McKeganey and Barnard (1996) discussed their strategies for conducting research into prostitutes and their clients. Their approach was largely that of observer-as-participant (see Figure 9.2), in that their research was based primarily on interviews with prostitutes and their clients, as well as some (frequently accidental) observation of interactions and overheard conversations. The interviews they conducted were especially important in gaining information on such areas as: how the prostitutes had moved into this line of work; permitted and prohibited sex acts; links with drug use; experience of violence; and the management of identity. In the following passage, a prostitute reconstructs her movement into prostitution:

> I was 14 and I'd run away from home. I ended up down in London where I met a pimp. . . . He'd got me a place to stay, buying me things and everything and I ended up sleeping with him as well. . . . One night we got really

drunk and stoned and he brought someone in. . . . [Then] after it happened I thought it was bad, I didn't like it but at least I was getting paid for it. I'd been abused by my granddad when I was 11 and it didn't seem a million miles from that anyway (1996: 25).

One area of particular concern to McKeganey and Barnard was the spread of HIV/AIDS infection and its implications for prostitutes and their work. This area was specifically addressed in interviews. For example:

> I've got a couple of punters who'll say 'I'll give you so and so if you'll do it without [a condom].' But never, I always use a condom for anal sex, oral sex and even for hand jobs; there's no way I'll let them come anywhere near me (1996: 66).
>
> You still get the bam-pots [idiots] asking for sex without. I had one the other night—I said, 'where have you been living—on a desert island?' (1996: 66).

---

converted to this eating strategy. For most people, vegetarianism is a matter that surfaces only at certain points, such as during meals and shopping. It is not feasible to carry out participant observation on something like this, which is so very episodic.

Reconstruction of events and future plans

A reconstruction of past events and future behaviour also cannot be accomplished through observation alone. Qualitative research frequently entails a reconstruction of events by asking interviewees to think back about how a series of past events created a current situation. Beardsworth and Keil (see Box 10.3) employed the symbolic interactionist notion of *career* to understand how people become vegetarians. Indeed most qualitative studies ask about events that occurred before the study began, to understand, for examples, the early family experiences of gang members, recent immigrants, and prostitutes. Some call this 'retrospective interviewing.' See Box 10.11 for a further example.

Reactive effects

The issue of reactive effects is by no means straightforward. As with structured observation (see Chapter

6), it can be anticipated that the presence of a participant observer will result in reactive effects (see Box 6.6). People's awareness that they are being observed can make them behave less naturally. However, participant observers, like researchers using structured observation, typically find that people become ac-

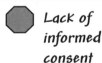

Ethical issue 10.3 — Lack of informed consent

McKeganey and Barnard's (1996; see Box 10.15) research was on negotiations between prostitute and client over the use of condoms in the light of threats of HIV/AIDS infection. It is not inconceivable that some prostitutes would have agreed to wear hidden 'wires' to capture and record these transactions. However, clients would not have been party to such agreements, so that ethical principles of informed consent and invasion of privacy would have been transgressed. As a result, the researchers relied on interviews about such negotiations or on prostitutes' stances on the matter and their reports of the views of some clients.

customed to their presence and begin to behave more naturally the longer they are around. Indeed, members of social settings sometimes express surprise when, on the verge of disengagement, participant observers announce their imminent departure.

Interviewers clearly do not suffer from the same kind of problem, but it can be argued that the unnatural character of the interview encounter is a context within which reactive effects may emerge. Participant observation also suffers from the related problem of observers disturbing the very situation being studied, because conversations and interactions occur, both with and about the observer, that otherwise would not happen. This is by no means easy to resolve and it is likely that both participant observation and qualitative interviewing set in motion reactive effects but of different kinds. Thus Potter (2003) got around the problem of reactivity by imagining hypothetical examples of poker games. He knew that real players would never allow him to walk behind them to observe strategy. Asking them directly would not work either; real players engage in concealment and deception by definition.

Less intrusive in people's lives

Participant observation can be costly in that the observer is likely to take up a lot more of peoples' time than an interview. Interviews in qualitative research can sometimes be very long and re-interviewing is not uncommon, but their impact is probably still less than having to take observers into account on a regular basis, though it is likely that this feature varies from situation to situation. Participant observation can be especially intrusive in terms of people's time when it occurs in organizational settings, for example, when the rhythm of work is disrupted.

Longitudinal research easier

One of the advantages of participant observation is its inherently longitudinal character, with the result that changes and connections between events can be observed. However, there are limits to the time that participant observers can devote to being away from their normal personal and other professional routines. Consequently, participant observation does not usually extend much beyond two to three years.

When participant observation is being conducted on a topic that is episodic, rather than requiring continued observation, a longer time period may be feasible.

Armstrong's (1993) research on football hooliganism, referred to several times in Chapters 8 and 9, entailed six years of participant observation, but, since football hooligans are not engaged full-time in this activity, the research did not require the researcher's continued absence from work and personal commitments. Interviewing can be carried out within a longitudinal research design somewhat more easily because repeat interviews may be easier to organize than repeat visits to participant observers' research settings. Following up on interviewees on several occasions is likely to be easier than returning to research sites on a regular basis.

Greater breadth of coverage

In participant observation, the researcher is invariably limited to a fairly restricted range of people, incidents, and localities. Participant observation in a large organization, for example, often means that knowledge of the organization, beyond the confines of the actual department (or other area) in which the observation is carried out, is unlikely to be very extensive. Interviewing allows access to a wider variety of people and situations.

Specific focus

As noted in Chapter 8, qualitative research sometimes begins with a specific focus, and indeed Silverman (1993) was critical of the notion that it should be regarded as an open-ended form of research. Qualitative interviewing seems to be better suited to such a situation, since the interview can be directed at a focus and its research questions. Thus, research by Bryman *et al.* (1996) had a very specific focus, in line with its funding—namely, conceptions of leadership among police officers. Because of its clear focus, it was more appropriate to conduct the research using a semi-structured interview guide rather than participant observation, since issues to do with leadership notions do not crop up on a regular basis, making observation a very extravagant method of data collection.

Overview

When Becker and Geer (1957: 28) proclaimed half a century ago that the 'most complete form of the sociological datum . . . is the form in which the participant observer gathers it,' Trow (1957: 33) reprimanded them for making such a universal claim. He argued that 'the problem under investigation properly dictates the methods of investigation.' The latter view is very much the one taken in this book. Specific research methods are appropriate for some studies but not others. The discussion of the merits and limitations of participant observation and qualitative interviews is meant simply to draw attention to some of the factors to take into account if given an opportunity to use one or the other in a study.

Equally, and to repeat, the comparison is a somewhat artificial exercise, because participant observation is usually carried out as part of ethnographic research and as such is usually accompanied by interviewing and other methods. In other words, participant observers frequently buttress their observations with methods of data collection giving them access to important areas not amenable to observation alone. However, the aim of the comparison is to provide a balance sheet in considering the strengths and limitations of a reliance on either participant observation or qualitative interview alone. Its aim is to draw attention to some of the factors to take into account in deciding how to plan a study and even how to evaluate existing research.

A checklist of issues to consider in qualitative interviewing

- ✓ Have you thought about how you will present yourself in the interview, such as how you will be dressed?

- ✓ Is there a clear and comprehensive/informative way of introducing the research to interviewees?

- ✓ Does the interview guide clearly relate to the research questions?

- ✓ Has a pilot test been done with some appropriate respondents and the interviewers (moderators) fully trained?

- ✓ Does the guide contain a good mixture of different kinds of questions, such as probing, specifying, and direct questions?

- ✓ Do the interviews allow novel or unexpected themes and issues to arise?

- ✓ Is the language in the questions clear, comprehensible, and free of unnecessary jargon?

- ✓ Are the questions relevant to those being interviewed?

- ✓ Have the questions been designed to elicit reflective discussions so that interviewees are not tempted to answer simply in 'yes' or 'no' terms?

- ✓ Do the questions offer a real prospect of seeing the world from the interviewees' point of view rather than imposing a frame of reference on them?

- ✓ Has the setting(s) in which the interviews will take place been checked out? Has the recording equipment been pre-tested and a dry run undertaken? Have all aids to be used (e.g., visual aids, segments of film, case studies) been pre-tested?

- ✓ Is there a plan in place if the interviewee does not turn up for the interview?

For a focus group:

- ✓ What is planned if some, but not all, participants turn up for the session?

- ✓ Have the questions been designed to encourage group interaction and discussion?

- ✓ Is there a strategy for dealing with silences and for particular participants who are reluctant to speak?

- ✓ Is there a strategy for dealing with participants who speak too much and hog the discussion?

- ✓ Is there a strategy for dealing with the discussion going off on a tangent?

K   KEY POINTS

- Interviewing in qualitative research is typically unstructured or semi-structured.

- Qualitative interviewing is meant to be flexible and to seek out the worldviews of research participants.

- If an interview guide is employed, it should not be too structured and allow some flexibility in the asking of questions.

- The qualitative interview should be recorded and then transcribed.

- Qualitative interviews can be adapted to online investigations.

- The focus group is a group interview. There is concern with the joint production of meaning.

- There are several issues concerning the recruitment of focus group participants— in particular, whether to use natural groups.

- The moderator generally tries to provide a relatively free rein to the discussion. However, there may be contexts where it is necessary to ask more specific questions.

- Group interaction is an important component of discussions.

- The growing use of the Internet offers significant opportunities for gaining access to a growing number of people, including focus group participants.

- A qualitative interview is a popular method of data collection in feminist studies and some writers view focus groups as well suited to a feminist standpoint.

- Whether to use participant observation or qualitative interviews depends in large part on the relative suitability to the research questions being addressed. Still, participant observers invariably conduct some interviews in their investigations.

Q   QUESTIONS FOR REVIEW

Differences between the structured interviews and qualitative interviews

- How does qualitative interviewing differ from structured interviewing?

Unstructured and semi-structured interviewing

- What are the differences between unstructured and semi-structured interviewing?

- Can semi-structured interviewing compromise the flexibility of qualitative research?

- What are the differences between life history and oral history interviews?

- What considerations need to be borne in mind when preparing an interview guide?

- What kinds of question can be asked in an interview guide?

- What skills does the interviewer need to develop for qualitative interviewing?

- Why is it important to record and transcribe qualitative interviews?

- What role can vignette questions play in qualitative interviewing?

Qualitative research using online personal interviews

- Can online personal interviews really be personal interviews? To what extent does the absence of direct contact mean that the online interview cannot be a true interview?

Introduction to focus groups

- What advantages can the focus group method offer in contrast to an individual qualitative interview?

Conducting focus groups

- Are there any circumstances in which it is a good idea to select participants who know each other?

Group interaction in focus group sessions

- Why is it important to examine group interaction when analyzing focus group data?

Limitations of focus groups

- Does the potential for loss of control over proceedings and group effects damage the potential utility of the focus group as a method?

Qualitative research using online focus groups

- How different is the role of the moderator in online, as against face-to-face, focus groups?

Feminist research and interviewing in qualitative research

- Why is the qualitative interview so prominent among feminist researchers?
- What dilemmas are posed for feminist researchers using qualitative interviewing?
- What dilemmas are posed for feminist researchers using focus groups?

Qualitative interviewing versus participant observation

- Outline the relative advantages and disadvantages of qualitative interviewing and participant observation.
- Is one method more in tune with the preoccupations of qualitative researchers than the other?

Part Four

Chapter 11 presents some of the options involved in choosing a sample. It also includes a bit of statistics, the topic of Chapter 12, to wet your feet. There the main tools needed to conduct quantitative data analysis are presented along with instructions on how to use SPSS computer software—a very widely used package of programs—to implement those techniques. Chapter 13 then examines different approaches to qualitative data analysis and offers advice on how it can be conducted using NVivo computer software.

11 Sampling

CHAPTER OVERVIEW

Sampling principles are not exclusively the concern of survey and other quantitative researchers; for example, sampling is relevant to the qualitative research you just read about in the last three chapters. That is why the chapter is placed here, unlike in most other texts in which sampling appears in the quantitative methods section. This placement reflects the shared character of qualitative and quantitative research, mentioned repeatedly in this book, and the specific focus of two future chapters. The chapter explores:

- the role of sampling in relation to the overall process of doing research;

- the related ideas of generalization (also known as external validity) and of a representative sample—the latter allows the researcher to generalize findings from a sample to a population;

- the idea of a *probability sample*—one using a random selection process;

- the main types of probability sample: simple random; systematic; stratified random; and the multi-stage cluster sample;

- the main issues involved in deciding sample size;

- different types of non-probability sample, including quota sampling, widely used in market research and opinion polls;

- potential sources of sampling error in survey research;

- sampling in structured observation research; with this method sampling is not just of people but also time and contexts;

- sampling strategies in ethnography, in particular *theoretical sampling*, which is associated with the grounded theory approach to qualitative data analysis;

- sampling in content analysis; and

- lowering non-response rates.

Introduction

This chapter is concerned with the issues involved in selecting individuals for research. Most students have wondered about the attitudes of fellow students on various matters, or about their behaviour in certain areas, or something about their backgrounds. To examine any of these three areas, structured interviews or mailed questionnaires would be appropriate. However, with let's say around 9000 students, it costs a great amount of money to send questionnaires to all 9000 and the time and energy to interview all of them would be prohibitive. It is almost certain that a *sample* of students from the total population of students would have to suffice.

The need to sample is almost invariably encountered in quantitative research. This chapter begins with matters relating to sampling in research involving data collection by structured interview or questionnaire. Other methods of quantitative research also involving sampling considerations follow. The principles of sampling involved there are more or less identical to those in the previous methods, but frequently other considerations come to the fore as well. Finally, sampling in qualitative research is ex-amined, followed by ways to lower non-response.

But for student work, will any sample suffice? Is it sufficient to stand in a central position on campus and then interview the students who come past and who agree to an interview? Alternatively, is it suffi-cient to move about in a central area, like the library, asking people to be interviewed, or to give question-naires to everyone taking a certain course?

The answer, of course, depends on whether the goal is to be able to *generalize* results to the entire stu-dent body at the university. If it is, it is very unlikely that any of the three sampling strategies just proposed would provide a *representative sample* of all students at the university and to generalize findings from a sam-ple to the population from which it was selected, the sample must be representative. Why? There are vari-ous reasons, but the following stand out:

- The first two approaches depend heavily on the availability of students during the times they are being sought out. Not all students are likely to be available at any one time; some are at work, so the sample cannot reflect these students.

- They also depend on the students going to the lo-cations. Not all students necessarily pass the data collection point or go to the library, or they may vary greatly in the frequency with which they do so. Their movements are likely to reflect such things as their classroom locations, where they live, and their social habits. Again, to rely on these locations would mean missing out on students who do not frequent them.

- It is possible, not to say likely, that decisions about whom to approach will be influenced by judgments about how friendly or cooperative prospective respondents look or by comfort in in-terviewing students of the same (or other) gender or race, as well as by many other factors.

- The problem with the third strategy is that all stu-dents taking the same course share at least that similarity, and anyone not taking the course is omitted. How many music or engineering majors take sociology, for instance?

In other words, in all three sampling approaches, decisions about whom to sample are influenced by

personal judgments and by prospective respondents' availability, both non-universal criteria. Such limita-tions mean, in the language of survey sampling, that the sample is *biased* and does not represent the pop-ulation from which it is selected. While it is incredi-bly difficult to remove bias altogether and to derive a truly representative sample, steps should be taken to keep that bias to an absolute minimum.

Three sources of bias can be identified (see Box 11.1 for an explanation of key terms):

- *If sampling is not random, chosen by chance, like numbers from a lottery cage.* In these instances there is a good possibility that human judgment affects the selection process, making some members of the population more likely to be selected than others, those nearer, less threatening, etc. This source of bias is eliminated through the use of probability/random sampling, described below.

- *If the sampling frame or list of potential subjects is in-adequate.* If the sampling frame is not comprehen-sive or is inaccurate, the sample derived cannot represent the population, even if a random/proba-bility sampling method is employed.

- *If some sample members refuse to participate or cannot be contacted—in other words, if there is non-response.* The problem with non-response is that those who agree to participate probably differ from those who do not agree to participate. The latter include those who de-liberately looked in the other direction or changed their path to avoid being asked to complete a ques-tionnaire. Are they holding down part-time jobs, thus limiting their time? Are they 'A' students with no time to waste? Some of these differences may be significant to the research question or questions.

If the data are available, a researcher can check how non-respondents differ from the population. It is often possible to do this in terms of characteristics such as gender or age, or, in the case of something like a sample of university students, whether the sample's characteristics reflect the entire sample in terms of fac-ulty membership. However, it is usually impossible to determine whether differences exist between the pop-ulation and the sample after non-response takes its toll in terms of 'deeper' factors, for example, attitudes toward separatism and patterns of smoking behaviour.

Box 11.1 Basic terms and concepts in sampling

- *Population*—basically, all of the units from which the sample is to be selected. The term 'units' is employed because not only people are sampled—the researcher may want to sample from a universe of nations, cities, regions, schools, firms, etc. Finch and Hayes (1994), for example, based part of their research on a random sample of wills of deceased people. Thus, 'population' has a much broader meaning than the everyday use of the term.

- *Sampling frame*—the listing of all units in the population from which the sample will be selected.

- *Sample*—the segment of the population selected for investigation, a subset of the population. The method of selection may be based on a probability or a non-probability approach (see below).

- *Representative sample*—a sample that is a microcosm of the population, reflecting it accurately. A sample like this is most likely when a probability sampling process is used (see next).

- *Probability sample*—a sample selected using a random process such that each unit in the population has a known chance of being selected. The aim of probability sampling is to keep *sampling error* (see below) to a minimum.

- *Non-probability sample*—a sample not selected using a random selection method. Essentially, this implies that some units in the population are more likely to be selected than are others.

- *Sampling error*—the difference between a sample and the population from which it is selected, even though a probability sample has been selected.

- *Non-sampling error*—difference between the population and the sample caused by either deficiencies in the sampling approach, such as an inadequate sampling frame or *non-response* (see below), or from such problems as poor question wording, poor interviewing, or flawed processing of data.

- *Non-response*—a source of non-sampling error that occurs whenever some members of the sample refuse to cooperate, cannot be contacted, or for some reason cannot supply the required data (perhaps because of mental incapacity).

- *Census*—if data are collected from *all* units rather than from a sample of units in a population, the data are treated as census data. The phrase '*the* census' typically refers to the complete enumeration of all members of the population of a nation state—that is, a national census.

Sampling error

To appreciate the significance of sampling error for achieving a representative sample, consider Figures 11.1 through 11.4. Imagine a population of 200 people and a sample of 50. Imagine as well that the topic is whether people watch soap operas, with the population equally divided between those who do (100) and those who do not (100). If the sample is representative, the sample of 50 should also be equally split in terms of this variable (see Figure 11.1). If there is a small amount of sampling error, so that there is one person too many who does not watch soap operas and one too few who does, it looks like Figure 11.2. Figure 11.3 shows a more serious overrepresentation in the sample of people who do not watch soaps. This time there are three too many who do not watch them and three too few who do. In Figure 11.4 there

is a very serious overrepresentation of people who do not watch soaps; there are 35 people in the sample who do not watch them, which is much larger than the 25 that would be expected in the sample.

It is important to appreciate that probability sampling *cannot* eliminate sampling error. Even with a well-crafted probability sample, a degree of sampling error is likely to creep in, just as in flipping a coin 100 times yields more 49Head/51Tail and 49Head/51Tail results *combined* than 50Head/50Tail results, which indeed though most probable, is highly unlikely. Take a minute to do this experiment in your class with 20 flips, and see the surprisingly large number of other than 10Head/10Tail results. However, probability sampling stands a better chance than non-probability sampling of minimizing such

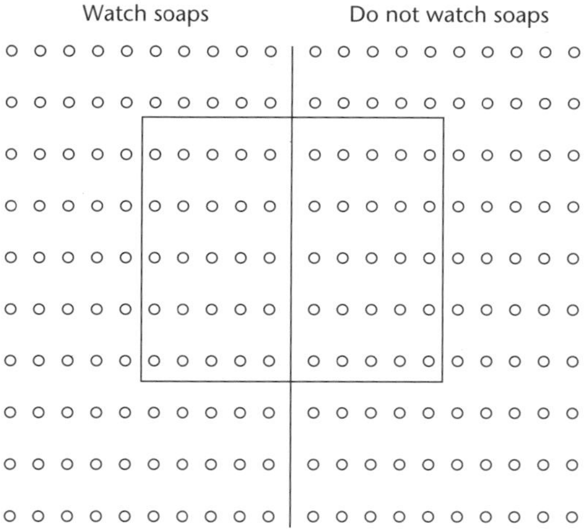

Watch soaps   Do not watch soaps

Figure 11.1 A sample with no sampling error

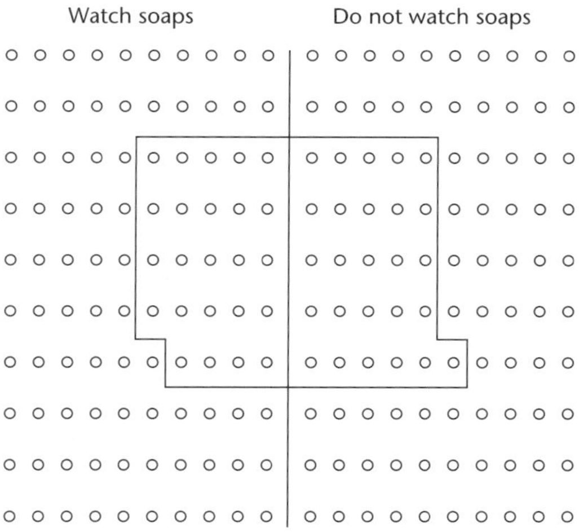

Watch soaps   Do not watch soaps

Figure 11.2 A sample with very little sampling error

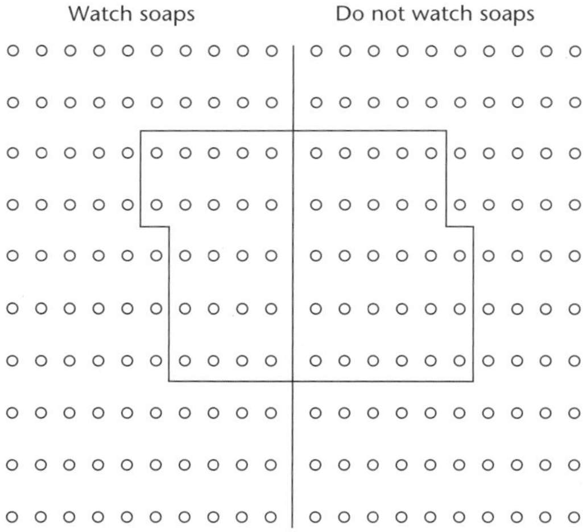

Watch soaps   Do not watch soaps

Figure 11.3 A sample with some sampling error

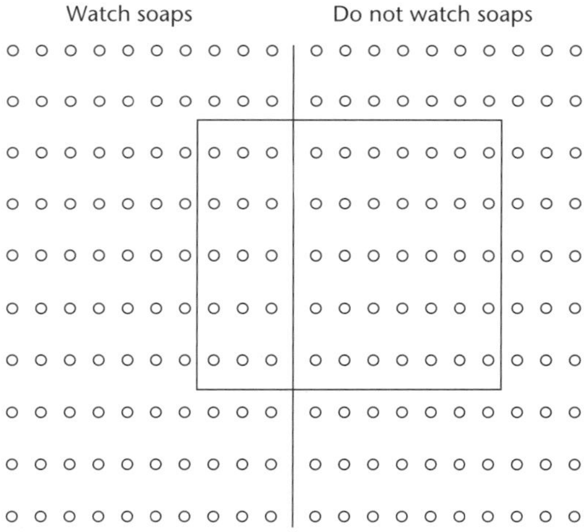

Watch soaps   Do not watch soaps

Figure 11.4 A sample with a lot of sampling error

sampling error so that it does not end up looking like Figure 11.4. Moreover, probability sampling allows the researcher to employ tests of statistical significance that permit inferences to be made about the sample from which the sample was selected. These will be addressed in Chapter 12.

Types of probability sample

Imagine a study among 9000 full-time university students on the social variables related to drinking. If the research is done at one nearby university, the population is all students in that university, which in turn means that results can be generalized only to students of that one university. A researcher simply cannot assume that level of alcohol consumption and its correlates are the same in other universities. Even at the selected university, results cannot be generalized to part-time students either.

Simple random sample

The simple random sample is the most basic form of probability sample. With it each unit of the population has an equal probability of inclusion in the sample. Suppose there is enough money to interview 450 students at the university. This means that the probability of inclusion in the sample is

$$\frac{450}{9000},\text{ that is, 1 in 20.}$$

This is known as the *sampling fraction* and is expressed as

$$\frac{n}{N}$$

where n is the sample size and N is the population size.

The key steps in devising a simple random sample can be represented as follows:

1. Define the population. This is all full-time students at the university, N, here 9000.

2. Select or devise a comprehensive sampling frame. Virtually all universities have an office that keeps student records; this will enable excluding those who do not meet criteria for inclusion, here the part-time students. As an aside, what ethical issue arises in this invasion of student privacy? But certainly it is not feasible to write to every student asking permission to view the list in order to devise a random sample. It would be just as easy to send everyone the questionnaire.

3. Decide sample size (n), here 450.

4. List all the students in the population and assign them consecutive numbers from 1 to N, here 1 to 9000.

5. Using a table of random numbers, or a computer program that can generate random numbers, select n (450) different random numbers that lie between 1 and N (9000).

6. The students who match the n (450) random numbers constitute the sample. Two points are striking about this process. First, there is almost no opportunity for human bias. Students are not selected on subjective criteria like looking friendly and approachable as in quota sampling below. Their selection is entirely mechanical. Second, the process is not dependent on students being available. They do not have to be walking in the interviewer's proximity to be included in the sample. The process of selection is done without their knowledge. Not until contacted by an interviewer do they know they are part of a social survey.

Step 5 mentions the possible use of a table of random numbers, found in the back of many statistics books or generated by simple computer software. The tables are made up of columns of five-digit numbers, such as:

09188	08358
90045	28306
73189	53840
75768	91757
54016	89415

The first thing to notice is that, since these are five-digit numbers and the population 9000, a four-digit number, none of the random numbers seems appropriate, except for 09188 and 08358, although the former is larger than the largest possible number.

The answer is to take just four digits in each number, for example, the last four, yielding the following:

9188	8358
0045	8306
3189	3840
5768	1757
4016	9415

Still two of the resulting numbers—9188 and 9415—exceed 9000; no student can match either number. The solution is simple: ignore these numbers. This means that the student assigned the number 45 will be the first to be included in the sample; the student assigned the number 3189 next; the student assigned 5768 next; and so on.

Not wanting to interview the same person twice, ignore any random number that appears more than once and replace it with another. This procedure produces a sample known as a simple random sample *without replacement:* no number is placed back in (replaced) for a second chance at inclusion. Virtually all simple random samples in social research are like this and so the qualifier 'without replacement' is invariably omitted. Strictly speaking, without replacement means the result is not a true simple random sample, as those chosen later have a greater chance of being selected than those selected earlier. Notice the first person chosen has one chance in 9000 of being included. Removing that person means person two has one chance in the remaining 8999. The last person chosen will have one chance out of the 8551 people remaining; 1/8551 is greater than the first chosen person's chance of being selected of 1/9000. Generally researchers overlook this problem, a small one compared with others in sampling.

Systematic sample

A variation on the simple random sample is the systematic sample that selects units directly from the sampling frame, without using a table of random numbers.

In the present case, 1 student in 20 is to be selected, 9000/450. With a systematic sample, take a random start between 1 and 20 inclusive, possibly by using the last two digits in a table of random numbers. With the 10 random numbers above, the first relevant one is 54016, since it is the first one where the last two digits yield a number of 20 or below, in this case, 16. This means that the 16th student in the sampling frame is first to be in the sample. Thereafter, take every 20th student on the list; so the sequence is: 16, 36, 56, 76, 96, 116, etc. Who is the last person in the sample? 8996.

This approach obviates the need to assign numbers to students' names and then to look up names of the students whose numbers have been drawn by the random selection process, thus saving time. It is important to ensure, however, that there is no inherent ordering in the sampling frame, since this biases the sample. If there is any order in the list, even alphabetization, the best solution is to remove it by rearranging the list. The result is a sample in which each individual has an equal chance of inclusion (all depending on that first random number).

Note that not every possible combination has an equal chance. Once that first number, here 16, is chosen everyone in the sample must end in six and no even numbered prefixes will qualify, like 26, 86, 166, etc. It is also be impossible to get two students with an unusual last name, as there would have to be 21 of them for both to be included if the required skipping of 20 names between choices is done. The simple random sample does not have this problem. The choice, as usual in research is between time available and data quality.

Stratified random sampling

In the imaginary study of university students, the student's discipline may be relevant to drinking and to other attitudes. Generating a simple random sample or a systematic sample *may* yield one in which, for example, the proportion of kinesiology students in the sample is the same as in the student population, but usually it is not an exact match. Thus, if there are 1800 students majoring in kinesiology, using a sampling fraction of 1 in 20 should mean 90 students in the sample from this faculty. However, because of sampling error, there may be, say, 85 or 93, from this faculty.

Because it is almost certain that the university includes in student records their faculty, or indeed may have separate sampling frames (lists) for each faculty, it is possible to ensure that students are exactly represented in terms of their faculty membership. In the language of sampling, this means stratifying the population by a criterion (in this case faculty) and selecting either a simple random sample or a systematic sample from each of the resulting strata. In the present example, five faculties mean five strata, with the sample in each stratum being one-twentieth of the total for each faculty, as in Table 11.1, which also shows a hypothetical outcome of a simple random sample, one that does not exactly mirror the population.

The advantage of stratified sampling is clear: it ensures that the resulting sample is distributed in the same way as the population in terms of the stratifying criterion. Using a simple random or systematic sampling approach *may* result in a distribution like that of the stratified sample, but it is unlikely. On the other hand, this strategy requires that the criteria for stratifying are known in advance of the research, something not always feasible.

Two more points are relevant here. Stratified sampling is sensible only when it is relatively easy to identify and allocate units to strata. Five strata based on exercise, from 'athletes' at one end to 'couch potatoes' at the other would be very hard to determine, requiring an initial study just to create the strata. Second, more than one stratifying criterion can be used at the same time. Thus here one could stratify by faculty and gender; or faculty, gender, and whether students are undergraduates or postgraduates, so long as the crite-

ria are easy to use and relevant to the research question. But such stratifying is really feasible only when the relevant information is available to identify members of the population in terms of the stratifying criterion (or criteria). At your school, is there a public list of female, undergraduate, engineering students?

Multi-stage cluster sampling

In the previous example, students to be interviewed attend a single university and there is not a lot of travel for interviewers. However, imagine a *national* sample of students. This would add a great deal to the time and cost to doing the research. This kind of problem can occur not only for national populations but even for a large city.

One way to deal with this problem is to employ *cluster sampling*. With cluster sampling, the primary sampling unit (the first stage of the sampling procedure) is not the individuals or units of the population to be interviewed, but an aggregate of them, known as *clusters*. Imagine a nationally representative sample of 5000 students. Using simple random or systematic sampling would yield a widely dispersed sample, and mean a great deal of travel for interviewers. One solution is to sample universities and then students from each of the sampled universities with a probability sample at each stage. Thus, randomly sample 10 universities from the entire population of universities, yielding 10 clusters, and then interview 500 randomly selected students at each of the 10 universities.

Table 11.1 The advantages of stratified sampling

Faculty	Population	Stratified sample	Hypothetical simple random or systematic sample
Humanities	1800	90	85
Social sciences	1200	60	70
Pure sciences	2000	100	120
Applied sciences	1800	90	84
Engineering	2200	110	91
TOTAL	9000	450	450

Suppose the result of sampling 10 universities is the following:

- Alberta
- McGill
- Simon Fraser
- Winnipeg
- Dalhousie
- Guelph
- Brandon
- University of Western Ontario
- Nippissing
- Toronto

This list is fine, but interviewers could still be involved in a great deal of travel, since the 10 universities are far from each other. And note the absence of universities in Saskatchewan, Newfoundland, and Prince Edward Island. An alternative solution to the one just presented is to group all universities by region, for example, Maritimes, Quebec, Ontario, Prairies, and BC and to randomly sample two regions. Five universities can then be sampled from each of the two lists of universities and then 500 students from each of the 10 universities. Thus, there are separate stages:

- group universities by region and sample two regions;

- sample 5 universities from each of the two regions; and

- sample 500 students from each of the 10 universities.

Cluster sampling is a multi-stage approach involving clusters first and then something else—either further clusters or population units. Doing so increases chances of having an unrepresentative sample but one that is cheaper to administer. Maximizing representativeness while minimizing cost cannot be achieved; a choice, usually a compromise, must be made. In another context, the same point is made. One can cluster telephone area codes, then exchanges, and then last four digits of phone numbers, randomly sampling each time. But since phone charges are now so low, the money saved is probably not worth the chance of missing whole area codes like the 905 belt around Toronto or Vancouver's 604.

Many examples of multi-stage cluster sampling entail stratification. One could, for example, stratify

---

> **Box 11.2** An example of a multi-stage cluster sample
>
> To study the influence of social class on voting in modern Canada, suppose the goal is to get 2000 interviews from a random selection of Canadian adults eligible to vote. This may involve:
>
> - *Sampling the 308 federal ridings*
>   - These are stratified by population size (not all ridings have the same number) into large, average, and small groupings; whether the riding is mostly rural or mostly urban; and dependence on federal transfer payments (high and low).
>   - 100 ridings are then sampled.
>
> - *Sampling polling districts*
>   - Two polling districts are chosen from each sampled riding.
>
> - *Sampling individuals*
>   - Ten addresses from each sampled polling district are systematically sampled.
>   - One person at each address is chosen according to some pre-defined rules, like oldest male, youngest female, etc.—in effect, another stratification.

universities in terms of whether they are 'new,' those receiving their charters after the great university expansion of the 1960s or 'old.' In each of the two regions, first group universities along the old/new university criterion and then select two or three universities from each of the two resulting strata per region.

Box 11.2 provides an example of a multi-stage cluster sample. It entailed four stages: the sampling of parliamentary constituencies, the sampling of polling districts, sampling of addresses, and the sampling of individuals. The advantage of multi-stage cluster sampling should be clear by now: it allows interviewers to be far more geographically concentrated than is the case of a simple random sample. Stratifying can then be a second step, within clusters. However, even when a very rigorous sampling strategy is employed, sampling error cannot be avoided, as the example in Box 11.3 shows.

Box 11.3 Generalizing from a random sample to the population

If an average of 9.7 units of alcohol is consumed in the previous seven days by respondents in a probability sample, would a similar figure be found in the population? The answer is complex but it is sketched out here and in Box 11.4. Even assuming the impossible task of taking an infinite number of random samples from a population, the sample means would not all exactly hit the population mean. One can never know that figure, but can imagine another study finding 9.6 units, another 9.8, and not the 9.7 above. These outcomes, as long as there are enough of them will take the form of a bell-shaped curve known as a *normal distribution* (see Figure 11.5) *with the sample means clustering at or around the population mean.* Half the sample means will be at or below the population mean; the other half will be at or above the population mean. Moving to the left (at or lower than the population mean) or the right (at or higher than the population mean), the curve tails off, reflecting the fewer and fewer samples generating means that depart considerably from the population mean. The variation of sample means around the population mean is the *sampling error* and is measured using a statistic known as the *standard error of the mean*. This is an estimate of the amount that a sample mean is likely to differ from the population mean.

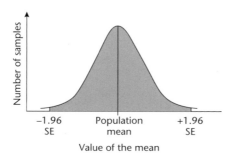

Figure 11.5 A distribution of sample means

Note: 95 per cent of sample means lie within the shaded area; SE = standard error of the mean.

This consideration is important because sampling theory tells us that 95 per cent of all sample means lie between + or – 1.96 standard errors from the population mean (see Box 11.4). Essentially, the criterion implies that one can be 95 per cent certain that the one sample mean found lies within + or – 1.96 standard errors from the population mean.

If a sample has been selected according to probability sampling principles, we know that we can be 95 per cent certain that the population mean lies between the sample mean plus or minus 1.96 multiplied by the standard error of the mean. This is known as the *confidence interval*. If the mean level of alcohol consumption in the previous seven days in our sample of 450 students is 9.7 units and the standard error of the mean is 1.3, one can be 95 per cent certain that the population mean lies between

$$9.7 - (1.96 \times 1.3)$$

and

$$9.7 + (1.96 \times 1.3)$$

that is, between 7.152 and 12.248.

With a stratified sample, the standard error of the mean is smaller than in other probability samples because the variation between strata sample in terms of the stratification criterion or criteria employed is essentially eliminated. This consideration demonstrates how stratification injects an extra increment of precision into the probability sampling process, since a possible source of sampling error is eliminated.

By contrast, a cluster sample without stratification exhibits a larger standard error of the mean than a comparable simple random sample. This occurs because a possible source of variability between students (i.e., going to one university rather than another, which may affect levels of alcohol consumption) is disregarded. If, for example, some universities have a culture of heavy drinking in which a large number of students participate, and if these universities are not selected because of the procedure for selecting clusters, an important source of variability is omitted.

The qualities of a probability sample

Many researchers prefer probability samples because they permit making inferences from information about a random sample to the population from which it is selected. In other words, they can generalize their findings from a sample to the population. This is not to say that the population and sample data are the same, but one can be used to estimate the other. In the example of alcohol consumption in the sample of 450 students, the mean number of units consumed by the sample ($\overline{X}$) can be used to estimate the population mean (μ) but with known margins of error. Greek letters are used for a population, our letters for the sample.

To address this point it is necessary to use some basic statistical ideas. These are presented in Box 11.4 and can be skipped if just a broad idea of sampling procedures is required.

Box 11.4 Sampling distribution

Assume a *population* of five cases (scores = 6, 8, 10, 12, 14) from which a random *sample* of two cases is selected. The five scores sum to 50 and therefore the mean of the population is 50/5, or 10. Taking all possible random samples of two cases with replacement (meaning that after a case is chosen it goes back into the pool, so that two 6's or two 14's are possible) and calculating the means of each sample of size two, the following results:

Value of First Observation in Sample

	6	8	10	12	14
6	6	7	8	9	10
8	7	8	9	10	11
10	8	9	10	11	12
12	9	10	11	12	13
14	10	11	12	13	14

Value of Second Observation in Sample

Thus the 7, where 6 and 8 meet, is the mean of 6 + 8/2 = 7; the 13 is where 12 and 14 meet, 12 + 14/2 = 13. Now count the number of the different sample means in the table; there are 25. There is only one mean of 14, in the bottom right corner but five means of 10 on the diagonal. Thus five of the 25 sample means, or 20 per cent of them, are 10, **the same as the population mean**. Sample means of 9 and 11 are the next most frequent at 32 per cent (16 + 16) of the means (see below). With 8 and 12, another 24 per cent (12 + 12) are now counted. So sample means of 8, 9, 10, 11, and 12 are 76 per cent of all possible sample means. The sample means furthest from the population mean, the 6 and 14, are the rarest, in each corner, at 4 per cent each.

Indeed all those percentages are really probabilities. The probability of getting a sample mean of 7 is 2 chances in 25, or as more usually expressed, 8 chances in 100, which gets back to the 8 per cent figure.

The logic of a confidence interval should now be more apparent. A researcher has only one sample but most random sample results stay close to the unknown population value. And just to make sure, an extension can be created on each side of the sample mean to make it even more likely that the one sample mean plus its extensions includes the population mean of 10. In this instance 76 per cent of the means +/– 2 (the extension) catch the population mean. When plotted, that is not exactly the bell

	SAMPLE	
Mean	Frequency	%
14	1	4
13	2	8
12	3	12
11	4	16
10	5	20
9	4	16
8	3	12
7	2	8
6	1	4
	Σ 25	100

curve shown in Box 11.3, but you can see the broad outline. Including more and more cases smoothes the lines into that curve.

With a real sample, randomly chosen and at least of size 100, 95 per cent of sample means +/– 1.96 Standard Errors, (the extensions around the one sample mean thus creating a band or what is called an interval), catch the population mean. Technically speaking, this does not mean there is a 95 per cent chance of having the population mean in that one range. It either is or it is not there and cannot be determined with just sample data. So statisticians turn it around and say: it is a safe bet that the one sample mean taken is one of the 95/100 samples +/– 1.96 SE that qualify. There is only a 5 per cent chance that the interval around the one sample mean calculated does not include the population mean.

This is basically how cheaters in professional sports are caught. They provide one sample (actually two, but one is a backup). The authorities have the data that would parallel the table above, although much more sophisticated. But pretend the above works. The population mean value for testosterone, for example, is 10. Athlete X comes in at 14. While that is a possible outcome, it is rare. So if the doping committee is willing to be wrong 4 per cent of the time (how often an honest 14 occurs), the athlete can be accused. Now with a reputation at stake, 4 per cent chance of an error is too high. That is why the tests probably allow only 1 chance in 10 000 that the results could be honest and not involve drugs.

Sample size

One question asked more than any other is 'how large should a sample be?' or 'is the sample large enough?' The decision about sample size is not straightforward. It depends on cost and time, of course, but after that it also depends on a number of considerations and thus there is no definitive answer. This situation is frequently a great disappointment to those who pose such questions. It is those further considerations that are now addressed.

Absolute and relative sample size

One of the most basic considerations, and possibly the most surprising, is that contrary to common expectation, it is the *absolute* size of a sample that is important, not its *relative* size. This means that a national probability sample of 1000 individuals in Canada has as much validity as a national probability sample of 1000 individuals in the US, even though the latter has a much larger population.

Increasing the size of a sample increases the precision of a sample; in effect this means that the 95 per cent confidence interval referred to in Box 11.3 is narrowed. However, a large sample cannot *guarantee* precision, so it is probably better to say that increasing the size of a sample increases the *likely* precision of a sample. This means that, as sample size increases, sampling error decreases. Common sample sizes are 100 (minimum) and then 400, 900,

1600, and 2500. They cut the sampling error in half, to a third, to a fourth, and to a fifth respectively. (You can ignore this, but if it helps, this is because square roots are involved in the denominator of the calculation; thus the original square root of 10 for a sample of 100, becomes 20, 30, 40, and 50 [square root of 2500], yielding the one-half, one-third, one-quarter, and one-fifth.) Notice how the increases in precision become less pronounced (going from 100 to 400 cuts it in half but 100 to 900 reduces it only to a third) and thus the rate of decline in the sample error of the mean declines. Considerations of sampling size are likely to be profoundly affected by matters of time and cost at such a juncture, since striving for smaller and smaller increments of precision becomes an increasingly uneconomic proposition, as ever-larger samples are decreasingly cost efficient.

Fowler (1993) warned against a simple acceptance of this size criterion and argued that it is not normal for researchers to be able to specify in advance 'a desired level of precision' (1993: 34). Moreover, since sampling error is only one component of any error entailed in an estimate, the notion of a desired level of precision is not realistic. Instead, to the extent that this notion affects decisions about sample size, it usually does so in a general rather than calculated way. And ultimately it is money that determines sample size.

Practical tip 👉 *Sample size and probability sampling for students*

As mentioned, the issue of sample size is a frequent concern. Basically, for most quantitative researchers size does matter, the bigger the sample the more representative it is likely to be (provided the sample is randomly selected), regardless of the size of the population from which it is drawn. However, students clearly need to do their research with very limited resources and a truly random sample may not be feasible. The crucial point is to be clear about and to justify what you have done. Explain the difficulties that you would have encountered in generating a random sample. Explain why you really

could not include any more in your sample of respondents. But above all, do not make claims about your sample that are not sustainable. Do not claim that it is representative or that you have a random sample when it is clearly the case that neither of these is true. In other words, be frank about what you have done. Also, there may be good features about your sample—the range of people included, the good response rate, the high level of honesty displayed. Make sure to play up these positive features at the same time as being honest about its limitations.

Non-response

However, considerations about sampling error do not end here. The problem of *non-response* should be borne in mind. In most research only some of the sample agrees to participate. If the aim is for 450 students and a prediction, based on other surveys, is for a 20 per cent rate of non-response, it may be advisable to sample 575 individuals, on the grounds that approximately 115 (20 per cent) will be non-respondents, leaving 460 and still room for some extra refusals.

The issue of refusal to participate is of particular significance because many researchers are experiencing declining response rates to social surveys (see Box 11.5) and not just in North America. In the US, estimates put it at about 30 per cent. So what looks like a 70/30 per cent split on something like approval of homosexual marriage can even out at 50/50 when these non-responders are counted after the fact. In the 2004 federal election, the 'don't know' response, a slightly different form of non-response, made pre-election predictions inaccurate. However, Smith (1995) showed that things like the subject matter of the research, the type of respondent, and the level of effort expended on improving the number of cooperating respondents affect non-response rates.

A further interesting issue in connection with non-response is that of how far researchers should go to boost response rates. Later in the chapter, a number of steps that can improve response rates to postal questionnaires, which are particularly prone to poor response rates, are discussed. However, boosting response rates can prove expensive. Teitler *et al.* (2003) presented a discussion of the steps taken to boost the response rate of a US sample that was hard to reach, namely, both of the unwed parents of newly-born children. They found that although increasing the sample from an initial 68 per cent to 80 per cent of all couples meant that the final sample resembled more closely the population from which the sample had been taken, diminishing returns set in. In other words, improvements in the characteristics of the sample necessitated a disproportionate outlay of resources. However, this is not to say that steps should not be taken to improve response rates. For example, following up respondents who do not initially respond to a postal questionnaire invariably results in an improved response rate at little additional cost.

Box 11.5 ⚪ *What is a response rate?*

A concern with *response rate* is common in social survey research; invariably some people in the sample refuse to participate. The response rate is the percentage of a sample that agrees to participate. Beagan's study (2001) of medical students made three attempts to get her 59 per cent response rate. However, its calculation is more complicated than this. First, not everyone who actually participates is included. If a large number of questions are not answered by a respondent or if it is clear that the interview or questionnaire was not taken seriously, some researchers exclude such a person and then employ only the number of *usable* interviews or questionnaires as the numerator. Similarly, not everyone in a sample turns out to be a suitable or appropriate respondent or can be contacted. Thus the response rate could be calculated as follows:

$$\frac{\text{number of usable questionnaires}}{\text{total sample} - \text{unsuitable or uncontactable members of the sample}} \times 100$$

The uncontactable must be examined, from whatever data exist on them, to see if they are different from those who are. Are they richer and on vacation? Are they ill and in hospital? Such differences may be important, depending on the research topic and should be taken into account in the analysis. Ironically, when research is based on a convenience sample it can be argued that a low response rate is less significant.

Heterogeneity of the population

Yet another consideration is the homogeneity and heterogeneity of the population from which the sample is to be taken. When a population is heterogeneous, like a whole country or city, the samples drawn are likely to be highly varied. When it is relatively homogeneous, such as a population of students or of members of an occupation, the amount of variation is less. The implication is that the greater the heterogeneity of a population, the larger a sample should be, to maximize the chance that all groups are represented.

Kind of analysis

Finally, researchers should bear in mind the *kind of analysis* intended. A case in point here is the contingency table showing the relationship between two variables in tabular form (see Chapter 12) or how variation in one variable relates to variation in another. In a 2 × 2 table there are four cells into which the data must fall, let's say gender (M/F) × whether voted in last election (Y/N). Suppose there were only 10 males and 10 females in the sample, and that 50 per cent of the men and 50 per cent of the women voted, showing no relationship. But suppose the sample by chance included one more woman who voted (rather than did not) and one man who did not. Now the figures are 40 per cent of men voted versus 60 per cent of women, quite a difference. To prevent this misinterpretation and for some stability a larger sample is required. Probably one would want to have at least 50 males and 50 females. Because there are approximately the same number of men and women, this is easy. But what if the variable is religion? Fifty Roman Catholics (or 50 Anglicans) are easy to find in any random sample of 1000. But what about 50 Jehovah's Witnesses or 50 Hindus? Here one strategy to achieve some stability of numbers is to randomly over-sample some of these small groups as Dinovitzer *et al.* (2003) did to guarantee sufficient social class variation.

Now suppose the variable related to voting is in which of Canada's provinces or territories one lives. The old sample size of 100 for gender is not looking so good. Even if they are grouped into five regions, a sample of 100 is insufficient, 250 better. And if a study is looking at both gender and region, the latter determines the sample size required. Thus, considerations of sample size should be sensitive to the planned analysis, here the number of cells in a table.

Types of non-probability sampling

Non-probability sampling is an umbrella term for all those forms of sampling not conducted according to the canons of probability sampling outlined above. It covers a wide range of different types of sampling strategy, at least one of which—the quota sample—is claimed by some practitioners to be almost as good as a probability sample. This section covers three main non-probability samples: the convenience sample; the snowball sample; and the quota sample.

Convenience sampling

A convenience sample is one that is simply available to the researcher by virtue of its accessibility. Imagine a researcher who teaches education at a university interested in the qualities teachers want in their principals and who administers a questionnaire to several classes of students, all of whom are teachers taking a part-time master's degree in education. The chances are that the researcher will receive all or almost all of the questionnaires back, for a good response rate. (Recall, however, the ethical question of asking people dependent on a grade from the researcher for their cooperation in research.) The findings may prove quite interesting, but the use of that sampling strategy makes it impossible to generalize the findings, because this sample is not representative but simply a group of teachers available to the researcher. They are almost certainly not representative of teachers as a whole—the very fact they are taking this degree program marks them off as different from teachers in general.

This is not to suggest that convenience samples should never be used. In fact they are used more often than suspected. Beagan's (2001) study of one class at a medical school and MacKinnon and Luke's (2002) study of cultural change involved a convenience sample of only 70 students. Convenience samples are also good for pilot studies. Pretend that the education professor is developing a battery of questions to measure the leadership preferences of teachers. Since it is highly desirable to pre-test such a research instrument before actually using it, administering it to a group not a part of the main study is a legitimate way of doing some preliminary analysis of such issues as whether respondents will reply honestly to questions on sensitive topics. In other words, for this purpose, a convenience sample is acceptable, except for the ethical issue raised above. A second context in which a convenience sample is acceptable is when it represents too good an opportunity to miss. The resulting data do not allow generalizable findings, but they can provide a springboard for further research or allow links to be forged with existing findings in an area. Box 11.6 contains an example of a convenience sample.

Box 11.6 A convenience sample

Suppose you want to study university undergraduates to find out the extent of their part-time employment while at school. To save time and effort you conduct the study at your school, that choice alone making the sample a convenience one, as it rules out all other universities in Canada. The choice within your university, however, can still be a probability sample but you think the problem not important enough to justify the cost. Thus, you choose five of the faculties there, and within each, one or two of the specific degree programs offered by the faculty. Pretend the final result is anthropology, art, chemistry, electrical engineering, French, kinesiology, media studies, and psychology. This choice of subjects is designed to maximize variety in the type of degree program and to provide similar numbers of males and females (since in particular degree programs one gender frequently predominates). Self-completion questionnaires can then be given to students in some first-, final-, and then either second- or third-year courses.

These procedures represent a very good attempt to generate a varied sample. It is a convenience sample, because the choice of university, faculty, and degree program is done purposively rather than randomly. Because of the way the questionnaires are administered (in class), there is a very high response rate. On the other hand, absentees from classes do not get a chance to fill out a questionnaire. An interesting question is whether absence from class is connected in some way to part-time working; in other words, is absence higher among students working at the time of the class or students perhaps too tired to go to the class because of their part-time work? Checking during the next scheduled class can provide some information here.

Box 11.7 A snowball sample of marijuana users

Becker (1963: 45–6) reported on how he generated a sample of marijuana users:

> I had been a professional dance musician . . . and my first interviews were with people I had met in the music business. I asked them to put me in contact with other [marijuana] users who would be willing to discuss their experiences with me. . . . Although in the end half of the fifty interviews were conducted with musicians, the other half covered a wide range of people, including labourers, machinists, and people in the professions.

Snowball sampling

Snowball sampling is a form of convenience sample, but worth distinguishing because it has attracted quite a lot of attention over the years. With this approach, the researcher makes initial contact with a small group of people who are relevant to the research topic and then uses them to establish contacts with others. Tastsoglou and Miedema (2003) used an approach like this to create a sample of immigrant women in the Maritimes. Box 11.7 describes the generation of a snowball sample of marijuana users for what is often regarded as a classic study of drug use.

Becker's comment on this method of creating a snowball sample is interesting: 'The sample is, of course, in no sense "random"; [indeed] it would not be possible to draw a random sample, since no one knows the nature of the universe from which it would have to be drawn' (Becker 1963: 46). What Becker is essentially saying here is there is no accessible sampling frame for the population from which the sample is to be taken. The difficulty of creating such a sampling frame means that a non-probability approach is the only feasible one. Moreover, even if one could create a sampling frame of marijuana users or of British visitors to Disney theme parks, it would almost certainly be inaccurate straightaway, because each is a shifting population. People become and cease being marijuana users, while new theme park visitors arrive every minute.

The problem with snowball sampling is that it is very unlikely to be representative of the population, though, as just suggested, the very notion of a population is problematic in some circumstances. However, by and large, snowball sampling is used not within a quantitative research strategy, but within a qualitative one: both Becker's and Bryman's studies used a qualitative research framework. Concerns about external validity and ability to generalize often do not loom large within a qualitative research strategy (see Chapters 3 and 8). Indeed Tastsoglou and Miedema (2003) warned the reader not to generalize from their 40 women to all immigrant women in the Maritimes, much less to those in the rest of Canada. This is not to suggest that snowball sampling is entirely irrelevant to quantitative research: when the researcher needs to focus upon relationships between people, tracing connections through snowball sampling can be a better approach than conventional probability sampling. Statistically small groups—such as gay left-handed lawyers, for a frivolous example—would be found with a snowball approach. Taking a random sample of all lawyers is too costly to find this small group.

Quota sampling

While quota sampling is infrequently used in academic social research, it is used intensively in commercial research, such as market research and political opinion polling. The aim of quota sampling is to produce a sample that reflects a population in terms of the relative proportions of people in different categories, such as gender, ethnicity, age groups, socioeconomic groups, and region of residence, and often in combinations of these categories. However, unlike a stratified sample, the sampling of individuals is not carried out randomly, since the final selection of people is left up to the interviewer. Information about the stratification of the Canadian population or about certain regions can be obtained from sources like the Census and from surveys based on probability samples such as the General Social Survey.

Once the categories and the number of people to be interviewed within each category (known as *quotas*) have been decided, interviewers merely have to select people who fit these categories. The quotas are typically interrelated. In a manner similar to strati-

fied sampling, the population may be divided into strata in terms of, for example, gender, employment, and age all at once (see Table 11.2). Census data can identify the number of people who should be in each subgroup; thus the numbers to be interviewed in each subgroup reflect the population. Interviewers then can seek out individuals who fit the subgroup quotas. Accordingly, an interviewer may be told to find and interview five 25- to 44-year-old unemployed females at an assigned location, such as a mall. Interviewers usually ask people who are available to them about those characteristics (though gender will presumably be self-evident) in order to determine their suitability for a particular subgroup. Once a subgroup quota (or a combination of subgroup quotas) is achieved, the interviewer is no longer concerned to locate individuals for that subgroup and moves on to another.

The choice of respondents is left to the interviewer, subject to the requirement of all quotas being filled, usually within a certain time period. Most Canadians have been approached in a mall by a person toting a clipboard and interview schedule and asked about their age, occupation, and so on, before being asked a series of questions about a product or whatever. That person is almost certainly an interviewer with a quota sample to fill. Sometimes, she will decide not to interview you because the quota of your group is already filled or you are in a group with no quota, for example, students who are often declared ineligible for inclusion.

Table 11.2 Strata for gender, age, and employment

Older, female, unemployed (5%)	Younger, female, unemployed (4%)
Older, female, employed (17%)	Younger, female, employed (20%)
Older, female, other (7%)	Younger, female, other (1%)
Older, male, unemployed (3%)	Younger, male, unemployed (6%)
Older, male, employed (15%)	Younger, male, employed (15%)
Older, male, other (6%)	Younger, male, other (1%)

A number of criticisms are frequently levelled at quota samples:

- Because the choice of respondent is left to the interviewer, the proponents of probability sampling argue that a quota sample cannot be representative. It may accurately reflect the population in terms of superficial characteristics, as defined by the quotas. However, in their choice of people to approach, interviewers may be unduly influenced by their perceptions of how friendly people are or by whether the people make eye contact with the interviewer (unlike many who look at the ground and shuffle past as quickly as possible, not wanting to be bothered).

- People who are in an interviewer's vicinity at interview times, therefore available to be approached, are not typical. There is a risk, for example, that people not in full-time paid work may be overrepresented, especially in malls, making the sample not representative.

- Judgments about eligibility may sometimes be incorrect, not usually for gender, but more so for age, and even more for social class. For example, someone who is actually eligible to be interviewed, but maybe younger than he or she looks, is not asked, because the quota of the older group is filled. In such a case, a possible element of bias is being introduced.

- It is not proper to calculate a standard error of the mean from a quota sample, making the use of many statistics inappropriate, because the range of possible values of a population cannot be determined.

All of this makes the quota sample look like a poor bet and there is no doubt that it is not favoured by academic social researchers. It does have some arguments in its favour, however:

- It is undoubtedly cheaper than a comparable probability sample. There is generally no travelling involved and it is easier to manage. It is unnecessary to keep track of people who need to be re-contacted or to keep track of refusals. Still patterns of refusal should be reported. For example, if it becomes apparent that most men (but not women) do not want to take part, this can signal bias in the results as those men who agree are truly a small minority.

- When speed is of the essence, a quota sample is invaluable. Newspapers frequently need to know how a sample of voters feels about a topic or how they intend to vote and conduct polls weekly or even more often as an election nears. Alternatively, a sudden major news event may require a more or less instant picture of the nation's views or responses. Again, a quota sample is much faster.

- As with convenience sampling, it is useful for conducting development work on new measures or research instruments or in exploratory work from which new theoretical ideas may be generated.

Structured observation and sampling

Just like survey research, structured observation necessitates decisions about sampling. However, with structured observation, issues surrounding sampling do not revolve solely around how to sample people and if they did, the considerations involved in probability sampling might not apply. Several other sampling issues are involved:

- public areas have no sampling frame. Thus people walking along a street and men who frequent tea-rooms do not permit random sampling. One can, however, choose the people by use of a table of random numbers, for example, the 3rd, then 7th, then 18th person seen on the street. That same table can be used to establish random samples of time, place, or activity where a sampling frame is more feasible.

- time sampling involves an observer recording whatever is happening at a time, for example, in a pub every 15 minutes after a random start. This can be done on one person or on several individuals at once and the 15 minutes figure can be varied using a table of random numbers. It is necessary that individuals watched on more than one occasion not be observed at the same time of the day; it is desirable for the observation periods to be randomly selected. For example, it would be an error to observe a certain pupil in a school classroom always at the end of the day when most students are tired. Being tired can give a false impression of that pupil's behaviour. Time sampling should be combined with the next strategy:

- a list of places can be randomly sampled, for example, in a pub near the phone, at the bar, by the pool table, outside where the smokers congregate, the washroom area, and the booths;

- 'behaviour sampling,' whereby an entire group is watched and the observer records a particular kind of behaviour. Thus in that same pub, one can observe the nth pick-up (second then fifth etc.) that occurs once the previous one has been observed, that n taken from a random number table.

Considerations relating to probability sampling derive largely from concerns about external validity. Such concerns are not necessarily totally addressed by resorting to probability sampling, however. For example, if a structured observation study is conducted over a relatively short span of time, issues of the stability or representativeness of the findings over time are likely to arise. If the research is conducted in schools, for example, observations conducted towards the end of the school year, when examinations are likely to loom large in the thinking of both teachers and students, may affect the results obtained compared to observations at a different point in the academic year. Consequently, consideration has to be given to the question of the timing of observation. Furthermore, how are the sites in which structured observation is to take place selected? Are they themselves representative? Clearly, a random sampling procedure for the selection of schools can assuage any worries in this connection. However, in view of the difficulty of securing access to settings such as schools and business organizations, it is likely that the organizations to which access is secured are not representative.

Limits to generalization

One point, often not fully appreciated, is that even when a sample is selected using probability sampling, any findings can be generalized *only* to the population from which that sample is taken. This is an obvious point, but it is easy to think that findings from a study have a broader applicability. In the imaginary study of alcohol consumption among students at a university, findings should be generalized only to that one university and not to students at other universities. There may be a higher (or lower) concentration of pubs in this one university's vicinity, there may be more (or less) of a culture of drinking at this university, or the university may recruit a higher (or lower) proportion of students with disposable income who can afford to drink. There may be many other factors too. Similarly, one should be cautious of overgeneralizing in terms of locality. What is true in Quebec is often not true in Saskatchewan.

One issue rarely discussed in this context and almost impossible to assess is whether there is a time limit on the findings generated. Quite aside from the fact that findings cannot (or at least should not) be generalized beyond the area sampled, is there a point at which one should say, 'Well, those findings applied *then* and maybe things have changed?' To take a simple example: no one assumes that the findings of a 1980 study of university students' budgeting and personal finance habits still apply to students in the early twenty-first century. Ever-increasing costs have changed how students finance their education, including perhaps a greater reliance on part-time work or parents and more loans. But, even when there is no definable or recognizable source of relevant change of this kind, there is still the possibility (or even likelihood) that findings are temporally specific. Thus there is a new meaning and reason for replication.

Sampling problems

There is some evidence that compared to random samples, quota samples are often biased. They underrepresent people in lower social strata, people who work in the private sector and manufacturing, and people at the extremes of income, and overrepresent women in households with children and people from larger households (Butcher 1994). On the other hand, probability samples are often biased too—for example, they underrepresent men and those in employment (Marsh and Scarbrough 1990) who may be both harder to contact and busier, thus less willing.

Other errors with respect to sampling (see Figure 11.6) include:

• *Sampling error.* See Box 11.1 for a definition. This kind of error arises because it is rare to end up with

Figure 11.6 Four sources of error in research

a truly representative sample, even when probability sampling is employed.

• *Sampling-related error* arises from activities or events related to the sampling process. Examples are an inaccurate sampling frame and non-response; each reduces generalizability or the external validity of findings.

Qualitative sampling

The sampling of informants in ethnographic research is often a combination of convenience sampling and snowball sampling, taking information from whatever sources are available. Very often they face opposition or at least indifference to their research and are relieved to glean information or views from whoever is prepared to divulge such details. This seems to have been the essence of Taylor's strategy; her female drug users were

> eventually obtained by a mix of 'snowballing techniques' . . . and my almost continuous presence in the area. . . . Rather than ask to be introduced or given names of others I could contact, when I met a woman I would spend as much time with her as she would allow, participating in her daily round, and through this come to meet others in her social circle. My continued presence in the area also led other women drug users to approach me when I was alone. . . . In addition, the drug worker in the area would mention my presence and interest to women with whom he came in contact and facilitate introductions where possible (1993: 16).

Ethnographers who take on a role that is closer to that of observer-as-participant rely somewhat more

on formally asking for names of others who may be relevant and who can be contacted.

Whichever strategy is adopted, the question is whether either results in a representative sample of informants. Probability sampling is almost never used in ethnographic research and is rarely employed even in qualitative research based on interviews. In many cases, it is not feasible to conduct a probability sampling exercise because it is difficult and often impossible to map 'the population' from which a random sample may be taken—that is, to create a sampling frame. Instead, ethnographers have to ensure that they gain access to as wide a range of individuals relevant to the research question as possible, so that many different perspectives and ranges of activity can become the focus of attention.

Theoretical sampling

An alternative strategy is *theoretical sampling* (see Box 11.8), advocated by Strauss and Corbin (1998). In their view, because of its reliance on statistical rather than theoretical criteria, probability sampling is not appropriate to qualitative research. Theoretical sam-

Box 11.8 🔆 *What is theoretical sampling?*

In theoretical sampling the researcher simultaneously collects and analyzes the data, decides what data to collect next and where to find them, and develops a theory as it emerges. The process of data collection is controlled by the emerging theory, whether substantive or formal. It is an ongoing process rather than a distinct and single stage, as it is, for example, in probability sampling.

For Charmaz (2000: 519), theoretical sampling is a 'defining property of grounded theory' and is concerned with the refinement of ideas, rather than boosting sample size (see Box 11.9).

Moreover, it is not just people that are the 'objects' of sampling, but also settings and events. This can be seen in a more recent definition: 'Data gathering driven by concepts derived from the evolving theory and based on the concept of "making comparisons," whose purpose is to go to places, people, or events that will maximize opportunities to discover variations among concepts and to identify categories in terms of their properties and dimensions' (Strauss and Corbin 1998: 201).

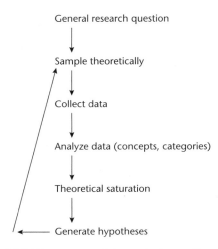

Figure 11.7 The process of theoretical sampling

generate hypotheses out of the categories that are building up and then move on to collecting data in relation to these hypotheses.

Proponents of grounded theory argue also that there is a great deal of redundancy in statistical sampling. For example, a commitment to interviewing a certain per cent of an organization's members may mean wasting time and resources because the significance of a concept and/or its connections with other concepts can sometimes be confirmed with a smaller sample. Instead, grounded theory advocates sam-

pling is meant to be an alternative strategy and 'done in order to discover categories and their properties and to suggest the interrelationships into a theory. Statistical sampling is done to obtain accurate evidence on distributions of people among categories to be used in descriptions and verifications' (Glaser and Strauss 1967: 62).

Figure 11.7 outlines the main steps in theoretical sampling. The reference in Box 11.8 to 'places, people, or events' is a reminder that, in ethnographic research, it is not just people who are being sampled but also events and contexts as well (see below).

In grounded theory, data collecting continues (observing, interviewing, and collecting documents) until the point of *theoretical saturation* (see Box 11.9). This means that previous interviews/observations have both formed the basis for the creation of a category and confirmed its importance. There is no longer a need to collect data in relation to that category. Instead, the researcher should move on and

Box 11.9 🔆 *What is theoretical saturation?*

The key is to carry on sampling theoretically until a category has been saturated with data. 'This means, until (a) no new or relevant data seem to be emerging regarding a category, (b) the category is well developed in terms of its properties and dimensions demonstrating variation, and (c) the relationships among categories are well established and validated' (Strauss and Corbin 1998: 212). In the language of grounded theory, a category operates at a somewhat higher level of abstraction than a concept in that it may group together several concepts that have common features denoted by the category. Theoretical saturation refers to the sampling, not just of people, but also of settings and events.

pling in terms of what is relevant to and meaningful for a theory up until a satiation point is reached.

Not just people

As pointed out in the last section, ethnographic sampling is not just about people but also about other things. Time and context may need consideration in the sampling process. Attending to *time* means that the ethnographer must make sure that people or events are observed at different times of the day and different days of the week, to avoid drawing inferences valid only for mornings or for weekdays rather than weekends, for example. It is impossible to be an ob-server at all times if only for the need to write up notes and body imperatives (eating, sleeping, and so on).

Because behaviour is influenced by contextual factors, it is also important to observe in a variety of locations. For example, football hooliganism is not a full-time occupation. To understand the culture and worldview of football hooligans, writers like Armstrong (1993) and Giulianotti (1995) had to en-sure that they interacted with them not just around the time of football matches, but also in a variety of contexts like pubs and when they engaged in gen-eral socializing. Rosenhan in his study of psychiatric hospitals would have to do the same (see Box 8.9).

Content analysis sampling

There are several phases in the selection of a sample for content analysis. The case of applying content analysis to the mass media is explored here but the basic principles have a broader relevance to other of its applications.

Sampling media

Many studies of the mass media specify a research problem in the form of 'examining the representation of *X* in the mass media.' The *X* may be trade unions, portrayal of women, food scares, crime, or drunk driv-ing. Thus Beharrell's (1993) study of the reporting and representation of AIDS/HIV concentrated on national newspapers over three years ended up with over 4000 news items. But which mass media to choose—news-papers, television, radio, or chat rooms? And, if news-papers, will it be tabloids, broadsheets, both? Will it include Sunday papers, free newspapers? Will feature articles and letters to the editor be included?

Sampling dates

Sometimes, the decision about dates is more or less dictated by the occurrence of a phenomenon. For example, the time for studying the growing presence of squeegee kids in Toronto was dictated by their ini-tial proliferation and then their legislated disappear-ance (Parnaby 2003). One could hardly examine the issue prior to their spread nor continue after their re-moval. With a research question that entails an on-going general phenomenon like crime, the matter of dates is more open. Probability sampling can be used here for sampling dates, for example, generating a systematic sample of dates by randomly selecting one day and then selecting every *n*th day thereafter.

The time span analyzed in content analysis thus depends on the research questions, and often the key decision becomes when to stop. For example, if Jagger (1998) had wanted to look for changes in how men and women represent themselves in dating advertise-ments (see Box 16.1) she would obviously have had to examine the columns of earlier years. She could have taken comparable samples from 10 and 20 years earlier. But she could have gone back even further. Warde (1997) was specifically interested in changes in representations of food (what should be eaten and how it should be eaten) in food columns in five of the most widely read women's weekly magazines. He looked at two years, 20 years apart, and within each year at the February, May, August, and November is-sues to ensure that seasonal factors did not overly in-fluence the findings. (If he had selected magazines just from November, there might have been a preoc-cupation with Christmas fare, while findings from a summer issue might have been affected by the greater availability of certain foods, such as particular fruit.) The final choice of years and months was somewhat arbitrary and reflects this issue of when to stop.

Reducing non-response

The question of whether response rates (see Box 11.5), are lower using the telephone than in person is unclear, in that there is little consistent evidence on this question (see Table 11.3). However, there is a general *belief* that telephone interviews achieve slightly lower rates than personal interviews (Shuy 2002; Frey 2004). Developments in telephone communications such as the growing use of call screening and of mobile phones have certainly had an adverse effect on telephone survey response.

Since interviewers represent the interface between the research and the respondent, they have an important role in maximizing the response rate for the survey. The following points should be borne in mind:

- Interviewers should be prepared to keep calling back if interviewees are out or unavailable. This requires taking into account people's likely work and leisure habits—for example, there is no point in daytime calling on people who work during the day. In addition, people living alone may be reluctant to answer the door, especially after dark.

- Be self-assured; a better response rate may result from presuming that people will agree to be interviewed rather than that they will refuse.

- Reassure people that you are not a salesperson. Because of the unethical tactics of organizations whose representatives say they are doing market or social research, many people have become very suspicious of people saying they would 'just like to ask a few questions.'

- Dress in a way that is acceptable to a wide spectrum of people.

- Make it clear that you are happy to find a time to suit the respondent.

Improving response rates to postal questionnaires

Mangione (1995: 60–1) provided the following classification of responses rate to postal questionnaires:

Over 85% excellent

70–85% very good

60–69% acceptable

50–59% barely acceptable

Below 50% not acceptable

Because of the tendency for postal questionnaire surveys to generate lower response rates than com-

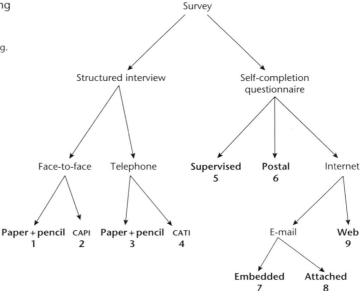

Figure 11.8 Main modes of administering a survey

CAPI is Computer-Assisted Personal Interviewing.
CATI is Computer-Assisted Telephone Interviewing.

Table 11.3 Comparing the strengths of different ways of contacting members of the chosen sample

	Mode of survey administration				
	Face-to-face interview	Telephone interview	Posted questionnaire	E-mail	Web
Resource issues					
Is the cost of the mode of administration relatively low?	✓	✓✓	✓✓✓	✓✓✓	✓ (unless access to low-cost software)
Is the speed of the mode of administration relatively fast?	✓	✓✓✓	✓✓✓	✓✓✓	✓✓✓
Is the cost of handling a dispersed sample relatively low?	✓ (✓✓ if clustered)	✓✓✓	✓✓✓	✓✓✓	✓✓✓
Sampling-related issues					
Does the mode of administration tend to produce a good response rate?	✓✓✓	✓✓	✓	✓	✓
Is the researcher able to control who responds (i.e., the person targeted is one who answers)?	✓✓✓	✓✓✓	✓✓	✓✓	✓✓
Is the mode of administration accessible to all sample members?	✓✓✓	✓✓	✓✓✓	✓ (because of need for respondents to be accessible online)	✓ (because of need for respondents to be accessible online)
Is the mode of administration less likely to result in non-response to some questions?	✓✓✓	✓✓✓	✓✓	✓✓	✓✓

Notes: Number of ticks indicates the strength of the mode of administration of a questionnaire in relation to each issue. More ticks correspond to more advantages in relation to each issue. A single tick implies that the mode of administering a questionnaire does not fare well in this area. Two ticks imply that it is acceptable and three ticks that it does very well. This table was influenced by Czaja and Blair (1996).

CAPI is Computer-Assisted Personal Interviewing; CATI is Computer-Assisted Telephone Interviewing.

parable structured interview surveys (and the implications this has for the validity of findings), a great deal of thought and research has gone into ways of improving survey response. The following steps are frequently suggested:

- Write a good covering letter explaining the reasons for the research, why it is important, and why the recipient has been selected; provide guarantees of confidentiality. Making it personal, by having the respondent's name and address in the covering letter and each letter individually signed cannot hurt.

- Postal questionnaires should always be accompanied by a stamped addressed envelope or, at the very least, return postage.

- Do not allow the questionnaire to appear unnecessarily bulky. Some researchers reduce the size of the questionnaire to fit a booklet format. As with structured interviewing (see Chapter 4), begin with questions more likely to be of interest to the respondent.

- Follow up individuals who do not reply at first, possibly with two or three further mailings. The importance of reminders cannot be overstated—they do work. One approach is to send out a reminder letter to non-respondents two weeks after the initial mailing, reasserting the nature and aims of the survey and suggesting that the person should contact a member of the research team to obtain a replacement copy of the questionnaire should the original one have been lost. Then, two

Practical tip 👉 Response rates

Response rates are important because the lower a response rate, the more questions are likely to be raised about how representative the achieved sample is. In a sense, this is likely to be an issue only with randomly selected samples. With samples not selected by probability sampling, it can be argued that the response rate is less of an issue because the sample is not representative of a population even if everyone participates. Postal questionnaire surveys in particular are often associated with low response rates and as Mangione's classification illustrates, according to some authorities a response rate below 50 per cent is not acceptable.

On the one hand, a great deal of published research achieves only a low response rate, so do not despair. The key point is to recognize and acknowledge its possible negative implications. On the other hand, many students find mail and other forms of questionnaire attractive because of their low cost and quick administration. The point of this discussion is not to be put off using such techniques just because of the prospect of a low response rate. There are other considerations.

weeks after that all continuing non-respondents should be sent another letter along with a further copy of the questionnaire. These reminders have a demonstrable effect on the response rate. Some writers argue for even more than two mailings of reminder letters to non-respondents. If a response rate is worryingly low, such further mailings are certainly desirable.

- Writing the cover letter to 'Occupant' loses most people; writing to a specific person is better. The downside is it may raise concerns: how did they know about me and will my responses really be confidential? Therefore, the researcher should try to deal with these potential fears in the letter.

- Providing monetary incentives increases the response rate but can be deemed unethical. They are more effective if the money comes with the questionnaire rather than if it is promised after its return. Apparently, respondents typically do not cynically take the money and discard the questionnaire. The evidence also suggests that quite small amounts of money have a positive impact on the response rate, but that larger amounts do not necessarily improve the response rate any further.

Virtual sampling issues

A major limitation of online surveys is that not everyone is online and has the technical ability to handle questionnaires online in either e-mail or web formats. Certain other features of online communications also make such surveys more problematic, such as:

- many people have more than one e-mail address;

- many people use more than one Internet Service Provider (ISP);

- a household may have one computer but several users;

- Internet users are a biased sample of the population in that they tend to be better educated, wealthier, younger, and not representative in ethnic terms (Couper 2000); and

- few sampling frames exist of the general online population and most of these are likely to be expensive to acquire since they are controlled by ISPs or may be confidential.

Such issues make the possibilities of conducting online surveys using probability sampling principles difficult to envisage. This is not to say that online surveys should not be considered. For example, in many organizations, most if not all non-manual workers are likely to be online and familiar with using e-mail and the Internet. Most university students are the same (Couper 2000).

The chief problem with virtual sampling strategies is having no idea about the representativeness of those who answer, for example, through a web survey questionnaire (though the same applies to the respondents of a paper-based questionnaire too). On the other hand, given incomplete knowledge and understanding of online behaviour and attitudes relating to online issues, it could reasonably be argued that some information about these areas is a lot better than none at all, provided the limitations of the findings in terms of their generalizability are appreciated.

There is growing evidence that online surveys typically generate lower response rates than mailed questionnaire surveys (Tse 1998; Sheehan 2001). In the early years, response rates for e-mail surveys were quite encouraging (Sheehan and Hoy 1999), but more recently they have been declining and are at lower levels than those for most mailed questionnaires (Sheehan 2001), though there are clear exceptions. Two factors may account for this decline: the novelty of e-mail surveys in the early years and a growing antipathy towards unsolicited e-mails among online communities. However, response rates can be boosted by following two simple strategies:

1. Contact prospective respondents before sending them a questionnaire. This is regarded as basic 'netiquette.'

2. As with postal questionnaire surveys, follow up non-respondents at least once.

The case for the first of these two strategies in boosting response rates is not entirely clear (Sheehan 2001), but seems to be generally advisable.

Overview

Online surveys are still in their infancy and have potential if only for their low cost. There is evidence that having a web survey or even an e-mail option can boost response rates to mailed questionnaires (Yun and Trumbo 2000). Several problems also have been identified with web and e-mail surveys but it is too early to dismiss them because methodologists are only beginning to get to grips with this approach to survey research and may gradually develop ways of overcoming the limitations being identified. Moreover, as pointed out, for certain kinds of populations (the young, wealthy, etc.) and as more and more people and organizations go online, some of the sampling-related problems will diminish.

One last point

Sampling decisions are the last step for most researchers before going into the field. Thus this may be a good time to review the ethical principles presented previously. They are included here for perusal.

Ethical issue 11.2 *A final checklist of ethical issues to consider just before going into the field to collect data*

- Have you read and incorporated your institution's ethical requirements for research? If only certain types of research need to be submitted for formal approval, is your research exempt or does it require clearance?

- Have you ensured that there is no prospect of any harm coming to participants?

- Does your research conform to the principle of informed consent, so that research participants understand:
  — what the research is about?
  — the purposes of the research?
  — who is sponsoring it?
  — the nature of their involvement in the research?
  — how long their participation is going to take?
  — that participation is voluntary?
  — that they can withdraw from participation at any time, even after the research starts?

  — what is going to happen to the data (e.g., how kept, when destroyed)?

- Are you sure that the privacy of the people involved in your research will not be violated and the confidentiality of data relating to your research participants will be maintained?

- If deception is involved, have you ensured that research participants will be debriefed, that is, explained its true purpose in a timely manner?

- After the data have been collected, have you ensured that the names of research participants and/or organizations involved will be made unidentifiable? Does the strategy for archiving data in electronic form comply with data protection legislation?

K KEY POINTS

- Probability sampling is a mechanism for reducing bias in sample selection.

- Become familiar with key technical terms in sampling such as: representative sample; random sample; non-response; population; sampling error; etc.

- Randomly selected samples are important because they permit generalizations to the population and because they have certain known qualities.

- Sampling error decreases as sample size increases.

- Quota samples can provide reasonable alternatives to random samples, but they have some deficiencies.

- Convenience samples can provide interesting data, but it is crucial to be aware of their limited generalizability.

- Sampling and sampling-related error are just two sources of error in social survey research.

- Sampling considerations in qualitative research differ from those addressed in quantitative research, in that issues of representativeness are less emphasized.

- Sampling in qualitative research must be done on people, places, times, even behaviours.

- Non-response rates vary by the medium of communication and most can be improved by persistent follow-up procedures.

Q QUESTIONS FOR REVIEW

- What do each of the following terms mean: population; non-probability sampling; sampling frame; representative sample; and non-sampling error?
- What are the goals of sampling?
- What are the main areas of potential bias in sampling?

Sampling error

- What is the significance of sampling error for achieving a representative sample?

Types of probability sample

- What is probability sampling and why is it important?
- What are the main types of probability sample?
- How does a stratified random sample offer greater precision than a simple random sample?
- To conduct an interview survey of around 500 people in Winnipeg, what type of probability sample would be best and why?
- A researcher positions herself on a street corner and asks every fifth person who walks by to be interviewed until she has a sample of 250. List some of the kinds of people to whom she should probably not generalize her results.

Sample size

- What factors should be taken into account in deciding the size needed for a probability sample?
- 'Non-response makes even most probability samples non-representative and thus not really worth the extra cost.' Discuss.

Types of non-probability sample

- Which form of non-probability sample is probably least useful and which most?
- What circumstances make snowball sampling appropriate?
- 'Both quota samples and true random samples generate representative samples, with little difference between them. This accounts for the widespread use of quota samples in market research and opinion polling.' Discuss.

Limits to generalization

- 'The problem of generalization to a population involves more than getting a representative sample.' Discuss.

Qualitative sampling

- What is theoretical sampling?
- How crucial is the idea of theoretical saturation to theoretical sampling?

Reducing non-response

- Realistically, what can you do to improve the response rate to a mailed questionnaire?

12 Quantitative data analysis

CHAPTER OVERVIEW

In this chapter some of the basic, but frequently used, methods for analyzing quantitative data analysis are presented. To illustrate them, a small imaginary data set on attendance at a gym is attached, the kind of small research project that is feasible for most undergraduates.

The chapter explores:

• the importance of anticipating questions of analysis early in the research process and certainly before all of the data have been collected;

• the different kinds of variables generated in quantitative research; knowing how to distinguish them is cru-

cial in the choice of a specific statistical method of analysis;

• methods for analyzing a single variable at a time (*univariate analysis*);

• methods for analyzing relationships between variables (*bivariate analysis*);

• analysis of relationships among three or more variables (*multivariate analysis*); and

• SPSS software procedures for accomplishing all three levels of analysis.

Introduction

In this chapter, some very basic techniques for analyzing quantitative data are examined; following that, sophisticated computer software (SPSS for Windows) for their calculation is introduced. The formulae that underpin them are not presented, since the necessary calculations can easily be done by SPSS, but some of the logic underlying them is. One chapter cannot do justice to these topics and readers are advised to consult books that provide more detailed and advanced treatments (e.g., Healey 2002).

Before beginning this exposition of techniques, a warning is appropriate. The biggest mistake in quantitative data analysis is to think that analysis decisions can wait until after the data collection is

complete. Analysis indeed does occur typically at a later and separate stage in the overall process. But, one should be fully aware of what techniques will be applied much earlier—for example, when designing the questionnaire, observation schedule, and coding frame. The two main reasons for this are as follows:

• Not just any technique can be applied to any variable but must be appropriately matched, thus requiring the researcher to be fully conversant with how different types of variable are classified.

• The size and nature of the sample also imposes limitations on the kinds of techniques suitable (recall Chapter 11).

A small research project

The discussion of quantitative data analysis is based on an imaginary piece of research carried out by an undergraduate for a senior thesis on leisure in modern society. She chose her topic because of her enthusiasm for gyms and workout facilities and an interest with how such venues are used and people's reasons for joining them. She had a hunch that they may be indicative of a 'civilizing process' and used this theory as a framework for her findings (Rojek 1995: 50–6). She was also interested in issues relating to gender and body image, and suspected that men and women differ in their reasons for going to a gym and in their activities there.

She secured the agreement of a gym close to her home to contact a sample of its members by post. The gym had 1200 members and she decided to take a simple random sample of 10 per cent of the membership (i.e., 120 members). She sent out postal questionnaires to members of the sample with a covering letter testifying to the gym's support of her research. One thing she wanted to know is how much time people spend on each of the three main classes of activity in the gym: cardiovascular equipment, weights, and exercises. She defined each of these carefully in the covering letter and asked members of the sample to keep a note of how long they spent on each of the three activities on their next visit. They were then requested to return the questionnaires to her in a prepaid reply envelope. She ended up with 90 questionnaires out of the 120—a response rate of 75 per cent.

The entire questionnaire ran to four pages; 12 of the questions along with the responses of a fictional respondent are provided in Box 12.1. Questions (1, 3, 4, 5, 6, 7, 8, and 9) were pre-coded and the respondent simply had to circle the appropriate code. With the others, specific figures were requested and simply transferred by a coder to the code column.

Box 12.1 **Part of a completed questionnaire on use of a gym**

Questionnaire

Code

1. Are you male or female? (please tick)

   Male __✓__ Female _____   ① 2

2. How old are you?

   __21__ Years   21

3. Which of the following best describes your *main* reason for going to the gym? (please circle one code only)

   Relaxation   _____   1
   Maintain or improve fitness   __✓__   ②
   Lose weight   _____   3
   Meet others   _____   4
   Build strength   _____   5
   Other (please specify)   _____   6

4. When you go to the gym, how often do you use the cardiovascular equipment (treadmill, step machine, bike, rower)? (please tick)

   Always   __✓__   ①
   Usually   _____   2
   Rarely   _____   3
   Never   _____   4

continued on next page

Box 12.1 *(continued)*

5. When you go to the gym, how often do you use the weights? (please tick)

Always	✓	①
Usually	___	2
Rarely	___	3
Never	___	4

6. Generally, how frequently do you go to the gym? (please tick)

Every day	___	1
4–6 days a week	___	2
2 or 3 days a week	✓	③
Once a week	___	4
2 or 3 times a month	___	5
Once a month	___	6
Less than once a month	___	7

7. Do you usually go with someone else to the gym or usually on your own? (please circle one code only)

On my own	✓	①
With a friend	___	2
With a partner/spouse	___	3

8. Do you have sources of regular exercise other than the gym?

Yes ___ No ✓   1 ②

*If you have answered **No** to this question, please proceed to question 10*

9. If you have replied **Yes** to question 9, please indicate the *main* source of regular exercise in the last six months from this list. (please circle one code only)

Sport	___	1
Cycling on the road	___	2
Jogging	___	3
Long walks	___	4
Other (please specify)	___	5

10. During your last visit to the gym, how many minutes did you spend on the cardiovascular equipment (treadmill, step machine, bike, rower)?

_33_ Minutes   33

11. During your last visit to the gym, how many minutes did you spend on weights?

_17_ Minutes   17

12. During your last visit to the gym, how many minutes did you spend on other activities (e.g., stretching exercises)?

_5_ Minutes   5

Missing data

The data for all 90 respondents are presented in Box 12.2. Each of the 12 questions is known for the time being as a variable (var00001, etc.); the number cor-responds to the question number in Box 12.1 (i.e., var00001 is question 1, var00002 is question 2, etc.). An important issue is how to handle the 'missing data' that arise when respondents fail to reply to a question—either by accident or because they do

Box 12.2 Gym survey data

Case	var00001	var00002	var00003	var00004	var00005	var00006	var00007	var00008	var00009	var00010	var00011	var00012
1	1	21	2	1	1	3	1	2	0	33	17	5
2	2	44	1	3	1	4	3	1	2	10	23	10
3	2	19	3	1	2	2	1	1	1	27	18	12
4	2	27	3	2	1	2	1	2	0	30	17	3
5	1	57	2	1	3	2	3	1	4	22	0	15
6	2	27	3	1	1	3	1	1	3	34	17	0
7	1	39	5	2	1	5	1	1	5	17	48	10
8	2	36	3	1	2	2	2	1	1	25	18	7
9	1	37	2	1	1	3	1	2	0	34	15	0
10	2	51	2	2	2	4	3	2	0	16	18	11
11	1	24	5	2	1	3	1	1	1	0	42	16
12	2	29	2	1	2	3	1	2	0	34	22	12
13	1	20	5	1	1	2	1	2	0	22	31	7
14	2	22	2	1	3	4	2	1	3	37	14	12
15	2	46	3	1	1	5	2	2	0	26	9	4
16	2	41	3	1	2	2	3	1	4	22	7	10
17	1	25	5	1	1	3	1	1	1	21	29	4
18	2	46	3	1	2	4	2	1	4	18	8	11
19	1	30	3	1	1	5	1	2	0	23	9	6
20	1	25	5	2	1	3	1	1	1	23	19	0
21	2	24	2	1	1	3	2	1	2	20	7	6
22	2	39	1	2	3	5	1	2	0	17	0	9
23	1	44	3	1	1	3	2	1	2	22	8	5
24	1	0	1	2	2	4	2	1	4	15	10	4
25	2	18	3	1	2	3	1	2	1	18	7	10
26	1	41	3	1	1	3	1	2	0	34	10	4
27	2	38	2	1	2	5	3	1	2	24	14	10
28	1	25	2	1	1	2	1	2	0	48	22	7
29	1	41	5	2	1	3	1	1	2	17	27	0
30	2	30	3	1	1	2	2	2	0	32	13	10
31	2	29	3	1	3	2	1	2	0	31	0	7
32	2	42	1	2	2	4	2	1	4	17	14	6
33	1	31	2	1	1	2	1	2	0	49	21	2
34	2	25	3	1	1	2	3	2	0	30	17	15
35	1	46	3	1	1	3	1	1	3	32	10	5
36	1	24	5	2	1	4	1	1	2	0	36	11
37	2	34	3	1	1	3	2	1	4	27	14	12
38	2	50	2	1	2	2	3	2	0	28	8	6
39	1	28	5	1	1	3	2	1	1	26	22	8
40	2	30	3	1	1	2	1	1	4	21	9	12
41	1	27	2	1	1	2	1	1	3	64	15	8
42	2	27	2	1	2	4	2	1	4	22	10	7
43	1	36	5	1	1	3	2	2	0	21	24	0
44	2	43	3	1	1	4	1	2	0	25	13	8
45	1	34	2	1	1	3	2	1	1	45	15	6
46	2	27	3	1	1	2	1	1	4	33	10	9
47	2	38	2	1	3	4	2	2	0	23	0	16
48	1	28	2	1	1	3	3	1	2	38	13	5
49	1	44	5	1	1	2	1	2	0	27	19	7
50	2	31	3	1	2	3	2	2	0	32	11	5
51	2	23	2	1	1	4	2	1	1	33	18	8
52	1	45	3	1	1	3	1	1	2	26	10	7
53	2	34	3	1	2	2	3	2	0	36	8	12
54	1	27	3	1	1	2	3	1	3	42	13	6
55	2	40	3	1	1	2	2	1	4	26	9	10
56	2	24	2	1	1	2	1	1	2	22	10	9

continued on next page

Box 12.2 *(continued)*

Case	var00001	var00002	var00003	var00004	var00005	var00006	var00007	var00008	var00009	var00010	var00011	var00012
57	1	37	2	1	1	5	2	2	0	21	11	0
58	1	22	5	1	1	4	1	1	1	23	17	6
59	2	31	3	1	2	3	1	1	4	40	16	12
60	1	37	2	1	1	2	3	2	0	54	12	3
61	2	33	1	2	2	4	2	2	0	17	10	5
62	1	23	5	1	1	3	1	1	1	41	27	8
63	1	28	3	1	1	3	3	2	0	27	11	8
64	2	29	2	1	2	5	2	1	2	24	9	9
65	2	43	3	1	1	2	1	2	0	36	17	12
66	1	28	5	1	1	3	1	1	1	22	15	4
67	1	48	2	1	1	5	1	1	4	25	11	7
68	2	32	2	2	2	4	2	2	0	27	13	11
69	1	28	5	1	1	2	2	2	0	15	23	7
70	2	23	2	1	1	5	1	1	4	14	11	5
71	2	43	2	1	2	5	1	2	0	18	7	3
72	1	28	2	1	1	4	3	1	2	34	18	8
73	2	23	3	1	1	2	1	2	0	37	17	17
74	2	36	1	2	2	4	2	1	4	18	12	4
75	1	50	2	1	1	3	1	1	2	28	14	3
76	1	37	3	1	1	2	2	2	0	26	14	9
77	2	41	3	1	1	2	1	1	4	24	11	4
78	1	26	5	2	1	5	1	1	1	23	19	8
79	2	28	3	1	1	4	1	2	0	27	12	4
80	2	35	2	1	1	3	1	1	1	28	14	0
81	1	28	5	1	1	2	1	1	2	20	24	12
82	2	36	2	1	1	3	2	2	0	26	9	14
83	2	29	3	1	1	4	1	1	4	23	13	4
84	1	34	1	2	2	4	2	1	0	24	12	3
85	1	53	2	1	1	3	3	1	1	32	17	6
86	2	30	3	1	1	4	1	2	0	24	10	9
87	1	43	2	1	1	2	1	1	2	24	14	10
88	2	26	5	2	1	4	1	1	1	16	23	7
89	2	44	1	1	1	4	2	2	0	27	18	6
90	1	45	1	2	2	3	3	2	0	20	14	5

not want to answer the question. Thus, respondent 24 failed to answer question 2 on age. This could be coded as a 99 and it is important to ensure that the computer software is notified of this fact, since it must not be counted as a 99-year-old gym participant. Also, question 9 has a large number of zeroes, because many people did not answer it, having been filtered out by the previous question (i.e., they do not have other sources of regular exercise). These can also be coded as nine to denote missing data, though strictly speaking their failure to reply is more indicative of the question not being applicable to them. Note also, that there are zeros for var00010, var00011, and var00012. These do *not* denote miss-

ing data but that the respondent spends zero minutes on the activity in question. Everyone has answered questions 10, 11, and 12, so there are no missing data for these variables. Were there any missing data, it would be necessary to code the missing data with a number that cannot also be a true figure. For example, nobody has spent 99 minutes on these activities, so this may be an appropriate number as it is easy to remember and cannot be read by the computer as anything other than missing data. Just to familiarize yourself with the data, please find a woman who goes alone and rarely uses weights but always uses cardiovascular equipment.

Getting started in SPSS

Introduction

To implement the techniques about to be presented one can do either of two things: learn the underlying procedures or formula for each technique and apply them to the data, or use computer software to accomplish the same task. The latter is the approach chosen in this book for two reasons: it is closer to real-life quantitative data analysis and it provides a useful transferable skill.

SPSS for Windows is the most widely used package of computer software for this kind of analysis, probably because it is relatively straightforward to use. SPSS, short for *Statistical Package for the Social Sciences*, has been in existence since the mid-1960s and over the years has undergone many revisions, particularly since the arrival of personal computers. The version used in preparing this section is Release 11. From this point on, when referring to SPSS for Windows in the text, it is called simply SPSS. The gym survey again is employed to illustrate.

SPSS operations are presented in **bold**, for example, <u>**Variable Name:**</u> and <u>**Analyze**</u>. Names given to variables are in ***bold italics***, for example, ***gender*** and ***reasons***. Labels given to values or to variables are also in bold but in a different font, for example, **reasons for visiting** and **male**. Box 12.3 presents a list of basic operations in SPPS. One further element

---

Box 12.3 Basic operations in SPSS for Windows

- The **SPSS Data Editor**. This is the sphere of SPSS into which data are entered and subsequently edited and defined. It is made up of two screens: the **Data Viewer** and the **Variable Viewer**. Move between these two viewers by selecting the appropriate tab at the bottom of the screen.

- The **Data Viewer**. This is the spreadsheet into which the data are entered. When starting up SPSS, the **Data Viewer** appears.

- The **Variable Viewer**. This is another spreadsheet, but this one displays information about each of the variables and allows changing that information. It is the platform from which to provide for each variable such information as: a variable name; a variable label; and value labels (see below).

- The **Output**. After an analysis or producing a diagram (called a 'chart' in SPSS), output is deposited here. The **Output Viewer** superimposes itself over the **Data Editor** after an analysis has been performed or a chart generated.

- A **Variable Name**. This is the name given to a variable, e.g., ***gender***. The name must be no more than eight characters. Until given a variable a name, it is referred to as ***var00001***, etc. When given a name, it appears in the column for that variable in the **Data View** window. It is generated from the **Variable Viewer**.

- A **Variable Label**. This is a (optional) label for a variable but not restricted to eight characters. Spaces can be used, e.g., **reasons for visiting**. The label appears in any output generated and comes from the **Variable Viewer**.

- A **Value Label**. This is a label attached to a code used when entering nominal and ordinal data. Thus, for **var00001**, one can attach the label **male** to 1 and **female** to 2. In output, such as a frequency table or chart, the labels for each value are presented, making the interpretation of output easier. It is generated from the **Variable Viewer**.

- **Missing Values...** If data for a particular variable is missing when entering data for a case, one must specify how missing values for that variable are recognized and omitted from calculations. Missing values are generated from the **Variable Viewer**.

- <u>**Analyze**</u>. This is the point on the menu bar above the **Data Editor** from which (via a drop-down menu) the method of analysis is selected. Note that, whenever an item on a menu appears with a right-pointing arrow after it, a further sub-menu is available.

- <u>**Graphs**</u>. This is the point on the menu bar above the **Data Editor** from which (via a drop-down menu) charts are selected.

- **Chart Editor**. A graph can be edited with the **Chart Editor**. To activate this editor, double-click anywhere in the graph. A small chart editor window appears along with an opaque version of the main graph and stays until the Editor is exited. From the Editor, various changes and enhancements to the graph can be made.

in the presentation is that a right-pointing arrow → denotes 'click once with the left-hand button of mouse' to make selections.

To start SPSS, double click on the **spsswin** icon on the computer screen. If there is no icon, → the **Start** button in the bottom left-hand corner of the screen and select from the menu of programs, → **SPSS for Windows**. A follow-on menu appears: select **SPSS 11.0 for Windows**. If after SPSS loads an opening dialogue box with the title 'What do you want to do?' and a list of options appears, disable it. It is not important in the following exposition, so → **Cancel**, leading to the **SPSS Data Editor**, made up of two components: **Data View** and **Variable View**. In the following discussion, these two screens are referred to as the **Data Viewer** and the **Variable Viewer**. Move between these two viewers by selecting the appropriate tab at the bottom of the screen. The **Data Viewer** is in the form of a spreadsheet grid into which data are entered. The columns represent *vari-*

ables—in other words, information about characteristics of each person in the gym study sample, like gender and age. Until data are entered, each column simply has **var** as its heading. The rows represent *cases*, which can be people (as in this example) or other units of analysis. Each block in the grid is referred to as a 'cell.' Note also that when the data are in the SPSS spreadsheet, they look different, for example, 1 is 1.00.

Entering data in the Data Viewer

To input the data into the **Data Viewer**, make sure that the top left-hand cell in the grid is highlighted (Plate 12.1). If it is not, simply click once in that cell. Then, type the appropriate figure for that cell—that is, 1. This number goes directly into that cell and into the box beneath the toolbar. As an alternative to using the mouse, many people find it easier to use the arrow keys on their keyboard to move from cell to

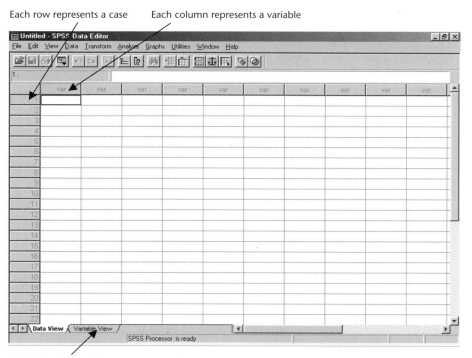

Each row represents a case   Each column represents a variable

For the **Variable View** to examine each variable in detail, click on this tab

Plate 12.1 The SPSS for Windows **Data Viewer**

cell. If a mistake is made, simply click once in the cell in question, type in the correct value, and click once more in that cell. The last piece of data goes into the bottom right-hand cell of what will be a perfect rectangle of data. Plate 12.2 shows the **Data Viewer** with the data from the gym survey entered (though only part of the set of data is visible, in that only the first 22 respondents and 10 of the 12 variables are visible). The first row of data contains the coded answers from the completed questionnaire in Box 12.1.

To proceed further, SPSS works in the following typical sequence for defining variables and analyzing data.

1. Make a selection from the menu bar at the top of the screen, for example, ➔ **Analyze**.

2. From the menu that will appear, make a selection, for example, ➔ **Descriptive Statistics**.

3. This will bring up a *dialogue box* in which to inform SPSS of something to do—for example, the variables to be analyzed.

4. Very often, further information is needed; ➔ a button that brings up a *sub-dialogue box*.

5. Provide the information in the sub-dialogue box and then go back to the dialogue box. Sometimes, a further sub-dialogue box is required before going back to the dialogue box.

When finished going through the entire procedure, ➔ **OK**. The toolbar beneath the menu bar allows shortcut access to certain SPSS operations.

Defining variables: variable names, missing values, variable labels, and value labels

Once finished entering the data, prepare the variables. The following steps allow this:

1. ➔ the **Variable View** tab at the bottom of the **Data Viewer** (opens the **Variable Viewer** shown in Plate 12.3).

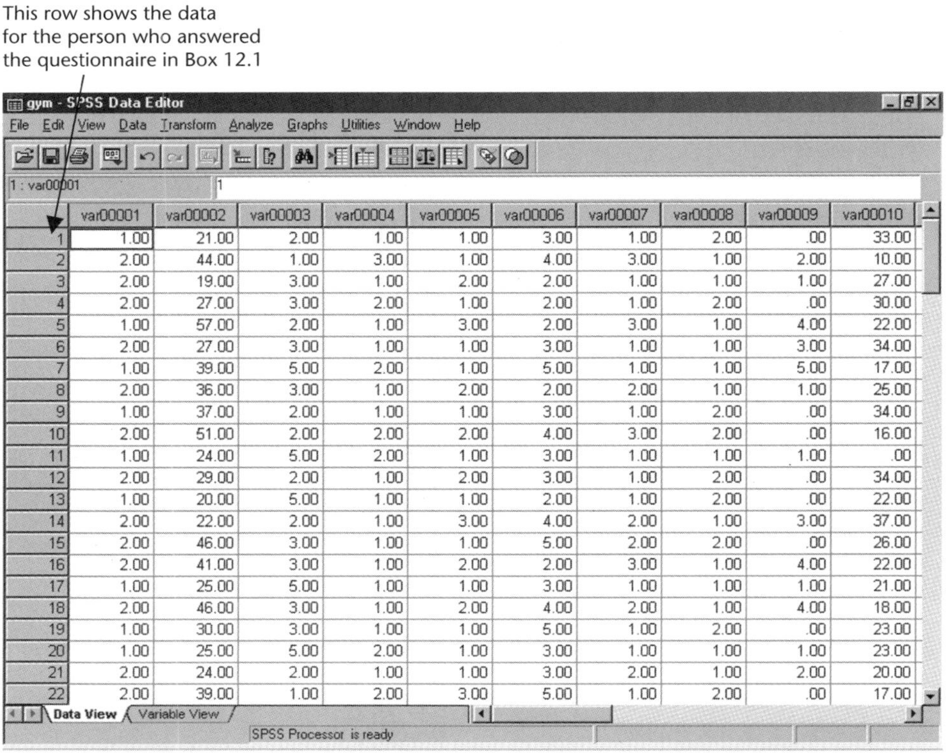

This row shows the data for the person who answered the questionnaire in Box 12.1

Plate 12.2 The **Data Viewer** with 'gym study' data entered

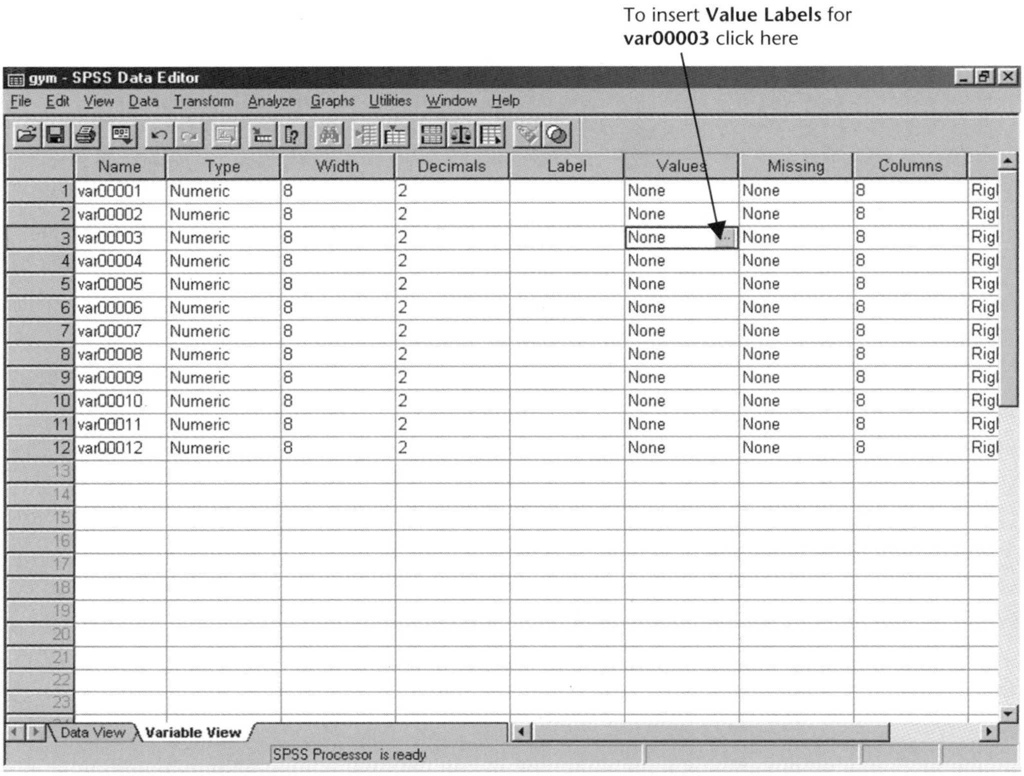

To insert **Value Labels** for **var00003** click here

Plate 12.3 The **Variable Viewer** dialogue box

2. To provide a variable name, click on the current variable name (e.g., **var00003**) and type a name for it (e.g., *reasons*). This name must be no more than eight characters and can*not* include spaces. This name is the identification needed for instructing the computer to perform any analysis. It is arbitrary and really can be anything, but an appropriate name is best.

3. Give the variable a more detailed name, known in SPSS as a variable label. To do this, → cell in the **Label** column relating to the variable getting a variable label. Then, simply type in the variable label (e.g., **reasons for visiting**). This label is not arbitrary and will actually appear on printouts, just like a designer label appears on clothes. It is what the study is about. But it is also optional if in a hurry.

4. Provide 'value labels' for variables that have been given names. The procedure generally applies to

variables that are not interval/ratio variables. The latter, which are numeric variables, do not need to be coded (unless grouping them in some way). To assign value labels, → in the **Values** column relating to the variable in question. A small button with three dots on it appears. → the button. The **Value Labels** dialogue box appears (Plate 12.4). → the box to the right of **Val**u**e** and begin to define the value labels. To do this, enter the value (e.g., **1**) in the area to the right of **Val**u**e** and then the value label (e.g., **relaxation**) in the area to the right of **Val**u**e Label**. Then → **Add**. Do this for each value. When finished → **OK**. To repeat, a variable name for question one on the questionnaire could be var00001, the variable label 'gender,' and the value labels, male and female. The computer reads only numbers so that male is a 1, the female a 2. So the value labels, strictly speaking, are optional. If omitted the data will tell you about the 1's and 2's instead.

Value Labels

Value: 6

Value Label: other

Add	1.00 = "relaxation"
Change	2.00 = "fitness"
	3.00 = "lose weight"
Remove	4.00 = "meet others"
	5.00 = "build strength"

OK
Cancel
Help

Remember to click here after entering
each **Value** and **Value Label**

Plate 12.4 The **Value Labels** dialogue box

5. Inform SPSS of the value given for each variable to indicate a missing value. In the case of *reasons*, the value is 0 (zero). To assign the missing value, → the cell for this variable in the **Missing** column. Again, → the button that will appear with three dots on it. This will generate the **Missing Values** dialogue box (Plate 12.5). In the **Missing Values** dialogue box, enter the missing value (0) below **Discrete missing value:** and then → **OK**.

To simplify the following presentation, *reasons* is the only variable for which a variable label is defined.

Saving the data

To save the data for future use, make sure that the **Data Editor** is the active window. Then,

→ **File** → **Save As...**

The **Save Data As** dialogue box then appears. It needs a name for the data, which is placed after **File name:** and a place to save the data—for example, onto a floppy disk. To select the destination drive, → the downward pointing arrow to the right of the box by **Save in**. Then choose the drive on which to save the data and → **Save**.

This procedure saves the data *and* any work done on it—for example, value labels and recoded variables. If subsequently doing more work on the data, such as creating a new variable, the data must be saved again or the new work will be lost. SPSS gives a choice of renaming the data, in which case there are two files of data (one with the original data and one with original data as changed), or keeping the same name. In that instance the original file is lost but its name retained and now applied to the modified file.

Plate 12.5 The **Missing Values** dialogue box

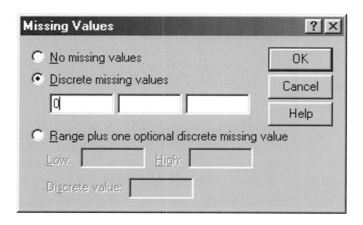

Missing Values

○ No missing values

● Discrete missing values

`0`

○ Range plus one optional discrete missing value

Low: 　　　　 High: 　　　　

Discrete value: 　　　　

OK
Cancel
Help

Retrieving data

To retrieve a data file, ➔ **File** ➔ **Open**... The **Open File** dialogue box will appear. Go to the location in which the data are deposited to retrieve the file containing the data and then ➔ **Open**.

Now at last, analysis of the data that has been entered can begin!

Types of variables

Look at the different questions and notice that some of them call for answers in terms of real numbers: questions 2 (age), and 10, 11, and 12. Questions 1 (gender) and 8 yield either/or answers, which are called dichotomies (only two possible responses). The rest of the questions take the form of lists of categories, but there are also differences among them. Some of the answers can be ranked in order: see questions 4, 5, and 6. Thus one can say for question 6 that the category 'every day' implies greater frequency than '4–6 days a week,' which in turn is a greater frequency than '2 or 3 days a week,' and so on. Compare this to questions 3, 7, and 9 where the categories can*not* be rank ordered. One cannot say in the case of question 3 that 'relaxation' is more or less of something than 'maintain or improve fitness' is.

This introduction leads to a classification of the different types of variables generated in the course of research. The four main types are distinguished by looking at the relationship between the categories of the variable *as manifested by any one individual*. The four are:

- *Nominal variables*. These variables, also known as *categorical variables*, are comprised of categories that have no relationship to one another except to say that they are *different*. Religion is an example. There are Roman Catholic, Anglican, Presbyterian, Other Christian, non-Christian, and non-believers. Two research participants either have the same religion (equal) or they have different (not equal) religions, the only kind of comparison possible. This also means that the list of categories is arbitrary: the above list could have begun with the non-believers or the Presbyterians or indeed any other religion and ended with the Roman Catholics. Switching order has no implication.

- *Ordinal variables*. These variables include the idea from nominal above of equal or not equal but the categories can also be ranked or ordered, > more than and < less than, meaning that order is more important as in Question 5. One can say that 'always' is more frequent than 'usually,' which is more frequent than 'rarely,' etc. and it would be somewhat illogical to order them as: always, never, sometimes, usually.

Spaces between the categories, however, may not be equal across the range. Thus the difference between the category 'always' and 'usually' is probably not the same as the difference between 'usually' and 'rarely,' and so on. This is because there is no unit of attendance in the question. These ordinal variables are those in prose with a comparative 'er' or superlative 'est' attached to them, as in slim, slimmer, and slimmest. More and most, less and least come here too but not fewer, and fewest, because they are saved for the next level which counts units.

- *Interval/ratio variables*. These are variables where a unit exists and thus the distances between the categories can be made identical across the range of categories. These involve not nominal, nor ordinal, but cardinal numbers, as 1, 2, 16, etc. In the case of variables var00010 to var00012, the unit is the minute and the distance between the categories is a one-minute interval. Thus, a person who spends 32 minutes on cardiovascular equipment is spending one minute more than someone who spends 31. That difference is the same as the difference between someone who spends 8 minutes and another who spends 9 minutes on the equipment. These last two instances really involved *subtracting* (32 − 31 = 1) and *adding* (8 + 1 = 9). So, at this level, one can say, equal or not equal from the nominal level, 32 NE 31, more or less than from the ordinal level, 32>31, 8<9, and how much more or less from the interval level, +1 and −1.

Ratio variables are interval variables with a fixed and non-arbitrary zero point, as in wind speed of

0 kilometres per hour. Since many social science variables exhibit this quality (e.g., income, age, years of school completed), they are not being distinguished here. But to understand, take two incomes: $30K and $45K. They are nominally unequal and the first is < the second, in fact $15K less. But with that real 0, one can also say the first is 2/3 of the second (or the second is 1.5 times the first). What is really happening here is *dividing and multiplying*. The first income to the second income also has a 2:3 *ratio*. This is the highest level of measurement, one allowing the widest range of analysis techniques including addition, subtraction, multiplication, and division. See Box 12.4 for a description of creating a new interval/ratio variable.

The four main types of variable and illustrations from the gym survey are provided in Table 12.1. Strictly speaking multiple-indicator (or multiple-item) measures of concepts, like Likert scales (see Box 3.4), produce ordinal variables. However, many writers argue that they can be treated as though they produce interval/ratio variables, because of the relatively

---

Box 12.4 Computing a new variable

A person's total amount of time spent in the gym is made up of three variables: *cardmins*, *weimins*, and *othmins*. Adding them up gives the total number of minutes spent on activities in the gym, and a new variable *totalmin*. (Why can it not be totalmins?) To do this, this procedure should be followed:

1 → Transform → Compute... [opens the Compute Variable dialogue box shown in Plate 12.6]

2 under Target Variable: type *totalmin*

3 select SUM[numexpr,numexpr,...] from the list underneath Functions: and click on the button with an upward-pointing arrowhead to send it into the box underneath Numeric Expression:

4 from the list of variables at the left, → *cardmins* → ▶ button [puts *cardmins* in box after SUM]; → *weimins* → ▶ button [puts *weimins* in box after cardmins]; → *othmins* → ▶ button [puts *othmins* in box after weimins]

5 → OK

The new variable *totalmin* is created and appears in the Data Editor.

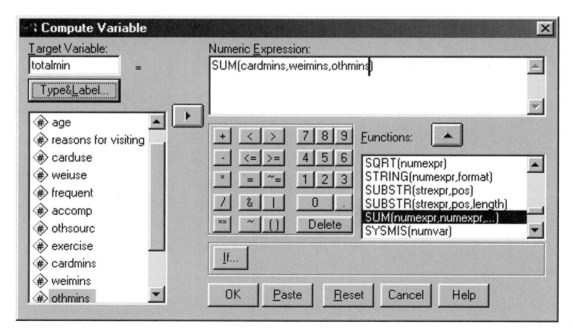

Plate 12.6 The Compute Variable dialogue box

Table 12.1 Types of variable

Type	Description	Examples in gym study	Variable Name in SPSS
Nominal	Variables whose categories cannot be rank ordered; also known as *categorical*	var00001 var00003 var00007 var00008 var00009	gender reasons accomp othsourc exercise
Ordinal	Variables whose categories can be rank ordered but the distances between the categories are not equal across the range	var00004 var00005 var00006	carduse weiuse frequent
Interval/ratio	Variables where the distances between the categories are identical across the range	var00002 var00010 var00011 var00012	age cardmins weimins othmins

large number of categories they generate. For a brief discussion of this issue, see Bryman and Cramer, who distinguish between 'true' interval/ratio variables and those produced by multiple-indicator measures (2001: 58–9). See Box 12.5 for an opposite issue, reducing an interval/ratio level to an ordinal or even nominal level. Figure 12.1 provides guidance about how to identify variables of each type.

Box 12.5 Recoding variables

Sometimes one needs to recode variables—for example, to group codes together, as was done to produce a table like Table 12.3 for an interval/ratio variable there **var00002**, now given the variable name *age*. SPSS offers two choices: recode *age* so that it is changed in the **Data Viewer**, or keep *age* as it is and create a new variable. This latter option is desirable to preserve the original variable as well as create a new one, here called *agegp*, for age groups, with five age bands, as in Table 12.3.

1 → **T**ransform → **R**ecode → **Into Different Variables** [opens **Recode into Different Variables** dialogue box shown in Plate 12.7]

2 → age → ▶ button [puts *age* in **Numeric Variable** → **Output Variable:** box] → box beneath **Output Variable Name:** and type *agegp* → **C**hange [puts *agegp* in the **Numeric Variable** → **Output Variable:** box] → **O**ld and New Values... [opens **Recode into Different Variables: Old and New Values** sub-dialogue box shown in Plate 12.8]

3 → the circle by **System- or user-missing** and by **System-missing** under New Value, if there are missing values for a variable, which is the case for this variable

4 → circle by **Range: Lowest Through** and type 20 in the box → box by **Value in New Value** and type 1 → **A**dd [the new value appears in the **O**ld → **New:** box]

5 → first box by **R**a**ng**e: and type 21 and in box after **through** type 30 → box by **Value in New Value** and type 2 → **A**dd

6 → first box by **R**a**ng**e: and type 31 and in box after **through** type 40 → box by **Value in New Value** and type 3 → **A**dd

7 → first box by **R**a**ng**e: and type 41 and in box after **through** type 50 → box by **Value in New Value** and type 4 → **A**dd

8 → circle by **Range: through highest** and type 51 in the box → box by **Value in New Value** and type 5 → **A**dd → **Continue** [closes the **Recode into Different Variables: Old and New Values** sub-dialogue box shown in Plate 12.8 and returns to the **Recode into Different Variables** shown in Plate 12.7]

9 → OK

The new variable *agegp* is created and appears in the **Data Viewer**. To generate **value labels** for the five age bands and possibly a **variable label**, repeat the approach described above.

continued

Box 12.5 *(continued)*

Original name of variable   Recoded name of variable

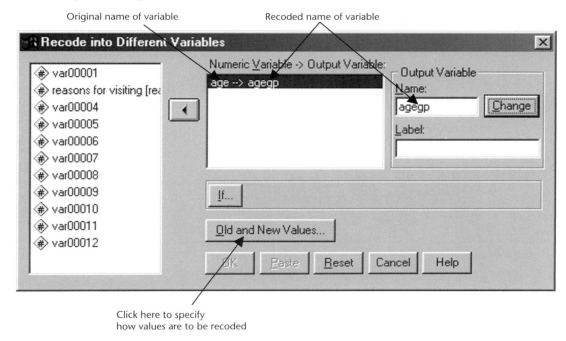

Click here to specify
how values are to be recoded

Plate 12.7 The **Recode into Different Variables** dialogue box

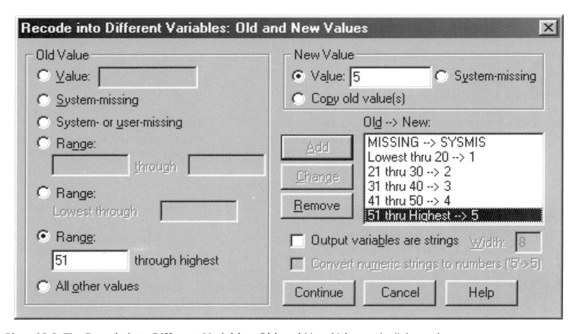

Plate 12.8 The **Recode into Different Variables: Old and New Values** sub-dialogue box

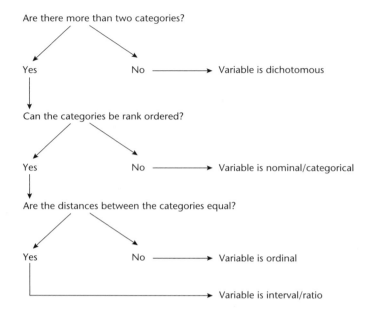

Figure 12.1 Deciding how to categorize a variable

Univariate analysis

Univariate analysis refers to the examination of one variable at a time and in this next section, several common approaches are outlined.

Frequency tables

A frequency table provides the number of people and the percentage belonging to each of the categories of the variable in question and can be created for all three variable types. An example of a frequency table for a nominal variable is provided for var00003 in Table 12.2. The table shows, for example, that 33 members of the sample go the gym to lose weight and that they represent 37 per cent (percentages are often rounded up and down in frequency tables) of the entire sample. This is calculated by the simple formula: n in category/TOTAL N. Nobody chose two possible answers—'meet others' and 'other.'

When an interval/ratio variable (like people's ages) is put in frequency-table format, invariably some of the categories, because they contain so few

cases, need to be combined in some way. When grouping in this way, take care to ensure that the categories created do not overlap (for example as do, 20–30, 30–40, 40–50, etc.). This violates the *mutually exclusive rule* (required for telling whether two cases are equal or not equal) meaning that no one should be able to fall into two categories. Where does a 30 year old go, the first or second category? Also recall from coding, the *exhaustive rule*: everyone must

Table 12.2 Frequency table showing reasons for visiting the gym

Reason	n	per cent
Relaxation	9	10
Maintain or improve fitness	31	34
Lose weight	33	37
Build strength	17	19
TOTAL	90	100

Table 12.3 Frequency table showing age of gym members

Age	n	per cent
20 and under	3	3
21–30	39	44
31–40	23	26
41–50	21	24
51 and over	3	3
TOTAL	89	100

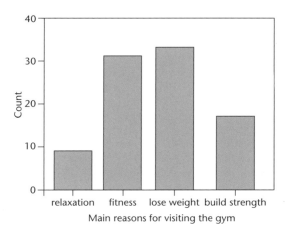

Figure 12.2 Bar chart showing main reasons for visiting the gym (SPSS output)

have a category, even if it is one for missing data or not applicable.

An example of a frequency table for an interval/ratio variable is shown in Table 12.3, var00002, age of gym visitors. Not to group people in terms of age ranges would mean 34 different categories, which is too many to meaningfully describe. By creating 5 categories, the distribution of ages is easier to comprehend. Notice that the sample totals 89 and that the percentages are based on a total of 89 rather than 90. This is because this variable contains one missing value (respondent 24).

The procedures for creating categories are a bit vague but there are two general rules: there should not be more than 10 categories, probably fewer, and each one should be relatively homogeneous. So a category for house prices of $250K+ would be inappropriate. First it has no top limit, and second a $250K house is not the same as one going for $5.6M. They should not share a category. As an exercise, think of the categories for the price of new shoes, given that the last category is $300–500 and then see Box 12.6 (on page 256).

Diagrams

Diagrams are sometimes used to display quantitative data. With nominal or ordinal variables, the *bar chart* and the *pie chart* are two of the easiest to use. A bar chart of the same data in Table 12.2 is presented in Figure 12.2. Each bar represents the number of

people in each category. This figure and the next two were produced with SPSS for Windows.

Another way of displaying the same data is in a pie chart, like the one in Figure 12.3. This also shows the size of the different categories but more clearly brings out the size of each relative to the total sample. The percentage that each slice represents of the whole sample is also given in this diagram.

To display an interval/ratio variable, like var00002, a *histogram* is likely to be employed. Figure 12.4 uses the same data and categories as Table 12.3. As with the bar chart, the bars represent the relative size of each of the age bands but in a histogram, there is no space between the bars. This is to distinguish histograms,

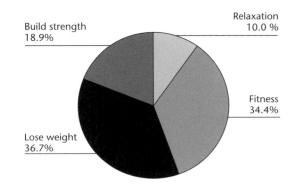

Figure 12.3 Pie chart showing main reasons for visiting the gym (SPSS output)

Box 12.6 Losing information

When one groups an interval/ratio variable like var00002, which refers to people's age, into categories (e.g., 20 and under; 21–30; 31–40; 41–50; 51 and over), an interval variable is being transformed into an ordinal variable. No longer can the data be added as is possible at the interval/ratio level. Thus researchers try to avoid such moving down levels of measurement. Dinovitzer *et al.* (2003), however, did transform years of education, a ratio variable, into a four-level ordinal variable. In effect, they were saying, for example, that those with one to eight years of education are basically similar and that differentiating a person with four years from one with five is not necessary. They are all 'low.'

If variables contain data that have only two categories (e.g., male/female for the variable gender) they are often called *dichotomous variables*. Ordinal (middle-class vs. working class) and interval/ratio (smart vs. dumb or hot vs. cold) variables can also be dichotomous but this is infrequent, as to do so loses so much information that is potentially there, how hot, how smart, how poor, etc. Moreover with just two points, a trend line, which needs a minimum of three points, cannot be discerned. If the data come that way, it is probably safest to treat them for most purposes as if they were ordinary nominal variables.

Sometimes researchers, especially students, have no choice but to give up some information. They just do not have enough cases for the detail they want. For example, examine the following data. Note how in some instances (see the West Secede), where most people strongly disagree and only a few agree, feel neutral, or disagree there could be only two people in neutral and four in agree, too few for making any generalizations. In such instances, one can collapse the data into a dichotomy (two parts) or trichotomy, remembering the rule about homogeneity.

	Gun-control (%)	Pro-choice (%)	NAFTA (%)	West Secede (%)
Strongly agree	36	45	21	12
Agree	17	23	10	4
Neutral	2	1	40	2
Disagree	18	10	6	8
Strongly Disagree	27	21	23	74

Gun control can easily be dichotomized into 'for' (36 + 17 = 53 per cent) and 'against' (18 + 27 = 45 per cent). The 2 per cent can be omitted or added to the against side as it is the smaller group. To trichotomize, it can be SA alone at 36 per cent; Agree, Neutral, and Disagree together at 37 per cent; and SD alone at 27 per cent. This appears to violate the homogeneity rule unless gun control is conceived of as an issue where people hold very strong opinions either way, and what remains is a soft middle. Pro-choice dichotomized is 68 per cent combining any agree vs. 32 per cent others. As a trichotomy, it can be SA alone at 45 per cent, Agree and Neutral at 24 per cent, and any disagree at 31 per cent. In addition to maintaining some sense of homogeneity, the rule is to maximize the smallest cell. Try it on NAFTA. The trichotomy is easy at 31 per cent, 40 per cent, and 29 per cent. What about the dichotomy? The only question is the Neutrals. Adding them to the 'agrees' gives that category 71 per cent versus 29 per cent for 'disagrees.' Adding them to the 'disagrees' makes it 69 per cent and 31 per cent. Maximizing the smallest rule says to give the Neutrals to the 'disagrees.' Finally, concerning whether the West should secede, probably the only thing to do is to dichotomize —absolutely opposed at 74 per cent and 26 per cent at less than that. A trichotomy does not make for much improvement in the data.

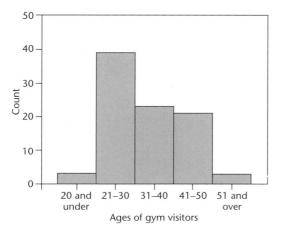

Figure 12.4 Histogram showing the ages of gym visitors (SPSS output)

produced for interval/ratio variables, and the bar charts produced for nominal and ordinal variables.

This is a good point to continue with SPSS for Windows, the software package that produced the diagrams just presented. The discussion begins with a general introduction followed by instructions on how to generate those charts. Then the chapter moves back to forms of analysis, with SPSS instructions for generating them interspersed in the text as appropriate. Learning new software requires some perseverance and at times it does not seem to be worth the learning process. But it is. It would take far longer to perform calculations on a sample of even 90 than to learn the software. With more advanced techniques and larger samples, the time saved is even more substantial.

Data analysis with SPSS

Generating a frequency table

To produce a frequency table like the one in Table 12.2:

1. → **Analyze** → **Descriptive Statistics** → **Frequencies...** [opens the **Frequencies** dialogue box shown in Plate 12.9].

2. → **reasons for visiting** → ▶ button [puts **reasons for visiting** in **Variable[s]:** box]

3. → **OK**

The table then appears in the **Output Viewer** (see Plate 12.10)

Note that in the **Frequencies** dialogue box, labels appear for those variables with labels previously

Select variable(s) to be analyzed from here

Click here to send selected variable(s) into **Variable[s]:** list

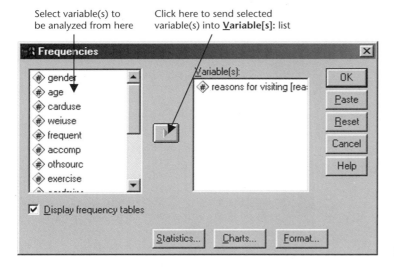

Plate 12.9 The **Frequencies** dialogue box

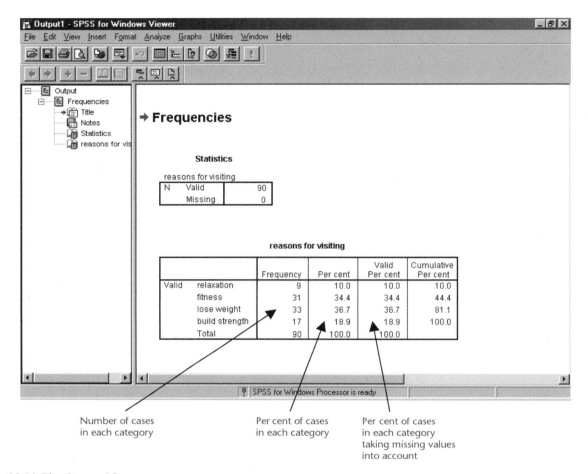

Plate 12.10 The **Output Viewer**

assigned like gender; those not assigned labels appear in terms of their variable names like var000XX. This is a feature of all dialogue boxes produced via **Analyze** and **Graphs** (see below).

Generating a bar chart

To produce a bar chart like the one in Figure 12.2:

1. → **Graphs** → **Bar...** [opens **Bar Charts** dialogue box]

2. → **Simple** → **Summaries for groups of cases** → **Define** [opens **Define Simple Bar: Summaries for Groups of Cases** sub-dialogue box shown in Plate 12.11]

3. **reasons for visiting** → ▶ button by **Category Axis** [**reasons for visiting** appears in the box] → **N of cases** beneath **Bars Represent** [*if* this has not already been selected, otherwise continue without doing this]

4. → OK

Generating a pie chart

To produce a pie chart like the one in Figure 12.3:

1. → **Graphs** → **Pie...** [opens the **Pie Charts** dialogue box] → **Summaries for groups of cases** → **Define** [opens the **Define Pie: Summaries for Groups of Cases** sub-dialogue box]

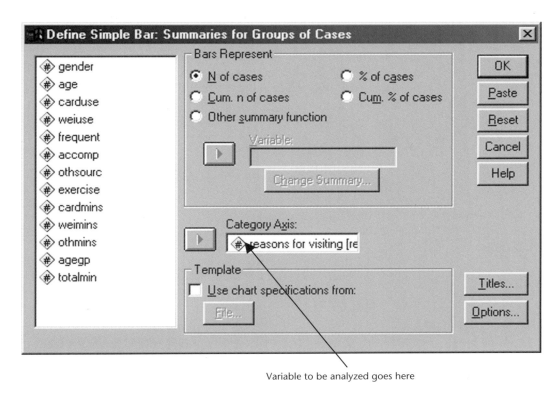

Variable to be analyzed goes here

Plate 12.11 The **Define Simple Bar: Summaries for Groups of Cases** sub-dialogue box

2. → **reasons for visiting** → ▶ button by **Define slices by** [**reasons for visiting** appears in the box] → **N of cases** beneath **Slices Represent:** [if this has *not* already been selected, otherwise continue without doing this]

3. → OK

To include percentages, as in Figure 12.3, *double-click* anywhere in the chart to bring up the **Chart Editor** (Plate 12.12). The chart appears in the **Chart Editor** and the main figure becomes opaque. Then → **Chart** and then → **Options...** and then place a tick by **Percents** [there should also be a tick by **Text**].

The chart is in colour, but, if access is only to a monochrome printer, change the pie chart into patterns, which allows the slices to be clearer. When the **SPSS for Windows Chart Editor** is open, all figures can be edited. Figures 12.2, 12.3, and 12.4 were produced by changing the bars or slices to white and

then introducing patterns. When in the **SPSS for Windows Chart Editor**, one can experiment by → **Format** and then selecting from the choices there. This procedure applies to all charts.

Generating a histogram

Producing a histogram like the one in Figure 12.4 is just as simple except that it requires defining the ages to be grouped (or using the newly created agegp variable). So instead create a histogram for another interval/ratio variable, minutes spent doing other activities at the gym, via → **Graphs** → **Histogram** and then selecting var00012. Another reason for spending less time on this is that there are usually other ways to describe interval/ratio data, like measures of central tendency and dispersion (below).

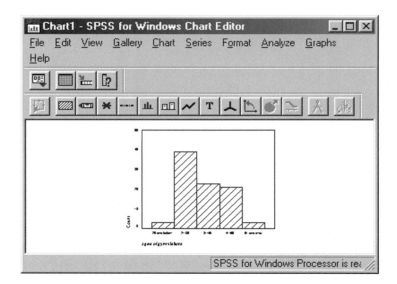

Plate 12.12 The **Chart Editor**

Printing output

To print all the output in the **SPSS for Windows Output Viewer**, make sure that the **Viewer** is the active window and then → **File** → **Print...** The **Print** dialogue box appears and then → **OK**. To print just some of the output, hold down the Ctrl button on the keyboard and click once on the parts to print. The easiest way to do this is to select the elements from the output summary in the left-hand segment of the **Output Viewer** shown in Plate 12.10. Then bring up the **Print** dialogue box. When the **Print** dialogue box appears, make sure **Selection** under **Print Range** is selected.

More univariate analysis and SPSS

Measures of central tendency

Measures of central tendency encapsulate, in one figure, a value that is typical or 'average' for a whole distribution of values. Three different forms of average are recognized: the mode, median, and the mean each most appropriate to a different level of measurement

- *Mode*. This is the value that occurs most frequently in a distribution. The mode for var00002 is 28. The mode can be employed in relation to all types of variable but is most applicable to nominal data.

- *Median*. This is the mid-point in a distribution of values, derived by arraying all the values in a distribution from the smallest to the largest and then finding the middle point. If there is an even num-

ber of values, the median is calculated by taking the halfway point between the two middle numbers of the distribution. In the case of var00002, the median is 31. The median can be employed in relation to both interval/ratio and ordinal variables but not nominal which lacks any sense of ranking from low to high. At that level things are either equal or not equal but not less or more than.

- *Arithmetic mean*. This is the average as understood in everyday use—that is, the sum of all values in a distribution divided by the number of values. Thus, the arithmetic mean (or more simply the *mean*) for var00002 is 33.6, meaning that the average age of gym visitors is nearly 34 years of age and calculated by *adding* all of the ages together and dividing by the number of ages, here 89. (The *adding* should have alerted you of the need for interval level data at least. Ordinal data lacks a unit and cannot be added or subtracted.) This is slightly higher than the median because a few considerably older members (especially respondents 5 and 10) inflate it. The mean is vulnerable to such *outliers* (extreme values at either end of the distribution), which exert considerable upward or downward pressure on the mean. In such instances, the median is recommended, as it is not affected in this way. (If there is only one outlier, or several out of a thousand, some researchers exclude it [them] and then calculate the mean, noting the removal in the text.)

One final point: the computer reads numbers only. So it can give a mean value for gender by adding up all of the 1's males and 2's females. A mean of 1.5 means equal numbers of each. What does an average of 1.6 mean? It signifies more females than males but strictly speaking such calculations should not be done. Before leaving this topic, imagine that the percentage of females in a school's faculty is 38 per cent. Is that more than 28 per cent? Is it 10 per cent more? Is the ratio of the two 38:28? The answer to all three questions is yes.

So is gender an interval ratio variable? No, it is not. Gender is a nominal variable, with only equal and not equal comparisons appropriate. What is occurring here is that the variable in question is not being examined at the *individual* level as required in the definition of level of measurement, but at the *group* level. Any nominal variable can become interval ratio if so transformed, as in 24 per cent come alone to the gym, which is 6 per cent less than the 30 per cent who come with a friend, etc.

Measures of dispersion

The amount of variation in a sample can be just as interesting as the typical value of a distribution. Two in-class tests can have the same mean of 60 per cent, but on one most people get between 50 and 70, while for the other the grades are evenly dispersed from the low 20's to 100 per cent. (In testing it is said that the first test does not discriminate; the brightest and least bright students get fairly close marks.) In the gym study, is there more or less variability in the amount of time spent on cardiovascular equipment compared with weights?

The most obvious way of measuring dispersion is by the *range*. This is simply the difference between the maximum and the minimum value in a distribution of values associated with an interval/ratio variable. (It can be applied to an ordinal variable too, but is more definitional there [a range from upper class to working class] than descriptive.) The range for the two types of equipment is 64 minutes for the cardiovascular equipment and 48 minutes for the weights. This suggests that there is more variability in the amount of time spent on the former, probably because some people spend almost no time on cardiovascular equipment. However, like the mean, the range is influenced by outliers, such as respondent 60 on var00010.

Another measure of dispersion is the *standard deviation*, which is essentially a measure of variation around the mean. Basically it is calculated by taking the difference between each value in a distribution and the mean, squaring it, dividing the total of these differences by the number of values, and then taking the square root. The standard deviation for var00010 is 9.9 minutes and for var00011 it is 8 minutes. Thus, not only is the average amount of time spent on the cardiovascular equipment higher than for the weights, there is more spread too. The standard deviation is also affected by outliers and, if omitted in calculating the mean, they are also omitted here.

Generating the arithmetic mean, median, standard deviation, and range

SPSS uses the following typical sequence for analyzing data.

1. Make a selection from the menu bar at the top of the screen, for example, → **Analyze**.

2. From the menu that appears, make a selection, for example, → **Descriptive Statistics**. They describe data as opposed to *inferential* statistics presented later.

3. This brings up a *dialogue box* for telling SPSS what is needed, for example, the specific variables to be analyzed.

4. Very often, SPSS needs further information; → a button to bring up a *sub-dialogue box*.

5. Provide the information in the sub-dialogue box and then go back to the dialogue box. Sometimes, a further sub-dialogue box appears and when finished go back to the dialogue box.

When finished with the entire procedure, → **OK**. The toolbar beneath the menu bar allows shortcut access to certain SPSS operations.

To produce the mean, median, standard deviation, and the range for an interval/ratio variable like *age*, follow these steps:

1. → **A**nalyze → D**e**scriptive Statistics → **E**xplore... [opens the **Explore** dialogue box]

2. → *age* → ▶ button to the left of **Dependent List:** [puts *age* in the **Dependent List:** box] → S**ta**tistics under **Display** → **OK**

The output also includes the 95 per cent confidence interval for the mean, which is based on the standard error of the mean. The output is in Table 12.4

Table 12.4 Explore output for **age** (SPSS output)

Explore

Case Processing Summary

	Cases					
	Valid		Missing		Total	
	N	Per cent	N	Per cent	N	Per cent
AGE	89	98.9%	1	1.1%	90	100.0%

Descriptives

			Statistic	Std. Error
AGE	Mean		33.5955	.9420
	95% Confidence	Lower bound	31.7235	
	Interval for mean	Upper bound	35.4675	
	5% Trimmed mean		33.3159	
	Median		31.0000	
	Variance		78.971	
	Std. Deviation		8.8866	
	Minimum		18.00	
	Maximum		57.00	
	Range		39.00	
	Interquartile Range		14.0000	
	Skewness		.446	.255
	Kurtosis		−.645	.506

Bivariate analysis

Bivariate analysis examines two variables simultaneously, to look for a relationship between them, searching for evidence that variation in one variable coincides with variation in the other. Several techniques are available for examining relationships, but their use depends on the nature of the two variables being analyzed. Figure 12.5 details the main types of bivariate analysis according to the types of variable involved.

Contingency tables

Contingency tables are probably the most flexible of all methods of analyzing relationships in that they can be employed in relation to any pair of variables, from nominal to interval. They are not, however, the most efficient method, especially for interval pairs, which is the reason why the method is not recommended in all of the cells in Figure 12.5. A contingency table is like a frequency table but it allows two variables to be simultaneously analyzed so that relationships between them can be examined. It is normal for contingency tables to include percentages, since they make the tables easier to interpret. Table 12.5 examines the relationship between gender and reasons for visiting the gym from the gym survey. Gender is the presumed independent variable and for

that reason becomes the column variable, a general preference among most researchers. Reasons are the presumed dependent or row variable (but see Box 12.7). In this case, gender influences reasons for going to the gym; reasons for going to the gym cannot influence gender. The percentages are *column percentages*, that is, those for *the independent variable*. The number in each cell is calculated as a percentage of the total number in its column. Thus, to take the top

Table 12.5 Contingency table showing the relationship between gender and reasons for visiting the gym

| | Gender | | | |
| | Male | | Female | |
Reasons	No.	%	No.	%
Relaxation	3	7	6	13
Fitness	15	36	16	33
Lose weight	8	19	25	52
Build strength	16	38	1	2
TOTAL	42		48	

Note: $\chi^2 = 22.726$ $p < .0001$, Cramér's $V = .50$.

	Nominal	Ordinal	Interval/ratio
Nominal	Contingency table + chi-square (χ^2) + Cramér's *V*	Contingency table + chi-square (χ^2) + Cramér's *V*	Contingency table + chi-square (χ^2) + Cramér's *V*. If the interval/ratio variable can be identified as the dependent variable, compare means with eta.
Ordinal	Contingency table + chi-square (χ^2) + Cramér's *V*	Kendall's tau-b	Kendall's tau-b
Interval/ratio	Contingency table + chi-square (χ^2) + Cramér's *V*. If the interval/ratio variable can be identified as the dependent variable, compare means with eta.	Kendall's tau-b	Pearson's *r*

Figure 12.5 Methods of bivariate analysis, one variable on top, other variable on side

left-hand cell, the 3 men who go to the gym for relaxation out of 42 men in total, make 3/42 or 7 per cent of the men in the sample. The procedure for generating a contingency table with SPSS is described below.

Contingency tables are generated to look for patterns of association. In this case, there are clear gender differences in reasons for visiting the gym. As our student anticipated, females are much more likely than men to go to the gym to lose weight. They are also somewhat more likely to go to the gym for relaxation. By contrast, men are much more likely to go to the gym to build strength. There is little gender difference in terms of fitness as a reason. The next section outlines how to generate a contingency table using SPSS. That is immediately followed by the alternatives available in SPSS to summarize those tables, the exact choice dependent on the type of variables involved in the bivariate relationship.

Generating a contingency table

To generate a contingency table, like Table 12.5, follow this procedure:

1. ➔ **Analyze** ➔ **D̲escriptive Statistics** ➔ **C̲rosstabs...** [opens the **Crosstabs** dialogue box shown in Plate 12.13]

2. ➔ **reasons for visiting** ➔ ► button by **R̲ow[s]** [**reasons for visiting** appears in the **R̲ow[s]:** box] ➔ *gender* ➔ ► button by **C̲olumn[s]:** [*gender* appears in the **C̲olumn[s]:** box] ➔ **C̲ells** [opens **Crosstabs: Cell Display** sub-dialogue box shown in Plate 12.14]

3. Make sure **O̲bserved** in the **Counts** box is selected. Make sure **C̲olumn** under **Percentages** is selected. If either of these was not selected, simply click at the relevant point. ➔ **Continue** [closes **Crosstabs: Cell Display** sub-dialogue box and return to the **Crosstabs** dialogue box shown in Plate 12.13]

4. ➔ **Statistics...** [opens the **Crosstabs: Statistics** sub-dialogue box shown in Plate 12.15]. For example suppose Cramér's *V* is needed (because of having two nominal variables).

5. ➔ **C̲hi-square** ➔ **P̲hi and Cramér's V** ➔ **Continue** [closes **Crosstabs: Statistics** sub-dialogue box and returns to the **Crosstabs** dialogue box shown in Plate 12.13]

6. ➔ **OK**

The resulting output is in Table 12.6. Cramér's *V* is just one of the available statistics.

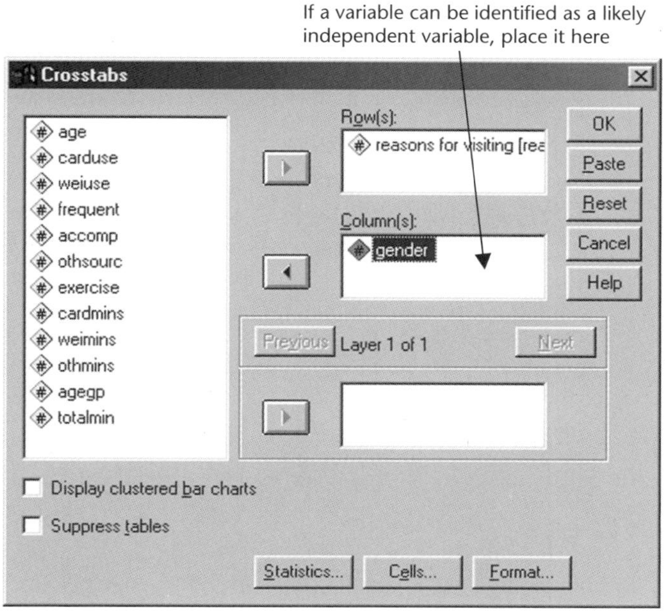

If a variable can be identified as a likely independent variable, place it here

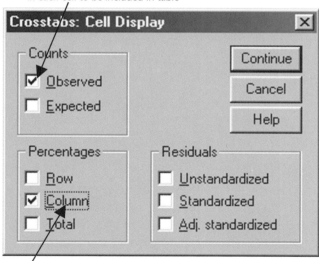

Plate 12.13 The **Crosstabs** dialogue box

Must be selected for number of cases in each cell to be included in table

Select to give the percentage of cases of each category of the column variable

Plate 12.14 The **Crosstabs: Cell Display** sub-dialogue box

Select to provide the χ^2 statistic for the contingency table

Select to generate phi/Cramér's *V*

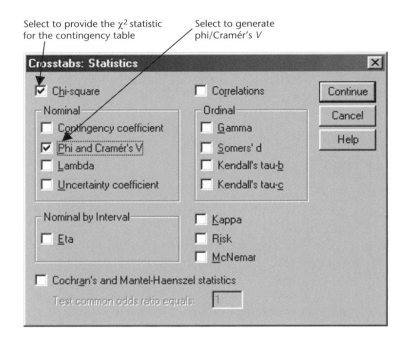

Plate 12.15 The **Crosstabs: Statistics** sub-dialogue box

Table 12.6 Contingency table for **reasons for visiting** by *gender* (SPSS output)

Crosstabs

Case Processing Summary

	Cases					
	Valid		Missing		Total	
	N	Per cent	N	Per cent	N	Per cent
reasons for visiting * GENDER	90	100.0%	0	.0%	90	100.0%

reasons for visiting * GENDER Crosstabulation

			GENDER		Total
			male	female	
reasons for visiting	relaxation	Count	3	6	9
		% within GENDER	7.1%	12.5%	10.0%
	fitness	Count	15	16	31
		% within GENDER	35.7%	33.3%	34.4%
	lose weight	Count	8	25	33
		% within GENDER	19.0%	52.1%	36.7%
	build strength	Count	16	1	17
		% within GENDER	38.1%	2.1%	18.9%
Total		Count	42	48	90
		% within GENDER	100.0%	100.0%	100.0%

continued

Table 12.6 *(continued)*

Chi-Square Tests

	Value	df	Asymp. Sig. [(2-sided)]
Pearson Chi-Square	22.726[a]	3	.000
Likelihood Ratio	25.805	3	.000
Linear-by-Linear Association	9.716	1	.002
N of Valid Cases	90		

[a] 2 cells (25.0%) have expected count less than 5. The minimum expected count is 4.20.

This is the χ^2 value referred to in the text

Symmetric Measures

		Value	Approx. Sig.
Nominal by Nominal	Phi	.503	.000
	Cramer's *V*	.503	.000
N of Valid Cases		90	

[a] Not assuming the null hypothesis.
[b] Using the asymptotic standard error assuming the null hypothesis.

Since this is not a 2 × 2 table, interpret Cramér's *V*

Shows strength of relationship

Shows level of statistical significance of computed value of Cramér's *V*

Pearson's *r*

Pearson's *r* is a statistic for examining relationships between two interval/ratio variables; its chief features are:

- the coefficient lies between 0 (zero or no relationship between the two variables) and 1 (a perfect relationship);
- the closer the coefficient is to 1, the stronger the relationship; the closer it is to zero, the weaker the relationship;
- the coefficient is either positive or negative—this indicates the *direction* of a relationship. Negative means one variable is going up while the other is going down; it does not matter which is which. Positive means the two are going in the same direction, either both up or both down.

To be able to use Pearson's *r*, the relationship between the two variables must be broadly *linear*—that

is, when plotted on a scatter diagram, the values of the two variables approximate a straight line (even though they may be scattered as in Figure 12.9) and do not curve. To check on this requires a scatter diagram.

Generating scatter diagrams

The production of scatter diagrams, known as *scatterplots* in SPSS, is illustrated in the relationship between *age* and *cardmins*. If one variable can be identified as likely to be the independent variable, it is by convention placed on the *X*-axis, the horizontal axis. Since *age* is bound to be the independent variable, follow these steps:

1. → **Graphs** → **Scatter...** [opens the **Scatter Plot** dialogue box]
2. → **Simple** [usually this has been automatically selected] → **Define** [opens the **Simple Scatterplot** sub-dialogue box shown in Plate 12.16]

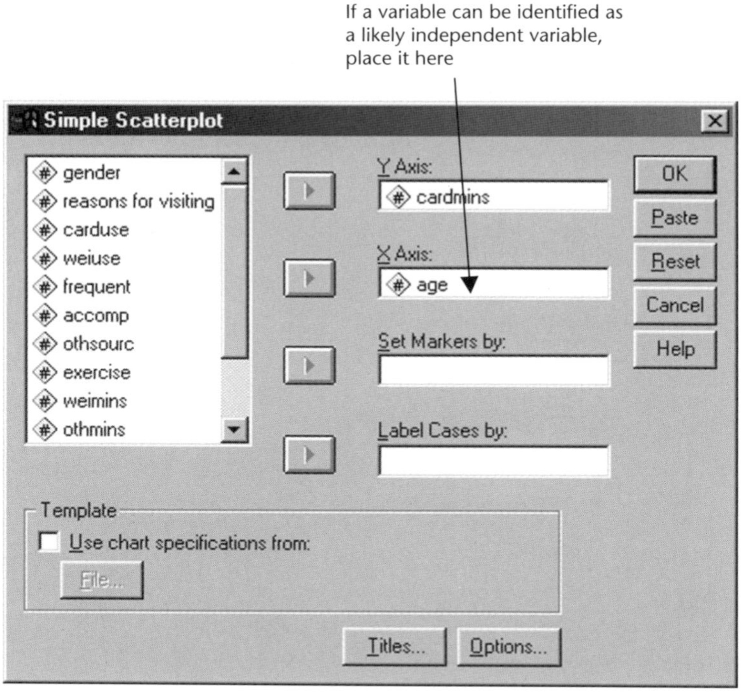

If a variable can be identified as a likely independent variable, place it here

Plate 12.16 The **Simple Scatterplot** sub-dialogue box

3. → *cardmins* → ▶ button by <u>Y</u> Axis: → *age* → ▶ button by <u>X</u> Axis: → OK

To illustrate these features consider Box 12.8, which gives imaginary data for five variables, and the scatter diagrams in Figures 12.6 to 12.9, which look at the relationship between pairs of interval/ratio variables. The scatter diagram for variables 1 and 2 is presented in Figure 12.6 and shows a perfect positive relationship, which yields a Pearson's *r* correlation of +1. This means that, as one variable increases, the other variable increases and probably that no other variable is affecting the relationship between them. If the correlation is below 1, at least one other variable is active, maybe even affecting variable 1 as well as variable 2.

The scatter diagram for variables 2 and 3 (Figure 12.7) shows a perfect negative relationship, which yields a Pearson's *r* correlation of –1. This means that, as one variable increases the other variable decreases and that no other variable is needed to explain that relationship. In both this and the prior instance, +/– 1.0, the line could be extended beyond the data to make predictions of what would happen

to either variable if the other moved beyond the range shown. Sociology rarely makes those extrapolations, as a mature science, with most things already known, is a prerequisite. Social data usually exhibit so many exceptions that few cases fall ex-

---

Box 12.8 Imaginary data from five variables to show different types of relationship

	Variables			
1	2	3	4	5
1	10	50	7	9
2	12	45	13	23
3	14	40	18	7
4	16	35	14	15
5	18	30	16	6
6	20	25	23	22
7	22	20	19	12
8	24	15	24	8
9	26	10	22	18
10	28	5	24	10

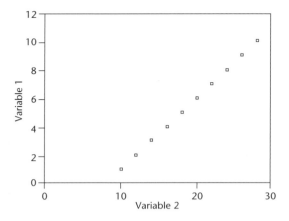

Figure 12.6 Scatter diagram showing a perfect positive relationship

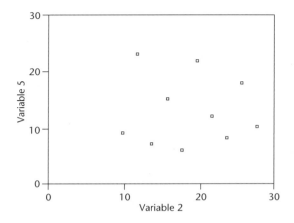

Figure 12.8 Scatter diagram showing two variables that are not related

actly on the line and thus require more general and less specific predictions.

No apparent pattern in the scatter diagram, as in the relationship between variables 2 and 5, means no or virtually no correlation between the variables. The correlation is virtually zero, at –.041. This means that the variation in the dependent variable is probably associated with variables other than the one used in this analysis. Figure 12.8 shows the appropriate scatter diagram.

If a relationship is strong, a clear patterning to the variables is evident. This is the case with variables 2 and 4, whose scatter diagram appears in

Figure 12.9. There is clearly a positive relationship and in fact the Pearson's r is +.88 (usually, positive correlations are presented without the + sign). This means that the variation in the two variables is very closely connected, but that there is also some influence of other variables.

Going back to the gym survey, the correlation between age (var00002) and the amount of time spent on weights (var00011) is –.27, a weak negative relationship. This suggests a tendency for older people to spend less time on such equipment, but that other variables clearly influence that amount of time.

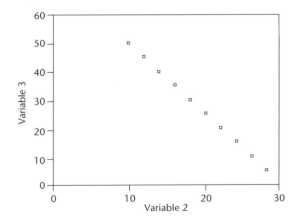

Figure 12.7 Scatter diagram showing a perfect negative relationship

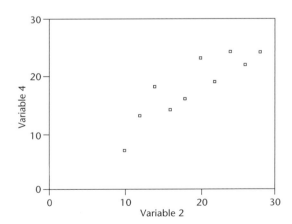

Figure 12.9 Scatter diagram showing a strong positive relationship

Generating Pearson's *r*

To produce Pearson's *r*, or the correlation between *age*, *weimins*, and *cardmins*, follow these steps:

1. → **A̲nalyze** → **C̲orrelate** → **B̲ivariate...** [opens **Bivariate Correlations** dialogue box shown in Plate 12.17]

2. → **age** → ▶ button → *cardmins* → ▶ button → *weimins* → ▶ button [*age, cardmins*, and *weimins* should now be in the **V̲ariables:** box] → **Pearso̲n** [*if* not already selected] → **OK**

The resulting output is in Table 12.7.

To produce Kendall's tau-b, follow the same procedures but instead of selecting **Pearson**, → **Kendall's tau-b̲**. Somer's d and Kendall's tau-c are other options, but for clarity not explained here.

Generating Kendall's tau-b

Kendall's tau-b is designed for pairs of ordinal variables, but is also used, as suggested by Figure 12.5, when one variable is ordinal and the other is interval/ratio. Notice the general rule of how data can be moved down a level, interval into ordinal, but not up. Thus Pearson's *r* is not calculated, as it would require a move from ordinal *up* to interval. It is exactly the same as Pearson's *r* in terms of the outcome of calculating it, in that the computed value of Kendall's tau-b is either positive or negative and varies between 0 and 1. In the gym study there are three ordinal variables: var00004, var00005, and var00006 (see Table 12.1). Using Kendall's tau-b to calculate the correlation between the first two variables, var00004 and var00005—frequency of use of the cardiovascular and weights equipment—it is very low. A slightly stronger relationship is found between var00006 (frequency of going to the gym) and var00010 (amount of time spent on the cardiovascular equipment), close to .4. The latter variable is an interval/ratio variable but to repeat the important point, for Pearson's *r* both variables must be at the interval/ratio level of measurement. Instead, Kendall's tau-b must be used (see Figure 12.5). The SPSS procedure is the same as described above for Pearson's. Note too that Spearman's rho, another option, can be used if relating two ordinal variables but only for a small number (< 30) of cases with few or

Plate 12.17 The **Bivariate Correlations** dialogue box

All variable(s) to be correlated go here

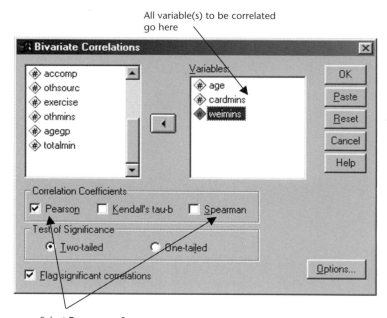

Select **Pearson** or **S̲pearman** depending on the kinds of variables being analyzed

Table 12.7 Correlations output for *age*, *weimins*, and *cardmins* (SPSS output)

Correlations

Correlations of $p < 0.05$ are 'flagged' with asterisks

Correlations

		AGE	WEIMINS	CARDMINS
AGE	Pearson Correlation	1.000	−.273 **	−.109
	Sig. (2-tailed)	.	.010	.311
	N	89	89	89
WEIMINS	Pearson Correlation	−.273 **	1.000	−.161
	Sig. (2-tailed)	.010	.	.130
	N	89	90	90
CARDMINS	Pearson Correlation	−.109	−.161	1.000
	Sig. (2-tailed)	.311	.130	.
	N	89	90	90

** Correlation is significant at the 0.01 level (2-tailed).

Shows strength of relationship as indicated by Pearson's *r*

Shows level of statistical significance of computed value of Pearson's *r*

Shows number of cases, less any cases for which there are missing data for either or both variables

no ties. It ranges from –1, a perfect negative relationship, to +1, a perfect positive relationship. For example, look at the participation rank (A) and popularity rank (B) of a group of seven people.

Person	Mary	John	Bill	Sally	Kim	Susan	Joe
A	1	2	3	4	5	6	7
B	1	2	3	4	5	6	7

Spearman's rho is 1.0; knowing a person's participation rank perfectly reveals the popularity rank. It is called rank-order correlation to remind you of its ordinal character and to distinguish it from Pearson's *r*.

Generating Cramér's *V*

Cramér's *V* is suitable for examining the strength of relationship between two nominal variables (see Figure 12.5). It ranges from 0 to 1 but is always positive as nominal data have no idea of < or > and thus positive and negative make no sense.

The value of Cramér's *V* associated with the analysis presented in Table 12.6 is .50, a moderate relationship. Cramér's *V* is usually reported along with a contingency table and a chi-square test (see below).

It is not normally presented on its own. The procedure for generating it with SPSS is merely to click it (see Plate 12.15).

Comparing means and eta

There are other statistics but we must stop and present just one more, sort of as a summary. To examine the relationship between an interval/ratio variable and a nominal variable, and if the latter can be relatively unambiguously identified as the independent variable, a potentially fruitful approach is to compare the means of the interval/ratio variable for each subgroup of the nominal variable. As an example, consider Table 12.8, which presents the mean number of minutes spent on cardiovascular equipment (var00010) for each of the four categories of reasons for going to the gym (var00003). The four means shown suggest that people who go to the gym for fitness or to lose weight spend considerably more time on this equipment than people who go to the gym to relax or to build strength.

This procedure is often accompanied by a test of association between variables called *eta*. This statistic expresses the level of association between the two variables and, as one is only nominal, meaning no

Table 12.8 Comparing subgroup means: time spent on cardiovascular equipment by reasons for going to the gym

Time		Reasons			
	Relaxation	Fitness	Lose weight	Build strength	Total
Mean number of minutes spent on cardiovascular equipment	18.33	30.55	28.36	19.65	26.47
n	9	31	33	17	90

ordering, like Cramér's *V* it is always positive. The eta for the data in Table 12.8 is .48, a moderate relationship between the two variables. Eta is a very flexible method for exploring the relationship between two variables, because it can be employed when one variable is nominal and the other interval/ratio. Also, it does not make the assumption that the relationship between variables is linear.

To test your general understanding of strength of relationships, look at these results from a Run's test, another statistic. M is for man, W for woman and it shows in a line who is more tolerant of same-sex marriages (left end), the scores from Likert items. Which is

the perfect relationship, where knowing gender perfectly predicts tolerance, and which shows no relationship? Result one: WWWWWWWWMMMMMMMM; result two: WMWMWMWMWMWMWMW. Result one is the perfect relationship; all women are more tolerant than men. In result two, gender does not help to predict as the tolerance of men and women is totally interspersed.

To produce a table like Table 12.8, follow these steps:

1. → <u>A</u>nalyze → Compare <u>M</u>eans → <u>M</u>eans... [opens the **Means** dialogue box shown in Plate 12.18]

2. → *cardmins* → ▶ button to the left of **Dependent List:** → **reasons for visiting** → ▶ button to the

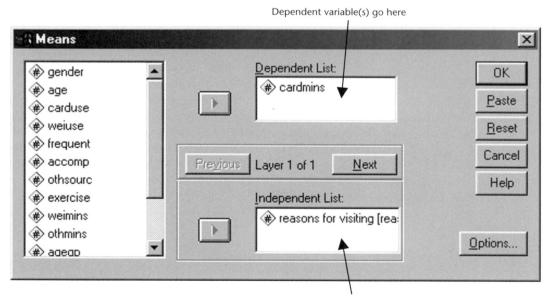

Dependent variable(s) go here

Independent variable(s) go here

Plate 12.18 The **Means** dialogue box

left of **Independent List:** ➔ **Options** [opens the **Means: Options** sub-dialogue box]

3. ➔ <u>A</u>**nova table and eta** underneath **Statistics for First Layer** ➔ **Continue** [closes the **Means: Options** sub-dialogue box and return to the **Means** dialogue box shown in Plate 12.18] ➔ **OK**

Amount of explained variance

Squaring eta, Kendall's tau-b, Spearman's rho, and Pearson's *r* yields a further useful statistic: how much of the variation in one variable is due to the other variable. Thus, if *r* is −.27, r^2 is .0729. This can be expressed as a percentage by multiplying r^2 by 100. The product of this exercise is 7 per cent. This means that 7 per cent of the variation in the use of cardiovascular equipment is accounted for by age. This also shows that a strong correlation like .7 explains only 49 per cent of the variance. For nominal data, squaring Cramér's *V* (.50) gives a close enough approximation, meaning that 25 per cent of the variation in reasons for visiting the gym is attributable to gender.

Statistical significance and inferential statistics

One difficulty with working on sample data is a lingering worry about whether the findings are generalizable to the population from which the sample is drawn. As seen in Chapter 11, there is always the possibility of *sampling error* (difference between the population and the sample chosen), even when probability-sampling procedures (as in the gym survey) are followed. If this happens, the sample is unrepresentative of the wider population and therefore findings lack external validity. To make matters worse, there is no feasible way of finding out whether they do in fact apply to the population as no one has the time or money to check this out. That is why sampling occurs in the first place. This is where statistical significance and the various tests of *statistical significance* come in; they provide an indication of confidence in the findings. They should, however, never be confused with substantive significance.

A technique that allows establishing that confidence and the risk of making that inference is needed. These two elements—confidence and risk—lie at the heart of tests of statistical significance (see Box 12.9). However, it is important to appreciate that tests of statistical significance are appropriate only in relation to probability samples. The fact that most researchers cheat on this rule is only noted here.

Chapter 11 (see Box 11.3), in the discussion of the standard error of the mean, revealed some of the ideas behind statistical significance. For example, the mean age of the gym sample is 33.6. Using the concept of the standard error of the mean, the 95 per cent confidence interval for the population mean is between 31.72 and 35.47. We think that this range is not one of the 5 in 100 sample ranges that do not include the population mean. The rest of this section looks at tests for determining the degree of confidence for measures of relationships

---

Box 12.9 **What is a test of statistical significance?**

A test of statistical significance allows the analyst to estimate a level of confidence that the results from a study based on a randomly selected sample are generalizable to the population from which the sample was drawn. It measures the risk of concluding that there is a relationship in the population when there is no such relationship in the population. On the other hand, if an analysis reveals a statistically significant finding, this does not mean that that finding is intrinsically significant or important. Statistical significance is solely concerned with the confidence researchers can have that their sample findings reflect a population. It does not mean that a statistically significant finding is substantively significant. And recall that statistical significance gets easier to achieve as sample size goes up. So a study of 200 independent vs. 400 fleet cabbies can show a statistically significant difference in tips of 15 cents a day in favour of the independents. That is not a reason for mortgaging a house to buy an independent cab, as 15 cents a day is of little substantive significance.

between variables. All of the tests have a common structure.

- *Set up a null hypothesis.* This is an hypothesis to be disproved. Scientists do not know the future, not even all of the past. Thus they can only be 99 per cent sure that something like the law of gravity is proved. It takes only one apple falling from the ground up to the tree to disprove the law. So just to be careful they say that the law of gravity has *not yet been disproved.* In the current example, the null hypothesis stipulates that two variables are not related in the population—for example, that there is *no* relationship between gender and visiting the gym in the population from which the sample is selected. Disproving that gives indirect support to the *research hypothesis* that there is a relationship in the population. For clarity, reread this paragraph.

- *Establish an acceptable level of statistical significance.* This is essentially a measure of the risk of rejecting the null hypothesis (implying that there *is* a relationship in the population) when it should not be rejected (implying that there is no relationship in the population). Levels of statistical significance are expressed as probability levels—that is, the probability of rejecting the null hypothesis when it should be confirmed (or, failing to reject it, in the unusual language of science and its avoidance of proving anything). See Box 12.10 on this issue. The convention among most social researchers is that the maximum acceptable level of statistical significance is $p < .05$, meaning that there are fewer than 5 chances in 100 that the sample shows a relationship not also found in the population. This risk level varies. Five errors in 100 are too high for testing a drug for its efficacy, especially a drug with side effects. Probably p would be set at .00001, accepting only one chance in 100 000 of an error.

- *Determine the statistical significance of the findings* (i.e., use a statistical test like chi-square).

- If the findings are statistically significant at the .05 level—so that the risk of getting a relationship as strong as the one found, when there is *no* relationship in the population, is no higher than 5 in 100—*reject* the null hypothesis. The results are unlikely to have occurred by *chance*.

Box 12.10 🔅 *What is the level of statistical significance?*

The level of statistical significance is the maximum level of risk one is prepared to take, conventionally in the social sciences up to 5 chances in 100, of falsely concluding that there is a relationship when there is not one in the population from which the sample is taken. This means that, in 100 samples, as many as 5 of them may exhibit a relationship when there is not one in the population. Any one sample of the 100 samples may be one of those five, but the risk is fairly small. This significance level is denoted by $p < .05$ (p means *probability*).

A significance level of $p < .1$ means accepting the possibility that as many as 10 in 100 samples may show a relationship where none exists in the population. Therefore, one would have less confidence in generalizing than with $p = .05$. But, if one wants a more stringent test, perhaps because worried about the use that may be made of the results, one can choose the $p < .01$ level. This means being prepared to accept a risk of only 1 in 100 that the results could have arisen by chance (that is, due to sampling error). Therefore, even if the results, following administration of a test, are statistically significant at the $p < .05$ level, but *not* the $p < .01$ level, the null hypothesis should not be rejected. In what other cases would this be appropriate?

There are in fact two possible types of error when inferring statistical significance, known as Type I and Type II errors (see Figure 12.10). A Type I error occurs when a true null hypothesis is rejected. This means that the results are too likely to have arisen by chance; concluding that there is a relationship in the population is wrong because there probably is not one.

A $p < .05$ level of significance means being more likely to make a Type I error than when using a $p < .01$ level of significance. This is because with .01 there is less chance of wrongly rejecting the null hypothesis. One is more likely to confirm the null hypothesis when the significance level is .01 (1 in 100) than when it is .05 (1 in 20). However, in doing so, the chance of a Type II error (accepting the null hypothesis when it should be rejected) is increased.

The two types of error cannot be minimized at the same time. Statisticians make the conservative choice of minimizing the Type I error, as this means more often failing to reject the null and thus less acceptance of the research hypothesis. As an aid in remembering this, what is worse, a criminal going free or an innocent person imprisoned? Most think it is the latter. The null hypothesis is innocence. The courts want to be truly sure before they reject that and perhaps send someone to jail. Of course reducing that problem, a Type I error, increases Type II, someone who is guilty getting off. Again both cannot be minimized at the same time.

Correlation and statistical significance

Examining the statistical significance of a correlation from a randomly selected sample provides information about the likelihood of a correlation in the population from which the sample was taken. Thus, with a correlation r of $-.62$ in the sample, what is the likelihood that there is no relationship between the two variables in the population? How likely is a $-.62$ to arise by chance, due to sampling error?

A correlation coefficient r that large, $-.62$, in that sized sample, if the two variables are not related in the population is rare; the significance level is actually $p < .05$ and most researchers would reject the null hypothesis of no relationship in the population. There are only 5 chances in 100 that a correlation of at least $-.62$ could have arisen by chance alone. In any one study a researcher *could* have 1 of

the 5 samples in 100 that shows a relationship when there is not one in the population, but the degree of risk is reasonably small. If, say, it was found that $r = -.62$ and $p < .1$, there could be as many as 10 chances in 100 that there is no correlation in the population. This would *not* be an acceptable level of risk for most purposes. It would mean that in as many as 1 sample in 10 a correlation of $-.62$ could occur when there is a zero correlation in the population. If $r = -.62$ and $p < .001$, there is only 1 chance in 1000 that a zero correlation exists in the population. There would be a very low level of risk in making the inference that the correlation had not arisen by chance.

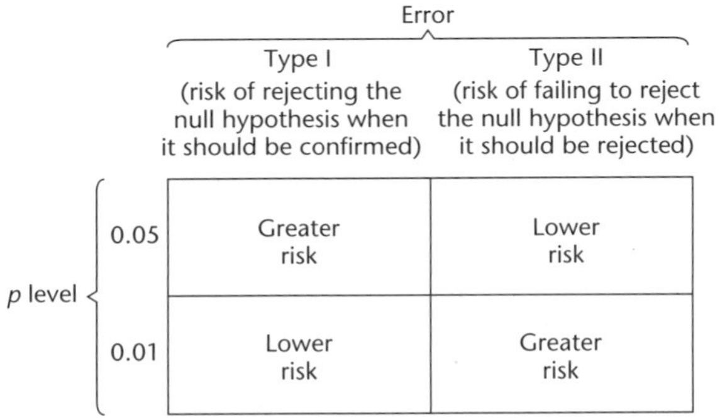

Whether a correlation coefficient is statistically significant or not is affected by two factors:

- the size of the computed coefficient, and
- the size of the sample.

This second factor may appear surprising. Basically, the larger a sample, the more likely it is that a computed correlation coefficient is statistically significant. Thus, even though the correlation between age and the amount of time spent on weights machines in the gym survey is just $-.27$, a fairly weak relationship, it is statistically significant at the $p < .01$ level. This means that there is only one chance in 100 that there is no relationship between age and weights in the population. Because the question of whether a correlation coefficient is statistically significant depends so much on the sample size, it is important always to examine *both* the correlation coefficient *and* the significance level. This is true for any calculated statistic.

This treatment of correlation and statistical significance applies to both Pearson's r and Kendall's tau-b. A similar interpretation can also be applied to Cramér's V in the chi-square test.

The chi-square test

The chi-square (χ^2) test is applied to contingency tables like Table 12.5. It is a measure of confidence that a relationship between two variables in a sample also would be found in the population. The test works by calculating for each cell in the table an expected frequency or value—that is, one that would

Error

	Type I (risk of rejecting the null hypothesis when it should be confirmed)	Type II (risk of failing to reject the null hypothesis when it should be rejected)
0.05	Greater risk	Lower risk
0.01	Lower risk	Greater risk

p level

Figure 12.10 Type I and Type II errors

occur on the basis of chance alone. Think of the days of the week and crime: one might expect that 14.28 per cent of all crimes would occur on Monday, 14.28 per cent on Saturday, in fact 14.28 per cent on each day of the week. That is what would be *expected* if there is no relationship between day of the week and crime. The real observed data say otherwise; there is a relationship with more crimes on Friday and Saturday. The chi-square value, which in Table 12.6 is 22.726, is calculated by taking the differences between the actual and expected values for each cell in the table and then summing those differences (it is slightly more complicated than this, but the details need not be of concern here). The chi-square value means nothing by itself and can be meaningfully interpreted only in relation to its associated level of statistical significance, which in this case is $p < .0001$. This means that there is only one chance in 10 000 of rejecting the null hypothesis (that is, inferring that there *is* a relationship in the population when there is no such relationship in the population). One can be extremely confident that there is a relationship between gender and reasons for visiting the gym among all gym members, since the chance of obtaining a sample that shows that relationship when there is no relationship among all gym members is 1 in 10 000.

But a chi-square value is also affected by the number of cases. While one wants a large chi-square to reject a null hypothesis, a larger N makes this easier to achieve. This is why it is necessary to look at the data and not just at the final statistic. Examine the three parts below of Table 12.9. All examine the relationship between sports played, contact, non-contact, none as the independent variable across the top, and self-esteem, high, medium, and low. Because the independent variable is nominal, chi-square is more appropriate than Kendall's tau-b.

The first two parts of Table 12.9, A and B, show that just by doubling the size of the sample, the results change from very likely due to chance in A (thus the null hypothesis cannot be rejected) to being less than 5 chances in 100 that they occurred by chance in B and thus a rejection of the null. Not only is this problematic, as it suggests collecting more and more data until the null can be rejected, but in any substantive world the null really should be rejected in B too: at any level of sports participation, half the respondents have low self-esteem. Sport participation does not really explain self-esteem in any important way. Now look at the last part of the table, C. Why was it included? It shows that chi-square is calculated only with numbers, not value labels; when the data from B for high and low self-esteem are switched around in C, which in most instances should mean something, chi-square stays the same. It deals with statistical significance, not practical, and has no substantive meaning.

Comparing means and statistical significance

A test of statistical significance can also be applied to the comparison of means in Table 12.8. This proce-

Table 12.9 How chi-square is affected by increasing the size of N and not affected by changes to column headings

Self-esteem	A			B			C		
	Contact	n/c	None	Contact	n/c	None	Contact	n/c	None
H	7	3	10	14	6	20	24	26	50
M	5	10	15	10	20	30	10	20	30
L	12	13	25	24	26	50	14	6	20
	$\chi^2 = 1.93$, not sig.			$\chi^2 = 5.08$, $p < .05$			$\chi^2 = 5.08$, $p < .05$		

Note: n/c means No Contact

dure entails treating the total amount of variation in the dependent variable—amount of time spent on cardiovascular equipment—as made up of two types: variation *within* each of the four subgroups that make up the independent variable and variation *between* them. The latter is often called the *explained variance* (explained by the group one is in) and the former the *error variance*. A test of statistical significance for the comparison of means entails relating the two types of variance to form what is known as an F statistic, which expresses the amount of explained variance in relation to the amount of error variance. In the case of the data in Table 12.8, the resulting F statistic is statistically significant at the $p <$ .001 level. This finding suggests that there is only one chance in 1000 that there is no relationship between the two variables among all gym members. SPSS produces information regarding the F statistic and its statistical significance if the procedures described earlier for eta are followed.

Multivariate analysis

Multivariate analysis entails the simultaneous analysis of three or more variables, and can only be introduced here. It is sometimes called *elaboration* as it is more complicated and creates a more valuable picture than does bivariate analysis. It is recommended that readers examine a textbook on quantitative data analysis for an exposition of techniques (e.g., Healey 2002). There are three main contexts within which multivariate analysis is employed. Each is explained below.

Is the relationship spurious?

To establish a relationship between two variables, not only must there be logical and temporal evidence of a relationship but the relationship must be shown to be *non-spurious*. A spurious relationship exists when there appears to be a relationship between two variables, but the relationship is not real: it is being produced because each variable is itself related to a third variable. For example, in a relationship between income and voting behaviour, is the relationship due to age (see Figure 12.11)? The older one is, the more likely one is to have a higher salary, while age is known to influence voting behaviour. If age is producing the apparent relationship between income and voting behaviour, that relationship is spurious. The easiest way to remember spuriousness is to think about the positive relationship between the number of fire engines at a fire and fire damage: the more engines, the greater the devastation. Does this mean that when you discover a fire you should call for only one fire engine? Of course not. The size of the fire accounts for both the number of engines responding and the damage. As an exercise, think about the positive relationship between the accumulative money spent on dates and sexual behaviour.

Is there an intervening variable?

If it is not spurious, *why* is there a relationship between income and voting? One possibility is that people of different incomes vary in their political attitudes, which in turn has implications for their voting behaviour. Political attitudes is then an *intervening variable,* coming between:

income ➔ political attitudes ➔ voting behaviour.

An intervening variable suggests that the relationship between the original two variables is not a direct one. If this is true, what should happen to the relationship to the relationship when its influence is controlled? Just looking at the three variables and arrows it should be apparent that cutting out the middle link

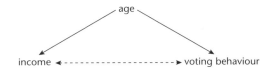

Figure 12.11 A spurious relationship

in the chain weakens it. On the other hand, suppose the third variable is race: race → income → voting behaviour. Race is *antecedent* to income. Again just looking at the chain suggests that if race is removed from the model, the other two remain connected and that is correct. The purpose of adding these third variables is to statistically control for them. See the control word? Yes, the purpose is to make cross-sectional research more like an experiment where random assignment makes all other things equal or controlled. Altogether there are six types of these third variables, called *test factors*. A final one is covered below, the others left for another course.

Does a third variable affect the relationship?

If the relationship between two variables holds for some groups but not for others the relationship is said to be specified, or moderated. In the gym study, for example, is the relationship between age and whether visitors have other sources of regular exercise (var00008) moderated by gender? Table 12.10 shows the relationship between age and other sources of exercise and includes both men and women. (Age has been broken down into just three age bands to make the table easier to read.) The table suggests that the 31 to 40 age group is less likely to have other sources of regular exercise than the 30 and under and 41 and over age groups. However, Table 12.11, which breaks the relationship down by gender, suggests that the pattern for males and females is somewhat different. Among males, the pattern shown in Table 12.10 is very pronounced, but for females the likelihood of having other sources of exercise declines with age. Thus the relationship between age and other sources of exercise is moderated by gender. This example merely illustrates how contingency tables can be employed for multivariate analysis. There are many other techniques.

Table 12.10 Contingency table showing the relationship between age and whether gym visitors have other sources of regular exercise (percentages)

Other source of exercise	Age		
	30 and under	31–40	41 and over
Other source	64	43	58
No other source	36	57	42
n	42	23	24

Table 12.11 Contingency table showing the relationship between age and whether gym visitors have other sources of regular exercise for males and females (percentages)

	Gender					
	Male			Female		
Other source of exercise	30 and under	31–40	41 and over	30 and under	31–40	41 and over
Other source	70	33	75	59	50	42
No other source	30	67	25	41	50	58
n	20	9	12	22	14	12

Generating a contingency table with three variables

To create a table like Table 12.11, do as follows:

1. ➔ **A**nalyze ➔ **D**escriptive Statistics ➔ **C**rosstabs... [opens the **Crosstabs** dialogue box shown in Plate 12.13]

2. ➔ *othsourc* ➔ ▶ button by **R**ow[s] [*othsourc* appears in the **R**ow[s]: box]

3. ➔ *age3* [this is the name given to the newly created variable with *age* recoded into three categories] ➔ ▶ button by **C**olumn[s]: [*age3* appears in the **C**olumn[s]: box] ➔ *gender* ➔ ▶ button beneath **Pre**v**ious** [*gender* appears in the box underneath **Layer 1 of 1**] ➔ **C**ells [opens **Crosstabs:**

Cell Display sub-dialogue box shown in Plate 12.14]

4. Make sure **O**bserved in the **Counts** box has been selected. Make sure **Column** under **Percentages** has been selected. If either has not, simply click at the relevant point. ➔ **Continue** [closes **Crosstabs: Cell Display** sub-dialogue box and returns to the **Crosstabs** dialogue box shown in Plate 12.13]

5. ➔ OK

The resulting table looks somewhat different from Table 12.11 in that *gender* appears as a row rather than as a column variable. This topic is saved for another course. Now it is time to move on to computer-assisted qualitative analysis.

Checklist on doing and writing up quantitative data analysis

☑ Do missing data have a code?

☑ If using a Likert scale with reversed items, are they reverse-coded?

☑ Are the statistical techniques appropriate to the level of the variables (i.e., whether nominal, ordinal, or interval/ratio)?

☑ Are the most appropriate and powerful techniques for answering the research questions used?

☑ If the sample is *not* randomly selected, are inferences about a population avoided (or at least if included, their limitations outlined)?

☑ If the data come from a cross-sectional design, are unsustainable inferences about causality resisted?

☑ Does the analysis go beyond univariate to include bivariate, even multivariate analyses?

☑ Are the research questions answered and only those analyses relevant to them presented?

K KEY POINTS

- **Think about data analysis before designing research instruments.**

- **Know the difference between nominal, ordinal, and interval/ratio variables. Techniques of data analysis are applicable to some types of variable and not others.**

- **Become familiar with computer software like SPSS before designing research instruments, to be aware early of potential difficulties using it.**

- **The basic message, then, is not to leave these considerations until the data have been collected, tempting though it may be.**

- **Do not confuse statistical significance with substantive significance.**

Q QUESTIONS FOR REVIEW

- What are missing data and why do they arise?

Getting started in SPSS

- Outline differences among: variable names, variable labels, and value labels.

- In what circumstances is it appropriate to recode a variable?

- In what circumstances is it appropriate to create a new variable?

Types of variables

- Make sure to know the differences among the three types of variable outlined in this chapter: interval/ratio; ordinal; and nominal.

- Why is it important to be able to distinguish among them?

- Imagine the kinds of answers to the following four questions in an interview survey. What kind of variable would each generate: nominal; ordinal; or interval/ratio?

  1. Do you enjoy going shopping?

     Yes

     Unsure

     No

  2. How many times have you shopped in the last month? Please write the number here _____ .

  3. For what items do you most enjoy shopping? Please tick one only.

     Clothes (including shoes)

     Food

     Things for the house

     Presents or gifts

     Entertainment (CDs, videos, etc.)

  4. How important is it to you to buy clothes with designer labels?

     Very important

     Fairly important

     Not very important

     Not at all important

Univariate analysis

- What is an outlier and how does having one affect the mean and the range?

- In conjunction with which measure of central tendency is the standard deviation usually reported: the mean; the median; or the mode?

Bivariate analysis

- Can one infer causality from bivariate analysis?

- Why are percentages crucial when presenting contingency tables?

- In what circumstances does one use each of the following: Pearson's *r*; Kendall's tau-b; Cramér's *V*; Spearman's rho; eta?

Data analysis with SPSS

Using the gym survey data, create:

- a frequency table for *exercise*;
- a bar chart and pie chart for *exercise* and compare their usefulness;
- a histogram for *cardmins*;
- measures of central tendency and dispersion for *cardmins*;
- a contingency table and Cramér's *V* for *gender* and *exercise*;
- a scatter diagram for *age* and *cardmins*;
- Pearson's *r* for *age* and *cardmins*;
- Kendall's tau-b for *carduse* and *weiuse*; and
- a difference of means analysis for **reasons for visiting** and *totalmin*.

Statistical significance

- What does statistical significance mean and how does it differ from substantive significance?
- What is a significance level?
- What does the chi-square test achieve?
- What does it mean to say that an eta of .42 is statistically significant at $p < .05$?

Multivariate analysis

- What is a spurious relationship?
- How can one tell the difference between an intervening variable and an antecedent one?
- What does it mean to say that a relationship is specified or moderated?

13 Qualitative data analysis

CHAPTER OVERVIEW

Because qualitative data from interviews or participant observation typically take the form of a large body of unstructured textual material, their analysis is not straightforward. Moreover, unlike quantitative data analysis, clear-cut rules about how to conduct qualitative data analysis have not been developed. In this chapter, some general approaches to qualitative data analysis are examined, along with *coding*, its main feature. The most significant recent development in qualitative research is computer software for these procedures. This software, often referred to as computer-assisted qualitative data analysis software (CAQDAS), removes many if not most of the clerical tasks associated with the manual coding and retrieving of data. There is no industry leader among the different programs (in the sense that SPSS holds this position among quantitative data analysis software). This chapter introduces a relatively new entrant that is having a big impact—QSR NVivo (the version discussed in this chapter is NVivo 2).

The chapter explores:

- *grounded theory* as a general strategy of qualitative data analysis; probably the most prominent of the general approaches to that analysis, its main features, processes, and outcomes are presented along with some criticisms of the approach;

- *coding* as a key process in grounded theory and in qualitative data analysis more generally; it is the focus of an extended discussion in terms of what it entails and some of its limitations;

- how to set up research materials for analysis with NVivo;

- how to code using NVivo, how to retrieve coded text, and how to create memos;

- some of the debates about the desirability of using CAQDAS;

- a criticism of coding in relation to qualitative data because it tends to fragment data; and

- the idea of *narrative analysis,* an approach that is gaining a following because it reduces that fragmentation.

Introduction

Because of its reliance on prose, in the form of field notes, interview transcripts, or documents, qualitative research rapidly generates a large, cumbersome database. Miles (1979) described qualitative data as an 'attractive nuisance'—attractive because of its richness but also a nuisance because that very richness can lead to a failure to examine the data in their wider scientific significance.

Yet, finding a path through the thicket of prose is not an easy matter, even baffling to many researchers confronting such data for the first time. 'What do I do with it now?' is a common refrain. In large part this is because there are few well-established and widely accepted rules for the analysis of qualitative data. Although learning the techniques of quantitative data analysis in a statistics course may seem painful at the time, it does provide an un-ambiguous set of rules about how to handle data. Analyses still must be interpreted, but at least there are relatively clear rules for getting to that point. Analytic procedures for qualitative data analysis have not reached this degree of codification and many argue that they are undesirable anyway (cf. Bryman and Burgess 1994*b*). What *can* be provided are broad guidelines (Okely 1994), and it is in this spirit that this chapter continues.

It has two main sections:

- *General strategies of qualitative data analysis*: grounded theory and *analytic induction*, its predecessor (see Box 13.1).

- *Basic operations in qualitative data analysis*: coding and narrative analysis, the latter different in style from the emphasis on coding seen in both grounded theory and secondary analysis of qualitative data. The chapter includes an outline of the use of computers in qualitative data analysis.

General strategies of qualitative data analysis

One difference between qualitative and quantitative data analysis is that, with the latter, analysis invariably occurs after, not before, the data have been collected. The process, as noted in Chapter 8, is often *iterative*, meaning that analysis starts after some of the data have been collected and then implications of that analysis shape any further data collection.

Grounded theory

Grounded theory (see Box 13.2) is by far the most widely used framework for analyzing qualitative data. There is, however, considerable controversy about what grounded theory entails (Charmaz 2000). For example, it is still vague on certain points, such as the difference between concepts and categories (see later). The term

---

Box 13.1 ⌁(✶)⌁ *What is analytic induction?*

Analytic induction begins with a rough definition of a research question, proceeds to a hypothetical explanation of that problem, and then collects data (examines cases). What makes it unique is that analytic induction seeks universal explanations of phenomena that permit no exception. If a case inconsistent with the hypothesis is encountered, the analyst *either* redefines the hypothesis to exclude the deviant or negative case *or* reformulates the hypothesis and proceeds with further data collection. With each new deviant case found, the analyst must choose again between reformulation and redefinition. Data collection continues until no new inconsistent piece of evidence is found. It is, in effect, a special case of grounded theory, one that holds 100 per cent of the time, but also rare, as the requirement to be able to explain all cases means that the explanation becomes too broad and less useful. Thus, while analytic induction is an extremely rigorous method of analysis, it is not in favour

by current qualitative researchers and indeed most of the examples used in textbooks to illustrate analytic induction are not recent. A Canadian exception is research by Whitehead and Carpenter (1999) on unsafe sexual behaviour in the military, an environment where condoms are thought of exclusively in terms of protection from disease, with no relation to pregnancy. They found that the greater the social and cultural distance between participants, the greater the likelihood of use of condoms. As similarity between them increases, condom use decreases, since it is perceived as only for disease prevention anyway.

One further problem with analytic induction is that it does not provide useful guidelines (unlike grounded theory) on the number of cases required before the absence of negative cases can be assumed and the validity of the hypothetical explanation (whether reformulated or not) can be confirmed.

> **Box 13.2** 💡 *What is grounded theory?*
>
> In its most recent incarnation, grounded theory is defined as 'theory derived from systematically gathered data, arising through the research process' (Strauss and Corbin 1998: 12). Its two central features are its development of theory out of data *and* an *iterative* approach, or *recursive* as it is sometimes called, meaning that data collection and analysis proceed in tandem, repeatedly referring back to each other.

'categories' is increasingly being employed rather than concepts but inconsistent use of key terms is not helpful to people trying to understand the overall process.

Against such a background, writing about the essential ingredients of grounded theory is not easy. As well, grounded theory cannot be described here in all its facets; instead, its main features are outlined, beginning with a distinction between *tools* and *outcomes* in grounded theory.

Tools of grounded theory

Some of the tools of grounded theory have been referred to in previous chapters.

- *Coding*—the key process in grounded theory, whereby data are broken down into component parts, and given names. It begins soon after the collection of initial data. As Charmaz put it: 'Unlike quantitative research that requires data to fit into *preconceived* standardized codes, the researcher's interpretations of data shape his or her emergent codes in grounded theory' (2000: 515; emphasis in original). In grounded theory, different types, or levels, of coding are recognized (see Box 13.3).

- *Theoretical saturation*—theoretical saturation means reaching a point at which there is no more point in reviewing old data or collecting new to see how they fit with concepts or categories; new data are no longer illuminating.

- *Constant comparison*—refers to a process of maintaining a close connection between data and conceptualization, so that the correspondence between concepts and categories with their indicators is not lost. More specifically, attention to the procedure of constant comparison enjoins the researcher continually to compare phenomena being coded under a certain category so that a theoretical elaboration of that category can emerge. Glaser and Strauss (1967) advised writing a *memo* (see later in this chapter) on the category after a few phenomena have been coded. It also entails being sensitive to contrasts between emerging categories.

Outcomes of grounded theory

The following are the products of different phases of grounded theory.

- *Concepts*—are the 'building blocks of theory' (Strauss and Corbin 1998: 101) and refer to labels given to discrete phenomena; they are produced through *open coding* (see Box 13.3).

- *Category, categories*—at a higher level of abstraction than concepts, a category subsumes two or more concepts. An especially crucial category may become a *core category* around which other categories pivot (see Boxes 13.3 and 13.4).

- *Properties*—attributes or aspects of a category.

- *Hypotheses*—initial hunches about relationships between concepts.

- *Theory*—according to Strauss and Corbin (1998: 22): 'a set of well-developed categories . . . that are systematically related through statements of relationship to form a theoretical framework that explains some social . . . or other phenomenon.' In grounded theory there are two levels of theory: *substantive theory* and *formal theory*. The former relates to theory in a certain *empirical* instance, for example, racial prejudice in a hospital setting (see Box 14.1). A formal theory is at a higher level of abstraction and has a wider range of applicability, to several substantive areas, such as prejudice generally and in a number of spheres. The generation of formal theory requires data collection in contrasting settings.

Box 13.3 Coding in grounded theory

Coding is one of the most central processes in grounded theory. It entails reviewing transcripts and/or field notes and giving labels (names) to items that seem to be of potential theoretical significance and/or that appear to be particularly salient within the social worlds of those being studied. As Charmaz (1983: 186) put it: 'Codes . . . serve as shorthand devices to *label, separate, compile,* and *organize* data' (emphases in original). This coding is a somewhat different process from coding quantitative data, such as social survey data. While in quantitative analysis coding is more or less a way of managing data, in grounded theory, and indeed in approaches to qualitative data analysis that do not subscribe to the approach, it is an important first step in the *generation* of theory. Coding in grounded theory is also somewhat more tentative than for quantitative data, and codes are less fixed. Coding in qualitative data analysis tends to be in a constant state of potential revision and fluidity. The data are treated as potential indicators of concepts and the indicators are *constantly compared* to see with which concepts they best fit. *Ad hoc* compromises may have to be made when two researchers are doing the coding (Tastsoglou and Miedema 2003).

Strauss and Corbin, drawing on their grounded theory approach, distinguished among three types of coding:

- *Open coding*—'the process of breaking down, examining, comparing, conceptualizing, and categorizing data' (1990: 61); this process stays very close to the data and yields the concepts later grouped and turned into categories. Noting various emotions, like anger, jealousy, affection, etc., is an example.

- *Axial coding*—'a set of procedures whereby data are put back together in new ways after open coding, by making connections between categories' (1990: 96). This is done by linking codes to contexts, to consequences, to patterns of interaction, and to causes. The category of emotion from above could be linked to contexts in which it is expressed, as in times of hardship or loss.

- *Selective coding*—'the procedure of selecting the core category, systematically relating it to other categories, validating those relationships, and filling in categories

that need further refinement and development' (1990: 116). A *core category* is the focus around which other categories are integrated, what Strauss and Corbin called the *storyline* that frames the account. 'Adaptation' could turn out to be core category in our example.

The three types of coding are really different levels of coding and each relates to a different point in the elaboration of categories in grounded theory. Not all grounded theory practitioners operate with this threefold distinction and indeed the notion of axial coding has been especially controversial because it is sometimes perceived as closing off too quickly the flexible and exploratory character of coding in qualitative data analysis. Charmaz (2004) preferred to distinguish between open or initial coding and selective or focused coding. The former tends to be very detailed and may even result in a code per line of text. It is crucial at this stage to be open-minded and to generate as many new ideas and hence codes as necessary to encapsulate the data. Selective or focused coding entails emphasizing the most common codes and those seen as most revealing about the data. Combining those initial codes generates new codes. The data are then re-explored and re-evaluated in terms of these selected codes. Pidgeon and Henwood (2004: 638) provided a useful example in their study of 60 mother-daughter relationships:

> The initial coding led to the development of a long and varied, but highly unwieldy, list of instances under the label 'Relational Closeness.' . . . [A] closer reading and comparison of the individual instances indicated a much more mixed view of the emotional intensity of the relationships, ranging from a welcome but painful sense of gratitude and debt to a stance of hypersensitivity and a desire to flee from a relationship which involved 'confinement' or 'smothering.' . . . [T]his subdivision was retained and coded through their respective labels 'Closeness' and 'Overcloseness.'

Coding thus involves a movement from generating codes that stay very close to the data to more selective and abstract ways of conceptualizing the phenomenon of interest.

Box 13.4 Categories in grounded theory

Orona's (1997) study of sufferers of Alzheimer's disease and in particular of their relatives exemplifies many features of grounded theory. She began with an interest in the decision-making process that leads relatives to place Alzheimer sufferers in a home. She gradually realized from coding her interview transcripts that this is not as crucial a feature for relatives as she had anticipated, not least because many of them simply feel they have no choice. Instead, she was slowly taken by the significance for relatives of the 'identity loss' sufferers are deemed to experience. This gradually became her core category. She conducted further interviews to flesh this notion out and reread existing transcripts in light of it. The link between indicators and category can be seen in relatives' references to the sufferer as 'gone,' 'different,' 'not the same person,' and as a 'stranger.' Orona was able to unearth four major themes that emerged around the process of identity loss. The theme of 'temporality' was particularly significant in Orona's emerging theoretical reflections and is revealed in such comments in transcripts as:

At the beginning . . .

It got much worse *later on.*

More and more, he was leaning on me.

Before she would never have been like that.

She *used to* love coffee (Orona 1997: 179–80).

In other words, such comments allowed the category 'temporality' to be built up. The issue of temporality was significant in Orona's emerging analysis, because it relates to the core category of identity loss. Relatives seek to help sufferers maintain their identities. Gradually, however, crucial events mean that the relatives can no longer deny the sufferers' identity loss.

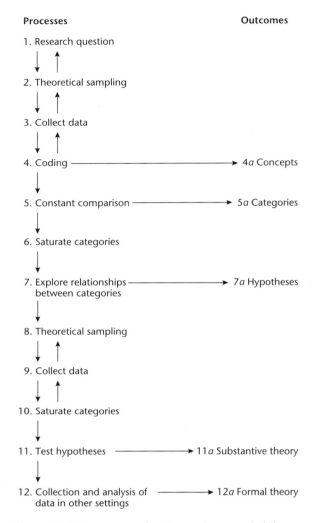

Figure 13.1 Processes and outcomes in grounded theory

The different elements are portrayed in Figure 13.1. As with any diagram, it is only a representation, but particularly so in this instance because different versions of the approach do not readily permit a more definitive rendition. Also, it is difficult to get across diagrammatically the iterative nature of grounded theory—in particular its commitment that data collection and analysis occur in parallel. This is achieved in the diagram with arrows pointing in both directions. The figure implies the following:

- The researcher begins with a general research question (step 1).
- Relevant people and/or incidents are theoretically sampled (step 2).
- Relevant data are collected (step 3).
- Data are coded (step 4), which may, at the level of open coding, generate concepts (step 4a).
- There is a constant movement backwards and forwards among the first four steps, so that early cod-

ing suggests a need for new data, which results in a need to theoretically sample, and so on.

- Through a constant comparison of indicators and concepts (step 5) categories are generated (step 5*a*). It is crucial to ensure a fit between indicators and concepts.

- Categories are saturated during the coding process (step 6).

- Relationships between categories are explored (step 7) in such a way that hypotheses about connections between categories emerge (step 7*a*).

- Further data are collected via theoretical sampling (steps 8 and 9).

- The collection of data is likely to be governed by the theoretical saturation principle (step 10) and by the testing of the emerging hypotheses (step 11), which lead to a specification of substantive theory (step 11*a*). See Box 13.5 for an illustration.

- The substantive theory is explored using grounded theory processes in a different setting from that in which it was generated (step 12), so that formal theory can be generated (step 12*a*). A formal theory relates to more abstract categories not specifically concerned with the research area in question (e.g., to chronically ill men).

Step 12 is relatively unusual in grounded theory, because researchers typically concentrate on a certain setting.

Concepts and categories are perhaps the key elements in grounded theory. Indeed, it is sometimes suggested that, as a qualitative data analysis strategy, it is better for generating categories than theory. In part, this is because studies claiming to use the approach often fail to generate grounded theory as such. Concepts and categories are nonetheless at the heart of the approach, and key processes such as coding, theoretical sampling, and theoretical saturation are designed to guide their generation. Again, Box 13.5 provides an illustration of a study that incorporates some key features of grounded theory.

Memos

One aid to conducting grounded theory is the *memo,* a note researchers write for themselves or colleagues concerning concepts and categories. Memos serve as

---

Box 13.5 Grounded theory in action

The research by Charmaz (1997) is concerned with the identity dilemmas of men who have chronic (but not terminal) illnesses. She outlined clearly the chief steps in her analysis:

- Interviews with men and a small number of women.

- Exploring the transcripts for gender differences.

- Searching for themes in the men's interviews and published personal accounts (e.g., autobiographies). An example is the theme of 'accommodation to uncertainty,' as men find ways of dealing with the unpredictable paths of their illnesses.

- Building 'analytic categories from men's definitions of and taken-for-granted assumptions about their situations' (1997: 39). Of particular significance in her work is the idea of 'identity dilemmas'—that is, the ways in which men approach and possibly resolve the assault on their traditionally masculine self-images. She showed that men often use strategies to re-establish earlier selves, so that for many audiences their identity (at least in their own eyes) can be preserved.

- Further interviews designed to refine the categories.

- Rereading personal accounts of chronic illness with a particular focus on gender.

- Reading a new group of personal accounts.

- Making 'comparisons with women on selected key points' (1997: 39).

Charmaz provided a substantive theory that helps to explain the importance of notions of masculinity for carving out an identity for chronically ill men.

---

reminders about what is meant by the terms used and provide building blocks for reflection. Memos are potentially very helpful to researchers in helping to crystallize ideas and not lose track of thoughts on various topics. An illustration of a memo is provided in Box 13.6.

Criticisms of grounded theory

Grounded theory has limitations, including:

- Some have suggested that, too often, claims of using grounded theory are unsubstantiated (Charmaz

Box 13.6 A memo

In their research into the bus industry Bryman *et al.* (1996) noticed that the managers frequently mentioned that their companies still followed officially discontinued rules and practices. They often referred to the idea of *inheriting* characteristics that held them back in trying to meet the new competitive environment they faced. As such, 'inheritance' is what Strauss (1987) called an *in vivo code* (one that derives from the language of people in the social context being studied), rather than what he called *sociologically constructed codes*, labels employing the analyst's own terminology. The following memo outlines the concept of inheritance, provides some illustrative quotations, and suggests some properties of the concept.

Memo for inheritance

Inheritance: many of our interviewees suggest that they have inherited certain company traits and traditions that would not be of their choosing. The key point about this inheritance is that our interviewees see it as hindering their ability to respond to a changing environment.

Inherited features include:

- expensive and often inappropriate fleets of vehicles and depots;

- the survival of attitudes and behaviour patterns, particularly among bus drivers, seen as inappropriate to the new environment (e.g., lack of concern for customer service) and which hinder service innovation;

- high wages from the earlier era; means that new competitors can more easily enter the market while paying drivers lower wages.

Sample comments:

'I suppose another major weakness is that we are very tied by conditions and practices we've *inherited*' (Commercial Director, Company G).

'We have what we've *inherited* and we now have a massive surplus of double decks. . . . We have to go on operating those' (Managing Director, Company B).

Managing Director of Company E said the company had inherited staff steeped in old attitudes: 'We don't have a staff where the message is "the customer is number one".'

Inheriting surplus capacity: such as too many buses or wrong size.

2000). Sometimes the term is used simply to imply that the analyst has grounded the theory in data but grounded theory is more than this. Other researchers appear to have used just one or two features of grounded theory but refer to having used the approach without qualification (Locke 1996). Moreover, the presence of competing accounts of the ingredients of grounded theory makes it difficult to criticize others for not having used it fully or correctly.

- Some question whether researchers can fully suspend awareness of existing relevant theories or concepts until that (quite late) stage of analysis when their theories emerge. Most social researchers are sensitive to the conceptual armoury of their disciplines and it seems unlikely that this awareness can be put aside. Indeed, today it is rarely accepted that theory-neutral observation is feasible. It is generally agreed that what is 'seen,' even in research, is conditioned by what is already

known about the social world being studied (in terms of both social scientific conceptualizations and as members of society). Also, many writers view this situation as desirable so that their investigations can build upon the work of others.

- There are practical difficulties with grounded theory. The time to transcribe recordings of interviews, for example, can make it difficult for researchers, especially with tight deadlines, to carry out a genuine grounded theory analysis, with its requisite constant interplay of data collection and conceptualization.

- It is doubtful whether grounded theory in many instances really results in *theory*. As previously suggested, it provides a rigorous approach to the generation of concepts, but it is often difficult to see what theory, in the sense of an explanation of something, is put forward. Moreover, in spite of frequent lip-service paid to generating formal theory, most grounded theories are substantive; in other words, they pertain to the specific social phenomenon being examined and not to a broader range of phenomena (though, of course, they *may* have such broader applicability).

- Grounded theory often invites researchers to code the data into discrete chunks. However, in the eyes of some, this kind of fragmentation results in a loss of context and narrative flow (Coffey and Atkinson 1996), a point returned to later.

Nonetheless, grounded theory today probably represents the most influential general strategy for conducting qualitative data analysis, though how far the approach is followed varies from study to study. What can be said is that many of its core processes, such as coding, memos, and the very idea of allowing theoretical ideas to emerge out of the data, have been very influential. Indeed, it is striking that one of the main developments in qualitative data analysis in recent years—computer-assisted qualitative data analysis—has implicitly promoted many of these processes, because the software programs have often been written with grounded theory in mind (Lonkila 1995).

Basic operations in qualitative data analysis

Coding is the starting point for most forms of qualitative data analysis, although some writers prefer to call it *indexing* rather than coding. The principles involved have been well developed by writers on grounded theory and others. Some of their considerations in developing codes (cf. Lofland and Lofland 1995) are:

- Of what general category is this item of data an instance?
- What does this item of data represent?
- What is this item of data about?
- Of what topic is this item of data an instance?
- What question does this item of data suggest?
- What sort of answer to such a question does this item of data imply?
- What is happening here?
- What are people doing?
- What do people say they are doing?
- What kind of event is going on?

Steps and considerations in coding

The following considerations are helpful in preparing for and during coding:

- *Code as soon as possible, as data are collected, as grounded theory suggests.* This may sharpen an understanding of the data and help with theoretical

sampling. Also, it can help to alleviate the feeling of being swamped by the data. At the very least, begin transcription of any recorded interviews at a relatively early stage.

- *Read through initial set of transcripts, field notes, documents, etc.,* without taking any notes or considering an interpretation; perhaps at the end jot down a few general notes about what seems especially interesting, important, or significant.

- *Do it again.* Read through the data again, but this time make marginal notes about significant remarks or observations, as many as possible. Initially, they will be very basic—perhaps keywords used by respondents or themes in the data. This is *coding*—generating terms that will help in interpreting the data.

- *Do not worry about generating what seem to be too many codes*—at least in the early stages of analysis; some will be fruitful, others not. The important thing is to be as inventive and imaginative as possible; tidying up can be done later. Remember that any one piece of data can, and often should, be coded in more than one way. An outburst of anger can be seen as an emotion, a cause of stress, or the beginning of a new level of integration.

- *Review the codes, possibly in relation to the transcripts.* Are two or more words or phrases being used to describe the same phenomenon? If so, remove one of them. Do some of the codes relate to concepts and categories in the existing literature? If so, is it sensible to use those instead? Are there connections between the codes? Is there evidence that respondents believe that one thing tends to be associated with or caused by something else?

- *Consider more general theoretical ideas in relation to codes and data.* At this point, generate some general theoretical ideas about the data. Try to outline connections between concepts and any developing categories. Consider in more detail how they relate to the existing literature. Develop hypotheses about linkages being made and go back to the data to see if they can be confirmed.

- *Finally, keep coding in perspective.* It is not analysis, only an important part of it. It is a mechanism for thinking about the meaning of the data *and* for reducing their vast amount to manageable size. The larger task of interpretation awaits including forging interconnections between codes, reflecting on the overall importance of the findings for the re-

search literature, and pondering the significance of the coded material for the lives of those studied.

Turning data into fragments

The coding of such materials as interview transcripts typically entails writing marginal notes on them and gradually refining those notes into codes and then cutting and pasting in the literal sense of using scissors and paste. It entails cutting up transcripts into files of chunks of data (and of course carefully identifying the origins of the chunk with, for example, name, position, date) for later data retrieval. Word processing programs can accomplish this but CAQDAS software is increasingly being used to perform these tasks (see Box 13.7).

There is no one correct approach to coding your data. As Box 13.3 suggests, grounded theory conceives of different types of code. Coffey and Atkinson (1996) pointed to three different levels of coding

---

Box 13.7 Introduction to CAQDAS

One of the most notable developments in qualitative research in recent years has been the development of computer software to facilitate the analysis of qualitative data. Computer-Assisted Qualitative Data Analysis Software, or CAQDAS as usually abbreviated, has been a growth area in terms of both the proliferation of programs that perform such analysis and the number of people using them.

Most of the best-known programs allow analysts to code text and later to retrieve it, tasks once done manually. For example, the software can search for all chunks of text relating to a code, and then cut and paste them together. Human input is still crucial. CAQDAS does not and cannot help with decisions about the codes or coding of textual materials or interpret findings. However, this situation is really little different (if at all) from the use quantitative data analysis software like SPSS where someone must still choose the variables to be analyzed and the specific techniques of analysis and then make sense of the results. Each form of software requires creativity. CAQDAS differs from SPSS largely in terms of its data.

With quantitative data analysis, SPSS is the industry leader. No parallel situation exists with regard to CAQDAS but NUD*IST (Non-numerical Unstructured Data Indexing Searching and Theorizing) is a package that most re-

searchers at least would know by name and one used by Tastsoglou and Miedema (2003). It became very popular in the 1990s and has been improved with the emergence of QSR NUD*IST Vivo, known as NVivo. This software is the one featured in this chapter and draws upon many features in NUD*IST, so that, if access is only to NUD*IST, much of the chapter is still applicable.

To use or not to use CAQDAS? With a very small data set, it is probably not worth the time and trouble navigating around new software. Catterall and Maclaran (1997) have argued that CAQDAS is not very suitable for focus group data because the code and retrieve function tends to hide the communication process that goes on there. On the other hand, learning new software provides useful skills that may be transferable on a future occasion. It is likely to be too expensive for personal purchase, though there are student and educational discounts. Demonstration copies of some of the main packages can be downloaded from the distributor's Internet site; they are full working programs but require purchase for actual use.

This chapter provides an introduction to NVivo using qualitative data from a study of visitors to Disney theme parks.

here applied to a passage from an interview first appearing in Box 10.7.

- First there is a very basic coding, which, in the passage in Box 10.7, can be liking or disliking the visit to a Disney theme park. However, such a coding scheme is unlikely to provide anything but a superficial analysis.

- A second level comprises a deeper awareness of the content of what is said and is organized around the focus of the research. An example is countries 'well-represented' and 'missing.'

- A third level moves slightly away from a close association with what the respondent says to a concern with broader analytic themes. This is how the passage in Box 10.7 was coded in terms of such features as whether a response: is fully enthusiastic ('uncritical enthusiasm') or is not critical of the Disney Corporation ('not critical of Disney'); reveals comments made about typical visitors ('visitors' ethnicity'); and makes critical comments ('aesthetic critique,' 'ethnicity critique,' 'nationality critique'). Interestingly, the passage also reveals the potential for a code employed by Coffey and Atkinson (1996: 43–5), the use of a 'contrastive rhetoric' which occurs when a person makes a point about something by comparing it to something else. This feature occurred when the husband made a point about the representation of British culture, which he regarded as poor, compared to that of China, which he regarded as good.

Practical tip ☞ *Too many codes*

Charmaz (2004) recommended, as a first stage in coding for grounded theory, 'line by line coding,' whereby virtually every line in a transcript or other source of data has a code attached to it. She argued that this process means that the qualitative researcher does not lose contact with the data and perspectives and interpretations of those being studied. While this process almost always results in a proliferation of codes, this should not be alarming. What the analyst of qualitative data needs to do is ask questions about what these codes have in common so that they can be combined into higher-order and more abstract codes. This has been illustrated elsewhere in the chapter.

As Coffey and Atkinson (1996) observed, following Strauss and Corbin's account (1990) of grounded theory, codes should not be thought of purely as mechanisms for the fragmentation and retrieval of text. They can do more than simply manage the data gathered. For example, an examination of the interconnections between codes may reveal that some are dimensions of a broader phenomenon. For example, 'ethnicity critique' came to be seen as a dimension of 'ideology critique,' along with 'class critique' and 'gender critique.' In this way, a map of the more general or formal properties of concepts being developed can be started.

Learning NVivo

This exposition of NVivo and its functions addresses just its most basic features; tutorials have been included to assist learners. In the following account, as in Chapter 12, ➔ signifies 'click once with the left-hand button of your mouse'—that is, select.

On opening NVivo, a welcome screen is presented (known as the **Launch Pad**), offering four options: create a project; open a project; open tutorial project; and exit NVivo. If starting a new project, as in the example that follows, select the first one. The next option is opening either a 'typical' or a 'cus-

tom' project. First-time users are strongly advised to select the former and this selection is made for this example. Then comes a screen offering an opportunity to name the project, here 'Disney Project.' Then, ➔ **Next** >. The details of the Project are then presented and, if happy with them, ➔ **Finish**.

Next appears a window, known as the **Project Pad** (see Plate 13.1), offering several options. In the example the aim is to import, into NVivo, documents originally created in Word. This is probably the most common route to creating documents for

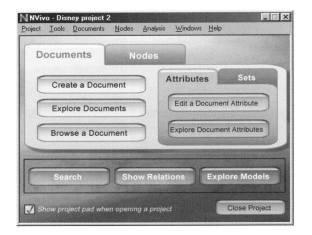

Plate 13.1 The **Project Pad**

processing by NVivo. The **Project Pad** can be hidden so that only the menu bar is visible (➔ **Windows** and then **Project Pad**). All functions on the Project Pad are still available from the menu bar left behind, but when learning NVivo it is reassuring to have the **Project Pad** visible.

To keep word-processed, project documents for later importing, save them as either .txt files (plain text files) or .rtf files (rich text files, which contain the text with some formatting features retained, like bold or italics). To do this in Word, ➔ **Save As....** Then in the box at the bottom of the dialogue box, which is called **Save as type**, ➔ the downward-pointing arrow and select **Rich Text Format**. Doing this does not change the existing document into an '.rtf' one. Instead, two documents will exist: the original Word one and the .rtf one. It is best to give them clearly different names. Then:

1. From the **Project Pad** (Plate 13.1) ➔ **Create a Document** [the **New Document Wizard: Creation** dialogue box opens].

2. ➔ **Locate and import readable external text file[s]** ➔ **Next >** [the **Select file to read** dialogue box in Plate 13.2 opens].

3. Select the file(s) for use; more than one can be selected by holding down the Ctrl key and selecting files.

4. ➔ **Open** [the **New Document Wizard: Obtain Name** dialogue box opens].

5. ➔ **Use the source file name as the document name**.

6. ➔ **Finish**.

The selected files are then copied into the NVivo project, returning to the **Project Pad** (Plate 13.1). At this point, editing of any of the documents entered is possible by selecting **Browse a Document**. The **Choose Document** dialogue box opens. Select the wanted document and then ➔ **Open**. This opens the **Document Browser** (Plate 13.3). From the **Document Browser**, the document can be edited as if using a word processor.

Plate 13.2 The **Select file to read** dialogue box

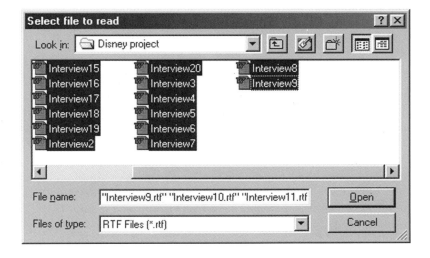

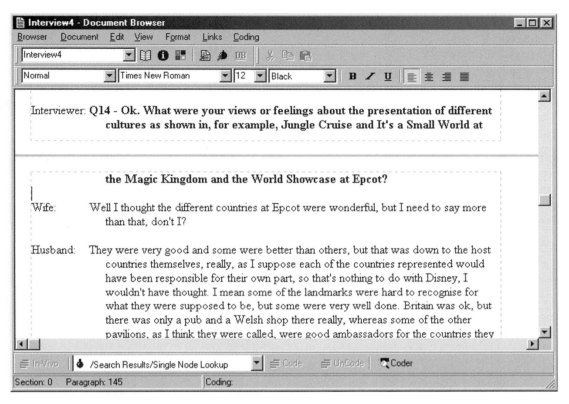

Plate 13.3 The **Document Browser**

Coding

Coding data is obviously one of the key phases in the whole process of qualitative data analysis. For NVivo, coding is accomplished through nodes (see Box 13.8).

There are several ways of coding in NVivo. The approach taken in the Disney Project was to:

1. Read through the interviews both in printed form and in the **Document Browser** (Plate 13.3).

2. Work out some codes that seem relevant to the documents.

3. Go back into the documents and code them using the **Node Browser** (see later).

An alternative strategy is to code while browsing the documents.

Box 13.8 *What is a node?*

NVivo's help system defines coding as 'the process of marking passages of text in a project's documents with *nodes*' (emphasis added). Nodes, therefore, map the coding route for a particular project: the items created to represent concepts, behaviours, indeed anything at all of interest. When a document has been coded, the node incorporates references to where in the documents the code appears. Once established, nodes can be changed or deleted. Nodes can be held in any of three ways, but only two are covered in this chapter. First, there are *tree nodes*, implying connections between them, allowing related nodes to be grouped together. The other type is *free nodes*, which stand alone, independent of any tree.

Creating nodes

The nodes used relevant to the passage in Box 10.7 are presented in Figure 13.2. Notice that there are two *free nodes* and three groups of *tree nodes*. With the latter, each node point—the equivalent of a code—has a unique number. These numbers have been inserted in Figure 13.2. The nodes and their associated numbers can be created in the following way.

1. Bring up the **Project Pad** again by exiting the document browser (click on the 'close' button).

2. → the tab titled **Nodes**. The **Project Pad** looks just like the one in Plate 13.1, but refers to nodes rather than to documents.

3. → **Create a Node** [opens the **Create Node** dialogue box shown in Plate 13.4].

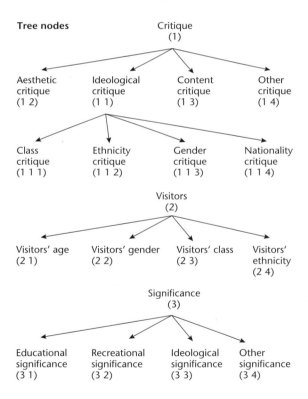

Tree nodes

Critique (1)

Aesthetic critique (1 2) Ideological critique (1 1) Content critique (1 3) Other critique (1 4)

Class critique (1 1 1) Ethnicity critique (1 1 2) Gender critique (1 1 3) Nationality critique (1 1 4)

Visitors (2)

Visitors' age (2 1) Visitors' gender (2 2) Visitors' class (2 3) Visitors' ethnicity (2 4)

Significance (3)

Educational significance (3 1) Recreational significance (3 2) Ideological significance (3 3) Other significance (3 4)

Free nodes

Uncritical enthusiasm
Not critical of Disney

Figure 13.2 Nodes used in the Disney Project

4. • To form a *free node*, make sure the appropriate dialogue box is on screen (see Plate 13.4). If not, simply → the **Free** tab.

   • Place the name of the free node in the box to the right of **Title:**, which in Plate 13.4 is **Not critical of Disney**. Note that the box also shows any existing free nodes (Plate 13.4 shows one called **Uncritical enthusiasm**).

   • In the box under **Description:** place a brief summary of what the node is about. This is not essential but can be useful as a reminder and when creating memos (see below on the procedure for creating memos).

   • → **Create**.

5. • To form a *tree node*, make sure the appropriate dialogue box is on screen (see Plate 13.5). To activate it, simply → the **Tree** tab.

   • Anticipate what a good Tree Node should look like. Place the starting point of the tree in the box by **Title** (in this case it is **Critique**) and then → **Create**. This Node then moves into the large box under **Tree Nodes:**.

   • As with free nodes, in the box under **Description:** place a brief summary of what the node is about.

   • Then double-click on the new tree node so that it appears in the small box under **Tree Nodes:**. Then place in the box by **Title:** the name of the first 'child' (as it is known in NVivo language) of the 'parent.' In this case, the parent is **Critique** and the first child is **Ideological Critique**. Make sure that it is in the box by **Address:** the number is that of the parent (in this case 1) and the child (**1**, so that it is **1 1**). Carry on doing this until all the children have been dealt with. For 'grandchildren,' here the four children of **Ideological Critique**, simply double-click on **Ideological Critique** and follow the same procedure as for the children.

   • When each child has been created, remember to → **Create**.

6. When finished, close the dialogue box. Remember one can always create new nodes using this procedure or else add them later during coding.

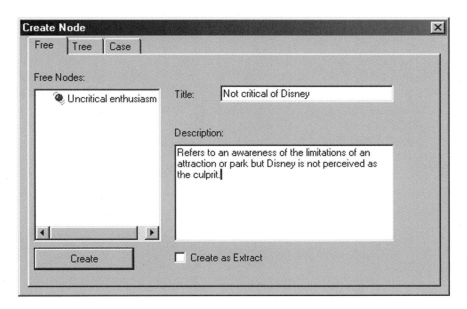

Plate 13.4 The **Create Node** dialogue box (free nodes)

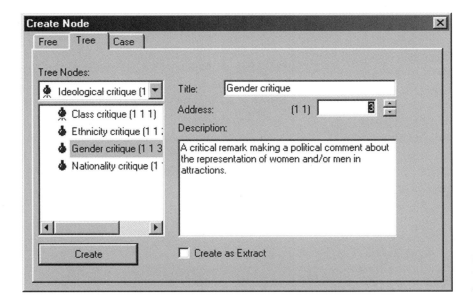

Plate 13.5 The **Create Node** dialogue box (tree nodes)

Editing and browsing

Browse and edit nodes as needed. To browse nodes, from the **Project Pad → Explore Nodes**. The **Node Explorer** dialogue box appears (see Plate 13.6). Selecting a node reveals its children or parents and any descriptions previously provided. Nodes already used at some point in coding documents appear in **bold**.

From the **Node Explorer** one can delete or change the names of nodes. To delete a node, simply click once on it and then → **Tools** and → **Cut**. To change the name of a Node, click once on the node and then click again after a short pause (i.e., *not* a double-click). The node then appears in outline and a new name can be provided. Once having carried out some coding, the **Node Explorer** reveals such

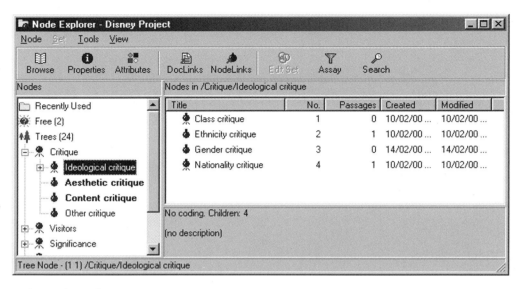

Plate 13.6 The **Node Explorer**

details as the number of occurrences (**Passages**) of that Node.

A child or sibling of a Node can be created by ➔ **Browse a Node** on the **Project Pad** (Plate 13.1). The **Choose Node** sub-dialogue box (see Plate 13.7) appears. This dialogue box also provides useful information about the nodes, but clicking on the ✳ button gives the option of creating a child or sibling node for the node selected.

Applying nodes in the coding process

Coding applies nodes to segments of text. Once some nodes have been set (and remember they can be added or altered at any time), follow this procedure:

1. ➔ the **Documents** tab on the **Project Pad** (Plate 13.1).

2. ➔ **Browse a Document** [opens the **Choose Document** dialogue box].

3. Select the document for coding, which in this case is **Interview4**, since it contains the passage in Box 10.7 that is the focus here, and then ➔ **OK**.

4. Highlight the passage to be coded.

5. Then ➔ **Coding** and then ➔ **Coder...** *or* simply ➔ **Coder** on the bar at the bottom of the screen

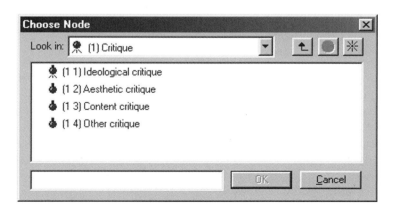

Plate 13.7 The **Choose Node** sub-dialogue box

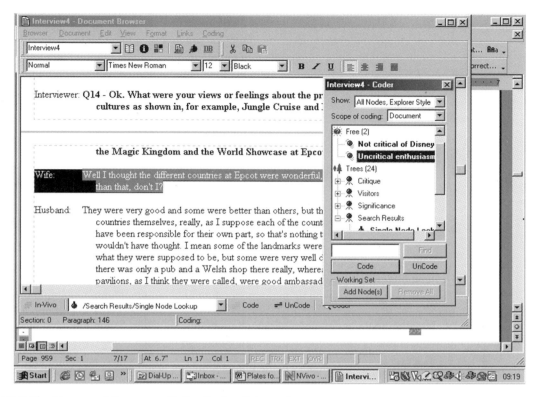

Plate 13.8 The **Document Browser** with the **Coder** dialogue box

[opens the **Coder** dialogue box—see Plate 13.8, which shows the **Document Browser** and the **Coder** dialogue box].

6. Select the node to be applied to the selected (highlighted) text and then → **Code**.

To *uncode* at any point, simply highlight the passage to be uncoded, and from the Coder dialogue box → **UnCode** or simply choose **UnCode** from the toolbar at the bottom of the screen.

These instructions apply to the application of *both* free nodes and tree nodes.

Coding stripes

It is helpful to see the areas of text coded and the nodes applied to them. NVivo has a very useful aid to this procedure called *coding stripes*. Selecting it produces multi-coloured stripes that represent portions of coded text and the nodes used. Overlapping codes do not represent a problem at all.

To activate this facility, → **View** and then → **Coding Stripes**. The screen then splits and the right-hand section contains the coding stripes. Plate 13.9 shows these stripes. Notice the segment coded with two nodes—*visitors ethnicity* and *ethnicity critique*. All the nodes used are clearly visible even when the **Coder** dialogue box is open.

Speed coding

At the bottom of the **Document Browser** is the *speed coding* bar (see Plate 13.9). If coding a passage or series of passages using recurring nodes, it may be easier to use this facility. A click on the downward pointing arrow to the immediate right of the box by it shows the most recently used nodes. Select the appropriate node and then → **Code** to the right of the selected node to code a highlighted text.

Another useful facility on this bar is an opportunity to generate *in vivo codes* (see Box 13.6 for an example). This is a code derived from the language of

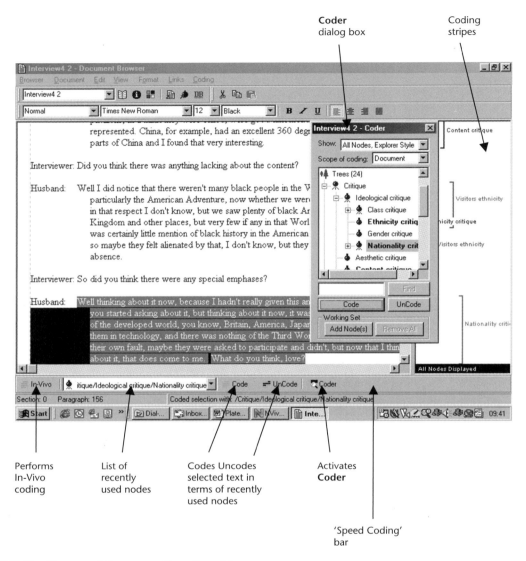

Coder dialog box

Coding stripes

Performs In-Vivo coding

List of recently used nodes

Codes Uncodes selected text in terms of recently used nodes

Activates **Coder**

'Speed Coding' bar

Plate 13.9 The **Document Browser** with coding stripes

research participants and found in the interview transcripts or field notes. To create an in vivo code, highlight the word or short passage that seems significant and from which to create a node. An example might be 'black history,' which can be seen in the unhighlighted passage in Plate 13.9. Once having highlighted the word or passage, ➔ the **InVivo** button, thus creating a new node entitled ***black history***. This is a free node and NVivo adjusts the list of free nodes accordingly. Highlight the area for coding in this new free node and then code it, using either the speed-coding bar or the **Coder** dialogue box.

Searching text

Once the data are coded, however preliminary that may be, a search of the data should be conducted. To do this, ➔ **Search** on the **Project Pad**. This brings

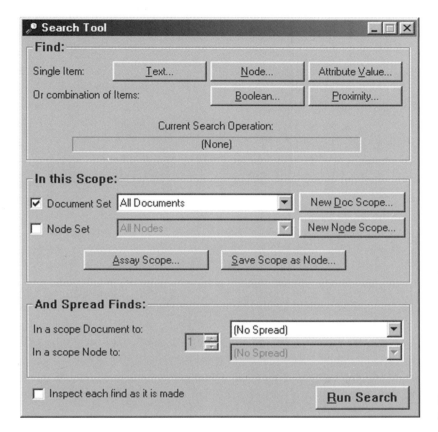

Plate 13.10 The **Search Tool** dialogue box

up the **Search Tool** dialogue box (see Plate 13.10), which facilitates a variety of searches, but just three simple ones are presented below.

To search for occurrences of a single node

These steps describe how to conduct a search for sequences of text that have been coded in terms of the node 'ethnicity critique.'

1. While in the **Search Tool** dialogue box, ➔ the **Node...** button to the right of **Single Item:** [opens the Single Node Lookup dialogue box shown in Plate 13.11].

2. Enter the name of the desired node in the window beneath **Search for text coded by this node:** and then ➔ OK.

3. If the name of the node is unknown or forgotten, ➔ **Choose** [opens the **Choose Node** sub-dialogue box—see Plate 13.12] and then ➔ the downward

pointing arrowhead to the right of the window by **Look in:**. Find the desired node. It is listed as either a free or a tree node. If the latter, simply keep clicking on the appropriate branches until finding the node of interest. Then ➔ OK.

Plate 13.11 The **Single Node Lookup** dialogue box

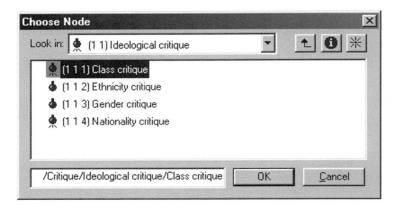

Plate 13.12 The **Choose Node** sub-
dialogue box

4. Redefine the scope of the search. The default in
   NVivo is **All Documents**.

5. → <u>R</u>un Search.

To search for the intersection of two or more nodes

These steps describe how to conduct a search for
sequences of text coded in terms of two nodes: *aesthetic critique* and *not critical of Disney*. This type of
search is known as a 'Boolean search.' It will locate
text coded in terms of the two nodes together (that

is, where they intersect) and ignore where each appears singly. The following steps are required:

1. In the **Search Tool** dialogue box (Plate 13.10) →
   Boolean [opens the **Boolean Search** dialogue box
   shown in Plate 13.13].

2. → **Choose Nodes** [opens the **Choose Nodes** dialogue box shown in Plate 13.14].

3. Select a node and → the **Node** button underneath
   Add:. Do this for the second node and any other
   nodes.

Plate 13.13 The **Boolean Search**
dialogue box for two or more nodes

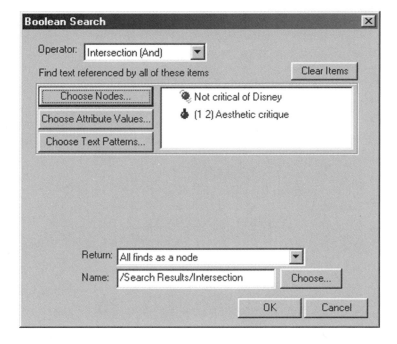

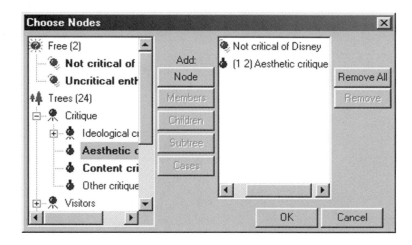

Plate 13.14 The **Choose Nodes** dialogue box for two or more nodes

4. ➔ **OK**, which returns to the **Boolean Search** dialogue box (Plate 13.13).

5. ➔ **OK**, which returns to the **Search Tool** dialogue box (Plate 13.10).

6. ➔ **OK**.

To search for specific text

NVivo can also perform searches for specific words or phrases, often referred to as 'strings' in computer jargon. For example, to search for *Magic Kingdom*, the following steps are appropriate:

1. In the **Search Tool** dialogue box (Plate 13.10) ➔ **Text...** [opens the **Text Search** dialogue box shown in Plate 13.15].

2. After **Search for this Text:**, type in the text sought (e.g., *Magic Kingdom*).

3. ➔ **OK**, which returns to the **Search Tool** dialogue box (see Plate 13.10).

4. ➔ **OK**.

Text searching can be useful for locating possible in vivo codes. They require going back to the documents to conduct in vivo coding.

Plate 13.15 The **Text Search** dialogue box

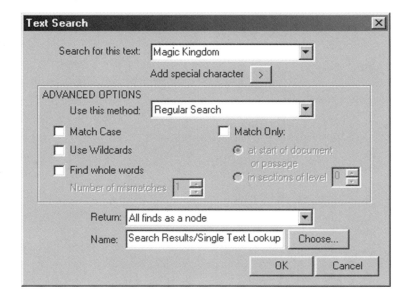

Output

The default for each search is to create a node into which the results of the search are printed. These results can be inspected before printing by using the **Node Browser**. Plate 13.16 shows the results of a search for the node *ethnicity critique* in Interview4.

Memos

Earlier it was noted that one feature of the grounded theory approach to qualitative data analysis is the use of memos in which ideas and illustrations are stored. Memos can be easily created in NVivo, but it is important to realize that the software makes no distinction between memos and other kinds of document. In other words, when creating a memo, so far as NVivo is concerned, it is indistinguishable from the original data (e.g., interview transcripts or field notes) and as such becomes part of the data set. Thus keep them separate and clearly marked. Memos can be created in the **Document Browser** (see Plate 13.17 for an example) via the following steps:

1. On the **Project Pad** → **Create a Document** [opens the **New Document Wizard: Creation** dialogue box].

2. → **Make a new blank document** and → **Create document as a memo**.

3. → **Next** > [opens the **New Document Wizard: Name** dialogue box].

4. After **Name:**, type in a name for the document (e.g., *gender critique memo*). Also provide a brief description of the document in the window under **Description**.

5. → **Finish**.

6. On the **Project Pad** → **Browse a Document** [opens the **Choose Document** dialogue box].

7. → the name of the document just created (e.g., *gender critique memo*); then provide the kind of description needed to clarify the code or concepts being developed (see Plate 13.17).

8. → **Browser**

9. → **Close**

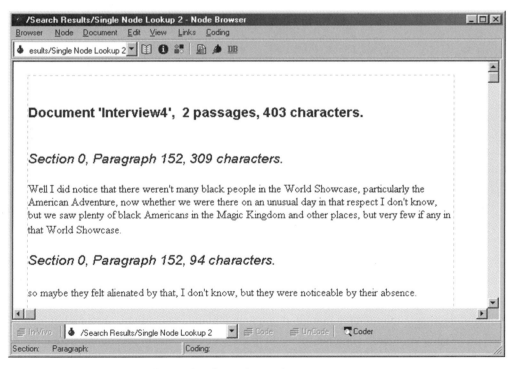

Plate 13.16 The **Node Browser** with the results of a node search

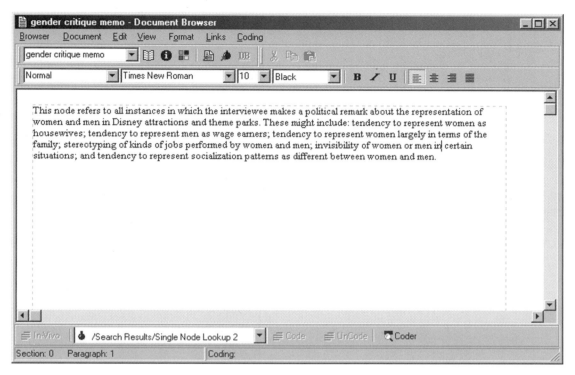

Plate 13.17 The **Document Browser** with a memo

A brief description may be adequate, in which case steps 1 to 5 are sufficient.

Saving and retrieving an NVivo project

When finished working on the data, it must be saved for future use. To do this, on the **Project Pad →** **Close Project** leading to a prompt to save the changes. Say yes, **→ Yes** which leads to exiting NVivo. To retrieve a project, at the welcome screen, **→ Open Project NVivo** opening a dialogue box. Select the project; if there is only one, it comes up as the default as in Plate 13.18. Then **→ OK**. The **Project Pad** then appears (see Plate 13.1).

Problems with coding

One of the most common criticisms of coding qualitative data is the possibility of losing the context of what is said. (For a more general critique of qualita-

tive data analysis packages see Box 13.9.) By plucking chunks of text out of the context within which they appear, such as a particular interview transcript, the social setting can be lost. A second criticism is that it results in a fragmentation of data, so that the narrative flow of what people say is lost (Coffey and Atkinson 1996). Sensitivity to this issue has been heightened since the late 1980s by a growing interest in narrative analysis (below). Riessman (1993: vi) became concerned about fragmentation when coding themes in her structured interview study on divorce and gender.

Some [interviewees] developed long accounts of what had happened in their marriages to justify their divorces. I did not realize these were narratives until I struggled to code them. Applying traditional qualitative methods, I searched the texts for common thematic elements. But some individuals knotted together several themes into long accounts that had coherence and sequence, defying easy categorization. I found myself not wanting to fragment the long accounts into distinct thematic categories.

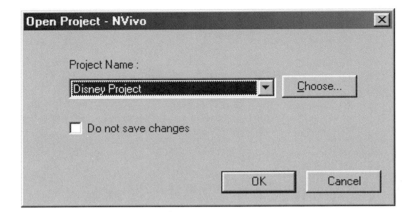

Plate 13.18 The **Open Project**
dialogue box

Box 13.9 Lack of agreement about the utility of CAQDAS

Unlike the almost universal use of computer software in quantitative data analysis, among qualitative data analysts use of software is often avoided, for several reasons.

- Some writers are concerned that the ease with which coded text can be quantified with qualitative data analysis packages means that qualitative research will be colonized by the reliability and validity criteria of quantitative research (Hesse-Biber 1995).

- Others feel that CAQDAS reinforces and even exaggerates the tendency toward a fragmentation of the textual materials (Weaver and Atkinson 1995), destroying any narrative flow of interview transcripts and field notes. In addition, an awareness of context is crucial to many qualitative researchers and the prospect of this element being sidelined is not attractive.

- Stanley and Temple (1995) suggested that most of the coding and retrieval features needed for qualitative data analysis, such as search, cut, and paste, already exist in word-processing software. Using Word for Windows, for example, thus not only saves money but also reduces time spent in learning new software.

- Coffey *et al.* (1996) argued that the style of qualitative data analysis in most CAQDAS software both presumes and is predicated on a certain style of analysis—one based on coding and retrieving text—that owes a great deal to grounded theory. Coffey *et al.* argued

that the emergence of grounded theory as a new standard is inconsistent with the very strength of qualitative research, its flexibility.

On the other hand, several writers have sought to extol the virtues of such packages on a variety of grounds:

- CAQDAS, like NVivo, invites thought about 'trees' of interrelated ideas, a useful feature, in that it urges the analyst to consider possible connections between variables.

- Quantitative researchers often criticize the tendency towards 'anecdotalism' found in much qualitative research—that is, the tendency to use quotations from interview transcripts or field notes but with little sense of their frequency or prevalence, that is, generalizability. CAQDAS invariably offers the opportunity to count the frequency with which a form of behaviour occurs or a viewpoint is expressed in interviews.

- CAQDAS enhances the transparency of qualitative data analysis. It is often noted how the way in which qualitative data were analyzed is unclear in published reports (Bryman and Burgess 1994b). CAQDAS may force researchers to be more explicit and reflective about the process of analysis and indirectly encourage replication, the feature so often lacking in qualitative analysis.

Riessman's account is interesting because it suggests several possibilities: that the coding method of qualitative data analysis fragments data; that some forms of data may be unsuitable for the coding; and that researchers can turn narrative analysis on themselves, since what she provided in this passage is precisely a narrative. Interest in narrative analysis certainly shows signs of growing and in large part this trend parallels the rebirth of interest in the life history approach (see Box 10.4). Nonetheless, the coding method is unlikely to become less prominent, because of several factors: its widespread acceptance in the research community; not all analysts are interested in research questions that lend themselves to narratives; the influence of grounded theory and its associated techniques; and the growing use and acceptance of computer software for qualitative data analysis, which frequently invites a coding approach.

Regardless of analytical strategy, it is unacceptable to simply say: 'this is what my subjects said and did, isn't that incredibly interesting?' Interpretation and theorizing are necessary. Many researchers are wary of this—they worry that, in doing so they may fail to do justice to what they have seen and heard or that they may contaminate their subjects' words and behaviour. This is a risk, but it has to be balanced against the fact that findings acquire significance in an intellectual community only when they have been subject to that reflection. The researcher is not there as a mere mouthpiece.

Final thoughts

As with the discussion of SPSS (Chapter 12), an even shorter one like this can provide only the most basic features of the software and a brief impression of what it is like. Doubtless, some readers will decide it is not for them and that the tried-and-tested scissors and paste or perhaps a modified Word search can do the trick. On the other hand, the software warrants serious consideration because of its power and flexibility.

Box 13.10 *What is narrative analysis?*

Narrative analysis is a term that covers a wide variety of approaches concerned with the search for and analysis of stories that people employ to understand their lives and the world around them. It has become particularly prominent in connection with the life history or biographical approach (see Box 13.11 for an example of this feature). However, as Box 13.12 shows, narrative analysis is not exclusively concerned with telling life histories. As Roberts (2002) observed, the term 'narrative analysis' is often employed to refer to both an approach—one that emphasizes the examination of the storied nature of human recounting of lives and events—and to the sources themselves, that is, the stories that people tell in recounting their lives. While there is little consensus on what narrative analysis entails, at the very least it entails a sensitivity to: the connections in people's accounts of past, present, and future events and states of affairs; people's sense of their place within those events and states of affairs; the stories they generate about them; and the significance of context for the unfolding of events and people's sense of their role within them. It is the way people organize and forge connections between events and the sense they make of those connections that provides the raw material of narrative analysis. Riessman (2004b) helpfully distinguished four models of narrative analysis:

- *Thematic analysis*—an emphasis on *what* is said rather than on *how* it is said.

- *Structural analysis*—an emphasis on the *way* a story is related. Issues of content do not disappear but there is an emphasis on the use of narrative mechanisms for increasing the persuasiveness of a story.

- *Interactional analysis*—an emphasis on the dialogue between the teller of a story and the listener. Especially prominent is the co-construction of meaning by the two parties, though content and form are by no means marginalized.

- *Performative analysis*—an emphasis on narrative as a performance that explores the use of words and gestures to get across a story. This model of narrative analysis includes an examination of audience responses to the narrative.

Narrative analysis

Narrative analysis, just referred to, is an approach both to eliciting and to analyzing data sensitive to the temporal sequence that people, as tellers of stories about their lives or events around them, detect in their lives and surrounding episodes and inject into their accounts (see Box 13.10). With narrative analysis, attention shifts from 'what actually happened?' to 'how do people make sense of what happened?' Proponents of narrative analysis argue that most approaches to the collection and analysis of data neglect the fact that people perceive their lives in terms of continuity and process and that attempts to understand social life not attuned to this feature neglect the perspective of those being studied (see Box 13.11). Life history research (Box 10.4) is an obvious location for the application of a narrative analysis, but its use can be much broader. For example, narrative analysis can relate not just to the life span but also to accounts of shorter episodes and to their interconnections.

Some researchers apply narrative analysis to interview accounts. For example, in her account of her 'click moment' as a narrative researcher, Riessman described how she applied narrative analysis to conventional interview transcript material and then began to uncover the stories her interviewees were telling her. In this case, Riessman was applying a narrative approach to materials gathered in a conventional way for conventional purposes. Other re-searchers start out with the intention of conducting a narrative analysis and deliberately ask people to recount stories (e.g., Miller 2000). Thus, while stories can arise out of answers to questions not designed to elicit a narrative, certain kinds of question are especially likely to do so. Riessman (2004a) suggested that a question like 'tell me what happened' followed with 'and then what happened' is much more likely to provide a narrative account than 'when did X happen?' While some narrative researchers prefer simply to start people off by asking them to tell their story about an event, Riessman argued that it is usually necessary to keep asking follow-up questions to stimulate the flow of details and impressions. For example, in her study of divorce, she often asked 'Can you remember a time when . . .?' and then followed it up with 'What happened that makes you remember that particular moment in your marriage?'

Coffey and Atkinson (1996) argued that a narrative should be viewed in terms of the functions that the narrative serves for the teller. The aim of narrative interviews is to elicit interviewees' reconstructed accounts of connections between events and between events and contexts (see Box 13.12 for an example). A narrative analysis seeks out the forms and functions of narrative. Miller (2000) proposed that narrative interviews in life story or biographical research are far more concerned with eliciting the interviewee's perspective as revealed in the telling of the story of his or her life or family than with the facts of that life. There is a concern with how that perspective changes in relation to different contexts. Box 13.12 provides an example of narrative analysis to a context with potential beyond the life story context. In this case, the author explored competing narratives in accounting for the failed implementation of an information technology system in a hospital.

Narrative analysis, then, is an approach to the analysis of qualitative data that emphasizes the stories that people use to explain events. It can be applied to data that have been created through a variety of research methods (notably semi-structured and unstructured interviewing and participant observation), but it has also become an interviewing approach in its own right, that is, the narrative interview in which

---

Box 13.11 Tattoo narratives

As part of a three-year participation observation study of tattoos, Atkinson (2002, 2004) elicited tattoo narratives from the women he interviewed. The great increase in the numbers of women getting tattoos had firmly challenged the older masculinity explanations for men who engage in that behaviour. Drawing upon feminist theories about bodies, he found that these women are not misfits and instead they use tattoos to signify their 'established' or 'outsider' constructions of femininity. Ideas about femininity, including conformity to and resistance against cultural norms, are crucial in explaining women's tattooing.

Box 13.12 An example of organizational narratives in a hospital

Brown (1998) examined the competing narratives involved in the aftermath of the introduction of new information technology (IT) in a hospital. The implementation was largely seen as unsuccessful because of the absence of clear clinical benefits and because of cost overruns. Drawing on his unstructured and semi-structured interviews with key actors regarding the IT implementation and its aftermath, Brown presented contrasting narratives of the three main groups in the implementation: the ward narrative; the laboratory narrative; and the implementation team's narrative.

The three contrasting narratives provide a very clear sense of the organizational as a political arena in which groups and individuals contest the legitimacy of others' interpretations of events. Thus, while the three groups had similar but not the same motivations for participating in the IT initiative, largely in terms of the espousal of an ethic of patient care, they had rather different latent motivations and interpretations of what went wrong (Brown 1998: 49).

In terms of the former, whereas the ward narrative implied a latent motivation to save doctors and nurses' time, the laboratory team emphasized the importance of retaining the existing IT systems, and the implementation team emphasized the possible advantages for their own careers, in large part by the increased dependence on their skills. In terms of the contrasting narratives of what went wrong, the ward narrative looked at the failure of the implementation team to co-ordinate the initiative and meet deadlines and the laboratory team emphasized the tendency for the implementation team not to listen or communicate. For their part, the implementation team's diagnosis pointed to the ward staff failing to communicate their needs, lack of cooperation from the laboratory staff, and poorly written software.

the researcher sets out to elicit stories. Also, as will be seen in connection with the writing of ethnographic research (see section on 'Writing ethnography' in Chapter 17) there is growing recognition of the ethnography (in the sense of the written product of a period of participant observation) as a narrative designed to tell a story about a way of life.

As an approach to the analysis of qualitative data, narrative analysis has not gone uncriticized. Bury (2001), while noting the growing interest in *illness narratives* (stories that people tell about the causes of in particular chronic illnesses they and/or others experience and their impact on their and others' lives), argued that there has been a tendency for narrative researchers to treat the stories they are told uncritically.

For example, he suggested that the frequent recourse in illness narratives to coping with and 'normalizing' chronic illness may in large part be an attempt to convince the audience (e.g., an interviewer or the reader of a book about someone's struggle with illness) of competence, more to do with wanting to be seen as a fully functioning member of society than a realistic account of coming to terms with a medical condition. However, as Bury recognized, the social conditions that prompt such narratives and the form the narratives take are themselves revealing. In drawing attention to the motives that lie behind illness narratives, he was not seeking to undermine narrative analysis but to draw attention to what narratives are supposed to reveal to the researcher.

K KEY POINTS

- **The collection of qualitative data frequently results in the accumulation of a large volume of information.**

- **Qualitative data analysis is not governed by codified rules in the same way as quantitative data analysis.**

- **There are different approaches to qualitative data analysis; grounded theory is probably the most prominent.**

- Coding is a key process in most qualitative data analysis strategies, but it is sometimes accused of fragmenting and decontextualizing text.

- Narrative analysis emphasizes the stories that people tell in the course of interactions with a qualitative researcher; it has become a distinct strategy in its own right for analyzing qualitative data.

Q   QUESTIONS FOR REVIEW

- What is meant by suggesting that qualitative data are an 'attractive nuisance'?

General strategies of qualitative data analysis

- What are the main ingredients of analytic induction?
- What are the main ingredients of grounded theory?
- What is the role of coding in grounded theory and what are the different types of coding?
- What is the role of memos in grounded theory?
- Charmaz wrote that theoretical sampling 'represents a defining property of grounded theory' (2000: 519). Why do you think she feels this way?
- What are some of the main criticisms of grounded theory?

Basic operations in qualitative data analysis

- Is coding associated solely with grounded theory?
- What are the main steps in coding?
- To what extent does coding result in the fragmentation of data?

Learning NVivo

- What is a node?
- What is the difference between a free node and a tree node?
- What is in vivo coding?
- Do nodes have to be set up in advance?
- What is speed coding?
- In NVivo, what is the difference between a document and a memo?
- How does one search for a single node or the intersection of two nodes?
- Why is it useful to display coding stripes?
- How does one search for specific text?

Narrative analysis

- To what extent does narrative analysis provide a solution to data fragmentation?
- How does the emphasis on stories in narrative analysis provide a distinctive approach to the analysis of qualitative data?
- Can narrative analysis be applied to all kinds of qualitative interviews?

Part Five

Part Five explores areas that transcend the quantitative/qualitative distinction. Chapter 14 invites readers to consider how useful the distinction is. This may seem a contrary thing to do, since the book has been organized around the quantitative/qualitative divide. However, the aim is to show that the distinction is not a hard-and-fast one. Chapter 15 considers the different ways in which quantitative and qualitative research can be combined. Such combinations are referred to as *multi-strategy research*. Chapter 16 examines content analysis, the study of media and other text, and applies qualitative, including conversation analysis and discourse analysis, and quantitative aspects. Chapter 17 looks at issues relating to the writing-up of social research and explores some features of good writing in both quantitative and qualitative research. Chapter 18 offers advice to students faced with the often daunting prospect of writing a dissertation. It is also helpful to those who have to do mini-projects as part of coursework requirements.

These chapters draw together certain issues from previous parts, but they also address others already raised, this time in much greater depth. In addition, they offer advice for students confronted with the need to produce a lengthy piece of work, an increasingly common requirement in many programs of study.

Breaking down the quantitative/qualitative divide

CHAPTER OVERVIEW

This chapter is concerned with the degree to which the quantitative/qualitative divide should be regarded as hard and fast. It shows that, while there are many differences between the two research strategies, there is also much research that transcends the distinction. One way this occurs is through combining quantitative and qualitative research, the focus of the next chapter. The present chapter is concerned with points of overlap between them and explores:

- aspects of qualitative research that can contain elements of the natural science model;

- aspects of quantitative research that can contain elements of interpretivism;

- how research methods are more independent of epistemological and ontological assumptions than sometimes supposed;

- ways in which aspects of the quantitative/qualitative contrast may break down;

- studies in which both research strategies are employed, so that qualitative research is used to analyze quantitative research and vice versa; and

- the use of quantification in qualitative research.

Introduction

With this book structured thus far around a distinction between quantitative and qualitative research, it may appear perverse to raise at this stage the prospect that the distinction is overblown. But the distinction has been maintained so far for two main reasons:

- There *are* differences between quantitative and qualitative research strategy and many researchers and writers on research methodology perceive this distinction.

- It is a useful means of organizing research methods and approaches to data analysis.

However, while epistemological and ontological commitments may be associated with certain research methods—such as the often-cited links between a natural science epistemology (in particular,

positivism) and social survey research, or between an interpretivist epistemology (e.g., phenomenology) and qualitative interviewing—the connections are neither fixed nor deterministic. In other words, while qualitative interviews may be predisposed towards an interpretivist and constructionist position, this is not always or fully the case, as the study of raves (Wilson 2002) reveals. This means that the connections posited in Chapter 1 between epistemology and ontology, on the one hand, and research method, on the other, are best thought of as tendencies rather than as definitive connections. Such connections were implied by the suggestion that within each of the two research strategies—quantitative and qualitative—there is a distinctive mix of epistemology, ontology, and research methods (see Table 1.1). Thus one cannot say that the use of a structured interview or self-completion questionnaire *necessarily* implies a commitment to a natural scientific model or that ethnographic research *must* mean an interpretivist epistemology. One should not be surprised at this: after all, quantitative research teaches that it is rare to find perfect associations between variables.

Research methods are much more free-floating than is sometimes supposed. A method of data collection like participant observation can be employed such that it is in tune with constructionism, but equally it can be used in a manner that reveals an objectivist orientation. Also, it is easy to underemphasize the significance of practical considerations in how social research is conducted. Conducting a study of drug dealers by mailed questionnaire is not impossible, but it is unlikely to succeed in terms of yielding valid answers to questions. The rest of the chapter demonstrates why the contrast between quantitative and qualitative research should not be overdrawn.

The natural science model and qualitative research

One of the chief difficulties in linking issues of epistemology and research method is the frequent characterization of the natural sciences as inherently positivist in orientation. There are three notable difficulties here:

- There is no agreement on the epistemological basis of the natural sciences. As noted in Chapter 1, positivism is but one version of the nature of the natural sciences, *realism* being one alternative account.

- Most of the discussions of natural science assume a close correspondence between their practices (what they actually do) and those that appear in their written accounts of what they do. But studies by social researchers of scientists' practices suggest that there is often a disparity between their work behaviour and their writings.

- The term 'positivism' (see Box 1.8) is frequently employed in a polemical way, usually as a negative and unhelpful criticism of another's work.

Quite aside from these difficulties linking a natural science model and positivism, there are also problems with associating the two terms solely with quantitative research. Qualitative research frequently exhibits features associated with a natural science model. This tendency is revealed in several ways:

- *Empiricist overtones*. Although empiricism (see Chapter 1) is typically associated with quantitative research, many qualitative researchers display a similar emphasis on the importance of direct contact with social reality as the springboard for any investigation. Thus, they frequently stress the importance of direct experience of social settings and understanding a social reality via that contact. The very idea that theory is to be grounded in data (recall Chapter 8) seems to constitute a manifesto for empiricism, and it is unsurprising, therefore, that some writers claim to detect 'covert positivism' in qualitative research.

Another example of empiricist overtones is the suggestion that social reality must be studied from the vantage of research participants, for the only way to gain access to those interpretations is through extended contact with them, implying that their meanings are accessible to the senses of researchers. The empiricism of qualitative research is perhaps most notable in conversation analysis, examined in Chapter 16, an approach that takes precise transcriptions of talk as its starting point and applies rules of analysis to such data. The analyst is actively discouraged from engaging in speculations about intention or context that might derive from an appreciation of the social setting.

- *A specific problem focus*. As noted, qualitative research can investigate quite specific, tightly defined research questions of the kind normally associated with a natural science model.

- *Hypothesis- and theory-testing*. Following from the last point, qualitative researchers typically test hypotheses or theories generated in the course of conducting their research, as in analytic induction or grounded theory. However, there is no obvious reason why this cannot occur in relation to previously specified hypotheses or theories. Wilson's qualitative study of raves (2002) used theory as a departure point. The somewhat infamous classic research by Festinger *et al.* (1956) on a millenarian religious cult used participant observation, a qualitative technique, to test a theory about how people respond when a belief they zealously endorse is disconfirmed. The authors argued that it is possible to imagine a number of conditions that, if met, could result in the belief being held *more* fervently after its disconfirmation. They thought that a local religious cult that believed that the end of the world was imminent (and thus were planning to wait on a mountaintop for a saviour) would provide an ideal opportunity for testing their ideas.

The researchers and hired observers pretended to be converts and joined the group, thereby gaining access to first-hand observations for testing the theory. Clearly assuming that the prediction of the end of the world would not in fact come true, the researchers gathered data before the fateful day on the members' levels of conviction and behaviour and then afterwards on their adaptation to the thwarted prophecy and falsification of a cherished belief. What they found was that the faithful were not dissuaded by the world not ending as predicted. Instead they decided that their faith had saved the world and they went out to proselytize for it.

- *Realism.* Realism (Box 1.9) is one way in which the epistemological basis of the natural sciences has been construed. It has entered into the social sciences in a number of ways, but one of the most significant of these is *critical realism.* This approach accepts neither a constructionist nor objectivist ontology and instead takes the view that while social phenomena are produced by real mechanisms, they are not directly observable and actually discernible only through their effects. For critical realism the task of social research is to construct hypotheses about such mechanisms and to seek their effects. Porter's (1993) critical realist ethnography is interesting in this connection (see

---

Box 14.1 Critical realist ethnography

Porter (1993, 2002) used a critical realist stance in his ethnographic study of a large Irish hospital where he spent three months as a staff nurse. His interest was in racism in this setting and one of his hypotheses was that the hospital setting would affect how the racism is expressed. Porter found that racism exists in the form of racist remarks made behind the backs of members of racial minorities. It does not, however, intrude into work relationships, because of the greater weight given to people's achievements and performance (such as qualifications and medical skills) rather than their ascriptive qualities (that is, 'race') when judging members of professions. In part, this is due to how black or Asian doctors make a point of emphasizing their knowledge and qualifications during their interactions with whites so that their professional credentials are confirmed. In terms of critical realism, one possible structural mechanism (racism) is countered by the operation of another structural mechanism (professional ideology). Only on rare occasions does tension between the two surface, as when a minority doctor conducted a religious observance on his knees in the middle of a hospital unit (Porter 2002).

Box 14.1), because it demonstrates the use of ethnography in connection with an epistemological position that derives from the natural sciences. It also relates to the previous point in providing a further illustration of hypothesis-testing qualitative research.

In addition, some qualitative researchers include some quantitative elements in their research. Miller (2000), for example, in what he called a *neo-positivism* (Box 10.4) made theoretically based predictions about people's lives in the life history method which is associated with qualitative rather than quantitative research. Another illustration is Charmaz's (2000) suggestion that in spite of the differences that developed between Glaser (1992) and Strauss (e.g., Strauss and Corbin 1998), the major writers on grounded theory, both held to the view of an objective, external reality. In other words, each saw a social world beyond the researcher, whose job it is to reveal its nature and functioning.

Quantitative research and interpretivism

Qualitative research would seem to have a near-monopoly on the ability to study meaning. Its proponents essentially claim that only qualitative research allows the social world of individuals to be studied through their own eyes. But this contention seems rather at odds with the widespread study of *attitudes* in social surveys based on interviews and questionnaires. In fact, it would seem that in this research quantitative researchers frequently address meanings. An example is the well-known concept of 'visible minority.' Some groups included in governmental designations, like the Chinese, may prefer not to see themselves as qualifying, rejecting its underdog connotation; other groups not included may think they should be.

The widespread inclusion of questions about attitudes in social surveys suggests that quantitative researchers are interested in matters of meaning and not only in verbal reports of behaviour. It may be objected that survey questions do not really tap issues of meaning because they are based on categories devised by the designers of the interview schedule or questionnaire and not by the subjects themselves. Two points are relevant here. First, the notion that qualitative research is better at gaining access to the point of view of those being studied than quantitative research is generally *assumed rather than demonstrated*. Qualitative researchers frequently claim to have tapped into participants' worldviews because, for example, of their extensive participation in the daily life of those they study, the length of time they spend in the setting being studied, or the lengthy and intensive interviews conducted. However, the explicit demonstration that interpretative understanding has been accomplished—for example, through any respondent validation (see Box 8.3)—is rarely undertaken. Second, if the design of attitude questions is based on prior questioning that seeks to bring out the range of possible attitudinal positions on an issue, attitudinal questions can come closer to gaining access to meaning.

Also the practice in much survey research of asking respondents the reasons for their actions also implies that quantitative researchers are frequently concerned to uncover issues of meaning. For example, in the research on delinquency in Box 1.4, the boys were asked to give reasons for their actions in their own words and then to choose the sociological theories that came closest to explaining them. Examples such as these point further to the possibility that the gulf between quantitative and qualitative research is not as wide as is sometimes supposed.

Quantitative research and constructionism

It was noted in Chapter 1 that a keynote of constructionism is a concern with representation, as it plays an important role in the construction of the social world. Qualitative content analysis plays an important role in developing just such an understanding, in the same way discourse analysis (Chapter 16) does in the social construction of events and meanings in newspaper reports and television programs. However, it is easy to forget that conventional quantitative content analysis can also be useful in this way.

Lantz and Booth's (1998) research on the social construction of breast cancer (see Box 1.14) provides an example of its use. As Box 1.14 makes clear, much of their understanding of the representation of breast cancer came from a qualitative content analysis, but they employed a quantitative content analysis as well. For example, a content analysis of the photographs of women linked to each article revealed that 80 per cent are of women under age 50; 85 per cent of the anecdotes and case stories also relate to women in this age group. This emphasis on younger women helps to create the impression that they are those most at risk. In fact, fewer than 20 per cent of new cases of breast cancer are in women under 50 and the mean age at diagnosis is 65. This inconsistency allowed Lantz and Booth to uncover how the media draw a connection between youthful lifestyles (working outside of the home, postponing parenthood, greater sexuality) and breast cancer, one consistent with the 'blame the victim' theme that the articles convey. Thus, the quantitative content analysis of articles on breast cancer played an important part in revealing the social construction of the disease. More generally, this example shows how quantitative research can play a significant role in a constructionist stance.

Research methods and epistemological and ontological considerations

To review the argument so far, it is suggested that:

- there are differences between quantitative and qualitative research in their epistemological and ontological commitments, *but*
- the connection between research strategy, on the one hand, and epistemological and ontological commitments, on the other, is not deterministic. In other words, there is a *tendency* for quantitative and qualitative research to be associated with the epistemological and ontological positions outlined in Table 1.1, but the connections are not perfect.

However, some writers suggest that research methods carry with them a full cluster of epistemological and ontological commitments such that to choose a self-completion questionnaire as a research option is more or less simultaneously to select a natural science model and an objectivist worldview. Similarly, the use of participant observation is often taken to imply a commitment to interpretivism and constructionism. The difficulty with such views is that there is no perfect correspondence between research strategy and matters of epistemology and ontology and thus any notion that a method inherently carries certain wider assumptions about knowledge and the nature of social reality begins to founder.

In fact, research methods are much more 'free-floating' in terms of epistemology and ontology than often supposed. This can be demonstrated in studies on social research itself. For example, Platt's (1986) historical research on American sociology suggested that the alleged connection between conservative functionalist theory, itself often associated with positivism, and the social survey is greatly exaggerated. Her research suggested that 'the two originated independently, and that leading functionalists had no special propensity to use surveys and leading surveyors no special propensity for functionalism' (1986: 527). Moreover, Platt's general conclusion on the use of research methods in American sociology between 1920 and 1960 is very revealing:

> Research methods may on the level of theory, when theory is consciously involved at all, reflect intellectual . . . *post hoc* justifications rather than . . . carefully chosen fundamental assumptions. Frequently methodological choices are steered by considerations of a practical nature . . . and are just slogans and aspirations . . . (1996: 275).

Again, even when there are discernible links between research methods and assumptions about knowledge, the connections are not absolute.

Further evidence of the autonomy of research methods is the fact that both quantitative and qualitative research methods are often employed within a single piece of research. This issue will be the focus of Chapter 15.

Problems with the quantitative/qualitative contrast

The contrasts between quantitative and qualitative research drawn in Chapter 8 suggest a somewhat hard-and-fast set of distinctions and differences (see, in particular, Table 8.1). Here are some distinctions to demonstrate that the split is exaggerated.

Behaviour versus meaning

A distinction is sometimes drawn between a quantitative focus on behaviour and a qualitative focus on meanings. But quantitative research frequently attempts to study meanings in the form of attitude scales. 'To what social class do you think you belong? Upper, upper middle, middle, lower middle, working.' Qualitative researchers counter and argue that the five pre-formulated alternatives offered respondents mean that actual meanings are sometimes missed, for example, for someone who would choose a sixth (poor) or an in-between option (upper-upper-middle). Also, somewhat ironically, quantitative research's social surveys using questionnaires and interviews have been shown not to reflect people's actual behaviour (see, e.g., Box 3.12), meaning they may fail on both points.

Looking at the other side of the divide, qualitative research frequently, if not invariably, examines behaviour in context. Qualitative researchers often want to interpret people's behaviour in terms of the norms, values, and culture of the group or community in question. In other words, quantitative and qualitative researchers are typically interested in both what people do and what they think, but go about the investigation of these areas in different ways. Therefore, the degree to which the behaviour versus meaning contrast coincides with quantitative and qualitative research should not be overstated.

Theory and concepts tested in research versus their emerging from the data

A related point relates to the characterization of quantitative research as driven by theory testing.

While experimental investigations probably fit this model well, survey-based studies are often more exploratory than this view implies. Although concepts have to be measured, the nature of their interconnections and specific hypotheses are frequently not specified in advance. There are so many questions asked, so many possible correlations, and multiple ways of organizing the findings that many hypotheses are designed after and not before data collection. Even here, however, they come before the analysis, but the general point is still valid that the analysis of quantitative social survey data is often more exploratory than is generally appreciated and consequently offers opportunities for generating theories.

The common depiction of quantitative research as solely an exercise in theory testing also fails to appreciate the degree to which findings frequently suggest new departures and theoretical contributions. Reflecting on his career in social survey research, Glock (1988: 45–6) provided the following example from his research on American church involvement, that women, older persons, the poorer, and family-less are more religiously active than their counterparts. These results, he pointed out, may mean those categories have more time on their hands to become involved. Alternatively or in addition, these people may be compensating for their being deprived relative to their counterparts, a conflict view that Marx would have preferred. He could not rule out either explanation with his data so he collected *new* data to test them, thus allowing his original quantitative data to lead to new research ideas.

Numbers versus words

Even perhaps this most basic distinction between quantitative and qualitative research has problems. Qualitative researchers sometimes undertake a limited amount of quantification of their data in an attempt to uncover the generality of the phenomena being described. While observing doctor–patient interactions in public and private oncology clinics, for example, Silverman (1985) quantified some of his data to show that patients in private clinics have a greater influence over what goes on in the consultations. However, Silverman warned that such quantification still should reflect the research participants' own ways of understanding their social world.

In any case, it has often been noted that qualitative researchers engage in 'quasi-quantification' through the use of terms like 'many,' 'often,' and 'some' (see later in this chapter). All that is happening in cases of the kind described by Silverman is that the researcher is injecting greater precision into such estimates of frequency.

Artificial versus natural

The artificial/natural contrast can similarly be criticized. It is often assumed that because much quantitative research employs research instruments that are applied (as in questionnaires) to the people being studied, it provides an artificial account of how the social world operates. Qualitative research is often viewed as more naturalistic (see Box 2.3 on naturalism). Ethnographic research in particular would seem to exhibit this quality, because the participant observer studies people in their normal social worlds and contexts—in other words, as they go about normal activities. However, when qualitative research is based on interviews (such as semi- and unstructured interviewing and focus groups), the depiction 'natural' is less applicable. Interviews still have to be arranged and interviewees have to be taken away from activities they would otherwise be engaged in, even when the interviewing style is of the more conversational kind. Little is known about interviewees' reactions to and feelings about being interviewed.

Phoenix (1994) reported on the responses of interviewees to in-depth interviews in connection with two studies—one concerned with mothers under the age of 20 and the other with the social identities of young people. While many of her interviewees apparently quite enjoyed being interviewed, it is equally clear that they were conscious of the fact that they had been engaged in interviews rather than conversations. This is revealed in the replies

quoted by Phoenix for some of the interviewees: one young black woman is reported as saying that she liked the interview and added: 'I had the chance to explain how I feel about certain things and I don't really get the opportunity to do that much.' And another interviewee said it was a 'good interview' and added: 'I have never talked so much about myself for a long time, too busy talking about kids and their problems' (1994: 61). While the interviews are clearly valuable in allowing the perspectives of people whose voices are normally silent to surface, they are by their own words not naturalistic. Thus it is inaccurate to conclude that artificiality is a problem only in quantitative research.

As noted in Chapter 10, focus group research is often described as more natural than qualitative interviewing because it emulates the way people discuss issues in real life. Natural groupings are often used to emphasize this element. However, whether this is how group participants view the nature of their participation is unclear. In particular, since people in focus groups are often paid strangers who have travelled some distance to discuss topics they rarely if ever talk about, it is clear that the naturalism of focus groups is more assumed than demonstrated.

In participant observation, the researcher can be a source of interference thus making the research situation less natural than it may superficially appear to be. It is difficult to estimate the degree to which this reactivity has an impact on what is found, but once again the naturalism of such research is often assumed rather than demonstrated, although it is likely that it is less artificial than the methods associated with quantitative research. However, when the ethnographer also engages in interviewing (as opposed to casual conversations), the naturalistic quality is definitely compromised.

These observations cast doubt on the rigidity of the quantitative/qualitative contrast. Once again, this is not to suggest that the contrast is unhelpful, but that it should not be exaggerated and students should not view quantitative and qualitative research as two absolutely divergent research strategies.

The mutual analysis of quantitative and qualitative research

The barriers between quantitative and qualitative research are also undermined when one approach is used to analyze the other.

A qualitative research approach to quantitative research

There has been a growing interest in examining quantitative research using some of the methods associated with qualitative research. In part, this trend is an extension of the growing interest among qualitative researchers in ethnography. The attention to quantitative research is very much part of this trend because it reveals that the written account of research constitutes both the presentation of findings and an attempt to persuade the reader of the credibility of those findings. This is true of the natural sciences too; for example, research by Gilbert and Mulkay (1984) showed how scientists employ an empiricist repertoire when writing up their findings to demonstrate how proper procedures were followed in a systematic and linear way. However, Gilbert and Mulkay also demonstrated that, when the scientists are interviewed on how they do their research, it is clear that the process is influenced by their personal biographies.

One way in which a qualitative research approach to quantitative research is manifested is through what Gephart (1988: 9) called *ethnostatistics*, 'the study of the construction, interpretation, and display of statistics in quantitative social research.' Gephart showed that there are a number of ways in which the idea of ethnostatistics can be realized, but it is just one—approaching statistics as rhetoric—that is presented here. Indeed, the very use of statistics itself can be regarded as a rhetorical device because quantification means that social research can look more like a natural science and perhaps achieve greater legitimacy and credibility by virtue of that association. Some of the rhetorical strategies identified by analysts are presented in Box 17.3.

However, the chief point here is that the nature of quantitative research can be illuminated from the vantage of qualitative research.

A quantitative research approach to qualitative research

In Chapter 16, Hodson's (1996) content analysis of workplace ethnographies will be given quite a lot of attention (see Box 16.7). Essentially, Hodson applied a quantitative content analysis to qualitative research. This form of research, sometimes called a *meta-ethnography*, may have potential in other areas of social research in which ethnography has been a popular method; Hodson (1999) suggested that the study of social movements is one such field and religious sects and cults are another. Hodson's research is treated as a solution to the problem of making comparisons between ethnographic studies in a given area. The only obvious downside is that it makes a choice and largely ignores contextual factors in order to explore relationships between variables abstracted from the ethnographies.

Certain key issues need to be resolved when conducting analyses of this kind. One relates to conducting an exhaustive literature search for suitable studies. Hodson chose to analyze just books, rather than articles, because of the limited amount of information usually included in the latter. Even then, criteria for the inclusion of a book needed to be stipulated. Hodson employed three: '(a) the book had to be based on ethnographic methods of observation over a period of at least 6 months, (b) the observations had to be in a single organization, and (c) the book had to focus on at least one clearly identified group of workers . . .' (Hodson 1999: 22). The application of these criteria resulted in the exclusion of 279 out of 365 books uncovered. A second crucial area related to the coding of the studies. Hodson stressed the importance of having considerable knowledge of the subject area, adopting clear coding rules, and pilot testing the coding schedule. In addition, he recommended checking the *reliability* of coding by having 10 per cent of the documents coded by two people. The process of coding was time-consuming; each book-length ethnography took 40 or more hours to code.

The approach has many attractions, not the least of which is the impossibility of any one quantitative researcher being able to conduct investigations in such a varied set of organizations. Also, it means that more data of much greater depth can be used than can typically be gathered by quantitative researchers and allows hypotheses derived from established theories to be tested, such as the 'technological implications' approach, which sees technology as having an impact on the experience of work (Hodson 1996). However, the loss of a sense of social context is likely to be unattractive to many qualitative researchers.

Of particular significance for this discussion is the remark that 'the fundamental contribution of the systematic analysis of documentary accounts is that it creates an analytic link between the in-depth accounts of professional observers and the statistical methods of quantitative researchers' (Hodson 1999: 68). In other words, the application of quantitative methods to qualitative research may provide a meeting ground for the two research strategies.

Quantification in qualitative research

As noted in Chapter 8, the numbers versus words contrast is perhaps the most basic difference between quantitative and qualitative research. However, in most instances there is quantification in qualitative research. Quite aside from the issue of combining quantitative and qualitative research, three observations are worth making about quantification in the analysis and writing-up of qualitative data.

Thematic analysis

In Chapter 8, it was observed that a very common approach to qualitative data analysis is a search for themes in transcripts or field notes. The choice of themes, however, is often determined by how often certain incidents, words, phrases, and so on that denote a theme recur. This process may also account for the prominence given to some themes over others. In other words, a kind of implicit quantification probably influences both the identification of themes and the elevation of some over others.

Quasi-quantification in qualitative research

It has often been noted that qualitative researchers engage in 'quasi-quantification' through the use of terms such as 'many,' 'frequently,' 'rarely,' and 'some,' which by definition are based on the relative frequency of some phenomenon. However, as expressions of quantities, they are imprecise, and it is often difficult to discern why they are being used at all. A limited use of actual numbers, when appropriate, can support their arguments better and this point leads directly to the next section.

Combating anecdotalism through limited quantification

One of the criticisms often levelled against qualitative research is its anecdotal evidence, giving the reader little guidance as to their generalizability. The widespread use of brief sequences of conversation, snippets from interview transcripts, and accounts of encounters between people provides little sense of the prevalence of whatever such items of evidence are supposed to indicate. There is the related risk that a particularly striking statement by someone or an unexpected activity may be given more significance by the researcher than warranted.

At least partly in response to these problems, qualitative researchers sometimes undertake a limited amount of quantification of their data. Gabriel's (1998) research collected stories about organization culture, altogether 377 of them in the course of 126 interviews in five organizations. Gabriel showed that the stories were of different types and he counted them, such as: 108 comic stories (which were usually a mechanism for disparagement of others); 82 epic stories (survival against the odds); 53 tragic stories (undeserved misfortune); 40 gripes (personal injustices); and so on. The types of stories could have been treated in an anecdotal way, but the use of such simple counting conveyed a clearer sense of their relative prevalence.

Exercises like this can counter the criticism that presenting qualitative data is often too anecdotal, giving readers too little sense of the *extent* to which certain beliefs are held or a certain form of behav-

iour occurs. Their greater precision is also superior to the estimates of frequency that must be inferred from quasi-quantification terms like 'some' or 'many.' Moreover, there may be greater use of limited amounts of quantification in qualitative research in the future as a result of the growing use of computers for qualitative data analysis like CAQDAS. Most of the major software programs include a facility for the analyst to produce simple counts of such things as the frequency with which a word or a coded theme occurs. In many cases, they can also produce simple cross-tabulations—for example, relating gender of author to the frequency of imperatives or whether men or women more often use the passive voice.

K KEY POINTS

- It is important not to exaggerate differences between quantitative and qualitative research.
- Connections between epistemology and ontology, on the one hand, and research methods, on the other, are not deterministic.
- Qualitative research can exhibit features normally associated with a natural science model.
- Quantitative research includes on occasions an interpretivist stance.
- Research methods are more autonomous in relation to epistemological commitments than is often appreciated.
- The artificial/natural contrast used to distinguish quantitative and qualitative research is often exaggerated.
- A quantitative research approach can be used to analyze qualitative data and a qualitative research approach can be used to analyze the rhetoric of quantitative researchers.
- Some qualitative researchers employ quantification in their work.

Q QUESTIONS FOR REVIEW

The natural science model and qualitative research

- Are all of the natural sciences equally positivist?
- How can some qualitative research exhibit a natural science model?

Quantitative research and interpretivism

- How can some quantitative research exhibit characteristics of interpretivism?

Quantitative research and constructionism

- How can some quantitative research exhibit characteristics of constructionism?

Research methods and epistemological and ontological considerations

- How closely tied are research methods and epistemological and ontological implications?

Problems with the quantitative/qualitative contrast

- Outline some of the ways in which the quantitative/qualitative contrast is not as hard and fast as often supposed.

The mutual analysis of quantitative and qualitative research

- What are some implications of Gilbert and Mulkay's research for the qualitative analysis of quantitative research?
- Assess the significance of ethnostatistics.
- Assess the significance of Hodson's research.

Quantification in qualitative research

- To what extent is quantification a feature of qualitative research?

15 Combining quantitative and qualitative research

CHAPTER OVERVIEW

This chapter is about research that combines quantitative and qualitative elements. While this may seem a straightforward way of breaking down the divide between the two research strategies, there may be practical difficulties and it is not without controversy. This chapter explores:

- arguments against the combination of quantitative and qualitative research; two arguments are distinguished: embedded methods and paradigm;

- two versions of the debate on combining quantitative and qualitative research, one concentrating on methods of research and the other on epistemological issues;

- different ways in which multi-strategy research has been carried out; and

- the need to recognize that multi-strategy research is not inherently superior to research employing a single research strategy.

Introduction

So far the book has emphasized the strengths and weaknesses of research methods associated with quantitative and qualitative research. One possible response to this recognition is combining them, to allow their various strengths to be capitalized on and their weaknesses compensated for. Indeed, the amount of combined research has been increasing since the early 1980s. However, not all research methodologists would agree that such integration is either desirable or feasible. Therefore, in discussing the combination of quantitative and qualitative research, this chapter looks at three main issues:

- an examination of the general arguments against integrating quantitative and qualitative research;

- the different ways in which quantitative and qualitative research have been combined; and

- an assessment of whether combined research is necessarily superior to investigations relying on

just one research strategy and whether there are any additional problems deriving from it.

This chapter uses the term *multi-strategy research* for research that integrates quantitative and qualitative research within a single project. Of course, there is research that, for example, combines structured interviewing with structured observation or ethnography with semi-structured interviewing. Wilson (2002), for example, recommended a broader definition of ethnography, one that would use multiple sources to investigate the rave subculture. Pratt and Valverde (2002) used newspaper reports, court decisions, an MA thesis, and a 'few experts close to the situation.' However, these are instances of the combination of research methods associated with just one (qualitative) research strategy. In the current discussion, multi-strategy research refers to research that combines research methods across the two research strategies.

The argument against multi-strategy research

The argument against multi-strategy research tends to be based on either or both of two assumptions:

- the idea that research methods carry epistemological commitments; and
- the idea that quantitative and qualitative research are separate *paradigms*.

These two positions are briefly reviewed here.

The embedded methods argument

This first position, outlined in Chapter 14, implies that research methods are permanently rooted in epistemological and ontological commitments, as can be discerned in statements such as the following:

> every research tool or procedure is inextricably embedded in commitments to particular versions of . . . knowing th[e] world. To use a questionnaire . . . to take the role of participant observer, to select a random sample . . . and so on, is to be involved in conceptions of the world which allow [the use] of these instruments (Hughes 1990: 11).

According to this view, a decision to employ, for example, participant observation is not simply a choice about data collection but a commitment to an epistemological position that is consistent with interpretivism and unacceptable to positivism.

This view even has led some writers to argue that multi-strategy research is not feasible. An ethnographer may collect questionnaire data about a slice of social life not amenable to participant observation, but this does not represent an integration of quantitative and qualitative research, because the epistemological positions of the two methods constitute irreconcilable views about how social reality should be studied. The chief difficulty with this kind of argument is, as noted in Chapter 14, that the idea of research methods carrying with them fixed epistemological and ontological implications is very difficult to sustain. They are capable of being put to a wide variety of tasks.

The paradigm argument

The paradigm argument is closely related to the previous one. It conceives of quantitative and qualitative research as *paradigms* (see Box 15.1) in which epistemological assumptions, values, and methods are inextricably intertwined and are incompatible between paradigms (Morgan 1998*b*). Therefore, when researchers combine participant observation with a questionnaire, they are not really combining quantitative and qualitative research, since the paradigms are incompatible: the integration is only at a superficial level and within a single paradigm.

The problem with the paradigm argument is that it rests, as with embedded methods, on an interconnection of method and epistemology that cannot, in the case of social research, be demonstrated. Moreover, while Kuhn (1970) certainly argued that paradigms share no common measures, it is by no means clear that quantitative research and qualitative research are in fact paradigms. As suggested in Chapter 14, there are areas of overlap and commonality between them.

Box 15.1   *What is a paradigm?*

A paradigm is a set of beliefs and norms telling scientists in a particular discipline what should be studied, in what way, and how results should be interpreted. Kuhn (1970) popularized the term in his analysis of natural science as going through periods of revolution, whereby 'normal' science (science carried out in terms of the prevailing paradigm) is increasingly challenged by new findings inconsistent with the assumptions and established findings in the discipline. The increasing frequency of such anomalies eventually gives way to a crisis in the discipline, which in turn occasions a revolution. The period of revolution is resolved when a new paradigm gains acceptance and a period of the new 'normal' science sets in. An important feature of paradigms is that they are *incommensurable*, that is, inconsistent with each other because of their divergent assumptions and methods. Disciplines in which no paradigm has emerged as pre-eminent, such as the social sciences, are deemed pre-paradigmatic, in that they feature competing paradigms.

Two versions of the debate about quantitative and qualitative research

There seem to be two different versions about the nature of quantitative and qualitative research, each with different implications for whether the two can be combined.

- An *epistemological version*, as in the embedded methods and paradigm arguments, sees quantitative and qualitative research as grounded in incompatible epistemological principles (and ontological ones too, but these tend to be given less attention). According to this version multi-strategy research is not possible.

- A *technical version*, the position taken by most researchers whose work is mentioned in the next section, gives greater prominence to the strengths of the data-collection and data-analysis techniques with which quantitative and qualitative research are each associated and sees them as capable of being fused. There is recognition that quantitative and qualitative research are each connected with distinctive epistemological and ontological assumptions but the connections are not viewed as fixed and unchangeable. Research methods are perceived, unlike in the epistemological version, as autonomous. A research method from one research strategy can be pressed into the service of another. Moreover, in some instances, as seen in the next section, the notion of a 'leading' research strategy in a multi-strategy investigation may not apply in some cases.

The technical version of the nature of quantitative and qualitative research essentially views the two research strategies as compatible. As a result, multi-strategy research becomes both feasible and desirable. It is in that spirit that the chapter now turns, to a discussion of the ways in which quantitative and qualitative research can be combined.

Approaches to multi-strategy research

This section is structured in terms of a classification developed many years ago of the different ways in which multi-strategy research has been undertaken (Bryman 1992). Several other ways of classifying such investigations have been proposed by others, and two are presented in Boxes 15.2 and 15.3.

The logic of triangulation

The idea of triangulation, Box 15.4, when applied to the present context implies that the results of an investigation employing a method associated with one research strategy are cross-checked against the results using a method associated with the other research strategy. It is an adaptation of the argument by writers such as Webb *et al.* (1966) that measuring a concept in more than one way can enhance confidence in the findings from a study using a quantitative research strategy.

An illustration of a triangulation approach is the Hughes *et al.* (1997) study of consumption by young people of 'designer drinks,' the fortified wines and strong white ciders that became popular in the 1990s. The authors used two main research methods:

- a qualitative research method: eight focus groups with 56 children and young adults. Each discussion lasted around two hours.

- a quantitative research method: a questionnaire administered in two parts to a multi-stage cluster sample (824) of 12–17 year olds. The first part was an interview and the second, to elicit more sensitive information, self-administered.

Box 15.2 Hammersley's approaches to multi-strategy research

Hammersley (1996) proposed three approaches to multi-strategy research:

- *Triangulation*—the use of quantitative research to corroborate qualitative research findings or vice versa.
- *Facilitation*—the use of one research strategy to aid research using another.
- *Complementarity*—the use of two research strategies so that different aspects of an investigation can be dovetailed.

The overall tenor of the results of the combined use of the two research strategies was mutually reinforcing. The qualitative findings showed age differences in attitudes towards designer drinks and other forms of alcoholic drink: the youngest (12–13) tend

Box 15.3 Morgan's classification of approaches to multi-strategy research

Morgan (1998b) proposed four approaches to multi-strategy research. His classification is based on two criteria:

- *The priority decision.* Is a qualitative or quantitative method the principal data-gathering tool?
- *The sequence decision.* Which method is used first?

These criteria yield four possible types:

		Priority	
		Quantitative	Qualitative
Sequence	Preliminary	M1	M2
	Follow-up	M3	M4

One difficulty with this scheme is being able to identify clearly *both* that either quantitative or quantitative research had priority and indeed that one came first. The research in Box 15.4 used both strategies and several methods but no single one was dominant.

to adopt a generally experimental approach; the 14 and 15 year olds think of drinking as a means of having fun and losing inhibitions and feel that designer drinks meet their needs well; the oldest group (16 and 17 year olds) are mainly concerned to appear mature and to establish relationships with the other sex, and tend to think of designer drinks as immature, targeted at younger drinkers. These connections with age were confirmed by the quantitative evidence, which also corroborated the suggestion from the qualitative evidence that designer drinks are largely associated with a desire to get drunk.

In this research, two features are worth noting: the use of a triangulation strategy seems to have been planned by the researchers and the two sets of results are broadly consistent. However, researchers may carry out multi-strategy research for other purposes, but in the course of doing so discover that they have generated quantitative and qualitative findings on related issues, so that they can treat such overlapping findings as a triangulation exercise. Second, whether planned or unplanned, when a triangulation exercise is undertaken the possibility of a failure to corroborate findings always exists. This raises the issue of how to deal with inconsistent results. One approach is to treat one set of results as definitive, usually the qualitative for their greater richness and depth, coupled with the ethnographer's greater proximity to the people studied. However, arbitrarily favouring one set of findings over another is not an ideal approach to reconciling conflicting findings deriving from a triangulation exercise.

Deacon *et al.* (1998) gathered data through several quantitative and qualitative research methods (see Box 15.5) but had not intended a triangulation exercise. The analysis of their data revealed an inconsistency: the quantitative data suggested broadly consensual relationships between journalists and social scientists, but the qualitative findings suggested a greater collision of approaches and values between them. Rather than opt for one set of findings over the other, the data were re-examined revealing that a major component of the discrepancy is the tendency for social scientists, when answering survey questions about coverage of their research, to reply with relief that it is not as bad as expected. However, in interviews, social scientists tend to make much more

Box 15.4 ⌁ *What is triangulation?*

Triangulation entails using more than one method in the study of social phenomena. The term has been employed somewhat more broadly by Denzin (1970: 310) to refer to an approach that uses 'multiple observers, theoretical perspectives, sources of data, and methodologies,' but the emphasis has tended to be on methods of investigation and sources of data. One of the reasons for the advocacy by Webb *et al.* (1966) of greater use of unobtrusive methods is their potential for triangulation (see Box 6.6). Triangulation can operate within and across research strategies. It was originally conceptualized by Webb *et al.* (1966) as using one method to develop subsequent measures, resulting in greater confidence in findings, and was very much associated with a quantitative research strategy. However, triangulation can also take place within a qualitative research strategy. In fact, ethnographers often check their observations with interview questions to look for any misunderstanding of what they had seen. Bloor (1997) reported that he tackled the process of death certification in two ways: interviews with clinicians responsible for certifying causes of deaths, and asking the same people to complete dummy death certificates based on case summaries he had prepared. Increasingly, triangulation refers to a process of cross-checking findings deriving from both quantitative and qualitative research (Deacon *et al.* 1998).

source of hypotheses that can be subsequently tested using a quantitative strategy. An example is Phelan's (1987) research on incest. She conducted qualitative interviews and conversations with family members attending a treatment program for incest. After a considerable amount of qualitative data had been collected, she became aware of differences in the meaning of incest for biological fathers compared with stepfathers. Quantifiable data were collected through interviews with families' counsellors that supported her hypothesis that 'the process of incest in structurally different families may vary' (Phelan 1987: 39).

- *Aiding measurement.* The in-depth knowledge of social contexts acquired through qualitative research can be used to inform the design of survey questions for structured interviewing and self-completion questionnaires. Johnson *et al.* (2003) used data from unstructured interviews to develop highly structured questions for later interviews with adolescent smokers. Walklate (2000) explained that for her research on fear of crime and safety issues in high-crime areas, a survey using traditional questions about victimization was used. However, the questions were amended to reflect the local context following six months of gaining a detailed knowledge of the areas through interviews, ethnography, and examination of local newspapers.

of what Deacon *et al.* called 'war stories'—that is, memorable and often highly wounding encounters with the media. Thus, in general, the questionnaires revealed that social scientists are relatively pleased with the reporting of their research, but, when encouraged to reflect on specific problems in the past, their replies are more negative.

Qualitative research facilitates quantitative research

There are several ways qualitative research can guide quantitative research:

- *Providing hypotheses.* Because of its tendency towards an unstructured, open-ended approach to data collection, qualitative research is often a

Quantitative research facilitates qualitative research

One of the chief ways quantitative research can prepare the ground for qualitative research is through the selection of people to be interviewed. This can occur in several ways. In the case of the research on the reporting of social science research in the mass media (see Box 15.5), a content analysis of media content (method 1) was used as a source of data in its own right. However, it also served as a means of identifying journalists who had reported relevant research (method 5). In addition, replies to questions in the general survey of social scientists (method 2) were used to help identify two groups of social scientists, those with particularly high and those with low levels of media coverage of their research, who were then interviewed with a semi-structured approach (method 4).

Jamieson (2000) administered a self-completion questionnaire to a sample of young men on their criminal activity. On the basis of their replies, equal numbers of young men were interviewed using qualitative interviewing in each of three categories: those who did not offend; those who had offended but not recently; and persistent offenders. A similar use of multi-strategy research can be seen in the example in Box 15.5.

Filling in the gaps

This approach to multi-strategy research occurs when the researcher cannot rely on either a quantitative or a qualitative method alone. Its most typical form is when ethnographers employ structured interviewing or possibly a self-completion questionnaire, because not everything they need to know about is accessible through direct observation, like past behaviour, or because of the difficulty of gaining access to certain groups of people.

Static and process features

One of the contrasts suggested by Table 8.1 is that quantitative research tends to bring out a static picture of social life and qualitative research shows more about process. While the term 'static' is often viewed in a negative light, in fact, it uncovers the regularities that allow the analysis of process. A multi-strategy research approach offers the prospect of being able to combine both elements. An illustration is provided by MacKinnon and Luke's (2002) study of cultural change from 1981–95. Their main method of data collection was survey research, but in addition they examined other data (census and public opinion) and newspapers articles on historical events to complete the picture. They found a reduced homophobia and anti-Semitism but also a reduced sympathy for First Nations over that time period. They cautioned that their small sample (70) and what were essentially 'good guesses' meant that their conclusions, 'like the interpretations of an ethnographer . . . are subject to alternative interpretations by others' (2002: 332).

> **Box 15.5** Research methods used in a study of the reporting of social science research in the mass media
>
> In their research on how social science research is reported in the mass media, Fenton *et al.* (1998) employed quantitative and qualitative methods:
>
> 1 content analysis of news and current affairs coverage (local and national newspapers, TV, and radio);
>
> 2 mailed questionnaire survey of 674 social scientists' views about media coverage and their own practices;
>
> 3 mailed questionnaire survey of 123 social scientists who, as identified in the content analysis, received media coverage;
>
> 4 semi-structured interviews with 20 social scientists who, as identified in the content analysis, received coverage;
>
> 5 semi-structured interviews with 34 journalists identified in the content analysis;
>
> 6 semi-structured interviews with 27 representatives of funding bodies and government;
>
> 7 tracking of journalists at three conferences; and
>
> 8 focus group analysis of audience reception of media items (13 focus groups).

Researcher and participant perspectives

Sometimes, researchers want to gather two kinds of data: qualitative data that shows the general perspectives of their subjects and quantitative data for exploring specific issues. For example, Milkman (1997) was interested in the meaning of industrial work and whether 1990 factory conditions had changed from the negative portrayals of such work in the 1950s. She employed semi-structured interviews and focus groups with GM car-production workers to elicit data relevant to this aspect of her work. However, in addition she had some specific interests in a 'buyout' plan that the company's management introduced in the mid-1980s after it had initiated a variety of changes to work practices. The plan gave workers the opportunity to give up their jobs for a substantial cash payment. In 1988 and again in 1991, Milkman carried out a questionnaire survey of workers who had taken up the company's buyout offer. The reason for the surveys was her interest in the buyout scheme, such as reasons for taking the buyout, how those taking it had fared since leaving General Motors, how they felt about their current employment, and differences among social groups (in particular ethnic groups) in current earnings relative to those at General Motors.

The problem of generality

As noted in Chapter 14, a problem of qualitative research is the tendency for findings to be presented in an anecdotal fashion with insufficient sense of the relative importance of the themes identified. Partly to counter this criticism, Tastsoglou and Miedema (2003) used quantitative national data on women's volunteering to compare it to their admittedly non-random sample of immigrant women, and found that their women actually volunteer more.

Qualitative research may help to interpret the relationship between variables

One of the problems that frequently confront quantitative researchers is how to explain relationships between variables. One strategy is to look for what is called an intervening variable, one that is influenced by the independent variable but in turn has an effect on the dependent variable. Thus, in a relationship between ethnicity and occupation, education may be an intervening variable:

> ethnicity → education → occupation.

This sequence implies that the variable ethnicity has an impact on education (for example, ethnic groups differ in their levels of education), which in turn has implications for the jobs that people of different ethnic groups attain. An alternative approach is to explore the relationship further in a qualitative study.

An illustration is provided by research on HIV-related risk behaviour among drug injectors. Data from structured interviews with 503 injectors re-vealed that 'females report significantly higher levels of needle sharing, sexual activity, and AIDS awareness than their male counterparts. Furthermore, women who are co-habiting with sexual partners who are themselves injectors, are particularly likely to report high levels of risk behaviour and also AIDS awareness' (Barnard and Frischer 1995: 357). What produces this relationship among gender, risk behaviour, and co-habitation? Semi-structured interviews with 73 injectors revealed that the relationship among these variables 'can be explained by the tendency for women to be in sexual relationships with men who themselves inject and with whom they are unlikely to use condoms' (1995: 360). Thus, here is an instance of light being shed on relationships among variables derived from quantitative research by a related qualitative one.

Studying different aspects of a phenomenon

There is a tendency to think of quantitative research as most suited to the investigation of 'macro' phenomena (such as social mobility, social stratification) and qualitative research as better suited to 'micro' ones (such as small-scale interaction). The macro/micro distinction can also be discerned in Table 8.1. In the example shown in Box 15.7, Wajcman and Martin (2002) used quantitative methods in the form of a questionnaire survey to explore career patterns of male and female managers. However, they also carried out qualitative, semi-structured interviews to explore how managers *made sense* of their career patterns in terms of their identity; the choice of methods was therefore determined by the particular aspect of career orientation of interest.

The category 'stages in the research process' draws attention to the possibility that quantitative and qualitative research may be suited to different phases in a study. However, these may simply be aspects of a more general tendency for quantitative research and qualitative researchers to examine different aspects of a common area of interest.

An illustration of the use of multi-strategy research to study different aspects of a phenomenon is the family-obligations study by Finch (1985). This

---

Box 15.6 Research methods used in a study of gender and organization

Halford *et al.* (1997) conducted research on the role and significance of gender in organizational contexts in two contrasting British labour markets, an economically buoyant new town experiencing problems of recruitment and a larger metropolitan area suffering from manufacturing decline and high unemployment. They examined contrasting organizations in each in these areas: local government organizations, a bank branch, and a hospital. In other words, their design was comparative in terms of both area (contracting and expanding in economic terms) and type of organization.

Three sources of data were employed. First, key informants supplied overall views on gender and career-related issues in all of the organizations and supplied documentary materials. Second, a mailed questionnaire surveyed nearly 1000 employees, with a response rate around 50 per cent. The questionnaire 'was designed to provide broad descriptive information about employees, careers, and [employees'] attitudes to their organization and to opportunities for women in particular' (Halford *et al.* 1997: 56). This material was used 'to describe broad patterns of response across a range of areas, such as occupational mobility, for different subgroups of the sample . . . or attitudes to the organization.' Third, between 25 and 35 employees in each of the three sectors were interviewed using a semi-structured interview as 'a filter for choosing people to interview in-depth' (1997: 56). Interviewees were selected from those who indicated on their questionnaires their willingness to be interviewed so that there were equal numbers of men and women and roughly equal numbers across career grades. The researchers said that they 'frequently found the information provided by in-depth interviews more revealing' (1997: 59).

---

research was concerned with the distribution within families of the obligation to care for relatives. It comprised two main data collection elements: a survey of a sample of nearly 1000 people by structured interview and semi-structured interviewing with 88 people. A major component of the survey interviewing was the use of the vignette technique described in Box 5.10. Mason described the purpose of integrating quantitative and qualitative research as follows:

> From the beginning . . . we were using the two parts of our study to ask different sets of questions about family obligations. Not only were we employing different methods to generate different types of data, but we also anticipated that these would tell us about different aspects of family-obligations. . . . [O]ur view was that an understanding of kin obligations *in practice* would require an analysis of the relationship between the two data sets and the social processes they expressed (Mason 1994: 90–1).

What were the sets of research questions to which Mason referred? The survey was designed to provide information about the degree to which there is a consensus about '"the proper thing to do" for relatives in a variety of circumstances' (1994: 90). Through the semi-structured interviews, Finch and Mason tried 'to discover what people actually did in practice for their own relatives, and also the processes by which they came to do it and make sense of it: did a sense of obligation or responsibility have a role in the process? How did people in practice work out what to do for their kin, or ask of their kin?' (Mason 1994: 90).

In such research, then, multi-strategy research is geared to addressing different kinds of research questions. The research on the reporting of social science research in the British mass media (Box 15.5) is a further example of a project designed to use quantitative and qualitative research to answer different research questions, for example:

- Questions about coverage, such as: How much coverage is there of social science research? What gets covered? Where? (method 1).

- Questions about the production of media items, such as: What kinds of attributes do journalists look for when thinking about whether to write an item on social science research? (methods 5 and 7).

- Questions about social scientists' attitudes to media reports of research in general (method 2) and to the reporting of their own research (methods 3 and 4). Method 4 was designed to allow the findings derived from method 3 to be elaborated and more fully understood.

- Questions about reception, such as: How do readers/viewers interpret media reporting of social science research? (method 8).

- Questions about the communication environment, such as: What are the policies of universities, government departments, and funding bodies concerning the media reporting of research? (method 6).

This form of multi-strategy research entails making decisions about which kinds of research question are best answered using a quantitative research method and which by a qualitative research method and about how best to interweave the different elements, especially since, as suggested in the context of the discussion about triangulation, the outcomes of mixing methods are not always predictable.

Solving a puzzle

The outcomes of research are, as suggested by the last sentence, not always easy to anticipate. Although people sometimes cynically suggest that social scientists find what they want to find, or that social scientists just convey the obvious, the capacity of the obvious to provide puzzling surprises should never be underestimated. When this occurs, employing a research method associated with the research strategy not initially used can be helpful. One context in which this may occur is when qualitative research is used as a salvage operation if an anticipated set of results from a quantitative investigation fails to materialize (Weinholtz *et al.* 1995). Box 15.7 provides an interesting illustration of this use of multi-strategy research.

Like unplanned triangulation, this category of multi-strategy research is more or less impossible to plan in advance. It essentially provides the quantita-

> ### Box 15.7 Combining survey research and qualitative interviewing in a study of managers
>
> Wajcman and Martin (2002) conducted survey research using a questionnaire on male and female managers (470 in total) in six Australian companies and conducted semi-structured interviews with 136 managers in each company. The survey evidence showed that male and female managers are generally more similar than different in terms of career orientations and attitudes. Thus, contrary to what many had anticipated, women's career experiences and orientations are *not* distinctive. They then examined the qualitative interviews in terms of narratives of identity and found that both male and female managers depict their careers in 'market' terms (as needing to respond to the requirements of the managerial labour market to develop their skills, experience, and hence career). *But* whereas for men narratives of career mesh seamlessly with narratives of domestic life, for women there is a disjuncture. Female managers find it harder to reconcile managerial identities with domestic ones and more often have to opt for one or the other. Thus, choices about career and family are still gendered. This research shows how a multi-strategy research approach can reveal much more than could have been gleaned through one approach alone.

tive researcher with an alternative to either reconstruct a hypothesis (see Ethical issue 15.1) or to file the results away (and probably never look at them again) when findings are inconsistent with a hypothesis. There may also be other instances in which a quantitative study can shed light on puzzling findings from a qualitative investigation.

Ethical issue 15.1 *Revising the hypothesis to fit the data in positivist research*

Suppose your reading of the literature led to the hypothesis that boys report their being sexually assaulted less than girl victims do. But analysis of your data reveals the counterintuitive opposite. What do you do? One unethical path would be to pretend that you always expected the boys to report more, perhaps due to recent publicity on the issue in private schools and churches. The review of literature can be rewritten to reflect this expectation. Another would be

to pretend the study was an inductive one right from the beginning, a perfectly acceptable approach to research.

The ethical path is to leave the literature and hypothesis intact and then in the discussion add commentary on why the hypothesis is not supported. Here the issue of publicity can be mentioned meaning that in 'normal' times of little publicity, the usual pattern of girls reporting more than boys should reappear.

Reflections on multi-strategy research

There can be little doubt that multi-strategy research is becoming more frequent. Two particularly significant factors in this development are:

- a growing preparedness to view research methods as techniques of data collection less encumbered by epistemological and ontological baggage; and

- a softening in the attitude towards quantitative research among feminist researchers, who previously had been highly resistant to its use (see Chapter 8 for a discussion of this point).

Other factors are doubtlessly relevant, but these two developments seem especially significant. An example of their operation can be found in research on audience reception of media and cultural texts, an area mentioned on several occasions in this book and predominantly studied using qualitative research methods (in particular, focus groups; see Chapter 10). Some researchers in this area have called for a rethinking of the field's attitude to quantitative research. Lingering unease among some qualitative researchers in this area, particularly regarding reliability and generalizability of findings, has led to calls for a possible use of quantitative research in tandem with qualitative methods (e.g., Schrøder 1999).

It is important to realize that multi-strategy research, like this, is not intrinsically superior to one-method or one-strategy research, tempting as that view is. Three points must be borne in mind. Just as in one-method research:

- Multi-strategy research must be competently designed and conducted. Poorly conducted research yields suspect findings no matter how many methods are employed.

- Multi-strategy research must be appropriate and dovetailed to the research questions. There is no point to collecting more data simply on the basis that 'more is better.' Indeed it is likely to take considerably more time and financial resources than research relying on just one method and can even dilute the research effort in both areas, since resources would be thinly spread.

- Not all researchers have the skills and training to carry out both quantitative and qualitative research, so that their 'trained incapacities' may act as a barrier to integration.

In other words, multi-strategy research should not be considered as a panacea. It may provide a better understanding of a phenomenon than if just one method is used. It may also frequently enhance confidence in the findings, for example, when a triangulation exercise is conducted. It may even improve chances of access to settings; Milkman (1997: 192), for example, suggested, in her research on a General Motors factory, that her promise of 'hard,' quantitative data facilitated her access even though she had no experience with this method. But the general point remains that multi-strategy research, while offering great potential in many instances, is subject to similar constraints and considerations as research relying on a single research strategy.

K KEY POINTS

- While there has been a growth in the amount of multi-strategy research, not all writers support its use.

- A view that there are epistemological and ontological impediments to the combination of quantitative and qualitative research is a barrier to multi-strategy research.

- There are several different ways of combining quantitative and qualitative research, both planned and unplanned, and of representing multi-strategy research.

Q QUESTIONS FOR REVIEW

- What is multi-strategy research?

The argument against multi-strategy research

- What are the implications for multi-strategy research of the embedded methods vs. the paradigm arguments?

Two versions of the debate about quantitative and qualitative research

- What are the main elements of the technical and epistemological versions of the debate about quantitative and qualitative research? What are their implications for multi-strategy research?

Approaches to multi-strategy research

- What are the chief ways quantitative and qualitative research have been combined?
- What is the logic of triangulation?
- Traditionally, qualitative research is depicted as having a preparatory role in relation to quantitative research. To what extent do the different forms of multi-strategy research reflect this view?

Reflections on multi-strategy research

- Why has multi-strategy research become more prominent?
- Is multi-strategy research necessarily superior to single strategy research?

16 Content analysis

CHAPTER OVERVIEW

Content analysis examines media, documents, and texts (which may be printed, visual, aural, or virtual) and can be quantitative, coding data into predetermined categories in a systematic and easily replicable manner or qualitative, seeking deeper meanings. It is because of this flexibility that the chapter is placed after the previous two that examined reducing the divide between qualitative and quantitative research. This chapter explores:

- the kinds of research question content analysis can answer;

- what features of the documents or texts are generally counted;

- how to code, probably the central stage of a content analysis;

- semiotics and hermeneutics;

- audiences, active and passive;

- the roots of conversation analysis in ethnomethodology;

- some of its rules and principles;

- the assumptions of discourse analysis;

- some of its analytic strategies;

- points of difference between the two approaches; and

- the advantages and disadvantages of content analysis.

Introduction

Imagine an interest in the amount and nature of newspaper coverage of crime. It could lead to such questions as:

- Do certain newspapers report more crimes than others?

- How much crime is reported and where in the paper—front page, inside page?

- Do columnists as well as reporters deal with the issues?

- Are some crimes given more attention, perhaps in more detail or accompanied by pictures?

- Do more crime stories appear during the week or on weekends?

- What crime predominates: crime against the person, property crime, crimes in which society is the victim?

Most content analysis is likely to entail several research questions, generally revolving around: *who* (does the reporting); *what* (gets reported); *where* (does the issue get reported); *why* (does the issue get reported); and *when* (it gets reported)—the same five *W*'s of any news report. But the researchers are also interested in omissions in coverage. For example, interviews with the family of the accused are rare; such inattention is itself notable, revealing what is and is not important to publishers.

Another issue frequently encountered in content analysis is change in the coverage an issue gets over time. For example, Miller and Reilly (1995) studied newspaper coverage of a 'food scare' about salmonella in eggs and found a massive amount of newspaper coverage for about 20 days following government statements on a particularly controversial incident. In the subsequent 12 months, the amount of coverage was sharply lower and it petered out further over the next 4 years, in spite of public health evidence that *the incidence of salmonella poisoning was increasing*. What apparently was lacking was another 'headlining' incident.

Such content analyses yield a quantitative description of the characteristics of a communication. Like other quantitative approaches, content analysis claims to be objective and systematic, but recall that objective really means intersubjective: in a replication others should find similar results, for example, agreeing that robbery gets more coverage than sexual assault on front pages. Systematic means reliable—that the results are consistent. Both mean that, as with something like an observation schedule (Chapter 6), rules are clearly specified, in advance, for the assignment of the raw material (such as crime stories) to categories. There is a transparency in the coding procedures so that personal biases intrude as little as possible. The rules in question may, of course, reflect the researcher's interests and concerns and therefore be a product of subjective bias, but once formulated, the rules can be (or should be capable of being) applied without bias.

Content analysis can also be applied to unstructured information, such as transcripts of semi- and unstructured interviews and even qualitative case studies of organizations (e.g., Hodson 1996). Nor is it necessary for the medium analyzed to be print. It can be websites. Research has been conducted, for example, on:

- visual images of women's and men's magazines to look at how messages about bodily appearance are gendered (Malkin *et al.* 1999);
- gender roles in animated cartoons (Thompson and Zerbinos 1995); and
- lyrics of popular songs to look for changes in the representation of women (Marcic 2002).

However, until now the main use of content analysis has been the examination of mass media printed texts and documents; it is one of a number of approaches for investigating text.

What is to be counted?

Obviously, decisions about what should be counted in a content analysis are determined by specific research questions. In quantitative research these are usually clearly specified in advance to guide both the selection of the media to be analyzed and the coding schedule so as not to omit some key dimensions. However, the following are frequently a focus of attention.

Words

While it may seem a dull activity, counting the frequency of certain words is often the first step in content analysis. Jagger's (1998) study of dating advertisements (see Box 16.1), for example, counted the words 'slim' and 'non-smoker' to uncover the characteristics deemed desirable. This enumeration can also reveal emphasis, style, even the overplaying of certain events. For example, Dunning *et al.* (1988) noted a tendency for the British press to sensationalize the reporting of disturbances at soccer matches. The use of such emotive words as 'hooligan' and 'lout,' along with inferences about 'war,' are clearly significant; less dramatic terms like 'fan' and 'hard-fought contest' would have encouraged different emotions among readers.

A variation on the search for the occurrence of certain words is the examination of the pairing of keywords. The growing availability of the printed news media in electronic form, such as on CD-ROM, greatly facilitates this search. For example, Hier (2002) found rave and drug use linked, giving an appearance of greater urgency to controlling raves. Parnaby (2003), on the other hand, noted how squeegee kids and homelessness were not paired, thus encouraging a simpler solution to a more complex problem. The examination of such accompanying keywords can then be a springboard for a more thematic analysis.

Box 16.1 Finding love

Jagger (1998) reported a content analysis of 1094 dating advertisements in four newspapers with a general readership. The sample was chosen over two four-week periods: March 1996 and May 1996 and three research questions drove the study:

- What is 'the relative significance of monetary resources and lifestyle choices as identity markers and desirable attributes for men and women'?
- How do men and women vary in how they market themselves and describe their preferred (or ideal) partners in terms of the body?
- How much are 'traditional stereotypes of masculinity and femininity . . . still in operation' (1998: 799)?

Jagger particularly noted the tendency for a considerable percentage of both men and women to market themselves in terms of their lifestyle choices. She also found that women are far more likely than men to stress the importance of economic and other resources in a preferred partner. There is also a somewhat greater propensity for women to market themselves in terms of physical appearance. As an aside, men are just as likely to market themselves as 'slim,' suggesting a bias on the part of both men and women against heavier people and further that certain norms of bodily shape may no longer be exclusive to one gender. More generally, her results pointed to the significance of the body in identity construction in modern society for both men and women. In a later publication, Jagger (2001) reported the findings from a qualitative content analysis of a sub-sample of the sample of 1094 advertisements.

Subjects and themes

Frequently in a content analysis the researcher wants to code text in terms of certain subjects and themes, thus requiring a more interpretative approach. At this point, the analyst is searching not just for the obvious or *manifest* content but also for some of the underlying or *latent* content as well. It becomes necessary to probe beneath the surface to ask deeper questions about what is happening. In the reports on crime, for example, who is portrayed as to blame—the accused, as expected, or is the victim also blamed? Another example is when the occupation of an accused or victim is not stated; is it implied in other material, like the address or the picture? Why in reports of a man being mugged, late at night in a downtown park, do you think that his marital status is sometimes included? In seeking to answer these questions what may begin as a quantitative content analysis is starting to take on qualitative overtones.

Dispositions

A further level of interpretation is likely when the researcher seeks to demonstrate a disposition in the texts being analyzed. For example, the researcher may want to establish whether journalists, in the reporting of crime in the news media, are sympathetic or hostile to the criminal. Is there something to show that the blame is on the accused, and thus punishment the solution, or on social conditions and thus on a chance for rehabilitation? If there are no manifest indications of such value positions, can inferences be made from the latent content?

Another way in which dispositions are revealed in content analysis is through the coding of ideologies, beliefs, and principles. Jagger (1998) coded dating advertisements in terms of whether gendered stereotypical categories of masculinity and femininity are employed when advertisers describe themselves (see Box 16.1). She found that women are more likely than men to advertise themselves in terms of a masculine stereotype (focus on appearance), while men are more likely to advertise themselves in terms of a feminine stereotype (on employment). It seems each knows its audience.

Coding

As the foregoing has implied, coding is a crucial stage in content analysis. There are two main elements to a content analysis coding scheme: designing a coding schedule and creating a coding manual. To illustrate, imagine a student interested in crime reporting in a local newspaper. To simplify, the fictional study is limited to crimes where the victim is a person rather than an organization and it considers just these variables:

1. nature of the offence;
2. gender of perpetrator;
3. occupation of perpetrator;
4. age of perpetrator;
5. gender of victim;
6. occupation of victim;
7. age of victim;
8. victim precipitation; and
9. position of news item in the paper.

Content analysts are normally interested in a much larger number of variables than this, but this simple illustration can help to get across how a coding schedule and coding manual operate.

Coding schedule

The coding schedule is a form onto which the data are entered (see Figure 16.1). The schedule is very much simplified to facilitate the discussion of the principles of coding in content analysis and of the construction of a coding schedule in particular.

Each of the columns in Figure 16.1 is a dimension (indicated by the column heading) being coded. The blank cells on the coding form are the places in which codes are to be written. One row is used for each media item coded. The codes can then be transferred to a computer data file for analysis with a software package like SPSS.

Coding manual

On the face of it, the coding schedule in Figure 16.1 seems bare, providing little information about what

is to be done or where. This is where the coding manual comes in as it is a set of instructions to coders that includes all possible categories for each dimension being coded. It provides: a list of all the dimensions; the different categories subsumed under each dimension; the numbers (i.e., *codes*) that correspond to each category; and guidance to coders on what should be taken into account in allocating any particular code to each dimension. Figure 16.2 provides the coding manual that might correspond to the coding schedule in Figure 16.1.

Our coding manual includes the occupation of both the perpetrator and the victim using a simple social-class scheme. The offences are categorized in terms of those used by the police in recording crimes. Their statistics have been criticized for reliability and validity (recall Chapter 7) so a comparison between police data and the reporting of crime in local newspapers is a possible research topic. Finer distinctions can be used, but, since the student may not be planning to examine a large sample of news items, broader categories are preferable. Note also that the coding schedule and manual permit two offences to be recorded for any incident. The student should treat the one featured in the article as the first offence. If more than two, the student has to make a judgment concerning the two most significant offences.

The coding manual is crucial because it provides a complete listing of all categories for each dimension being coded and guidance about how to interpret the dimensions. It is on the basis of these lists and guidance that a coding schedule of the kind presented in Figure 16.1 is made. Even a lone researcher should spend a lot of time providing detailed instructions about how to code. While here there is no problem of inter-coder reliability, the issue of intra-coder reliability is still significant (see page 337).

Case number	Day	Month	Nature of offence I	Gender of perpetrator	Occupation of perpetrator	Age of perpetrator	Gender of victim	Occupation of victim	Age of victim	Depiction of victim	Nature of offence II

Figure 16.1 Coding schedule

Nature of offence I

01. Violence against the person
02. Sexual offences
03. Robbery
04. Burglary in a dwelling
05. Burglary other than in a dwelling
06. Theft from a person
07. Theft of bicycle
08. Theft from shops
09. Theft from vehicle
10. Theft of motor vehicle
11. Other theft and handling stolen goods
12. Fraud and forgery
13. Drug offences
14. Other offences

Gender of perpetrator

1. Male
2. Female
3. Unknown

Occupation of perpetrator

01. Professionals, administrators, officials and managers in large establishments; large proprietors
02. Lower-grade professionals, administrators, and officials; higher-grade technicians; managers in small business and industrial establishments; supervisors of non-manual employees
03. Routine non-manual employees in administration and commerce
04. Personal service workers
05. Small proprietors, artisans, etc., with employees
06. Small proprietors, artisans, etc., without employees
07. Farmers and smallholders; self-employed fishermen
08. Lower-grade technicians, supervisors of manual workers
09. Skilled manual workers
10. Semi-skilled and unskilled manual workers (not in agriculture)

11. Agricultural workers
12. Other
13. Unemployed
14. Homemaker
15. Student
16. Retired
17. Unknown

Age of perpetrator

Record age (–1 if unknown)

Gender of victim

1. Male
2. Female
3. Unknown

Occupation of victim

Same as for occupation of perpetrator
If not applicable, code as 99

Age of victim

Record age (–1 if unknown)

Depiction of victim

1. Victim responsible for crime
2. Victim partly responsible for crime
3. Victim not at all responsible for crime
4. Not applicable

Nature of offence II (code if second offence mentioned in relation to the same incident; code 0 if no second offence)
Same as for Nature of offence I

Position of news item

1. Front page
2. Inside
3. Back page

Figure 16.2 Coding manual

Here is a news report of a fictional road rage incident. Two male motorists, one a retired school-teacher aged 68, the other a 26-year-old assembly-line worker, got into an argument and the worker punched the retired man, causing him to fall, hit his head, and suffer a concussion. There was no second offence. The coding of the incident would then appear as in Figure 16.3 and the data would be entered into a computer program like SPSS as follows:

Case number	Day	Month	Nature of offence I	Gender of perpetrator	Occupation of perpetrator	Age of perpetrator	Gender of victim	Occupation of victim	Age of victim	Depiction of victim	Nature of offence II	Position of news item
001	24	11	01	1	10	26	1	13	68	2	00	2

Figure 16.3 Completed coding schedule

Case number	Day	Month	Nature of offence I	Gender of perpetrator	Occupation of perpetrator	Age of perpetrator	Gender of victim	Occupation of victim	Age of victim	Depiction of victim	Nature of offence II	Position of news item
002	25	12	06	1	13	34	2	16	86	3	01	2

Figure 16.4 Completed coding schedule with errors

Suppose a second article, appearing the next day, described how an unemployed 34-year-old female pickpocket took a wallet from an 86-year-old woman and then knocked her down. The code is provided above but with a few errors. Can you spot them? Forms like these would be completed for each news item within the chosen period(s) of study.

Potential pitfalls in devising coding schemes

The potential dangers in devising a content analysis coding scheme are similar to those involved in designing structured interview and structured observation schedules. Points to recall include:

- *Mutually exclusive categories.* There should be no overlap in the categories supplied for each dimension. If the categories are not mutually exclusive, coders are unsure about how to code an item.
- *Exhaustive.* Every possible dimension should have a category.
- *Clear instructions.* Coders should be clear about what factors to take into account when assigning codes. Sometimes these have to be very elaborate. In quantitative content analysis, coders generally have little or no discretion in how to code the units of analysis.
- *A clear unit of analysis.* For example, in the imaginary study of the media reporting of crime in the local press, there is both the media item (e.g.,one newspaper article) and the topic being coded (one of two offences). In practice, a researcher is interested in both but needs to keep the distinction in mind.

To enhance the quality of a coding scheme, it is advisable to conduct a pilot study on early versions to identify difficulties in applying the coding scheme, such as discovering that no code is available to cover a particular case (not exhaustive). Pilot tests also help to reveal if one category of a dimension includes an extremely large percentage of items. When this occurs, it may be necessary to consider breaking that category down so that it allows greater discrimination in the items being analyzed. Reliability of coding is a further concern. An important part of pre-testing the coding scheme is examining consistency between coders (*inter-coder reliability*) and, if time permits, intra-coder reliability. The process of gauging reliability is more or less identical to that briefly covered in the context of structured observation in Box 6.2.

Qualitative content analysis

Qualitative content analysis comprises a search for underlying themes in the materials analyzed and can be discerned in several of the studies referred to earlier, such as Beharrell's study of the reporting of AIDS in the press (1993) and the Giulianotti (1997) study of hooligans. The processes through which the themes are extracted are often left implicit and the extracted themes are usually illustrated—for example, with brief quotations from a newspaper article or magazine. Thus, Lynch and Bogen (1997) examined core sociological textbooks to show that they contain key recurring themes that present an upbeat and scientific view of the discipline that is, ironically in the researchers' view, a biased one in that it is a value-laden account of the discipline. Most texts are slanted toward positivism and contain an idealization of how natural science is practised. For another example, Seale (2002: 109) examined newspaper reports about people with cancer. One of the phases of his analysis entailed an 'NVivo coding exercise, in which sections of text concerning themes of interest were identified and retrieved.' He was especially interested in gender differences in how sufferers are represented and demonstrated that stories about men are much more likely than those about women to discuss how a person's character is important in dealing with the disease.

Altheide (1996) outlined an approach he called *ethnographic content analysis* (ECA) representing a codification of procedures that can be viewed as typical of qualitative content analysis. He described his approach as differing from traditional quantitative content analysis in that the researcher is constantly revising the themes or categories distilled from the examination of documents. As he put it:

> ECA follows a recursive and reflexive movement between concept development-sampling-data, collection-data, coding-data, and analysis-interpretation. The aim is to be systematic and analytic but not rigid. Categories and variables initially guide the study, but others are allowed and expected to emerge during the study, including an orientation to *constant discovery* and *constant comparison* of relevant situations, settings, styles, images, meanings, and nuances (1996: 16; emphases in original).

Thus while quantitative analysis typically entails applying predefined categories to the sources, ECA allows a greater refinement of those categories and the generation of new ones. For example, Parnaby's (2003) examination of squeegee kids included a reflexive examination of documents done while still forming and verifying theoretical concepts. It was a process of constant discovery and constant comparison. In addition, ECA emphasizes the context within which documents are generated, so that a study of newspaper reports of crime would also require an appreciation of things like news organizations and the work of journalists (Altheide 2004).

Semiotics

Another form of qualitative content analysis is semiotics, the *science of signs*, an approach to the analysis

of symbols in everyday life. As such it can be employed in relation not only to documentary sources, but also to all kinds of data because of its commitment to treating phenomena as texts. The main terms employed in semiotics are as follows:

- the *sign* is something that stands for something else, such as a yellow traffic light; it is made up of a signifier and the signified;
- the *signifier* is the thing that points to an underlying meaning, the yellow light itself;
- the *signified* is the meaning to which the signifier points, to stop if possible;
- a *denotative meaning* is the manifest or more obvious meaning of a signifier and as such indicates its function, to stop traffic;
- a *connotative meaning* is a meaning associated with a certain social context that can arise in addition to its denotative meaning, for example, to speed up to beat the anticipated red light; and
- *polysemy* refers to a quality of signs—namely, that they can be interpreted in many ways.

Semiotics seeks to uncover the hidden meanings that reside in texts as broadly defined. Consider, by way of illustration, the curriculum vitae (CV) in academic life. The typical academic CV contains such features as personal details; education; previous and current posts; administrative responsibilities and experience; teaching experience; research experience; research grants acquired; and publications. One can treat the CV as a system of interlocking signifiers denotatively meaning a summary of the individual's experience (its sign function) or at the connotative level as an indication of an individual's value, particularly in connection with chances for prospective employability. Each CV is capable of being interpreted in different ways and is therefore polysemic, but there is a code whereby certain attributes of CVs are seen as especially desirable and therefore less contentious in terms of an agreed attribution of meaning. Indeed, applicants for posts know this and devise their CVs to highlight desired qualities and to downplay others, so that the CV becomes a presentation of self as Miller and Morgan (1993) suggested.

Box 16.2 provides an illustration of a semiotic study of Disneyland as a text. The chief strength of semiotics

Box 16.2 A semiotic Disneyland

Gottdiener (1997: 108–15) proposed that California's Disneyland can be fruitfully analyzed through a semiotic analysis, thus treating it as a text. He concluded that Disneyland's meaning is based on its opposition to the alienated daily lives of nearby Los Angeles residents. He identified, through this principle, several *sign systems* contrasting the park and its surrounding environment: transportation, food, clothing, shelter, entertainment, social control, economics, politics, and family. Thus, the first of these sign systems—transportation—reveals a contrast between the Disneyland visitor as pedestrian (walking with others in a group) and the Los Angeles passenger (a car is necessary; danger on the congested freeways). A further component of his analysis entailed an analysis of the connotations of the different 'lands' that make up the park. He suggested that each land is associated with signifiers of capitalism, for example:

- Frontierland—predatory capital, conquering;
- Adventureland—colonialism/imperialism; and
- Tomorrowland—state capital for space exploration.

Hermeneutics

Hermeneutics is an approach originally devised for understanding theological texts in particular. It was influential in the general formulation of interpretivism as an epistemology (see Chapter 1, where the idea of hermeneutics was briefly encountered) and is more or less synonymous with Weber's notion of *Verstehen*. The central idea behind hermeneutics is that the analyst of a text must seek to bring out the meanings of a text from the perspective of its author. This entails attention to the social and historical context within which a text is produced. Qualitative content analysis and semiotics are hermeneutic when they are sensitive to this context and can be applied both to texts as documents and for the analysis of non-documentary phenomena. What is crucial is the link between understanding text from its author's point of view and the social and historical context of its production. Indeed, in many respects, for a hermeneutic approach, the latter is a precondition of the former.

Their hermeneutic study of corporate image advertisements of a Canadian synthetic crude oil company was a 'formal analysis of the structural and conventional aspects of the text' (Phillips and Brown 1993: 1563). For them this meant examining texts in terms of their constituent parts and the writing conventions employed. This can involve the use of any of several techniques, such as semiotics or discourse analysis (more about this later in the chapter), but Phillips and Brown used the former. They also employed a large database of magazine and newspaper articles relating to the company, giving them additional documentary materials. They showed how corporate image advertisements are attempts to mobilize support for company activities from government (and the public unfamiliar with the company) at a time of intense competition for funding and to ward off the environmental legislation that threatens them.

lies in its invitation to see beyond and beneath the apparent ordinariness of everyday life and its manifestations. The main difficulty one often feels with a semiotic analysis is that, although it invariably results in a compelling exposition of a facet of the quotidian, it is difficult to escape a sense of the arbitrariness of the analysis provided. However, in all probability this sense is unfair to the approach, because the results of a semiotic analysis are probably no more arbitrary than any interpretation of documentary materials or any other data, such as a thematic qualitative content analysis of the kind described earlier. Indeed, it would be surprising not to be struck by a sense of arbitrariness in interpretation, in view of the principle of polysemy that lies at the heart of semiotics.

Readers and audiences—active or passive?

Audience reception is a prominent area of inquiry in media and cultural studies. The key point is whether audiences/readers are active interpreters of what they see or hear. Do they passively derive the meanings that authors or designers infuse into their texts, as in the oil company advertisements just described, or do they resist those meanings and arrive at independent readings, or do they arrive at a middle point that incorporates both passive and active elements? Much research on this issue suggests that audiences frequently come up with readings different than those intended by authors (see Fenton *et al.* 1998 for a summary of some of this research).

Although the idea of the 'active audience' has not gone unchallenged (e.g., McGuigan 1992), the stream of research is so strong to have placed a question mark over the readings of texts by social scientists. This suggests caution in accepting whether their interpretations, such as in Giulianotti's (1997) study of 'fanzines' or Hier's (2002) examination of minutes of city council meetings to understand the rave issue, are the same as those another social scientist would make, or match those of the original readers or audiences of these outputs. The social researcher is always providing a personal 'spin' on the texts analyzed. The same is true of all social science data: the conclusions derived from questionnaire or ethnographic data are always going to be one particular interpretation. Thus, the main point is that close scrutiny and a withholding of judgment are required when reading researchers' renditions of any kind of text.

Two approaches to the study of language

In this section two approaches that treat language as the central focus are examined, conversation analysis (CA) and discourse analysis (DA). While CA and DA do not exhaust the range of possibilities for studying language, they do represent two of the most prominent approaches and each includes what are usually thought of as quantitative and qualitative assumptions. Each has evolved a technical vocabulary and set of techniques. This section outlines some of their basic elements and draws attention to contrasting features. But each is also more complicated and thus the discussion just scratches the surface.

Conversation analysis

The roots of CA lie in ethnomethodology, a sociological position that focuses on the 'practical, commonsense reasoning' people use in their everyday life. It includes their science of cause and effect and the generalizations (if I do this, then that will happen) that allow them to go about their social life and through which social order is accomplished. Social order is not seen as a pre-existing force constraining individual action, but as something that is worked at and accomplished by people through interaction. As Garfinkel, one of its founders, pointed out, the role of sociology is not to uncover 'objective' social facts as Durkheim suggested, but to see them as an accomplishment, as the eventually taken for granted patterns arising from the concerted activities of the daily life of ordinary people (Garfinkel 1967: vii).

Two ideas are particularly central to ethnomethodology and find clear expression in CA: *indexicality* and *reflexivity*. The former means that the meaning of spoken words or utterances, including pauses and sounds, depends on the context in which they are used. (Actually these words can also be written, as in chat rooms.) Reflexivity means that spoken words constitute the social world in which they are located; in other words, talk is not a 'mere' representation of the social world, standing for something else, but a reality. In these ways, ethnomethodology fits fairly squarely with two aspects of qualitative research—a preference for a contextual understanding of action (see Chapter 8) and an ontological position associated with constructionism (see Chapter 1).

In the years following its introduction, ethnomethodological research sought to conduct fine-grained analyses of the sequences of interaction revealed in conversations recorded in naturally occurring contexts. As such, CA is a multifaceted approach—part theory, part method of data acquisition, part method of analysis. The predilection for the analysis of talk gleaned from naturally occurring situations suggests that CA fits well with another preoccupation among qualitative researchers —namely, a commitment to naturalism (see Box 2.3 and Box 8.1).

Conversation analysts have developed a variety of procedures to study talk in interaction. Psathas (1995: 1) described them as 'rigorous, systematic procedures' that can 'provide reproducible results.' Such a framework smacks of a commitment to the codification of procedures that generate the valid, reliable, and replicable findings that mark quantitative research. It is not surprising, therefore, that CA is sometimes described as having a positivist orientation. Thus, a cluster of features that are broadly in tune with qualitative research (contextual, naturalistic, studying the social world in its own terms, and without prior theoretical commitments) are married to traits that are resonant of quantitative research.

However, the emphasis on context in CA is somewhat at variance with the way in which contextual understanding is normally conceptualized in qualitative research. For CA practitioners, context refers to the specific here-and-now context of immediately preceding talk, whereas for most qualitative researchers it has a much wider focus, encompassing things like the broader culture of the group within which action occurs, including their values, beliefs, and typical modes of behaviour. This is precisely the kind of attribution which CA practitioners seek to avoid. To import elements that are not specifically grounded in the here and now of what has just been said during a conversation risks implanting an understanding that is not grounded in participants' own terms. It is no wonder, therefore, that writers like Gubrium and Holstein (1997) treated it as a sep-

arate tradition within qualitative research (see Box 8.1), while Silverman (1993) found it difficult to fit CA into broad descriptions of qualitative research.

Assumptions of conversation analysis

An initial route into CA often begins with the analyst noticing something significant about how a speaker says something, a recognition that generates an interest in the function the turn of phrase serves. Clayman and Gill (2004) gave the example of how children often begin a question by saying 'You know what, Daddy [or whoever]?' when among adults. The question generally produces a 'What?' reply that allows the child to find a slot in a sequence of conversation or to inaugurate such a sequence. The use of this strategy, instead of a straight declarative statement, may reflect a child's lesser power.

Once such a focus has been identified, conversation analysts typically follow certain basic assumptions. Heritage (1984, 1987) proposed three:

- *Talk is structured.* Talk comprises patterns, and participants are implicitly aware of the rules that underpin these patterns. As a result, conversation analysts do not attempt to infer motivations of speakers from what they say or to ascribe their talk to purely personal characteristics. Such information is unnecessary, since the conversation analyst is oriented to the underlying structures of action, as revealed in talk, in its pauses, emphases, questions usually preceding answers, etc.

- *Talk is forged contextually.* Talk must be analyzed in terms of its context and understood in terms of the talk that has preceded it.

- *Analysis is grounded in data.* Conversation analysts shun prior theoretical schemes and instead argue that characteristics of talk and of the constitutive nature of social order in each empirical instance must be induced out of data, a qualitative preference.

In doing a project based on CA, do not be tempted to collect too much data. The real work of CA goes into the painstaking analysis that its underlying theoretical stance requires. It may be that just one or two portions of transcribed text will allow addressing the research questions.

Transcription and attention to detail

The transcript in Box 16.3 includes some basic symbols employed by conversation analysts:

> We:ll A colon indicates that the sound that occurs directly before the colon is prolonged. More than one colon means further prolongation (e.g., : : : :).

> .hh h's preceded by a dot indicate an intake of breath. If no dot is present, it means breathing out.

> (0.8) A figure in parentheses indicates a period of silence, usually measured in tenths of one second. Thus, (0.8) signals eight-tenths of a second of silence.

> you and I An underline indicates an emphasis in the speaker's talk.

> (.) Indicates a very slight pause.

The attention to detail in the sequence of talk in Box 16.3 is striking but what is significant in it? Silverman (1994) drew two main inferences. First, *P* initially tries to deflect any suggestion that there may be a special reason that she needs an HIV test. As a result, any disclosure that she has been engaging

in potentially risky behaviour is delayed. Second, *P*'s use of '*you*' depersonalizes her behaviour. Silverman argued that sequences like these show how 'people receiving HIV counselling skilfully manage their talk about delicate topics' (1994: 75). The hesitations are designed by patients to establish that issues like these are not the subject of normal conversation; the rather general replies to questions indicate that the speaker is not the kind of person who immediately launches into a discussion about difficult sexual matters with a stranger. As an aside, Silverman suggested that *P*'s hesitancy and depersonalization are minimal. Others stall more, lie, or refuse totally to answer (1994: 76).

Some basic tools of conversation analysis

There are recurring features in how talk is organized that can be regarded as tools that can be applied to sequences of conversation. The following tools are presented merely to provide a flavour of the ways in which CA proceeds.

Turn-taking

One of the most basic ideas in CA is that taking turns is one of the ways in which order is achieved in everyday conversation. This is a particularly important tool of conversation analysis, because it illustrates that talk depends on shared codes indicating the ends of utterances. If such codes did not exist, there would not be smooth transitions in conversation. Hutchby and Wooffitt (1998: 47) summarized this model as indicating that only one speaker tends to talk at a time, the other listening, and turns are taken with as little gap between them as possible.

Of course, things do go wrong in conversations, as occurs when there is overlapping of people talking. Silverman (1993: 132) noted several repair mechanisms for instances in which turn-taking conventions are not followed:

- when someone starts to speak before the other has finished, the interrupted speaker stops talking before completing his or her turn;

- when a turn transfer does not occur at an appropriate point (e.g., when someone does not re-

---

Box 16.3 Conversation analysis showing a question and answer adjacency pair

Silverman (1994: 72) provided the following extract from a conversation between an HIV counsellor (*C*) and a patient (*P*):

1 C Can I just briefly ask why: you thought about having

2 an HIV test done:

3 P .hh We:ll I mean it's something that you have these

4 I mean that you have to think about these da: ys, and

5 I just uh: m felt (0.8) you- you have had sex with

6 several people and you just don't want to go on (.)

7 not knowing.

spond to a question), the speaker may speak again, perhaps reinforcing the need for the other person to speak (e.g., by re-phrasing the question).

The crucial point to note about such repair mechanisms is that they allow the rules of turn-taking to be maintained in spite of the fact that they have been breached.

Adjacency pairs

One of the ways in which turn-taking is revealed is through the examination of *adjacency pairs*, the well-attested tendency for some kinds of activity, as revealed in talk, to involve two linked phases: a question followed by an answer, as in Box 16.3; an invitation followed by a response (accept/decline); or a greeting followed by a returned greeting. The first phase invariably implies that the other part of the adjacency pair will be forthcoming, for example, that an invitation will get a response. The second phase is of interest to the conversation analyst not just because it becomes a springboard for a response in its own right but because compliance indicates an appreciation of the apparent normative structure, or how one is supposed to respond to the initial phase. In this way 'intersubjective understandings' are continuously reinforced. This is not to imply that the second phase *always* follows the first; indeed, the response to a failure to comply with the expected response, as when one answers a question with another question, has itself been the focus of attention by conversation analysts.

Preference organization

But some responses are clearly preferential to others. An example is when an invitation or a request is proffered: acceptance is the *preferred response* and refusal the *non-preferred response*. For example, Potter (1996: 59) contrasted a sequence in which an offer is met with a straightforward acceptance—'thank you' —with the sequence in Box 16.4, in which an invitation is declined.

Potter argued that this kind of response by *A* is fairly typical of acceptance rejections, which are, of course, non-preferred responses, drawing attention to several features that contrast strikingly with the unequivocal preferred response of acceptance, a 'thank you.' For example, *A* delays the start of the re-

---

> **Box 16.4 Conversation analysis in action: a non-preferred response**
>
> 1 *B*: Uh if you'd care to come over and visit a little while
>
> 2 this morning I'll give you a cup of <u>co</u>ffee.
>
> 3 *A*: hehh
>
> 4 Well
>
> 5 that's awfully sweet of you,
>
> 6 I don't think I can make it this morning. hh uhm
>
> 7 I'm running an ad in the paper and-and uh I have to
>
> 8 stay near the phone (Potter 1996: 59).

---

sponse and fills it with 'hehh.' Also, the rejection is 'softened' by *A* saying that he or she doesn't 'think' he or she can make it (leaving a chance that an acceptance is still possible) and is accompanied by an explanation for failing to provide the preferred response. The key point is that the participants recognize the preference structure of this kind of adjacency pairing and this affects the response (that is, hesitancy, acknowledgment of the invitation, and providing an explanation) in the case of declining the offer. An acceptance does not have to be justified, whereas a refusal generally does, to allow the relationship between the two parties to be unharmed by *A*'s non-preferred response.

Research can then be done by students on things like repair mechanisms, to see if different groups, like men and women, students and professors, etc., exhibit varying patterns; for example, it can determine who are the interrupters, who defer to the interrupters, and who do not, etc. Your class could go to an eating area on campus to collect such data, each student watching different conversations. To catch body movements, video recordings can supplement CA's toolkit of methods (Heath 1997).

A final note

CA sees any attribution of cultural motives and meanings to understanding a conversation as illegitimate.

Although such an extension carries risks of misunderstanding, an approach that prohibits such speculation is potentially restrictive. As well, for the participants of an exchange, much of their talk is informed by their mutual knowledge of contexts. The analyst is restricted from taking those additional components of the context into account if they are not specifically part of the organization of talk. Again, this admonition seems to restrict the analyst more than is desirable and to consign CA to those research questions that are amenable to locating meaning in talk alone. On the other hand, CA reduces the risk of making unwarranted speculations about what is happening in social interaction and has contributed much to understanding the accomplishment of social order, one of the classic concerns of social theory.

Discourse analysis

Although it incorporates aspects of CA, discourse analysis goes beyond CA and can be applied to forms of communication other than talk, such as newspaper articles, and is in this respect more flexible than CA. Moreover, in DA there is less emphasis on naturally occurring talk, so that the talk in research interviews can be a legitimate target for analysis. According to Potter, DA 'emphasizes the way versions of the world, of society, events and inner psychological worlds are produced in discourse' (1997: 146). For continental philosophers like Foucault (1926–84), discourse is a term for the way a particular set of linguistic categories relating to an object and the ways of depicting it frame the way people comprehend that object. The discourse forms a version of it and moreover, the version of an object comes to *constitute* it.

For example, a certain discourse concerning mental illness comes to make concepts of what mentally ill persons are like, the nature of their illness, how they should be treated, and who is legitimately entitled to treat them. The discourse then can become a framework for justifying the power of practitioners concerned with the mentally ill and for their treatment regimens. In this way, a discourse is much more than language: it is constitutive of the social world that is a focus of interest or concern. Foucault's approach was to take a broad historical approach to the study of discourse. Discourse analysts, in integrating insights from CA, however, derive much more fine-grained analyses of talk and texts than is a feature of Foucault's approach.

Also, unlike CA, there are several different approaches labelled as DA (Potter 1997). The version discussed here is one that has been of special interest to social researchers and is associated with such writers as Potter (1997), Potter and Wetherell (1994), and Billig (1991). This version of DA exhibits two distinctive features at the level of epistemology and ontology (Potter 1997).

- It is generally *anti-realist*; in other words, it denies that there is an external reality awaiting a definitive portrayal by the researcher. It therefore disavows the notion that researchers can arrive at privileged accounts of the social world.

- It is *constructionist*; in other words, the emphasis is placed on the versions of reality propounded by members of the social setting being investigated and on their renditions of that reality (see Box 1.13). More specifically, the constructionist emphasis recognizes that discourse entails a selection from many viable renditions. For example, is a person who speaks to himself dangerous or harmless, more in need of treatment than a handout or the opposite? In the process a particular reality is built up.

Thus, discourse is not simply a neutral device for imparting meaning. People seek to accomplish things when they talk or when they write; DA is concerned with the strategies they employ in trying to create different kinds of effect. This version of DA is therefore action-oriented, revealed in three basic discourse-analytic questions:

- What is this discourse doing?

- How is this discourse constructed to make this happen?

- What resources are available to perform this activity? (Potter 2004: 609).

This action orientation is revealed in a study of the first few moments of telephone calls to a National Society for the Prevention of Cruelty to Children helpline. Through an analysis of these call openings, Potter and Hepburn (2004) showed that these first few moments perform certain actions:

- They are a springboard for the caller to specify details of his or her concerns.

- They seek to establish that the child protection officer who receives the call is someone who, as an expert, can verify the caller's concerns.

- The caller makes it clear that he or she is concerned but not so concerned or certain about the status of the situation as to contact the police.

- The child protection officer shows an ability to treat the report as serious without having to presuppose the truth or seriousness of the report.

Thus, through an analysis of these brief moments of conversation, the flow of discourse achieves a number of objectives for both parties and is therefore action. On the other hand, as Gill (1996) suggested, what is said is always a way of *not* saying something else. In other words, either total silence on a topic, or formulating an argument in a conversation in one way rather than in another way, is a crucial component of seeing discourse as a solution to a problem.

In addition, DA shares with CA a preference for locating contextual understanding in terms of the situational specifics of talk. As Potter (1997: 158) put it, discourse analysts prefer 'to see things as things that are worked up, attended to, and made relevant in interaction rather than being external determinants.' However, DA practitioners are less wedded to this principle than are conversation analysts.

Discourse analysts resist the idea of codifying their practices and indeed argue that such a codification is probably impossible. Instead, they prefer to see their style of research as an 'analytic mentality' and as such as 'a craft skill, more like bike riding or chicken sexing than following the recipe for a mild chicken *rogan josh*' (Potter 1997: 147–8). One useful point of departure for DA research is to treat the way that something is said as being 'a solution to a problem' (Widdicombe 1993: 97). Gill (2000) suggested

in addition adopting a posture of 'skeptical reading.' This means searching for a purpose lurking behind the way things are said or presented. Gill proposed that DA can be usefully thought of as comprising four main themes, outlined in Box 16.5.

The bulk of the exposition of DA that follows is based on a study of a television program demonstrating how claims about success in the treatment of cancer can be boosted or undermined through the use of quantification (see Box 16.6).

Box 16.5 Four themes in discourse analysis

Gill (2000) drew attention to four prominent themes in DA:

1 *Discourse is a topic.* This means that discourse is a focus of inquiry itself and not just a means of gaining access to aspects of social reality that lie behind it. Such a view contrasts with a traditional research interview in which language is a way of revealing what interviewees think about a topic or their behaviour and the reasons for that behaviour.

2 *Language is constructive.* This means that discourse is a way of constituting a particular view of social reality. Moreover, in rendering that view, choices are made regarding the most appropriate way of presenting it and these reflect the disposition of the person responsible for devising it.

3 *Discourse is a form of action.* As Gill put it, language is viewed 'as a practice in its own right' (2000: 175). Language is a way of accomplishing acts, such as attributing blame, presenting oneself in a particular way, or getting an argument across. Moreover, a person's discourse is affected by the context that he or she is confronting. Thus, an account of reasons for wanting a job may vary according to whether addressing interviewees in a job interview, family members, or friends.

4 *Discourse is rhetorically organized.* This means that DA practitioners recognize that discourse is concerned with 'establishing one version of the world in the face of competing versions' (Gill 2000: 176). In other words there is a recognition that people want to persuade others when they present a version of events.

Box 16.6 Discourse analysis in action: producing facts through quantification rhetoric

The study of the representation of facts in the television program *Cancer: Your Money or Your Life* (Potter *et al.* 1991; Potter and Wetherell 1994) used a variety of different sources, including:

- a video recording of the program;
- observations of one of the people making the program, who acted as a participant observer while it was being made;
- drafts of the script, shooting schedules, and recordings of editing sessions;
- the entire interviews with the various people interviewed for the program (such as cancer research specialists and heads of charities); and
- additional research interviews with some of the latter people and with some of the people involved in making the program.

One of the phases of the analysis entailed the 'coding' of the various sources collected. The authors said:

> We made a list of about a dozen keywords and phrases that related to the sequence—percentage, cure rates, death rates, 1 per cent, etc.—and then ran through each of the interview and interaction files, looking for them with a standard word-processor. . . . Whenever we got a 'hit' we would read the surrounding text to see if it had relevance to our target sequence. When it did we would copy it across to an already opened coding file . . . noting the transcript page numbers at the same time. If we were not sure if the sequence was relevant we copied it anyway, for, unlike the sorts of coding that take place in traditional content analysis, the coding is not the analysis itself but a preliminary to make the task of analysis manageable (Potter and Wetherell 1994: 52).

Here is a prominent sequence used in the research. It occurred roughly halfway through the program, following the interviews with cancer scientists who had cast doubt on whether their research, much of it funded by charities, results in successful treatment:

> COMMENTARY: The message from these scientists is clear—exactly like the public—they hope their basic research

will lead to cures in the future—although at the moment they can't say how this will happen. In the meantime, their aim is to increase scientific knowledge on a broad front and they're certainly achieving this. But do their results justify them getting so much of the money that has been given to help fight cancer? When faced with this challenge the first thing the charities point to is the small number of cancers which are now effectively curable.

[on screen: DR NIGEL KEMP CANCER RESEARCH CAMPAIGN]

> KEMP: The outlook for individuals suffering from a number of types of cancer has been totally revolutionized. I mean for example—children suffering from acute leukemia—in the old days if they lived six months they were lucky—now more than half the children with it are cured. And the same applies to a number of other cancers—Hodgkin's Disease in young people and testicular tumours in young men (Potter and Wetherell 1994: 52–3).

At this point a table showing the annual incidence of 34 types of cancer begins to scroll on the screen. The total incidence is 243 000 and the individual incidences range from placenta (20) to lung (41 400). The three forms of cancer mentioned by Kemp and levels of incidence are highlighted in yellow: childhood leukemia (350), testis (1000), and Hodgkin's Disease (1400). The program continues while the table is scrolling.

> COMMENTARY: But those three curable types are amongst the rarest cancers—they represent around 1 per cent of a quarter of a million cases of cancers diagnosed each year. Most deaths are caused by a small number of very common cancers.

> KEMP: We are well aware of the fact that [pause] once people develop lung cancer or stomach cancer or cancer of the bowel sometimes—the outlook is very bad and obviously one is frustrated by the s[low], relatively slow rate of progress on the one hand but equally I think there are a lot of real opportunities and positive signs that advances can be made—even in the more intractable cancers (Potter and Wetherell 1994: 53).

Producing facts

In this section about discourse analytic research, the emphasis is on the resources employed in conveying allegedly factual knowledge. The researchers were especially interested in the role of what they call *quantification rhetoric*, by which is meant the ways in which numerical and non-numerical statements are made to support or refute arguments. The interest in this issue lies in part in the importance of quantification in everyday life and in part in the tendency for many social scientists to make use of this strategy themselves (John 1992). The specific focus of the research was a study of a television program entitled *Cancer: Your Money or Your Life* (Potter *et al.* 1991; Potter and Wetherell 1994). Among other things, the program claimed to show that the huge amounts of money donated by the public to cancer charities are doing little to 'cure' the disease. The details of the materials used in the research and an outline of the process of analysis are provided in Box 16.6. In their analysis of their data, such as the portions of transcript also in Box 16.6, Potter and Wetherell employed several devices.

Using variation as a lever

The authors drew attention to the phrase '1 per cent of a quarter of a million,' because it incorporates two quantitative expressions: a relative expression (a percentage) and an absolute frequency (quarter of a million). First, the change in portraying quantification is important, because it allows the program-makers to make their case about the low cure levels (just 1 per cent) compared with the large number of new cases of cancer. Second, they could have pointed to the absolute number of people who are cured (2500), but the impact would have been less. Also, the 1 per cent is not being contrasted with 243 000 but with a quarter of a million. Not only does this citation allow the figure to grow by 7000 but also quarter of a million sounds larger.

Reading the detail

Discourse analysts incorporate the CA preference for attention to the details of discourse. For example, Potter and Wetherell suggested that the description of the three 'curable cancers' as 'amongst the rarest cancers' is deployed to imply that these are atypical cancers, so that it is unwise to generalize from them to all cancers.

Looking for rhetorical detail

Attention to rhetorical detail entails being sensitive to how arguments are constructed. Thus, during the editing of the film, the program-makers' discourse suggested they were looking for ways to provide a convincing argument for their case that cancer re-

mains largely intractable in spite of the money spent on it. The program-makers very consciously devised the strategy outlined in the discussion of 'using variation as a lever' of playing down the numerical significance of those cancers amenable to treatment. Moreover, Potter *et al.* (1991) pointed out that one element of their argument is to employ a tactic they call a 'preformulation,' whereby a possible counter-argument is discounted in the course of presenting an argument, as when the commentary says: 'When faced with this challenge the first thing the charities point to are the small number of cancers which are now effectively curable.'

Overview

DA draws on insights from CA, particularly when analyzing strings of talk. The CA injunction to focus on the talk itself and the ways in which intersubjective meaning is accomplished in sequences of talk is also incorporated into DA. It sometimes seems as though DA practitioners come perilously close to invoking speculations not directly discernible in the sequences being analyzed—that is, speculations about motives. DA is in certain respects a more flexible approach to language in social research than CA, because it is not solely concerned with the analysis of naturally occurring talk and it permits the intrusion of understandings of what is going on that are not specific to the immediacy of previous utterances. It is precisely this to which conversation analysts object, as when Schegloff (1997: 183) wrote about DA: 'Discourse is too often made subservient to contexts not of its participants' making, but of its analysts' insistence.' For their part, discourse analysts object to the restriction that this injunction imposes, because it means that conversation analysts 'rarely raise their eyes from the next turn in the conversation, and, further, this is not an entire conversation or sizeable slice of social life but usually a tiny fragment' (Wetherell 1998: 402).

Both CA and DA practitioners sideline the notion of a pre-existing material reality that can constrain individual behaviour. This anti-realist inclination has been a source of controversy as this lack of attention to a material reality, which lies behind and underpins discourse, has proved too abstracted for some social researchers and theorists. Writing from a critical realist position (see Box 1.9), Reed (2000) argued that discourses should be examined in relation to social structures, such as power relationships, that are responsible for the occasioning of those discourses. For another example, Hier (2002) described his focus on Toronto City Council minutes for his work on raves as critical discourse analysis. In each attention is focused on the ways in which dis-courses work through existing structures, transforming the concept of discourse from a self-referential sphere in which nothing of significance exists outside it into a 'generative mechanism.' Thus while many DA practitioners are anti-realist, an alternative, realist position in relation to discourse is feasible. Such an alternative position is perhaps closer to the classic concerns of the social sciences than an anti-realist stance.

Advantages of content analysis

Content analysis has several advantages, outlined here.

- In its most quantitative form, it is a very transparent research method, making replication easy. It is this transparency that often causes content analysis to be referred to as an 'objective' method of analysis.

- It allows for a longitudinal analysis with relative ease. For example, the crime study can be expanded to examine changes in newspaper crime reporting over two perhaps very different periods.

- Content analysis is often referred to favourably as an *unobtrusive method*, a term previously defined (Webb *et al.* 1966) meaning that the method does not change the behaviours of participants in any way. It is therefore a *non-reactive method* (see Box 6.6). Newspaper articles and television scripts are generally not written with an expectation that a content analysis may one day be carried out on them. On the other hand, if the content analysis is being conducted on interview transcripts or ethnographies (e.g., Box 16.7), the documents may have at least partly been influenced by the

---

Box 16.7 A content analysis of qualitative research on the workplace

Hodson reported the results of a content analysis of 'book-length ethnographic studies using sustained periods of direct observation' (1996: 724). The idea of ethnography was explored in detail in Chapter 9. As a method, ethnography entails a long period of participant observation in order to understand the culture of a social group. Hodson (1996) performed a content analysis on ethnographic studies of workplaces published in book form (articles were excluded because they rarely included sufficient detail). Thousands of case studies from around the world were assessed for possible inclusion in the sample, but in the end 86 ethnographies were selected and 106 cases analyzed (several published ethnographies were of more than one case). Each case was coded into one of five types of workplace organization: craft, direct supervision, assembly line, bureaucratic, and worker participation. This was the independent variable. Various dependent variables were also coded. Here is one of the variables and its codes:

Autonomy

1 = none (workers' tasks are completely determined by others, by machinery, or by organizational rules); 2 = little (workers occasionally have a chance to select among procedures or priorities); 3 = average (regular opportunities to select procedures or to set priorities within definite limits); 4 = high (significant latitude in determining procedures and setting priorities); 5 = very high (significant personal interpretation is needed by the worker to reach broadly specified goals) (Hodson 1996: 728).

Hodson's findings suggest that some pessimistic accounts of worker participation schemes (e.g., that they do not genuinely permit participation and do not necessarily have a beneficial impact on the worker) are incomplete. A more detailed treatment of this research is in Hodson (1999).

anticipation of such scrutiny and thus contain some reactive error.

- It is a highly flexible method, applicable to a wide variety of different kinds of unstructured information. While content analysis is primarily associated with the analysis of mass media outputs, it has a much broader applicability. Box 16.8 illustrates a rather unusual but still interesting application.

- Content analysis can allow looking at social groups that are difficult to access. For example, much of the knowledge of the social backgrounds of elite groups, such as senior clergy, company directors, and top military personnel, comes from content analyses of such publications as *Who's Who* and also of business pages.

Box 16.8 Just burp the cover and you get a perfect seal

Vincent (2003) conducted a particularly interesting example of combining qualitative and quantitative strategies in her study of Tupperware. She looked at all of the literature by the company and about it, from its inception to today, using a qualitative content analysis to do so. What image of women did the company show? A housewife who really did not work outside the home and could use selling Tupperware for a bit of pin money? A woman too busy juggling career and family and thus in need of time-saving and economical Tupperware? Vincent then went to census data to look for parallels in women's roles, especially their working in the public sphere.

Disadvantages of content analysis

Like all research techniques, content analysis suffers from certain limitations:

- A content analysis can only be as good as the documents on which the practitioner works. Recall that Scott (1990) recommended assessing documents in terms of criteria such as: authenticity (that the document is what it purports to be); credibility (that there are no grounds for thinking that the contents of the document have been or are distorted in some way); and representativeness (that the specific documents examined are representative of all possible relevant documents; if certain kinds of document are unavailable or no longer exist, generalizability is jeopardized). These considerations are especially important in a content analysis of documents like letters. These issues were explored in Chapter 7.

- Even in quantitative content analysis it is almost impossible to devise coding manuals that do not require some coder interpretation. To the extent that this occurs, it is questionable to assume a perfect correspondence of interpretation between the persons responsible for producing the documents being analyzed and those coders.

- Particular problems are likely to arise when the aim is to impute *latent* meanings that lie beneath the superficial indicators of content rather than the more readily apparent *manifest* content. In searching for traditional markers of masculinity and femininity (see Box 16.1), the potential for an invalid conjecture was magnified. A related distinction is sometimes made between a more mechanical analysis (in particular, counting certain words) and an emphasis on themes in the text, which entails a higher level of abstraction and a corresponding greater chance of invalidity.

- It can be difficult to ascertain answers to 'why?' questions through content analysis. For example, Jagger found that 'the body of their partner, its attractiveness, shape and size, is of less importance to advertisers when in the buying mode [advertising for a partner]' (1998: 807) than when selling oneself (see Box 16.1). But why? And finding that this is true of both men and women is, as Jagger suggested, even more surprising. Again, why? Answers are usually speculations at best. Similarly, Fenton *et al.* (1998) found that sociology was only the fourth most common discipline referred to when social science research is being reported in the mass media, but by far the most frequently *inferred* discipline. Again, while interesting, the reasons for it are only speculative (Fenton *et al.* 1998). Sometimes, users of content analysis have been able to shed some light on 'why?' questions raised by their investigations by conducting additional data collection exercises and/or interviews with journalists and others (e.g., Fenton *et al.* 1998).

- Some content analytic studies are accused of being atheoretical and it is easy to see why. The emphasis in content analysis on measurement can easily and unwittingly result in a focus on what is measurable rather than what is theoretically significant or important. However, content analysis is not necessarily atheoretical. Jagger (1998) placed her findings on dating advertisements in the context of current ideas about consumerism and the body. Hodson's (1996) content analysis of workplace ethnographies (Box 16.7) was underpinned by theoretical ideas deriving from research concerning developments in workplace organization and their impact on workers.

K KEY POINTS

- Frequently content analysis is located within the quantitative research tradition of emphasizing the specification of clear rules to increase reliability, but content analysis can be qualitative as well.

- While traditionally associated with analysis of mass media content, it is in fact a flexible method applicable to a wide range of phenomena.

- It is important to be clear about research questions and about what is to be counted in order to be certain about units of analysis and what exactly is to be analyzed.

- The coding schedule and coding manual are crucial early stages in the preparation for a content analysis.

- Content analysis can become particularly controversial when it is used to search for latent meaning and themes.

- Semiotics and hermeneutics can also be considered as qualitative approaches to content analysis.

- Research exists on the extent to which readers of documents are active or passive consumers.

- Both CA and DA approaches see language itself as a focus of interest.

- CA is a systematic approach to conversation that sees talk as structured in the sense of following rules.

- Practitioners of CA avoid making inferences about talk that are not grounded in its immediate context.

- DA shares many features with CA but comes in several different versions and can be applied to a wider variety of phenomena than CA, which is limited to naturally occurring talk.

- Discourse is conceived of as a means of conveying meaning and generally relates meaning in talk to contextual factors.

- As with all research methods, there are advantages and disadvantages of content analysis.

Q QUESTIONS FOR REVIEW

- To what kinds of documents and media can content analysis be best applied?
- What is the difference between manifest and latent content? What are the implications of the distinction for content analysis?

What are the research questions?

- Why are precise research questions especially crucial in content analysis?

What is to be counted?

- What kinds of things can be counted in a content analysis?
- To what extent is it necessary to infer latent content when going beyond counting units, like words, inches of coverage, size of pictures?

Coding

- What is the difference between a coding schedule and a coding manual?
- What potential pitfalls need to be guarded against when devising coding schedules and manuals?

Qualitative content analysis

- What is a sign? How central is it to semiotics?
- What is the difference between denotative and connotative meaning?
- What lessons can be learned from the hermeneutic approach used by Phillips and Brown?

Conversation analysis

- What is meant by each of the following: turn-taking, adjacency pair, preference organization, repair mechanism? How do they relate to the production of social order?
- Evaluate the argument that CA reduces the need to examine a participant's motives?

Discourse analysis

- What is the significance of saying that DA is anti-realist and constructionist?
- What are the chief differences between CA and DA?

Advantages of content analysis

- 'One of the most significant virtues of content analysis is its flexibility, that it can be applied to a wide variety of documents.' Discuss.

Disadvantages of content analysis

- To what extent does the need for coders to interpret meaning undermine latent content analysis?
- Must content analysis be atheoretical?

17 Writing up social research

CHAPTER OVERVIEW

One of the main stages in any research project, regardless of its size, is reporting the findings. Writing is crucial, because an audience must be persuaded about the credibility and importance of the research. This chapter presents some of the characteristics of the writing-up of social research and explores:

• why writing, and especially good writing, is important to social research;

• using examples, how quantitative and qualitative research are composed;

• the influence and implications of postmodernism for writing; and

• key issues in the writing of ethnography, an area in which discussions about writing have been especially prominent.

Introduction

The aim of this chapter is to examine some of the strategies of writing up social research. Initially, it explores whether quantitative and qualitative research need different approaches. As will be seen, the similarities are frequently more striking and apparent than the differences. However, the main point of this chapter is to extract some principles of good practice that can be developed and incorporated into student writing. This is an important issue, since many find writing up research more difficult than carrying it out and others treat the writing-up stage as relatively unproblematic. But no matter how well research is conducted, readers have to be convinced about the credibility of the knowledge claims being made. Good writing helps in developing a style that it is *persuasive* and *convincing*. Flat, lifeless, uncertain writing does not have the power to persuade and convince. In exploring these issues, rhetorical strategies in the writing of social research are briefly examined (see Box 17.1). As Atkinson (1990: 2) observed about social research, 'the conventions of text and rhetoric are among the ways in which reality is *constructed.*'

This chapter reviews some basic ideas about structuring written work. Two published articles are examined to uncover some helpful features, one based on quantitative research and the other on qualitative research. When Bryman (1998) compared qualitative and quantitative research articles, he found the differences between them less pronounced than anticipated from his reading of the methodological literature on the comparison. One difference he did

---

Box 17.1 What is rhetoric?

The study of rhetoric is fundamentally concerned with attempts to convince or persuade an audience. Often encountered in a negative context, such as 'mere rhetoric,' rhetoric is an essential ingredient of writing. To suggest that rhetoric should be suppressed makes little sense, since it is in fact a basic feature of writing. The examination of rhetorical strategies in social research writing is an attempt to identify rhetorical techniques designed to convince and persuade others about the credibility of the knowledge claims presented.

notice, however, is that in journals quantitative researchers often give more detailed accounts of their research design, research methods, and approaches to analysis than do qualitative researchers. This is surprising, because in *books* reporting their research, qualitative researchers provide detailed accounts of these areas. Wolcott (1990: 27) also noticed this tendency: 'Our [qualitative researchers] failure to render full and complete disclosure about our data-gathering procedures gives our methodologically-oriented colleagues fits. And rightly so, especially for those among them willing to accept our contributions if we would only provide more careful data about our data.' Being informed that a study is based on a year's participant observation or a number of semi-structured interviews is not enough to claim the credibility that a writer may wish.

However, this point aside, in the discussion that follows illustrating one article based on quantitative research and one based on qualitative research, do not be too surprised if they turn out to be more similar than may have been expected.

Writing up quantitative research: an example

To illustrate some of the characteristics of writing up quantitative research for academic journals, take the article by Kelley and De Graaf (1997), referred to in several chapters (see especially Boxes 1.6 and 3.5). The article is based on a secondary analysis of survey data on religion in 15 nations and was accepted for publication in one of the most prestigious journals in sociology—the *American Sociological Review*. The vast majority of published articles in academic journals have undergone a blind review process, being read by two or three peers, who comment on the article and give the editors a judgment about its merits and therefore whether it is worthy of publication.

Most articles submitted are rejected. With highly prestigious journals, that is the fate of more than 90 per cent of articles. Moreover, it is unusual for an article to be accepted on its first submission. Usually, the referees suggest areas that need revising and the author is expected to respond to that feedback. Revised versions of articles are usually sent back to the referees for further comment and this process may result in the author having to revise the draft yet again. It may even result in rejection. Therefore, an article like Kelley and De Graaf's is not just the culmination of a research process but is also the outcome of a feedback process. The fact that it was accepted for publication, when so many others are rejected, testifies to its merits as having met the standards of the journal. That is not to say it is perfect, but the refereeing process is an indication that it does possess certain crucial qualities.

The article has the following components, aside from the abstract and bibliography:

1. introduction;
2. theory;
3. data;
4. measurement;
5. methods and models;
6. results; and
7. conclusion.

Introduction

Right at the beginning of the introduction, the opening four sentences attempt to grab the reader's attention, to give a clear indication of the article's focus, and to provide an indication of the likely significance of the findings. This is what the authors wrote (Kelley and De Graaf 1997: 639):

Religion remains a central element of modern life, shaping people's world-views, moral standards, family lives, and in many nations, their politics. But in many Western nations, modernization and secularization may be eroding Christian beliefs, with profound consequences that have intrigued sociologists since Durkheim. Yet this much touted secularization may be overstated—certainly it varies widely among nations and is absent in the United States (Benson, Donahue, and Erickson 1989: 154–7; Felling, Peters, and Schreuder 1991; Firebaugh and Harley 1991; Stark and Iannaccone

1994). We explore the degree to which religious beliefs are passed on from generation to generation in different nations.

This is an impressive start, because, in just over one hundred words, the authors set out what the article is about and its significance. Look at what each sentence achieves:

- The first sentence locates the research focus as addressing an important aspect of modern society, one which touches on many people's lives.

- The second sentence notes that there is variety among Western nations in the importance of religion and that the variations may have 'profound consequences.' But this sentence does more than the first sentence: it also suggests that this topic has long been of interest to sociologists. To support this point Durkheim, one of sociology's most venerated figures, is mentioned.

- The third sentence suggests that there is a problem with the notion of secularization, a research focus for many sociologists of religion. Several fairly recent articles are cited to support the authors' contention that some commentators exaggerate secularization. In this sentence, the authors are moving towards a rationale for their article that is more in terms of sociological concerns than pointing just to social changes, which are the main concern of the two opening sentences.

- Then in the fourth sentence the authors set up their specific contribution to this area, the exploration of the passing on of religious beliefs between generations.

So, by the end of four sentences, the contribution the article is claiming to make to understand religion in modern society has been outlined and situated within an established literature on the topic. This is quite a powerful start to the article, because the reader knows what the article is about and the particular case the authors are making for their contribution to the literature on the subject.

Theory

In this section, existing ideas and research on the topic of religious socialization are presented. The authors point to the impact of parents and other people on children's religious beliefs, but then assert that 'a person's religious environment is also shaped by factors other than their own and their parents' religious beliefs, and hence is a potential cause of those beliefs . . .' (1997: 641). This suggestion is then justified, which prompts the authors to argue that 'prominent among these "unchosen" aspects of one's religious environment is birthplace' (1997: 641). Kelley and De Graaf's ruminations on this issue lead them to propose a first hypothesis, which stipulates that contextual factors have an impact on religious beliefs. This leads them to suggest in two related hypotheses that, in predominantly secular societies, family background has a greater impact on a person's religious beliefs than in predominantly devout societies, because in the former parents and other family members are more likely to isolate children from those threatening secular influences. However, in devout societies this insulation process is less necessary and the influence of national factors greater. Thus, it ends up with very clear research questions, arrived at by reflecting on existing ideas and research in the area.

Data

In this section, the authors outline the data sets used for their research. The sampling procedures are outlined along with sample sizes and response rates.

Measurement

In this section, Kelley and De Graaf explained how the main concepts in their research are measured. The concepts are: *religious belief* (the questionnaire items used are in Box 3.5); *parents' church attendance*; *secular and religious nations* (that is, the scoring procedure for indicating the degree to which a nation is religious or secular in orientation on a five-point scale); *other contextual characteristics of nations* (e.g., whether or not a former Communist nation); and *individual characteristics* (e.g., age and gender).

Methods and models

This is a very technical section, which outlines the different ways in which the relationships between the variables can be conceptualized and the implications of using different mutivariate analysis approaches for the ensuing findings.

Results

The authors provide a general description of their findings and then consider whether the hypotheses *are* supported. In fact, it turns out they are. The significance of other contextual characteristics of nations and individual differences are separately explored.

Conclusions

In this final section, Kelley and De Graaf return to the issues that have been driving their investigation, those presented in the Introduction and Theory sections. They began this section with a strong statement of their findings: 'The religious environment of a nation has a major impact on the beliefs of its citizens: people living in religious nations acquire, in proportion to the orthodoxy of their fellow citizens, more orthodox beliefs than those living in secular nations' (Kelley and De Graaf 1997: 654). They then reflected on the implications of the confirmation of their hypotheses for understanding the process of religious socialization and religious beliefs. They also addressed the implications of their findings for those theories about religious beliefs in modern society outlined in their Theory section:

> Our results also speak to the long-running debate about US exceptionalism (Warner 1993): They support the view that the United States is unusually religious. . . . Our results do not support Stark and Iannaccone's (1994) 'supply-side' analysis of differences between nations which argues that nations with religious monopolies have substantial unmet religious needs, while churches in religiously competitive nations like the US do a better job of meeting diverse religious needs (Kelley and De Graaf 1997: 655).

The final paragraph spelled out inferences about the impact of social change on a nation's level of religious belief. The authors suggested that factors such as modernization and the growth of education depress levels of religious belief resulting in a precipitous rather than gradual fall in levels of religiosity.

In their final three sentences, they went on to write about societies undergoing such change:

> The offspring of devout families mostly remain devout, but the offspring of more secular families now strongly tend to be secular. A self-reinforcing spiral of secularization then sets in, shifting the nation's average religiosity ever further away from orthodoxy. So after generations of stability, religious belief declines abruptly in the course of a few generations to the modest levels seen in many Western nations (Kelley and De Graaf 1997: 656).

It may be argued that these reflections are somewhat risky, because the data from which the authors derived their findings are cross-sectional rather than longitudinal. They were clearly extrapolating from their scoring of the 15 nations in terms of levels of modernization to the impact of social changes on national levels of religiosity. However, these final sentences make for a strong conclusion, which itself may form a springboard for further research.

Lessons

What lessons can be learned from Kelley and De Graaf's article? To some extent, they have been alluded to in the above exposition but are still worth spelling out.

- There is a clear attempt to grab the reader's attention with strong opening statements, which also act as signposts to what the article is about.

- The authors spell out clearly the rationale of their research. This entails pointing to the continued significance of religion in many societies and to the literature on religious beliefs and secularization.

- The research questions are clearly spelled out, in fact with fairly specific hypotheses. As noted in Chapter 3, by no means is all quantitative research driven by hypotheses, despite implications that it is. Nonetheless, Kelley and De Graaf chose to frame their research questions in this form.

- The nature of the data, the measurement of concepts, the sampling, the research methods employed, and the approaches to the analysis of the data are clearly and explicitly summarized in sections 3, 4, and 5.

Box 17.2 ⌇(☀)⌇ *An empiricist repertoire?*

Papers written for social science journals display certain features that suggest an inevitability to the outcome of the research. In other words, the reader is given a sense that, in following the rigorous procedures outlined in the article, the researchers logically arrived at their conclusions. Others attempting a replication would too. This series of linked stages leading to an inescapable culmination is to a large extent a reconstruction of events, designed to persuade referees and editors (who, of course, use the same tactics themselves) of the credibility and importance of one's social scientific findings. This means that the conventions about writing up a quantitative research project, some outlined in this chapter, are in many ways an invitation to reconstruct an investigation in a particular way.

The whole issue of how the writing-up of research represents a means of persuading others of the credibility of knowledge claims has been a particular preoccupation among qualitative researchers (see below) and has been greatly influenced by the surge of interest in postmodernism. However, in Box 17.3, some of the rhetorical strategies involved in writing up quantitative social research are outlined. Three points are worth making about these strategies in the present context. First, they are characteristic of an empiricist repertoire. Second, although the writing of qualitative research has been a recent focus (see below), some attention has also been paid to quantitative research. Third, when Bryman (1998) compared the writing of quantitative and qualitative research articles, he found they are not as dissimilar in terms of rhetorical strategies as sometimes thought. However, he did find greater use of a management metaphor (see Box 17.3), one also evident in Kelley and De Graaf's article; for example, '*we excluded* the deviant cases from our analysis' (1997: 646) and '*we divided* the nations into five groups' (1997: 647; emphasis added).

- The presentation of the findings in section 6 is oriented very specifically to the research questions that drive the research.

- The conclusion returns to the research questions and spells out the implications of the findings for them and for the theories examined in section 2. This is an important element. It is easy to forget that the research process closes a circle when it returns unambiguously to its research questions. There is no point inserting extraneous findings that do not illuminate the research questions. Digressions of this kind can be confusing to readers.

There is also a clear sequential process moving from the formulation of the research questions through the exposition of the nature of the data and the presentation of the findings to the conclusions. Each stage is linked to and follows on from its predecessor (but see Box 17.2). The structure used by Kelley and De Graaf is one commonly used in quantitative research in social science academic journals. Sometimes, there is a separate Discussion section that appears between the Results and the Conclusion.

Writing up qualitative research: an example

Now look at an example of a journal article based on qualitative research. Not really representative, it does however exhibit features often regarded as desirable qualities in terms of presentation and structure. The article is one that has been referred to in several previous chapters (especially Boxes 2.15 and 10.3): a study of vegetarianism by Beardsworth and Keil (1992). The study is based on semi-structured interviews and was published in the *Sociological Review*, a leading British journal.

The structure runs as follows:

1. introduction;

2. the analysis of the social dimensions of food and eating;

3. studies of vegetarianism;

4. the design of the study;

5. the findings of the study;

6. explaining contemporary vegetarianism; and

7. conclusions.

What is immediately striking about the structure is that it is not dissimilar to Kelley and De Graaf's (1997). Nor should this be so surprising. After all, a structure that runs

Introduction → Literature review → Research design/
methods → Results → Discussion → Conclusions

is not obviously associated with one research strategy rather than the other. One difference from quantitative research articles is that the presentation of the results and their discussion are frequently rather more interwoven in qualitative research articles, as is seen in Beardsworth and Keil's article. As with Kelley and De Graaf's article, the writing is examined in terms of the article's structure.

Introduction

The first four sentences give an immediate sense of what the article is about and its focus:

The purpose of this paper is to offer a contribution to the analysis of the cultural and sociological factors that influence patterns of food selection and food avoidance. The specific focus is contemporary vegetarianism, a complex of inter-related beliefs, attitudes and nutritional practices which has to date received comparatively little attention from social scientists. Vegetarians in Western cultures, in most instances, are not life-long practitioners but converts. They are individuals who have subjected more traditional foodways to critical scrutiny, and subsequently made a deliberate decision to change their eating habits, sometimes in a radical fashion (Beardsworth and Keil 1992: 253).

Like Kelley and De Graaf's, this is a strong introduction. Again look at what each sentence achieves:

• The first sentence makes it clear that the research is concerned with the study of food.

• The second sentence provides a specific research focus, the study of vegetarianism, and makes a claim for attention by suggesting that this topic has been underresearched by sociologists. Interest-

ingly, this is almost the opposite of the claim made by Kelley and De Graaf in their second sentence, in that they pointed to a line of sociological interest in religion going back to Durkheim. Each is a legitimate textual strategy for gaining the attention of readers.

• Attention is jolted even more by an interesting assertion that begins to draw the reader into one of the article's primary themes, the idea of vegetarians as converts.

• The fourth sentence elaborates on the idea that for most people vegetarianism is an issue of choice rather than a tradition into which one is born.

Thus, after around one hundred words, the reader has a clear idea of the focus of the research and has been led to anticipate that there is unlikely to be a great deal of pre-existing social research on this issue.

The analysis of the social dimensions of food and eating

This and the next section review existing theory and research; the contributions of various social scientists to social aspects of food and eating are discussed. The literature reviewed acts as a backcloth to the issue of vegetarianism. Beardsworth and Keil proposed that 'there exists a range of theoretical and empirical resources which can be brought to bear upon the issue of contemporary vegetarianism' (1992: 255). This point is important, as they noted once again at the end of the section, that vegetarianism has received little attention from social scientists.

Studies of vegetarianism

This section examines the social scientific literature on vegetarianism. The review includes: opinion poll and survey data, which point to the likely percentage of vegetarians in the British population; debates about animal rights; sociological analysis of vegetarian ideas; and a reference to a dated survey research study (Dwyer *et al.*, 1974) of vegetarians in the US. In the final paragraph of this section, the authors indicated the contribution of some of the literature they covered.

The design of the study

The first sentence of this section forges a useful link with the preceding one: 'The themes outlined above appear to warrant further investigation, preferably in a manner which allows for a much more richly detailed examination of motivations and experiences than is apparent in the study by Dwyer *et al.*' (Beardsworth and Keil 1992: 260). This opening gambit allowed the authors to suggest that the literature in this area is scant and that there are many unanswered questions. Also, they distanced themselves from the one sociological study of vegetarians, which in turn led them to set up the grounds for preferring qualitative research. The authors then outlined:

- who was to be studied and why;
- how respondents were recruited and the difficulties encountered;
- the semi-structured interviewing approach (see Box 10.2) and its rationale;
- the number of people interviewed and the interview context; and
- the approach to analyzing the interview transcripts, largely through identifying themes.

The findings of the study

The chief findings are outlined under separate headings: respondents' characteristics, types of vegetarianism, the process of conversion, motivations, nutritional beliefs, social relations, and dilemmas. The presentation of the results is carried out so that the discussion of their meaning or significance leads to the next section, which provides, exclusively, a discussion of them. For example, in the final sentence reporting findings relating to nutritional beliefs, the authors wrote (Beardsworth and Keil 1992: 276):

> Just as meat tended to imply strongly negative connotations for respondents, concepts like 'fruit' and 'vegetable' tended to elicit positive reactions, although less frequently and in a more muted form than might have been anticipated on the basis of the analysis of the ideological underpinnings of 'wholefoods' consumption put forward by Atkinson (1980, 1983), or on the basis of

the analysis of vegetarian food symbolism advanced by Twigg (1983: 28).

In this way, the presentation of the results pointed to some themes taken up in the following sections and demonstrated the significance of certain findings for some of the previously discussed literature.

Explaining contemporary vegetarianism

This section discussed the findings in light of the study's research questions on food selection and avoidance. The results were also related to many of the ideas encountered in the two literature sections. The authors developed an idea emerging from their research, which they called 'food ambivalence.' This concept encapsulated for them the anxieties and paradoxes concerning food that can be discerned in the interview transcripts (e.g., food can be construed both as necessary for strength and energy and simultaneously as a source of illness). Vegetarianism is in many respects a response to the dilemmas associated with food ambivalence.

Conclusions

In this section, the authors returned to many of the ideas and themes that drove their research. They spelled out the significance of the idea of food ambivalence, which is probably the article's main contribution to research in this area. The final paragraph outlined the importance of food ambivalence for vegetarians, but the authors were careful not to imply that it is the sole reason for the adoption of vegetarianism. In the final sentence they wrote: 'However, for a significant segment of the population [vegetarianism] appears to represent a viable device for re-establishing some degree of peace of mind when contemplating some of the darker implications of the carefully arranged message on the dinner plate' (Beardsworth and Keil 1992: 290). The sentence neatly encapsulated one of the article's main themes, vegetarianism as a response to food ambivalence, and alluded through the reference to 'the carefully arranged message' to semiotic analyses of meat and food.

Lessons

As with Kelley and De Graaf's article, it is useful to review some of the lessons learned from this examination of Beardsworth and Keil's article.

- Just like the illustration of quantitative research writing, there are strong opening sentences, which attract attention and give a clear indication of the nature and content of the article.

- The rationale of the research is clearly identified. To a large extent, this revolves around identifying the sociological study of food and eating as a growing area of research but also noting the paucity of investigations of vegetarianism.

- Research questions are specified but they are somewhat more open-ended than in Kelley and De Graaf's article, which is in keeping with the general orientation of qualitative researchers. The research questions revolve around the issue of vegetarianism as a dietary choice and the motivations for that choice.

- The research design and methods are outlined and an indication given of the approach to analysis. The section in which these issues are discussed demonstrates greater transparency than may be the case with other qualitative research articles.

- The presentation and discussion of the findings in sections 5 and 6 are geared to the broad research questions that motivated the researchers' interest in vegetarianism. However, section 6 also represents the major opportunity for the idea of food ambivalence and its dimensions to be articulated. The inductive nature of qualitative research means that the concepts and theories generated from an investigation must be clearly identified and discussed, as in this case.

- The conclusion elucidates in a more specific way the significance of the results for the research questions. It also explores the implications of food ambivalence for vegetarians, so that one of the article's major theoretical contributions is clearly identified and emphasized.

Postmodernism and its implications for writing

Postmodernism is an extremely difficult idea to pin down. In one sense, it can be seen as a questioning of the taken-for-granted. It questions the very notion of dispassionate social scientists seeking to uncover a pre-given external reality and it views their accounts as only one among many ways of rendering social reality to audiences. As a result, 'knowledge' of the social world is relative; as Rosenau (1992: 8) put it, postmodernists 'offer "readings" not "observations," "interpretations" not "findings" . . .'

For postmodernists, reporting findings in a journal article provides merely one version of the social reality investigated; thus they adopt an attitude of investigating the bases and forms of those knowledge claims. While the writing of all types of social science is potentially in the postmodernist's firing line, it has been the texts produced by ethnographers that have been a particular focus. The ethno-

graphic text 'presumes a world out there (the real) that can be captured by a "knowing" author through the careful transcription and analysis of field materials (interviews, notes, etc.).' Postmodernism makes such accounts problematic because there 'can never be a final, accurate representation of what was meant or said, only different textual representations of different experiences' (Denzin 1994: 296).

However, it is wrong to depict the growing attention to ethnographic writing as exclusively a product of postmodernism. Atkinson and Coffey (1995) argued that other intellectual trends in the social sciences also stimulated this interest. One is concerned with distinctions between rhetoric and logic and between the observer and the observed, another with doubts about the possibility of a neutral language through which the natural and social worlds can be revealed. Illustrations of these issues can be dis-

Box 17.3 Rhetorical strategies in writing up quantitative research

The rhetorical strategies used by quantitative researchers include the following:

- There is a tendency to remove the researcher from the text as an active agent of the research process to convey an impression of objectivity of findings—that is, as part of an *external* reality, one independent of the researcher.

- The researcher surfaces in the text only to demonstrate ingenuity in overcoming obstacles (Bryman 1998).

- Key figures in the field are routinely cited to bestow credibility on the research.

- The research process is presented as a linear one to convey an air of inevitability about the results.

- The use of a *management metaphor* is common in the presentation of findings in which the researcher is depicted as ingeniously '"designing" research, "controlling" variables, "managing" data and "generating" tables' (Bryman 1998: 146). See Richardson (1990) on this point.

cerned in Boxes 17.2 and 17.3. Atkinson and Coffey also pointed to the antipathy within feminism towards the image of the neutral 'observer-author' who assumes a privileged stance in relation to members of the social setting being studied. This stance is regarded as one of domination of the observer-author over the observed that is inconsistent with the goals of feminism (revisit Chapter 8 for an elaboration of this general point). This concern has led to an interest in how privilege is conveyed in ethnographic texts and how voices, particularly of marginal groups, are suppressed.

The concerns within these and other traditions (including postmodernism) have led to experiments in writing ethnography (Richardson 1994). An example is the use of a 'dialogic' form of writing that seeks to raise the profile of the multiplicity of voices that can be heard in the course of fieldwork. As Lincoln and Denzin (1994: 584) put it: 'Slowly it dawns on us that there may . . . be . . . not one

"voice," but polyvocality; not one story, but many tales, dramas, pieces of fiction, fables, memories, histories, autobiographies, poems, and other texts to inform our sense of lifeways, to extend our understandings of the Other . . .'

Manning (1995) cited, as an example of the postmodern preference for allowing a variety of voices to come through within an ethnographic text, Stoller's (1989) research in Africa. Manning (1995: 260) described the text as a dialogue, not a monologue by the ethnographer, one 'shaped by interactions between informants or "the other" and the observer.' This postmodern preference for seeking out multiple voices and for turning the ethnographer into a 'bit player' reflects the mistrust among postmodernists of 'meta-narratives,' that is, positions or grand accounts that they think implicitly question the possibility of alternative versions of reality. On the other hand, 'mini-narratives, micro-narratives, local narratives are just stories that make no truth claims and are therefore more acceptable to postmodernists' (Rosenau 1992: xiii).

Postmodernism has also encouraged a growing reflexivity about the conduct of social research and the growing interest in the writing of ethnography is very much a manifestation of this trend (see Box 17.4). This reflexivity can be discerned in how many ethnographers turn inwards to examine the truth claims inscribed in their own classic texts, the focus of the next section.

In the end, what postmodernism gives, despite its recent decline, is an acute sense of uncertainty. It raises the issue of how one can ever know or capture a social reality that belongs to another. In so doing it points to an unresolvable tension that will not go away and is further revealed in the issues raised in the next section. To quote Lincoln and Denzin (1994: 582) again: 'On the one hand there is the concern for validity, or certainty in the text as a form of . . . authenticity. On the other hand there is the sure and certain knowledge that all texts are socially, historically, politically, and culturally located. Researchers, like the texts they write, can never be transcendent.' At the same time, of course, such a view renders problematic the very idea of what social scientific knowledge is or comprises.

Box 17.4 :⚡: *What is reflexivity?*

Reflexivity has several meanings in social science. To ethnomethodologists it refers to the way in which speech and action do more than merely act as indicators of deeper phenomena (see Chapter 16). Its other meaning carries the connotation that social researchers should reflect on the implications of their methods, values, biases, and decisions on the knowledge of the social world that they generate. Related, reflexivity entails a sensitivity to the researcher's cultural, political, and social context. As such, 'knowledge' from a reflexive position is always a reflection of a researcher's location in time and social space. This notion is especially explicit in Pink's (2001) formulation of a reflexive approach to the use of visual images (see Chapter 9).

There has been a growing reflexivity in social research, documented in books that collect details on the nuts and bolts of the actual research process as distinct from the often sanitized portrayal in research articles (e.g., Bryman 1988). The confessional tales referred to in Box 17.5 are invariably manifestations of this same development. Therefore, the rise of reflexivity largely predates the growing awareness of postmodern thinking. What distinguishes the reflexivity that has followed in the wake of postmodernism is a greater acknowledgment of the role of the researcher in the construction of knowledge. A researcher is not just someone who extracts knowledge from observations and conversations with others and then transmits knowledge to an audience. The researcher is viewed as implicated in the construction of knowledge both through the observer stance assumed in relation to the observed and through the ways in which an account is transmitted in the form of a written text.

Writing up ethnography

The term 'ethnography,' as noted in Chapter 9, is interesting, because it refers to both a method of social research and the finished product of ethnographic research. Thus, writing seems to be at the heart of the ethnographic enterprise. In recent years, the production of ethnographic texts has become a focus of interest in its own right and particularly in the rhetorical conventions employed in their production.

Ethnographic texts are designed to convince readers of the *reality* of the events and situations described, and the plausibility of the analyst's explanations. The ethnographic text does not simply present a set of findings: it must provide an 'authoritative' account, with strong claims to truth, of the group or culture in question. Stylistic and rhetorical devices persuading the reader to enter into a shared framework of facts and interpretations, observations, and reflections permeate the ethnographic text. Just like the writing found in reports of quantitative social research, the ethnographer typically uses a writing strategy imbued with *realism*. This simply means that the researcher presents an authoritative, dispassionate account to represent an external, objective reality. In this respect, there is very little difference between the writing styles of quantitative and qualitative researchers. Van Maanen (1988) called ethnography texts that conform to these characteristics *realist tales*. These are the most common ethnographic writings, though he distinguished other types (see Box 17.5). However, the *form* that this realism takes differs. Van Maanen distinguished four characteristics of realist tales: experiential authority, typical forms, the native's point of view, and interpretive omnipotence.

Experiential authority

Just as in much quantitative research writing, the author disappears from view. Readers are told what the members of a group, the only people directly visible in the text, say and do. An invisible author provides the narrative, giving the impression that the findings presented are what any reasonable, similarly placed researcher would have found. Readers have to accept that this is what the ethnographer

Box 17.5 Three forms of ethnographic writing

Van Maanen (1988) distinguished three major types of ethnographic writing:

- *Realist tales*—apparently definitive, confident, and dispassionate third-person accounts of a culture and of the behaviour of its members. This is the most prevalent form of ethnographic writing.

- *Confessional tales*—personalized accounts in which the ethnographer is fully implicated in the data-gathering and writing-up processes. These are warts-and-all accounts of the trials and tribulations of doing ethnography. They have become more prominent since the 1970s and reflect a growing emphasis on reflexivity in qualitative research in particular. Several of the sources referred to in Chapter 10 are confessional tales (e.g., Armstrong 1993; Giulianotti 1995). However, confessional tales are more concerned with detailing how research is carried out than with presenting findings. Very often the confessional tale is told in one context (such as an invited chapter in a book of similar tales) but the main findings are written up in realist tale form.

- *Impressionist tales*—accounts that feature 'words, metaphors, phrasings, and . . . the expansive recall of fieldwork experience' (1988: 102). There is an emphasis on stories of dramatic events that provide 'a representational means of cracking open the culture and the fieldworker's way of knowing it' (1988: 102). However, as Van Maanen noted, impressionist tales 'are typically enclosed within realist, or perhaps more frequently, confessional tales' (1988: 106).

saw and heard. This strategy essentially plays down any suggestion of bias arising from the personal subjectivity of the author/ethnographer, for example, that the fieldworker may have become too involved with the people being studied. To this end, when writing up their ethnographic work, authors play up their academic credentials and qualifications, their previous experience, and so on. All this enhances the degree to which their accounts can be relied upon and the authors/ethnographers appear as reliable witnesses.

A further element of experiential authority is that, when describing their methods, ethnographers invariably make a great deal of the intensity of the research—they spent so many months in the field, had conversations and interviews with countless individuals, worked hard to establish rapport, and so on. Drawing the reader's attention to such hardships of the fieldwork—the danger, the poor food, the disruptive effect on normal life, the feelings of isolation and loneliness, and so on creates a sympathy for the author, or less charitably, deflects potential criticism of the findings.

Also worth mentioning are the extensive quotations from conversations and interviews that invariably form part of the ethnographic report. These are also important ingredients in the author's use of *evidence* to support the points made. However, they are also a mechanism for establishing the credibility of the report in that they demonstrate the author's ability to encourage people to talk. The copious descriptive details—of places, patterns of behaviour, contexts, and so on—can also be viewed as a means of piling on the sense of the author being an ideally placed witness for all the findings uncovered.

Typical forms

The author often generalizes about a number of recurring features of the group in question to create a typical form of the feature. Examples based on particular incidents or people may be used, but basically the emphasis is upon recurrent patterns of behaviour. For example, in her conclusion to her ethnographic research on female drug users, cited several times in Chapter 9, Taylor wrote: 'Yet the control exercised over women through the threat to remove their children highlights a major factor differentiating female and male drug users. Unlike male drug users, female drug users, like many other women, have two careers: one in the public sphere and one in the private, domestic sphere' (1993: 154). This statement portrays a pattern among women drug users, making any individual woman important only insofar as she can illustrate such general tendencies.

The natives' points of view

A commitment to seeing through the eyes of the people being studied is important for qualitative researchers because it is part of a strategy of getting at the meaning of social reality from the perspectives of those being studied. However, it also represents an important element in creating a sense of authority on the part of the ethnographer. After all, claiming to have taken the natives' points of view implies being in an excellent position to speak authoritatively about the group in question. Ethnographies frequently include numerous references to the steps taken by the ethnographer to get close to the people studied and success in this regard. Thus, for her research on female drug users, Taylor (1993: 16) wrote:

> Events I witnessed or took part in ranged from the very routine (sitting around drinking coffee and eating junk food) to accompanying various women on visits to . . . the HIV clinic; I accompanied them when they were in court, and even went flat-hunting with one woman. I went shopping with some, helping them choose clothes for their children and presents for their friends. I visited them in their homes, rehabilitation centres, and maternity wards, sat with them through withdrawals, watched them using drugs, and accompanied them when they went 'scoring' (buying drugs).

Interpretative omnipotence

When writing an ethnography, the author rarely presents possible alternative interpretations of an event or pattern of behaviour. Instead, the phenomenon in question is presented as having a single meaning or significance, which the fieldworker alone has cracked. Indeed, the evidence provided is carefully marshalled to support the singular interpretation placed on the event or pattern of behaviour. It seems obvious or inevitable that anyone would draw the same inferences the author drew when faced with such clear-cut evidence.

These four characteristics of realist tales imply that what researchers are doing as researchers is only one part of creating a sense of having figured out the nature of a culture. Creating that understanding also has very much to do with how the researchers, in their written ethnography, *represent* what they did in the field. But in the end recall that for postmodernists any realist tale is merely one 'spin'—that is one version that can be or has been formulated in relation to the culture in question.

Bibliography

No one likes to make bibliography entries and that is why most bibliographies include an error or two. The problem with errors is that they show a lack of attention on the author's part. Here is a bibliography taken from an earlier version of this text with errors deliberately added. Look all of the entries over first, to see the form, and then see how many errors you can find. Errors in bibliography entries will not stop true scholars from finding your source, just slow them down a bit. The answers are at the end of the next chapter.

Practical tip **Referring to websites**

It is a common practice in academic work when referring to websites to include the date(s) consulted. This convention has arisen because a subsequent researcher, perhaps wanting to follow up some findings, may find that the websites are no longer there or that they have changed.

Abraham, J. (1994), 'Bias in Science and Medical Knowledge: The Opren controversy,' *Sociology*, 28: 717–36.

Armstrong, D, Gosling, A., Weinman, J., and Marteau, T. (1997), 'The Place of Inter-Rater Reliability in Qualitative Research: an Empirical Study,' *Sociology*, 31: 597-606

Atkinson, R. (1998), *The Life Story Interview* (Thousand Oaks, CA: Sage).

Barnard, M., and Frischer, M. (1995), 'Combining Quantitative and Qualitative Approaches: Researching HIV-Related Risk Behaviours among Drug Injectors', *Addiction Research,* 351–62.

Barter, C., and E. Renold (1999) 'The Use of Vignettes in Qualitative Research,' *Social Research Update*, 25.

Blaikie, A. (2001), 'Photographs in the Cultural Account: Contested Narratives and Collective Memory in the Scottish Islands,' *Sociological Review*, 49- 345–67.

Buchanan, D. R. (1992), 'An Uneasy Alliance: Combining Qualitative And Quantitative Research Methods,' *Health Education Quarterly*, **19**: 117–35.

Charmaz, K., (2000), 'Grounded Theory: Objectivist and Constructivist Methods,' in Denzin, N.K. and Lincoln, Y.S. (eds.), *Handbook of Qualitative Research*, 2nd ed. (Thousand Oaks, CA: Sage).

B. Czarniawska. (1998), *A Narrative Approach to Organization Studies* (Thousand Oaks, XA: Sage).

Giulianotti, R. (1995), 'Participant Observation and Research into Football Hooliganism: Reflections on the Problems of Entrée and Everyday Risks,' *Sociology of Sport Journal*, 12: 1–20.

Reinharz, S, 1992, *Feminist Methods in Social Research* (New York).

Okely, J. (1994), 'Thinking through Fieldwork, in A. Bryman and R G. Burgess (eds.), *Analyzing Qualitative Data* (London: Routledge).

Sheehan, K. (2001), 'E-Mail survey response rates: A review,' *Journal of Computer-Mediated Communication*, 6. www.ascusc.org/jcmc/vol6/issue2/sheehan.html

DO NOT ALPHABETIZE authors in items with multiple authors. The order reflects their choice, or at least the choice of the most powerful in the group. What ethical issues arise in determining authorship order? Some online bibliographies include only the first author, as does part of *Social Science Citation Index*. Is alphabetical listing a good compromise?

K KEY POINTS

- Good writing is probably just as important as good research practice. Indeed, it is probably better thought of as a part of good research practice.

- A clear structure and statement of research questions are important components of writing up research.

- The study of rhetoric and writing strategies generally reveals that the writings of social scientists do more than simply report findings; they are designed to convince and to persuade.

- The emphasis on rhetoric is not meant to imply that there is no external social reality; it merely suggests that understanding that reality is profoundly influenced by the ways writers represent it.

- While postmodernism has exerted a particular influence on this last point, writers working within other traditions have also contributed to it.

- The basic structure of and the rhetorical strategies employed in most quantitative and qualitative research articles are broadly similar.

- Rhetoric and the desire to persuade others of the validity of research is not always a bad thing. Everyone wants to get points across and to persuade readers that the conclusions are right. The question is how well it is done. Is the best possible case made? Bearing in mind the significance of writing strategy increases chances of that success.

Q QUESTIONS FOR REVIEW

- Why is it important to consider the ways in which social research is written up?

Writing up quantitative research: an example

- Read an article based on quantitative research in a Canadian sociology journal. To what extent does it exhibit the same characteristics as Kelley and De Graaf's article?

- What is meant by rhetorical strategy? Why are rhetorical strategies important in writing up social research?

- Do Kelley and De Graaf employ an empiricist repertoire?

Writing up qualitative research: an example

- Read an article based on quantitative research in a Canadian sociology journal. How far does it exhibit the same characteristics as Beardsworth and Keil's article?

- How is the structure of Beardsworth and Keil's article different from Kelley and De Graaf's?

Postmodernism and its implications for writing

- Why has postmodernism produced a growth of interest in the writing of social research?

- What is reflexivity?

Writing up ethnography

- Is it true that typical ethnographic writing is imbued with realism?

- What forms of ethnographic writing other than realist tales can be found?

- What are the main characteristics of realist tales?

18 Conducting a research project

CHAPTER OVERVIEW

The goal here is to provide advice to students on some of the issues to consider in conducting a relatively small-scale project as part of their degree requirements. In addition to needing help with the conduct of research, which it is hoped has been provided by the bulk of this book up to this point, more specific advice on tactics in doing and writing up social research for such a task can be useful.

The chapter explores a wide variety of issues such as:

- advice on timing;
- advice on generating research questions;
- dealing with existing literature on the subject; and
- advice on writing to help produce compelling findings.

Introduction

This chapter provides some advice for those readers carrying out their own small-scale project. The previous 17 chapters should have provided helpful information about the choices available and how to implement them. But beyond this, how might you go about conducting a small project of your own and writing a senior research paper of about 10 000 to 15 000 words, an increasingly common requirement for undergraduate social science degree programs. Students in postgraduate degree programs will also find some of the observations helpful. Finally, the advice is tailored for students engaged in empirical research, in which they collect new data or perhaps conduct a secondary analysis of existing data.

Know what is expected by your institution

Your institution or department will have specific requirements concerning a wide variety of different features that a dissertation should comprise and a range of other matters. These include such things as: the form of binding, how it is to be presented, whether an abstract is required, the size of page margins, the format

for referencing, number of words, perhaps the structure of the presentation, plagiarism, deadlines, and so on.

The advice here is simple: *follow the requirements, instructions, and information provided*. If anything in this book conflicts with your institution's guidelines and requirements, ignore this book.

Identifying research questions

Many students want to conduct research in areas of personal interest. This is not a bad thing; as noted in Chapter 1, many social researchers start from this point as well (see also Lofland and Lofland 1995: 11–14). However, this beginning must progress to developing research questions, in qualitative research as well as quantitative. Even though Chapter 8 said that qualitative research is more open-ended than quantitative research, and Chapter 9 referred to some notable studies not driven by specific research questions, totally open-ended research is risky. It can lead to collecting too much data and, when writing it up, to a confused focus. So, unless your supervisor advises to the contrary, formulate some research questions. In other words, what is it about your area of interest that you want to know?

Research questions are, therefore, important. They provide a focus that will

- guide the literature search;
- limit the scope of the exercise (see Figure 18.1);
- guide decisions about what data must be collected;
- guide the analysis of data;
- guide the writing up of data; and

- reduce chances of going off in unnecessary directions and tangents.

Therefore, research questions have many uses and it is helpful to resist any temptation to delay their formulation.

Research questions should exhibit the following characteristics:

- They should be clear, in the sense of being intelligible.

- They should be researchable, thus not formulated in terms so abstract that they cannot be investigated. Nor should they be so grand in scope to be unrealistic, given the time frame.

- They should have some connection(s) with established theory and research. This means that there should be an existing literature both to help illuminate how the research questions should be approached and to connect them with the larger discipline. Even with a topic scarcely addressed by social scientists, it is unlikely that there will be no relevant literature (e.g., on related or parallel topics).

- Since an argument should be developed in the paper, research questions should be linked to each

Research area
(Concerns about risk)
↓

Select aspect of research area
(Variations in concerns about risk)
↓

Research questions
(What areas of risk are of greatest concern among people? Do age, gender, social class, and education affect risk? Do parents worry more than non-parents about risk? What is the main source—newspapers, television, family—of peoples' knowledge about issues relating to risk? Do concerns about risk have an impact on how people conduct their daily lives and if so in what ways? Do worries about risk result in fatalism?)
↓

Select research questions
(What areas of risk are of greatest concern among people? Do age, gender, social class, and education affect risk? Do parents tend to worry about risk more than non-parents do?)

Figure 18.1 Steps in selecting research questions

Box 18.1 Marx's (not Karl) sources of research questions

Marx (1997) suggested the following possible sources of research questions:

- Intellectual puzzles and contradictions.
- The existing literature.
- Replication.
- A feeling that a certain theoretical perspective or notable piece of work is misguided. Your work presents the reasons for your opposition.
- A social problem. Remember that this is just a source of a research question, one needing the identification of social scientific (for example, sociological) issues in relation to it.
- 'Gaps between official versions of reality and the facts on the ground' (1997: 113). An example here is some-

thing like Parnaby's (2003) ethnographic investigation of how squeegee kids were turned into a 'disease' invading private space, and one needing legislation.

- The counterintuitive. For example, when common sense seems to fly in the face of social scientific truths, as it did when those awaiting an end of the world that did not occur began to proselytize rather than slink away in embarrassment.
- Related 'empirical examples that trigger amazement' (1997: 114). He gave as examples deviant cases and atypical events.
- New methods and theories. How can they be applied in new settings?
- 'New social and technical developments and social trends' (1997: 114).

other. Constructing a single argument for unrelated research questions is almost impossible, even for experienced researchers.

- They should at the very least hold out the prospect of being able to make an original contribution—however small—to the topic.

If stuck about how to formulate research questions (or indeed other phases of the research), look at journal articles or research monographs to see how others have formulated them. Look at past student papers for ideas as well. Marx (1997) suggested a wide range of sources of research questions (see Box 18.1).

Using a supervisor

Most institutions that require a project like this allocate students to supervisors but institutions vary greatly in the kind and amount of assistance that can be expected of these supervisors. Equally, students vary in how frequently and for what they will see their supervisors. The advice here is simple: use a supervisor to the fullest extent allowable and follow the pointers given. The supervisor is usually well versed in the research process and can provide help and feedback at all stages of the research, subject to your institution's strictures in this regard. If the supervisor is critical of your research questions, interview schedule, early drafts, or whatever, try to respond positively. It is not a personal attack. The criticisms invariably are accompanied by reasons for

them and suggestions for revision. Be thankful for the opportunity to address deficiencies *before* your work is formally examined. Supervisors regularly have to go through the same process themselves, when they submit an article to a peer-refereed journal or apply for a research grant.

Also relevant here is that students stuck at the start, or behind in their work, sometimes respond by avoiding their supervisors. They then get caught up in a vicious circle that results in their work being neglected and then rushed at the end. Try to avoid this situation by confronting any difficulties, especially, for example, in getting going or falling behind, the worst two, and seek out your supervisor for advice immediately.

Managing time and resources: start thinking early about the research area

Most students are asked to start thinking about a potential topic well before being required to start actual work on the project. It is worth taking that advantage, because all research is constrained by time. Two points are relevant here:

- Work out a timetable, preferably with your supervisor, detailing the different stages of the research (including the review of literature and writing-up). The timetable should specify the different stages and the specific dates for starting and finishing them (see Figure 18.2 for an example of a quantitative research outline). Some stages are likely to be ongoing—for example, searching the literature for new references (see below)—but that should not delay developing a timetable.

- Find out what, if any, resources are available for carrying out your research. For example, can the institution help with such things as photocopying, postage, stationery, and so on? Can it lend hardware, such as recording equipment and transcription machines, to record and transcribe interviews? Has it got the necessary software, such as SPSS or a qualitative data analysis package like NVivo? This kind of information helps to establish if the research design and methods are financially feasible and practical. The imaginary 'gym study' in Chapter 12 is an example of an investigation feasible within the kind of time frame usually allocated to undergraduate dissertations. However, it would require such facilities as: photocopying covering letters and questionnaires; postage for sending the questionnaires out and for any follow-up letters to non-respondents; return postage for the questionnaires; and the availability of a quantitative data analysis package like SPSS.

Searching the existing literature

Online bibliographical databases accessible at most university libraries are an invaluable source of references. The best one for students probably is *Sociological Abstracts*. It allows searches by keyword (topic), author, title, journal, and other descriptors. Focus is then easily made narrower by specifying language, year, and type of presentation. Thus, only 'English, post-1998, articles' can be searched and listed from latest to earliest. That 'articles only' restriction removes papers presented at meetings and dissertations—too hard for most students to access in any event. The searches use Boolean combinations of 'and,' 'or,' and 'not.' Therefore a student can search keywords for articles on 'sexism and universities' to find articles that deal with both topics in the same piece. Choosing 'sexism or universities' gets those articles just referred to plus articles on either one alone, on sexism alone, and on universities alone.

That is probably not a good choice—it's too broad; but 'universities and sexism or prejudice' is as it expands the first option above to cover university prejudice in addition to university sexism. Finally 'not' restricts the search. 'Sexism not universities' finds articles about sexism in places other than universities. Students should experiment with the use of keywords and Boolean options, and if unsuccessful, a librarian can help.

The output of these procedures gives details of journal articles in which the keyword (or journal, or year, etc.) appears. It may provide an abstract (if the journal concerned includes them) and full details of the article including references. Other indices are more specialized, for example, the *Canadian Periodical Index* and the *Population Index*, as are collections of abstracts, for example, *Sage Race Relations Abstracts* and *Women's Studies Abstracts*. The *Readers'*

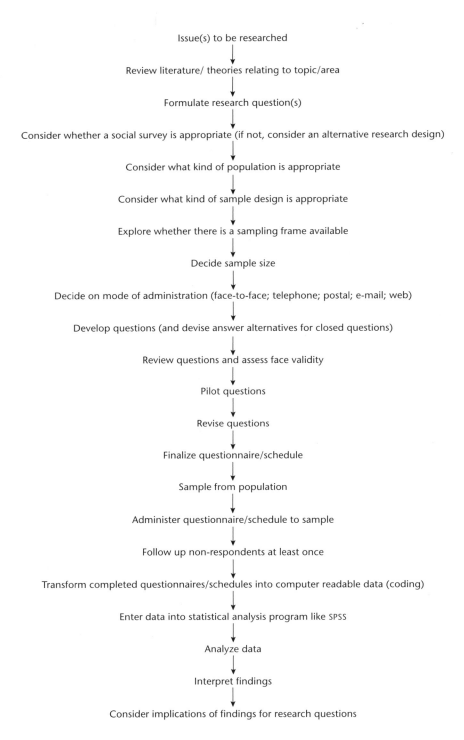

Figure 18.2 Steps in conducting a social survey

Guide to Periodical Literature gives more popular pieces, those that would appear in magazines, etc., and it is generally not a source for serious scholars. Mark the records you want and e-mail them to yourself for a permanent record.

The bibliographies in the articles found can then provide additional sources to examine. A particularly interesting tool is the *Social Sciences Citation Index* that looks forward from the original articles to later ones that cite the original. Therefore what others later think of the earlier piece can be revealed. Perhaps they are critical of the original, or perhaps they accept and add to it. A history of research in the area of interest is thus built up. Recalling Chapter 16, that is the denotative meaning of the citation index. Connotatively, to some professors it is a place to see how often they have been cited. To those granting tenure and raises, it can be a crude source of merit: 'more citations, better researcher,' followed by lengthy battles on measurement validity and other of the quantitative/qualitative issues discussed in this book.

The library catalogue is an obvious route to finding books, even to the holdings of other universities. Again, ask a librarian. Too often, however, the books are checked out, dated, or contain too much information for student papers, so the above sources may be preferable. The rule of thumb is to stop searching when the same items keep on appearing; this is similar to the idea of theoretical saturation mentioned in connection with qualitative research.

The existing literature should be explored to identify the following issues:

- What is already known about this area?
- What concepts and theories are relevant?
- What research methods and strategies have been employed in studying this area?
- Are there any significant controversies?
- Are there any inconsistencies in findings relating to this area?
- Are there any unanswered research questions?

Why review the existing literature? The most obvious reason is to know what is already known about the area of interest and so avoid 'reinventing the wheel.' You will be able to revise and refine your research questions in the process of reviewing the literature. Beyond this, using the existing literature on a topic is a way to develop an argument about the significance of your research and where it will lead. The simile of a *story* is sometimes used in this context (see below).

A competent review of the literature is also at least, in part, a means of affirming your credibility as someone knowledgeable in your chosen area. Thus, when reading the existing literature, try to do the following:

- Take good notes, including details of the full citation of the material. It is infuriating to find that you forgot to record the volume number of an article needed in your Bibliography.
- Develop critical reading skills. The written review of the literature should be critical rather than descriptive. This involves not simply criticizing the work of others but asking questions about the significance of the work, such as: How does it relate to other things you have read? Is it contradictory? Are there any apparent strengths and deficien-

---

Practical tip *Reasons for writing a literature review*

The following are reasons for writing a literature review:

1 To know what is already known in a research area and thus avoid being accused of reinventing the wheel.

2 To learn from other researchers' mistakes and avoid them.

3 To reveal different theoretical and methodological approaches to the research area.

4 For help in developing an analytic framework.

5 To find additional variables to add to the research.

6 To suggest further research questions.

7 For help with the interpretation of the findings.

8 To give some pegs on which to hang those findings.

9 It is expected.

cies—perhaps in terms of method or in terms of the credibility of the conclusions drawn? What theoretical ideas have influenced the item?

In some areas of research, there are very many references. Try to identify the major ones and work outwards from there. Move on to the next stage of the research at the point you identified in your timetable (see earlier) so that you can dig yourself out of the library. This is not to say that your search for the literature will cease, but that you need to force yourself to move on. Seek out your supervisor's advice on whether you need to search the literature more.

Preparing for research

Do not begin your data collection until you have identified your research questions fairly clearly. Develop data collection instruments with these research questions at the forefront of your thinking. If at all possible, conduct a small pilot study to see how well your research instruments work. You will also need to think about access and sampling issues. If the research requires access to or the cooperation of one or more closed settings like an organization, you need to confirm at the earliest opportunity the necessary permission to conduct your work. This usually takes so long that I advise not using closed settings for student research. You also need to consider how you will go about gaining access to people. This issue leads you into sampling considerations, such as the following:

- Whom do you need to study to investigate the research questions?
- How easy is access to a sampling frame?
- What kind of sampling strategy is feasible (e.g., probability sampling, quota sampling, theoretical sampling, or convenience sampling)?
- Can this choice of sampling method be defended?

Also, while preparing for data collection, consider whether there are possible ethical problems associated with your research methods or approach to contacting people.

Doing research and analyzing results

This is what the bulk of this book has been about, so it seems superfluous to go over this ground again. Here are some useful practical reminders:

- Keep good records. A research diary can be helpful here, but there are several other things to bear in mind. For example, in a mailed questionnaire survey keep good records of who replied, to know who needs a reminder. If participant observation is a component of the research, it is imperative to keep good field notes and not rely on memory.

- Become thoroughly familiar with any hardware to be used in collecting your data, such as tape recorders for interviewing, and make sure they are in good working order (e.g., with batteries not close to being flat).

- Do not wait until all your data have been collected to begin coding. This recommendation applies to both quantitative and qualitative research. If using a questionnaire survey, begin coding data and entering them into SPSS, or an alternative package, after accumulating a reasonable number of completed questionnaires. In the case of qualitative data, such as interview transcripts, the same point applies; indeed, it is a specific recommendation of the proponents of grounded theory that data collection and analysis should be intertwined.

Box 18.2 Safety in research

In 2002, a 19-year-old British female sociology student, thought to have gone to interview a homeless person, was reported missing. Because of safety concerns, her advisor had advised her to take a friend and to conduct the interview in a public place. In fact, she had not gone to conduct the interview and to everyone's relief turned up abroad (see Barkham and Jenkins, 'Fears for Fresher Who Vanished on Mission to Talk to the Homeless,' *The Times*, 13 December 2002).

There is an important lesson in this incident: social research may on occasion place you in potentially dangerous situations. You should avoid taking personal risks at all costs and you should resist any attempts that place you in situations where personal harm is a real possibility. Just as you should ensure that no harm comes to research participants (as prescribed in the discussion of ethical principles throughout the book), individuals involved in directing research should not place students and researchers in situations in which they may come to harm.

Equally, lone researchers should avoid such situations. The advice given by the student's tutor—to take someone with her and to conduct the interview in a public place—is sensible. If you have a cell phone, keep it nearby and switched on. Establish a routine whereby you keep in regular contact. Even in situations in which there is no obvious reason to think a situation could be dangerous, a researcher can be faced with a sudden outburst of abuse or threatening behaviour. This can arise when people react relatively unpredictably to an interview question or to being observed. If there are signs that such behaviour is imminent (e.g., through body language) begin a withdrawal from the research situation. Further guidelines on these issues can be found in Craig (2004).

Lee (2004) drew an important distinction between two kinds of danger in fieldwork: *ambient* and *situational*. The former refers to situations that are avoidable, in that one can choose another topic, and in which danger is an ingredient of the context. Fieldwork in conflict situations of the kind encountered by the researcher who took on the role of a bouncer (Winlow *et al.* 2001) is an example. Situational danger occurs when a researcher attracts aggression, hostility, or violence from particular participants, even in a safe setting (Lee 2004). It is less easy to foresee than is ambient danger which is not to say that ambient danger is entirely predictable. It was only some time after she began her research in a hospital laboratory that Lankshear (2000) realized the possibility of her being exposed to dangerous pathogens.

- Remember that the transcription of recorded interviews takes a long time. Allow at least six hours transcription for every one hour of recorded talk, at least in the early stages of transcription.

- Become familiar with any data analysis packages as early as possible. This familiarity establishes or refutes a need for them and, if the former, ensure mastering them *before* they are needed for the analysis.

- Do not at any time take risks with personal safety (see Box 18.2).

Writing up research

It is easy to neglect the writing stage in the research process because of difficulties encountered earlier. But, obvious though this point be, a paper has to be written. Findings must be conveyed to an audience, something that all researchers have to face. The first bit of advice is . . .

Start early

It is easy to view the writing-up of your research findings as something you can think about after you have collected and analyzed your data. There is, of course, a grain of truth here, in that you can hardly write up your findings until you know what they are. However, there are good reasons for beginning writing early on, since it forces you to start thinking about such issues as how best to present and justify the research questions driving your research or how to structure the theoretical and research literature used to frame the research questions. A further reason is an entirely practical one: many people find it difficult to get started and employ (probably unwittingly) procrastination strategies to put off the inevitable. This tendency can result in rushed, last-minute writing. Writing under this kind of pressure is not ideal. How you represent your findings and conclusions is a crucial stage in the research process. Not providing a convincing account of the research does not do it justice.

Be persuasive

This point is crucial. Writing up research is not simply a matter of reporting findings and drawing some conclusions. Writing contains many other features, such as referring to the literature used, explaining how the research was carried out, and outlining how the analysis was conducted. But above all, it must be *persuasive*, convincing readers of the credibility of the conclusions. Simply saying 'isn't it interesting' is not enough. Readers must be persuaded that the findings and conclusion are both plausible and significant.

Get feedback

Try to get as much feedback on your writing as possible and respond positively to the points made. Your supervisor is likely to be the main source of feedback; provide your supervisor with drafts of your work to the fullest extent that regulations allow, giving plenty of time to provide feedback. There are others like you who want your supervisor to comment on their work, and, if rushed, the comments may be less helpful. Also, you can ask others in your same degree program to read your drafts and comment on them and they may ask you to do the same. Their comments may be very useful, but, by and large, your supervisor's comments are the main ones you should seek.

Avoid sexist, racist, and other prejudicial language

Remember that writing should be free of sexist, racist, and other prejudicial language. The Social Science and Humanities Research Council of Canada publication *On the Treatment of the Sexes in Social Research* by M. Eichler and J. Lapointe is helpful.

Structure your writing

The following is typical of the structure of a 10 000- to 15 000-word research project entailing data collection.

Title page

Examine your institution's rules about what should be included here.

Acknowledgments

You may want to acknowledge the help of various people, such as gatekeepers who gave you access to an organization, people who have read your drafts and provided you with feedback, or your supervisor for his or her advice.

List of contents

Your institution may have recommendations or prescriptions about the form this should take.

Practical tip  *Non-sexist writing*

One of the biggest problems (but by no means the only one) when trying to write in a non-sexist way is avoiding those 'her/his' and 'his/her' formulations. The easiest way of dealing with this is to write in the plural in such circumstances. For example:

- 'I wanted to give each respondent the opportunity to complete the questionnaire in his or her own time and in a location that was convenient for him or her.'

This sentence, although grammatically correct, can be rephrased as:

- 'I wanted to give respondents the opportunity to complete their questionnaires in their own time and in a location that was convenient for them.'

An abstract

This is a brief summary of your work. Not all institutions ask for this component, so see if it is required. Journal articles usually have abstracts; draw on them for how to approach this task.

Introduction

- You should explain what you are writing about and why it is important. Saying simply that you had a long-standing personal interest is not enough.

- You might indicate in general terms the theoretical approach or perspective you used and why.

- You should also at this point outline your research questions. In the case of dissertations based on qualitative research, research questions are often more open-ended than is the case with quantitative research. But do try to identify some research questions.

- The opening sentence or sentences are often the most difficult of all. Becker (1986) advised strongly against opening sentences that he described as 'vacuous.' He gave the example of 'This study deals with the problem of careers,' and adds that this kind of sentence 'is evasive, pointing to something without saying anything, or anything much, about it. *What* about careers?' (Becker 1986: 51). He suggested that such evasions arise from a concern of giving away the plot. In fact, he argued, it is much better to give readers a quick and clear indication of what is going to be presented and how. Kelley and De Graaf's and Beardsworth and Keil's opening sentences do rather well in this regard.

Literature review

This chapter reviews the main ideas and research on the area of interest. However, it should do more than simply summarize the relevant literature.

- You should, whenever appropriate, be critical in your approach.

- You should use your review of the literature to show why your research questions are important. For example, if the basis for your research questions is the point that although a lot of research has been done on X (a general topic or area, such as food consumption or football hooliganism), lit-

tle research has been done on X_1 (an aspect of X), the literature review is where you justify this assertion. Alternatively, it may be that there are two competing positions with regard to X_1 and you are going to investigate which one provides a better understanding. In the literature review, you should outline the nature of the differences between the competing positions. The literature review, then, locates your own research within a tradition of related research.

- Bear in mind that you want to return to much of the literature examined here in your discussion of findings and conclusion.

- Do not try to get everything you read into a literature review. Trying to force it all in (because of the great effort involved in uncovering and reading the material) is not going to help. The literature review is there to assist in developing an argument, and bringing in material of passing relevance may undermine your ability to get your argument across.

- Recall that reading the relevant literature should continue more or less throughout your research. This means that a literature review written before the data collection is provisional. Indeed, you may want to revise the initial review *but not to make the new review conform to unexpected, but now known, findings*. It did, after all, inform your research. Recall Ethical issue 10.1.

- Further thoughts on different ways of construing the literature are presented in Box 18.3. They were derived from a review of qualitative studies of organizations, but have a much broader applicability, including to quantitative research.

Research methods

The term 'research methods' is meant here as a kind of catch-all for several issues that need to be outlined: research design; sampling approach; how access was achieved if relevant; the procedures used (such as, if sending out a mail questionnaire, did it include a follow up of non-respondents); the nature of the questionnaire, interview schedule, participant observation role, observation schedule, coding frame, or whatever (these usually appear in an appendix, but you should comment on such things as your

---

Box 18.3 Presenting the qualitative research literature

Further useful advice on relating work to the literature can be gleaned from examining how articles based on qualitative research on organizations are composed. In their examination of such articles, Golden-Biddle and Locke (1993, 1997) argued that good articles in this area develop a story; that is, a clear and compelling framework around which the writing is structured. This idea is very much in tune with Wolcott's (1990: 18) recommendation to 'determine the basic story you are going to tell.' Golden-Biddle and Locke's research suggested that the presentation of the author's position in relation to the literature is an important component of storytelling and distinguished two ways in conveying the literature.

- **Constructing inter-textual coherence**—the author shows how existing contributions to the literature relate to each other and the research reported. The techniques are:
  - *synthesized coherence*—theory and research previously regarded as unconnected are pieced together;
  - *progressive coherence*—portrays the building-up of an area of knowledge around which there is considerable consensus;
  - *non-coherence*—recognition that there has been considerable disagreement in the many contributions to a certain research program.

Each of these strategies is designed to leave room for a contribution to be made.

- **Problematizing the situation**—the literature is then subverted by locating a problem. The following techniques are identified:
  - *incomplete*—the existing literature is not fully complete; there is a gap;
  - *inadequate*—the existing literature on the phenomenon has overlooked ways of looking at it that can greatly improve understanding it; alternative perspectives or frameworks are then introduced.

The key point about Golden-Biddle and Locke's account, of how literature is construed in research, is its use by writers to achieve a number of things.

- They demonstrate their knowledge and competence by referring to prominent writings in the field.
- They develop their version of the literature in such a way to lead up to the contribution they are making in the article.
- The gap or problem in the literature identified corresponds to the research questions.
- The idea of writing up research as storytelling serves as a useful reminder that reviewing the literature, which is part of the story, should link seamlessly with the rest of the article and not be considered a separate element.

---

style of questioning or observation and why you asked the things you did); problems of non-response; note-taking; issues of access and cooperation; coding issues; and analysis procedures. When discussing each, describe and defend the choices made, such as why a mailed questionnaire rather than a structured interview approach was used, or why a particular population was chosen for sampling.

Results

In this chapter you present the bulk of your findings. If you have a separate Discussion chapter, the results are generally presented with little commentary in terms of the literature or implications. If there is no Discussion chapter, you need to provide some reflections on the significance of your findings

for your research questions and for the literature. Bear these points in mind:

- Whichever approach is taken, remember not to include *all* your results. You should present and discuss only those findings that relate to your research questions. This may mean a rather painful process of leaving out many findings, but it is necessary, so that the thread of the argument is not lost.

- Your writing should point to particularly salient aspects of the tables, graphs, or other forms of analysis you present. Do not just summarize what a table shows; direct the reader to the component(s) of it that is especially striking from the point of view of your research questions. Try to ask yourself what story you want the table to convey and then relay it to your readers.

- Another sin to be avoided is simply presenting a graph or table without any comment whatsoever, leaving the reader to wonder why you think the finding is important.

- A particular problem in qualitative research for students is the need to leave out large parts of their data. As one experienced qualitative researcher put it: 'The major problem we face in qualitative inquiry is not to get data, but to get rid of it!' (Wolcott 1990: 18). You simply have to recognize that much of the rich data accumulated have to be jettisoned, or any sense of an argument in your work is likely to be lost. There is also the risk that your account of your findings will appear too descriptive and lack an analytical edge. This is why it is important to use research questions as a focus and to orient the presentation of findings to them.

Discussion

In the Discussion, you reflect on the implications of the findings for the research questions that drove the research. In other words, how do the results illuminate the research questions? If you have specified hypotheses, as Kelley and De Graaf (1997) did, the discussion revolves around whether the hypotheses were confirmed or not. If not, you might speculate about some possible reasons for, and the implications of, why they were not supported. Was the sample too small? Did you forget a key variable? In the case of Beardsworth and Keil's (1992) article, section 6 acts as a discussion section, and it is there that they brought out the main theoretical contribution of their research—the idea of food ambivalence—and explored its implications.

Conclusion

The main points here are as follows:

- A Conclusion is not the same as a summary. However, it is frequently useful to bring out, in the opening paragraph of the Conclusion, your argument thus far. This means relating your findings and your discussion of them to the original research questions. Thus, your brief summary should be a way to hammer home to readers the significance of what you have done. However, the Conclusion should do more than merely summarize.

- It should make clear the implications of the findings for your research questions.

- You may also suggest some ways in which your findings have implications for theories relating to your area of interest.

- You may also draw attention to any limitations of your research, now apparent with the benefit of hindsight, and suggest improvements for further research.

- It is often valuable to propose those areas of further research that are suggested by your findings.

Two things to avoid are engaging in speculations that take you too far away from your data or that cannot be substantiated by the data, and discussing issues or ideas not previously introduced.

Appendices

In appendices you may want to include such things as the questionnaire, coding frame, or observation schedule, letters sent to those sampled, and letters sent to and received from gatekeepers where the co-operation of an organization was required.

References

Include here all references cited in the text. For the format of the References section you should follow the one prescribed by your department. The format is usually a variation of the method employed in this book.

Finally

Remember to fulfil any obligations, such as supplying a copy of your dissertation, if, for example, your access to an organization was predicated on providing one; maintain the confidentiality of information given and the anonymity of informants and other research participants by securing and later destroying all of the primary data.

Checklist of issues to consider for writing up research

☑ Is there a good correspondence between the title of the project and its contents?

☑ Have you clearly specified your research questions?

☑ Have you clearly linked the literature cited to your research questions?

☑ Is your discussion of the literature critical and organized so that it is not just a summary of what you have read?

☑ Have you clearly outlined your research design and your research methods, including:
— why you chose a particular research design?
— why you chose a particular research method?
— why you implemented your research in a particular way (e.g., how the interview questions relate to the research questions or why you observed participants in particular situations)?
— how you selected your research participants?
— whether there were any issues to do with cooperation (e.g., response rates)?
— if your research required access to an organization, how and on what basis was agreement for access forthcoming?
— any difficulties encountered in implementing your research?
— steps taken to ensure that the research was ethically responsible?
— how data were analyzed?

☑ Have you presented your data so it relates to your research questions?

☑ Are the interpretations of your data fully supported with tables, figures, or segments from transcripts?

☑ Are those tables and/or figures properly labelled with a title and number?

☑ Does the discussion of the findings relate to the research questions?

☑ Does that discussion show how they shed light on the literature presented?

☑ If presenting tables and/or figures, are they commented upon in the discussion?

☑ Do the conclusions clearly allow the reader to establish what your research contributes to the literature?

☑ Have you explained the limitations of your study?

☑ Do your conclusions consist solely of a summary of findings? If so, rewrite them.

☑ Do the conclusions make clear the answers to your research questions?

☑ Have you broken up the text in each chapter with appropriate subheadings?

☑ Do you provide clear signposts in the course of writing, so that readers are clear about what to expect next, and why it is there?

☑ Does the writing avoid sexist, racist, and other prejudicial language?

☑ Have you checked to ensure that there is not excessive use of jargon?

☑ Have you included all necessary appendices (e.g., interview schedule, letters requesting access, communications with research participants)?

☑ Does the list of references include *all* items referred to in your text?

☑ Does the form for references follow precisely the style your institution requires?

☑ Have you ensured that your institution's requirements for submitting projects are fully met on such issues as number of words (so that it is neither too long nor too short) and whether an abstract and table of contents are required?

☑ Have you ensured that you do not quote excessively when presenting the literature?

☑ Have you fully acknowledged the work of others so that you cannot be accused of plagiarism?

☑ Have you acknowledged, probably in a preface, the help of others where appropriate (e.g., your supervisor, people who may have helped with interviews, people who read drafts)?

☑ Finally, go back and check for consistency of style. Is the tense consistent, the margins, pagination, and capitalization? Many forms are acceptable; the key is that they be consistently applied.

Ethical issue 18.1 *Ethical approval for student work*

By this point you have read many of the ethical issues involved in social research. Generally, for the type of work being described in this chapter, securing ethical approval is not necessary. Schools usually designate your supervisor as the person who should stop any unethical practices. Still it is your work and you should pay attention to the rules, flexible though they are. Supervisors have limited time to oversee your work and situations arise in the field in which you may have to make an immediate decision. In the end although you sign nothing, the ethical responsibility is yours.

Following are some examples of tricky ethical issues from actual research. To refresh your memory, see if you can spot them.

- You are supposed to interview Ms Jones. Her mother answers the door and asks to be interviewed. She is lonely so you interview her and throw away the data; later you interview Ms Jones.

- Introductory psychology students are told to participate in two experiments during the year. They do not have to do so, but if not, they have to write a five-page paper.

- To reduce lying, rather than asking, 'Have you ever masturbated?' the question is rephrased as 'At what age did you begin masturbating?'

- To see if answers in an interview are truthful, some questions are repeated. In a variation, respondents are asked about reading books or seeing movies that do not exist.

- Respondents are told that a questionnaire is anonymous. Actually, the questionnaire can be identified by little pinholes in the last page, done to keep track of non-respondents needing a reminder. This will save a lot of paper.

- A respondent asks after the interview is completely over that her case not be used.

And then in real life:

- Crown attorneys conduct a survey to find out who is sympathetic to sexual assault victims. The defence does the opposite. Each then tries to stack the jury.

- Survey researchers poll voters in different parts of the country for their attitudes. Candidates then tailor their speeches in specific locations to reflect those local findings.

Bibliography errors in Chapter 17 are found at *X*.

Abraham, J. (1994), 'Bias in Science and Medical Knowledge: The Opren *X*controversy,' *Sociology*, 28: 717–36.

Armstrong, D, Gosling, A., Weinman, J., and Marteau, T. (1997), 'The Place of Inter-Rater Reliability in Qualitative Research: *X*an Empirical Study,' *Sociology*, 31: 597-606*X*.

Atkinson, R. (1998), *The Life Story Interview* (Thousand Oaks, CA: Sage).

Barnard, M., and Frischer, M. (1995), 'Combining Quantitative and Qualitative Approaches: Researching HIV-Related Risk Behaviours among Drug Injectors',*X* *Addiction Research, X*351–62.

Barter, C., and *X*E. Renold (1999)*X* 'The Use of Vignettes in Qualitative Research,' *Social Research Update*, 25*X*.

Blaikie, A. (2001), 'Photographs in the Cultural Account: Contested *X* Narratives and Collective Memory in the Scottish Islands,' *Sociological Review*, 49*X*- 345-67.

Buchanan, D. R. (1992), 'An Uneasy Alliance: Combining Qualitative *X*And Quantitative Research Methods,' *Health Education Quarterly*, *X(font)*19: 117–35.

Charmaz, K., (2000), 'Grounded Theory: Objectivist and Constructivist Methods,' in Denzin, *X*N.K. and Lincoln, *X*Y.S. (eds.), *Handbook of Qualitative Research*, 2nd ed. (Thousand Oaks, CA: Sage).

*X*B. Czarniawska. (1998), *A Narrative Approach to Organization Studies* (Thousand Oaks, *X*XA: Sage).

SPACING*X*

Giulianotti, R. (1995), 'Participant Observation and Research into Football Hooliganism: Reflections on the Problems of Entrée and Everyday Risks,' *Sociology of Sport Journal*, 12: 1–20.

Reinharz, S. *X*1992, *Feminist Methods in Social Research* (New York*X*).

*X*ALPHABETIZATION

Okely, J. (1994), 'Thinking through Fieldwork*X*, in A. Bryman and R*X* G. Burgess (eds.), *Analyzing Qualitative Data* (London: Routledge).

Sheehan, K. (2001), 'E-Mail *X*survey *X*response *X*rates: A *X*review,' *Journal of Computer-Mediated Communication*, 6*X*. www.ascusc.org/jcmc/vol6/issue2/sheehan.html

Glossary

Terms appearing elsewhere in the Glossary are in *italic*.

Action research Approach in which the researcher and client collaborate to diagnose a problem and develop a solution based on the diagnosis.

Adjacency pair The tendency for certain kinds of talk activity to be linked.

Analytic induction Approach to the analysis of qualitative data in which collection of data continues and the hypothesis is modified until no cases inconsistent with it, no more deviant or negative cases of a phenomenon, are found.

Arithmetic mean Also known simply as the **mean**, this is the everyday average—namely, the total of a distribution of values divided by the number of values.

Biographical method See **life history method**.

Bivariate analysis The examination of the relationship between two variables, as in *contingency tables; correlation*.

CAQDAS An abbreviation of **c**omputer-**a**ssisted (or -aided) **q**ualitative **d**ata **a**nalysis **s**oftware.

Case study A *research design* that entails a detailed and intensive analysis of a single case or at most two or three cases for comparative purposes.

Causality A concern with establishing causal connections between variables, rather than mere *correlation* between them.

Cell The area in a table, such as a *contingency table*, where the rows and columns intersect and data are inserted.

Census The enumeration of an entire *population*; unlike a *sample*, which comprises a count of some units in a population, a census relates to all of them.

Chi-square test Chi-square (χ^2) is a test of *statistical significance*, employed to establish confidence that a finding displayed in a *contingency table* can be generalized from a *probability sample* to the *population* from which it is drawn.

Closed question A question employed in an *interview schedule* or *self-completion questionnaire* that presents the respondent with a fixed set of possible answers to choose from; also called **fixed-choice question**.

Cluster sample A sampling procedure in which the researcher first samples areas (i.e., clusters) and then samples units from within these clusters, usually using a *probability sampling* method.

Code, coding In *quantitative research*, codes act as tags to assign the data on each *variable* to a category of the variable in question. Numbers are then assigned to each category to allow easier computer processing. In *qualitative research*, coding breaks data down into component parts, which are then given names.

Coding frame A listing of the codes used in the analysis of data. For answers to a structured interview schedule or questionnaire, the coding frame delineates the categories used for each *open question*. With *closed questions*, the coding frame is essentially incorporated into the pre-given answers, hence the frequent use of the term 'pre-coded question' to describe such questions.

Coding manual This is the statement of instructions to coders that outlines all the possible categories for each dimension being coded.

Concept A name given to a category that organizes observations and ideas by virtue of their possessing common features.

Concurrent validity One of the main approaches to establishing *measurement validity*. It entails relating a measure to an existing criterion on which cases (e.g., people) are known to differ and that is relevant to the *concept* in question.

Connotation A term used in *semiotics* to refer to the meanings of a *sign* associated with the social context within which it operates: a sign's connotations are supplementary to and less immediately apparent than its *denotation*.

Constant An attribute on which cases do not differ; compare with *variable*.

Constructionism, constructionist An *ontological* position (often referred to as **constructivism**) that asserts that social phenomena and their meanings are continually being accomplished by social actors. It is antithetical to *objectivism* and *essentialism*.

Content analysis An approach to the analysis of documents and texts that seeks to quantify content in terms of predetermined categories and in a systematic and replicable manner. The term is sometimes used in connection with qualitative research as well—see *qualitative content analysis*.

Contingency table A table, comprising rows and columns, that shows the *relationship* between two *variables*. Usually, at least one of the variables is a *nominal variable*. Each *cell* in the table shows the number (usually percentage) of cases for that specific combination of the two variables.

Control group See experiment.

Convenience sample A sample that is selected because of its availability to the researcher; a form of *non-probability sample*.

Conversation analysis The fine-grained analysis of (recorded and then transcribed) talk as it occurs in naturally occurring situations, to uncover the underlying structures in interaction that make social order possible. Conversation analysis is grounded in *ethnomethodology*.

Correlation An approach to the analysis of relationships between *interval/ratio variables* and/or *ordinal variables* that seeks to assess the strength and direction of the relationship between the variables concerned. *Pearson's* r and *Spearman's rho* are both correlational measures. With *nominal* variables, the corresponding term is **measure of association**.

Covert research A term frequently used in connection with *ethnographic* research in which the researcher does not reveal his or her true identity. Such research violates the ethical principle of *informed consent*.

Cramér's V A statistical measure for assessing the strength of the relationship between two *nominal* variables.

Critical realism A *realist* epistemology that asserts that the study of the social world should be concerned with the identification of the structures that generate that world in order to change them, so that inequalities and injustices may be counteracted. Unlike a *positivist* epistemology that is *empiricist*, critical realism accepts that the structures may not be amenable to the senses.

Cross-sectional design A *research design* that entails the collection of data on more than one case (usually quite a lot more than one) and at a single point in time in order to collect a body of quantitative or quantifiable data in connection with two or more variables (usually many more than two), which are then examined to detect patterns of relationship.

Deductive An approach to the relationship between theory and research in which the latter is conducted with reference to hypotheses and ideas inferred from the theory; compare with *inductive*.

Denotation A term used in *semiotics* to refer to the principal and most manifest meaning of a *sign;* compare with *connotation*.

Dependent variable A *variable* that is caused by an *independent variable*.

Diary A term that in social research can mean different things. Three types can be distinguished: diaries written at the behest of a researcher; spontaneously produced personal diaries that can be analyzed as a *personal document*; and diaries written by researchers to log their activities and reflections.

Dichotomous variable A variable with just two categories.

Dimension An aspect of a *concept*.

Discourse analysis An approach to the analysis of talk and other forms of discourse that emphasizes the way language creates versions of reality.

Ecological fallacy The error of assuming that inferences about individuals can be made from aggregate data.

Ecological validity A concern with the question of whether social scientific findings are applicable to people's everyday, natural social settings.

Empiricism An approach to the study of reality that suggests that only knowledge gained through experience and the senses is acceptable.

Epistemology, epistemological A theory of knowledge, particularly employed in this book to refer to a stance on what should pass as acceptable knowledge; see *positivism*, *realism*, and *interpretivism*.

Essentialism A position that has close affinities with naive *realism*. Essentialism suggests that objects have essences that denote their authentic nature; compare with *constructionism*.

Eta A test of the strength of the *relationship* between two *variables*. The *independent variable* is usually a *nominal variable* while the *dependent variable* must be an *interval variable* or *ratio variable*.

Ethnography, ethnographer Like *participant observation*, a research method in which the researcher is immersed in a social setting for an extended period of time, observing behaviour, listening to what is said in conversations both between others and with the fieldworker, and asking questions. However, the term has a more inclusive sense than participant observation, which seems to emphasize the observational component. Also, the term is frequently used to refer to the written output of ethnographic research.

Ethnomethodology A sociological perspective concerned with the way in which social order is accomplished through talk and interaction. It provides the intellectual foundations of *conversation analysis*.

Evaluation research The kind that is concerned with the evaluation of real-life interventions, such as policy changes, in the social world.

Experiment A *research design* that rules out alternative explanations of findings deriving from it (i.e., possesses *internal validity*) by having at least (*a*) an experimental group, which is exposed to a treatment, and a control group, which is not, and (*b*) *random assignment* to the two groups.

Experimental group See experiment.

External validity A concern with the question of whether the results of a study can be generalized beyond the specific research context in which they were generated.

Face validity A concern with whether an *indicator* appears to reflect the content of the *concept* in question.

Facilitator See moderator.

Factor analysis A statistical technique used for large numbers of *variables* to establish whether there is a tendency for groups of them to be interrelated. It is often used with *multiple-indicator measures* to see if they cluster into one or more groups (factors) of indicators.

Field experiment A study in which the researcher directly intervenes in and/or manipulates a natural setting to observe what happens as a consequence.

Field notes A detailed chronicle by an *ethnographer* of events, conversations, and behaviour and the researcher's initial reflections on them.

Focus group A form of group interview in which: there are several participants (in addition to the *moderator/facilitator*); there is an emphasis in the questioning on a particular fairly tightly defined topic; and the emphasis is on interaction within the group and the joint construction of meaning.

Frequency table A table that displays the number and/or percentage of units (e.g., people) in different categories of a variable.

Gatekeeper A non-researcher who controls researcher access to a research setting.

Generalization, generalizability A concern with the *external validity* of research findings.

Grounded theory An approach to the analysis of qualitative data that aims to generate theory out of research data by achieving a close fit between the two.

Hermeneutics A term taken from theology, it is concerned with the theory and method of the interpretation of human action and emphasizes the need to understand from the perspective of the social actor.

Hypothesis An informed speculation, which is set up to be tested, about the possible relationship between two or more variables.

Independent variable A *variable* that has a causal impact on a *dependent variable*.

Index See scale.

Indicator A measure employed to refer to a *concept* when no direct measure is available.

Inductive An approach to the relationship between theory and research in which the former is generated out of the latter; compare with *deductive*.

Informed consent A key principle in social research ethics, it implies that prospective participants should be given as much information as needed to make an informed decision about whether to participate in a study.

Inter-coder reliability The degree to which two or more individuals agree about the *coding* of an item; likely to be an issue when *coding* answers to *open questions* in research based on *questionnaires* or *structured interviews*.

Internal reliability Degree to which indicators that make up a *scale* are consistent.

Internal validity A concern with the soundness of making a *causal* relationship between two or more variables.

Interpretivism An *epistemological* position that requires the social scientist to grasp the subjective meaning of social action.

Interval variable A *variable* where the distances between the categories are identical across its range of categories.

Intervening variable A *variable* that is affected by another one and that in turn has a causal impact on yet a third variable. Taking an intervening variable into account often facilitates the understanding of the relationship between two variables. It is Y in the following: $X \rightarrow Y \rightarrow Z$.

Interview guide A rather vague term used to refer to the brief list of memory prompts of areas to be covered that is often employed in *unstructured* and less often even in *semi-structured interviewing*.

Interview schedule A collection of questions designed to be asked by an interviewer; one is always used in a *structured interview*.

Intra-coder reliability The degree to which an individual differs over time in the *coding* of an item; likely to be an issue when *coding* answers to *open questions* in research based on *questionnaires* or *structured interviews*.

Kendall's tau A test of the strength of the *relationship* between two (generally) *ordinal variables*.

Key informant Someone who offers the researcher, usually in an *ethnography*, perceptive information about the social setting, important events, and individuals.

Life history interview Similar to the *oral history interview*, but the aim of this type of *unstructured interview* is to glean information on the entire biography of each respondent.

Life history method Also often referred to as the *biographical method*, this method emphasizes the inner experience of individuals and its connections with changing events and phases throughout the life course. The method usually entails *life history interviews* and the use of *personal documents* as data.

Likert scale A widely used format in which respondents are typically asked their degree of agreement with a series of attitude statements that together form a *multiple-indicator* measure. The scale is deemed to measure the intensity of respondents' feelings about an issue.

Longitudinal research A *research design* in which data are collected on a *sample* (of people, documents, etc.) on at least two occasions.

Mail questionnaire Traditionally this term was synonymous with the *postal questionnaire,* but with the arrival of e-mail-based questionnaires, either embedded or attached, many prefer to refer to them as postal rather than as mail.

Mean See arithmetic mean.

Measure of central tendency A measure, like the *arithmetic mean*, *median*, or *mode*, that summarizes a set or distribution of values.

Measure of dispersion A measure, like the *range* or *standard deviation* that summarizes the amount of variation in a set or distribution of values.

Measurement validity The degree to which a measure of a concept truly reflects that concept; see also *face validity* and *concurrent validity*.

Median The mid-point in a set or distribution of values.

Meta-analysis A method for determining the relationship between variables by drawing together the findings from several, often many, research studies. It is typically achieved through quantitative measurement and the use of statistical procedures.

Missing data Data relating to a case that are not available, for example, when a respondent in *social survey* research does not answer a question. These are referred to as 'missing values' in SPSS.

Mode The value that occurs most frequently in a set or distribution of values.

Moderated relationship A *relationship* between two *variables* is said to be moderated when it holds for some, but not all, categories of a third variable.

Moderator The person who guides the questioning of a *focus group*, also called a *facilitator*.

Multiple-indicator measure A measure that employs more than one *indicator* to measure a *concept*.

Multi-strategy research A term used to describe research that combines *quantitative* and *qualitative research*.

Multivariate analysis The examination of relationships among three or more *variables*.

Narrative analysis An approach that is sensitive to the temporal sequence that people, as tellers of stories about their lives or events around them, detect in their lives and thus inject into their accounts.

Naturalism A confusing term that has at least three distinct meanings: a commitment to adopting the principles of natural scientific method; being true to the nature of the phenomenon being investigated; and a style of research that seeks to minimize the intrusion of artificial methods of data collection.

Negative relationship A *relationship* between two *variables*, whereby as one increases the other decreases.

Nominal variable Also known as a *categorical variable*, it is comprised of categories that cannot be ranked.

Non-probability sample A sample not selected using a random sampling method. Essentially, this implies that some units in the population are more likely than others to be selected.

Non-response A source of *non-sampling error* that occurs when someone in a sample refuses to cooperate, cannot be contacted, or for some other reason cannot supply the required data.

Non-sampling error Differences between the *population* and a *sample* that arise either from deficiencies in the sampling approach, such as an inadequate *sampling frame* or *non-response*, or from such problems as poor question wording, poor interviewing, or a flawed data processing.

Null hypothesis A *hypothesis* of no relationship between two variables, the one you hope to disprove.

Objectivism An *ontological* position that asserts that the meaning of social phenomena have an existence independent of social actors; compare with *constructionism*.

Observation schedule A device used in *structured observation* that specifies the categories of behaviour that are to be observed and gives instructions on how behaviour should be allocated to those categories.

Official statistics Data compiled by or on behalf of state agencies in the course of conducting their business.

Ontology, ontological A theory of whether social entities can and should be considered objective entities with a reality external to specific social actors, or as social constructions built up from the perceptions and actions of these actors. See *objectivism* and *inductivism*.

Open question In an *interview schedule* or *self-completion questionnaire,* one that does not present the respondent with a set of possible answers to choose from and thus they must decide how to answer; compare with *closed question.*

Operational definition The definition of a *concept* in terms of the operations to be carried out in its measurement.

Operationism, operationalism A doctrine, mainly associated with a version of physics, that emphasizes the search for *operational definitions* of *concepts.*

Oral history interview A largely *unstructured interview* in which respondents are asked to recall and to reflect on events.

Ordinal variable A variable whose categories can be ranked (as in the case of *interval* and *ratio variables*), but the distances between the categories are not equal or known across the range.

Outlier An extreme value in a distribution of values. If a *variable* has one—either very high or very low—the *arithmetic mean* or the *range* will be distorted by it.

Paradigm A term deriving from the history of science, used to describe a cluster of beliefs that dictates for scientists in a particular discipline what should be studied, how research should be done, and how results should be interpreted.

Participant observation Research in which the researcher is immersed in a social setting for an extended period of time, observing behaviour, listening to what is said in conversations both between others and with the fieldworker, and asking questions. It usually includes interviewing *key informants* and studying documents and as such is difficult to distinguish from *ethnography.* In this book, participant observation is employed to refer to the observational aspect of *ethnography.*

Pearson's r A measure of the strength and direction of the *relationship* between two *interval/ratio variables.*

Personal documents Things such as *diaries,* letters, and autobiographies not written for an official purpose; they provide first-person accounts of the writer's life and events within it.

Phenomenology A philosophy concerned with how individuals make sense of the world around them and how, in particular, philosophers should keep separate any preconceptions concerning their grasp of that world.

Population The universe of units from which a *sample* is selected.

Positive relationship A *relationship* between two *variables,* whereby as one increases the other increases as well, or both simultaneously decrease.

Positivism An *epistemological* position that advocates the application of the methods of the natural sciences to the study of social reality.

Postal questionnaire A form of *self-completion questionnaire* sent to respondents and usually returned by them by mail.

Postmodernism A position with a distaste for both master-narratives and a *realist* orientation. Postmodernists display a preference for qualitative methods and a special concern with how research findings are represented in claims about truth.

Pre-coded question Another name for a *closed question,* but often preferred, because it shows the lack of necessity of a *coding frame;* the range of answers is predetermined and a numerical *code* pre-assigned, even pre-printed, for each possible answer.

Probability sample One selected using *random sampling* and in which each unit in the population has a known probability of being selected.

QSR NVivo A *CAQDAS* package that derives from, but then goes beyond NUD*IST (Non-numerical Unstructured Data Indexing Searching and Theorizing).

Qualitative content analysis An approach to constructing the meaning of documents and text that allows categories to emerge out of data and recognizes the significance of the context in which an item being analyzed (and the categories derived from it) appear.

Qualitative research Such research usually emphasizes words rather than quantification in the collection and analysis of data. As a *research strategy* it is *inductivist, constructivist,* and *interpretivist,* but qualitative researchers do not always subscribe to all three features; compare with *quantitative research.*

Quantitative research One that usually emphasizes quantification in the collection and analysis of data. As a *research strategy* it is *deductivist* and *objectivist* and incorporates a natural science model of the research process (in particular, one influenced by *positivism*), but quantitative researchers do not always subscribe to all three features; compare with *qualitative research.*

Quasi-experiment A *research design* that is close to being an *experiment* but that does not meet the requirements fully and therefore does not exhibit complete *internal validity.*

Questionnaire A collection of questions administered to respondents; when used on its own, the term usually denotes a *self-completion questionnaire.*

Quota sample A type of *non-probability sample,* it samples a *population* to match the relative proportions of people in different categories.

Random assignment A term used in connection in *experiments* to refer to allocation of research participants to the experimental or control group.

Random sampling The form in which the inclusion of any unit of a *population* occurs entirely by chance.

Range The difference between the maximum and the minimum value in a set or distribution of values associated with an *interval* or *ratio variable.*

Ratio variable An *interval variable* with a true zero point.

Reactivity, reactive effect A term used to describe the effect on research participants of knowing that they are being studied, which may result in atypical behaviour.

Realism An epistemological position that acknowledges a reality independent of the senses but accessible to the researcher's tools and theoretical speculations. It implies that the categories created by scientists refer to real objects in the natural or social worlds; see also *critical realism.*

Reflexivity A term used to refer to reflections by social researchers about the implications, for the knowledge of the social world they generate, of their methods, values, biases, decisions, and mere presence in the very situations they investigate.

Relationship An association between two variables whereby the variation in one variable coincides with variation in another variable.

Reliability The degree to which a measure of a concept is stable.

Replication, replicability The degree to which the results of a study can be reproduced. See also *internal reliability.*

Representative sample One that reflects the population accurately, so that it is a microcosm of the *population.*

Research design This term is employed in this book to refer to a framework for the collection and analysis of data. A choice of research design reflects decisions about the priority being given to a range of dimensions of the research process (such as *causality* and *generalization*).

Research strategy A term used in this book to refer to a general orientation to the conduct of social research (see *quantitative research* and *qualitative research*).

Respondent validation Sometimes called **member validation**, a process whereby researchers provide the people on whom they conducted research with an account of their findings and requests feedback on that account.

Response set The tendency among some respondents to *multiple-indicator measures* to reply in the same way to each constituent item, even if such a pattern is unlikely, or even contradictory.

Rhetoric A concern with how appeals to convince or persuade are devised.

Sample The segment of the population selected for research, a subset of the *population.* The selection may be based on *probability* or *non-probability sampling.*

Sampling error Differences in data between a *random sample* and the *population* from which it is selected.

Sampling frame A listing of all units in a *population* from which a *sample* is to be selected.

Scale A term usually used interchangeably with **index** to refer to a *multiple-indicator measure* in which the score a person gives for each component *indicator* is summed to provide a composite score for that person.

Secondary analysis The analysis of quantitative or qualitative data by researchers not involved in their original collection, often for purposes that may not have been envisaged by those responsible for the original data collection.

Self-completion questionnaire One that the respondent answers without the aid of an interviewer; sometimes called a **self-administered questionnaire.**

Semiotics An approach to the analysis of documents and related phenomena that emphasizes the importance of *signs;* it seeks out their deeper meaning and reveals how signs are designed to have an effect on consumers of those signs.

Semi-structured interview A term that covers a wide range of types, it typically refers to a context in which the interviewer has a series of questions in the general form of an *interview guide* but is able to vary the sequence of questions. The questions are frequently somewhat more general than those typically found in a *structured interview* schedule and the interviewer usually has some latitude to ask further questions in response to what are seen as significant replies.

Sensitizing concept A term to refer to a preference for treating a *concept* as a guide in an investigation, so that it points in a general way to what is relevant or important. This position contrasts with the idea of an *operational definition,* in which the meaning of a concept is fixed in advance of the investigation.

Sign A term employed in *semiotics.* A sign is made up of a signifier (manifestation of a sign) and the signified (that deeper meaning to which the signifier refers).

Simple random sample A *sample* in which each unit of the *population* has been selected entirely by chance and has an equal probability of being included.

Snowball sample A *non-probability sample* in which the researcher makes initial contact with a small group of people who are relevant to the research topic and then uses them to establish contacts with others.

Social desirability bias A distortion of data caused by respondents' attempts to construct accounts that conform to a socially acceptable model of behaviour.

Spearman's rho (ρ) A measure of the strength and direction of the *relationship* between two *ordinal variables*.

SPSS Originally short for **S**tatistical **P**ackage for the **S**ocial **S**ciences, it is a widely used computer program that allows quantitative data to be managed and analyzed.

Spurious relationship A *relationship* between two *variables* is said to be spurious if it is being produced by the impact of a common third variable on each of the two variables. When the third variable is controlled, the relationship disappears.

Standard deviation A measure of dispersion around the *mean*.

Standard error of the mean An estimate of the amount that a sample mean is likely to differ from the population mean.

Statistical significance (test of) Allows analysts to estimate their confidence that the results of a study of a randomly selected *sample* are generalizable to the *population* from which the sample was drawn. Such a test has nothing to do with substantive significance or importance. The *chi-square test* is an example of this kind of test. Using a test of statistical significance to generalize from a sample to a population is known as **statistical inference**.

Stratified random sample A *sample* in which units are *randomly sampled* from a *population* that has been previously divided into categories (strata).

Structured interview One in which all respondents are asked exactly the same questions in the same order with the aid of a formal *interview schedule*.

Structured observation Often called *systematic observation*, it is a technique in which the researchers employ explicitly formulated rules for what they should look for, including when and where, and how they should record behaviour.

Survey research A *cross-sectional design* in which data are collected from respondents, predominantly by *self-completion questionnaire* or by *structured interview* at *a single point in time* in order to collect a body of usually quantifiable data in connection with two or more *variables* (usually more than two) which are then examined to detect patterns of *relationship* among them.

Symbolic interactionism A theoretical perspective in sociology that views social interaction as taking place in terms of the meanings actors attach to their action and context.

Systematic sample A *probability sampling* method in which units are selected from a *sampling frame* according to fixed intervals, such as every fifth unit.

Text A term either in the conventional sense of a written work or in more recent years to refer to a wide range of phenomena, such as culture and even Disneyland.

Theoretical sampling A term used mainly in relation to *grounded theory* for sampling carried out in such a way that the emerging theoretical considerations guide the selection of cases and/or research participants. It is supposed to continue until a point of *theoretical saturation* is reached.

Theoretical saturation In *grounded theory*, the point when emerging *concepts* have been fully explored and no new insights are being generated. See also *theoretical sampling*.

Thick description A term devised by Geertz to refer to detailed accounts of a social setting that can form the basis for creating general statements about a culture and its significance in peoples' social lives.

Transcription, transcript The written translation of a recorded *interview* or *focus group* session.

Triangulation The use of more than one method or source of data in the study of a social phenomenon so that findings may be cross-checked.

Trustworthiness A set of criteria advocated by some writers for assessing the quality of *qualitative research*.

Turn-taking The notion from *conversation analysis* that order in everyday conversation is achieved through taking turns in conversations.

Univariate analysis The analysis of a single *variable* at a time.

Unobtrusive methods Those that do not make research participants aware of their being studied and therefore are not subject to *reactivity*.

Unstructured interview One in which the interviewer typically has only a list of topics, often called an *interview guide*. The questioning is usually informal and the phrasing and sequencing of questions vary from interview to interview.

Validity A concern with the integrity of the conclusions generated from a piece of research. There are different aspects of validity. See, in particular, *measurement validity*, *internal validity*, *external validity*, and *ecological validity*. When used on its own, *validity* is usually taken to refer to *measurement validity*.

Variable An attribute in terms of which cases differ or vary. See also *dependent variable* and *independent variable*; compare with *constant*.

Vignette techniques A method involving the presentation of hypothetical stimuli to individuals, which are interpreted by the researcher to reveal the underlying characteristics of the individual; also called **projective techniques**.

References

Abraham, J. (1994), 'Bias in Science and Medical Knowledge: The Opren Controversy,' *Sociology*, 28: 717–36.

Achille, M., and Ogloff J. (1997), 'When Is a Request for Assisted Suicide Legitimate?' *Canadian Jour. of Behavioural Sci.* 29: 19–27.

Adams, M. (2003), *Fire and Ice* (Toronto: Penguin).

Adriaenssens, C., and Cadman, L. (1999), 'An Adaptation of Moderated E-mail Focus Groups to Assess the Potential of a New Online (Internet) Financial Services Offer in the UK,' *Jour. of the Market Research Society*, 41: 417–24.

Altheide, D.L. (1996), *Qualitative Media Analysis* (Thousand Oaks, CA: Sage).

———— (2004), 'Ethnographic Content Analysis,' in M. Lewis-Beck, A. Bryman, and T. Liao (eds.), *The Sage Encycl. of Soc. Sci. Research Methods* (Thousand Oaks, CA: Sage).

Armstrong, D., Gosling, A., Weinman, J., and Marteau, T. (1997), 'The Place of Inter-Rater Reliability in Qualitative Research: An Empirical Study,' *Sociology*, 31: 597–606.

Armstrong, G. (1993), 'Like that Desmond Morris?' in D. Hobbs and T. May (eds.), *Interpreting the Field: Accounts of Ethnography* (Oxford: Clarendon Press).

———— (1998), *Football Hooligans: Knowing the Score* (Oxford: Berg).

Atkinson, M. (2002), 'Pretty in Ink: Conformity, Resistance and Negotiation in Women's Tattooing,' *Sex Roles*, 47: 219–35.

———— (2004), 'Tattooing and Civilizing Processes,' *Canadian Rev. of Sociology and Anthropology*, 41: 125–46.

Atkinson, P. (1981), *The Clinical Experience* (Farnborough: Gower).

———— (1990), *The Ethnographic Imagination: Textual Constructions of Society* (London: Routledge).

———— (2004), 'Life Story Interview,' in M. Lewis-Beck, A. Bryman, and T. Liao (eds.), *The Sage Encycl. of Soc. Sci. Research Methods* (Thousand Oaks, CA: Sage).

———— and Coffey, A. (1995), 'Realism and Its Discontents: On the Crisis of Cultural Representation in Ethnographic Texts,' in B. Adam and S. Allan (eds.), *Theorizing Culture: An Interdisciplinary Critique after Postmodernism* (London: UCL Press).

Baer, D., Curtis, J., and Grabb, E. (2001), 'Has Voluntary Association Membership Declined? Cross-national Analyses for Fifteen Countries,' *Canadian Rev. of Sociology*, 38: 249–74.

Bahr, H., Caplow, T., and Chadwick, B. (1983), 'Middletown III: Problems of Replication, Longitudinal Measurement, and Triangulation,' *Annual Rev. of Sociology*, 9: 243–64.

Bales, Robert (1951), *Interaction Process Analysis* (Cambridge, MA: Addison-Wesley).

Bampton, R., and Cowton, C.J. (2002), 'The E-Interview,' *Forum Qual. Social Research*, 3 (2): www.Qual.-research.net/fqs/.

Barnard, M., and Frischer, M. (1995), 'Combining Quantitative and Qualitative Approaches: Researching HIV-Related Risk Behaviours among Drug Injectors,' *Addiction Research*, 2: 351–62.

Barter, C., and Renold, E. (1999), 'The Use of Vignettes in Qualitative Research,' *Social Research Update*, 25.

Beagan, B. (2001), 'Micro Inequities and Everyday Inequalities: "Race," Gender, Sexuality and Class in Medical School,' *Canadian Jour. of Sociology*, 26: 583–610.

Beardsworth, A., and Keil, T. (1992), 'The Vegetarian Option: Varieties, Conversions, Motives and Careers,' *Sociological Rev.*, 40: 253–93.

———— ———— (1997), *Sociology on the Menu: An Invitation to the Study of Food and Society* (London: Routledge).

———— Bryman, A., Ford, J., and Keil, T. (n.d.), '"The Dark Figure" in Statistics of Unemployment and Vacancies: Some Sociological Implications,' discussion paper, Department of Social Sciences, Loughborough Univ.

———— ———— Keil, T., Goode, J., Haslam, C., and Lancashire, E. (2002), 'Women, Men and Food: The Significance of Gender for Nutritional Attitudes and Choices,' *Brit. Food Jour.*, 104: 470–91.

Becker, H. (1958), 'Problems of Inference and Proof in Participant Observation,' *Amer. Sociological Rev.*, 23: 652–60.

———— (1963), *Outsiders: Studies in the Sociology of Deviance* (NY: Free Press).

———— (1967), 'Whose Side Are We On?' *Social Problems*, 14: 239–47.

———— (1970), 'Practitioners of Vice and Crime,' in R. Habenstein (ed.), *Pathways to Data* (Chicago: Aldine).

———— (1986), *Writing for Social Scientists: How to Start and Finish Your Thesis, Book, or Article* (Chicago: Univ. of Chicago Press).

———— and Geer, B. (1957), 'Participant Observation and Interviewing: A Comparison,' *Human Organization*, 16: 28–32.

Beharrell, P. (1993), 'AIDS and the British Press,' in J. Eldridge (ed.), *Getting the Message: News, Truth and Power* (London: Routledge).

Belk, R., Sherry, J., and Wallendorf, M. (1988), 'A Naturalistic Inquiry into Buyer and Seller Behaviour at a Swap Meet,' *Jour. of Consumer Research*, 14: 449–70.

Berthoud, R. (2000a), 'Introduction: The Dynamics of Social Change,' in R. Berthoud and J. Gershuny (eds.), *Seven Years in the Lives of British Families: Evidence on the Dynamics of Social Change from the British Household Panel Survey* (Bristol: Policy Press).

—— (2000b), 'A Measure of Changing Health,' in R. Berthoud and J. Gershuny (eds.), *Seven Years in the Lives of British Families: Evidence on the Dynamics of Social Change from the British Household Panel Survey* (Bristol: Policy Press).

Bhaskar, R. (1989), *Reclaiming Reality: A Critical Introduction to Contemporary Philosophy* (London: Verso).

Billig, M. (1991), *Ideology and Opinions: Studies in Rhetorical Psychology* (Cambridge: Cambridge Univ. Press).

Blaikie, A. (2001), 'Photographs in the Cultural Account: Contested Narratives and Collective Memory in the Scottish Islands,' *Sociological Rev.*, 49: 345–67.

Blaxter, M. (1990), *Health and Lifestyles* (London: Routledge).

Bloor, M. (1997), 'Addressing Social Problems through Qualitative Research,' in D. Silverman (ed.), *Qualitative Research: Theory, Method and Practice* (London: Sage).

——, Frankland, S., Thomas, M., and Robson, K. (2001), *Focus Groups in Social Research* (London: Sage).

Blumer, H. (1954), 'What Is Wrong with Social Theory?' *Amer. Sociological Rev.*, 19: 3–10.

—— (1956), 'Sociological Analysis and the "Variable,"' *Amer. Sociological Rev.*, 21: 683–90.

—— (1962), 'Society as Symbolic Interaction,' in A. Rose (ed.), *Human Behavior and Social Processes* (London: Routledge & Kegan Paul).

Bottomore, T.B., and Rubel, M. (1963), *Karl Marx: Selected Writings in Sociology and Social Philosophy* (Harmondsworth, UK: Penguin).

Brannigan, A., Gemmell, W., Pevalin, D., and Wade, T. (2002), 'Self-control and Social Control in Childhood Misconduct and Aggression: The Role of Family Structure and Hyperactivity,' *Canadian Jour. of Criminology*, 44: 119–42.

Braverman, H. (1974), *Labour and Monopoly Capital: The Degradation of Work in the Twentieth Century* (London: Monthly Rev. Press).

Brayfield, A., and Rothe, H. (1951), 'An Index of Job Satisfaction,' *Jour. of Applied Psych.*, 35: 307–11.

Bridgman, P. (1927), *The Logic of Modern Physics* (NY: Macmillan).

Brown, A. (1998), 'Narrative, Politics and Legitimacy in an IT Implementation,' *Jour. of Management Studies*, 35: 35–58.

Brown, S., and Lightfoot, G. (2002), 'Presence, Absence, and Accountability: E-mail and the Mediation of Organizational Memory,' in S. Woolgar (ed.), *Virtual Society? Technology, Cyperbole, Reality* (Oxford: Oxford Univ. Press).

Bryman, A. (1988a), *Quantity and Quality in Social Research* (London: Routledge).

—— (1992), 'Quantitative and Qualitative Research: Further Reflections on Their Integration,' in J. Brannen (ed.), *Mixing Methods: Qualitative and Quantitative Research* (Aldershot: Avebury).

—— (1994), 'The Mead/Freeman Controversy: Some Implications for Qualitative Researchers,' in R. Burgess (ed.), *Studies in Qual. Methodology, Volume 4* (Greenwich, CT: JAI Press).

—— (1995), *Disney and His Worlds* (London: Routledge).

—— (1998), 'Quantitative and Qualitative Research Strategies in Knowing the Social World,' in T. May and M. Williams (eds.), *Knowing the Social World* (Buckingham: Open Univ. Press).

—— (1999), 'Global Disney,' in P. Taylor and D. Slater (eds.), *The American Century* (Oxford: Blackwell).

—— and Burgess, R. (1994a), 'Developments in Qualitative Data Analysis: An Introduction,' in A. Bryman and R. Burgess (eds.), *Analyzing Qualitative Data* (London: Routledge).

—— —— (1994b), 'Reflections on Qualitative Data Analysis,' in A. Bryman and R. Burgess (eds.), *Analyzing Qualitative Data* (London: Routledge).

—— —— (1999), 'Introduction: Qualitative Research Methodology: A Review,' in A. Bryman and R. Burgess (eds.), *Qualitative Research* (London: Sage).

—— and Cramer, D. (2001), *Quantitative Data Analysis with SPSS Release 10 for Windows: A Guide for Social Scientists* (London: Routledge).

—— —— (2004), 'Constructing Variables,' in M. Hardy and A. Bryman (eds.), *Handbook of Data Analysis* (London: Sage).

—— Haslam, C., and Webb, A. (1994), 'Performance Appraisal in UK Universities: A Case of Procedural Compliance?' *Assessment and Evaluation in Higher Educ.*, 19: 175–88.

—— Stephens, M., and Campo, C. (1996), 'The Importance of Context: Qualitative Research and the Study of Leadership,' *Leadership Quarterly*, 7: 353–70.

Buckle, A., and Farrington, D. (1994), 'Measuring Shoplifting by Systematic Observation,' *Psych., Crime and Law*, 1: 133–41.

Bulmer, M. (1980), 'Why Don't Sociologists Make More Use of Official Statistics?' *Sociology*, 14: 505–23.

—— (1984), 'Facts, Concepts, Theories and Problems,' in M. Bulmer (ed.), *Social Research Methods* (London: Macmillan).

Burman, M., Batchelor, S., and Brown, J. (2001), 'Researching Girls and Violence: Facing the Dilemmas of Fieldwork,' *Brit. Jour. of Criminology*, 41: 443–59.

Burrell, I., and Leppard, D. (1994), 'Fall in Crime a Myth as Police Chiefs Massage the Figures,' *Sunday Times*, 16 Oct., 1, 5.

Bury, M. (2001), 'Illness Narratives: Fact or Fiction?' *Sociology of Health and Illness*, 23: 263–85.

Buston, K. (1997), 'NUD*IST in Action: Its Use and Its Usefulness in a Study of Chronic Illness in Young People,'

Sociological Research Online, 2: www.socresonline.org.uk/socresonline/2/3/6.html.

Butcher, B. (1994), 'Sampling Methods: An Overview and Review,' *Survey Methods Centre Newsletter*, 15: 4–8.

Camerer, C. (1997), 'Taxi Drivers and Beauty Contests,' *Engineering and Sci.*, 60: 11–19.

Catterall, M., and Maclaran, P. (1997), 'Focus Group Data and Qualitative Analysis Programs: Coding the Moving Picture as well as Snapshots,' *Sociological Research Online*, 2: www.socresonline.org.uk/socresonline/2/1/6.html.

Charles, N., and Kerr, N. (1988), *Women, Food and Families* (Manchester: Manchester Univ. Press).

Charlton, T., Gunter, B., and Coles, D. (1998), 'Broadcast Television as a Cause of Aggression? Recent Findings from a Naturalistic Study,' *Emotional and Behavioural Difficulties*, 3: 5–13.

—— Coles, D., Panting, C., and Hannan, A. (1999), 'Behaviour of Nursery Class Children before and after the Availability of Broadcast Television: A Naturalistic Study of Two Cohorts in a Remote Community,' *Jour. of Social Behaviour and Personality*, 14: 315–24.

Charmaz, K. (1983), 'The Grounded Theory Method: An Explication and Interpretation,' in R. Emerson (ed.), *Contemporary Field Research: A Collection of Readings* (Boston: Little, Brown).

—— (1997), 'Identity Dilemmas of Chronically Ill Men,' in A. Strauss and J. Corbin (eds.), *Grounded Theory in Practice* (Thousand Oaks, CA: Sage).

—— (2000), 'Grounded Theory: Objectivist and Constructivist Methods,' in N. Denzin and Y. Lincoln (eds.), *Handbook of Qualitative Research*, 2nd ed. (Thousand Oaks, CA: Sage).

—— (2002), 'Qualitative Interviewing and Grounded Theory Analysis,' in J. Gubrium and J. Holstein (eds.), *Handbook of Interview Research: Context and Method* (Thousand Oaks, CA: Sage).

—— (2004), 'Grounded Theory,' in M. Lewis-Beck, A. Bryman, and T. Liao (eds.), *The Sage Encycl. of Soc. Sci. Research Methods* (Thousand Oaks, CA: Sage).

Chin, M., Fisak, B., and Sims, V. (2002), 'Development of the Attitudes Toward Vegetarianism Scale,' *Anthrozoös*, 15: 333–42.

Cicourel, A. (1964), *Method and Measurement in Sociology* (NY: Free Press).

—— (1982), 'Interviews, Surveys, and the Problem of Ecological Validity,' *Amer. Sociologist*, 17: 11–20.

Clairborn, W. (1969), 'Expectancy Effects in the Classroom: A Failure to Replicate,' *Jour. of Educational Psych.*, 60: 377–83.

Clancey, W. (2001), 'Field Science Ethnography: Methods for Systematic Observation of an Arctic Expedition,' *Field Methods*, 13: 223–43.

Clapper, D., and Massey, A. (1996), 'Electronic Focus Groups: A Framework for Exploration,' *Information and Management*, 30: 43–50.

Clayman, S., and Gill, V.T. (2004), 'Conversation Analysis,' in M. Hardy and A. Bryman (eds.), *Handbook of Data Analysis* (London: Sage).

Cobanoglu, C., Ward, B., and Moreo, P.J. (2001), 'A Comparison of Mail, Fax and Web-based Survey Methods,' *Intnatl. Jour. of Market Research*, 43: 441–52

Coffey, A. (1999), *The Ethnographic Self: Fieldwork and the Representation of Reality* (London: Sage).

—— and Atkinson, P. (1996), *Making Sense of Qualitative Data: Complementary Research Strategies* (Thousand Oaks, CA: Sage).

—— Holbrook, B., and Atkinson, P. (1996), 'Qualitative Data Analysis: Technologies and Representations,' *Sociological Research Online*, 2: www.socresonline.org.uk/socresonline/1/1/4.html.

Coleman, C., and Moynihan, J. (1996), *Understanding Crime Data: Haunted by the Dark Figure* (Buckingham: Open Univ. Press).

Coleman, H., Grant, C., and Collins, J. (2001), 'Inhalant Use by Canadian Aboriginal Youth,' *Jour. of Child and Adolescent Substance Abuse*, 10: 1–20.

Collins, M. (1997), 'Interviewer Variability: A Review of the Problem,' *Jour. of the Market Research Society*, 39: 67–84.

Collins, R. (1994), *Four Sociological Traditions*, rev. ed. (NY: Oxford Univ. Press).

Conger, J., and Kanungo, R. (1998), *Charismatic Leadership in Organizations* (Thousand Oaks, CA: Sage).

Cook, T., and Campbell, D. (1979), *Quasi-Experimentation: Design and Analysis for Field Settings* (Boston, MA: Houghton Mifflin).

Corti, L. (1993), 'Using Diaries in Social Research,' *Social Research Update*, 2.

Coté, J., and Allahar, A. (1994), *Generation on Hold: Coming of Age in the Late Twentieth Century* (Toronto: Stoddart).

Couper, M. (2000), 'Web Surveys: A Review of Issues and Approaches,' *Public Opinion Quarterly*, 64: 464–94.

—— and Hansen, S. (2002), 'Computer-assisted Interviewing,' in J. Gubrium and J. Holstein (eds.), *Handbook of Interview Research: Context and Method* (Thousand Oaks, CA: Sage).

Coxon, A. (1994), 'Diaries and Sexual Behaviour: The Use of Sexual Diaries as Method and Substance in Researching Gay Men's Response to HIV/AIDS,' in M. Boulton (ed.), *Challenge and Innovation: Methodological Advances in Social Research on HIV/AIDS* (London: Taylor & Francis).

Craig, G. (2004), 'Managing Safety in Policy Research,' in S. Becker and A. Bryman (eds.), *Understanding Research for Social Policy and Practice: Themes, Methods, and Approaches* (Bristol: Policy Press).

Cramer, D. (1998), *Fundamental Statistics for Social Research* (London: Routledge).

Crook, C., and Light, P. (2002), 'Virtual Society and the Cultural Practice of Study,' in S. Woolgar (ed.), *Virtual Society? Technology, Cyperbole, Reality* (Oxford: Oxford Univ. Press).

Curasi, C. (2001) 'A Critical Exploration of Face-to-face Interviewing vs. Computer-mediated Interviewing,' *Intnatl. Jour. of Market Research*, 43: 361–75.

Czaja, R., and Blair, J. (1996), *Designing Surveys: A Guide to Decisions and Procedures* (Thousand Oaks, CA: Sage).

Dale, A., Arber, S., and Proctor, M. (1988), *Doing Secondary Analysis* (London: Unwin Hyman).

Davies, P. (2000), 'Doing Interviews with Female Offenders,' in V. Jupp, P. Davies, and P. Francis (eds.), *Doing Criminological Research* (London: Sage).

Deacon, D., Bryman, A., and Fenton, N. (1998), 'Collision or Collusion? A Discussion of the Unplanned Triangulation of Quantitative and Qualitative Research Methods,' *Intnatl. Jour. of Social Research Methodology*, 1: 47–63.

——, Pickering, M., Golding, P., and Murdock, G. (1999), *Researching Communications: A Practical Guide to Methods in Media and Cultural Analysis* (London: Arnold).

Demers, A. (1996), 'Effect of Support Groups on Family Caregivers to the Frail Elderly,' *Canadian Jour. on Aging*, 15: 129–44.

Denzin, N. (1970), *The Research Act in Sociology* (Chicago: Aldine).

—— (1994), 'Evaluating Qualitative Research in the Poststructural Moment: The Lessons James Joyce Teaches Us,' *Intnatl. Jour. of Qual. Studies in Educ.*, 7: 295–308.

Desroches, F. (1990), 'Tearoom Trade: A Research Update,' *Qual. Sociology* 13: 39–61.

Dickinson, H. (1993), 'Accounting for Augustus Lamb: Theoretical and Methodological Issues in Biography and Historical Sociology,' *Sociology*, 27: 121–32.

Dinovitzer, R., Hagan, J., and Parker, P. (2003), 'Choice and Circumstance: Social Capital and Planful Competence in the Attainments of Immigrant Youth,' *Canadian Jour. of Sociology*, 28: 463–88.

Ditton, J. (1977), *Part-time Crime: An Ethnography of Fiddling and Pilferage* (London: Macmillan).

Dommeyer, C., and Moriarty, E. (2000), 'Comparison of Two Forms of an E-Mail Survey: Embedded vs. Attached,' *Intnatl. Jour. of Market Research*, 42: 39–50.

Dunning, E., Murphy, P., and Williams, J. (1988), *The Roots of Football Hooliganism: An Historical and Sociological Study* (London: Routledge).

Durkheim, E. (1938), *The Rules of Sociological Method*, trans. S. Solavay and J. Mueller (NY: Free Press).

—— (1952), *Suicide: A Study in Sociology*, trans. J. Spaulding and G. Simpson (London: Routledge & Kegan Paul).

Dwyer, J., Mayer, L., Dowd, K., Kandel, R., and Mayer, J. (1974), 'The New Vegetarians: The Natural High?' *Jour. of the Amer. Dietetic Assoc.*, 65: 529–36.

Dyer, W., and Wilkins, A. (1991), 'Better Stories, Not Better Constructs, to Generate Better Theory: A Rejoinder to Eisenhardt,' *Academy of Management Rev.*, 16: 613–19.

Elliott, H. (1997), 'The Use of Diaries in Sociological Research on Health Experience,' *Sociological Research Online*, 2, http://www.socresonline.org.uk/socresonline/2/2/7.html.

Fenton, N., Bryman, A., and Deacon, D. (1998), *Mediating Social Science* (London: Sage).

Festinger, L., Riecken, H., and Schachter, S. (1956), *When Prophecy Fails* (NY: Harper & Row).

Finch, J. (1985), '"It's Great to Have Someone to Talk to": The Ethics and Politics of Interviewing Women,' in C. Bell and H. Roberts (eds.), *Social Researching: Politics, Problems, Practice* (London: Routledge & Kegan Paul).

—— (1987), 'The Vignette Technique in Survey Research,' *Sociology*, 21: 105–14.

—— and Hayes, L. (1994), 'Inheritance, Death and the Concept of the Home,' *Sociology*, 28: 417–33.

—— and Mason, J. (1990), 'Decision Taking in the Fieldwork Process: Theoretical Sampling and Collaborative Working,' in R. Burgess (ed.), *Studies in Qual. Methodology*, 2: 25–50.

Fine, G. (1996), 'Justifying Work: Occupational Rhetorics as Resources in Kitchen Restaurants,' *Administrative Sci. Quarterly*, 41: 90–115.

Foddy, W. (1993), *Constructing Questions for Interviews and Questionnaires: Theory and Practice in Social Research* (Cambridge: Cambridge Univ. Press).

Forster, N. (1994), 'The Analysis of Company Documentation,' in C. Cassell and G. Symon (eds.), *Qualitative Methods in Organizational Research* (London: Sage).

Foster, J. (1995), 'Informal Social Control and Community Crime Prevention,' *Brit. Jour. of Criminology*, 35: 563–83.

Fowler, F. (1993), *Survey Research Methods*, 2nd ed. (Newbury Park, CA: Sage).

—— and Mangione, T. (1990), *Standardized Survey Interviewing: Minimizing Interviewer-Related Error* (Beverly Hills, CA: Sage).

Frazer, R., and Wiersma, U. (2001), 'Prejudice vs. Discrimination in the Employment Interview: We May Hire Equally, but Our Memories Harbour Prejudice,' *Human Relations*, 54: 173–91.

Frean, A. (1998), 'Children Read More after Arrival of TV,' *The Times*, 29 April: 7.

Frey, J. (2004), 'Telephone Surveys,' in M. Lewis-Beck, A. Bryman, and T. Liao (eds.), *The Sage Encycl. of Soc. Sci. Research Methods* (Thousand Oaks, CA: Sage).

Frohlich, K., Potvin, L., Chabot, P., and Corin, E. (2002), 'A Theoretical and Empirical Analysis of Context: Neighbourhoods, Smoking, and Youth,' *Social Sci. and Medicine*, 54: 1401–17.

Gabor, T., Hung, K., Mihorean, S., and St-Onge, C. (2002), 'Canadian Homicide Rates: A Comparison of Two Data Sets,' *Canadian Jour. of Criminology*, 44: 351–63.

Gabriel, Y. (1998), 'The Use of Stories,' in G. Symon and C. Cassell (eds.), *Qualitative Methods and Analysis in Organizational Research* (London: Sage).

Gans, H. J. (1962), *The Urban Villagers* (NY: Free Press).

—— (1968), 'The Participant-Observer as Human Being: Observations on the Personal Aspects of Field Work,' in H. Becker (ed.), *Institutions and the Person: Papers Presented to Everett C. Hughes* (Chicago: Aldine).

Garfinkel, H. (1967), *Studies in Ethnomethodology* (Englewood Cliffs, NJ: Prentice-Hall).

Gazso-Windlej, A., and McMullin, J. (2003), 'Doing Domestic Labour: Strategising in a Gendered Domain,' *Canadian Jour. of Sociology*, 28: 341–66.

Geertz, C. (1973), 'Thick Description: Toward an Interpretive Theory of Culture,' in C. Geertz, *The Interpretation of Cultures* (NY: Basic Books).

Gephart, R. (1988), *Ethnostatistics: Qualitative Foundations for Quantitative Research* (Newbury Park, CA: Sage).

Gerson, K., and Horowitz, R. (2002), 'Observation and Interviewing: Options and Choices,' in T. May (ed.), *Qualitative Research in Action* (London: Sage).

Giddens, A. (1984), *The Constitution of Society* (Cambridge, UK: Polity).

Gilbert, G., and Mulkay, M. (1984), *Opening Pandora's Box: A Sociological Analysis of Scientists' Discourse* (Cambridge: Cambridge Univ. Press).

Gill, R. (1996), 'Discourse Analysis: Practical Implementation,' in J. Richardson (ed.), *Handbook of Qualitative Research Methods for Psychology and the Social Sciences* (Leicester: BPS Books).

—— (2000), 'Discourse Analysis,' in M. Bauer and G. Gaskell (eds.), *Qualitative Researching with Text, Image and Sound* (London: Sage).

Ginn, J., and Arber, S. (1995), 'Exploring Mid-life Women's Employment,' *Sociology*, 29: 73–94.

Giulianotti, R. (1995), 'Participant Observation and Research into Football Hooliganism: Reflections on the Problems of Entrée and Everyday Risks,' *Sociology of Sport Jour.*, 12: 1–20.

—— (1997), 'Enlightening the North: Aberdeen Fanzines and Local Football Identity,' in G. Armstrong and R. Giulianotti (eds.), *Entering the Field: New Perspectives on World Football* (Oxford: Berg).

Gladney, A., Ayars, C., Taylor, W., Liehr, P., and Meininger, J. (2003), 'Consistency of Findings Produced by Two Multidisciplinary Research Teams,' *Sociology*, 37: 297–313.

Glaser, B. (1992), *Basics of Grounded Theory Analysis* (Mill Valley, CA: Sociology Press).

—— and Strauss, A. (1967), *The Discovery of Grounded Theory: Strategies for Qualitative Research* (Chicago: Aldine).

Glock, C. (1988), 'Reflections on Doing Survey Research,' in H. O'Gorman (ed.), *Surveying Social Life* (Middletown, CT: Wesleyan Univ. Press).

Glucksmann, M. (1994), 'The Work of Knowledge and the Knowledge of Women's Work,' in M. Maynard and J. Purvis (eds.), *Researching Women's Lives from a Feminist Perspective* (London: Taylor & Francis).

Goffman, E. (1956), *The Presentation of Self in Everyday Life* (NY: Doubleday).

—— (1963), *Stigma: Notes on the Management of Spoiled Identity* (Harmondsworth, UK: Penguin).

Gold, R. (1958), 'Roles in Sociological Fieldwork,' *Social Forces*, 36: 217–23.

Golden-Biddle, K., and Locke, K. (1993), 'Appealing Work: An Investigation of how Ethnographic Texts Convince,' *Organization Sci.*, 4: 595–616.

—— (1997), *Composing Qualitative Research* (Thousand Oaks, CA: Sage).

Goode, E. (1996), 'The Ethics of Deception in Social Research: A Case Study,' *Qual. Sociology*, 19: 11–33.

Gottdiener, M. (1997), *The Theming of America: Dreams, Visions and Commercial Spaces* (Boulder, CO: Westview Press).

Gouldner, A. (1968), 'The Sociologist as Partisan,' *Amer. Sociologist*, 3: 103–16.

Goyder, J., Guppy, N., and Thompson, M. (2003), 'The Allocation of Male and Female Occupational Prestige in an Ontario Urban Area: A Quarter-century Replication,' *Canadian Rev. of Sociology and Anthropology,* 40: 417–39.

Grabb, E., and Curtis, J. (2004), *Regions Apart: The Four Societies of Canada and the U.S.* (Don Mills, ON: Oxford University Press).

Greene, J. (1994), 'Qualitative Program Evaluation: Practice and Promise,' in N. Denzin and Y. Lincoln (eds.), *Handbook of Qual. Research* (Thousand Oaks, CA: Sage).

—— (2000), 'Understanding Social Programs through Evaluation,' in N. Denzin and Y. Lincoln (eds.), *Handbook of Qual. Research*, 2nd ed. (Thousand Oaks, CA: Sage).

Griffin, J. (1961), *Black Like Me* (Boston: Houghton Mifflin).

Guba, E., and Lincoln, Y. (1994), 'Competing Paradigms in Qualitative Research,' in N. Denzin and Y. Lincoln (eds.), *Handbook of Qual. Research* (Thousand Oaks, CA: Sage).

Gubrium, J., and Holstein, J. (1997), *The New Language of Qualitative Method* (NY: Oxford Univ. Press).

Halford, S., Savage, M., and Witz, A. (1997), *Gender, Careers and Organisations: Current Developments in Banking, Nursing and Local Government* (London: Sage).

Hammersley, M. (1992*a*), 'By What Criteria Should Ethnographic Research Be Judged?' in M. Hammersley, *What's Wrong with Ethnography* (London: Routledge).

—— (1992*b*), 'Deconstructing the Qualitative-Quantitative Divide,' in M. Hammersley, *What's Wrong with Ethnography* (London: Routledge).

—— (1996), 'The Relationship between Qualitative and Quantitative Research: Paradigm Loyalty versus Methodological Eclecticism,' in J. Richardson (ed.), *Handbook of*

Research Methods for Psychology and the Social Sciences (Leicester: BPS Books).

——— (1997), 'Qualitative Data Archiving: Some Reflections on Its Prospects and Problems,' *Sociology*, 31: 131–42.

——— and Atkinson, P. (1995), *Ethnography: Principles in Practice*, 2nd ed. (London: Routledge).

——— Scarth, J., and Webb, S. (1985), 'Developing and Testing Theory: The Case of Research on Pupil Learning,' in R. Burgess (ed.), *Issues in Educational Research: Qualitative Methods* (London: Farwin).

Healey, J. (2002), *Statistics: A Tool for Social Research,* 6th ed. (Belmont, CA: Wadsworth).

Heath, C. (1997), 'The Analysis of Activities in Face to Face Interaction Using Video,' in D. Silverman (ed.), *Qualitative Research: Theory, Method and Practice* (London: Sage).

Heritage, J. (1984), *Garfinkel and Ethnomethodology* (Cambridge, UK: Polity).

——— (1987), 'Ethnomethodology,' in A. Giddens and J. Turner (eds.), *Social Theory Today* (Cambridge, UK: Polity).

Hesse-Biber, S. (1995), 'Unleashing Frankenstein's Monster? The Use of Computers in Qualitative Research,' *Studies in Qual. Methodology*, 5: 25–41.

Hessler, R., Downing, J., Beltz, C., Pelliccio, A., Powell, M., and Vale, W. (2003), 'Qualitative Research on Adolescent Risk Using E-mail: A Methodological Assessment,' *Qual. Sociology*, 26: 111–24.

Hier, S. (2000), 'The Contemporary Structure of Canadian Racial Supremacism; Networks, Strategies, and New Technologies,' *Canadian Jour. of Sociology*, 25: 471–94.

——— (2002), 'Raves and the Ecstacy Panic: A Case Study in the Subversive Nature of Moral Regulation,' *Canadian Jour. of Sociology*, 27: 33–57.

Hiller, H., and DiLuzio, L. (2004), 'The Interviewee and the Research Interview: Analyzing a Neglected Dimension in Research,' *Canadian Rev. of Sociology and Anthropology,* 41: 1–26.

Hine, V. (2000), *Virtual Ethnography* (London: Sage).

Hirsch, J. (1981), *Family Photographs* (NY: Oxford Univ. Press).

Ho, K., Baber, Z., and Khondker, H. (2002) 'Sites of Resistance: Alternative Websites and State-society Relations,' *Brit. Jour. of Sociology*, 53: 127–48.

Hobbs, D. (1988), *Doing the Business: Entrepreneurship, the Working Class and Detectives in the East End of London* (Oxford: Oxford Univ. Press).

——— (1993), 'Peers, Careers, and Academic Fears: Writing as Field-work,' in D. Hobbs and T. May (eds.), *Interpreting the Field: Accounts of Ethnography* (Oxford: Clarendon Press).

———, Hadfield, P., Lister, S., and Winlow, S. (2003), *Bouncers: Violence and Governance in the Night-time Economy* (Oxford: Oxford Univ. Press).

Hochschild, A. (1983), *The Managed Heart* (Berkeley and Los Angeles: Univ. of California Press).

Hodson, R. (1996), 'Dignity in the Workplace under Participative Management,' *Amer. Sociological Rev.*, 61: 719–38.

——— (1999), *Analyzing Documentary Accounts* (Thousand Oaks, CA: Sage).

Holbrook, A., Green, M., and Krosnick, J. (2003), 'Telephone Versus Face-to-face Interviewing of National Probability Samples with Long Questionnaires: Comparisons of Respondent Satisficing and Social Desirability Response Bias,' *Public Opinion Quarterly*, 67: 79–125.

Holbrook, B., and Jackson, B. (1996), 'Shopping Around: Focus Group Research in North London,' *Area*, 28: 136–42.

Homan, R. (1991), *The Ethics of Social Research* (London: Longman).

——— and Bulmer, M. (1982), 'On the Merits of Covert Methods: A Dialogue,' in M. Bulmer (ed.), *Social Research Ethics* (London: Macmillan).

Houghton, E. (1998), 'Sex Is Good for You,' *Guardian*, 92 (Jan.): 14–15.

Howell, J., and Frost, P. (1989), 'A Laboratory Study of Charismatic Leadership,' *Organizational Behavior and Human Decision Processes*, 43: 243–69.

Huey, L. (2003), 'Explaining Odlin Road: Insecurity and Exclusivity,' *Canadian Jour. of Sociology*, 28: 367–86.

Hughes, E. (1943), *French Canada in Transition* (Chicago: Univ. of Chicago Press).

Hughes, G. (2000), 'Understanding the Politics of Criminological Research,' in V. Jupp, P. Davies, and P. Francis (eds.), *Doing Criminological Research* (London: Sage).

Hughes, J. (1990), *The Philosophy of Social Research*, 2nd ed. (Harlow: Longman).

Hughes, K., MacKintosh, A. M., Hastings, G., Wheeler, C., Watson, J., and Inglis, J. (1997), 'Young People, Alcohol, and Designer Drinks: A Quantitative and Qualitative Study,' *Brit. Medical Jour.*, 314: 414–18.

Hughes, R. (1998), 'Considering the Vignette Technique and its Application to a Study of Drug Injecting and HIV Risk and Safer Behaviour,' *Sociology of Health and Illness*, 20: 381–400.

Humphreys, L. (1970), *Tearoom Trade: Impersonal Sex in Public Places* (Chicago: Aldine).

Hutchby, I., and Wooffitt, R. (1998), *Conversation Analysis* (Cambridge, UK: Polity).

Jagger, E. (1998), 'Marketing the Self, Buying an Other: Dating in a Post Modern, Consumer Society,' *Sociology*, 32: 795–814.

——— (2001), 'Marketing Molly and Melville: Dating in a Postmodern, Consumer Society,' *Sociology*, 35: 39–57.

Jamieson, J. (2000), 'Negotiating Danger in Fieldwork on Crime: A Researcher's Tale,' in G. Lee-Treweek and S. Linkogle (eds.), *Danger in the Field: Risk and Ethics in Social Research* (London: Routledge).

Jayaratne, T., and Stewart, A. (1991), 'Quantitative and Qualitative Methods in the Social Sciences: Current Feminist

Issues and Practical Strategies,' in M. Fonow and J. Cook (eds.), *Beyond Methodology: Feminist Scholarship as Lived Research* (Bloomington, IN: Indiana Univ. Press).

John, I.D. (1992), 'Statistics as Rhetoric in Psychology,' *Australian Psychologist*, 27: 144–9.

Johnson, J., Bottorff, J., Moffat, B., Ratner, P., Shoveller, J., and Lovato, C. (2003), 'Tobacco Dependence: Adolescents' Perspectives on the Need to Smoke,' *Social Sci. and Medicine*, 56: 1481–92.

Jones, K. (2000), 'Constructing rBST in Canada: Biotechnology, Instability, and the Management of Nature,' *Canadian Jour. of Sociology*, 25: 311–41.

Kanayama, T. (2003), 'Ethnographic Research on the Experience of Japanese Elderly People Online,' *New Media and Society*, 5: 267–88.

Karabanow, J. (2002), 'Open for Business: Exploring the Life Stages of Two Canadian Street Youth Shelters,' *Jour. of Sociology and Social Welfare,* 29: 99–116.

Katz, J. (2002), 'From How to Why: On Luminous Description and Causal Inference in Ethnography (Part 2),' *Ethnography*, 3: 63–90.

Katz, J., Kuffel, S., and Coblentz, A. (2002), 'Are There Gender Differences in Sustaining Dating Violence?' *Jour. of Family Violence,* 17: 247–71.

Kelley, J., and De Graaf, N. (1997), 'National Context, Parental Socialization, and Religious Belief: Results from 15 Nations,' *Amer. Sociological Rev.*, 62: 639–59.

Kelly, L., Burton, S., and Regan, L. (1994), 'Researching Women's Lives or Studying Women's Oppression? Reflections on What Constitutes Feminist Research,' in M. Maynard and J. Purvis (eds.), *Researching Women's Lives from a Feminist Perspective* (London: Taylor & Francis).

Kendall, L. (1999), 'Recontextualizing "Cyberspace": Methodological Considerations for On-line Research,' in S. Jones (ed.), *Doing Internet Research: Critical Issues and Methods for Examining the Net* (Thousand Oaks, CA: Sage).

Kent, R., and Lee, M. (1999), 'Using the Internet for Market Research: A Study of Private Trading on the Internet,' *Jour. of the Market Research Society*, 41: 377–85.

Kerr, D. (2004), 'Family Transformations and the Well-being of Children: Recent Evidence from Canadian Longitudinal Data,' *Jour. of Comparative Family Studies*, 35: 73–90.

Kimmel, A. (1988), *Ethics and Values in Applied Social Research* (Newbury Park, CA: Sage).

Kitzinger, J. (1993), 'Understanding AIDS: Researching Audience Perceptions of Acquired Immune Deficiency Syndrome,' in J. Eldridge (ed.), *Getting the Message: News, Truth and Power* (London: Routledge).

—— (1994), 'The Methodology of Focus Groups: The Importance of Interaction between Research Participants,' *Sociology of Health and Illness*, 16, 1994: 103–21.

Krosnick, J., Holbrook, A. *et al.* (2002), 'The Impact of "No Opinion" Response Options on Data Quality: Non-Attitude Reduction or an Invitation to Satisfice?' *Public Opinion Quarterly*, 66: 371–403.

Krueger, R. (1998), *Moderating Focus Groups* (Thousand Oaks, CA: Sage).

Kuhn, T. (1970), *The Structure of Scientific Revolutions*, 2nd ed. (Chicago: Univ. of Chicago Press).

Kusow, A. (2003), 'Beyond Indigenous Authenticity: Reflections on the Insider/ Outsider Debate in Immigration Research,' *Symbolic Interaction*, 26: 591–9.

Kvale, S. (1996), *InterViews: An Introduction to Qualitative Research Interviewing* (Thousand Oaks, CA: Sage).

Lankshear, G. (2000), 'Bacteria and Babies: A Personal Reflection on Researcher's Risk in a Hospital,' in G. Lee-Treweek and S. Linkogle (eds.), *Danger in the Field: Risk and Ethics in Social Research* (London: Routledge).

Lantz, P., and Booth, K. (1998), 'The Social Construction of the Breast Cancer Epidemic,' *Social Sci. and Medicine*, 46: 907–18.

LaPiere, R.T. (1934), 'Attitudes vs. Actions,' *Social Forces*, 13: 230–7.

Lauder, M. (2003), 'Covert Participant Observation of a Deviant Community: Justifying the Use of Deception,' *Jour. of Contemporary Religion* 18: 185–96.

Layder, D. (1993), *New Strategies in Social Research* (Cambridge, UK: Polity).

——, Ashton, D., and Sung. J. (1991), 'The Empirical Correlates of Action and Structure: The Transition from School to Work,' *Sociology*, 25: 447–64.

Leake, J. (1998), 'Police Figures Hide Poor Clear-up Rate,' *The Times*, 21 June: 1.

LeCompte, M., and Goetz, J. (1982), 'Problems of Reliability and Validity in Ethnographic Research,' *Rev. of Educational Research*, 52: 31–60.

Lee, R.M. (2000), *Unobtrusive Methods in Social Research* (Buckingham: Open Univ. Press).

—— (2004), 'Danger in Research,' in M. Lewis-Beck, A. Bryman, and T. Liao (eds.), *The Sage Encycl. of Soc. Sci. Research Methods* (Thousand Oaks, CA: Sage).

Lee-Treweek, G. (2000), 'The Insight of Emotional Danger: Research Experiences in a Home for the Elderly,' in G. Lee-Treweek and S. Linkogle (eds.), *Danger in the Field: Risk and Ethics in Social Research* (London: Routledge).

Leidner, R. (1993), *Fast Food, Fast Talk: Service Work and the Routinization of Everyday Life* (Berkeley and Los Angeles: Univ. of California Press).

Levitas, R., and Guy, W. (1996), in R. Levitas and W. Guy (eds.), *Interpreting Official Statistics* (London: Routledge).

Lewis, O. (1961), *The Children of Sánchez* (NY: Vintage).

Li, P. (2003), 'Initial Earnings and Catch-up Capacity of Immigrants,' *Can. Public Policy*, 29: 319–37.

Liebling, A. (2001), 'Whose Side Are We On? Theory, Practice and Allegiances in Prisons Research,' *Brit. Jour. of Criminology*, 41: 472-84.

Lincoln, Y., and Denzin, N. (1994), 'The Fifth Moment,' in N. Denzin and Y. Lincoln (eds.), *Handbook of Qual. Research* (Thousand Oaks, CA: Sage).

——— and Guba, E. (1985), *Naturalistic Inquiry* (Beverly Hills, CA: Sage).

Little, M. (2001), 'A Litmus Test for Democracy: The Impact of Ontario Welfare Changes for Single Mothers,' *Studies in Political Economy*, 66: 9–36.

Locke, K. (1996), 'Rewriting *The Discovery of Grounded Theory* after 25 Years?' *Jour. of Management Inquiry*, 5: 239–45.

Lofland, J., and Lofland, L. (1995), *Analyzing Social Settings: A Guide to Qualitative Observation and Analysis*, 3rd ed. (Belmont, CA: Wadsworth).

Lonkila, M. (1995), 'Grounded Theory as an Emergent Paradigm for Computer-Assisted Qualitative Data Analysis,' in U. Kelle (ed.), *Computer-aided Qualitative Data Analysis* (London: Sage).

Lupton, D. (1996), *Food, the Body and the Self* (London: Sage).

Lynch, M., and Bogen, D. (1997), 'Sociology's Asociological "Core": An Examination of Textbook Sociology in the Light of The Sociology of Scientific Knowledge,' *Amer. Sociological Rev.*, 62: 481–93.

Lynd, R., and Lynd, H. (1929), *Middletown: A Study in Contemporary American Culture* (NY: Harcourt Brace).

——— ——— (1937), *Middletown in Transition: A Study in Cultural Conflicts* (NY: Harcourt Brace).

McCall, M.J. (1984), 'Structured Field Observation,' *Annual Rev. of Sociology*, 10: 263–82.

McGuigan, J. (1992), *Cultural Populism* (London: Routledge).

McKee, L., and Bell, C. (1985), 'Marital and Family Relations in Times of Male Unemployment,' in B. Roberts, R. Finnegan, and D. Gallie (eds.), *New Approaches to Economic Life* (Manchester: Manchester Univ. Press).

McKeganey, N., and Barnard, M. (1996), *Sex Work on the Streets* (Buckingham: Open Univ. Press).

MacKinnon, N., and Luke, A. (2002), 'Changes in Identity Attitudes as Reflections of Social and Cultural Change,' *Canadian Jour. of Sociology*, 27: 299–338.

Macnaghten, P., and Jacobs, M. (1997), 'Public Identification with Sustainable Development: Investigating Cultural Barriers to Participation,' *Global Environmental Change*, 7: 5–24.

Madge, C., and O'Connor, H. (2002), 'On-line with E-Mums: Exploring the Internet as a Medium of Research,' *Area*, 34: 92–102.

Madriz, M. (2000), 'Focus Groups in Feminist Research,' in N. Denzin and Y. Lincoln (eds.), *Handbook of Qual. Research*, 2nd ed. (Thousand Oaks, CA: Sage).

Malbon, B. (1999), *Clubbing: Dancing, Ecstasy and Vitality* (London: Routledge).

Malinowski, B. (1967), *A Diary in the Strict Sense of the Term* (London: Routledge & Kegan Paul).

Malkin, A.R., Wornian, K., and Chrisler, J.C. (1999), 'Women and Weight: Gendered Messages on Magazine Covers,' *Sex Roles*, 40: 647–55.

Mangione, T.W. (1995), *Mail Surveys: Improving the Quality* (Thousand Oaks, CA: Sage).

Mann, C., and Stewart, F. (2000), *Internet Communication and Qualitative Research: A Handbook for Researching Online* (London: Sage).

Manning, P. (1995), 'The Challenge of Postmodernism,' in J. Van Maanen (ed.), *Representation in Ethnography* (Thousand Oaks, CA: Sage).

Marcic, D. (2002), *Respect: Women and Popular Music* (NY: Texere).

Markham, A. (1998), *Life Online: Researching the Real Experience in Virtual Space* (London and Walnut Creek, CA: AltaMira Press).

Marsh, C., and Scarbrough, E. (1990), 'Testing Nine Hypotheses about Quota Sampling,' *Jour. of the Market Research Society*, 32: 485–506.

Marshall, G., Newby, H., and Vogler, C. (1988), *Social Class in Modern Britain* (London: Unwin Hyman).

Marx, G.T. (1997), 'Of Methods and Manners for Aspiring Sociologists: 37 Moral Imperatives,' *Amer. Sociologist*, 102–25.

Mason, J. (1994), 'Linking Qualitative and Quantitative Data Analysis,' in A. Bryman and R. Burgess (eds.), *Analyzing Qualitative Data* (London: Routledge).

——— (1996), *Qualitative Researching* (London: Sage).

——— (2002), 'Qualitative Interviewing: Asking, Listening, Interpreting,' in T. May (ed.), *Qualitative Research in Action* (London: Sage).

Mauthner, N., Parry, O., and Backett-Milburn, K. (1998), 'The Data Are Out There, or Are They? Implications for Archiving and Revisiting Qualitative Data,' *Sociology*, 32: 733–45.

Mayhew, P. (2000), 'Researching the State of Crime' in R. King and E. Wincup (eds.), *Doing Research on Crime and Justice* (Oxford: Oxford Univ. Press).

Maynard, M. (1994), 'Methods, Practice and Epistemology: The Debate about Feminism and Research,' in M. Maynard and J. Purvis (eds.), *Researching Women's Lives from a Feminist Perspective* (London: Taylor & Francis).

——— (1998), 'Feminists' Knowledge and the Knowledge of Feminisms: Epistemology, Theory, Methodology and Method,' in T. May and M. Williams (eds.), *Knowing the Social World* (Buckingham: Open Univ. Press).

Mead, M. (1928), *Coming of Age in Samoa* (NY: Morrow).

Menard, S. (1991), *Longitudinal Research* (Newbury Park, CA: Sage).

Merton, R. (1938), 'Social Structure and Anomie,' *Amer. Sociological Rev.*, 3: 672–82.

——— (1967), *On Theoretical Sociology* (NY: Free Press).

Midgley, C. (1998), 'TV Violence has Little Impact on Children, Study Finds,' *The Times*, 12 Jan.: 5.

Mies, M. (1993), 'Towards a Methodology for Feminist Research,' in M. Hammersley (ed.), *Social Research: Philosophy, Politics and Practice* (London: Sage).

Miles, M.B. (1979), 'Qualitative Data as an Attractive Nuisance,' *Administrative Sci. Quarterly*, 24: 590–601.

Milgram, S. (1963), 'A Behavioural Study of Obedience,' *Jour. of Abnormal and Social Psych.*, 67: 371–8.

Milkman, R. (1997), *Farewell to the Factory: Auto Workers in the Late Twentieth Century* (Los Angeles: Univ. of California Press).

Millen, D. (1997), 'Some Methodological and Epistemological Issues Raised by Doing Feminist Research on Non-Feminist Women,' *Sociological Research Online*, 2: www.socresonline.org.uk/socresonline/2/3/3.html.

Miller, D., and Reilly, J. (1995), 'Making an Issue of Food Safety: The Media, Pressure Groups, and the Public Sphere,' in D. Maurer and J. Sobal (eds.), *Food and Nutrition as Social Problems* (NY: Aldine de Gruyter).

Miller, D. Disney (1956), *The Story of Walt Disney* (NY: Dell).

Miller, N., and Morgan, D. (1993), 'Called to Account: The CV as an Autobiographical Practice,' *Sociology*, 27: 133–43.

Miller, R.L. (2000), *Researching Life Stories and Family Histories* (London: Sage).

Miraftab, F. (2000), 'Sheltering Refugees: The Housing Experience of Refugees in Metropolitan Vancouver, Canada,' *Canadian Jour. of Urban Research*, 9: 42–63.

Morgan, D. (1998*a*), *Planning Focus Groups* (Thousand Oaks, CA: Sage).

—— (1998*b*), 'Practical Strategies for Combining Qualitative and Quantitative Methods: Applications for Health Research,' *Qual. Health Research*, 8: 362–76.

—— (2002), 'Focus Group Interviewing,' in J. Gubrium and J. Holstein (eds.), *Handbook of Interview Research: Context and Method* (Thousand Oaks, CA: Sage).

—— and Spanish, M. (1985), 'Social Interaction and the Cognitive Organization of Health-relevant Behaviour,' *Sociology of Health and Illness*, 7: 401–22.

Morgan, R. (2000), 'The Politics of Criminological Research,' in R. King and E. Wincup (eds.), *Doing Research on Crime and Justice* (Oxford: Oxford Univ. Press).

Myles, J., and Hou, F. (2004), 'Changing Colours: Spatial Assimilation and New Racial Minority Immigrants,' *Canadian Jour. of Sociology*, 29: 28–58.

Nettleton, S., Pleace, N., Burrows, R., Muncer, S., and Loader, B. (2002), 'The Reality of Virtual Social Support,' in S. Woolgar (ed.), *Virtual Society? Technology, Cyperbole, Reality* (Oxford: Oxford Univ. Press).

Neuman, W.L. (2003), *Social Research Methods* (Toronto: Pearson Canada).

Nixon, K., Tutty, L., Downe, P., Gorkoff, K., and Ursel, J. (2002), 'The Everyday Occurrence: Violence in the Lives of Girls Exploited through Prostitution?' *Violence against Women*, 8: 1016–43.

Norris, C. (1993), 'Some Ethical Considerations on Fieldwork with the Police,' in D. Hobbs and T. May (eds.), *Interpreting the Field: Accounts of Ethnography* (Oxford: Clarendon Press).

Oakley, A. (1981), 'Interviewing Women: A Contradiction in Terms,' in H. Roberts (ed.), *Doing Feminist Research* (London: Routledge & Kegan Paul).

—— (1998), 'Gender, Methodology and People's Ways of Knowing: Some Problems with Feminism and the Paradigm Debate in Social Science,' *Sociology*, 32: 707–31.

O'Connell Davidson, J., and Layder, D. (1994), *Methods, Sex, and Madness* (London: Routledge).

O'Connor, H., and Madge, C. (2001), 'Cyber-Mothers: Online Synchronous Interviewing Using Conferencing Software,' *Sociological Research Online*, 5: www.socresonline.org.uk/5/4/o'connor.html.

—— —— (2003), '"Focus Groups in Cyberspace": Using the Internet for Qualitative Research,' *Qual. Market Research*, 6: 133–43.

Okely, J. (1994), 'Thinking through Fieldwork,' in A. Bryman and R. Burgess (eds.), *Analyzing Qualitative Data* (London: Routledge).

O'Reilly, K. (2000), *The British on the Costa del Sol: Transnational Identities and Local Communities* (London: Routledge).

Orona, C.J. (1997), 'Temporality and Identity Loss due to Alzheimer's Disease,' in A. Strauss and J. Corbin (eds.), *Grounded Theory in Practice* (Thousand Oaks, CA: Sage).

Pahl, J. (1990), 'Household Spending, Personal Spending and the Control of Money in Marriage,' *Sociology*, 24: 119–38.

Parker, M. (2000), *Organizational Culture and Identity* (London: Sage).

Parnaby, P. (2003), 'Disaster through Dirty Windshields: Law, Order and Toronto's Squeegee Kids,' *Canadian Jour. of Sociology*, 28: 281–307.

Pawson, R., and Tilley, N. (1997), *Realistic Evaluation* (London: Sage).

Peñaloza, L. (1999), 'Just Doing It: A Visual Ethnographic Study of Spectacular Consumption at Niketown,' *Consumption, Market, and Culture*, 2: 337–400.

Perrucci, R., Belshaw, R., DeMerritt, A., Frazier, B., Jones, J., Kimbrough, J., Loney, K., Pappas, J., Parker, J., Trottier, B., and Williams, B. (2000), 'The Two Faces of Racialized Space at a Predominantly White University,' *International Jour. of Contemporary Sociology*, 37: 230–44.

Pettigrew, A. (1997), 'What Is a Processual Analysis?' *Scandinavian Jour. of Management*, 13: 337–48.

—— and Whipp, R. (1991), *Managing Change for Competitive Success* (Oxford: Blackwell).

Phelan, P. (1987), 'Comparability of Qualitative and Quantitative Methods: Studying Child Sexual Abuse in America,' *Educ. and Urban Society*, 20: 35–41.

Phillips, N., and Brown, J. (1993), 'Analyzing Communications in and around Organizations: A Critical Hermeneutic Approach,' *Academy of Management Jour.*, 36: 1547–76.

Phoenix, A. (1994), 'Practising Feminist Research: The Intersection of Gender and "Race" in the Research Process,' in M. Maynard and J. Purvis (eds.), *Researching Women's Lives from a Feminist Perspective* (London: Taylor & Francis).

Pidgeon, N., and Henwood, K. (2004), 'Grounded Theory,' in M. Hardy and A. Bryman (eds.), *Handbook of Data Analysis* (London: Sage).

Pink, S. (2001), *Visual Ethnography* (London: Sage).

Platt, J. (1986), 'Functionalism and the Survey: The Relation of Theory and Method,' *Sociological Rev.*, 34: 501–36.

—— (1996), *A History of Sociological Research Methods in America 1920–1960* (Cambridge: Cambridge Univ. Press).

Podsakoff, P., and Dalton, D. (1987), 'Research Methodology in Organizational Studies,' *Jour. of Management*, 13: 419–44.

Poland, B.D. (1995), 'Transcription Quality as an Aspect of Rigor in Qualitative Research,' *Qual. Inquiry*, 1: 290–310.

Porter, S. (1993), 'Critical Realist Ethnography: The Case of Racism and Professionalism in a Medical Setting,' *Sociology*, 27: 591–609.

—— (2002), 'Critical Realist Ethnography,' in T. May (ed.), *Qual. Research in Action* (London: Sage).

Potter, G. (2003), '*Sui generis* Micro Social Structures: The Heuristic Example of Poker,' *Canadian Jour. of Sociology*, 28: 171–202.

Potter, J. (1996), *Representing Reality: Discourse, Rhetoric and Social Construction* (London: Sage).

—— (1997), 'Discourse Analysis as a Way of Analysing Naturally Occurring Talk,' in D. Silverman (ed.), *Qual. Research: Theory, Method and Practice* (London: Sage).

—— (2004), 'Discourse Analysis,' in M. Hardy and A. Bryman (eds.), *Handbook of Data Analysis* (London: Sage).

—— and Hepburn, A. (2004), 'The Analysis of NSPCC Call Openings,' in S. Becker and A. Bryman (eds.), *Understanding Research for Social Policy and Practice: Themes, Methods, and Approaches* (Bristol: Policy Press).

—— and Wetherell, M. (1994), 'Analyzing Discourse,' in A. Bryman and R. Burgess (eds.), *Analyzing Qualitative Data* (London: Routledge).

—— —— and Chitty, A. (1991), 'Quantification Rhetoric—Cancer on Television,' *Discourse and Society*, 2: 333–65.

Pratt, A., and Valverde, M. (2002), 'From Deserving Victims to "Masters of Confusion": Redefining Refugees in the 1900s,' *Canadian Jour. of Sociology*, 27: 135–62.

Psathas, G. (1995), *Conversation Analysis: The Study of Talk-in-Interaction* (Thousand Oaks, CA: Sage).

Punch, M. (1994), 'Politics and Ethics in Qualitative Research,' in N. Denzin and Y. Lincoln (eds.), *Handbook of Qual. Research* (Thousand Oaks, CA: Sage).

Radley, A., and Chamberlain, K. (2001), 'Health Psychology and the Study of the Case: From Method to Analytic Concern,' *Social Sci. and Medicine*, 53: 321–32.

—— and Taylor, D. (2003*a*), 'Images of Recovery: a Photo-Elicitation Study on the Hospital Ward,' *Qual. Health Research*, 13: 77–99.

—— —— (2003*b*), 'Remembering One's Stay in Hospital: A Study in Photography, Recovery and Forgetting,' *Health: An Interdisciplinary Jour. for the Social Study of Health, Illness and Medicine*, 7: 129–59.

Rafaeli, A., Dutton, J., Harquail, C.V., and Mackie-Lewis, S. (1997), 'Navigating by Attire: The Use of Dress by Female Administrative Employees,' *Academy of Management Jour.*, 40: 9–45.

Reed, M. (2000), 'The Limits of Discourse Analysis in Organizational Analysis,' *Organization*, 7: 524–30.

Reiner, R. (2000*a*), 'Crime and Control in Britain,' *Sociology*, 34: 71–94.

—— (2000*b*), 'Police Research,' in R. King and E. Wincup (eds.), *Doing Research on Crime and Justice* (Oxford: Oxford Univ. Press).

Reinharz, S. (1992), *Feminist Methods in Social Research* (NY: Oxford Univ. Press).

Richardson, L. (1990), 'Narrative and Sociology,' *Jour. of Contemporary Ethnography*, 19: 116–35.

—— (1994), 'Writing: A Method of Inquiry,' in N. Denzin and Y. Lincoln (eds.), *Handbook of Qual. Research* (Thousand Oaks, CA: Sage).

Riches, G., and Dawson, P. (1998), 'Lost Children, Living Memories: The Role of Photographs in Processes of Grief and Adjustment Among Bereaved Parents,' *Death Studies*, 22: 121–40.

Riessman, C.K. (1993), *Narrative Analysis* (Newbury Park, CA: Sage).

—— (2004*a*), 'Narrative Interviewing,' in M. Lewis-Beck, A. Bryman, and T. Liao (eds.), *The Sage Encycl. of Soc. Sci. Research Methods* (Thousand Oaks, CA: Sage).

—— (2004*b*), 'Narrative Analysis,' in M. Lewis-Beck, A. Bryman, and T. Liao (eds.), *The Sage Encycl. of Soc. Sci. Research Methods* (Thousand Oaks, CA: Sage).

Rinehart, J. (1996), *The Tyranny of Work*, 3rd ed. (Toronto: Harcourt Brace).

——, Huxley, C., and Robertson, D. (1998), *Not Just Another Auto Plant* (Ithaca, NY: Cornell Univ. Press).

Ristock, J. (2001), 'Decentring Heterosexuality: Responses of Feminist Counsellors to Abuse in Lesbian Relationships,' *Women and Therapy*, 23: 59–72.

Roberts, B. (2002), *Biographical Research* (Buckingham: Open Univ. Press).

Rojek, C. (1995), *Decentring Leisure: Rethinking Leisure Theory* (London: Sage).

Rose, G. (2001), *Visual Methodologies* (London: Sage).

Rosenau, P.M. (1992), *Post-Modernism and the Social Sciences: Insights, Inroads, and Intrusions* (Princeton: Princeton Univ. Press).

Rosenhan, D.L. (1973), 'On Being Sane in Insane Places,' *Science*, 179: 350–8.

Rosenthal, R., and Jacobson, L. (1968), *Pygmalion in the Classroom: Teacher Expectation and Pupils' Intellectual Development* (NY: Holt, Rinehart & Winston).

Rosnow, R.L., and Rosenthal, R. (1997), *People Studying People: Artefacts and Ethics in Behavioral Research* (NY: W.H. Freeman).

Rubin, H.J., and Rubin, I.S. (1995), *Qualitative Interviewing: The Art of Hearing Data* (Thousand Oaks, CA: Sage).

Rushton, J. (2000), *Race, Evolution and Behaviour: A Life History Perspective* (Port Huron, MI: Charles Darwin Research Institute).

Russell, R., and Tyler, M. (2002), 'Thank Heaven for Little Girls: "Girl Heaven" and the Commercial Context of Feminine Childhood,' *Sociology*, 36: 619–37.

Sampson, H., and Thomas, M. (2003), 'Lone Researchers at Sea: Gender, Risk and Responsibility,' *Qual. Research*, 3: 165–89.

Sanjek, R. (1990), 'A Vocabulary for Fieldnotes,' in R. Sanjek (ed.), *Fieldnotes: The Making of Anthropology* (Ithaca, NY: Cornell Univ. Press).

Sarsby, J. (1984), 'The Fieldwork Experience,' in R. Ellen (ed.), *Ethnographic Research: A Guide to General Conduct* (London: Academic Press).

Schaeffer, D., and Dillman, D. (1998), 'Development of a Standard E-mail Methodology,' *Public Opinion Quarterly*, 62: 378–97.

Schegloff, E. (1997), 'Whose Text? Whose Context?' *Discourse and Society*, 8: 165–87.

Schlesinger, P., Dobash, R.E., Dobash, R.P., and Weaver, C. (1992), *Women Viewing Violence* (London: British Film Institute).

Schrøder, K.C. (1999), 'The Best of Both Worlds? Media Audience Research between Rival Paradigms,' in P. Alasuutari (ed.), *Rethinking the Media Audience* (London: Sage).

Schuman, H., and Presser, S. (1981), *Questions and Answers in Attitude Surveys: Experiments on Question Form, Wording, and Context* (San Diego, CA: Academic Press).

Schutz, A. (1962), *Collected Papers I: The Problem of Social Reality* (The Hague: Martinus Nijhof).

Scott, J. (1990), *A Matter of Record* (Cambridge, UK: Polity).

Seale, C. (1999), *The Quality of Qualitative Research* (London: Sage).

—— (2002), 'Cancer Heroics: A Study of News Reports with Particular Reference to Gender,' *Sociology*, 36: 107–26.

Shalla, V. (2002), 'Jettisoned by Design? The Truncated Employment Relationship of Customer Sales and Service Agents under Airline Restructuring,' *Canadian Jour. of Sociology*, 27: 1–32.

Sharf, B.F. (1999), 'Beyond Netiquette: The Ethics of Doing Naturalistic Discourse Research on the Internet,' in S. Jones (ed.), *Doing Internet Research: Critical Issues and Methods for Examining the Net* (Thousand Oaks, CA: Sage).

Sharpe, K. (2000), 'Sad, Bad, and (Sometimes) Dangerous to Know: Street Corner Research with Prostitutes, Punters, and the Police,' in R. King and E. Wincup (eds.), *Doing Research on Crime and Justice* (Oxford: Oxford Univ. Press).

Sheehan, K. (2001), 'E-mail Survey Response Rates: A Review,' *Jour. of Computer-Mediated Communication*, 6: www.ascusc.org/jcmc/vol6/issue2/sheehan.html.

—— and Hoy, M. (1999), 'Using E-mail to Survey Internet Users in the United States: Methodology and Assessment,' *Jour. of Computer-Mediated Communication*, 4: www.ascusc.org/jcmc/vol4/issue3/sheehan.html.

Shuy, R.W. (2002), 'In-person versus Telephone Interviewing,' in J.F. Gubrium and J.A. Holstein (eds.), *Handbook of Interview Research: Context and Method* (Thousand Oaks, CA: Sage).

Silverman, D. (1984), 'Going Private: Ceremonial Forms in a Private Oncology Clinic,' *Sociology*, 18: 191–204.

—— (1985), *Qualitative Methodology and Sociology: Describing the Social World* (Aldershot: Gower).

—— (1993), *Interpreting Qualitative Data: Methods for Analysing Qualitative Data* (London: Sage).

—— (1994), 'Analysing Naturally Occurring Data on AIDS Counselling: Some Methodological and Practical Issues,' in M. Boulton (ed.), *Challenge and Innovation: Methodological Advances in Social Research on HIV/AIDS* (London: Taylor & Francis).

Silverman, R., Sacco, V., and Teevan, J. (2000), *Crime in Canadian Society* (Toronto: Harcourt Canada).

Skeggs, B. (1994), 'Situating the Production of Feminist Ethnography,' in M. Maynard and J. Purvis (eds.), *Researching Women's Lives from a Feminist Perspective* (London: Taylor & Francis).

—— (1997), *Formations of Class and Gender* (London: Sage).

—— (2001), 'Feminist Ethnography,' in P. Atkinson, A. Coffey, S. Delamont, J. Lofland, and L. Lofland (eds.), *Handbook of Ethnography* (London: Sage).

Smith, D.J., and McVie, S. (2003), 'Theory and Method in the Edinburgh Study of Youth Transitions and Crime,' *Brit. Jour. of Criminology*, 43: 169–95.

Smith, N., Lister, R., and Middleton, S. (2004), 'Longitudinal Qualitative Research,' in S. Becker and A. Bryman (eds.), *Understanding Research for Social Policy and Practice: Themes, Methods, and Approaches* (Bristol: Policy Press).

Smith, T.W. (1995), 'Trends in Non-response Rates,' *Intnatl. Jour. of Public Opinion Research*, 7: 157–71.

Stacey, J. (1988), 'Can There Be a Feminist Ethnography?' *Women's Intnatl. Studies Forum*, 11: 21–7.

Stake, R.E. (1995), *The Art of Case Study Research* (Thousand Oaks, CA: Sage).

Stanley, L., and Temple, B. (1995), 'Doing the Business? Evaluating Software Packages to Aid the Analysis of Qualitative Data Sets,' *Studies in Qual. Methodology*, 5: 169–97.

Stoller, P. (1989), *The Taste of Ethnographic Things* (Philadelphia: Univ. of Pennsylvania Press).

Strauss, A. (1987), *Qualitative Analysis for Social Scientists* (NY: Cambridge Univ. Press).

—— (1998), *Basics of Qualitative Research: Techniques and Procedures for Developing Grounded Theory* (Thousand Oaks, CA: Sage).

—— and Corbin, J. (1990), *Basics of Qualitative Research: Grounded Theory Procedures and Techniques* (Newbury Park, CA: Sage).

—— Schatzman, L., Ehrich, D., Bucher, R., and Sabshin, M. (1973), 'The Hospital and Its Negotiated Order,' in G. Salaman and K. Thompson (eds.), *People and Organizations* (London: Longman).

Sudman, S., and Bradburn, N. (1982), *Asking Questions: A Practical Guide to Questionnaire Design* (San Francisco: Jossey-Bass).

Sugiman, P. (2004), 'Memories of the Internment: Narrating Japanese-Canadian Women's Life Stories,' *Canadian Jour. of Sociology*, 29: 359–88.

Sullivan, O. (1996), 'Time Co-ordination, the Domestic Division of Labour and Affective Relations: Time Use and the Enjoyment of Activities within Couples,' *Sociology*, 30: 79–100.

Sutton, R.I. (1992), 'Feelings about a Disneyland Visit: Photography and the Reconstruction of Bygone Emotions,' *Jour. of Management Inquiry*, 1: 278–87.

—— and Rafaeli, A. (1988), 'Untangling the Relationship between Displayed Emotions and Organizational Sales: The Case of Convenience Stores,' *Academy of Management Jour.*, 31: 461–87.

—— —— (1992), 'How We Untangled the Relationship between Displayed Emotion and Organizational Sales: A Tale of Bickering and Optimism,' in P. Frost and R. Stablein (eds.), *Doing Exemplary Research* (Newbury Park, CA: Sage).

Sweet, C. (2001), 'Designing and Conducting Virtual Focus Groups,' *Qual. Market Research*, 4: 130–5.

Tastsoglou, E., and Miedema, B. (2003), 'Immigrant Women and Community Development in the Canadian Maritimes: Outsiders Within?' *Canadian Jour. of Sociology*, 28: 203–34.

Taylor, A. (1993), *Women Drug Users: An Ethnography of an Injecting Community* (Oxford: Clarendon Press).

Taylor, S. (1999), 'Covert Participant Observation: Unguarded Moments in Organizational Research,' *Notework: The Newsletter of the Standing Conference on Organizational Symbolism*, May: 8–18.

Teitler, J., Reichman, N., and Sprachman, S. (2003), 'Costs and Benefits of Improving Response Rates for a Hard-to-reach Population,' *Public Opinion Quarterly*, 67: 126–38.

Thompson, T., and Zerbinos, E. (1995), 'Gender Roles in Animated Cartoons: Has the Picture Changed in 20 Years?' *Sex Roles*, 32: 651–73.

Tilley, N. (2000), 'Doing Realistic Evaluation of Criminal Justice,' in V. Jupp, P. Davies, and P. Francis (eds.), *Doing Criminological Research* (London: Sage).

Totten, M. (2001) 'Legal, Ethical, and Clinical Implications of Doing Fieldwork with Youth Gang Members Who Engage in Serious Violence,' *Jour. of Gang Research*, 8: 35–49.

Tourangeau, R., and Smith, T.W. (1996), 'Asking Sensitive Questions: The Impact of Data Collection Mode, Question Format, and Question Context,' *Public Opinion Quarterly*, 60: 275–304.

Trow, M. (1957), 'Comment on "Participant Observation and Interviewing: A Comparison,"' *Human Organization*, 16: 33–5.

Tse, A. (1998), 'Comparing the Response Rate, Response Speed and Response Quality of Two Methods of Sending Questionnaires: E-mail vs. Mail,' *Jour. of the Market Research Society*, 40: 353–61.

—— (1999), 'Conducting Electronic Focus Group Discussions among Chinese Respondents,' *Jour. of the Market Research Society*, 41: 407–15.

Turnbull, P. (1973), *The Mountain People* (London: Cape).

Van Den Hoonaard, W.C. (2001), 'Is Research-ethics Review a Moral Panic?' *Canadian Rev. of Sociology and Anthropology*, 38: 19–36.

Van Maanen, J. (1988), *Tales of the Field: On Writing Ethnography* (Chicago: Univ. of Chicago Press).

—— (1991*a*), 'Playing Back the Tape: Early Days in the Field,' in W. Shaffir and R. Stebbins (eds.), *Experiencing Fieldwork: An Inside View of Qualitative Research* (Newbury Park, CA: Sage).

—— (1991*b*), 'The Smile Factory: Work at Disneyland,' in P. Frost, L. Moore *et al.* (eds.), *Reframing Organizational Culture* (Newbury Park, CA: Sage).

Vidich, A., and Bensman, J. (1968), *Small Town in Mass Society* (Princeton, NJ: Princeton Univ. Press).

Vincent, S. (2003), 'Preserving Domesticity,' *Canadian Rev. of Sociology and Anthropology*, 40: 171–96.

Wachholz, S., and Miedema, B. (2000), 'Risk, Fear, Harm: Immigrant Women's Perceptions of the "Policing Solution" to Woman Abuse,' *Crime, Law, and Social Change*, 34: 301–17.

Wacjman, J., and Martin, B. (2002), 'Narratives of Identity in Modern Management,' *Sociology*, 36: 985–1002.

Walby, S., and Myhill, A. (2001), 'New Survey Methodologies in Researching Violence against Women,' *Brit. Jour. of Criminology*, 41: 502–22.

Walklate, S. (2000), 'Researching Victims,' in R. King and E. Wincup (eds.), *Doing Research on Crime and Justice* (Oxford: Oxford Univ. Press).

Walsh, M., Hickey, C., and Duffy, J. (1999), 'Influence of Item Content and Stereotype Situation on Gender Differences in Mathematical Problem,' *Sex Roles*, 41: 219–40.

Walters, D. (2004), 'A Comparison of Labour Market Outcomes of Post-secondary Graduates of Various Levels and Fields over a Four-cohort Period,' *Canadian Jour. of Sociology*, 29: 1–27.

Warde, A. (1997), *Consumption, Food and Taste* (London: Sage).

Weaver, A., and Atkinson, P. (1995), *Microcomputing and Qualitative Data Analysis* (Aldershot: Avebury).

Webb, E.J., Campbell, D.T., Schwartz, R.D., and Sechrest, L. (1966), *Unobtrusive Measures: Non-reactive Measures in the Social Sciences* (Chicago: Rand McNally).

Weber, M. (1947), *The Theory of Social and Economic Organization*, trans. A.M. Henderson and T. Parsons (NY: Free Press).

Weick, K.E. (1990), 'The Vulnerable System: An Analysis of the Tenerife Air Disaster,' *Jour. of Management*, 16: 571–93.

Weinholtz, D., Kacer, B., and Rocklin, T. (1995), 'Salvaging Quantitative Research with Qualitative Data,' *Qual. Health Research*, 5: 388–97.

Westergaard, J., Noble, I., and Walker, A. (1989), *After Redundancy: The Experience of Economic Insecurity* (Cambridge, UK: Polity).

Wetherell, M. (1998), 'Positioning and Interpretative Repertoires: Conversation Analysis and Post-structuralism in Dialogue,' *Discourse and Society*, 9: 387–412.

White, J. (1990), *Hospital Strike* (Toronto: Thompson Educ. Publishing).

Whitehead, P., and Carpenter, D. (1999), 'Explaining Unsafe Sexual Behaviour: Cultural Definitions and Health in the Military,' *Culture, Health, and Sexuality*, 1: 303–15.

Whyte, W.F. (1955), *Street Corner Society*, 2nd ed. (Chicago: Univ. of Chicago Press).

Widdicombe, S. (1993), 'Autobiography and Change: Rhetoric and Authenticity of "Gothic" Style,' in E. Burman and I. Parker (eds.), *Discourse Analytic Research: Readings and Repertoires of Text* (London: Routledge).

Wilkinson, P., and Whitworth, D. (1998), 'Fat Is Fanciable, Says the Body of Evidence,' *The Times*, 7 Jan.: 3.

Wilkinson, S. (1998), 'Focus Groups in Feminist Research: Power, Interaction, and the Co-production of Meaning,' *Women's Studies Intnatl. Forum*, 21: 111–25.

—— (1999*a*), 'Focus Group Methodology: A Review,' *Intnatl. Jour. of Social Research Methodology*, 1: 181–203.

—— (1999*b*), 'Focus Groups: A Feminist Method,' *Psych. of Women Quarterly*, 23: 221–44.

Williams, M. (2000), 'Interpretivism and Generalization,' *Sociology*, 34: 209–24.

Wilson, B. (2002), 'The Canadian Rave Scene and Five Theses on Youth Resistance,' *Canadian Jour. of Sociology*, 27: 373–412.

Winkler, C. (1995), 'The Ethnography of the Ethnographer,' in C. Nordstrom and A. Robben (eds.), *Fieldwork under Fire: Contemporary Studies of Violence and Survival* (Berkeley: Univ. of California Press).

Winlow, S., Hobbs, D., Lister, S., and Hadfield, P. (2001), 'Get Ready to Duck: Bouncers and the Realities of Ethnographic Research on Violent Groups,' *Brit. Jour. of Criminology*, 41: 536–48.

Wolcott, H. (1990), *Writing up Qualitative Research* (Newbury Park, CA: Sage).

Wolf, D. (1991), 'High Risk Methodology: Reflections on Leaving an Outlaw Society,' in W. Shaffir and R. Stebbins (eds.), *Experiencing Fieldwork: An Inside View of Qualitative Research* (Newbury Park, CA: Sage).

Yin, R. (1984), *Case Study Research: Design and Methods* (Beverly Hills, CA: Sage).

Yun, G.W., and Trumbo, C.W. (2000) 'Comparative Response to a Survey Executed by Post, E-mail, and Web Form,' *Jour. of Computer-mediated Communication*, 6: www.ascusc.org/jcmc/vol6/issue1/yun.html.

Index